ELEANOR

David Michaelis

SIMON & SCHUSTER
New York   London   Toronto   Sydney   New Delhi

Simon & Schuster
1230 Avenue of the Americas
New York, NY 10020

First Simon & Schuster hardcover edition October 2020

SIMON & SCHUSTER and colophon are registered trademarks of Simon & Schuster, Inc.

Grateful acknowledgment is made to HarperCollins Publishers for permission to quote from *The Autobiography of Eleanor Roosevelt* by Eleanor Roosevelt. Copyright © 1937, 1949, 1958, 1961 by Anna Eleanor Roosevelt. Copyright © 1958 by Curtis Publishing Company. Copyright renewed 1989 by Franklin A. Roosevelt. Afterword copyright © 2014 by Nancy Roosevelt Ireland. Used by permission of HarperCollins Publishers.

And for permission to quote from *The Autobiography of Eleanor Roosevelt: This I Remember* by Eleanor Roosevelt. Copyright © 1937, 1949, 1958, 1961 by Anna Eleanor Roosevelt. Copyright © 1958 by Curtis Publishing Company. Copyright renewed 1989 by Franklin A. Roosevelt. Afterword copyright © 2014 by Nancy Roosevelt Ireland. Used by permission of HarperCollins Publishers.

And for permission to quote from *The Autobiography of Eleanor Roosevelt: This Is My Story* by Eleanor Roosevelt. Copyright © 1937, 1949, 1958, 1961 by Anna Eleanor Roosevelt. Copyright © 1958 by Curtis Publishing Company. Copyright renewed 1989 by Franklin A. Roosevelt. Afterword copyright © 2014 by Nancy Roosevelt Ireland. Used by permission of HarperCollins Publishers.

And for permission to quote from *You Learn By Living* by Eleanor Roosevelt. Copyright ©1960 by Eleanor Roosevelt. Copyright Renewed 1988 by Franklin A. Roosevelt. Used by permission of HarperCollins Publishers.

For information about special discounts for bulk purchases, please contact Simon & Schuster Special Sales at 1-866-506-1949 or business@simonandschuster.com.

The Simon & Schuster Speakers Bureau can bring authors to your live event. For more information or to book an event, contact the Simon & Schuster Speakers Bureau at 1-866-248-3049 or visit our website at www.simonspeakers.com.

Interior design by Carly Loman

Manufactured in the United States of America

10   9   8   7   6   5   4

Library of Congress Cataloging-in-Publication Data has been applied for.

ISBN 978-1-4391-9201-6
ISBN 978-1-4391-9205-4 (ebook)

To Nan

I felt obliged to notice everything.

E.R.

CONTENTS

V. MRS. ROOSEVELT

VI. AGITATOR

VII. WORLDMAKER

PRINCIPAL CHARACTERS

(in order of appearance)

I. GRANNY (1884–1892)

ANNA REBECCA HALL ROOSEVELT (1863–1892); Anna
   Mother
ELLIOTT BULLOCH ROOSEVELT (1860–1894); Nell
   Father
CORINNE ROOSEVELT ROBINSON (1861–1933); Auntie Corinne
   Father's younger sister
ANNA ROOSEVELT COWLES (1853–1931); Bamie, Auntie Bye
   Father's older sister; political guru to three generations of
   Roosevelts
THEODORE ROOSEVELT (1858–1919); Uncle Ted; TR
   Father's older brother; 26th U.S. President
MARTHA BULLOCH ROOSEVELT (1835–1884); Mittie
   Father's mother
ALICE LEE ROOSEVELT LONGWORTH (1884–1980); Cousin Alice
   Family rival
ANNA ELEANOR ROOSEVELT (1884–1962); Little Nell, Granny, Totty,
   Babs, Eleanor, ER, Grandmère
SARA DELANO ROOSEVELT (1854–1941); Cousin Sallie, Ma-mà
   Mother-in-law
JAMES ROOSEVELT (1828–1900); Squire James
   Father-in-law
FRANKLIN DELANO ROOSEVELT (1882–1945); FDR
   Fifth cousin; spouse; 32nd U.S. President
EDITH KERMIT CAROW ROOSEVELT (1861–1948); Aunt Edith
   TR's (second) spouse; first lady of the United States

THEODORE ROOSEVELT, JR. (1887–1944); Cousin Ted
  Political rival, New York State

ELIZABETH LIVINGSTON HALL MORTIMER (1865–1944); Aunt Tissie
  Godmother; guardian abroad

ANNA BULLOCH GRACIE (1833–1893); Aunt Gracie
  Father's aunt; guardian at home

JAMES KING GRACIE (1840–1903); Uncle Bunkle
  Great-uncle

ELLIOTT ROOSEVELT, JR. (1889–1893); Ellie
  Brother

GRACIE HALL ROOSEVELT (1891–1941); Hall
  Brother

CATHARINE MANN (1862–1941); Katie
  Domestic worker; mother of Eleanor's half brother

ELLIOTT ROOSEVELT MANN (1891–1976); Robert
  Half brother

DOUGLAS ROBINSON, JR. (1855–1918); Uncle Douglas
  Aunt Corinne's spouse

SUSAN LUDLOW PARISH (1865–1950); Cousin Susie
  Mother's cousin; guardian

EDITH LIVINGSTON HALL MORGAN (1873–1920); Aunt Pussie
  Mother's sister; shape-shifting mentor

MAUDE LIVINGSTON HALL GRAY (1877–1952); Aunt Maude
  Mother's sister; family ally

VALENTINE HALL III (1867–1934); Uncle Vallie
  Mother's brother; U.S. National Lawn Tennis Champion

EDWARD LUDLOW HALL (1872–1932); Uncle Eddie
  Mother's brother; U.S. National Lawn Tennis Champion

CORINNE ROBINSON ALSOP COLE (1886–1971); Cousin Corinnie
  Family ally

II. ORPHAN (1892–1905)

MARY LIVINGSTON LUDLOW HALL (1843–1919); G'ma
  Maternal grandmother; legal guardian

MARIE CLAIRE SOUVESTRE (1835–1905); Mademoiselle
>Teacher; mentor

HELEN AGNES POST (1885–1962); Nelly
>School friend

BLANCHE SPRING (1871–1922)
>Nurse; ally

ANNA (1906–1975)
>Daughter

JAMES (1907–1991); Jimmy
>Oldest son

FIRST FRANKLIN JR. (1909–1909); Baby Franklin
>Lost child

ELLIOTT ROOSEVELT (1910–1990)
>Favored son

III. MISSUS (1905–1922)

JENNIE WALTERS DELANO (1853–1922)
>FDR's aunt Jennie; spouse of Warren Delano III (1852–1920); family ally

FRANKLIN D. ROOSEVELT, JR. (1914–1988); Brud
>Favorite son of the FDR family

JOHN ASPINWALL ROOSEVELT (1916–1981)
>Youngest son

CHARLES FRANCIS MURPHY (1858–1924); "Silent Charlie"
>Head of New York City's Tammany Hall, 1902–1924

LOUIS McHENRY HOWE (1871–1936); Louie
>Chief adviser

LUCY MERCER RUTHERFURD (1891–1948)
>Social secretary

W. SHEFFIELD COWLES, JR. (1898–1986); Cousin Sheffield
>Auntie Bye's son; FDR's naval assistant, First World War

ROBERT W. LOVETT (1859–1924)
>Orthopedic surgeon; world's foremost authority on polio rehabilitation, 1921

GEORGE DRAPER (1880–1959)
  FDR's personal physician
ELIZABETH READ (1872–1943); Lizzie
  Mentor; legal adviser
MARGUERITE ALICE LEHAND (1896–1944); Missy
  FDR's closest companion, protector
KERMIT ROOSEVELT (1889–1943); Cousin Kermit
  Soldier, explorer, writer

IV. STATE-WOMAN (1922–1932)

ESTHER LAPE (1881–1981)
  Mentor; social activist and administrator
NANCY COOK (1884–1962); Nan
  Political ally; friend; managing partner, Val-Kill Industries
MARION DICKERMAN (1890–1983)
  Politician; friend; head, Todhunter School
CURTIS B. DALL (1896–1991); Curt
  Anna's (first) spouse; father, Ellie and Curtis
EARL MILLER (1897–1973)
  New York State Trooper; bodyguard
MALVINA CYNTHIA THOMPSON SCHEIDER (1893–1953); Tommy
  Executive assistant; chief of first lady's secretariat, 1932–1945
ELINOR FATMAN MORGENTHAU (1892–1949)
  Friend; political associate; spouse, Treasury Secretary Henry
  Morgenthau, Jr.
ALFRED EMANUEL SMITH (1873–1944); Al
  Governor of New York, 1923–1928
BELLE MOSKOWITZ (1877–1933)
  Associate in New York State government
MOLLY DEWSON (1874–1962); "Little General"
  Lieutenant on Al Smith's 1928 presidential campaign; head of
  Democratic National Committee's Women's Division, 1936
FRANCES PERKINS (1880–1965)
  Social activist; U.S. secretary of labor

BERNARD MANNES BARUCH (1870–1965)
   Financial backer
JOHN BOETTIGER (1900–1950)
   Favored son-in-law; Anna's (second) spouse
LORENA ALICE HICKOK (1893–1968); Hick
   Associate Press reporter; secret romantic partner

V. MRS. ROOSEVELT (1933–1941)

HARRY L. HOPKINS (1890–1946)
   Settlement social worker; New Deal administrator; FDR's
   wartime consigliere
JOSEPH P. LASH (1909–1987); Joe
   Student leader; activist; intimate friend and adviser;
   posthumous biographer
HENRIETTA NESBITT (1874–1963); Mrs. Nesbitt
   Housekeeper
EDITH BENHAM HELM (1874–1962); Mrs. Helm
   Social secretary
STEPHEN T. EARLY (1889–1951); Steve
   Secretary to the President
ELEANOR ROOSEVELT [DALL] SEAGRAVES (1927–); Sistie, Ellie
   Oldest grandchild
CURTIS ROOSEVELT [DALL] (1930–2016); Buzzie
   Grandson
ELIZABETH BROWNING DONNER ROOSEVELT (1911–1980); Betty
   Elliott's (first) spouse; mother, Billy Roosevelt
WILLIAM DONNER ROOSEVELT (1932–2003); Billy
   Grandson
BETSEY CUSHING ROOSEVELT WHITNEY (1909–1998)
   Jimmy's (first) spouse
ROMELLE THERESA SCHNEIDER ROOSEVELT (1915–2002); Rommie
   Jimmy's (second) spouse
ETHEL DU PONT (1916–1965)
   Franklin Jr.'s (first) spouse

HENRY A. WALLACE (1888–1965)
U.S. secretary of agriculture, 1933–1940; U.S. vice president, 1940–1944; U.S. secretary of commerce, 1944–1946

MARY McLEOD BETHUNE (1875–1955); Mrs. Bethune
"First Lady of the Struggle"

HAROLD L. ICKES (1874–1952)
U. S. secretary of the interior

WALTER F. WHITE (1893–1955)
Leader of the National Association for the Advancement of Colored People (NAACP)

BRECKINRIDGE LONG (1881–1958)
Career diplomat; architect of U.S. State Department's anti-Semitic and racist anti-immigration policy

VI. AGITATOR (1941–1946)

LAURA FRANKLIN DELANO (1885–1972); Aunt Polly
FDR's cousin

BELLE WILLARD ROOSEVELT (1892–1968); Belle
Family ally; spouse of cousin Kermit Roosevelt

MARGARET LYNCH SUCKLEY (1891–1991); Daisy
FDR's cousin

WINSTON S. CHURCHILL (1874–1965)
Prime minister of England, 1940–1945, 1951–1955

FIORELLO H. LA GUARDIA (1882–1947)
Mayor of New York, 1934–1945; ranking codirector, Office of Civilian Defense

GILBERT A. HARRISON (1915–2008)
Director, OCD Division of Youth Activities

MAYRIS CHANEY (1906–2003)
Dancer; OCD director of children's activities

HARRY S. TRUMAN (1884–1972)
FDR's third vice president; former senator from Missouri; succeeded to the presidency upon FDR's death

DURWARD V. SANDIFER (1900–1981)
Principal UNO adviser to ER

RALPH BUNCHE (1904–1971)
Adviser to first U.S. delegation to UNO; winner, 1950 Nobel
Peace Prize

ANDREY YANUARYEVICH VYSHINSKY (1883–1954)
Soviet politician; former state prosecutor of Stalin's Moscow
trials; ER's UN nemesis

ADLAI E. STEVENSON II (1900–1965)
Governor of Illinois; Democratic nominee for President, 1952,
1956

VII. WORLDMAKER (1947–1962)

ARNO DAVID GUREWITSCH (1902–1974); David
Personal physician; intimate friend

NEMONE BALFOUR (1906–1989)
Musician, singer; David Gurewitsch's (first) spouse

EDNA PERKEL GUREWITSCH (1924–)
Art gallery curator; David's (second) spouse

MARTHA GELLHORN (1908–1998)
Journalist; war correspondent

GEORGE C. MARSHALL (1880–1959)
U.S. secretary of state, 1947–1949

ANNE LINDSAY CLARK (1916–1973)
John's (first) spouse

ANNA STURGIS ROOSEVELT GIBSON (1942–); Nina
Granddaughter

SARAH DELANO ROOSEVELT (1946–1960); Sally
Granddaughter

FRANCIS SPELLMAN (1889–1967)
Catholic prelate, cardinal archbishop of New York

JOHN FITZGERALD KENNEDY (1917–1963)
35th U.S. President

CARMINE DE SAPIO (1908–2004)
Last Tammany boss, 1949–1961

ALLARD K. LOWENSTEIN (1929–1980)
   Democratic activist; politician
HENRY MORGENTHAU III (1917–2018)
   Television producer, *Prospects of Mankind*, 1959–1962
MAUREEN CORR (1917–2009)
   Last personal secretary
DAVID GRAY (1870–1968); Uncle David
   Aunt Maude's (second) spouse; family ally
JAMES A. HALSTED (1905–1984)
   Anna's (third) spouse; medical doctor; pioneer of group medical
   practice

I

GRANNY

I seemed like a little old woman.

E.R.[1]

ONE

I n February 1884, just as Anna Hall Roosevelt learned that she was pregnant, a blinding fog closed over Manhattan. Thicker and heavier than any in recent memory, it shut the city down for days.[1]

Late on February 12, the fifth straight night of precautionary bells tolling along rails and rivers,[2] Anna's husband, Elliott Roosevelt, was summoned through the filthy gray cloud to the family townhouse at 6 West Fifty-Seventh Street. His brother Theodore's "flower-like" young wife,[3] Alice Lee Roosevelt, had given birth to their first child, also Alice. Elliott wired the happy news to Albany, where Theodore, only twenty-five, was in his third term as the blond, side-whiskered "Cyclone Assemblyman," crusading against machine politics, corruption, and "that most dangerous of all dangerous classes, the wealthy criminal class."[4]

But delivery had gravely weakened the mother, and by next evening everything was falling apart. "There is a curse on this house," groaned Elliott to his younger sister, Corinne.[5] By the time Theodore burst through the front door, his wife was semi-comatose from Bright's disease while, a floor below, his mother, fifty-year-old Mittie Bulloch Roosevelt, sank beneath acute typhoid fever. By three in the morning, Mittie was gone.

By two that afternoon Alice had died in Theodore's arms, only twenty-two. It was St. Valentine's Day.

The double catastrophe knocked the surviving Roosevelts entirely off course. Putting the city of death behind him, Theodore stumbled west to his Dakota ranch, leaving his older sister, Anna, known as Bamie (pronounced "BAM-ie"), to take care of little Alice.

For Elliott, twenty-four and unmoored by the loss of his mother, Alice Lee Roosevelt's death cast a dread of fatherhood over his wife's recently established pregnancy. Anna herself now feared that child-

birth would kill her. The whole family was wracked with apprehensions.[6]

LESS THAN EIGHT MONTHS LATER, on a fair, breezy Saturday, October 11, 1884, Anna and Elliott's little girl was born—at eleven in
the morning, behind the brownstone front of 29 East Thirty-Eighth
Street.[7] Her birth coincided with the last rusty quarter of October's
"blood moon," an orange rind rising over Gotham that night at ten
minutes past eleven.[8]

In years to come, when editing her father's letters, she would introduce her birth into the family epic as the first clear footprint in a
dark trail: "Life treads so closely on the heels of death!"[9] So painfully
did she associate labor and delivery with inescapable doom that when
she recalled bearing her first child in 1906, she dwelled on the resignation that closed over her: "This was something I could do nothing
about—the child would come when it would come, as inevitably as
death itself."[10]

She had no birth certificate. Her parents somehow let her arrival
go unrecorded in the municipal archives,[11] instead marking her name
in a family Bible, at the head of a new page of births: *Anna*, for her
mother and her father's elder sister; *Eleanor*, from Elliott's childhood
nicknames, Ellie and Nell.

Her father embraced her as a "miracle from Heaven," though Elliott and Anna had been hoping for a male heir, a "precious boy jr"[12] to
put an end to the Roosevelt clan's "plague," as one biographer would
term the family's recent "sending of girls."[13] Time was on Anna's side.
She was twenty-one, with a healthy baby,[14] a dashing husband, and her
horizons open wide.

BUT THE YOUNG PARENTS HAD already begun to drift.

Their first discovery was that each was set on being the loved
one. Each deeply needed the other's attention and esteem: both were
acutely sensitive to disapproval.[15] One or the other was always pouting
in a dark room, injustice hanging its sulky cloud in the hallways, meals
on trays creaking with reproachful indignation upstairs.

Time, if still on their side, was carelessly weaponized. Elliott never came home in the evening when he had said he would, and Anna on no occasion appeared downstairs before nine in the morning. To compound her punishment of his lateness, she was eternally declining a previously accepted invitation with the excuse that she was "not feeling my best and . . . on my back."[16] One languorous midafternoon Anna admitted, "If I followed my own inclinations I would never move off the piazza," nevertheless ruefully conceding: "But this I know would not do."

Elliott, bounding off to a drag-hunt, was always just getting back freshly bandaged from a fall. At one Wednesday match in 1885, his mallet went into his eyeglasses, leaving glass particles in his right eye. He raised eyecup after eyecup to cleanse it, suffering agonies until Thursday morning, when a doctor could at last come to pluck out the grit. "It still continues to be very painful," reported Anna to Bamie, notably on the letterhead of HOTEL SHELBURN, FIFTH AVENUE, N.Y., where she retreated the following Monday.[17]

The summer of '85 passed in bouts of moody concealment alternated with bursts of almost willed gaiety. Elliott's letters are frantic, forever repeating lines already written, oblivious of what he has said to whom. Amid his frothing, not one mention of Eleanor, now ten months old. Instead, both parents endlessly analyze the quality of polo being played, while Elliott is privately consumed by Anna's snobbery, brittleness, headaches.

At summer's end, finally, after some "very pleasant old time days" at Oak Lawn, the Halls' summer house on the Hudson's east bank above Tivoli, we encounter the first recorded appearance of a one-day-to-be-world-famous feature: "Little Eleanor is looking so well, and her four little pearly front teeth have altered the entire expression of the face to quite a pretty one."[18]

HER FATHER AND MOTHER TOOK their little girl upriver from Manhattan to visit Elliott's elder Dutchess County cousin, James Roosevelt; his young second wife, Sara; and their son, Franklin, who was, Eleanor later liked to say, the first person she remembered.[19]

The Hyde Park Roosevelts awaited the Oyster Bay Roosevelts at their ornamental farmhouse overlooking the river. Six years before, the widowed James, fifty-two, had met Sara Delano, twenty-six, introduced by Elliott's sister Bamie at a family dinner celebrating Theodore's Harvard commencement. They married four months later, sailing for Liverpool on the same ship aboard which Elliott was staging his passage to India. The mixed-age newlyweds were only too happy to leave the impression of being the twenty-year-old Elliott's "aunt and uncle"[20] and to make their London hotel suite the wayfarer's headquarters. Barely had he returned in March 1882 than he stood godfather to the newborn Franklin; and now, still dashing, he pressed a gold watch fob on his four-year-old godson.[21] "Generosity," Eleanor would write, "actuated him."[22]

In the nursery at Hyde Park, the children played horsie, Franklin on all fours, gamely or under protest (the story would be told both ways) trotting Eleanor off to Boston. Afterward, they were called down to tea. Eleanor, a grave little girl with bangs falling over a worried brow, would be mocked by her mother again and again in these years for her unsmiling seriousness.

Anna wanted her daughter to be precisely as she, Anna, was; saving that, a fine reflection. "Eleanor, I hardly know what's to happen to you," she would say, in legend, if not in fact. "You're so plain that you really have nothing to do except *be good*."[23] But good as she was, and saddled in Anna's eyes by what Henry Adams with flat New England relish called "the Roosevelt coarseness of feature and figure,"[24] she could not satisfy her mother's requirements. Her one legitimate and physiological flaw was a curvature of the spine, which would be fitted with a back brace and require painful treatment at the special hospital that her grandfather had established.[25]

Whether or not the discomfort of the brace contributed to Eleanor's awkwardness on this visit, she was, by her own account, made nervous that day. Eleanor's lifelong eagerness to deprecate her childhood self as "a rather ugly little girl"[26] is contradicted by such contemporaneous sources as *Frank Leslie's Illustrated Newspaper*, out of which pops "a lovely little daughter, a dainty little maid."[27]

But that afternoon in Hyde Park—as so often in these years—

Eleanor almost at once lowered her eyes, as if just by being there she was disgracing her mother. Summoned to tea in the library, she stood head-down by the door. Franklin's parents became early witnesses to the ritualized humiliation that would be inflicted upon her in the years just ahead, as often as not in front of company.

"Come in," called Anna, focusing all eyes on Eleanor. "Come in, *Granny*."[28]

"From then on," Eleanor would write, "what she had said was constantly in my mind."[29] The shame she carried shaped her relationships all her early life.

THE YEAR 1886 BISECTED THE thirty-year span in which the nation's industrial wealth soared from $30 billion to nearly $127 billion.[30] As Vanderbilt, Morgan, and Rockefeller combined their respective interests into a new kind of beast—frighteningly large corporations sucking up and pumping out yet more hundreds of millions; wealth, in short, as an end in itself—such old-guard Knickerbockers as the Roosevelts and the Halls could do little better than run in place. Or run poorly for mayor, as Theodore had impetuously done, not waiting his turn, and finishing a humiliating third.[31] Or they could subscribe to newly emerging closed-gate institutions—chiefly the New York *Social Register*, launched in 1887—which fortified their former distinction and encouraged the almost primitive use of a "stud book," as the *Social Register* came to be called, to choose a mate with whom to maintain the "purity" of the tribe.[32]

Anna's family, the Halls, were still comfortable in town and country, but not so relatively rich as when they had been in full possession of one of the larger real estate fortunes in brownstone New York.[33] Anna's grandfather Valentine Hall, Sr., among the most respected of Gotham real estate magnates, had become richer still by marrying his partner's daughter. Anna's father, Valentine Hall, Jr., and aunt, Margaret, consolidated the family's upswing by marrying siblings from the still-feudal Hudson Valley gentry, the Ludlow branch of Livingstons, which took great pride in tracing its bloodline to the best-known Revolutionary-era Livingstons.

Anna's mother, Mary Livingston Ludlow Hall, herself the only daughter of a highly esteemed Manhattan real estate broker, Dr. Edward Hunter Ludlow, had been reassured by her lawyer in November 1883 that she and her children were in very good shape. Mary, known as G'ma, or Grandmother Hall, was living on income from about $200,000 in investments, and the children's inheritances of several million each had "not only been preserved for them wholly unimpaired, but, taken as a whole, [had] actually quite largely increased in value, and this, too, during times of extraordinary adversity and ruinous falling in prices."[34]

So for the moment Anna had enough to feel secure[35]—but only just: some $15,000 a year with Elliott's income added in.[36] But Elliott was in trouble. His agile, sporting dandyism only made him *look* successful. Increasingly he was drawn not to his office downtown but out to Long Island—to foxhunt and play polo at the Meadow Brook Hunt Club, newly established at the edge of the Hempstead Plains. For young men like Elliott and Theodore—children during the Civil War—foxhunting in the 1880s was a test of horsemanship and, therefore, of warrior courage. Riding to hounds was their generation's chance to practice martial leadership.

The Roosevelts had been in New York since 1649. Their fortune traced back to Eleanor's great-grandfather Cornelius Van Schaack "CVS" Roosevelt, who became one of Manhattan's five richest landowners and a founder of the Chemical National Bank, the city's only financial institution that never failed to honor its obligations in gold. Dying in 1871, CVS left the largest fortune ever probated in Manhattan—ten million dollars ($222 million in today's money). His four sons carried the Roosevelt enterprise from the old Dutch merchant community of Maiden Lane into twentieth-century investment banking, especially as key members of the great underwriting syndicates for transport and communications bonds, notably those of the Great Northern Railroad and the American Atlantic and Central and South American Cable companies, the latter acquired by the All-America Cable Company, which in turn would be snapped up by the future International Telephone and Telegraph (I.T.T.);[37] all reflecting the city's own story, as a consolidating New York flowered into the financial capital of the greatest industrial civilization ever seen. The Roosevelts came to embody, in serious part, what Edith Wharton, voice of the understated old patriciate, would denounce as "this modern newspaper rubbish about a New York aristocracy," sharply reminding her readers in 1920 that "our grandfathers and great-grandfathers were just respectable English or Dutch merchants."[38]

Sometimes styled the "Oyster Bay Roosevelts" from the summer colony CVS had established thirty-four miles eastward on the north shore of Long Island, Eleanor's father's family was identified by a curious dark complexion;[39] startlingly pale-blue eyes; intense, captivating interest in those they met; heated, almost frothy, excitements within the family circle alongside their confidently demanding criticisms of one another; a set determination to hold on where others let go; a gift for overdoing things; and, above all other impulses, the resolve to transform private misfortune into public well-being.

WHILE ELLIOTT MORE AND MORE sloughed off his city business, Uncle Ted returned from London—where he had quietly and happily married their childhood playmate Edith Kermit Carow—and took up residence at Sagamore Hill, the Queen Anne shingle-style house he had built on Cove Neck, northeast of Oyster Bay village, overlooking Long Island's north shore. The first of five children, Theodore Jr., arrived in September 1887, and by the following summer Edith was pregnant again.[40]

By 1887, meanwhile, Elliott was still trying to be a New York gentleman of 1870. Booze was one test: to maintain control while poisoning oneself. Steeplechases were another: he whose hand trembled first, or whose boot slipped the stirrup, showed himself a weakling. But was it horsemanship that saw him over each of sixty post-and-rail fences, or just the headlong flight of a man too soused to be killed? Even during these good years, his polo was jaggedly uneven. Meadow Brook teammates Stanley Y. Mortimer, who would marry Anna's sister Tissie, and Winthrop Rutherfurd, future husband of Lucy Mercer, had to be counted on for the winning goal—since, as Anna now wincingly noticed, "Elliott can barely stay on his pony."[41]

"Poor Nell, I was so awfully sorry for you last night," she wrote, reminding him of his "promise not to touch any champagne tonight. It is poison truly & how I dread seeing you suffer."[42] The more he indulged, the less Anna could be his partner, instead obliged to serve in the dominant strict-nurse role that Elliott loved best to maneuver beneath and around. "You know a chap loves to be ruled over by a lovely woman," he once confessed to Corinne.[43]

In Theodore's head-on male view, Anna was sissifying his brother.[44] As for Anna's habit of ordering dresses from Worth in Paris, Theodore felt certain that her "utterly frivolous life" was "[eating] into her character like an acid." Cousin John Ellis Roosevelt, himself having chosen two wrong wives, "wondered why he married her"[45] and blamed Anna for "making" Elliott "play in with the fast Meadow Brook set."

In fact, Elliott had already lost more ground than his Oyster Bay clan knew, not just in the money game or at the club bar. His confidence wore away as he found himself less and less able to metabolize his abundant energies into lasting satisfactions. His acute imagination briefly moved him to gather his notes and letters from India to turn into a book, but he got no further than an article for Boone and Crockett, the hunting club he and Theodore helped found.[46] He, too, saw a place for himself in Republican politics, not far behind that which his brother had already won, but he could not get going—and, not having to do anything, he did nothing, except marinate in his own simmering feelings. He took a connoisseur's pleasure in victimized unfulfillment.

Greater planets than Elliott Roosevelt were rising. Shivering in his own shadow, he planned another solution to the overripe Long Island life of risk and liquor: to sail for Liverpool in the spring of 1887—and thereafter, who knew? He, Anna, and Anna's closest sister, Tissie, now a ravishing twenty-one, along with the two-and-a-half-year-old Eleanor and a nursemaid, could well become Whartonian "continental wanderers."[47]

Which in their case meant that, late in the afternoon of May 19, the Roosevelts found themselves lost in another fog nearly four hundred miles southeast of Nantucket, as two White Star liners misguidedly steamed full ahead,[48] bells clanging.[49]

ALL DAY THE WEATHER HAD been calm, the sea smooth. Since eleven the night before a dense whiteness had blanketed the seaways.[50] The 5,004-ton flagship *Britannic*,[51] a day from New York, held course for England. The 3,867-ton *Celtic*, outbound from Liverpool, had veered south to avoid the Long Island shoals, and was by now sixty miles off her scheduled track. By 5:25 p.m., these square-rigged sailing steamers had drawn to within three hundred muffled yards of each other, the fog banking so mountainously as to hide even their towering black masts from each other's lookouts.

On the uppermost deck, *Britannic*'s first-class passengers were gathering at the rail for the thrill of seeing two mutually invisible White Star consorts maneuvering past each other through a North Atlantic pea-souper. Most captains still considered it sound practice to accelerate through fog, or in this case to race to safety beyond the other vessel. The superior classes, who had just taken tea, interpreted this contretemps as a kind of transoceanic sporting diversion. In pairs they rallied on deck to cheer on their peppery-bearded captain before retiring to dress for dinner.

In their gilded White Star stateroom, Elliott and Anna sensed no danger whatsoever as the fog whistles shrilled back and forth. They left Eleanor in her nurse's care and proceeded with their dinner preparations. More than forty years after the maritime drama, Eleanor would still write, "I never liked fog."[52]

OUT OF THE SHROUDED SEA like a shark's fin drove the *Celtic*'s bow.[53] Panicked, Captain Perry gave the order to put on all steam.[54] Luckily the first blow struck just behind the engine room—a second earlier, and *Britannic* would have gone straight down. Perry's gamble in maintaining top speed had in that respect paid off. Still, it was a direct hit, and no two steamships had ever collided without one sinking.[55]

Celtic rebounded on her own momentum. The second blow struck at a perfect right angle to split *Britannic*'s quarterdeck rail, scoop away three lifeboats, topple rigging, demolish 180 feet of steerage deck, and mutilate passengers as her prow cut ten feet into an aft steerage compartment.[56] Still under her own full steam, *Britannic* dragged *Celtic* some hundred yards forward,[57] only to sustain one more swipe as *Celtic* staggered away, leaving a last long gash at the waterline and opening *Britannic*'s No. 4 hold to the sea. In the stove-in steerage compartment, where four passengers had been killed outright, "all was the wildest confusion."[58]

Britannic was taking on water. *Celtic*, uninjured except for a dramatically holed bow that would be patched with mattresses, got lifeboats away for *Britannic* soon enough.[59] Captain Perry had given the order for lifebelts and lifeboats, but panic had already swept the ship: *She was on her way to the bottom.*[60]

AMONG THE LIFEBELTED LADIES ON Promenade Deck it had taken a few minutes for grim dismay to pass into tight-lipped resolution. "The strain," Anna Roosevelt would recall, "was fearful though there were no screams and no milling about. Everyone was perfectly quiet."[61]

Anna's response to crisis, whether aboard a panic-ridden steamer or at home whispering over some society scandal in *Town Topics*,[62] was to conduct herself with a coldly unassailable elegance. Passionately dispassionate, her one enthusiasm lay in refusing to concede that she was subject to intense feeling, even if her husband was intemperate—as was beginning to be murmured—and most especially if two decks below lay the hideously congealing remains of a man cut in two by a force-pump.

Historians would be tempted to find in Eleanor's diminutive presence on the sinking, class-bound *Britannic* a magically receptive eyewitness, uniquely able to perceive distress. But what she grasped from the chaos of the collision (along with a lifelong preference for dry land, and chronic anxiety about open water and boats and swimming and heights) was the same frightened impression that fellow passengers reported: "I remember only that there was wild confusion."[63]

For the next hour, the waters steadily brought down *Britannic*'s riven stern—first two, then six, then eight feet into the slapping sea, pitching the bow ever more steeply upward. Women and children waited to be taken off in orderly clusters, while the men around them panicked.[64] More than thirty minutes went by before the distressed vessel got a single lifeboat free.[65]

When the first fully loaded boat jammed on the port side, sailors spent fifteen minutes hunting for a blade to cut it loose. The Hall-Roosevelt women were put into a lifeboat commanded by Third Officer Mencken, and Eleanor's turn to board came. She had to be passed down over water, which terrified her. She fought, shrieking frantically as she hung over the side, then locked onto a sailor's neck, making it impossible to lower her down the hull to her father, who was standing in the boat below, shouting encouragement with upstretched arms.

But how had Elliott got into the lifeboat? Other family men like him were duty-bound to remain on board, obeying the spine-stiffening statutes of the Birkenhead Drill, which had established the doctrine of "women and children first" specifically to head off the rushes that had overwhelmed so many lifeboats. One eyewitness saw the shorthanded Third Officer Mencken order Elliott into the boat, not just to catch his daughter but to help row the survivors to safety. Elliott was remembered to have been cool, collected, and generous in his assistance to the third officer; and Mencken later said that had Roosevelt *not* followed his command, Mencken would have had to make what then looked to be a 350-mile row with one oar short.[66]

Collis P. Huntington, dynamo of California's Big Four railroad and industrial oligarchy, saw it differently: through the eyes of a sixty-five-year-old big wheel, who had repeatedly proved himself through ruthless self-reliance.[67] His anger against Knickerbocker exclusiveness may have distorted his take on Elliott's conduct.[68] Huntington was then negotiating to raise a Fifth Avenue castle a few doors from the Roosevelts, but this cutthroat Western kingpin so threatened Vanderbilt railroad interests that he and his second wife had been barred from that apex of New York society where Anna shone brightest.

Whatever private animus Huntington may have felt, he took every advantage as First Mogul of the ship to tell the *New York World* that Roosevelt and a fellow passenger, the Wall Street banker John Paton, had lost their heads and forced their way into a boat.[69] Paton had in fact been ordered by the captain aboard a lifeboat with *his* wife and daughter, but unlike Roosevelt, the well-known Scotsman had refused[70]—as men like them were expected to—and would take the trouble to clear himself of the charges publicly.

All this whipsawed Elliott, exposing him to gloating innuendo at this moment of putting New York and Oyster Bay behind him. By following orders and fleeing to safety, Elliott had submitted to a lesser fate, with its endless sour consequences.

NEITHER *BRITANNIC* NOR *CELTIC* WENT down. Patched up but still leaking, the liners limped back to New York in consort, crawling in after two harrowing days and three tense nights. Huntington's smear had winged ahead to the *World*, filling the news vacuum with excited rumor and speculation as multitudes awaited the ships' maimed return. Society columns in the *New York Times* held that Elliott's conduct had not been a straightforward matter of obedience to duty: "The etiquette of disasters at sea had better be compiled at once," took up the *Times*, "for there seems to be a wide difference of opinion as to the course a man should pursue, placed as Mr. Roosevelt was."[71]

Tugboats dispatched to meet the ships brought the survivors in off the bar, passing the strangely reassuring new colossus just raised by Frédéric-Auguste Bartholdi—a handsome giantess lifting her arm to welcome anyone seeking refuge from a world of accident and trouble.

Back on dry land, the Roosevelts and Aunt Tissie paused barely a day before boarding the next ship for Liverpool. Elliott, now being called "the only man to leave the *Britannic*,"[72] was determined to sail at once. But Eleanor would not go. She wept at the first mention of another crossing; by one account, she "shook at even the thought of going to sea again."[73] She was certain that nothing but terror awaited her on open water. Nor was she by any means alone in her feelings: on May 23, the *New York Times* urged *all* prospective transatlantic tourists to take "serious thoughts" before sailing again.[74]

But, as so often in her girlhood, it was she who was made to feel disgraced and guilty for being "a terrified and determined little girl."[75] Going by the story that would be "told [her] many times," Eleanor imagined that she had been responsible for putting her father's honor on the line. Moreover, by her commonsense refusal to go back to sea, she had now cast herself as the family coward, and would ever after put herself into the collision narrative as a "timid child," an obstacle to her parents' smoothly resumed passage.[76]

Happily, one adult in the family showed every sign of being able to understand and vindicate her response. Her grandmother Roosevelt's half sister, Aunt Annie Gracie, saw that Eleanor was "so little and gentle & had made such a narrow escape out of the great ocean . . . it made her seem doubly helpless & pathetic to us," and shepherded Eleanor out to Oyster Bay. Anna Louisa Bulloch and her husband, the kindly New York broker James King Gracie,[77] had served Eleanor's father's generation as "an extra set of parents."[78] Now Eleanor's great-aunt would be the first in her long line of surrogate mothers.

Two or three times on the way out to Long Island, she asked where her mother and father and Aunt Tissie were. As soon as she was settled at Gracewood,[79] the architecturally daring shingle "cottage" which Uncle and Aunt Gracie had just built, her aunt gave her tea on the new piazza: "the best tea I could, to make up to her for her little lonely table with only one little person at it."[80]

Eleanor sat quietly eating her aunt's stewed prunes, oatmeal biscuits, and bread and butter. But whenever she glimpsed a sail on the Sound, or heard the slopping of the sea, or later, whenever her aunt and uncle took her on a drive along the shore, she quavered, "Baby does not want to go in the water. Not in a boat."[81]

From across the open Atlantic, Anna confided to "Aunt Annie" that she ached at having deserted Eleanor, "but know it was wiser to leave her."[82] Safely installed at the St. James's Club, Piccadilly, Elliott could now report: "I have been delighted with our trip so far, though the Hall girls are a large contract to handle for a boy of my age and weight."[83] After shopping sprees in leafy Victorian London, sojourns at country houses, coaching parties, river-punting, and fashionably cosmopolitan dinners, Elliott marveled at "the girls'" social successes, at which he was "content with a back seat."[84]

The rest of her parents' summer jottings are notable only for their entire self-absorption, the triviality of Elliott's pursuits, and at least one six-hour British Isles edition of Anna's headaches.[85] On her side of the ocean, Eleanor asked her aunt: "Where is baby's home now?"[86] Even more pressing and unutterable: Who in the world was going to raise Eleanor?

TWO

W HEN THEY CAME FOR THEIR child, after "a very good September in Scotland," Eleanor's parents had settled on where to
live.[1] Their town address for the New York season would be 56 West
Thirty-Seventh Street, and Elliott would join Uncle Gracie's banking
and brokerage house. The following spring, that of 1888, they broke
ground for a country place near Hempstead, Long Island.[2] By mid-
July, Elliott could report to Bamie: "It looks fairly under way now and
promises well. Baby Eleanor goes up to look after it every day and calls
it hers."[3]

Eleanor's childhood-home-to-be—"a very fine country seat . . . a
spacious and expensive mansion," enthused *Frank Leslie's Illustrated
Weekly*[4]—was slowly rising on ten acres freshly carved from the
wooded upland of Meadow Brook Park.[5] Her parents called the place
Half-Way Nirvana—a joke encapsulating its incompleteness as much
as their own.

Through all family movements that summer, Eleanor remained
cheerful as a finch, so long as she could be on dry land with her father.
To be close to him was bliss. "I wanted," she later conceded, "to be
loved so badly, and most of all I wanted to be loved by my father."[6]
In pictures from this time, Elliott turns to Eleanor, as completely absorbed as a mother in a Mary Cassatt painting. He liked to lean close,
so that their foreheads met. Then, with a soulful gaze into her eyes,
he would say, "Let's have a Chinese kiss," and they would rub noses.[7]

Eleanor had pets at Half-Way Nirvana, and lessons with wonderful Aunt Gracie,[8] and regularly scheduled picnics and playtimes with
her slightly older but scary and often sassy Cousin Alice, which she
enjoyed. On these dates, as was so often the case, her mother's approval
lay with the other child. But so long as Father kept his eyes on her—
and she could dance for him and the other gentlemen around the din-

ner table, pirouetting until her father swept her high in his arms, their eyes fixed into each other's in the twirling ecstasy of the moment—her happiness flowed.

"Our happy family life on Long Island," she would caption this brief spell.[9]

ON ELEANOR'S BIG DAY, OCTOBER 11, 1887, Anna moved herself to send from wherever she was "just a line to wish you a very happy birthday & many of them. Write me all about how you spend the day & give Mother's love to Aunty and Uncle. Mother wishes she could be with you to see all the fun and play some of the games. I enclose a letter from Father to you. With fond love from your devoted Mother."[10]

The recipient was three.

The pathos of Eleanor's early childhood is that of "the little old woman"—a warm, dependable senior adult, a "Granny"—who must mother herself.

"I don't believe her mother treated her as a human being at all," recalled one childhood playmate.[11]

Eleanor, in turn, treated Anna as an immortal, a "distant and beautiful thing that I couldn't possibly get close to"[12] but which could be "admired inordinately" as a "vision" clad in garments and adornments that she felt "grateful to be allowed to touch."[13]

The following October 11, 1888, her father observed, "The funny little tot had a happy little birthday, and ended by telling me, when saying good-night (after Anna heard her say her prayers) that she loved everybody and everybody loved her. Was it not cunning?"[14]

It was his spell. *She* had something to give *him*.

FIRST THING EVERY MORNING, SHE tiptoed into Elliott's bedroom and enacted their ritual of making sure that he was up. As often as not he would be still in bed, and it was Eleanor's job to warn him that he was late for breakfast, and to get him on his feet.[15]

Eleanor, at four, understood the wayward boy Elliott better than Anna ever wanted to. Daughter managed father as his nurse-companion, and the reversal fascinated Elliott. Playfully, he used Eleanor's sweet concern to reprove himself; he had a painting made from a

favorite photograph of his tiny guardian, in which the wise child Eleanor appears with a straight bang across her forehead, finger raised in
admonition—an image he canonized as "Little Nell scolding Elliott."[16]

These morning rituals projected a hopeful existence in which she
was loved by the man who was "the center of my world."[17] They were
the singular deliverance from a childhood that would appear in the
adult Eleanor's memory as "one long battle against fear."[18]

Her terror of ships and the sea was nothing compared with the
vertiginous panic that overtook her on being swung into the saddle.
The morning her father announced that it was time she learned to
ride, the world below her booted feet fell away like the sea below *Britannic*. But there was nothing for her to do but walk the pony on—
Elliott Roosevelt's daughter was going to be a horsewoman. When
he complimented her at the end of that first session, she knew no
greater happiness. Going out on horseback never got easier, but the
more she learned to accept her fear of it, the less she dreaded disappointing him.

Her father was the kind of alcoholic upon whom the first drink of
the day never failed to effect a complete transformation.[19] At this stage
of addiction, however, he was not yet slumped in a chair from breakfast onward, brandy and water and tincture of opium by his side. But
neither had he conceded that alcohol and medications were vigilantly
waiting to roll him over. "Do dear throw your horrid cocktails away,"
Anna dared to plead, yet carefully equivocating, "I wonder if this last
is asking too much."[20]

That spring of 1889, he could leave such entreaties unanswered,
having persuaded himself that he was still the master of his glass, that
he could take it or leave it—and take it he did, counting on a drunk
man's luck to bounce him through the next steeplechase, but really
waiting for the game to get him.

Anna struggled to know how to respond to her husband's smash-
ups. And did as she did with all things: she took a step back. "I do
love you so and want you to be my darling strong boy," she affirmed.
"I think I would be the happiest woman living if you would ever be
well and give up all wines and medicines."[21] But when Anna kept her
distance, Eleanor jumped to fill the gap. The messier side of her fa-

ther's life as a sportsman became her special domain.[22] Looking after the dressings for a broken collarbone or pulled muscle, she showed herself uncannily gifted at responding to each fresh hurt.[23]

IT WAS A DOUBLE SOMERSAULT in dress rehearsal for James Waterbury's lavish Society Circus that got him.[24] On sight, Dr. Keyes diagnosed a sprain, bandaged his foot, and sent Elliott home. But the swelling never went down, the throbbing never lessened, and after two grim weeks, he went to his own Dr. Shaffer, who took off the first bandage and, amid the resulting sour stench, informed Elliott that Keyes's mishandling had put him in a good way to getting "a fine Club foot."[25]

One morning late in June, Eleanor came to his room and was confided something that terrified her. The foot, still not healing properly, would have to be re-broken and reset. Dr. Shaffer was waiting downstairs to take him away for surgery. Helpless, Eleanor watched her father rise and hobble out. This was the turning point: "From this illness, my father never quite recovered."[26]

Had there been any possibility of Eleanor's experiencing the joys or even routine of childhood, that time was now passing. In August, she was sent away to Grandmother Hall's, and at Tivoli learned that her brother Elliott Roosevelt, Jr., had been born on September 29. She wrote a letter to her father, in which she wished her parents well, offered advice to the baby's nurse should the newborn cry, then came straight to the crucial question about any child of Anna Roosevelt's: "How does he look? Some people tell me he looks like an elephant and some say he is like a bunny."[27]

Except for one pitiable moment at Half-Way Nirvana when Eleanor identified an Angora kitten as an "Angostura,"[28] those aromatic bitters that flavored her father's liquor, she showed few signs of registering the impact of addiction on their lives. "Little Eleanor is as happy as the day is long," Elliott convinced himself during the heavy self-medicated month following his accident: "Plays with her kitten, the puppy & the chickens all the time & is very dirty as a general rule. I am the only 'off' member of the family."[29]

By year's end, her father was in free fall, taking a cure somewhere in the South. He disappeared without saying good-bye, leaving Eleanor hurrying daily to greet the postman. "I told her," Anna wrote Elliott, "you would not be here for two weeks and she seemed awfully disappointed, but was quite satisfied when I told her you were getting well."[30] Even more than wellness, Anna wanted nothing to seem wrong.

That winter of 1890, she stood at last within reach of her goal. The old social hurdle of Mrs. Astor's guest list of "four hundred" had dissolved as New York increasingly became the clearinghouse for industrial prosperity, and every manufacturing mogul from the Middle West or mining king from the Rockies now hurried to *the* American city to add his own marble fortress to the steam-wreathed skyline of Vanderbilt and Morgan. More than a thousand millionaires could now claim crowns on the king line of the Gotham playing board;[31] and as the new game opened at the New Year's Eve Ball, held for the first time at the Metropolitan Opera,[32] Anna stood as a social leader of the new age, receiving as one of three patronesses representing the old sovereign houses—the Astors, the Vanderbilts, the Roosevelts.[33]

Elliott's winter rest cure had meanwhile failed. To maintain basic equilibrium and bodily function he now depended on tipping the laudanum bottle, droplet by blood-muddy droplet. Laudanum was sold without a prescription, as readily available as a cough-suppressant or sleeping potion.[34] When he resumed such life as was possible at home, Anna noticed that his excitements had risen to the level of the "unnatural,"[35] and his riding had become so erratic that during one spill he for the first time was kicked in the head.[36] His night side was unloosed by the alcohol-laudanum regimen. Loaded, he rambled the sleeping house; no one knew whom he would next awaken.[37]

"What do you mean when you say he threatens awful things?" asked Theodore of Bamie.

"He has long talked of suicide," she replied.[38]

Three times that spring he vowed to end his life,[39] each crisis staging up from domestic incidents. When he turned up unannounced and jittery during tea at Aunt Gracie's or dinner at Corinne's, he inflamed the company with his agitated talk, then ran off again, leaving his aunt and sister in anguish. Even the smallest tender gesture now struck them as "the old Elliott."[40]

His boyish excitability still surfaced, but all too quickly escalated through irritability to brutal fury to stormy exits. "He was manic-depressive and went off on these terrific binges," recalled Cousin Corinnie. "Yet there was nobody that my mother loved better or that Mrs. Gracie loved better. He must have had something that was specially attractive and appealing."[41]

Elliott's flair for stirring up the females of his family manifests throughout the Roosevelt archives, starting with the long-distance caressing of his eternally girlish mother and ending on the same note with his prematurely aged daughter. Even a parental admonition to Eleanor to stop chewing her fingernails came tricked out in the snuggling pillow talk that Elliott could never resist: "Take good care of those cunning wee hands that Father so loves to be petted by."[42]

When the servants at Half-Way Nirvana began to tease Catharine "Katie" Mann, the Roosevelts' twenty-seven-year-old German housemaid, about Elliott's interest in her, Anna ignored the chatter. The family lawyer would soon learn that Elliott had given Katie Mann a gold locket,[43] written her letters professing love, and somehow formalized the notion[44] of Katie as his "spiritual wife."[45] The servants' idea that Miss Mann had "been a good deal in [Elliott's] room"[46] was true; as was, yet more indefensibly, their suspicion that Elliott's voice had one night been heard in her room.[47]

Anna's refusal to acknowledge the facts, her fixed smile as terrible things now regularly unfolded and were just as regularly shoveled under the carpet, shielded Eleanor from some of the collateral damage of her father's decline. Telling the story of her childhood in later life, she described what it had been like to see her father dead drunk, even as she insisted that he had never shown *her* "any treatment or behavior that was horrifying in any way."[48]

But by then rumors were circulating. Elliott's more staid contemporaries eyed him askance. Ominous insinuations landed ever closer to the truth.[49] "Sometimes they would whisper," wrote Corinne, "saying, 'Poor fellow, he will die some day with [his] boots on, in some cheap and drunken brawl.'"[50] Practical warnings reached as far off as Washington, where Elizabeth Sherman Cameron observed to Henry Adams: "Elliott seems to be quite out of his head."[51]

In July, Anna finally put her foot down and announced that they would all leave for San Moritz at once. Tissie would have them at her villa, where she was now expanding into the international high life as Mrs. Stanley Mortimer. They exiled themselves on July 21, embarking from the lower-visibility piers of Boston, and giving the reporters to understand that they were going abroad to treat Elliott's unhealed foot.

IN THE VIENNA OF SIGMUND Freud's new "talking cure," Elliott consulted with a rising star of pathological anatomy, Dr. Erwin von Graff,[52] who committed him (none too hopefully) to the Mariengrund sanitarium. Bamie, her patience tried once too often, refused to let him out of her sight. She persuaded the spa officials to overlook the rules and rent her a room, from which she informed Theodore: "It apparently never occurs to his mind for one instant that he is in any way responsible for anything he does, or, for what he brings on Anna."[53]

Within days, Elliott had abruptly terminated treatment, hastily packing the family off for Paris. Anna, pregnant again, was advised by her doctor to break the journey into three, perhaps four, stages; but Elliott rejected this "poppycock," and arranged to go right through.[54]

"Anna is always in a terribly hard position," decided Bamie, "for while she may have made many mistakes in judgment I do not see how she can cope with such an utterly impossible person."[55]

In New York, Katie Mann gave birth to a boy, whom she named Elliott and calmly presented for examination to a phrenological expert hired by the Roosevelt family lawyer. She wanted $10,000 to help support Elliott Roosevelt Mann[56]—a sum far closer in 1891 dollars to capital investment than to upkeep of a working-class mother and child. Yet if the Roosevelts did not come up with this, she would bring suit and take the scandal public. Elliott disputed the claim, crying blackmail, but privately confessed to Anna that he could not say for certain whether or not he had fathered the boy.[57]

Anna took a house in Neuilly-sur-Seine, just inside the Paris limits—to be closer to the "very noted" French doctor whom Bamie had engaged for her prenatal care and delivery.[58] But the doctor refused to make calls after dark; and it was only because he had fallen in love with Anna that he made himself available when a boy, Gracie

Hall Roosevelt, to be known as Hall, was delivered without harm on June 2, 1891.

That summer, when the professional investigator of "likenesses" declared Katie Mann's baby to be Elliott's as well, it became clear that if the case went to court any jury's sympathies would be with the mother. "The character of the man is taken much into account," warned Theodore, now one of the three civil service commissioners reforming the spoils system in Washington. "Elliott must consider whether he is fit to go on a witness stand and be cross-examined as to his whole way of living—his habits in drinking, opiates, going out of his head and acting in a wild and foolish way, etc."[59]

In Washington, Theodore and Edith braced for Theodore to become publicly ensnared. But the Wall Street banker James Alfred Roosevelt's fear for the family name proved greater, and he paid Katie Mann and her lawyers the full sum expected of Elliott.

Meanwhile, in Paris, Elliott detonated again, this time in violence as he accused Anna of an affair with the doctor at Neuilly. Bamie reported to Theodore further "hideous revelations" of another order of awfulness, certain letters among which supported the judgment that it was now dangerous for Eleanor to be left with her father. Whatever grave wrong Elliott had committed, Theodore and Edith locked these letters away,[60] never to be seen again; and Eleanor herself was packed off to a convent.[61]

SHE HAD BEEN TAKING DAILY French lessons, supplementing what she had picked up from her first nurse. But language was far less a barrier over these next three months than religion and isolation. Among the convent's patrician Catholic mademoiselles Protestant Eleanor was cast in her familiar role of fish out of water. She was not permitted to help beautify the saints' shrine given into her classmates' care, but at such moments was kept firmly apart, left to wander by herself in the walled garden as spring came on.

One such day, one of the little Madeleines lapsed from grace and accidentally swallowed a penny, bringing onto herself Mother Superior's contempt and a torrent of stern prayers.[62] Eleanor soon announced that she, too, had swallowed a coin, but this time the sisters brushed her off as a liar, and no matter how harshly Mother Superior chastised her, she stuck obstinately to her story. Anna, already more than enough troubled, disgustedly took her sinful brat back to Neuilly.

Eleanor would remember the drive home as one of utter agony and bafflement. Anna would not absolve Eleanor—"Granny, how could you disgrace me so?"[63]—and Eleanor suffered acutely. She could bear any physical punishment, the colder and swifter the better, compared to another scalding of her mother's disappointment.[64] "Fear of not measuring up to what Mother wished me to be was with me from then on."[65]

Her father's indulgence of the penny episode freeze-framed his Rhett Butler myth, for this was the last she saw of him among the family or with a loving sparkle in his eye. Eleanor knew that he was in disgrace with Uncle Ted and Aunt Edith and her mother, but this forfeiture of standing only made her more protective.[66] Because he defended her in the parable of the penny, treating Eleanor not "as a criminal," but as a daughter worthy of her parents' love and respect, Father remained unsullied. "He had no faults and no weaknesses," she would recall believing, the logical next step being that "for many years he embodied all the qualities I looked for in a man."[67]

Reality was, however, building to its grimmest stage. Delirium and its demons now surfaced in the June weeks following Hall's birth. The clouds swelled over Paris as one more of Elliott's disturbing binges reached crisis point at the end of July. Bamie set herself up as a tribunal of one, and, on the 27th,[68] "had him seized."[69] Elliott would describe this as a kidnapping,[70] watching through child's eyes as he was carried over the Seine and through the cool groves, past the broad allées, and onto a rough lawn where he was manhandled up and over the verandah and into the care of Dr. Honoré Saury and the alienist Dr. Victor Revertégat at the great white Château de Suresnes.[71]

LEAVING HER HUSBAND TO THE doctors and Theodore to petition the New York Supreme Court to declare Elliott legally insane and freeze his assets,[72] Anna shepherded the children back to the Halls' river refuge at Tivoli. Newspaper headlines once again accompanied their homecoming, this time screaming the family's shame: ELLIOTT ROO-

SEVELT INSANE[73]. . . THEODORE ROOSEVELT'S BROTHER ELLIOTT
WRECKED BY RUM . . . DEMENTED FROM DRINK . . . HIS WIFE
FEARED FOR HER LIFE.[74]

After six months, Theodore hurdled the Atlantic to browbeat
the now remorse-stricken Elliott into surrendering two-thirds of his
$175,000 fortune,[75] including a $60,000 trust,[76] for the benefit of Anna
and the children. His timing proved singularly fortunate. In a year, Elliott's attorney, Francis H. Weeks, would be exposed and sent to prison
for embezzling just such trusts as Elliott's.[77]

Anna reestablished the children in Manhattan, moving them into
a house on East Sixty-First Street and flurrying them off to Tivoli and
Bar Harbor according to the usual patterns. When Elliott returned to
America that first winter, Anna enforced a two-year trial separation,[78]
committing herself not to seek a divorce if he entered a sensational new
drying-out program in the prairie railroad town of Dwight, Illinois.[79]
For three weeks in February 1892, Elliott submitted to four-times-
daily injections of the "Double Chloride Gold Cure,"[80] an aversion
therapy administered in combination with whiskey or morphine, pioneered by former railroad surgeon Leslie E. Keeley.

The treatment, which cost as much as $300,[81] did indeed smother
the addict's desire for drink or opiates, but only by violently nauseating
him with atropine and two other alkaloids of deadly nightshade. Elliott
waxed rapturous about sobering up in sea-to-shining-sea brotherhood,
but for him the Keeley Cure was paradoxical to the point of perversity.
Doubling down on his chemical dependencies, the treatment upheld
his certainty that he could control addiction by modifying excessive
intake of one destructive substance with excess of another.

Detoxified, Elliott asked to see Eleanor and the boys. But Anna,
backed by Theodore, held her ground. She wished for reconciliation,
she told him, but could not endure for herself or the children another
failed attempt to make the family whole. She would require proof of at
least one year's sobriety before conceding any kind of reunion.

Brother-in-law Douglas Robinson offered Elliott a position in
southwestern Virginia as overseer of the Douglas Land Company's
sixty thousand acres,[82] beneath which ran two or more valuable bands
of brown iron ore that the family intended to mine.[83] In the meantime,

as one cousin recalled, the foothills tract was being "used as a place to store family drunkards."[84]

There, in the small town of Abingdon, less than ten miles from the Tennessee border, Elliott rented rooms from a judge's widow and set about rehabilitating himself in Anna's eyes "out in the great hills and the wild forests with no companion but my horse."[85]

ELEANOR WAS ALSO TRYING HARD to win Anna's approval. But as she reoriented herself to her mother's more social Manhattan, people noticed that "I had not inherited the almost incredible beauty of my mother."[86] At children's parties, the old Knickerbocker families— Iselins, Sloanes, van Rensselaers—seemed to have raised much more attractive and confident children than she.

Eleanor yearned to dress beautifully. She should have been graduated to dresses, but her mother (who took far greater interest in ordering Elliott Jr.'s first trousers)[87] kept Eleanor uniformed in a little girl's white muslin dimity. One contemporary remembered Eleanor Roosevelt as "a big girl with a pigtail"—and could tell that she was "very lonely."[88]

By Eleanor's own account, her happiest times were rainy afternoons spent in the maid's sewing room at Auntie Bye's, two blocks from the new brownstone at 52 East Sixty-First, where she feasted on cambric tea with cookies and no one bothered her.[89] It was her only refuge from a growing hostility toward herself. Eleanor furtively did whatever she could to retaliate against her mother who, so far as she knew, had closed the family's doors on her beloved father. She now lied to get what she wanted; and she began to steal: first candy meant for grown-up dinner parties, then forbidden sugar to top her cereal, until her nanny caught and punished her.[90]

The household's secrets, however, kept their sugarcoating. Certainly no one told Eleanor the truth about her father, or bothered to correct her "strange and garbled idea of the troubles which were going on around me."[91] Whenever her mother was in her best mood—dressing to go out to a dinner and talking to her maid—Eleanor learned to eavesdrop for information about her father's exile.

* * *

ELEANOR WAS SEVEN THAT SUMMER of 1892. She slept in her mother's bedroom in Lynam House,[92] the Bar Harbor hotel favored by New Yorkers,[93] where the two drew briefly close as she cared for Anna. Devastating headaches were plaguing her mother under the dread prospect of Elliott's reappearance: "I hate everything and everyone," Anna confided in Bamie.

In August, a hopeful word had come from Virginia: "The poison seems to have gone clean out of my system."[94] But Anna had heard such guarantees before.

All her life, Eleanor believed that she had to earn love—by pleasing others, by undertaking ever more numberless duties, by one more tour of useful Rooseveltian *doing*. Comforting her mother that August for "hours on end," soothing Anna's scalp with long, tender fingers at the head of her bed, assured her that she might not be useless after all. To be capable of lightening burdens, she later understood, was "the greatest joy I experienced."[95]

In the external world, she still seemed able only to tarnish Anna's new start. At Tivoli, Great-Aunt Maggie Ludlow discovered that Eleanor had no educational or domestic foundation whatsoever, and immediately sent over her own companion to give reading lessons. Taken to task for this maternal failure, Anna set herself to teach Eleanor to spell, while harshly reprimanding the boys' Alsatian nurse, Madeleine,[96] whom she deputized to supervise Eleanor's remedial exercises in sewing and darning. Madeleine considered this an imposition— two small boys were enough—and presided over Eleanor's attempts at mending with a primitive vengeance, scissoring out hours of work for a single misweaving in a stocking heel.[97]

On the first day that fall of the fashionable Frederic Roser classes, held at whichever Fifth Avenue or Gramercy Park household could find a spare upstairs room, Eleanor was asked to stand and spell several simple words.[98] This was her moment to shine, and she knew it.

Nine pupils made up the class—all eyes now upon Eleanor Roosevelt—and, most chilling of all, Anna herself had come to watch. Chatter died away. Into the stillness Eleanor rose, only to find herself unable to open her mouth, let alone to spell the plain word *horse*. Her "shyness" had struck her dumb, and she slumped back in trembling disgrace, a failure so complete that her mother could not even mock her, but took her aside afterward in gravest disgust to make clear that she could not imagine what would happen if Eleanor did not "mend [her] ways."[99]

"Because of this and similar incidents," Eleanor would write in later years, "I became less and less confident. Even my father's approval of my horseback riding did not banish my feeling that I was a failure."[100] So powerful was her sense of being inadequate that even when, in Anna's remaining days, Eleanor managed a singular feat of classroom heroics—standing before the others to recite the aptly chosen "The Revenge," Tennyson's 118-line ballad of gritty defense[101]—not a word of it remains in Eleanor Roosevelt's memory of her childhood.

As autumn swept in, Anna seemed driven by a demon of time. "Why, we must know about the moon, and all the recent discoveries in the planets!" she said a little breathlessly, the week before attending a lecture at Carnegie Hall on Giovanni Schiaparelli's misinterpreted "canals" on Mars and mapping of a "twilight zone" between the sunlit and dark sides of Mercury. "I must know all this for my children's sake at least," cried Anna.[102]

Urgency hovered over the third-floor family room's tea table, at which Anna was trying to counteract past damage by reestablishing familiar routines, such as a children's hour before supper—although Anna called it "mother's hour."[103] Curtains drawn, a wood fire burning brightly, the silver teakettle simmering away, Anna played horse or tag or read to the boys, cuddling and kissing them on her lap, while moving into position a footstool on which she meant Eleanor to sit at her feet.[104]

Three-year-old Ellie had grown to become "a saintlike child . . . so loving and attractive," as Anna described her firstborn son; indeed, Eleanor also believed him "so good he never had to be reproved."[105] Baby Hall, a "lovely boy with a strong will" was just sixteen months old.[106] Having been consigned to look on from her footrest on the periphery of this charmed circle, Eleanor later described her mother's unfathomable meanness as "a curious barrier between myself and these three."[107]

Undeterred, Eleanor was thrilled by her brothers. Even when their mother showed a lasting preference for Ellie, Eleanor's sibling pride overrode jealousy. Her friend Helen Cutting would remember her showing off her little darling: "There it was lying on a great big bed. I thought what an awful-looking creature, but oh how Eleanor adored that baby."[108]

Her mother's few remaining grains were fast running out. Only six weeks into the new regime, Anna had to submit to an operation about which Eleanor was told little. The boys were so young that they had to remain at Sixty-First Street; and Eleanor was packed off, first to Aunt Gracie and Uncle Bunkle, with whom she observed her eighth birthday, then to Oak Lawn and Grandmother Hall.

The procedure, so far as can be known, was not life-threatening. But the ether, taking its first twilight effects, cast Anna loose from months of self-imposed restraint, and she cried out that she no longer wished to live. Life in the narrow margin between the extremes of Elliott Roosevelt was no longer life at all.

UP UNTIL THE LAST MINUTE, Mrs. Elliott Roosevelt's name had headed the invitations to the first Ladies' Assembly of the new season. The cards had just left the engraver's hands[109] when, on the afternoon of December 9, after funeral services at 52 East Sixty-First Street, the undertakers descended from a hearse behind black horses to bury her upriver at Tivoli.

It had all come quickly apart. In November, Anna had bounced back from the operation. Eleanor had returned home from Oak Lawn. Then, just before Thanksgiving, she was once more rushed out of the house—this time to her mother's double first cousin (and Eleanor's godmother), twenty-six-year-old "Cousin Susie" Parish.[110] A new disaster was upon them, grave enough for Ellie and Hall to be hurried to Great-Aunt Maggie's, and for Grandmother Hall to hasten up to Sixty-First Street to nurse her choking, shivering daughter.

Diphtheria, the neck-swelling infection against which there was then no antitoxin, took hold of Anna; and on December 7, 1892, three months short of thirty, she died a horrible strangulating death. The newspapers reported that Anna "died broken-hearted,"[111] making her "an easy prey" to opportunistic infection.[112]

Eleanor did not react as an eight-year-old was supposed to when faced with the sudden irrevocable loss of her mother. She did take it as catastrophic—"All my world seemed to have suddenly disintegrated around me"—but she also discovered: "and yet life went on." Upon this "first and most important lesson" the rest of her life would pivot: "No matter what happened to one in this world, one had to adjust to it."[113]

Eleanor shed no tears. With the world-changing news there came only the realization: *Now her father would be back*. Her mother would not—yet life would go on. Life *was going on*—and soon Father would be with her, for her to comfort *him*, for there was now "no hope of ever wiping out the sorrowful years he had brought upon my mother."[114]

ANNA HAD LEFT GRANDMOTHER HALL in charge of the children, with Theodore to serve as legal guardian.[115] And so, once Anna's will had been read, uncontested by Elliott, the children were installed at the Hall brownstone, 11 West Thirty-Seventh Street.

Eleanor quickly learned to suppress her excitement as she anticipated the arrival of "the person she loved best in the world."[116] When her father made one of his unpredictable visits, he gathered her close, and an almost frantic sense of togetherness bound father and daughter as Elliott outlined the life they would someday delight in together. "A life of our own," he called it; days and weeks that would "always" revolve just around the two of them; months spent traveling; years of building a household that would include the boys.

This last threw Eleanor into some confusion: "I did not understand whether my brothers were to be our children or whether he felt that they would be at school and college and later independent."[117]

Her father's vision came to sound like a widower molding a much younger wife to his taste. But from his instructions—"all those *little* things that will make my dear Girl so much more attractive if she attends to them, not forgetting the big ones: unselfishness, generosity, loving tenderness and cheerfulness"[118]—she took a kind of empowerment, transforming from "Granny" to the skillful "old child."

Elliott drew her into a transcendent illusion: "There started that day a feeling which never left me that he and I were very close together."[119] But, close—how? where? Not in the real world, wherein they were kept apart by the family elders; and where, the one time that Elliott managed to get Eleanor away from Grandmother and out for a stroll along Fifth Avenue, he then abandoned her with his three fox terriers in the dog room at the Knickerbocker Club. Upstairs in the bar, forgetting Eleanor completely, he left her and the dogs over the next six hours to fend for themselves.

HER FATHER'S LETTERS SIFTED UP from Abingdon to West Thirty-Seventh, or to Oak Lawn, or in the summers to staid Bar Harbor. "Write me soon little 'Grannie'—And don't forget to love me a little—I love you *so much*."[120] These were the epistles, Aunt Pussie later recorded, that Eleanor "loved & kissed before she went to bed."[121]

Sometimes Elliott intensified the romance with descriptions of how he was spoiling other children in far Virginia—girls who would "be so glad to know you in person; they say they know your photograph so well."[122] More than thirty years later at a White House reception, Eleanor would meet a woman who described a photograph taken in Abingdon of Elliott Roosevelt and an unknown little girl. Eleanor, however, could identify her immediately: "Miriam Trigg was her name, and when I was eight I felt as though I knew her and I was very envious because she could ride her pony with my father and I was in the north."[123]

To each of two girls, Lillian Lloyd and Emily Blair, Elliott gave dolls on which they bestowed names in a form that thousands would one day repeat, and for whom Eleanor sent doll[124] jewelry.[125] "Won't you come down and play with my pretty doll?" wrote Lillian. "I named my pretty doll Eleanor Roosevelt Lloyd."[126]

Elliott and the little girls of Abingdon were not the only ones shaping Eleanor Roosevelt into a nearly mythic figure. Eleanor's own "dream story" projected herself as prime executrix to a powerful, good-looking Great Roosevelt whose restrictions due to crippling illness could be magicked away as she managed his household and traveled a world that they themselves were bringing into being. It made her happy as nothing else ever had—to imagine herself into world-wide duty.[127]

*　*　*

HER MOTHER HAD BEEN DEAD less than a year when Eleanor's younger brother contracted scarlet fever, on top of which struck diphtheria; and so, on May 25, 1893, Elliott Jr. strangled to death.[128]

To add to the tragedy and their own fearful sorrow, Eleanor and Hall were strictly quarantined that spring. "No one would go near them,"[129] recalled Auntie Bye. Uncle Ted and Aunt Edith kept a firm distance; Aunt Corinne was forbidden by her husband to "see any of them"[130] or even to set foot in West Thirty-Seventh Street until the house was fumigated. None of the Roosevelts attended Ellie's funeral or the burial at Tivoli. "Elliott feels it very much and is very nervous," reported Douglas Robinson, after speaking with his brother-in-law from the safe side of the front door at the Hall brownstone.

The latest desolation drove Elliott into a relapse,[131] further compounded when, just fifteen days after his namesake son was snatched away, Aunt Annie Gracie, his life's "guardian angel," died three months short of her sixtieth birthday.[132]

HIS DRINKING WAS NOW VOLCANIC: every binge, leading to blackout, inexorably advancing the disease to its life-threatening stage. "Poor Elliott is wandering about New York," declared Edith. "Heaven knows where, he rarely spends a night in his rooms."[133]

To anyone who may have thought they knew him, it was impossible to believe that this shambling wreck was Elliott.[134] Unthinkable that this bundle of flesh and bone being carried out of the Knickerbocker Club—his feet dangling like the hooves of a brought-down buck when they levered him into a hansom—was the same human being whom Grandmother Hall called "the dearest man I ever knew, so gentle, and kindhearted."[135]

He had slipped back into uptown obscurity as "Mr. Eliot," leasing a townhouse at 313 West 102nd Street under the warm attentions of a certain "Mrs. Evans." He appeared sporadically in Eleanor's life, each visit making her once more a stranger to the house where she had just begun to feel at home. Aunt Corinne had to be asked to write her brother to remind him that he was persona non grata and had agreed to refrain from such visits "for the sake of the children."[136]

It was easy enough for Eleanor to daydream through her father's letters, because, fundamentally unreal, they canonized one reality: he was dependent on her. In January 1894, when for fifteen days he had heard nothing from her, he fumed: "Are you never going to let me have news of your dear little self and Brudie again?"[137]

To protect Eleanor from neediness run amok, Aunt Edith suggested she be sent away to a good boarding school. Eleanor had visited at Sagamore Hill that April 1894, and Aunt Edith, herself the daughter of an alcoholic, looked upon her with commiserative pity: "I do not feel she has much chance, poor little soul."[138] When the final blow fell, Edith was grateful that "little Eleanor can have loving and tender last words from her father to treasure."[139]

He had implored her to be a mother to Hall.[140] The problem, she later recalled, was that "if I ever wanted to mother anyone, it was my father."[141] She ever after equated her father with the iconic dead Christ laid across Mary's extended lap in Michelangelo's *Pietà*[142] for, just as Elliott had depicted father and daughter as coequals in their dream story, Michelangelo had portrayed the two generations as of the same age.[143]

Up to the afternoon of August 14, 1894, by Uncle Ted's agonized accounting, Elliott had been getting at least half a dozen bottles down every morning: brandy, anisette, champagne, crème de menthe. Trapped in his own mind, listening to his body hum—delirium set in, and "he wandered ceaselessly everywhere, never still, and he wrote again and again to us all, sending to me two telegrams and three notes. He was like some stricken, hunted creature."[144]

At ten in the evening, after falling from a window at West 102nd Street, Elliott at last fulfilled his endless repertoire of impossible demands. At the age of thirty-four, he plunged himself into nothingness, just as if a trapdoor between the worlds had dropped open beneath him.

IN BAR HARBOR, AT LYNAM'S, the old summer hotel where she had soothed her mother's headaches, Eleanor had posted a message on July 30: "Goodbye dear Father I send you a great deal of love. I am your little daughter Nell."[145]

Now, when the news from 102nd Street reached them, her mother's younger sisters, Edith ("Pussie") and Maude, came to Eleanor with voices thickened by grief. But she would not hear her father spoken of as dead.[146] "I simply refused to believe it, and while I wept long and went to bed still weeping, I finally went to sleep and began the next day living in my dream world as usual."[147]

"Poor child has had so much sorrow crowded into her short life she now takes everything very quietly," recorded her grandmother. "The only remark she made was, 'I did want to see Father once more.'"[148]

The adults, meanwhile, disagreed about where Elliott should be buried. There was no room in the old Ludlow mausoleum back of the church at Tivoli, and a new vault could not be built for another two months.[149] Theodore, upon hearing "this hideous plan," vetoed any final resting place but the Roosevelt plot in Brooklyn's vast Green-Wood Cemetery, "beside those who are associated with only his sweet innocent youth."[150]

Grandmother's decision to keep the children from Elliott's funeral meant that Eleanor had "no tangible thing to make death real to me."[151] Few kinfolk followed Elliott's coffin to Green-Wood Cemetery. Neither Auntie Bye nor Auntie Corinne nor Aunt Edith saw fit to attend,[152] so the carriages bore two Oyster Bay cousins, plus Elliott's mistress and some friends who ran a brothel.[153] Theodore, struck silent by laryngitis, held back.[154]

By nightfall on Friday, August 17, the freshly dug soil of Eleanor's father's grave had been shoveled back in, the plot later to be corked by a stone. And "from that time on I knew in my mind that my father was dead, and yet I lived with him more closely, probably, than I had when he was alive."[155] In her grand illusion, the vivid dream narrative "went on without a break"[156]—as did she herself.

THREE

ORPHANED, ELEANOR LIVED ON THE fourth floor, street side, of her grandmother's brownstone. "I've always lived in other people's houses," she later said. "I always had to take the worst room, and I couldn't make a fuss about it."[1]

Each morning renewed her struggle to recover the stimulant her father had given her: "the realest thing in my life."[2] When her grandmother engaged a string of French and German nannies for afternoon walks, she went along light-footedly on these outings, but took a subtle power and exhilaration from showing them who was in charge: "I walked them all off their feet. They always tried to talk to me, and I wished to be left alone to live in [the] dream world in which I was the heroine and my father the hero. Into this world I retired as soon as I went to bed and as soon as I woke in the morning, and all the time I was walking or when any one bored me."[3]

Ordered as a deck of cards, the hierarchy and routine at 11 West Thirty-Seventh Street dealt her into the here and now. Every morning before breakfast, the whole household, servants and coachman included, met for prayers in the dining room.[4] Sundays, Eleanor recited the day's collect to her grandmother (in French) and instructed the coachman's small daughter in Bible studies.[5] Twice every day, she was compelled to maintain her posture by walking to and fro holding a stick through her arms behind her back. She could not admit to being tired—it made her a burden to those she was with. Resentments were also unacceptable. Should someone upset her, the rule was that she must not tell anybody.[6]

Without complaint, she conformed to a regimen that frequently exasperated her but did not permit, as one friend said, "the sulks and the tantrums that children were allowed to have under the shelter of their [own] family."[7] Sorrow was undignified and undermining; grief, to be very briefly displayed, never to be indulged. "We don't cry where people are, we go and cry by ourselves" was her grandmother's firm principle. As for receiving bad news, if she absolutely *must* cry, she was to find a bathtub and weep into it.[8]

Grandmother Hall, soberly gowned in black brocade, silver watch proudly pinned above her bosom, imparted to Eleanor the principle that women of her station had a duty to exercise personal authority— though only over strictly delineated domestic spheres. A wellborn girl was in no way encouraged to a career in medicine or the law, but once married she could be the mistress of a household. In the meantime, Eleanor must master such tribal customs as would make her a success when presented to the matrons and potential husbands of Brownstone New York.[9]

"Until I entered my teens," recalled Eleanor, "this pattern did not trouble me."[10] From ten to fourteen she found no reason to question Grandmother Hall.[11] "I was in great awe of her."[12]

EVERY FIRST OF MAY, WHEN the Halls moved household,[13] they kept to the same ancient routine, migrating from Murray Hill to Tivoli as rigidly as horseshoe crabs scuttling to shallow coastal waters.[14] On that date, Eleanor switched over from winter's long flannel underwear (worn daily November through April, regardless of temperature) to summer's mandatory cover-up (itchy long black stockings, flannel pet-ticoat, tight high-button boots), leaving her schoolmates in the city to wonder why anyone would submit to wearing such monstrous relics. Jessie Sloane, her most beautiful and best-turned-out Roser classmate, was incredulous. Yet any offer to lend more comfortable clothing only made Eleanor martyr herself still more.[15]

In May of 1899, Eleanor's seventh spring of unquestioning subor-dination to Grandma, she had but one desire—to go west by rail with Jessie Sloane, whom she idolized. Jessie's father, Henry, having lately expanded the family furnishing company W. & J. Sloane, beyond the Rockies, was engaging a private car to carry the girls across the con-tinent to the Pacific coast.[16] Eleanor could not remember ever having wanted anything so much in her life, and long afterward she marked Grandmother Hall's refusal to let her go as one of the biggest disappointments of her adolescence.[17] Eleanor dared to appeal, but despite tearful pleadings,[18] the subject was dropped.

She was never told why Grandmother judged the trip morally "unwise."[19] Had she seen the newspaper that April 29,[20] she might have seen that Jessie's mother, heiress to a Brooklyn pharmaceutical fortune and one of the great beauties of her generation,[21] had cuckolded Jessie's father.[22] The previous afternoon, the State Supreme Court had deprived her of custody of her daughters, and further denied her access until they turned twenty-one.[23]

Out West, as Jessie's companion, Eleanor might have seen for herself that she was not so marked or shamed or indeed different from other "well-brought-up" girls. She was not alone in having parents who had been unable to come to terms with vastly advantaged lives. Instead, her grandmother's reserve condemned her to the suspicion that perhaps she, or Hall, could be vulnerable in their makeup to similar collapse.

From the New York Central depot, a large carriage lumbered them through the village of Madalin, north on the Woods Road, out to the gate lodge, through the stone gate, then along a leafy lane that opened onto the oak-shaded lawn and the great russet-brick mansion brooding in isolation above the Hudson.

Each morning in the new green season, Grandmother took Eleanor downstairs with her to unlock the storeroom and scoop from standing barrels those staples the cook would need the rest of the day. Carefully she apportioned each measure of flour or sugar or coffee into the bowl Eleanor held.[24] In the cellar, Eleanor was also encouraged to work alongside Mary Overhulse, cranking the washer, ironing handkerchiefs, napkins, and petticoats.[25] Mary Glaser Overhulse was then forty-seven, a cheerful woman of brutal good humor.[26] Eleanor had a formative experience in going home with the German cook and laundress to her farm in Clermont[27] and getting to know the Overhulse children, Anna and William, who were older but shy. Happy just to be noticed by them, Eleanor was happier still to be put to apple-picking in the orchard after supper, the evening star low over the Catskills peak called Round Top, the air filled with the fragrance of haying.[28]

In the hour after supper at Oak Lawn, she felt a similar gratitude to her unmarried aunts and uncles for dropping whatever they were doing to play tag or hide-and-seek or I Spy.[29] All her life she would recall running around the piazza and looking through the windows to catch a glimpse of someone inside.[30] Just as vivid were the Sunday evenings when she and Hall gathered with the others to sing hymns around the piano,[31] "and no matter how poor our voices were we could join in." Eleanor would describe those choral Sundays as "some of the pleasantest hours of my childhood."[32]

They loved the place—"*dear* Tivoli."[33] Vallie gave whole afternoons to showing Eleanor how to jump her pony; Eddie taught her the finer points of lawn tennis at the nearby Edgewood Club. Not unfairly, Vallie has come down to posterity as a family monster, the phantom of Oak Lawn, a crude Edwardian lush who sprayed buckshot from the mansard windows to terrorize neighborhood children. But in Eleanor's first years with the family, Valentine and Edward Hall were celebrated young sports heroes, having leapt and hammered their way to the highest standing in the new world of lawn tennis: Vallie shared the doubles championship of the United States in 1888 and 1890; together, the Hall brothers claimed the National Eastern Doubles prize for 1892.

Uncle Vallie and Uncle Eddie seemed to have everything: money, supreme confidence, endless prospects. One or the other was always to be found in the latest number of *Outing* magazine; Vallie was the acclaimed author of *Lawn Tennis in America*, the first book of its genre to look inside the game by analyzing players and the knottier points of rules and handicaps, all "written in the sprightly style of a novel."[34] But the wheel was turning. The pacesetting first national champions of the new game, Vallie and Eddie were already in danger of becoming the last of an old breed. Addiction, bad debts, bankruptcy, charges of violent and abusive behaviors transformed the Hall brothers from dashing men-about-town into feckless drunks protected by their very gentle mother.

The Hall sisters meanwhile sparkled in the society columns as "dazzling creatures"[35]—extravagant, unpredictable, deeply generous, and utterly impractical. Eleanor's oldest and most beautiful aunt,

Elizabeth ("Tissie"), a Venus of the opera box, was forever buying a half dozen watercolors by some needy and deserving but not wholly recognized artist.[36] The younger sisters, Edith ("Pussie") and Maude, were considered the wild ones for riding in hansom cabs alone, without their maids.[37] They all had the same featherlike poise and distinctive jawline, the underside shaped like a spade. Altogether they were a marvel, Gibson Girls who had floated free of Gibson: "The Hall sisters were always 'sumpin'!"[38] recited Eleanor. She was flattered when Pussie and Maude included her on carriage rides with their beaux and in frequent redecorations of the third floor—"at one period everything must be white!"[39] Best of all these liberties was the thrill of rising before the house stirred to wake up Pussie, filch slices of bread and butter thickly coated with brown sugar from the pantry, and boat to town to pick up the mail.

Many years later, Eleanor would write, "I shall never know any place, or any house as well as I know that one."[40]

OAK LAWN WAS ALMOST A lodge in the wild. No electric current sparked the place to life; no party-line telephone connected it to the other manors along the river. News of any kind arrived at least a day late. When an explosion sank the battleship USS *Maine* in Havana harbor in February 1898, killing 266 men and igniting the Spanish-American War, Eleanor had only the vaguest idea about why Uncle Ted was sailing for Cuba with his Rough Riders. Except for the family's sudden dismay when one of Pussie's young men died in a Florida troop camp, America's "splendid little war" barely reached Oak Lawn.[41]

"If I had not had books," Eleanor later realized, "I don't think I would have known anything about the world."[42]

She had noticed the way Uncle Eddie would saunter into the library, take down a work by Dickens or Scott, settle himself into a chair on the piazza, then read chapter after chapter straight through in a day, closing the book with a snap at sundown.[43] This she emulated, escaping to the arms of a cherry tree near the river bluff with Hector Mallet's *Sans Famille* (about another marginalized orphan); or lying on the front lawn with Dickens's *Oliver Twist* or *The Old Curiosity Shop*; or under the top-floor mansard roof with the popular Victorian novel

Misunderstood, which she absorbed in one sitting, "just crying a whole rainy afternoon through the book," as its seven-year-old waif, Humphrey Duncombe, paralyzed in a fall from a forbidden tree, blissfully reunites with his mother in another world.

Reading helped her see how the lives of those around her manifested "a certain story book quality,"[44] a stereopticon effect which recurred through these years: life and literature again and again combining to reveal an uncanny hyper-realism.[45] The volatile Pussie, increasingly consumed by the theatrics of finding a man and a fortune, became for Eleanor a figure from a novel, a study in self-sabotage. Indeed, Pussie was believed to be Edith Wharton's model for the tragic Lily Bart of *The House of Mirth*,[46] Wharton's portrait of the idle rich in Brownstone Society, where "fewer responsibilities attach to money with us than in other societies."[47]

Her brother Hall, too, came into focus in Oak Lawn isolation as Eleanor read *Robinson Crusoe* by lampwick. Girls didn't wander the woods putting their feet on the necks of their groveling little brothers, but at the height of Eleanor's first infatuated reading of Defoe,[48] she hauled her brother to a secret spot, a quarter of a mile away, where Hall served as Eleanor's "poor Friday."[49]

Fate had begun to show different plans for the two real-life castaways of Half-Way Nirvana. Hall had salvaged prodigious willfulness and charm from the wreck of the Elliott Roosevelts. He was bright, a quick study; but all too often in the years ahead, rather than applying himself to sustained pursuit of his goals, he would obstinately settle for pleasing others in the easiest way he knew how. His blond curls and little round face had made him Pussie's pet from the start. She dressed him in a black velvet suit, rode him around on her back, and called him "the Cherub."[50] Eleanor, rechristened "Totty," found herself jealous "because I could not aspire to any such name,"[51] still more so because Pussie "showed a real maternal affection for him." She was galled by how effectively Pussie exercised her flair for child's play with Hall, while Eleanor, the teenager, was forever paralyzed by a heavy sense of duty.

Meanwhile, neither Pussie nor Maude made any sort of maternal effort to teach Eleanor the names of flowers or trees, much less explain the menstrual onset of puberty. If she wanted to go on half-thinking that babies were "brought in the doctor's satchel,"[52] none of the aunts minded.[53]

She had a still harder time identifying feelings, or, yet more complicated, her needs. None of her surrogate mothers taught her how to say when enough was enough, or that too much was yet too little. She developed instead a fundamental capacity to oblige, to live subject to another's control; enduring authority by making herself more or less invisible. She seemed to "need" only to please, and to be good, strong, and brave for others, to be her surviving brother's caretaker—to focus on *his* needs as a means of meeting her own. If she did all those things, she believed, she would be the ideal child her father had called on her to be. But her imagination's power to give refuge was fading as she grew.

RIDING A BULKY FIFTH AVENUE stagecoach to her French lesson one morning, accompanied by her maid, Eleanor noticed among the well-dressed passengers a sick and impoverished-looking man. To her overwhelming dismay, he suddenly leapt up, snatched a woman's purse, and jumped off. Before she knew what she was doing, Eleanor flew to the door and also jumped from the moving coach, landing amid a cluster of passersby on the sidewalk and yells of "Stop thief!" For months afterward, the man's urgency and desperation "continued to come before me in my dreams."[54]

That same summer, a gray polo pony ran away with her twice in a single day. "And all my old fear of riding returned again. From that time on, I was never entirely free of it."[55]

Eleanor, at fourteen, was plagued by anxieties. The greatest of all her dreads was "the terror of displeasing the people I lived with." One night on West Thirty-Seventh Street, as Aunt Pussie lay sick in bed, calling for ice, Eleanor wished that she could refuse the call. But "if I did that, she would never again ask me to help her and I could not bear not to be asked." All alone in the dark brownstone, she fought herself forward step by fearful step.

Forbidden to complain, Eleanor unwillingly submitted to Hall's prickly Alsatian governess—a "terrifying character," as Cousin Corinne recalled her.[56] For Eleanor, the nightmare of Madeleine would resume whenever the governess grudgingly took on such "extra duties" as the nightly brushing and pinning of Eleanor's long golden hair. Even a minute's lateness for hair duty was punished with a tongue-lashing, then real humiliation once Madeleine had seen that the hall door was fastened. Hanging her head in the flickering candlelight, Eleanor had to brace herself, arms outstretched, knees quivering, against the proper count of brushstrokes. If she faltered through any of this, Madeleine would claw up a handful of her hair, and in furtive silence, almost daring Eleanor to cry out for someone to intervene, pull her closer—so gaggingly close that Eleanor could not but take in with each breath the nauseating after-fumes of her elder's evening wine ration.

Shamed self-consciousness seemed inescapable. She kept Madeleine's predations a secret until in the summer of 1898, when she confessed to Grandmother between sobs on a walk in the woods. Her tormentor's connection with her was at once severed, though Madeleine was kept on to look after Hall.

DEEP WATER REMAINED THE CHIEF devil among her raw fears, never more so than during a brief summer visit to Oyster Bay, where Uncle Ted dared her to jump off a waterfront dock. Expected to start paddling, she came up spluttering, only to be good-naturedly dunked by a cousin, at which point she panicked and sank like lead in the sea.[57] Asked in later life about her uncle's influence, she replied instantly: "He was the first person to throw me into the water to try to make me swim. And he had to fish me out again because I didn't swim. And he was very indignant."[58]

Cove Neck was one sink-or-swim test after another:[59] Uncle Ted cracking the whip down Cooper's Bluff, a sandy headland adjoining Sagamore Hill, then leading the charge back to the top; obstacle courses through haystacks in which who knew what lurked; snakes thrust upon her by male cousins; a tall, hollow tree into which Uncle Ted rappelled each child on a rope.[60] Every challenge surmounted seemed to ratify the child-conqueror as a rough and ready citizen of the United States. TR wanted the next generation to feel as he had as a boy: that every act in their daily lives was a significant part of their citizenship.[61] "But," for each dividend from this fascinating uncle, "there was a good deal of pain because I felt very inadequate to many of the things that we did."[62]

Eleanor wanted Uncle Ted's approval, though his hyperactivity frightened her.[63] She loved it when instead he presided over the piazza at sunset, identifying Sagamore Hill's birds from fragments of their song and glimpses of their feathers or nests; or when he gathered the children to read old Norse sagas aloud on rainy days in the Gun Room atop the house. Sometimes, in a volume of poetry, he would stop and repeat a line that especially pleased him. Later, at home, Eleanor found she could recall his favorite phrases word for word and say them aloud to herself.[64]

In these years, she had one disagreement with him that stayed with her the rest of her life. One day Uncle Ted told her that for all its horrors, war gave people access to qualities within themselves that peace kept hidden. "I rebelled at the time," recalled the later Eleanor, "and I still rebel at the thought that war alone can bring out the best in people."[65]

As another parentless Christmas bore down, she pretended to believe in Santa Claus, not wanting to spoil things for Hall. Pussie and Maude had gone right on treating him as their "Cherub" and her as their "Cinderella," leaving Eleanor to clean up their cheese-glazed Welsh rarebit pans after they'd frolicked an evening away with their swells. "You are a girl," Grandmother instilled in her, "and you have to be more sensible and thoughtful than your brother."[66] And, she might have added: yet more so than your aunts and uncles.

Grandma decided that because Eleanor was conspicuous—a long-limbed near six feet in heels—she should take ballet lessons, which put her in the current boom of dancing for young women. Eleanor herself had dreams of becoming a singer; stirrings of ambition filled her, too, whenever she attended the theater. Pussie had tried to satisfy her growing taste for the stage, taking her to see and afterward to meet the legendary Eleanora Duse.[67]

But with Grandma ever more shut away in her bedroom, and the aunts off in tumbling pursuit of husbands, the Hudson's shipping lanes and New York Central tracks were all that gave the house a pulse. From Eleanor's bedroom on windless nights, if she held her breath, she could hear the voices of seamen, carrying up to her window from long-hulled freight boats sailing upriver. Sometimes as orders issued in foreign accents, sometimes as salty laughter and snatches of song, the passage of mariners reached in from the "perpetually interesting river"[68]—almost as if radio and Mrs. Roosevelt and a world of millions in need had already been invented.

ALL YEAR SHE LOOKED FORWARD to Auntie Corinne's young people's holiday house party in Orange, New Jersey. But upon arriving that New Year's Eve at Overlook, the Robinsons' country house, she was chagrined to discover that she was no longer part of the fun.[69]

The others still saw one another regularly, were growing closer together. Their families had healed. Eleanor was like a graft that wasn't taking. (Who even remembered her *brother* Elliott?) Cousin Corinnie, always an ally, had been six when "Aunt Anna" died and eight the year of "Uncle Ellie's" death. To Corinnie, that branch of the family seemed almost to have been abolished.[70] Cousin Eleanor was "a person apart," a revenant Roosevelt: "She didn't have anyone who loved her."[71]

Uncle Ted and Auntie Bye remained powerfully mute on Eleanor's father Elliott, carrying forward the Roosevelt family tradition of "deleting relatives" who had brought disgrace on the others.[72] Only good-hearted Aunt Corinne spoke of her father in Eleanor's presence, and with great naturalness, evoking "the most charming man she ever knew."[73] But at that year's holiday festival, Aunt Corinne was saddened whenever she caught sight of her niece, feeling that "poor little Eleanor" seemed increasingly rigid, unable to enjoy life: "more Hall than Roosevelt."[74]

All through the holiday activities, she returned always to her "lonely chair," knowing that her most recent conversational partner was now making fun of her to the others. She was "afraid even to glance in their direction,"[75] and in her dread could not learn how to be anything *but* serious and sensitive, even a bit superior. If all that were not amply estranging, Eleanor's clothes once again proved wrong. She was expected to be suitably turned out for the various winter sports, and to fill up an engraved dance card at the climactic Essex County Country Club event. During the day, she joined the skating party on wobbly ankles, but when the others went off coasting, urging her to join them, she confined herself to watching in chilled isolation.

Worse was the heat of the evening's dance. Feeling stiff and prissy and uncertain of how and with whom to open up, she hovered awkwardly in her short white dress made of nainsook, a muslin fabric used for baby clothes. Cousins Alice and Corinne boasted new long gowns of tulle and fine organdy. Eleanor had passed up their imploring offers to wear one of their extras.[76] She would not live on sympathy; and, what was more, those dresses would not have fit. "Eleanor looked like someone at a fancy-dress party portraying a little child," recalled Corinne.[77]

In later years, Alice took issue with Eleanor's tendency to "make out that she was unattractive and rejected." Among the Oyster Bay Roosevelts, she claimed, "I was the ugly duckling, not Eleanor."[78] This stretched the truth, but Alice and Eleanor, the paired bookends of their fathers' *annus horribilis*, 1884, were both cast as odd-girl-out in their respective families. Each in her different way would master the distinctive power of the misunderstood outlier.

That night, a "tall, rather coltish-looking" Eleanor stepped onto the country club floor "with masses of pale, gold hair rippling to below her waist." Her "really lovely blue eyes"[79] flashed with the quiet determination to show everyone that she was no sidelined stray. Her distant cousin, Franklin Delano Roosevelt, had asked her to dance. This was their first moment of looking each other over. It mattered enough, when he returned to Groton School to complete his fifth form year, for Franklin to report to his mother—keeping her well off the scent from the start—"Cousin Eleanor has a fine mind."[80]

THE FOLLOWING SPRING AND SUMMER of 1899, Grandmother spotted that Eleanor was growing thinner, ever more wan and chalky. Taking into account her headaches, poor appetite, wakefulness at night, and general daytime gloom,[81] Grandmother concluded that Eleanor was being overstimulated. She blamed Pussie and Maude's many friends "constantly swarming in,"[82] leaving Eleanor the sympathetic ear to whichever belle poured out her latest disenchantment. "There I always was," an older Eleanor affirmed, "sitting in a corner of the sofa and missing nothing that was going on."[83]

Grandmother wrote to Marie Souvestre, cofounder (with her late romantic partner Caroline Dussaut) of Les Ruches, the French boarding school outside Paris where Auntie Bye had come into possession of her analytic mind. In an age when women's education was viewed as dangerous to the social order, harmful even to a girl's health and morality, Souvestre sought to give her students a greater sense of capability and opportunity. To every newcomer to the mansarded house at Les Ruches, she would demand, "Why was your mind given you, but to think things out for yourself?"[84]

Souvestre was an imperious sixty-three when she wrote to reassure Grandmother Hall of her interest in Eleanor—remembering her fondness for Bamie Roosevelt, and how she had met Eleanor's parents in Paris eight years before. By now, she had reestablished her school to the southwest of London, in a manor house around whose remaining acres the railway suburbs were just then popping up. Allenswood, as the bilingual academy was called, combined a no-nonsense French approach to teaching with a miniaturized version of English country house life.

The headmistress regularly drew as guest lecturers the same statesmen, intellectuals, and radical reformers who sent their daughters from Paris, London, Berlin, Rome, homeward from all corners of the British Empire. Among the international set of ruling families who colonized Allenswood, the unmarried Souvestre was hailed as more than a schoolmistress. Her private life as a gay woman silently passed over, she occupied the cultural place reserved for great actresses and women of shaman-like genius. To the high bourgeoisie of the Belle Époque, this was the school's cachet: the commanding presence of this highly cultivated woman of great forthrightness—*cette grande femme*, as Lytton Strachey called her.[85]

IN SEPTEMBER, JUST A FEW weeks before Eleanor's fifteenth birthday, Grandmother presented her with a ring that she had been given on reaching that age, which she had passed on to Eleanor's mother and then put away after Anna's death.[86] So Eleanor made the crossing wearing her Hall heirloom on her right hand, as she read and re-read her father's letters from the stash in her valise, habitually nibbling on her left thumbnail.

Aunt Tissie, her godmother, had volunteered as chaperone despite having her hands full, back on land, with a young daughter and a husband forever nursing the sprains of his sporting life. But no sooner had the ship dropped below Bedloe's Island than Tissie shut herself in her stateroom, admitting that she was a poor sailor and always took to her berth immediately after boarding. As always with her female elders, Eleanor subordinated her own energies and followed suit.

Shut away alongside her aunt, she missed everything from the Statue of Liberty out to open water. But Eleanor Roosevelt was soon to discover more of herself than she had ever known—under the torch of a mighty Frenchwoman with radical visions of liberty and justice.

II

ORPHAN

I was brought up in a rather peculiar way.

E.R.[1]

FOUR

T HE FOG CARRIED A WHIFF of tar from London's chimney pots. Behind this motionless curtain, a brick boundary wall greeted their arrival at Allenswood. At the center of a six-acre park and gardens hulked the Earl Spencer's Victorian Gothic manor house, converted for thirty-five or so international schoolgirls and their teachers to live in chilly dormered bedrooms. Mademoiselle's pupils attended classes in stove-heated dayrooms and took their meals in a formal dining room.

Within the gate, the lower branches of a lofty cedar of Lebanon pointed up the drive to the school portico. There, a regal woman with a head of snow-white hair came buzzing down the steps to welcome Eleanor. When their eyes met, the newcomer felt the headmistress's hard black stare drill "right through to my backbone."[1]

Eleanor would later poeticize her first impression as one of immediate liberation upon crossing the school's threshold.[2] Installed in her room, she discovered that Mlle. Souvestre, "with her instinctive understanding,"[3] had chosen her just the right roommate, Marjorie Bennett, a gentle English girl who showed Eleanor the ropes and helped her to realize that she was well prepared to meet the school's standards of honesty, diligence, and loyalty, not to mention its cardinal rule that every girl speak French throughout the day.

From her first school meal, Eleanor found her voice. Her old crushing loneliness had briefly ambushed her when Aunt Tissie departed, but once seated at the headmistress's table, she chatted in such a mature and fluent tone ("when we hardly dared open our mouths," recalled one classmate[4]), that Mademoiselle flooded the table with acclaim for the new student. Afterward, when several girls came to Eleanor—"Totty"[5]—for help with their required weekly compositions, her delight in their compliments went straight to her cheeks: "I was in a glow."[6]

The next morning, each girl turned out in the school uniform—white shirtwaist, striped school bow tie, ground-sweeping skirt, beribboned boater—and for once Eleanor eagerly took her place as the conspicuous tallest. Confident to be dressed correctly and like all the others, she felt that here, at last, she would be "free from all my former sins and traditions."[7]

JOYOUSLY ALIVE WITH FLOWERS THROUGHOUT the dayrooms in fall and spring, Allenswood had three special customs that immediately freed Eleanor from old hurts.

The first was "kissing time."[8] Every morning after room inspection and every night before bedtime, the girls gathered around the stove in the big study hall. At a signal, each would greet or say good night to every other girl with a kiss, as a way of supporting and sustaining a clique-free community of affectionate participants in a common cause—an ideal that Eleanor would seek to foster for the rest of her life.

Second, for a full hour and a half after the midday meal, a small selection of students would be called upon to lie down and fix their minds on a single thought that would then be discussed over tea with Mademoiselle—a practice that Eleanor would apply as the mother of a chronically ill child. Those chosen were expected to discourse freely and boldly on their insights; and once again Eleanor showed sense in ways that made her seem "so very much more grown up than we were," recalled one classmate.[9]

Finally, there were the evenings in Mademoiselle's library. Small, handpicked groups sat in little chairs on either side of the fireplace's crackling logs and beneath nudes painted by the French muralist Puvis de Chavannes, a friend of Mademoiselle's father, the writer and futurist Émile Souvestre. Reviewing such intimate subjects as race, religion,[10] or reactions to Toynbee Hall, the pioneering East London settlement house,[11] Mademoiselle urged each student to take active responsibility for her ideas.

The two precepts of these evening seminars were to think for oneself and to speak forthrightly—ferociously, if necessary—whether the subject was the British Empire's oppression of subject peoples, or "the plight of the Negro in America," or the innocence of Captain Alfred Dreyfus, the Jewish French army officer falsely convicted of espionage. Souvestre's sympathy for small nations, for trade unions, for innocents ruined by French justice, for underdogs in general—all came into play.

On October 11, 1899, Eleanor's fifteenth birthday, the British and the Boers went to war. The South African War, as viewed from Mademoiselle Souvestre's library southwest of the oppressor's capital city, exposed Eleanor to the reality of authority's miscalculations. A war that everyone in England supposed would be over by Christmas would end up becoming the longest, bloodiest, costliest, and most chastening conflict fought by Britain between 1815 and 1914.[12] "The debate as to whether that war was right or wrong gave me my first burning concern with a grave public issue," recalled Eleanor.[13]

The Boers also gave Eleanor a special place in Mlle. Souvestre's politics. Bitterly critical of the war and its motives, Souvestre did not just rail against the crude ruthlessness of British power; she analyzed the ethics of the warring governments. When her English students celebrated British victories, she tolerated their loud revels in the gym and withheld her own opinions from those pupils "whose parents might have considered them heretical, if not traitorous,"[14] while feeling free to unload privately in her study with Eleanor and the German, Swiss, Swedish, Russian, and Italian girls. This went on up to the evening of June 1, 1902, when word came that a peace treaty had been signed in Pretoria. Allenswood's English girls danced around the schoolrooms until Mlle. Souvestre, "perfectly furious," shut down the celebration, reminding them that an imperial nation had rounded up civilians and penned them into "concentration camps," where thousands had perished of starvation and disease.

That evening, the English girls trooped off to Thanksgiving service, while Eleanor remained with Mademoiselle.[15] "I often wish," she wrote in a distant future, "that I might take Mlle. Souvestre with me to the United Nations."[16]

Mademoiselle was merciless in her insistence that her advantaged pupils had been given truly unusual capacity and choice over others in a world still desperately poor. It would be a criminal waste not to put these gifts to the greater good. On any subject related to religious belief, she could be witheringly sarcastic. In one discussion, after asking for opinions on the question of "why it was good to pray," she challenged the beliefs of every girl until one dared to ask what *Mademoiselle* thought. Whereupon Souvestre drew herself up and declared that she never shared such aspects of private thought, and only liked to hear the opinions of children on religion because they amused her.[17]

Explosions—the word students used to describe both Mademoiselle's laughter[18] and her rage[19]—seemed to combust out of nowhere. Afterward, Souvestre withdrew into implacable silence. Behind closed doors, trays would be brought by the school's tiny adjunct power, Pauline Samaia, the Italian teacher who served Allenswood as housemother and business manager, and Souvestre as nurse, selfless companion, and emotional caretaker.

When Mademoiselle was away, everyone noticed the calm. Without that powerful voice and the action she churned up around her, quiet fell over the house.[20] But when Signorina Samaia went up to London even for the day, Mademoiselle became "restless and ragey," and positioned herself beside a heavily trafficked hallway door expressly to scold, and if possible to shame, any pupil who let it bang.[21] As for the loyal Samaia, one student remarked that Souvestre was apt to treat "Signorina" "just like a child."[22]

Some pupils felt exposed by Souvestre's physical assertion of authority: the snow-white hair, the onyx eyes, the erect spine, the charged probing. She seemed to penetrate so intently into her girls' concerns that some of them came to believe that she could read their minds, which only ensured that they kept her even more obsessively in mind. Some froze at the mere sound of her voice. Others stopped breathing when she approached.[23] One student, recalling this paralyzing awe, summarized: "We respected her and loved her but most of us were a little afraid of her. Totty never seemed to be, though."[24]

ON THE FIRST EVENING SESSION of every term, Souvestre read poetry aloud. Challenging the girls to listen carefully, she read out a favorite poem two or three times, lingering over lines she especially liked. Then she would call for a volunteer to stand and recite these lines back to her without looking at the printed page.[25]

On her first poetry night, Eleanor stood, finding that the lines came to her as naturally as Uncle Ted's old favorites from "The Charge of the Light Brigade."[26] In fact, she was a prodigy of aural memory, but at Oak Lawn no one had noticed these triumphs of the ear. At Allenswood, her talent shined.

The attention she captured intensified the next day when Mademoiselle praised her before a full assembly.[27] In her autobiography, Eleanor Roosevelt reflected, "This was the first time in all my life that all my fears left me."[28] But no sooner had she shown promise as a school exemplar than self-consciousness welled up behind her new public front.

This time, it started when Eleanor, anticipating a visit with a new friend's family, became "so homesick and woebegone that everyone was sorry for her."[29] The new comrade who triggered this episode was Helen Agnes "Nelly" Post,[30] a spirited, roguish girl who had been at school a full year longer. Eleanor would come to feel intimate with "Bennett," her sturdy roommate; and she increasingly admired the lovely German girl Carola de Passavant, and enjoyed her friends Avice Horn, sent "home" from Australia, and Hilda "Burky" Burkinshaw, back from India. But to Eleanor, mischievous Nelly Post was the tuning fork. Without even a knock—simply by bursting impishly through the door of Mademoiselle's library—Nelly set everyone around her vibrating.

From their first class together Eleanor found her irresistible. She "had a fine mind and a very warm heart," said Eleanor, but she also "had the most violent temper I have almost ever seen, and I doubt if anyone had ever tried to discipline her."[31] In Fraulein Petritsch's classroom, to Eleanor's horrified delight, Nelly's pranks and capers repeatedly brought the lesson to a complete standstill. She was a natural subversive—more like a Western American than an Easterner. Indeed, Nelly's family's ranch in the Texas Panhandle,[32] the vivid unseen promise of its wild "miles and miles of country to ride in"—525,000 acres, to be exact[33]—became one of their secretly shared subjects at Allenswood.[34]

The two Americans took history with Mademoiselle Souvestre, and though there were eight others in the headmistress's study, so far as Eleanor was concerned "there was no one but [Nelly]. This impression of mine was helped considerably by the fact that Mlle. Souvestre seemed to feel that there were only two members of her class—[Nelly] and myself."[35]

She was elated by the headmistress's recognition of their yin-and-yang closeness. Still more mystic chords seemed to have been struck from their startlingly similar backgrounds. Nelly's father, like Eleanor's, had been a much-loved New York sportsman—Arthur Post, who five months before Nelly was born had died in the Anglo-American sporting community of Pau. Nelly's mother, Lizzie Wadsworth, was fashionable, beautiful, and impersonal.[36]

Eleanor and Nelly made friends so quickly, and so immediately generated excitement as a pair, that when Nelly's family planned to drive out from London the very first Sunday afternoon, Nelly insisted that Eleanor come with them. She thought that it would be pleasant for Eleanor to "see some other Americans."[37]

All of a week earlier, Eleanor had felt wondrously free of her former life. Now, faced with the prospect of being exposed to family acquaintances as the laughably plain daughter of Anna Hall Roosevelt, she wanted to run and hide. Worse, any outing that involved horseback riding with gutsy Wadsworth women, as Nelly had gaily promised, could not help but reveal Eleanor's own fears.

No amount of coaxing could pull "Little Nell" out; she was spooked, once more diminished into the form of "a big girl with a pigtail."[38] When the polished carriage clattered up the drive with Nelly's cousins and half sister and glamorous mother, Eleanor stayed in her room. Nelly went out by herself to greet her family and tell them about her friend. Sixteen-year-old Harriet Wadsworth would recall her cousin describing "the little American girl who was so homesick," then going back inside to "lead out the most pathetic and awkward little girl you ever saw."

Eleanor said hello shyly, recalled Harriet, then "slunk back into the school."[39]

While these superb horsewomen could only remind her of her failures, she redeemed herself among other notable figures. When Mademoiselle had important guests to dinner—illustrious literary or artistic figures, as well as "one or two Prime Ministers of England and France" whom she sat on either side of herself—Eleanor had no trouble contributing from her place opposite the adults. Her classmates marveled at how "Totty" was "never awed by anyone"[40] and could "lead Mademoiselle off on almost any track and keep her going."[41]

Playing the part of Mademoiselle's mindful protégée allowed Eleanor to exercise her natural curiosity and to pick up material from the visiting adults, which she would blend into her own thinking and then sprinkle into related subjects at her next evening session with a delighted Souvestre. Eleanor ever after felt guilty of copycatting, believing herself to be simply mirroring her way into a position of pseudo-authority without sustained study.[42] When variations on this situation repeated in her adulthood, she made an art of being better informed and more carefully prepared than her colleagues.

By the end of first term, her report card showed enthusiastic endorsements from her teachers and high praise from the headmistress: "She is the most amiable girl I have ever met."[43] Eleanor could be counted upon "to influence others in the right direction."[44] And as time went on: "Eleanor has the warmest heart that I have ever encountered. As a pupil she is very satisfactory but even that is of small account when you compare it to the perfect quality of her soul."[45]

EVERY DECADE OR SO, MARIE Souvestre singled out a favorite not just to be admired or applauded as a school leader, but for a broader mission. More than a schoolroom pet, the favorite was to carry Souvestre's high culture to the world. Bamie Roosevelt had been such a one; Beatrice Chamberlain, another; Dorothy Strachey, a third. Implicit in Eleanor's fall-term victories was her chance to become their official successor.

That fall, as Nelly once again cut up in class, Eleanor took a place at her side as the steady one who had no quarrel with the system. Mademoiselle could see that Eleanor had a calming effect on Nelly: she was impartial and fair, not easily swayed, nor was she susceptible to "anything that was not perfectly straightforward and honest."[46] So Mademoiselle confidently put Nelly alone with Eleanor for an additional German tutorial, and all went well until the day that Fräulein Petritsch angered Nelly, who pitched a glass-and-metal inkstand at her.

Eleanor knew at once that this was unpardonable. Nelly had shown a raw force that Mademoiselle could not close her eyes to. If she were to give in, it would seem favoritism, cowardice, or truckling to the powerful Wadsworths. Mademoiselle was also fighting the stereotype that women achieved their ends by tantrum. To Souvestre, so personally volatile herself, calmness was true self-mastery. Here was an already favored Anglo-American, a girl of the Empire, violating Allenswood's core value of self-discipline.

Eleanor, completely heartbroken, went to ask the headmistress to show mercy.[47] But to no avail: Mademoiselle was adamant, Nelly was expelled, and a tearful Eleanor was once again alone.

For a number of years afterward, she tried to stay in touch with Nelly. Nelly's life as a maiden-in-waiting to several royal princesses occupied her completely, and they lost track of each other. Eleanor later heard that she had married a gentleman usher and groom-in-waiting to King Edward VII and had children. When she came to write about Nelly in her autobiography, extolling "a really fascinating girl," and casting their friendship as the relationship whose intensity "marked . . . the earliest months at Allenswood," she revealed a yearning to keep feelings for Nelly alive: "Her glamour is still with me, so that I would give much to see her walk into my room today."[48] When she wrote this—early January 1937—a White House invitation from Mrs. Franklin D. Roosevelt was all but guaranteed to bring people to her door. She could fairly easily have seen Nelly, soon to be Lady St. Germans,[49] had she been confident of the Nelly who would turn up.

Instead she made a secret of Nelly's name. Perhaps she was exercising an abundance of discretion since, by then, Nelly's husband, the 8th Earl of St. Germans, and her son (as a page), were honored intimates of the future King George VI.[50] Whatever the reason, in three volumes of autobiography, peopled by hundreds of notable figures, Eleanor Roosevelt felt the need to keep just one person's identity safe under a pseudonym. She memorialized Nelly as "Jane."[51]

SUMMER RETURNED. ELEANOR ENVIED THE girls with homes to go to. She was kept in Europe, and suffered a burden of guilt about not going home to look after her brother. To be sure, Hall did not lack for surrogate mothers, but he was Eleanor's special duty; and in Eleanor's first year's absence, Pussie had irritatingly taken Hall further under her wing. As always, Eleanor was carrying the new passion too far, energizing the relationship with pity—distinctly not what Hall needed—while keeping concealed her own needs for attachment.

During school breaks, Eleanor holidayed alone with Mademoiselle on the Continent. Here her mentor detected an executive drive in Eleanor and put her directly in charge of buying their tickets, securing hansoms, tipping porters, anticipating expenses. She insisted Eleanor take full responsibility for seeing each task through. These skills, which "gave me a kind of experience that was to be very useful when I had children of my own,"[52] encouraged her to put things in order and mobilize them in exciting ways.

Touring Italy the following two Easters and at Christmas came as a revelation. Wherever they went, Mademoiselle would sniff out the best of the local foods; reconnoiter the "one" cathedral worth spending time in; give high marks to some great thinker of the region. The only way to know an urban landscape, Mademoiselle insisted, was on foot. They walked everywhere and never stayed in the accepted hotels for Americans or Britons but instead lodged with the bourgeoisie, as when they spent several weeks in Florence at the house of a painter. For Eleanor, the elasticity of these days showed her how rigidly she had viewed life from Oak Lawn. Daily discussions with her Florentine painter host about how he was posing his models for a rendition of the Last Supper opened Eleanor to the idea that the Christ figures she had known in Doré's Bible in the library at Tivoli were not "a real likeness of a real man" but aspects of a collective and evolving consensus of sacred images. "Isn't it queer," she later wrote, "how children take things for granted until something wakes them up?"[53]

"It all served," she later realized of these awakenings, "to make you a citizen of the world, at home wherever you might go."[54]

Souvestre marveled that Eleanor never tired. She was "never out of sorts, never without a keen interest in all that she sees. I have rarely seen such a power of endurance."[55] For Eleanor, it was more a question of how to take it all in, when she was feeling "keener than I have probably ever been since."[56] On their first morning in maze-like Florence,

Mademoiselle saw at once that Eleanor would march her to exhaustion, and so put a guidebook in the sixteen-year-old's hand, letting her loose without a thought for conventional chaperonage or even safety. "Perhaps she realized that I had not the beauty which appeals to foreign men, and that I would be safe from their advances," Eleanor said self-deprecatingly in later years. "Being ugly and innocent, nothing disagreeable ever happened to me, and I never expected it to."[57]

Unsurprisingly, she could not see how appealing she was. She had a beautiful smile, but the face she turned to the tearooms and galleries of the ancient city was doleful. "Totty—so intelligent, so charming, so good," said Mademoiselle definitively, before throwing up her hands in exasperation: "*Mais elle n'est pas gaie!*"[58]

No evidence survives of any erotic attraction between teacher and student. Biographers would later ask if Eleanor was aware that her teacher was gay.[59] Souvestre did depend emotionally on Eleanor, who became more skilled at reading her mentor's moods the longer she remained at Mademoiselle's side—learning which were safe and thus allowed for spontaneity, and which were explosive and required her to improvise.

The possibility of Eleanor's failing to measure up was no longer on anyone's mind. The Totty Roosevelt who returned to Allenswood the next two falls became an intermediary, mediating tensions between her fellow students and Mademoiselle. She had tried to do this for Nelly Post; and though she had failed to save her friend, she came into her own as the beloved ombudsman for Allenswood's international student body.[60]

Mademoiselle privileged her further by assigning her to look after the girls who were ill, mothering them and administering medicines. Through damp English winters, Eleanor maintained the school's precautions against influenza by soaking pieces of cotton wool in eucalyptus oil and hanging the swatches from the chandeliers in study hall. She made school purchases, helped Signorina Samaia run the house, and welcomed new girls from Germany, France, Russia, nursing them through their struggles and adjustments, making them feel rapidly at ease in circumstances so different from their usual lives.

In September 1901, when the assassination of President McKinley transformed Vice President Theodore Roosevelt, at forty-two, into the youngest chief executive in American history, Eleanor sensed new eyes upon her. She would later admit that even with Uncle Ted now leading the nation, she did not "have the least idea how our government was run, nor did I have any curiosity about it."[61]

The more Allenswood kindled her instinct to serve others, the more she resisted going home to "come out" in society. Her youthful ideal—professional nursing—necessarily remained a dream. To Grandmother Hall's generation, the thought of nursing the public was vulgar; a well-bred girl taking her place in society was supposed to marry, not scrub the sick or empty bedpans; even caring for family members was best left to servants. College was also out of the question, since at Vassar or Bryn Mawr Eleanor would only become the kind of serious young woman no gentleman would ever look at. "All you need, child," rasped Grandmother, "are a few of the social graces to see you through life."[62] She insisted that Eleanor return for her debut in winter 1902.

Eleanor would remember Allenswood as the happiest time of her early life and Mademoiselle as her most profound influence, after her father.[63] She could imagine returning one day to Allenswood to teach alongside her mentor and to mediate between Souvestre and her latest worshipful followers. But Eleanor made no cult of her teacher; and the real education of Eleanor Roosevelt depended most on that part of herself that responded to misfortune as the super-adult everyone needed.[64]

This survival skill neatly dovetailed with the Souvestrian belief that whatever came her way was hers to handle. And without higher education or further training in social sciences, this alloy of universal responsibility would fill her life with commitments, often petty, sometimes damaging, always time-devouring. Years would pass before she could accurately take her own measure or discriminate among those causes and people vying for her help and her heart. For now, whatever and whomever was left on her doorstep was her responsibility.[65]

THAT JULY, 1901, AUNT PUSSIE—ELEANOR'S anti-Souvestre— landed in England to pursue yet another married man and, incidentally, to take Eleanor home from school.[66] Pussie was now, as Eleanor later commented, "a liberal education in how a person who is really probably emotionally unstable can make life miserable for the people around them."[67]

Unmarried and embittered at twenty-eight, Pussie seized new love as fiercely as if it were a revolver. Anxiously awaiting a proposal from her latest target, she checked herself and Eleanor into a London hotel for a night of "long discussions and tears."[68] As the hour of sailing approached and no word came, Eleanor assumed that the man "did not relish a scandal, and there was not going to be any further love story going on."[69] Pussie's obligation to bring Eleanor back left her no choice but to board the steamer home, her hopes put aside again.

As the sluggish Atlantic Transport Line vessel steamed for New York, Pussie restarted the melodrama, declaring this her last voyage, and vowing to throw herself overboard.[70] Eleanor took her at her word, jumping up every time she started for the cabin door, whereupon Pussie would mock Eleanor's newfound Allenswood-alpha-girl authority.[71]

Everyone agreed that she had become much comelier while abroad. One friend recalled the returning Eleanor as a "lovely appealing young girl—fresh from school in Europe—winning all hearts by her charm and seriousness, and exquisitely turned out [in] beautiful and chic clothes."[72] Another friend saw in her tall new presence a "Gibson-girl figure, a pensive dignity, the charm of tenderness, and the sweetness of youth."[73] Even Cousin Alice had to admit that there was "something loveable about her."[74]

Pussie may simply have been ashamed at being so needy as to have put her niece on protracted alert—her niece, moreover, who was about to bud into a debutante. Whatever the reason for her bile, when they both stayed at Northeast Harbor in July, Pussie took her revenge, turning on Eleanor the blast she kept threatening to use on herself.

The summer had been stormy on Mount Desert Island, the buoy in the harbor clanging on the afternoon Eleanor braved the windy, thundering walk from Cousin Susie Parish's to Aunt Maggie's cottage on the harbor shore. Inside, when tea was served, the talk of the day turned to Eleanor and what she would wear to the next of the summer's dances, which raised the subject of Mlle. Souvestre's tailor having fitted her for a stylish gown in Paris. Put out by this, Pussie wondered aloud if Eleanor wouldn't always look like a child dressed up? "You're so homely," Pussie told her, with point-blank relish, "that no man will ever want to marry you."[75]

This was suspect, coming from a famous beauty who was six years past the average age of marriage for women. But Pussie was too quick to be caught, and immediately let fly another round of live ammunition, sniping at Eleanor for her "neglect" of brother Hall. When Eleanor stoutly protested that her father had left *her* in charge of Hall, Pussie went in for the kill. "You're so innocent," she taunted, "you don't know anything about your father."[76]

She then grimly laid out for Eleanor the dire facts of Elliott's infamy seven summers before. Her father had died—not in Virginia, as the newspapers had said and as Eleanor had always believed—but in sordid surroundings: his mistress's apartment on West 102nd Street. Doping himself. Guzzling alcohol by the quart. Knocking on a neighbor's door during a fit of delirium tremens to ask if "Miss Eleanor Roosevelt were at home," and upon learning that she was not, asking the neighbor to "tell her her father is so sorry not to see her."[77] Then running violently up and down stairs. Then jumping from a parlor window.

Eleanor had a half brother, didn't she know? *Elliott Roosevelt Mann*,[78] later to change his name to Elliott *Robert* Mann to expunge his mother Katie Mann's early attempt to prove his paternity.[79] Eleanor's father had gotten the housemaid pregnant, bringing further shame on the family when this Katie Mann tried to blackmail the Roosevelts. Uncle James Alfred Roosevelt had paid off the woman, only to find that Katie reappeared, bastard in her arms, at the reading of Eleanor's father's will. But before Miss Mann could state further claims, the husband of a *Mrs. Evans*, Elliott's *newer* mistress, had brandished a loaded revolver, and this "Mr. Evans" had kept his finger on the trigger as he threatened to shoot up the Roosevelt family lawyer's office. . . .[80]

As if smiling through a curl of her own gunsmoke, Pussie finished: "That's the kind of father you had."

Elliott Roosevelt's death had stopped her nine-year-old life in its tracks. Now, seven years later, here it was blasting out of the back of her adolescence.

Pussie was cruel. "What right had she to make [me] so miserable?" volleyed an older Eleanor. "It seemed to me then that she was the most selfish person I had ever known."[81] But her authority was sufficient to cast a spiral of doubt that sickened Eleanor. Had *she* been the only one from whom the truth had been kept? "Father's little Golden Hair." Was she nothing special after all—just a *newer* Miss Roosevelt in El-liott Roosevelt's ongoing serial?

There seemed no bottom to the depths she must now reexamine. The new information undermined her most basic understanding of herself and her family, which now included a pitiable half brother. It embarrassed her to know that somewhere lived a disadvantaged little boy bearing her father's name.

After Cousin Susie corroborated Pussie's story, Eleanor limped back to Tivoli, clinging to the hope that Grandmother Hall would deny it. But Grandmother only intensified Eleanor's confusion when she further explained that Elliott's "weakness" had been the deciding factor in Anna's tragedy: "It ruined your mother's life."[82]

AND WITH THAT, HER DREAM was gone.

If she could only get back to Allenswood, where she could take refuge. What comfort to know that she had a third and final year under Mlle. Souvestre's wing. Even though she would have to come back and live with Pussie during her debut, it was heartening to know that she had a real mentor, upon whom she could now rely "as a guide for me—to think of what I could do, rather than about what I could not."[83] For if Pussie was right, and her father had been a bad man, El-eanor now understood that she could redeem him just as absolutely by being an extremely good woman.

No one would ride herself harder or adhere more closely to codes of conduct. She would show the Assembly Ball matriarchs—her moth-er's generation of matrons who had treated her in the wake of her fa-ther's death "like the daughter of a wicked, ruined man."[84] She would lecture roguish Cousin Alice on which presents were permissible to receive from gentlemen (flowers, books, cards; positively no jewelry), as Alice vaguely fingered a string of seed pearls she had won from a passing admirer the week before.[85]

More satisfying, she would show vampish Aunt Pussie how to expand into marriage, and banish forever the bad story of her parents, by putting virtue and a virtuous husband in her own. From now on, wrote Eleanor, "a certain kind of orthodox goodness was my ideal and ambition."[86]

FIVE

O
NE SUMMER AFTERNOON ON THE upriver local, Eleanor was
pleased to see Cousin Franklin Roosevelt gliding toward her.[1]

He had just finished his second year at college, stood a handsome
inch and a half over six feet, and met her smile with keen, closely set
blue eyes.[2] His manner was lighthearted, playful, and his delight in
needling her brought his smile, crowded with fanglike canine teeth,
"near to a predator's ecstasy."[3]

Franklin Roosevelt could be tricky. Strong-headed, superior—an
only child, infinitely beloved—he was the prince of his own domain
but a figure of ridicule among his peers.[4] Like Eleanor, Franklin felt
left out, and she understood this as few others did. When she had last
seen him at young people's parties arranged by his mother, Franklin
had regarded her as the one contemporary he could count on to "help
to fill out chinks"[5]—a canny recognition of another consummate insider living within herself as an outsider, developing an extra ear for
what was pointedly never uttered.

Franklin read the world by flashes of intuition and acted in a series
of lightning strikes. Now he invited Eleanor to come forward to the
Pullman to say hello to his mother, and she followed as if pulled by a
current.

Cousin Sallie, twenty months a widow, sat straight as a mast, covered from hat to floor by a black veil. She was genial and interested
and outspokenly fond of Eleanor's father, delighted to commemorate
Elliott in his most successful role as "Godfather to my boy."[6] Only
much later would Eleanor learn how harsh Cousin Sallie could be in
her judgments against her father and his "weakness."[7]

For now all was sweetness and music as they reminisced about
long-ago autumn dancing classes held by a Hyde Park neighbor for
the children from the river families. And now that everybody had no-

ticed how sensible and attractive Eleanor had grown, Cousin Sallie could join her nearest neighbors, the Newbolds, in commending her as "a true Roosevelt."[8] Cousin Sallie put it her own way: "Now take Eleanor," she would say. "She has lovely eyes and nose, but her mouth is decidedly Roosevelt." Franklin, she held, had "nothing of the Roosevelt in his looks." Her son was entirely "Delano in appearance."[9]

On this subject, Sara was absolute. Mother and son undeniably shared the Delano face: symmetric blunt chin and high, broad brow. More noteworthy, they shared a Delano *expression*, a look of unconsidered confidence and natural authority; and, if someone remarked on the similarity of their rich round, tenor voices, she would reply, "Of course we talk alike—I brought him up, didn't I?" Then, with a satisfied lifting of her chin: "Franklin's voice is like all the Delanos'."[10]

Cousin Sallie's family occupied an unusual position in American wealth, having oriented themselves toward maritime trade in the Pacific. Sara's father, Warren Delano II, had become rich as the chief American rival to English interests in the $38 million ($1.092 billion today) Pearl River Delta opium trade.[11] Twice making his fortune by peddling Turkish "black dirt," Delano never tried to justify a morally shameful enterprise but insisted that he had followed fair and honorable business practices established among his cohort of American "tea" traders.[12]

Sara adored her father as only a near-favorite can, suffering his prolonged absence. When Sara startled everyone by marrying, against her father's wishes, *his* contemporary James Roosevelt, the easygoing, side-whiskered Hudson Valley entrepreneur and good Union Democrat, she was consolidating adventurous Delano aspiration with landed Roosevelt respectability. As "Mrs. James," empress of Hyde Park and generalissima of Springwood,[13] the Roosevelt family home overlooking the Hudson River, Sara simply covered over her anxiety about partings and separations in the thick burlap of maternal stubbornness.[14]

She took great pride in becoming her only child's nurse, bathing Franklin until he was nearly nine years old. They were separated from each other just once in all of Franklin's childhood: on Eleanor's parents' wedding day. Franklin had been little more than a month shy of two on that December afternoon in 1883 when Mama (pronounced Ma-mà) left him with her family at Newburgh. When she appeared to be missing, Franklin was "unable to believe she could have left him behind." He searched the nursery but found only her jacket, then "buried his face in it . . . crying, 'Mama! Mama!'"[15]

Outwaiting by a full two years the other mothers who sent their twelve-year-olds to be schooled by Dr. Peabody at Groton, she ensured that Franklin's first venture into the world would be as odd man out.

James Roosevelt's death in December 1900 left Sara, at forty-six, a young widow. She saw herself and "her boy" simply going on as they always had—as "a loving couple," as their friends had called them in the days when mother and son toured museums and galleries hand-in-hand.[16] Franklin delighted in Mama's authority. "I wish him to be under the influence of his mother," decreed the last will of James Roosevelt, entirely superfluously. So far as mother and child were concerned, there was nobody else and would never be anyone else but Mama and Franklin.[17]

Hyde Park on Hudson remained mother and son's mighty fortress. Coming home and being home—"at the river," Franklin called it—meant that he and Mama were magnetically aligned at the secure center of their earth.[18] Home at the river meant the house commanding the high slope sweeping down to the Hudson.[19] Tall oaks creaked in the river wind, and a fifteen-foot-high hemlock hedge screened Mama's rose garden, an oval-shaped acre of Eden perfumed by the blooms of thirty-four separate rose beds and fertilized by cow flop, the secret ingredient that made Mrs. James's the brightest roses in the valley.[20] As soon as Franklin graduated and could come home with her from Cambridge, Mama planned for their family of two to resume this glorious idyll along the Hudson.

Franklin, however, was learning to deflect his mother's attention from inconvenient truths. Little over a month earlier, he had proposed marriage to a Boston debutante—"the loveliest of her year," recalled a wistful FDR in later life.[21] Alice Sohier was the lustrously beautiful seventeen-year-old daughter of a North Shore banker, to whose Republican family an exuberant Franklin had announced his ambition to be president. He had just as eagerly confessed to Alice his wish to have no fewer than six children—the very size of brood that Cousin Ted had just installed in the White House—and that pipe dream, as much as Franklin's romantic overreaching (he had to be slapped, *hard*, Alice later said) persuaded her to reject his proposal.

"I did not wish to be a cow," tossed off Alice to a friend.[22]

Franklin had not spoken a word of the close-call courtship to his mother; indeed, he had encoded his diary to prevent discovery. Marrying a Boston belle would have meant the end of Franklin and Mama and the home they loved. Had Alice accepted Franklin, he would now be preparing for a life of "settling down in the Back Bay to spend the rest of my days."[23]

Instead, just five weeks after his "narrow escape," here was the prince of the river, running home with Mama, deliberately bringing forward a cousin whom Sara had known with affection since babyhood.[24] Cousin Sallie was free to like Eleanor; and as the New York Central rolled them all homeward, Eleanor could not help liking her. That summer of 1902, when the Halls were now undergoing a kind of domestic chaos in which everyone was excused from being a responsible grown-up, Eleanor found a strange bliss in Franklin's mother's probity.[25]

OAK LAWN STOOD FURTHER APART than ever, not even linked to its neighbors by one of the new farm-line telephones. This had become especially hard on Hall, now eleven, a bright boy with only a tutor watching out for him. Grandmother Hall was still his legal guardian, but "somehow or other," grasped Eleanor, "the real responsibility for this young brother was slipping very rapidly from her hands into mine."

Intensely protective, she hated to leave Hall alone on the place, especially when Uncle Vallie, in an upstairs front bedroom, was far enough gone to poke a shotgun muzzle out the window and fire blasts of buckshot at River Road daredevils, real and imagined, dodging from tree to tree on the lawn. It was only a matter of time before his shaking hand *couldn't* be counted on to miss.

Captive to Vallie's binge cycles, Grandmother isolated herself. To Eleanor she looked ill and pale and "seemed quite old already,"[26] though Mary Hall was only just approaching sixty. "I feel my life has been so wasted," Grandma confessed to Aunt Maude, after Aunt Tissie reproached her during one of Uncle Eddie's disappearances. "I have never done anything for any of you."

For Eddie, a tennis champion's golden youth had given way to an especially pitiful adulthood. The turning point had come at a stag dinner celebrating his twenty-first birthday at the New York Athletic Club. Many wines had been poured; by one waiter's account, "quart after quart with the utmost regularity,"[27] until the young men began pitching glasses, bottles, cups and saucers across their third-floor private dining room. One waiter, Theodore Morgenthaler, was just coming into the room when a glass smashed into his left eye, a rush of blood flowing from the wound.[28]

In truth, Eddie himself had done this, but except for handing the man a twenty-dollar bill for "the cut" to be attended to,[29] took no further responsibility. Even when a doctor in the club found that the glass had severed the eyelid and penetrated iris and pupil; and a proper eye doctor then pronounced Morgenthaler blinded forever in the injured eye. Eddie went right on rolling out the high life until Morgenthaler sued him. Compelled to resign from his club, Eddie hurried off to Europe and plowed through the scandal that followed,[30] his denials enraging editorial writers at the *Brooklyn Eagle*: "When young men celebrate their inheritance of a large fortune by putting out the eyes of a waiter, socialists have plausible reasons for saying that the uneven distribution of wealth is productive of serious trouble."[31] For his part, Eddie squandered his inheritance (valued in today's dollars at more than $2.5 million); and after the sudden death of a young wife, became an alcoholic widower, selling poultry at Hempstead, Long Island, to make ends meet. Eleanor stuck loyally by her uncle, caring for his three daughters, later paying for their schooling,[32] and ordering Eddie's poultry for the Roosevelt household in Manhattan—until continual delays and evasions became intolerable and she realized she was doing nothing to help him, only facilitating his incapacity.

As for Vallie, Grandmother Hall went on covering his debts, each time returning to her darkened bedroom and carrying on in willed

silence until the next crash. During this phase, Vallie would peni-
tently abstain from liquor, work to restore trust with family members,
and maintain his thirty-five-year-old physique with strict exercise.
("His appearance was not of a dissipated man," said one woman he
assaulted.)[33] But once the next binge had started to roll, he became
treacherous, advancing through open bar tabs and unpaid hotel bills to
blackouts to arrests to nights in the local lockup. Finally, in June 1901,
he had been brought before a judge for more than $4,000 in personal
debt (about $145,000 now) and declared bankrupt. He denied all.

Eleanor had Allenswood schoolmates to stay the summer of '02,
and though they went home unharmed, she never again dared to bring
friends over. Franklin visited just once, played some tennis with Eleanor, and took a lion-tamer's pride in subduing Vallie. It was the beginning of the end of living under her grandmother's roof.

When the time came to enter Hall in the first form at boarding
school that autumn, she didn't hesitate. For the next six years, from
ages eighteen to twenty-three, Eleanor spent one weekend of every
term visiting Groton School with the much older parents of her
brother's classmates. On each of her trips, she stayed at the traditional
boardinghouse and conformed to code by dealing uncomplainingly
with Mrs. Whitney's hard beds and unheated rooms. From home she
wrote Hall every day, explaining to a friend, "I want him to feel he
belongs to somebody."[34]

But where would Hall come home to? Oak Lawn was no longer
safe, though Grandmother would not admit it. "I have heard," wrote
Auntie Bye to Aunt Corinne, "that things occur at the Tivoli house
and they are exactly what happened with Elliott."[35]

When three locks appeared inside Eleanor's bedroom door, and no
one said why, she showed no alarm—that would have been bad form.
Matter-of-factly she told a friend that the locks had been installed "to
keep my uncles out."

Eleanor's sentiments about the house and the women who had
raised her there never wavered. In a farewell hug with her aunt during
the Second World War, she imparted, "You, Tissie—I think you and
I and Maude are *Halls*."[36] Still later in life, she summed herself up as
"more of a Hall than a Roosevelt." And in midlife, musing on her girl-

hood days at Oak Lawn, she would reflect: "There are sad memories as well as happy ones, but I hope I shall be able to keep a few things near me which will always vividly bring before me ghosts of past days."

But ghosts arise from the dead, not the living, and at Oak Lawn it was the living who never went away.

TAKING HERSELF AND HER TRUNKS and books into the frantically rising city of the new Flatiron Building, Eleanor kept house with Aunt Pussie and a skeleton staff of cook and maid at diminished 11 West Thirty-Seventh Street. Whether Hall would nomadically follow her to this grim old brownstone shell, as she dimly hoped he would, remained one of her chief worries.

The pressure, meanwhile, was on. The debutante season featured five Roosevelts: Eleanor, Alice, Christine (daughter of Emlen), Dorothy (only child of Hilborne), and Helen (daughter of Franklin's half brother, Rosy)—a so-called Magic Five, among whom the U.S.[37] newspapers had already spotlighted *her* for having "more claims to good looks than any of the Roosevelt cousins," thanks to her Hall "inheritance." The *New York Times* predicted: "Miss Roosevelt will receive a warm welcome. Her mother was a charming woman and one of the most popular of matrons in New York society."[38]

When the season of formal dances got underway, Eleanor's anxiety slicked her palms with sweat. She did not know what to say. Even when she did conjure something to speak about, her voice betrayed her. It was, she believed, her great enemy.

Yet when she was with Cousin Franklin there were "no dreadful silences."[39] Franklin was both reader and collector, hunting and mastering information wherever he could find it, always insisting that *they* must find out more on this or that question. Each time she saw him in public—at the New York Horse Show, the traditional November start to society's season; or at Louis Sherry's restaurant and ballroom afterward; or at lunch together after Christine Roosevelt's dance; or at the house party given for Eleanor by U.S. diplomat Whitelaw Reid, father of her fellow debutante—Franklin wanted to know what she had been reading. Just between themselves: Did she think the author reliable? What book did she recommend for *him*?

She realized that he, much like herself, was strangely at odds with the system, and that he needed her help. This last reminded her of the all-important covenant she had had with her father: *she* had something to give *him*.

As the annual Assembly Ball loomed, her mother's Gilded Age nightmare had at last come true.[40] The Hall women could no longer manage what would have been the most meaningful part of Eleanor's coming out—the afternoon "at-home," or "letting-out," reception held under her grandmother's roof.[41]

Grandmother Hall hosted a tea, afterward sealing herself and Uncle Vallie into Oak Lawn as if into a pickling jar. By staying upriver throughout Eleanor's debut winter, she hoped to prevent the child's reputation being further contaminated; and so, she left it to Aunt Tissie to execute a theater party for sixty and supper afterward at Louis Sherry's, as well as to arrange for the sisters Callot, premier Parisian couturiers, to gown Eleanor for the ball. Mlle. Souvestre, meanwhile, despaired that "all this will estrange you from all that I knew you to be!"[42]

If the un-Souvestrian intention of the entire season was to secure a suitable husband with a handsome fortune, the real point of the Assembly Ball was to show the bosses of her own sex that she was now sufficiently well trained in the string-pulling ways of the woman's game of "Spend and Catch" to be of future use to them.

On December 11, Eleanor drew on long white gloves, gathered an opera cloak around her low-necked ivory satin gown, and forced herself to the massive old Waldorf on Fifth Avenue at Thirty-Fourth Street, accompanied by Cousin Susie and Uncle Henry Parish. There she joined the four other Roosevelt debutantes and mounted the stairs to the West Foyer, where the receiving committee stood before an embankment of Southern smilax and farleyence ferns.

Her mother's leading rival, Mrs. John Jacob Astor, held the center of the line. Eleanor was expected to enter gracefully, sweep the room with a demure smile, and make a deep curtsy without toppling over. Thirty-four years later, appearing at the Waldorf during a charity fundraiser, she would be hissed at by "a group of people whose names are extremely well known in Newport and Tuxedo Park."[43] Even after that, she called facing her mother's peers in 1902 the most difficult thing she had ever done.

Her own cohort was complicated enough. Heading the guest list were such reminders of past attacks of self-consciousness as her Allenswood crush Nelly Post's Wadsworth cousin, along with a figure from Eleanor's childhood desolation, her once-a-summer playmate Carola de Peyster, who would be engaged within a month.[44] Had she realized beforehand "what utter agony it was going to be," she "would never have had the courage to go."[45]

Darting off as quickly as she could, Eleanor bore home a single traditional gentleman's favor that night: a fancy straw garden hat trimmed with flowers and ribbons—from the kindly older Bob Ferguson, former Rough Rider and Roosevelt family friend. Aunt Pussie, meanwhile, swept in at dawn, her pompadour fallen to her shoulders, her arms heaped with satin boxes loaded with chocolates. Eleanor's sole Assembly keepsake proved Pussie right: "I knew I was the first girl in my mother's family who was not a belle, and though I never acknowledged it to any of them, I was deeply ashamed."[46]

Over the next months—"my unhappiest time of all"[47]—Eleanor had no authoritative female in her corner. Uncle Vallie's escapes from Oak Lawn had increased in frequency, as had his binges, the bitter end of which invariably found him tumbling into the Thirty-Seventh Street house to make an ugly scene, most recently in front of a dinner party hosted by Pussie and Eleanor.[48] When it was beyond question that "somebody must stop Vallie," Eleanor proved to be the one best able to speak to Captain O'Connor at the West Thirtieth Street Police Station. She was also steady with hotel clerks, who brought out the patronizing worst in her grandmother, and remained unfazed by Vallie's spewing of profanity, letting none of his storm of viciousness offend her, but calmly prevailed over his objections and brought him home to sleep it off.

To her Roosevelt aunts, it was clear that Eleanor would have to make a change "on account of her environment." Aunt Corinne was unhappy that her niece was living "almost entirely alone with Pussie in

Thirty-seventh Street in a most erratic way, and I think insensibly she has become less careful about things."[49]

In truth, each time she took charge, Eleanor sensed in herself "a certain kind of strength and determination which underlay my timidity."[50] She took naturally to any duty that drew her to the "less attractive and less agreeable sides of life,"[51] and felt most fulfilled when her handling of bad things won her the reward of further responsibility. But when she went to Aunt Corinne to talk over her situation, she choked out the terrible fact: "Auntie, I have no real home." She began to sob in such a pathetic way, recorded Corinne, "that my heart simply ached for her."[52]

For now, the facts remained: Eleanor was nineteen and belonged nowhere. She had no house from which to be courted, not even a bedroom to call her own.

The ever-watchful Auntie Bye, down in Washington, was "dreadfully worried about Eleanor,"[53] and when the President's niece arrived there after Christmas to join a young people's house party that Cousin Alice was hosting for the New Year's celebrations,[54] Bye pointedly reported: "She looks badly and is in a *very* difficult position."[55]

After a summer and fall of renovations, the clean, bright, modernized Roosevelt White House was ready for the one day on the official calendar when citizens of "all ages, colors, and sexes, and conditions"[56] were invited in to receive and return the greetings of the New Year.

Eleanor appeared cross and unyielding when she took her place in the receiving party. She girded herself to stand in polite semi-silence with the younger assistants. This was frustrating because she had much to say—and to report.

That debutante year, Eleanor's urge to be useful—to *do* something—had become for the first time stronger than her wish to please.

As a member of the newly created Junior League for the Promotion of Settlement Movements, founded by her friend Mary Harriman, she extended herself beyond Oak Lawn caretaking into the newly established social engineering of settlement houses. Founded as a progressive social movement in Victorian England, the settlement idea of mending industrial capitalism's inequalities by bringing the urban working class into neighborhood fellowship with college-educated reformers had come to the United States twelve years earlier, through social worker Jane Addams's Hull House in Chicago. Eleanor volunteered for daytime duty at the Rivington Street settlement, and rode the Second Avenue Elevated down to where the roaring cars almost touched the sides of the tenements.

Twice a week, Eleanor threaded her way through the bedlam of pushcarts to 95 Rivington Street, where a pleasant brownstone with a children's playground out back (one of the city's first) stood at the heart of the Tammany-protected red-light district. Beyond its stoop, prostitution thrived unchallenged.

Within this "lay convent,"[57] students wore uniforms, tapers lighted the dinner table, and Ionic columns upheld order. In front and back rooms joined by sliding mahogany doors, Eleanor learned to teach fancy dance and calisthenics to the daughters of Italian immigrants, accompanied on piano by her friend and fellow debutante Jean Reid, daughter of the proprietor of the *New York Tribune*, U.S. diplomat Whitelaw Reid. Once, when Jean fell ill, Eleanor taught alone, expecting to feel clumsy and insufficient, but surprising herself at how naturally she took command. Afterward, she enjoyed a comfortable rapport with two students who walked her to the Elevated.

Helpfulness was the green heart of "neighborhood work." Shoveling snow in winter. Bringing ice in summer. Painting floors, sewing carpets, washing windows.[58] "The most important part of our work is to be nice to people," advised the College Settlement Association.[59] Ideally, residents spent months at No. 95, lending a hand, listening to problems, responding to individual needs, "settling like a submarine into the life of the neighborhood."[60] When an opening for political change or legislative reform appeared, settlement workers could then broker[61] between state reformers and the more vocal of Rivington's newer Italians and older Germans and relatively new Polish Jews and Russians: rallying the many to stand for their rights as one.

Upon hearing of Eleanor's contributions to what he brushed away as "club work," Franklin exhibited a streak of trademark superiority.

His arrogance derived from the fact that most settlement programs were aimed at women and children, and that few, if any, of the great male reformers were identified with the leadership of the movement. For many male leaders of the coming generation settlement work was a port of call in the larger mission of reshaping society through organized social intelligence. For Franklin Roosevelt in 1903, this was not man-making stuff; good works were an assertion of his class and position. For Eleanor, they were a correction. What their class's unnoticing industrialists and merchant bankers knew of the lowest 10 percent centered upon the idea that "they" had "brought 'it' on themselves"—drinking, prostitution, the beating of wives, the overworking of children. A burgeoning literature of urban horror was only just beginning to back Uncle Ted in his progressive reforms. Eleanor's willingness to stick her neck out gave her a clear view of all that still needed doing.

One afternoon, she invited Franklin down to meet her students and see for himself why her sympathies had been stirred. To the children's delight, he made a dashing entrance, looking as if he had floated down the East River in his tailored suit, beribboned straw boater, and gold-rimmed pince-nez. At her next class meeting, her charges pressed her to learn if that had been her "feller," a term that had to be explained to Miss Roosevelt.[62] Once she understood, she had to smile.

When Franklin arrived at the settlement for one of their rendez-vous, Eleanor had a sick child in need of being taken home. Franklin went with her, the little girl in his arms, up three flights to reach the family's flat at the rear of a dumbbell tenement. They stood an awkward moment in the dim hallway, not knowing whether to try conversation in Eleanor's beginner's Italian or to nod along solemnly with the parents' limited English.

Franklin seemed preternaturally alert to the stunted figures within, bent over, shuffling, crippled from lack of nourishment. For Eleanor, it was like looking in on patients at the Orthopedic. From her childhood visits to her father's family's hospital, she had "always seen life personally."[63] Her interest and sympathy, even her indignation, was never aroused by an abstract cause but "by the plight of a single person whom I have seen with my own eyes." Through Eleanor, Franklin would hone his own instinct for reducing the general to the particular.

"My God," he said when they were back outside, "I didn't know people lived like that."[64]

AT THE NEW YEAR'S RECEPTION, Franklin stood among the President's inner circle with a confident, clean-shaven face. Franklin's longing to be closer to Cousin Ted could at last be gratified. For him, the Roosevelt White House was a dream come true.[65] He had attended Alice's debut the year before, spent three days in Washington at Auntie Bye's, and returned to the White House for a private talk with the President, who liked Franklin more and more. TR told Cousin Sallie: "I'm so fond of that boy, I'd be shot for him!"[66]

But Eleanor's Oyster Bay cousins were merciless on the subject of Franklin, whose initials, they joked, stood for "Feather Duster."[67] They mocked him for his pretty face and narrow-set eyes, but above all, for his too-easy assent to his mother's wishes. Alice declared him the kind of "good little mother's boy . . . you invited to the dance but not the dinner afterward."[68] Franklin did not appear in the least oppressed by Oyster Bay malice or commotions, as Eleanor was. Yet, despite—or because of—his smooth handling of being a "wrong" Roosevelt, he seemed to find his balance at Eleanor's side.

All through this visit in her uncle's White House, she felt Franklin looking not just *to* her, but *at* her. Indeed, all his life he would marvel, as if seeing her as she had been at this time and in this place, at how magnificent she looked in evening clothes, her gold-brown hair piled atop her head.

Meanwhile, as the months slipped by, Rivington gave her a chance to grasp that the great failure of the American experiment had been local government—corrupt, inefficient, unable to deliver basic municipal services. The nation was spreading itself with marvelous speed, opening up to millions of newcomers, but it couldn't govern its cities, and the cities were failing the neighborhoods of the poor, leaving the tribal chiefs of Tammany Hall to consolidate political power by providing for the needs of "million-footed Manhattan."[69]

For Eleanor, the neighborhood household was the one place her drive to be useful could mix practicality with progress. She had to admit, too, that it thrilled her that her fine-looking cousin cared enough to let his curiosity lead him this far downtown.

She liked that he had a strong "English" profile and was as handsome as any of Pussie's cavaliers but, crucially, not as popular—probably because he could be as quicksilver as Pussie herself. In the midst of one of his book boosts with Eleanor, having baited her with his interest in a novel that she was reading for pleasure, Franklin suddenly switched on her, turning wildly sarcastic about the author. She found it bewildering; but play she would, and back she came, earnestly defending book and author, only to be still more dismayed when Franklin about-faced yet again, insisting that he had enjoyed her book and only wanted to draw her out.

His manner, by turns inquisitive and droll, made him one minute cool, next all colors and warmth. His sense of humor had not developed much beyond boyhood chamberpot jokes, and he bridged awkward moments in mixed company with elaborate storytelling. His favorite social ploy was to tease; he was a skilled kidder, though his kidding was less that of "a feller" and more the needling of her mother, whom Franklin echoed when he ribbed Eleanor for being "grandmotherly."

Ice-yachting with Franklin aboard his *Hawk*, at speeds several times faster than the wind, Eleanor learned to hold on tight. Indoors, too, he challenged her. Why, for instance, did a couple of afternoons at a downtown settlement make her any more useful than the average socialite volunteer? Thanks to the new Junior League, plenty of virtuous girls now saw how distressing the world of need could be, but after being taken back uptown in their family carriages did not have to do anything more about it. Their duty was simply to be distressed. How would Eleanor's instruction of new immigrants' daughters in fancy dance steps improve their parents' chances of putting a better roof over their heads?

Eleanor knew that one of her chief tasks in preparing these Italian daughters to become American women was to pry them loose from their elders—to free them to be their most independent selves in their new world. Nonetheless, she agreed with Franklin. Even college-educated women were frustrated by the small part they had to play.

When Eleanor floated an alternative, that of taking rooms of her own downtown, Grandmother Hall declared it unthinkable, and Cousin Susie agreed that she would lose her reputation. Moreover, Cousin Susie insinuated that if Eleanor went on volunteering in the slums she risked bringing "their" diseases back into the house where her mother and younger brother had both died of diphtheria.

If she couldn't live at Rivington Street, she could deepen her commitment to the settlement "family." Her Roosevelt aunts would have been shocked to learn that Eleanor had gone without permission to a hall on Fourteenth Street where everybody sang workers' anthems. Also without anyone's consent, she went right ahead and signed up for a training lecture in practical sociology, which she attended with Helen Roosevelt, Franklin's half niece. When Franklin heard of it, she blurted, "Now don't laugh." The lecture, she insisted, "*was* interesting & very practical & if we are going down to the settlement we ought to know something."[70]

She was prepared to see bad things truthfully, but she needed training in turning her sympathy to action. When she joined the National Consumers League and was sent to investigate working conditions for salesgirls in department stores, it never occurred to her that girls might get tired standing behind counters all day long, or that employers *wouldn't* provide stools for them to take a rest. Working for the League's legislative committee on one of its campaigns to rewrite the housing code, she nerved herself to go into tenements in the West Village to document the misery of small children toiling in at-home sweatshops. From repeated inspections of ongoing violations, she grasped the part she could play as a "plain neighbor."[71] When Cousin Susie and Grandmother Hall insisted that Eleanor curtail her slum activities, it seemed impossible that she must stop serving the good but go on being Aunt Pussie's Cinderella.

All that now changed the weekend of the Harvard-Yale football game. Eleanor was visiting her brother at Groton, and she felt the community's special excitement when Franklin came out from Cambridge to attend Sunday vespers. Groton's chapel bound them tightly as a couple within the school's fellowship. It seemed entirely in the way of things that Franklin should walk Eleanor unchaperoned to the fir-banked Nashua River; and there, with the "Groton family" as inspiration for their future, he asked her to marry him and she accepted.

Back at Tivoli, Grandmother Hall asked if she was sure she was in love. Solemnly, Eleanor answered yes. "And yet," an older Eleanor could clearly see: "it was years later before I understood what being in love was or what loving really meant."[72]

For Eleanor, new happiness once again came accompanied by old pain and the sudden sorrow of "another link gone."[73] Upon Eleanor's return from Groton, James King Gracie, the "saint with whiskers" who with Great-Aunt Gracie had served as her childhood's "extra set of parents," died at his townhouse. He left her $15,000 in trust, a stable source of cash for her lifetime on top of her protected parental inheritance.

Franklin delayed until Thanksgiving before breaking their news. He took Mama for a walk in the garden behind the Delanos' family house at Fairhaven and tried to explain having gotten engaged, but Sara would not hear of it. Franklin simply could not have done such a thing without consulting her.

Mama declared a year's moratorium on engagement. She further hatched a plan for Eleanor to feign indifference whenever Franklin was present, and for the couple never to touch. Without complaint, Eleanor agreed to do as she wished, writing to Mama to reassure and to sympathize with "how hard it must be."[74] Franklin hastened to add that nothing would change, only that Mama would now have "two children"[75] who loved her.

That was their compact: Eleanor could be Franklin's wife, if Eleanor would be Sara's daughter, leaving Franklin free to keep his options open. It was their first magical illusion: Eleanor would step behind the curtain as the Other Woman and re-emerge as Mama's Filial Companion, a role for which Mlle. Souvestre had well prepared her.

For one so committed to straight-ahead "goodness," Eleanor was surprisingly effective at joining Franklin in Mama's flanking maneuvers. In this year under wraps, Eleanor and Franklin established themselves as a tremendously externalized couple. "Watch them," Harry Hopkins would many years later tell a friend. "Watch them because they do all their communication with each other in public."[76]

* * *

WHEN MAMA SENT THE SILVER to the bank and took Franklin on a winter cruise to the Caribbean in 1904, Eleanor was not invited.

She headed instead to Washington, to join a young people's New Year's house party hosted by Cousin Alice. Intimidated by invitations from Uncle Ted's White House, Eleanor felt easier staying with Auntie Bye. Her aunt gave her advice then that she tried ever after to live by: "You will never be able to please everyone. No matter what you do, my dear, some people are going to criticize you. But don't let what they say upset you. Just be entirely sure that you would not be ashamed to explain your actions to someone you love and who loves you. And if you are satisfied in your mind that you are right, then you need never worry about criticism."[77]

When mother and son returned from the Caribbean, they all met for tea at Auntie Bye's. Two days later, Eleanor fled to New York, leaving Franklin and his mother to dine at the White House. "I've come to the conclusion that I need someone to watch over my temper," Eleanor confided to Franklin, "it makes me so cross with myself to lose it and yet I am forever doing it."

In her darker, prickly moments, the thought of bright and breezy Franklin restored her better spirits. "I only hope," she told him, "that I shall bring you happiness. I don't seem to succeed in bringing it to most people, however, do I?"[78] On days when she did not see Franklin— "boy, dear," she had begun to call him[79]—she felt this gloom acutely. She let her yearning fill her pages: "I am hungry for you every moment, you are never out of my thoughts . . . I wish you were here, dear, to kiss me good-night."[80] She signed her letters, as she had to her father, "your devoted Little Nell."[81]

When the follies of Aunt Pussie's love life finally resolved in the capture of William Forbes Morgan, Jr., the nephew of J. P. Morgan who had attended Eleanor at her Assembly Ball, the marriage was celebrated in the twin townhouse adjacent to Cousin Susie's. On the day before the wedding, as Eleanor hurried about in bridesmaid tasks, she caught the bride-to-be spending the afternoon vamping around town in a motorcar with Bobby Goelet, a fashionable Manhattan rake. It was unfathomable to Eleanor: anyone truly in love, "spending the last afternoon like that."[82]

The wedding day went as planned. Eleanor did her part without complaint, but felt the more entitled to judge harshly—and to withdraw as soon as her duties were done, livid.[83] It did make her think: "It is a pretty solemn thing when it comes to the point of this getting married and I do not see how anyone who has not a great love in their heart can go through with it." She appealed to the Copey literature student in Franklin: "Have you ever read the service through Honey? I wish you would sometime for each time I hear it, I think it more beautiful and it means so much, one's whole life, in fact."[84]

THAT SPRING, SHE AND FRANKLIN saw each other constantly, and wherever Franklin was, there was the sun. By hitching herself to someone so different, Eleanor felt a sense of having been shut in and now breaking out. "I am so happy," she told him. "So *very* happy in your love, dearest, that all the world has changed for me."[85]

When Franklin became a dark horse for election to one of three prestigious marshal roles for his Harvard class, Eleanor knew exactly the day upon which the election fell. "Well, I wish you the very best of luck, boy dear," she wrote, sincerely, lightly teasing Franklin for taking the voting so seriously that she could imagine him "hanging around the polls."[86] As expected, he was trounced "after a hard struggle," as was the captain of the crew, but it was Franklin who bled in public when a faulty front-page *New York Times* story correctly headlined his setback but accidentally exposed his still-private wish: PRESIDENT ROOSEVELT'S NEPHEW DEFEATED.[87]

The next mail went off with Eleanor's confidence that he would have better luck in the next round of voting for the job of permanent class chairman, which would put him at the head of a university steering committee for years to come. At this he was victorious, earning himself as well a speaker's slot at the class dinner, the speech for which he began writing at once. "Don't forget," Eleanor reminded him, "you are to bring me the rough copy of your speech."[88]

In June, Franklin graduated, and Eleanor attended the Class Day exercises with Mama. During the summer, the couple exchanged visits at Tivoli and Hyde Park—her first visit there since Franklin had ridden her around the nursery and her mother had humiliated her at the library door. On hayrides and cliff walks and evening sails aboard *Half-Moon*, Eleanor sensed that Mama, sorry for her, had executively decided to do something for *their poor little Eleanor*. For once, however, this stirred the part of Eleanor that responded whenever she sensed a true ally in an older woman.

In August, it was off to Campobello, the Roosevelts' beloved Canadian island on the Bay of Fundy, where Franklin had summered all his life. Here, on her first visit to this faraway place, Eleanor realized that her beau was a far more serious collector than she had known. Whenever they passed a little antiques shop, whether in Welshpool or across the channel in Eastport, Franklin would pull up the horse and they would go in to look for stamps. "I am sorry to say that I felt critical about this," admitted Eleanor later. "For the life of me I couldn't see why he wanted more stamps when he already had his great-uncle's fine collection."[89]

Franklin was urgent in his pursuits. Whenever he was closing in on some long-sought treasure, a boundless exhilaration, almost a rapture, came over him as he spoke about it. Whatever he was after, he must get it at once, and he was not himself until mind or hand closed around the prize.

IN THE FALL, FRANKLIN STARTED at Columbia School of Law, which Cousin Theodore in his time had also picked. Harvard, his father's law school, remained closer to his own ideal, but neither Franklin nor his mother saw the law as his real profession. The future had social answers, so far as they were concerned; when the time came, levers were available for pulling. To clerk at one of the better Wall Street firms, mother and son addressed themselves to friends at the New York Yacht Club to make introductions; the Commodore was the senior partner of the firm that Franklin hired on to.

Eleanor knew how important being at the center of the action was to Franklin. Feeling responsible about limiting his social prospects, anxious as always about acceptance herself, and trying harder than ever to fit in with Mama, Eleanor thought nothing at the end of Franklin's first day of asking him whether he had "found any old acquaintances" on Morningside Heights, "or had only Jew Gentlemen to work with."[90]

On Eleanor's twentieth birthday—October 11, 1904—with their engagement still a secret, Franklin gave her a square princess-cut diamond with six sparkling side stones.[91] "I love it so," she burst out, "yet I know I shall find it hard to keep from wearing it!"[92] She was not allowed to show her ring to anyone, not even her best friend of this period, Isabella Selmes, a debutante from the West whose parents had known Uncle Ted in the Badlands.

That same day, Sara sent Eleanor a note: "I pray that my precious Franklin may make you very happy and [I] thank him for giving me such a loving daughter. I thank *you* also darling for being what you are to me already. This is straight from my heart."[93]

When it came to Franklin and Mama, there would always be strings attached. But the older, powerful Sara could see great potential in what young Eleanor had to give *her*; and it was to this part of the unspoken agreement that "Totty" could confidently cosign. She wanted to stop having to be the child-adult herself. She needed someone to take care of her, and all she had to do to win Sara's love was to be invisible.

The engagement, kept secret since August 1903, was made official on November 30, 1904, whereupon Eleanor fell ill with the flu. For the next two days, she remained "*very* weak," recorded Mama, "like a shadow."[94] On the third day she pulled herself together to accompany Franklin to their engagement dinner at the Parishes'. Next came the obligatory visit to the Delanos at Fairhaven, where Eleanor took comfort in being welcomed to a rational, well-managed household that would not be swept away by a deranged uncle, a drunken father, or even a hyperkinetic President of the United States.

Uncle Ted, elected that November to the great office in which fate first tossed him, wrote to Franklin: "I am as fond of Eleanor as if she were my daughter; and I like you, and trust you, and believe in you." As if he had read Franklin's mind or decoded his diary: "No other success in life—not the Presidency, or anything else—begins to compare with the joy and happiness that come in and from the love of the true man and the true woman, the love which never sinks lover and sweetheart in man and wife. You and Eleanor are true and brave, and I believe you love each other unselfishly; and golden years open before you."[95]

THE FOURTH OF MARCH 1905 celebrated a President who invoked the continent as a whole, fusing Industrial North and Old South through his childhood heritage, joining cosmopolitan East and cowboy West in his young manhood, tilting the center of federal power from the States and Capitol Hill to his own newly potent Executive end of Pennsylvania Avenue. There, linking Atlantic and Pacific Oceans on his office globe with one hand, TR doubled U.S. naval power and, through the "Roosevelt Corollary" to the Monroe Doctrine, redefined the United States as an international police power, ready to intervene and put an end to conflicts arising in the Western Hemisphere.

To the Oyster Bay family, the day felt "like a glorified Xmas, even more shiny inside than usual."[96] By noon, cold wind and threatening clouds had pulled back for TR to take his second oath of office in the sunshine of the Capitol platform. Turning to face the crowd packed under the trees across the plaza, he spoke briefly. Behind and above him, Eleanor and Franklin sat among the President's clan. "This was a great excitement to both of us," recalled Eleanor; "purely personal to me, but I think to my future husband very political, too."[97]

Franklin was still an upriver cousin little known by the press, appearing to the Inaugural public as Franklin "B." Roosevelt. He would never stop being a charmer with a bit of the sixth form bully, but he was wise enough to know (as only a boy nicknamed "Feather Duster" knows) that if his will to power was to be taken seriously, he needed a woman of urgency at his side.

Dancing at the Inaugural Ball, they appeared for the first time a born duo. Society editors were delighted to rack and re-rack the many billiard-ball combinations in this new game. Miss Eleanor Roosevelt, daughter of the President's late brother, was to be married to the son of Mrs. James Roosevelt, who had been introduced to her late husband by his fourth cousin, the President's oldest sister. Meanwhile, the prospective groom, godson of the late father of the bride, was also half brother to J. Roosevelt Roosevelt, whose daughter Helen, niece of Franklin, had recently wed a cousin of Eleanor, Theodore Robinson, a nephew of President Roosevelt, who happened also to be godfather to the bride, leaving one upstate newspaper to joke: "Puzzle: What relation will the lady be to herself after the wedding?"[98]

Aunt Edith offered the White House, "to do for you as we should for Alice."[99] Franklin looked right at home in Cousin Ted's Executive Mansion, which as the author H. G. Wells remarked, "was like visiting any large comfortable, leisurely, free-talking country house."[100] Eleanor felt more comfortable marrying in Manhattan, where Cousin Susie and Uncle Henry Parish's town house, adjoining that of Great-Aunt Maggie, had second-floor drawing rooms opening into each other through sliding doors, making it possible to wed "at home" yet have a fair number of guests. At the same time, she wanted Uncle Ted, her godfather, to stand in and give her away; and since he was coming up to New York to give speeches at annual St. Patrick's dinners, the President's schedule chose their date for them—coincidentally another hollow iteration of her mother's birthday.[101]

And so, by 7 a.m. on March 17, 1905—proclaimed in the national press "Roosevelt Day not St. Patrick's Day"[102]—the flag was lowered over the White House, to signify that the President was on his way, rolling to his native city.[103]

SIX

B UT SHE WAS SURE HE would not come. As the hour drew closer
and the parade grew louder—more than sixty thousand strong,[1]
marching past on Fifth Avenue—Eleanor became convinced that
Uncle Ted would be unable to get through. And not just the worried
bride: "Everyone was petrified."[2] Once the President of the United
States did arrive, top-hatted and beaming, offering Eleanor the crook
of his soldier's arm and Franklin his congratulations on "keeping the
name in the family,"[3] many of the guests were held outside at check-
points at either end of East Seventy-Sixth Street.

Inside, the bridal party, led by Cousins Alice and Corinne, glided
along an aisle formed by the ushers on the Ludlow side of the twin
rooms. The Reverend Dr. Endicott Peabody, Franklin's headmaster,
stood ready to officiate, as six bridesmaids advanced one by one in
cream taffeta and tulle veils above which swayed three white Prince
of Wales plumes tipped in silver—ornamentation usually reserved
for being presented at Buckingham Palace, but here representing the
ostrich-feather crest on the Roosevelt coat of arms.[4]

Franklin's taste for pomp and bloodlines, questionable in a democratic country,[5] had become positively grandiose with this merger of
Hyde Park and Oyster Bay. He had gone all out on his ushers' deco-
rations, seeing to it that the central graphic totem of *his* line's armo-
rial bearing—a trio of thorned roses—appeared in the diamond- and
pearl-encrusted stickpins he had designed for the groomsmen to dis-
play in their cravats.[6]

To Eleanor he gave a small gold chatelaine watch set with her initials and the tribe's three-feather crest in small diamonds.[7] One observer accurately noted that Franklin had made a wedding present of
"the sort of watch that German governesses used to wear."[8] Eleanor's
soon-to-be habitual gesture—cutting a hurried downward glance at

the watch face pinned to her blouse—made it seem as if in marriage to Franklin Roosevelt she would be a "Granny" after all. Appropriately, she—who would live to warn the world of the ticking of the atomic clock, and was beginning her married life in the same year that Einstein was formulating the theory that founded the atomic age—now went to the altar wearing time as a decoration over her heart.

AT FIVE O'CLOCK, THE FRANKLIN D. Roosevelts set off for Grand Central and a ten-day honeymoon in Hyde Park.[9] "I do hope they will be very happy," Cousin Corinne said in farewell, "for if anyone deserves it, [it] is Eleanor."[10] Marie Souvestre, days from dying of cancer, wired Eleanor a single word for the future: *Bonheur*.

At the Hyde Park depot, the family coachman met their train. It was a cold, clear evening, and Franklin trotted his bride along the Albany Post Road—for real now, not the nursery game of eighteen years before. Turning through stone gates, they clattered along the Roosevelts' quarter-mile avenue of maples to see that candles had been lighted in the windows for Franklin's homecoming. Dour Elspeth McEachern, the Scotch caretaker he called "Tiddle," met Eleanor at the door with a look of "wondering if I could come up to her expectations as the wife of 'her boy.'"[11]

All his life, those closest to Franklin Roosevelt almost unanimously concluded that in his inmost feelings he was unknowable. At the time of his marriage he was said to be "completely impenetrable."[12] Eleanor would spend much of the next fifteen years learning to accept that it was "part of his nature not to talk to anyone of intimate things."[13] Only that bread-crumb path of books led Eleanor a few steps into his "heavily forested interior."[14] The first morning, after breakfast, when he took his newly minted wife into the library and placed a prized first edition in her hands, encouraging her to admire the volume's pristine state, Eleanor felt he was putting into her safekeeping the finer part of himself.

She turned the leaves delicately, but when a small rip tore the edge of an uncut page, cold shivers raced down her spine. Uncertain what to say—she had done it, no question—she made herself confess at once.[15]

To her great surprise, Franklin insisted that books were to be read, not bronzed: "If you had not done it," he offered, "I probably would!"[16] Later, she marked his gallant response as "the beginning of my becoming more mature about my fears of displeasing people."

For the rest of that first spring, while law school pinned them to a hotel apartment on West Forty-Fifth Street, she struggled to show Franklin that he had married an efficient homemaker. "My ideas of a wife," mused a later, freer Eleanor, "were strictly concerned with the household."[17] Yet Grandmother Hall's lessons in pantry administration failed to translate for apartment-living newlyweds. Without cook or butler she had little idea how to feed her husband or herself. She was able to darn Franklin's socks, and to put some order to their linens and other wedding presents, but whenever she filled her new vases with spring flowers and left them on the table for her husband to enjoy, she could only watch in stunned silence as Mama swept up the bouquet with offers of a "lightening" touch.[18]

By the end of each week at the Hotel Webster, Eleanor was so distressed at the "depths of my ignorance,"[19] that she gladly surrendered; being invited to cheerful family parties in Mama's smoothly run household would at least make Franklin happy.

At Easter, the realization of her long-sustained hope for Hall to come home to a room of his own proved disappointing. The hotel layout was so confining that her quietly willful, six-foot-three, 225-pound brother "seemed to fill the whole apartment."[20] But over Hall's years of transition from Groton to Harvard, Franklin's facetious banter had its effect on this intelligent, secretive manchild home from school. It genuinely lightened Eleanor's heart—and household arrangements—to see how good her husband was with her brother.

PACKING STEAMER TRUNKS FOR THEIR summer-long European honeymoon brought back Eleanor's dread of Atlantic voyages. She was an efficient manager of steamer tickets and letters of credit, but the confidence of her Allenswood crossings evaporated when she imagined the humiliation of being seasick with "a husband to take note of my suffering, particularly one who seemed to think that sailing the ocean blue was a joy!"[21] The days and nights on shipboard could not fail to offer proof of how little she was cut out to be any kind of mate.

Auspiciously, RMS *Oceanic* crossed smoothly, the sea like a mirror. Eleanor had only to endure oppressive heat, and to live up to her position at dinner as the lady to Captain Cameron's right, or to follow along blindly when Franklin flattered the master of the ship into escorting the Roosevelts on a top-to-bottom tour. As always, she could not help noticing the fretful eyes and tightly held elbows of steerage passengers. But she asked no questions and exclaimed instead over how clean everything was.[22]

Whenever another woman responded to her husband's good looks, she put herself under similar restraint. During her engagement, she had agonized to a cousin, "I shall never be able to hold him, he is so attractive."[23] Popular feminine wisdom agreed, warning her that "by comparison you will seem twice as homely and as old as you are, and people will always wonder as they look upon you why he did it."[24]

In fact, Franklin sometimes looked and dressed and acted like an ass. Striped boaters and starched high collars, Turf Club jocularity, his habit of tipping back his head to peer down through pince-nez—it was hard to take him seriously. He had an attractive forgiving streak for the follies of such heavy-drinking eccentrics as were then treasured in English country life,[25] all of which made him seem even more the epitome of the adventuring American fop delighted to be taken for an English gentleman.

On the *Oceanic*, their stewardess gushed to Eleanor that her husband was "so handsome and has the real English profile."[26] Eleanor gladly received this homage and passed it along to Franklin—who flashed her a spiteful glare. Contrary to Anglophilic appearances, he loathed the British and wished to have people know him as a self-determining patriot, free of imperial vanities. His sole pride in European roots was as a latter-day "Dutchman," so deeply planted among Hudson Valley gentry that he liked to think himself "unsnubbable."[27]

In reality, social shocks from his time at Harvard had left enduring hurt. Before being blackballed by the Porcellian Club—both his father and Uncle Ted had been members—Franklin had never been denied anything fundamental. Now, when anything came easily, when he was admired or flattered for advantages he took for granted, frustration surfaced fast. Outside Paris, to a relation of his father's who cooed,

"Qu'il est beau, qu'il est charmant,"[28] Franklin bared his teeth and gave his most "severe" look.[29] When Eleanor then set down the curious scene in her newsletter to Mama, Franklin swiped the pen to scribble his petty protest: *This isn't true—Eleanor got buttered on both sides!*[30]

FLEET STREET HAILED THEIR ARRIVAL with a front-page photograph announcing the young couple as "President Roosevelt and Bride on Honeymoon."[31] Being taken for Uncle Ted, or as "the President's son," had a magic power that summer of TR's world-altering deeds. These climaxed in September with the American president's signing of the Portsmouth Treaty, ending Japan's first assertion of an Asian power surging onto the world stage in the Russo-Japanese War. Franklin boasted: "Everyone is talking about Cousin Theodore . . . the most prominent figure of present-day history," he assured his mother,[32] meanwhile taking delight in teasing her by quoting their royal suite at Brown's at a highly unlikely $1,000-a-day (more than $28,000 in current money).[33]

Eleanor's pretensions to economy made her even easier to bait. She hated spending money on herself. But, having protested the high cost of a dress, she then felt guilty *not* buying, and so bought things she didn't need, reproaching herself afterward for paying full price and opening herself to Franklin's mockery.

Her interim nickname, "Baby"—not yet shortened to the final teeth-clamped cigarette-holder diminution—*Babs!*—played off Franklin's idea that his "nursery" bride remained willfully immature in the things he himself had mastered.[34] This conceit dominated his breezy catch-up notes to Mama, in which he made a point of jovially sabotaging Eleanor's dutiful postings about doing "a little" shopping[35] with a belittling counternarrative that exaggerated their actual haul of furs, linens, fine furniture, "and other unmentionables."[36]

PELTING RAIN PENNED THEM INSIDE the royal suite, so they could not use the tickets for Saturday's polo matches or the open two-seated electric car that Nelly Post had kindly sent around for the newlyweds' first London weekend.[37] Eleanor's schoolgirl crush was now a sparkling figure in fashionable circles, her calendar apparently too crowded or the friendship too thinned to make sure they caught up.[38] Eleanor recorded no regrets about Nelly but acutely felt the loss of Marie Souvestre.[39]

She decided she must go out to Allenswood, yet with Mademoiselle gone, there seemed little point in bringing Franklin. It was strange enough when she arrived to find Mlle. Samaia all alone. Their melancholy reunion[40] shadowed Eleanor's newfound joy, and served as stark contrast to Franklin's elation the following weekend when he brought his bride to Osberton-in-Worksop,[41] one of Nottinghamshire's great estates,[42] which he had first visited as a bird-obsessed eleven-year-old fascinated by the household museum.[43]

Eleanor felt intimidated by the other guests in the oval-ceilinged drawing room—*overwhelmed*, she later acknowledged.[44] These were Mama's chessboard people, including a bishop and an earl and their hosts, the Earl and Countess of Liverpool. Eleanor was introduced to no one—she was presumed to know everyone—and could see with new eyes what her husband could do with a small group of essentially self-centered strangers. Among sportsmen and their wives, as well as with clergymen and lords, he was irresistible, as sparkling and desirable a companion as Elliott Roosevelt had been in similar circumstances.

Eleanor bluffed through a formal dinner, going along with her husband afterward to play highly competitive and monetized bridge at separate card tables. Franklin amused himself with a skillful, shrewd game, while Eleanor, tormented by falseness, angry with herself for thinking she could play at Franklin's games with Franklin's people, found herself shamefacedly settling losses with cash. She felt "like an animal in a trap," and ever after recalled this agonized evening as one of the unhappiest of her life.[45]

THE SEMI-ROYAL HONEYMOON ROLLED ON, cross-Channel to Paris, down to Milan, over to Venice, then gradually through the Dolomites and the Tirol in a carriage behind a pair of horses.[46] Their progress broke off at Ulm and Augsburg in southern Germany, then proceeded up through high Alpine passes to St. Moritz, and back to Paris, London, and on to the English and Scottish countrysides—a sustained expedition in accumulating treasure for Franklin's collections.

"Books, books," wrote Eleanor, "everywhere we went."[47]

Collecting left her cold; she went along to Parisian bookstalls as Franklin's translator but hoped he would see further acquisitions as "a waste of money and a lack of common sense."[48] If they were to make ends meet while he studied law, they must spend sensibly.

One night, Eleanor awakened to find her husband climbing through the window shutters, pawing at the glass. "I must get it," he was saying, "it is very rare."[49] Grabbing hold of his nightshirt, Eleanor asked what he was after. "I can't reach that book!" he protested, furious with her. *If I don't get it now, I may never get it at all!*"[50]

THEY HAD BEEN INSTALLED ON the Grand Canal a week when Franklin suffered the first of four honeymoon outbreaks of hives, which would include a ten-day siege in August. The gondolier recommended by Cousin Julia Delano zoomed the happy invalid to and fro across the Lagoon, the sea breezes a palliative for the pink algae-like blooms burning under his skin.

The gondola released Eleanor from cares of her own. Its swaying rhythm reminded her of her father and the charmed evening when Elliott had sung in waltz time with the circle of stripe-shirted men on the water.[51]

At the Lido, she kept a prudish distance from anything that looked risqué. One letter home crackled with criticism of the cut of a woman's bathing suit. In Paris, she disapproved of Gertrude Vanderbilt Whitney turning up at Voisin's with a man not her husband: indeed, with "Bertie" Goelet, the decadent brother of "Bobby," with whom Eleanor had caught Aunt Pussie having a last fling.[52] She abhorred the notion of flirtation becoming fashionable. Although her letters to Mama sincerely attempted to "carry lots of love," they appeared to Eleanor long, dull, and stupid when compared to Franklin's "amusing ones." The contrast made her feel "really quite ashamed."[53]

THEIR HONEYMOON ROUTE BRIMMED WITH romance, but Franklin failed to make Eleanor feel truly loveable. She found the sexual side of their marriage less than pleasant, and perhaps so did he. Just before they were to go north, another consignment of hives materialized, prompting Franklin to dash out for a last visit to a favorite new bookshop, where he gave in to impulse and bought an entire library, instructing the bookseller to pack up and send home his treasure in crates—an Astor-sized shipment of more than three thousand titles.[54]

On the same July day, their gondolier delighted Eleanor by presenting her with a single volume. The book had been in the Venetian's keeping for much of his adult life—a beautifully bound edition of the lyrics of sixteenth-century Italian poet Torquato Tasso, who had died just before the Pope was to crown him poet laureate. Her "benevolent bandit" wanted Eleanor to keep it to remember her nights on the canals.[55]

Eleanor was relieved and then yet more baffled when Franklin's heat-inflamed welts mysteriously disappeared only to reappear once more in the cool climate and chocolate-box scenery of Augsburg. She worried that Sara would think *her* to blame for the relapse.[56] Everywhere in the honeymoon correspondence is evidence that they all still believed Mama to be Franklin's greatest caretaker.

In the mountains of Cortina, after an easy trail walk to a teahouse, tension surfaced back at their hotel when Franklin put Eleanor on the spot, proposing at dinner that in the morning they attempt one of the most difficult climbs in the Faloria—four thousand feet above Cortina. Dining at their hotel was family style: opposite the Roosevelts sat the elderly Misses Van Bibber, friends of Mama's on Campobello.[57] Everyone awaited Eleanor's response.

Quietly she replied that she had done all the hiking she cared to do on this trip, but of course Franklin must have his climb.

To the company's dismay, Franklin then turned to their amusing table companion, stylish Kitty Gandy, a Manhattan millinery shop owner who had been cadging Franklin's cigarettes and promising him an ostrich-plumed winter hat in return. She was older than both Roosevelts but gamely took Franklin's challenge, and next morning at seven, Franklin provocatively set out with Kitty, leaving Eleanor to awaken alone.

At lunch, she had to answer to the table for her husband's unnatural and now ominous absence. This was the first example of Franklin treating Eleanor as inadequate. It enraged her. When the climbers finally returned after lunch, reveling in shared triumph and adventure, Eleanor greeted her husband coldly.

Franklin would have none of her silent treatment. There was no question of apology. After all, Franklin had asked Eleanor to climb and she had refused. If wrong was now being done to Eleanor, Eleanor was doing it to herself. And so they had their first "Patient Griselda" standoff, as Eleanor later dubbed these episodes in which she withdrew into icy silence and Franklin remained breezily forbearing.

The following evening, Franklin left her to her martyr's bed of nails while he joined the other guests and "had the time of my life," dancing with the cook and maids, twirling the hotel's proprietress, smoking with the porter: in short, putting his feline nature on full view as he played all around him off one another, then sat back to relish the results from an amused distance.

When they left the hotel the next day and drove out of the mountains, Eleanor sat erect in the carriage, her head held high and slightly forward—the surest sign that she was still troubled. Going over the Stevio Pass, Franklin explained that he was walking beside the carriage because he did not want to strain the horses. She knew he had backed off to let her anger cool, even as he himself went right on enjoying the world without her, glowing with the good brown color from the sun at high altitude.

When Franklin reached up and gave her a peace offering of wild mountain flowers, they smelled sweeter "than anything I have ever had."[58]

ONE STILL MORE CRITICAL PATTERN was set at honeymoon's end in the north and south of Scotland. They went north first——to Novar, Bob Ferguson's family place in the Highlands. During their stay, Eleanor was asked to open the village flower show. She had never spoken five words in public. "I could not do it," she insisted. "I was quite certain that I could never utter a word aloud in a public place."[59]

Franklin volunteered to substitute, but when the day arrived, Eleanor did an about-face. Perhaps the fresh news of Uncle Ted's triumph in Russo-Japanese statecraft inspired her courage—certainly not the anti-American riots that had followed in Japan. Perhaps it was simple one-upmanship with Franklin. A mutually motivating competitiveness had begun to play between them.

"*We* opened the flower show," emphasized Eleanor to Mama.[60]

"She opened it very well," countered Franklin, "and wasn't a bit rattled and spoke very clearly and well, but I had an awful time of it and wasn't even introduced." Nettled by this informality, Franklin had wandered up to the platform to do his bit on gardening and raising vegetables. "The foolishness of my smile," he told his mother, "was only equaled by the extreme idiocy of the remarks that followed."[61] But Franklin was sincerely taken aback, even hurt, by the feeble applause that saw him off the platform.

As he went, Franklin was asked by a crofter about American methods of *cooking* vegetables.[62] Casually, he advised "the tenantry"[63] to cook all their vegetables in cream—a Marie Antoinette tone-deafness that would have surprised a later world of radio millions. "I could not stop him," reported Eleanor.[64]

A related episode took place a few days later, when Eleanor and Franklin stayed briefly at Raith, the Fergusons' Lowlands estate across the Firth of Forth from Edinburgh. Their host was Bob's uncle, Sir Ronald Ferguson, who took Franklin under his wing, while Lady Helen showed Eleanor the special generosity of taking her seriously. Eleanor wished to impress her hostess, whom she knew to be "typical of the alert Englishwoman who knows the politics of the hour to the last detail."[65]

Lady Helen, daughter of Lord Dufferin, one of the most successful statesmen of Victorian England, had indeed served innumerable political campaigns. She spoke of British politicians and Britannic statecraft as an insider and had been applauded for her own work among the poor and the sick. Her one other guest was a formidable magistrate from Colonial India, Sir Frederick Nicholson, and soon enough Eleanor's ear was picking up details from these two veterans of parliamentary democracy. She in turn put on "my same old air of being well informed,"[66] as she had once described the "bad habit"[67] she had learned in order to live up to her special place at Mademoiselle Souvestre's table.

"There's one question I have always wanted to ask some Amer-

ican," interposed Lady Helen at afternoon tea, pouring and passing Eleanor's cup with the delighted air of having indeed found her
American—the President's niece, no less: "Will you please explain the
relationship between your states and your federal government? Both
seem to have so many separate functions that I do not understand the
ways they work together."

Eleanor was—her word—floored.[68] She had no sense of government, not even of belonging to a political party: Grandmother Hall
had seen to that. Except for Uncle Ted's leadership of the federal government, as before he had been at the head of New York State, she
knew nothing of what he himself called the "great machinery"[69] of the
American constitutional system.[70] Through what little she had done in
the Consumers League, she had a picture of expert lawyers drawing
up proposed legislation and codes to present to the state legislature
at Albany.[71] But as for who occupied its senate and assembly seats, or
how such a body played its part in the people's business, she was "quite
ignorant."[72] Lady Helen, meanwhile, waited for her answer.[73]

Eleanor fumbled, realizing full in the face that she had been caught.
Recalling her girlhood shamings before her mother, she "wished that
the ground would open up and swallow me."[74]

Luckily, Franklin appeared just then for tea. Eleanor looked to
him "frantically."[75] He had come to her rescue before and "knew my
problem quite well and his eyes twinkled as he gave the answer."[76]

An article of faith in their marriage would be that at such moments of public exposure, they would each do whatever they could
to protect the other. Eleanor had bluffed just as unconvincingly as
Franklin had done on the platform at Novar. She later explained in
her account of their honeymoon that their respective unprotected humiliations "righted the balance so far as our personal relationship was
concerned."[77] Her secret—their secret—was that she, too, had energy
and a great name and wanted to put this to some use.

Her humiliation at being caught in ignorance at Raith stayed with
her. She vowed to learn things for herself, and to look into things diligently, even if that meant working twice as hard as Franklin to master
the same subject.

*   *   *

After years of returning to her off-kilter Hall relatives, Eleanor was grateful to be swept home to Mama's well-ordered household at 200 Madison Avenue, thence to Hyde Park for the weekend. Rough seas on the homeward journey had left her ill, and Franklin was immediately preoccupied by two makeup exams for courses he had failed in first-year law school. They would not have the new house on East Thirty-Sixth Street for another month; mercifully so, as Eleanor had no hope of taking charge of the twelve-foot-wide, five-story brownstone that Mama had rented, decorated, and staffed.

Seeing no improvement after several days of her daughter-in-law's queasiness, Sara summoned the doctor, who examined Eleanor on October 11, as she turned twenty-one. He pronounced the diagnosis three days later: the younger Mrs. Roosevelt was three months pregnant.

SEVEN

FOUR MONTHS TO GO, HER belly "the size of the Great Pyramid,"[1] she did not feel entitled to put her feet up or to be cared for.

"She is wonderful," Mama recorded, "always bright and well."[2]

Eleanor would give birth four times in the next five years—and again in 1914 and 1916. With each pregnancy Franklin and Mama expected her to be "completely cheerful, completely self-controlled, not in the least worried about having a baby."[3] In consequence, Eleanor created powerful, self-renewing habits; never showing Franklin how despondent she felt, always concealing her fears from Mama. Instead of joining other expecting mothers in sisterly solidarity, she drove herself ever onward, alone.

When nausea struck in the last three months of her first pregnancy, she took it as a lesson in empathy: "It made me a little more understanding and sympathetic of the general illnesses human beings are subject to."[4] Otherwise, she suspected, she would be "more insufferable than I am."

"No matter how busy she is," observed her childhood friend Caroline Drayton Phillips,[5] "she is never nervous, or restless, but always perfectly calm & self-possessed." Long past the point when Caroline had made concessions to her own "confinement" during one of their parallel pregnancies, Eleanor, "strong as an ox," carried on all her usual activities.

"Don't you ever get tired?" objected Caroline.

"No," said Eleanor, "I feel very well, and I don't get tired at all."

"A *most* discouraging person," Caroline lamented to her diary.[6]

THE DAY ARRIVED—MAY 2, 1906—WHEN she blushingly began to feel contractions while playing cards after dinner. "E. had some discomfort," noted Mama.[7]

The next morning at nine, she began her "lying in" upstairs at 125 East Thirty-Sixth, attended by bespectacled Dr. Albert H. Ely and a well-trained pediatric nurse from St. Luke's Hospital called Blanche Spring. All through labor—through all *six* of her labors over these ten years—Eleanor held on to the same firm hand: not that of Franklin's mother, who kept vigil with her son downstairs, but of "the very lovely" Nurse Spring, working through illness of her own that first delivery but full of rare understanding.[8]

At 1:15 in the afternoon, the new mother pushed out a healthy baby girl, ten pounds, one ounce[9] —Anna Eleanor Roosevelt, named for Eleanor's mother and for herself.[10] As she looked down into the face of Anna, it was her newborn's complete helplessness that flushed out prenatal anxiety and startled Eleanor into seeing herself, however fleetingly, as something more than Sara and Franklin's birthing surrogate.

Breastfeeding went poorly, despite Nurse Spring's determination to get mother and child on a schedule. Mama had kept Franklin on the breast for more than a year; conversely, Eleanor would only have milk for the last of her babies.[11] Meanwhile, regular feedings and baths by additional nurses kept the new mother at an awkward distance from Anna, whom Franklin, a cuddly father and natural in the nursery, soon dubbed "Sis."

Eleanor drew closest in these weeks to Nurse Spring, in whose strong face, kind eyes, and luxurious, upswept golden pompadour she found a kind of double. Neither "newly-arrived Irish," nor "Scottish," nor for that matter "English,"[12] as she variously appears in Roosevelt biography, Blanche Spring was a thirty-five-year-old American, born in Maine. Her father, Jacob Spring of Brownfield, Maine, had struck it rich in Argentina as an exporter of wool and sent Blanche to the well-regarded St. Luke's Training School for Nurses in New York. Eleanor defied convention by treating Blanche as an admired equal: "a constant help in time of trouble, a friend and, for me, a great educational factor."[13]

When motherhood bewildered Eleanor with "a million and one situations in which no one ever prepared [her] to function,"[14] Blanche taught her how to make a bed and bathe a child; how to handle illnesses and accidents; how to use ventilation to safeguard the family against contagion.[15] Most important, Eleanor learned to recognize certain symptoms and not to be frightened when she didn't know what they meant.[16] Through Blanche she formed her clearest image of maternal duty: "A mother must learn to be almost a trained nurse."[17]

Blanche Spring was always with her. Each time the nurse returned, often for several months following a birth, or all through a dire illness, Eleanor's relief was intense. When Blanche left, a month after Anna's birth, the loss shook her. "Poor little Eleanor is upset by it," recorded Mama, "though she is brave."[18]

No sooner was Blanche gone than the baby had a convulsion accompanied by high fever. This was Anna's first summer at Hyde Park, and the distressed parents followed the accepted procedure: mustard bath, cold compresses. But neither Eleanor nor Franklin could be sure what afflicted their child, since convulsions in babies were known to signal measles, or pneumonia, or—the killers in Eleanor's line—scarlet fever and diphtheria.[19]

They worked well together in emergency. They had an equally strong need to solve problems rather than probe mysteries, and at once determined to take Anna to L. Emmett Holt, a pioneering pediatrician and Manhattan's most popular baby doctor. Mama, however, was at her most autocratic with family health. Sara understood that the city doctor was best, but her resentment at having to let Anna go made her declare a sudden run to New York unsafe.[20] They must all stay put—*she* would summon Dr. Ely, the family physician. By long habit, Franklin knew better than to oppose his mother directly on such questions, and left Eleanor to insist upon Dr. Holt.

As it worked out, Anna recovered quickly under the care of the great baby doctor, but Eleanor was left exhausted, her confidence worn through by these child-rearing "rubs and disagreements" between Mama and herself.[21] At such times, she took refuge with Aunt Jennie Delano,[22] who lived a few doors away with Franklin's fun-loving Uncle Warren, president of the Delano Coal Company in Pennsylvania. Aunt Jennie, an early feminist, hosted a reading group in her brownstone, which Eleanor attended, but it was the safe haven she provided that mattered most. After two hours with her broad-minded, affectionate Aunt Jennie, Eleanor would say, "I'm straightened out now," and could go back.[23]

At home, Mama went on issuing orders. To any question about the baby's diet and medicines, or clothing and fresh air, she had the answers; and she kept control by putting her own servants and policies into play without informing Eleanor of her instructions. The chain of command ran directly between "Mrs. James" and Anna's caregivers, bypassing Eleanor.

If Anna cried at night, Eleanor found herself beaten to the crib by Nurse Watson. Mama insisted that it was *Nurse's* job, not Eleanor's, to get out of bed to soothe the child; and Mama had no trouble cracking the whip on Nurse Watson.[24] If Anna lost her appetite, Eleanor first heard of it from the cook. She was given no time to judge for herself what course to take,[25] and when she spoke to Nurse Watson, she was told that Mrs. James had prescribed castor oil.

Once, when Anna fell ill, Eleanor suggested a course of calomel—the old mercury medicine of Grandmother Roosevelt's medicine chest. Mama pushed back and confidently awaited Dr. Ely's endorsement of castor oil, but when the doctor arrived and examined Anna, he sided with Eleanor and supplied the old toxin, which she went right on dispensing for the next ten years whenever a child had a digestive disorder.[26]

Otherwise, Eleanor positioned herself as one of Dr. Holt's "modern" mothers. Challenging Mama, she had the butler build from chicken wire and wooden batons one of the new *plein air* napping cages then coming into vogue. Every morning after Franklin went off to work, Eleanor placed Anna into her cage to be hung out the upstairs rear window for an hour's airing. But she miscalculated, forgetting the chill effect of the shaded side of the building. The Roosevelts' neighbors in the facing rear house were agitated by Anna's bawling cries, and before long Eleanor received a stinging rebuke from Mrs. Bayard Tuckerman, who threatened to report her to the Society for the Prevention of Cruelty to Children.[27]

But another neighbor, Lily Polk, was among a number of young matrons of this silk-stocking neighborhood who considered Eleanor the ideal modern mother. When they copied her airing method, "How daring we felt!"[28]

ALL THROUGH THE SUMMER OF 1906, Eleanor endured an excruciating case of hemorrhoids. Into the fall, she suffered this postpartum affliction with her usual reserve, and was so set against medical intervention that one of the children's governesses considered her "a Christian Scientist in spirit."[29]

By Christmas and New Year's, however, the pressure of social demands had fought her to a standstill, and on the 17th of January, she submitted to an operation considered by the medical establishment among the most agonizing and dangerous. Dr. Ely and a colleague performed the surgery in Eleanor's bedroom, using Blanche Spring as attending nurse. The first part of the procedure advanced without difficulty, but when the doctor tried to awaken his anesthetized patient, Eleanor showed no sign of coming to. From the black edge of consciousness, she heard one of the men ask Nurse Spring with no special urgency, "Is she gone? Can you feel her pulse?"[30]

The horror of helplessness stayed with her for years. She came through safely, but all through convalescence kept her windows wide open to the January air, as if to clear the sickish sweet reek of ether, which lingered as though oranges had rotted in the room. Whenever the door was opened, a biting wind snapped through, discouraging visitors. She pointedly refused conversation with anyone approaching her bedside. As Franklin and Mama and select family members came and went, Eleanor remained stiffly turned away, her condition more consistent with deep grief than postoperative bed rest.

"I imagine that they probably thought that I was far more ill than I really was," reflected Eleanor, later conceding: "My disposition was at fault rather than my physical condition."[31]

The pattern never changed. When hurt, she suppressed her feelings, and when anyone tried to come closer, whether to help or to hurt more, her only instrument of resistance was to turn away and sulk.

Not until Franklin's birthday on January 30 was she willing to have family and servants gather in her room for cake. Everybody had to wear overcoats and hats, but this made a sort of costume party of the occasion, and they all remained good-natured as the birthday candles shivered in the icy draft. Four days later, when Eleanor awakened to an accumulation of morning snow at the windowsill, she allowed herself to sit up. Mama visited for two hours. The siege was over.

IN A MONTH SHE WAS pregnant again, and when her waist measured thirty-four inches by September, she was sure it was twins. She gave birth just before Christmas 1907, and could hear Franklin greet his mother on the telephone with the announcement: "A son, all right, Mummy!"[32]

The coming of James meant displacing Hall from his room. On Christmas Eve, Eleanor made sure to fill and hang her brother's holiday stocking at Mama's house so that he would have it early, just as always. She also filled one for Blanche Spring, stuffing it with modest tributes and private jokes, but tried not to draw attention to the pleasure it gave her. Even so, when Mama came over with Hall to join the festivities, she did notice that treating Miss Spring to "a real Christmas stocking" was "rather an excitement" for Eleanor.[33] Later, in Mama's diary listing of those seated at Christmas lunch at Aunt Corinne's, she clearly disapproved of Eleanor's staying behind to help Nurse Spring with the baby.[34]

Mama had begun to hint at a change when Eleanor thought she might be having twins. Sara had always judged their "14-foot mansion" tiny,[35] but now, when visitors offered a courteous word about the house, she couldn't resist whispering as loudly as possible: "Too small!"[36] When Blanche Spring returned to nurse Eleanor through James's birth, the whispering campaign intensified. Then, on Christmas Day, Mama came right out with it and gave Franklin and Eleanor a new house.

She drew a charming picture of the place on a single sheet of letterhead: five stories tall, "19 or 20 feet wide," a well-proportioned townhouse with an arched street entrance and a chimney pluming smoke into the sky. The address of their happy home, explained Mama, was "not yet quite decided."[37]

Within weeks, she made the decision herself. Sara had a good alibi for wanting to move from 200 Madison Avenue: B. Altman's had come to the neighborhood, and in Sara's generation, when retail invaded, it was time to move uptown. Thirty blocks north, in the almost country quiet of East Sixty-Fifth Street, she went ahead and bought not one but *two* plots of land.[38] Tearing down the existing brownstones, Numbers 47 and 49, she commissioned the prominent New York architect Charles A. Platt to erect a neo-Georgian town house in buff brick trimmed with limestone and crowned by the Roosevelt family crest. Opening the iron-gated front entrance was like stepping into a Chinese box concealing two more front doors facing each other within.

The yuletide illusion that Franklin and Eleanor were the happy owners of a new house went up the chimneys for good. Franklin and *Sara* Roosevelt were the twosome in charge, soon to be officially recognized as such by the U.S. Census, which counted them as "heads of household," and Eleanor as "wife."[39]

Neighbors over the next decade referred to 47–49 East Sixty-Fifth Street as "Sara Roosevelt's townhouse."[40] Meanwhile, Aunt Jennie Delano, Eleanor's sensible family ally, heard of these arrangements and declared herself opposed. According to Aunt Jennie's daughter: "When Aunt Sallie built that double house on East Sixty-Fifth Street, my mother called it the most dreadful thing she knew of."[41]

"The basic trouble," summed up one of Eleanor's sons later on, "was that Granny, though she would have denied it indignantly had anyone accused her of it, never quite forgave Mother for marrying her boy."[42]

WEEKENDS AT HYDE PARK IN these years, Sara almost always recorded their arrival as an event exclusive to Franklin. "F. came," she would write in her diary,[43] as if her boy had motored home from the office. He was clerking at Carter, Ledyard and Milburn, a highly respected downtown firm then advising some of the world's biggest corporations on how to get around Theodore Roosevelt's antitrust laws.[44]

Home at Springwood, Franklin could play cat-and-mouse with

anyone who came to the door. He loved to lure city people into one of his country pastimes, then cut the earth from beneath them. If no other guests were "up from town," Eleanor functioned like the governess of a boy who felt entitled to take *her* as his fun.

One weekend, all innocently, he put Eleanor on Bobby—"dear Bobby," as Mama called the slower, more manageable horse that she had given Franklin's father when his heart trouble had worsened.[45] In recent years Franklin had retrained his father's gentle old mount; but without a word about that, off went Eleanor, trotting Bobby into the woods. All went well until she reached the neighbors' property and turned back for home. As she turned, Bobby bolted, running ahead at a death-defying gallop. Petrified, Eleanor hung on, trying every device to stop. When Bobby finally reached base, bringing her in pale and breathless, Franklin looked up.

Airily: "Oh, I forgot to tell you, I taught him to do that." Twinkle in his eye: "Of course you couldn't do anything with him."[46]

As a couple, they were foils. He endured her seriousness and intensity as she endured his pranks and swordplay. For Franklin, the princely, boyish world of his upbringing remained a source of entitlement all his life. He was not intentionally unkind, but he could be cold; his sense of fun was often cruel; and the more defenseless his victim, the less Franklin could resist the impulse to bully.[47]

For Eleanor, an "old" young woman married to an eternally young man, his latest mischief brought grim amusement. It was repeatedly said in these years that she had no sense of humor.[48] More accurately, she showed a deadpan accommodation of alarms set off by others. Imparted in sardonic asides and droll resignation, it shared a close relation to the morbid sense of humor developed in emergency professions, here applied to a husband's poker nights and treasure hunts and open-ended life of extended Tom Sawyer adventuring.

Often, however, in the early months of each of their children's lives, she could be solely grim. There was something untouchable about Eleanor as a mother of infants. It was work, with "very little sense of the joy which should have come with having babies," she lamented in later years.[49] When Franklin came home, sweeping up the chicks, bestowing nicknames like prizes ("Sis" for Anna, "Bunny" for Elliott, "Brud" for FDR Jr.), he gave his children (as he would his closest associates) the illusion of the personal. He left the hard work to Eleanor.

She meanwhile yearned for Franklin to be hers, yet could not find in her husband the exclusivity and closeness she had known from her father. Or, at least, from the Elliott Roosevelt who mesmerized her with grand plans for a shared life. Franklin had instead and no less thrillingly made her coauthor of his ambitions.

A YEAR PASSED BEFORE THEY moved uptown in December 1908.

Situated mid-block between Madison and Park Avenues, standing seven stories tall from cellar to roof, the freshly built mansion was not one house for one family—but two separate and mirroring ménages under one roof. The dining rooms and drawing rooms and fourth-floor bedrooms opened into one another through wide sliding doors.

As so often, Mama had gotten what she wanted through cleverness and guile. Having erected a stately home that worked like a magician's apparatus, she had technically not *moved in* with her "children," but instead installed herself and her two young satellites in this Siamese-twin complex. She nominally confined herself to 47, while Franklin and Eleanor housed themselves and their two children in 49, all with little discussion.

By December 17, they had settled in. That night, they dined with Mama—on her side.[50] Unsettlingly, when they passed back through to their side after dinner, Eleanor could not know when, day or night, or through which door, she would next see her mother-in-law.[51]

At night, lamplight from Mama's side banded the closed panels that joined the dining rooms and sitting rooms. But when Mama's lights were off and the panels were open and the rooms joined as one, the dark, merged spaces looked vast and disorienting. One young great-grandchild later crossed over from one side to the other and realized he did not know where he was or how to get back to safety. Bursting into tears, he sat down and waited "to be rescued."[52]

It was disorienting even for the adults to live this way. Mama might assert dominion over the connecting doors, or she might suddenly appear on one of the two elevators, six stairways, or in any one of twenty rooms, but her actual presence was not half so strange as the intangible sense of her *will* working its way into Eleanor's life through the house and its things.

While unpacking, which she preferred to do by herself, and right away, Eleanor made sure that a favorite blue vase could be seen on the brighter side of her drawing room mantel. "I think it was my early training which made me painfully tidy," she reflected. "I want everything around me in its place!"[53] But a day or so later Eleanor noticed that the blue vase had been moved to the other side of the mantel. She checked to be sure that neither Franklin nor the servants had made the shift, then moved it back; only to find it, the next time she entered the room, relocated again. It was like a stage illusion, the magician's assistant forever repositioning the vase, only to have the "powers" of an unseen impresario move it to where it "really belonged."[54]

Before the move, Eleanor's friends had noticed how entwined she had become with Sara, making herself into the perfect daughter-in-law, devoted, pliant, subordinate. They were aghast at how she would chant "Yes, Mama—No, Mama" three or four times in a row.[55] "She didn't always submit but she submitted too much," observed Helen Cutting,[56] who with several of Eleanor's bridesmaids kept trying to understand how she was doing it: "How Eleanor, with her character, could have been as subservient as she was, allowing her mother-in-law to do everything a wife should do—picking a house, hiring servants?"[57]

In the first house, it had been easier for her to let things go Mama's way. Now, with two children under three, and another on the way, the stakes had intensified, and the one time Eleanor lost control, she showed such livid fury that her cousin Helen Roosevelt Robinson called a doctor "for fear Eleanor would have a miscarriage."[58]

No one in the household ever told Mama to mind her own business, least of all Franklin. Had he been willing to redraw adult boundaries with his mother, their newly arriving family might have been Eleanor's to mother. But frustration had been set up from the start by Franklin's attachment to Sara and Sara's need to annex her son's life. And so, jealousy baked deeply into both women, the more so for remaining invisible in the hallways they shared.

One day, Franklin addressed a delicate matter when he announced to his mother that he and Eleanor had made arrangements to have their servants at No. 49 live out of the house, starting immediately.

Sara, aghast, argued for their staying put, but when she saw that Franklin was in earnest, and that Eleanor was prepared to stick to their guns, Sara threw a fit. "She was quite upset," reported Franklin.[59] Not yet done, Mama wrote to Eleanor on the topic, and when the balance shifted back to Franklin, he wavered: "I don't know quite what to say about it." Rehearsing the alternatives, he reasoned that with the holidays coming, "it would certainly be nice to have [the servants] there," but "on the other hand we have practically decided not to."[60]

Whereupon he left the whole matter, as if striding away from a see-saw, leaving Mama to teeter her way down to the satisfied position and Eleanor to dangle in midair. Over his shoulder he tossed off to Eleanor, "Do just as you think best, dearest, and you know I'll back you up!"[61]

A few weeks after the 1908 move, Eleanor's frustrations ambushed her. A sudden rush of tears, once started, wouldn't stop. "I did not quite know," Eleanor later wrote, "what was the matter with me."[62]

Franklin found her at her dressing table. She managed to get out that she did not like to live in a house that was not in any way hers.

Had she lost her mind? Did she remember, he wondered, how the two of them had worked together with Mr. Platt? Eleanor's insistence on Platt's lighting schedules? His placement of telephones, his intercom signals and doorbells?[63] And back in April, when she and Mama had looked at wallpapers . . .[64]

Eleanor choked out that, in any case, this was not the way she wanted to live. Franklin quietly replied that he was sure that once she gave it a chance she would feel differently. And with that, her husband left her to work it out.[65]

COME MARCH, THE DAY AFTER her fourth wedding anniversary, she had her hair washed and nails done, and at two in the afternoon took a drive with Mama, returning home at four. Franklin glided in forty-five minutes later, Dr. Ely knocked at five-thirty, and by then, Eleanor's cherished Blanche Spring had taken her accustomed place at her side. This time, she pushed out her baby in less than three hours—a second son, at eleven pounds the biggest and, Eleanor decided, "the most beautiful of all the babies."[66] They named him for his handsome father.

For once, motherhood was an idyll. That summer, she spent every new day on Campobello with her beautiful baby boy and the honey-headed Blanche Spring, whom she kept at her side more than five months, only with great regret seeing her off in August.[67]

That fall, they christened Baby Franklin and afterward left him at Mama's with his German governess and returned to New York for a week. Eleanor's hands were now frequently at work on a piece of knitting, a baby blanket or sweater. On the train to the city, the rhythmic action of her needles induced a mindful calm, easing the stress of leaving the children and their nurses with Mama. Her knitting bag became a constant companion.

On October 14, Eleanor went to town. On the 19th, Mama packed in the neighbors for a parlor lecture, journeyed to the city the next day for an American Red Cross meeting, and returned the day after to find Baby Franklin "not very well tho' he takes his food." Mama summoned a local doctor who diagnosed a heart murmur.[68] Eleanor hurried back to Hyde Park, needles clacking. She and Franklin saw the doctor, changed the baby's food, moved Franklin Junior and his nurse to a quieter room, then returned again to New York.

Suddenly, Mama was telephoning in emergency. Baby Franklin was sick. Eleanor rounded up Blanche Spring and together they raced to Hyde Park, reaching the struggling child that evening. By nine-thirty the next morning, they reversed direction and took the sick boy by train into the city for a second opinion, only to learn the worst. Baby Franklin's heart was failing.

Forty-eight tormenting hours followed at 49 East Sixty-Fifth. Two doctors and two nurses kept watch. From her room, where she lay, "useless," Eleanor could hear her seven-month-old baby crying.[69] All day on November 1, she sat by his bed, and for a few hours he seemed to be holding his own. Then his pulse became erratic, and she looked on helplessly as, a little before seven, Franklin telephoned to his mother's side of the house: "Better come, Mama, Baby is sinking." Twenty-five minutes later, the small child with the cupid-bow lips had ceased to breathe.

"No matter how little one's baby is," wrote Eleanor, years later, "something of oneself dies with it. It leaves an empty place in one's heart which nothing can ever fill again."[70]

SHE BELONGED TO THE LAST generation of women for whom burying an infant was not unusual. Helen Roosevelt, Franklin's half niece, lost a small baby to whooping cough in 1911. Eleanor's brother Hall, who like Eleanor married young in part to recover a sense of home, could not even say *what* had killed his firstborn. Thirty-seven years after the death of Franklin Junior, when asked what was the most moving letter she ever received—in a time when Eleanor received hundreds of thousands of letters a year—she still answered, "the one sent me after the death of our infant son, by a woman who had lost her only child at birth and never had another one."[71]

In 1909, bereaved mothers and fathers still followed separate protocols. Men were expected to show that the loss had hurt them and then put it aside; women were thought likely to magnify their grief such that its longevity might threaten their own lives. Franklin could go on without the child. For Eleanor, it was her own body being left there under the cold crust of earth.

"Sometimes I think I cannot bear the heartache which one little life has left behind but I realize," she told her old friend Isabella Ferguson, as she had said of pregnancy itself, "that it was meant for us to understand and to sympathize more deeply with all life's sorrows."

Yet she could not find sympathy for herself. A month after Franklin Junior's burial, she was pregnant again, and now, when fate might give her another chance, she held herself to blame. She stood convinced that instead of protecting her baby she had outright repeated the mistakes of her neglectful parents, leaving Franklin Junior vulnerable to her family's stalker, infection. Dr. Ely had fueled this suspicion; but Albert Ely, after all, was a leading gynecologist with a reputation to protect, not merely the "family doctor" of Mama and

Franklin's mythologies. He had suggested, heartlessly, that Baby Franklin might have been able to withstand his illness if he had been breast-fed.[72]

Following the Edwardian grief script, Franklin remained saddened but unhalted. Less than three months after the baby's death, on January 27, 1910, he made a speech to the New York Milk Committee, a nonprofit group seeking to improve the city's milk supply for infant feeding, in which he defended the right of upstate dairy farmers to recent price hikes.[73]

Eleanor's anguish intensified, spilling out in bitter reproach whenever Franklin tried to buck her up. She was unable to let go of her suspicion that Mama had cared too much and Franklin not enough. More and more frequently she withdrew into accusatory sulks. All through the winter, by her own later judgment, she behaved "idiotically."[74]

As the weeks went by and her belly grew as broad and hard as a dressmaker's dummy, she felt ashamed at the thought of a newborn replacing the lost child. Shame handed her a lash; and the more she inflicted upon herself, the more scared and worried and despairing she felt for the new life growing within her. She would ever after take the blame for her next son's psychological sufferings, pinning his manic depressive nature on her prenatal melancholy.

In June 1910, after more than a year's absence in Africa and Europe, Uncle Ted sailed into New York Harbor to a hero's welcome that launched him into a ticker-tape parade stretching five miles up Broadway. Franklin and Eleanor were among the family party ferrying TR ashore, and Franklin succeeded in getting Uncle Ted's blessing when he buttonholed him at the family luncheon to confide his hope to run for the state senate that fall—as a Democrat.[75]

When Poughkeepsie's party leaders came to Carter Ledyard's offices to recruit Roosevelt as their latest candidate for the traditionally Republican 26th state senatorial district—a biennial joke among Dutchess County Democrats—Franklin took the offer seriously. He said he needed twenty-four hours to think it over.[76]

That was October 3. He knew to avoid consulting his mother. Sara had no wish to see her son plunge into the "messy business," although with her Franklin involved, it would no longer be politics but statesmanship.

He huddled with Eleanor, but the decision, so far as she was concerned, had already been made. Ten days earlier, at 49 East Sixty-Fifth Street, she had given birth to the biggest Roosevelt baby yet, a boy weighing two ounces shy of a staggering twelve pounds, and onto his sturdy frame had fallen the fateful name Elliott.

Franklin explained that the Democratic sweep of the county the previous November had made the solidly Republican senate seat vulnerable for the first time in a generation. Their own visit to Uncle Ted's White House earlier that year had stirred and clarified Franklin's earliest dreams. He saw a day when he would have his chance to be president and could now see himself following the path that Uncle Ted had blazed: a seat in the state legislature, appointment as assistant secretary of the navy, election to the governorship of New York, and then, with any luck, the presidency.[77]

"I listened to all his plans with a great deal of interest," remembered Eleanor.[78] She approved of Franklin's independence in not following Uncle Ted's party, instead joining the Democrats. She believed in the scale of his ambition: a man starting small *should* think big. If Albany was in the cards, then she and the children would follow along, and do what they could to make a success of it. For Eleanor, however, nursing a healthy baby would now come first,[79] no matter how the vote went for Franklin. "It never occurred to me," she later wrote, "that I had any part to play."

On the last day of the campaign, at Tivoli, Eleanor heard Franklin make a political speech. She had attended only one other campaign meeting, and to her dismay, on this day he spoke haltingly, each pause in a line making her wonder if he really knew how to get to the end. She was struck, too, by the thinness in his face, and a high-strung nervousness that made him seem artificially thoughtful whenever he listened to someone's concern. She knew how interested he was in solving people's problems, but politics is money, and Franklin's boyish determination outweighed whatever scruples he or Eleanor might have had about bucketing some $2,500 of his own inheritance into the race, far outspending his opponent, and buying more newspaper advertisements than all the other Democratic candidates on the ballot.[80]

When the returns were in, Roosevelt carried the district, swept along by a national and statewide Democratic avalanche. Mama's diary parses the metrics: "Anna weighs 42.8; James 35.13. Franklin elected State Senator with about 1,500 majority."[81]

III

MISSUS

I have no profession—no training for anything.

E.R.[1]

EIGHT

Arriving in Albany with three small children, two maids, a wet nurse, and a household staff of three, Eleanor deployed a nomadic herder's skills to reestablish home base in a big rented brownstone on Capitol Hill.

She accompanied Franklin—decked out in a Prince Albert cutaway, spats, tall hat, and pince-nez—to the inauguration of John A. Dix, the first Democratic governor in eighteen years. The Roosevelts hurried back to greet constituents at a catered reception where, for "three solid hours," as Eleanor remembered it, more than four hundred guests wandered in and out of their open front door.[1]

Darkness came early those first days on the hill—a fast-lowering twilight that made Albany seem small and a little sinister. Her second morning, when a neighboring matron stopped Eleanor on the street with "You must be Mrs. Roosevelt, for your children are the only children I do not know," she was brought up short—shocked to realize, after living five years in a city of more than four million, that every woman on the block would now know her every move.[2]

She felt she had no room to make mistakes. Partly, this was the result of having been shoehorned by fate into constricted womanhood without the grace period of an American adolescence. Indirectly, the neighbor was pointing out how unusual it was for the young Roosevelts to have set up a fully staffed household. Most legislators spent their fifteen-hundred-dollar salary on boardinghouse rooms, going home to their families at session's end. The *New York Herald and Telegram*'s legislative correspondent, the gnomish Louis Howe, informed Eleanor that her husband's importance as an upstate Democrat was "somewhere between that of a janitor and a committee clerk."[3]

In Albany, political wives were all but unknown. If Eleanor so much as licked a stamp for constituent mail, she would be soiling her hands. Doing anything more than needlework, with the occasional sightseeing visit to the gallery of the senate or assembly chamber, would make her a meddler in affairs for which she had no qualification.[4] Day to day, she was not expected to involve herself in anything more public than marketing at the shops on a list approved by Albany's older Dutch families.[5]

But Eleanor's need to be needed had a direct effect on her husband's political future. She quietly found ways to manage their rental as an extension of Franklin's senate seat. The "Sheehan business," as Senator Roosevelt ever after called his celebrated stand against Tammany's upstate power, marked Franklin's first move for wider notice and the real beginning of Eleanor's political apprenticeship.

IN 1911, WITH THE UNITED STATES still two years away from the Seventeenth Amendment, New York chose its senators in the state legislature, which invested power in single-party caucuses, crooked lawmakers, rich corporate donors, and machine bosses. Since Tammany Hall had just elected the governor and ruled subservient Democratic legislators now in control of both houses, the election of a successor to U.S. Senator Chauncey M. Depew (whose term expired on March 4) put Tammany's famously inscrutable boss, Charles Francis Murphy, in position to extend his city rule through Albany to Washington.

From a makeshift wigwam in the Ten Eyck Hotel, Murphy quietly circulated word on Albany's Capitol Hill that he would grant no state patronage and no committee assignments until every Democrat attending the party's binding caucus pledged himself to the Tammany nominee. The likeliest candidate was William "Blue-eyed Billy" Sheehan, a famously corrupt Buffalo Democrat and former lieutenant governor,[6] now a rich New York City public-utilities lawyer to whom Murphy owed a political debt for his bundling of dozens of corporate contributions to Tammany's war chest.[7]

Attendance at the caucus subordinated lawmakers to the "Quiet Boss's"[8] supreme will. Open defiance was rare, but on January 3, Edmund Terry, an anti-Tammany assemblyman from Brooklyn, had had enough; he gathered a small band from both assembly and senate to bolt the meeting. Franklin became the first senator to join the insurgents, recruiting additional assemblymen to take their political future into their own hands. A total of twenty-one insurgents walked out—enough to leave Murphy's vote count short and the nomination in limbo.[9]

Their plan was to remain unbound by caucus decision, holding out until the floor session, when they would cast their unbossed votes with those of the Republicans to kill the Tammany nomination and put an end to "Murphyism." But striking a blow for freedom of conscience in public life was one thing. Remaining organized was another. The insurgents needed a headquarters near the Capitol, and Edmund Terry had no rooms large enough. Eleanor offered the State Street house, later remarking that "the rights and wrongs of that fight meant very little to me, though I think I probably contributed somewhat to its duration."[10]

As the first weeks of holding out against Tammany turned into a month, the house served the group, recalled Terry, as "a harbor of refuge."[11] The daily routine of feeding the press in his front parlor gave Franklin the job of team spokesman, which in turn encouraged the Albany press corps to cast young Senator Roosevelt as "the head and front of the insurgent movement that has caused Boss Murphy and his candidate for the Senate sleepless nights and riveted the attention of the entire country on Capitol Hill."[12]

This gave Franklin a chance not just to strike a blow against bossism, but to gain confidence from a source other than snobbery. Until now, his characteristic expression—chin up, mouth pursed, cold blue eyes peering through pince-nez—was pure condescension.[13] It took knowing Franklin as Eleanor did to understand that, deep down, he was fearful of being found ordinary and not so bright.[14]

"Shoot away quick," he commanded, inviting reporters' questions. "I must be back with my friends in five minutes." This was an improvement over calling a colleague *asinine*,[15] or giving off "chilly airs" to those asking his support on labor legislation.[16] According to the *New York Times*, "The young lawmaker said it rather quietly and in a softly modulated voice."[17]

The house-as-headquarters allowed Eleanor to join the men as an impartial aide-de-camp. She knew instinctively not to pretend that she was one of them. Instead she relaxed into their midst by knitting through their meetings, night after night, as the insurgency held out through a second month of the standoff.

Louis Howe, the *Herald and Telegram*'s legislative correspondent, called it "the most humanly interesting political fight for many years."[18]

INTO A THIRD MONTH, THE blue haze in the library fumed upward, choking the children in the nursery directly overhead. Eleanor moved Anna and James to the third floor, which meant carrying the thirty-five-pound James up an extra flight of stairs all that spring, since he had been diagnosed with a heart murmur and forbidden from climbing stairs.

The insurgents, meanwhile, had thwarted the Tammany candidate again and again, enraging Sheehan. He threatened to go into the counties represented by Franklin and his brother bolters and make their lives miserable.[19] Unless they ended their holdout at once, they would be "ruthlessly hunted out of public life."[20]

Eleanor had not expected this, and it frightened her.[21] Boss Murphy personally pressured Franklin, offering him plum appointments; and taking the occasion of the younger man's birthday to ask, with a "delightful smile," as Franklin saw it, if there was any chance of Roosevelt's coming around on Sheehan. Franklin stood on principle: by opposing Murphy's nominee he was honoring his constituents' objections to the big-city utilities lawyer's record of "bad faith, corruption, and faithless financing."[22]

Hearing this, Blue-eyed Billy claimed character assassination, and said he would give Roosevelt one last chance, insisting that they meet for a private sit-down the next day. Franklin countered by inviting Sheehan and his wife, Blanche, to lunch, informing Eleanor that she would have the Sheehans as their luncheon guests on February 2 at 248 State Street. "I shall never forget my feelings that day," wrote Eleanor in her autobiography.[23]

Eleanor Roosevelt had not yet disenthralled herself from anti-Semitic social thinking; the same kind of prejudice against Roman Catholics remained active in her view of Tammany villains. The old part of her that nursed superstitions expected Sheehan to be a monster.[24] Lunch, however, went smoothly. Blue-eyed Billy proved to be an urbane conversationalist; appreciative and complimentary, he charmed Eleanor.

Franklin was having none of it. He shepherded his opponent into the study, leaving Eleanor to entertain Blanche Sheehan, a respectable Buffalo matron draped in a fox stole. As high and low tones volleyed behind the door, the women were careful to employ polite parlor talk. At length the men emerged—Sheehan red-faced, Franklin pale—and the Roosevelts saw the Sheehans out. Many years later Eleanor would remember asking whether agreement had been reached, and how relieved she felt when her husband snapped off a brisk "Certainly not."[25]

After seventy-four days, however—the longest legislative deadlock in state history—State Supreme Court Judge James A. O'Gorman, a former grand sachem of Tammany Hall and therefore a compromise candidate's compromise candidate, was elected on the first of April, turning the siege into a victory for Murphy, who also got to fill O'Gorman's vacancy on the bench with his son-in-law. Franklin emerged as a champion of Progressivism, but Eleanor looked on appalled as Murphy and his thugs made good on Sheehan's vengeful threats.

Payback came fast. Franklin had established a new law firm with two Carter Ledyard colleagues, and Murphy personally saw to it that they lost their first client.[26] For others who had dared oppose Tammany, mortgages were foreclosed, loans called, notes mysteriously came due, privileges were canceled[27]—anything to sap their livelihoods. One man targeted for punishment was a country newspaper owner who depended on the printing of government notices to support his wife and two children. After ignoring months of persuasion and coercion, he had to stop his presses, fire his reporter, and eventually close his doors because local merchants had withdrawn their advertising and Murphy had diverted every notice to a competitor.

"That year taught me many things about politics," Eleanor later recalled, "and started me thinking along lines that were completely new."[28] The loss of privacy left her uneasy; she enrolled in a local class on how to relax the muscles, regulate breathing, and retire for a half hour each day into silence.[29]

* * *

THE NEW CENTURY UNFOLDED LIKE a series of stamps commemo-
rating heroic engineering feats that changed the world. Wireless radio
broadcasting.[30] The first passenger flight in an airplane.[31] A canal joining the Atlantic and Pacific Oceans across the Isthmus of Panama, the
monumental construction of which Franklin took a legislative recess
to witness. Meanwhile, in Albany, when a bulletin about the sinking
of *Titanic* reached Eleanor, it seemed from first reports that all aboard
the unsinkable ship had been saved. Then the "appalling and awful"
reality filtered in. She thought it "almost worse for the many women
who were saved and who would probably far rather have gone down
with their husbands and sons." She was glad that Franklin was "at
least out of the thick of ice bergs."[32]

He reached Panama as excavation of the daunting Culebra mountain ridge neared completion. "I can't begin to describe it and have
become so enthusiastic that if I didn't stop I would write all night,"
marveled the future builder of monumental engineering structures.[33]

In April Eleanor thrilled to hear Franklin boosted by Harriman
Railroad attorney Maxwell Evarts as a potential gubernatorial candidate to oppose former assembly speaker James W. Wadsworth, Jr.,[34]
uncle of her schoolgirl crush, Nelly Post, and soon to be a constant political antagonist. Franklin's renomination for the senate was far from
assured and his election in November equally uncertain. Tammany
was going all out to stop him. The Republicans thought him dangerous. His anti-Tammany statements, tagging its members "beasts of
prey" and "hopelessly stupid,"[35] had been distributed to make him
look anti-Irish and anti-Catholic.[36] Alfred E. Smith, the labor reform
champion from the Lower East Side, dismissed Roosevelt as "a damn
fool."[37] The 1912 race, moreover, was pitting him against not one but
two opponents, thanks to Uncle Ted's breakaway party.

In June, Colonel Roosevelt—fifty-four and stout, "fit as a bull
moose"—had emerged from premature retirement to smash the Republican Party in two when it failed to nominate him. TR launched
a third-party presidential candidacy under the National Progressive
Party banner, and his followers rallied to him as "Bull Moosers." Eleanor admitted to Isabel and Bob Ferguson that she secretly wished

Franklin "could be fighting now for Uncle Ted, for I feel he is in the party of the future."[38]

That month, her brother Hall, a junior at Harvard, had brought his fiancée, Margaret Richardson, to Campobello, then married her in a grand gathering of clans at King's Chapel, Boston.[39] Franklin served as best man; Auntie Corinne was the life of the party. Hall, not quite twenty-one, and Margaret, twenty, seemed to Eleanor "very young" as they sailed off to honeymoon in Paris, "but one must hope that all will go well!"[40] Within weeks, news of the death of Margaret's father, a revered Boston surgeon, cut short their happy days abroad.

Many years later, Hall's surviving children would recall that as a young man he had predicted his own death at fifty. To Eleanor, who loved Hall as a son and longed to be a person of real meaning in his life, her brother seemed to be on that schedule by the age of eighteen.[41] "From that time on," she later reflected, "the only way that anyone could hold him, was to let him go."[42]

At Harvard, Hall became a brilliant[43] and popular[44] member of the Class of 1913, graduating Phi Beta Kappa.[45] Eleanor sorted out his early drinking messes without protest, but as time went on, her interventions with Hall assumed a shape that she later regretted when the pattern reappeared in other relationships: "I give everyone the feeling that I've 'taken them on' & don't need anything from them & then when they naturally resent it & don't like to accept from me, I wonder why!"[46]

"I am sorry not to be in Boston when you pass through," Hall wrote in frustration in 1911, "but as you usually scorn all assistance I guess there is little difference."[47] Margaret echoed her husband's exasperation with Eleanor: "She tried to do so much and never would accept anything, and that's awfully hard for the others. She was always the doer."[48] Margaret later lamented that she could not seem to get close to Eleanor, an older woman wholly dedicated to her husband's career.[49]

By 1912, Franklin had directed his own people-pleasing: "Is F paying any attention to his family this summer," Hall asked Eleanor in July, "or is the bee buzzing as hard as ever?" The boy who had once served under Eleanor's Crusoe as her "man Friday" suggested that she "build a little cell for him at Campo and tie him down."[50]

Over these next eight years, Democratic party nominations for plum jobs were almost continually on offer: U.S. senator, governor of New York,[51] vice president of the United States—his to decide which would advance him on the royal road to the White House, hers to follow.[52]

SHE WAS WELL SCHOOLED NOW. It never occurred to her to question where they were to go, or what they were to do, or how they were to do it. "I simply knew that what we had to do we did, and my job was to make it easy."[53] In fact, at this stage, well beyond offering the State Street rental as insurgency headquarters, Eleanor made the national figure of Franklin Roosevelt possible. A man who looked as Franklin did and bore the Roosevelt name was seen without explanation as a leader. And being, as Franklin liked to say, "nephew by law" to the most famous man in the country had saved the Hyde Park yachtsman ten years of acquiring a name.

The job Franklin now coveted was Uncle Ted's old post: assistant secretary of the navy. In 1911, Franklin had met with the New Jersey governor and former Princeton University president Woodrow Wilson and subsequently organized his anti-machine New York Democrats into a formal bloc to support Wilson's bid for the presidency. Behind Roosevelt's clean, youthful, reformist leadership, that group had gone to the Democratic convention in Baltimore, where, without proper credentials, they were refused admittance.

But that was not the end of that. Several weeks before the convention, Franklin had gotten to know the manufacturer of the buttons that Wilson's arch opponent, Speaker of the House Champ Clark, was supplying to hundreds of *his* supporters so that they could pack the hall. In a flash of Roosevelt magic, he got hold of some three hundred buttons, distributed them among his Wilson brigade, and flooded the armory with cheering Wilson partisans to make what Franklin always claimed was the tide-turning moment in the many-balloted contest.[54]

Baltimore wilted in record-breaking heat, and the sweaty chaos of a convention in which she had no part to play irritated Eleanor. As often as not, she just sat down wherever she was and knitted, darting a glance every so often to notice "the contempt in which the New York delegation was held and the animosity shown toward the big financiers." These she reported to Aunt Maude, commenting, "If we are not going to find remedies in Progressivism, then I feel sure the next step will be Socialism."[55]

Before dashing for New York to scoop up the children and set off for Campobello, she had a taste of being married to a small national presence. Franklin, though only thirty and a first-term state senator, was now the promising Roosevelt. He was doing a serious job, organizing Wilson delegates, meeting and impressing such members of the Southern Democratic establishment as the owner and editor of the *Raleigh News and Observer*, Josephus Daniels, a close old friend of the party's great populist orator William Jennings Bryan and a passionate believer in Wilson for president. To Daniels, young Roosevelt was "as handsome a figure of an attractive young man as I had ever seen," and before they went their separate ways, Daniels took their chance meeting as "a case of love at first sight."[56]

Turning his attention to his district, Franklin hired a red touring car, draped it in bunting, and went out one clear July day to cover 150 miles. Over the course of his route, he discovered that Columbia County's bosses were against him and Putnam's were for him, and so, he concluded, with a favorite son's delight, "Dutchess must decide." Next came the nominating convention in Poughkeepsie, where he received his designation by unanimous vote and planned to start campaigning at once.

But after leaving the "chicks" with Mama at Hyde Park and coming to the city on the first of October, Franklin fell mysteriously ill. The next morning he had a high fever and intense stomach pain. Dr. Ely was puzzled by his symptoms and could only make a general guess at "some form of intestinal poison."

It was typhoid fever—the dirty water disease. Franklin and Eleanor had drunk from the stateroom water pitcher while brushing their teeth on the steamer hurrying home from Canada to kick off the campaign.

For the next four weeks, Franklin was slowly poisoned by *Salmonella typhi*. Before sulfa drugs and the dawn of modern antibiotics, sufferers of severe typhoid simply starved to death. The wasting killed one in five victims.

Eleanor cared for him in his third-floor back bedroom at 49 East Sixty-Fifth Street. She dispensed palliatives, ran trays up and down stairs, and made his bed with him in it, carrying on each of these duties as if put on earth to nurse Franklin D. Roosevelt at this turning point in his rise to power.

"All went well," she affirmed, "except that at certain times of the day I felt very peculiar."[57] The back of her head ached.

That night, when Mama arrived to look in on Franklin and give Eleanor a good night kiss, the heat radiating off Eleanor's forehead shocked her. Eleanor protested, declaring herself in tolerable good health, but agreed to sit still and take her own temperature.

She had 102, and by next afternoon, 104. Dr. Ely ran tests. For two full weeks Eleanor had been living uncomplainingly with typhoid fever.

As before, once she surrendered to the point of submitting to a sickbed, she let no one enter her room. "Poor lamb," crooned Mama, "how she hates being ill and giving up."[58] Aunt Tissie explained to Aunt Maude that Franklin's mother was on hand, "but E sees *no one.*" Her Hall aunts clucked sympathetically: "Typhoid is so treacherous," wrote Tissie, "that one can't *help* worrying, as you *never* know from day to day what may develop . . ."[59]

With only twenty-four days to the election, and Franklin too ill to campaign, he urgently needed someone who could stump the district. Franklin's illness, according to historian and biographer Frank Freidel, had "made the odds against Roosevelt's reelection to the state senate seem unsurmountable."[60]

Eleanor was the one to telephone Louis Howe at his house at Horseneck Beach, Massachusetts. To her relief, he agreed to come on the double, but when this single-minded, oppressive little man arrived in New York City, she was not so sure. He had big black staring eyes, the long, underslung jaw of a tortoise, and on his cheeks a rough pebbling of reptile skin. It was hard to imagine him kissing babies atop a hay wagon in Columbia County.

Yet off he went with Franklin's check, filling in the amount as needed. Sometimes called the sickbed campaign, Howe's success as Roosevelt's 1912 stand-in could as well be dubbed the "blank-check rescue." They trusted each other that much already, these alter egos in development.

To Eleanor, their arrangement seemed careless. Louis appeared weak and vague. Each time he came back to report on progress from the district, all he seemed to do was to fill Franklin's sickroom with a wall of cigarette smoke.

But Howe had set up his headquarters in a Poughkeepsie hotel, and he proceeded to cover the district in the jaunty red Maxwell. He had never run a local campaign but understood that people needed to see an avuncular face on a poster and to hear from Franklin Roosevelt in a letter. Howe's mimeographed formula, whether addressing apple growers or fishermen or hog farmers, expressed sympathy for every person's situation, and while promising nothing discussed specific jobs Roosevelt might help obtain.

His main strategy was the old trick of turning the candidate's weakness (unavailability, hauteur, insincerity) toward strength (personal contact, authenticity, warmth). Rushing at things half-cocked, letting his enthusiasm run away with him, Franklin appeared too easily swayed. Louis's air of authority, his acumen, and especially the deep focus of his intelligence, balanced Roosevelt's impulsiveness and made Franklin's arrogance read like youthful idealism.

Above all, as Eleanor came to recognize through the Sweet Caporal smokescreen, Louis was in control, and that more than any other quality was what *she* needed from anyone stepping into the magic triangle.

UP THROUGH ELECTION DAY 1912, Eleanor and Franklin traded the lead on whose infection remained more serious. When both fevers had broken for good, Franklin had been reelected to the state senate, Uncle Ted had been defeated, and Woodrow Wilson was the next President of the United States.

In January, Franklin met with the President-elect in Trenton. Roosevelt's willingness to fight Tammany, his field support for the New Jersey governor at the Baltimore convention, his organizing for

Wilson in the powerful Empire State, and his tasteful franchising of the most famous name in American politics had made him a likely appointee in the new administration. But nothing concrete had come of the meeting, and in March, when Eleanor accompanied Franklin to Washington for the Inauguration, they were still waiting to hear their fate.

The day before, March 3, 1913, more than five thousand women rallied for the largest suffrage demonstration the capital had ever seen. Eleanor, strongly *against* women having the right to vote, still viewed politics as an exclusively male preserve. Indeed, among all her nearest female friends and relatives, only Aunt Pussie advocated for suffrage, and had tried for several years to convert Eleanor to the suffragist cause, bringing out such a passionate counterattack from Eleanor that Hall reproached her for not having better self-control.[61]

Uncle Ted, writing in *Outlook*, observed that suffrage and concepts of female duty struck women as incompatible: "Most of the women I know best are against woman suffrage precisely because they approach life from the standpoint of duty." On the platform at Carnegie Hall he declared, "Go and convert my wife and daughters; I am the only one of my family who believes in woman suffrage!"[62]

In 1911, Franklin had resisted the appeals of Vassar College suffragists in his district. But when a vote on a constitutional amendment came before the legislature the following year, Franklin voted in favor, never failing to credit the lobbying of Inez Millholland, a young movement leader who was a practicing lawyer. Franklin liked to conjure the image of "America's prettiest suffragist" perched atop his desk in the senate chamber, flattering him, all but tickling him with her lady lawyer's arguments.

Now here was Millholland, astride her gray horse leading the "petticoat cavalry" up Pennsylvania Avenue.[63] As the parade's mounted herald, she held her head high no matter how often men in the crowd broke through passive police lines along the mile-long route, grabbing at the ladylike marchers, pulling at their clothes, harassing them with obscenities. Behind Millholland came a horse-drawn cart emblazoned with the demonstration's most important demand: Amendment to the

Constitution of the United States Enfranchising the Women of the Country.[64]

Eleanor responded to the spectacle with an impersonal eye. "Nice fat ladies," she remarked in a letter to Isabella Ferguson.[65]

IT HAD TAKEN THEODORE ROOSEVELT about fifteen years in the political trenches of Albany, New York City, and Washington to be appointed to the office for which the new navy secretary, Josephus Daniels, endorsed Franklin to President Wilson two days later behind closed doors.

"How well do you know Mr. Roosevelt?" asked Wilson, "and how well is he equipped?"

Daniels sketched his prospective deputy with great conviction as a singularly attractive, honorable, and brave anti-Tammany Democratic leader—not just a "coming man," but "one of our kind of liberal."[66]

Wilson agreed—Roosevelt was a "capital" choice.[67] He would give the President and the party "unexpected bragging rights."[68]

Before sending up the nomination, Daniels consulted the senators from Roosevelt's state. The first, James A. O'Gorman, the compromise candidate who owed his election to Franklin's Insurgents, surprised Daniels by being merely "agreeable."[69] Next came the respected Republican Elihu Root, whose face took on a "queer look" when he asked Daniels, "You know the Roosevelts, don't you?" Root had been McKinley's secretary of war and Theodore Roosevelt's secretary of state. He had seen TR "ride in front." It did not matter who was officially in charge—"being the lead horse in any team" was the Roosevelt way.

Daniels replied that an assistant secretary of the navy with a mind of his own could only strengthen a chief wise enough not to fear his subordinate. But Root was vehement: "Every person named Roosevelt wishes to run everything and [will] try to be the Secretary."[70]

Franklin had served just two legislative sessions and part of a third, returning briefly to Albany that spring to finish up pending business. When the U.S. Senate promptly confirmed his appointment, FDR traded legislative government and rural politics for the hot center of

Woodrow Wilson's New Freedom, the agenda that would establish, among other progressive reforms, antitrust regulation and the Federal Reserve System.

He was now the number two in the fifth department of the first Democratic government in sixteen years. Louis Howe came to Washington as special assistant, Mama obligingly remained behind with the children, and Eleanor planned to follow briefly before relocating the household to Campobello for the summer. Franklin was thirty-one, the navy's youngest-ever assistant secretary. Without any management experience, he had direct responsibility for budgets, procurement, and spending in a department whose 1913 budget, $143.5 million, amounted to more than a third of United States defense spending.

Eleanor felt "too much taken up with the family to give it much thought."[71] When she did think about Washington, it worried her that she "didn't know a soul." She was "afraid of [making] all kinds of stupid mistakes."[72]

Uncertain about her actual duties as the wife of the twentieth-ranking official in the Executive Branch, she took herself to Auntie Bye, protocol expert and now the wife of an admiral, who poured tea and urged "dearest, dearest Eleanor" to think of the navy itself as her duty. She must do what she could for young officers' wives trying to keep up their social position on small pay. Eleanor's weekly calls would be her big responsibility, and Bye commiserated with her over this tedious obligation.[73] She would do well, advised Bye, to "follow the form." Meanwhile, it gave her aunt a "homey sensation" to think ahead to Eleanor and Franklin moving that fall as renters into "1733," the Washington headquarters of the Oyster Bay clan on N Street Northwest.[74]

MARCH 17 FOUND ELEANOR IN Boston, visiting Hall and Margaret and their new baby.[75] Franklin, sworn in that morning, was attempting to look busy on the third floor of the big-boned State, War, and Navy Building, later known as the Old Executive Office Building. Between the office of the secretary of the navy and the White House intervened a mere tract of asphalt. Looking across West Executive Avenue to the West Wing and the gleaming mansion beyond, the new Roosevelt on the job could not help being keenly impressed by the "significance of it all." Only when the restrained excitements of his first official day waned, and the indolent hoofbeats of a passing horse could be heard,[76] did a still greater "significance" dawn on him.

Their eighth wedding anniversary.[77] Eleanor took the lapse in stride, having limited herself to ordering Franklin a modest, practical present "as we couldn't do anything else together!"[78]

When she next heard from her husband—two days later[79]— Franklin was in charge. Josephus Daniels had gone on an inspection tour, leaving his acting secretary free to greet a gang of newspapermen: "You remember what happened the last time a Roosevelt occupied this position?"[80]

Insubordination, for a start. As senior deputy on duty, Theodore Roosevelt had defied his superior and wired the famous order to Commodore George Dewey to maneuver the U.S. Navy's Asiatic squadron from Hong Kong into striking position of Manila Bay. When Spain then declared war, the strategic advantage of Roosevelt's surprise move won the Philippines for the United States, propelling TR into the Spanish-American War and ultimately the White House.

Josephus Daniels was proud of having loaded into the system "the Democratic Roosevelt," as he had dubbed Franklin at the convention in Baltimore. To his diary he mused, "May history repeat itself!"[81]

In 1913, Americans were trying to decide whether they intended to go on expanding as a world power or to shut themselves up in continental isolation. Daniels—a pacifist, religious fundamentalist, defender of the common man against vested interests, white supremacist, teetotaler, and slow-moving small-town Southern editor—had every reason to be suspicious of his deputy. Franklin—a Big Navy interventionist, fleet modernizer, Monroe Doctrine expansionist— could often be impetuous, sometimes reckless. Unable to keep under wraps his talent for authority—and obnoxiousness to superiors— Franklin sincerely believed he could run the department better than a newspaperman who meant *port* and *starboard* when he indicated *left* and *right* to his admirals. Daniels might be the President's man, but to Franklin it was *his* navy—time and the right-sized emergency would prove it.

Daniels took note, as Eleanor had during her young husband's sleepwalking episodes, that when Franklin Roosevelt decided he wanted something, he would stop at nothing to get it. Yet Daniels loved him. Franklin Roosevelt was the golden boy who could do no wrong.

IT TOOK ELEANOR TWO WEEKS to get her calling routine to six minutes a visit.[82]

Crossing as many as thirty addresses off her list each afternoon,[83] she hit up wives of the justices of the Supreme Court on Mondays; of the representatives in Congress, Tuesdays; of the cabinet, Wednesdays; and once a month, the wives of naval attachés and the women of the Navy Yard. Thursdays were for the lofty Senate ladies; Fridays, the diplomatic women of first and second rank; Saturdays, resident society, the "cave dwellers" in their Beaux Arts marble dens. She made a point, also, of calling on the President's wife, Ellen Axson Wilson.

Calling, or card-leaving, as the Washington ritual was known, required loading her children into the chauffeured car, buttoning her gloves, fixing her hat, gathering up her leather card case, and darting into the next house on her list to stammer out the formula: "How do you do, I'm Mrs. Franklin Roosevelt. My husband has just come as Assistant Secretary of the Navy."[84] By leaving her engraved calling card on the silver tray in the vestibule, she ensured both a return visit from her hostess and a place for the Franklin Roosevelts at that particular household's fêtes or among that department's season's dinners and dances.

On Wednesdays, she also received calls herself, or lent a hand to the secretary's wife—Addie Worth Bagley Daniels, a good-natured, easygoing North Carolina aristocrat of outspoken views[85]—until her feet ached and her voice rasped. Naval luncheons and official dinners given by the Navy League packed her calendar. Her executive capacity found outlet in further tasks of planning and hosting official dinners, where she gained recognition as one of the few Washington women who could speak French and translate for others, a not insignificant skill when France's Washington mission, led by Ambassador Jean Jules Jusserand, close friend of Uncle Ted's, was a formative presence in global diplomacy.[86]

Cousin Alice pronounced calling and card-leaving "a Washington mania that no sane human beings should let themselves in for."[87] It was also work: it took patience and stamina and kindness; Alice did not want the authority of donkey work, nor did she have the impulse to be kind. Her object was to be feared—to be the alpha female whose invitations to her own select circle were coveted.[88] Eleanor's authority rested on being in earnest and in her instinct for knowing just when someone needed a bunch of violets or a small present for a voyage to France. She never shirked from the toil of the card case; she never claimed "delicacy,"[89] or "a brief illness," code among official ladies for marital strain, excessive menstruation, or depression.[90]

She made one exception to her all-in cooperation as a naval wife. To staff the gloomy house on N Street, she had brought from New York four servants, all white, who joined Auntie Bye's two oldest retainers, both African-American. But Franklin's boss, devoutly Christian, had also been North Carolina's all too effective collaborator in resisting Reconstruction's political empowerment of formerly enslaved African Americans.[91] In 1898, as editor of the state's most prominent newspaper, Daniels served as the propaganda wing of a conspiracy to overthrow the elected multiracial government of Wilmington, North Carolina, and reclaim the state legislature in order to reestablish white supremacy as official government policy. Daniels's disinformation campaign in the *News and Observer* helped to incite voter intimidation and house-by-house terror, ultimately leading an armed white mob of 2,000 to execute more than sixty African-American citizens in the streets, force black city officials to resign or be butchered on the spot, and terrorize hundreds of women and children who had fled to the surrounding swamps and forests.

When the Daniels had the Roosevelts to dinner fifteen years after the carnage—a bloodbath so shameful it would remain for decades among the United States' most carefully hidden crimes against humanity—Eleanor appreciated her host asking the traditional bless-

ing before the meal, but had difficulty reconciling piety with the harsh
reprimand Daniels gave her that night at the dinner table.

Cloaked in his soft Piedmont voice, the secretary of the navy declared it unnatural for whites to assume a servile position in the house
of a white family; only Negroes could wait on their superiors. "Whom
else," he said, "could one kick?"[92]

Eleanor would never forget the "almost brutal feeling" of this cruelty.[93] Daniels stopped short of ordering Eleanor to send home her
New York domestics before they—and she—offended the social order
of what was to be, in these Wilson years, a nation's capital more deeply
divided than ever by skin color and only marginally more welcoming
to the advancement of women.[94]

COUSIN ALICE LONGWORTH WOULD LATER carp about Eleanor's
"do-goody and virtuous"[95] practices in Wilson's Washington. Yet little
that could be called public-spirited appears in this early record of her
thoughts or deeds concerning the groups and people that Eleanor Roosevelt spent her later life championing. During the Wilson years, she
was simply eager to be charitable, and gave money to the unfortunate
whom she knew. For example, having set up a bank account for the
baby of Elliott's Slovakian wet nurse, she conscientiously maintained
deposits.[96]

Eleanor's deeper desire to prove herself as Mrs. Franklin D. Roosevelt made social duties seem more important than social work.
Eleanor did not join Ellen Axson Wilson in her active concern for
improving conditions in Washington's system of housing. The city's
African American work force lived in disease-ridden alleyway hovels
converted from gardener's sheds originally attached to the city's big
houses. Upon Ellen Wilson's sudden death from Bright's disease in
August 1914, Congress at last responded out of respect, but too little
and too late, and the issue would lie waiting another twenty years for
Eleanor to correct her own earlier failure.

On social prejudices, she followed her caste-conscious mother-in-
law's lead. Up through the First World War, in complete contradiction
of her Souvestrian and Settlement House beliefs, Eleanor wore bigotry
as if it were a coat slipped on to suit an occasion. All too easily she

joined Mama in dinner-party anti-Semitism, expressing condescension for the people one might meet at a reception honoring the financier and soon-to-be War Industries Board chief Bernard Baruch: "I've got to go to the Harris party, which I'd rather be hung [*sic*] than seen at," she told Mama, adding: "Mostly Jews."[97]

Unchallenged by family or friends, Eleanor shamelessly reported such nasty postmortems as "The Jew party [was] appalling. . . . I never wish to hear money, jewels, or sables mentioned again."[98] Uncle Ted might have considered Felix Frankfurter "the most brilliant young man in America,"[99] but Eleanor saw no disgrace in adjudging Harvard's Vienna-born professor of law "an interesting little man but very Jew,"[100] because Mama was fine with that—and Henry Adams was fine with that. When President Wilson's appointment of Louis Brandeis to the Supreme Court erupted into conflict, Eleanor accepted the private consensus that anti-Semitism was naturally holding up Senate approval—Brandeis would be the court's first Jewish justice—whereas Senate Republican resistance to "the people's advocate" had more to do with the nominee's relentless and effective exposure of the criminal nature of banking oligarchs who controlled the nation's financial system.[101]

Wilson, meanwhile, had openly established racial segregation as the new administration's policy for federal workers. In his first year in office, the President granted the requests of his postmaster general and treasury secretary to rid their agencies of experienced African American civil servants. Positions held by Negroes in Republican administrations were now white-only. At a lower level, separate work spaces, dining tables, and restrooms divided white from black across the government; any black official unlucky enough to have white women under his supervision was fired.[102] Wilson issued no executive order, but defended his abandonment of equality and fairness, and dealt brusquely with objections such as those of one group of African American professionals led into Wilson's office by a Boston newspaper editor. "Segregation," asserted the President, "is not a humiliation but a benefit, and ought to be so regarded by you gentlemen."[103]

*   *   *

SOCIAL WASHINGTON REMAINED A REPUBLICAN stronghold. As Colonel Roosevelt's niece, Eleanor was favored by the hostesses and cave dwellers as one of the "right Roosevelts." She received special welcome at the embassies of Britain and France and from the old stalwarts of Uncle Ted and Aunt Edith's life in Washington. Henry Adams's niece Aileen Tone recalled that Eleanor rated a special respect from everyone who knew her. "She seemed more like a college girl then whose ideas were only beginning to bud. Her charm was of a very quiet, old-fashioned kind."[104]

At one dinner party, Eleanor's fellow Washington wife, the future novelist Nathalie Sedgwick Colby, noticed that Eleanor "came alive when she talked," and "talked a great deal." In the sitting room, when the men rejoined the women after cigars and brandy, Colby liked the way Eleanor "got up, a lady's way, as if people were the element in which she wheeled easiest."[105]

As for Franklin, a metamorphosis had begun that would transform the haughty state senator, celebrated local rival to matinee idols,[106] into a figure of immense physical and popular appeal— the Gay Cavalier, as Franklin Lane dubbed him.[107] Said Eleanor's Cousin Corinne: "I never knew anyone who grew so much more attractive with power."[108]

His job put him in charge of sixty-five thousand men, made him an authority on the construction and operation of the biggest warships in history, and demonstrated his proficiency in the procurement and maintenance of weapons, explosives, ammunition, and equipment. In the department, Roosevelt presented himself as the one real seaman capable of taking charge. He worked hard, and the sailors in shore stations and foremen in the navy yards soon realized that only when Josephus Daniels went on vacation did they get the materials they needed or the orders that got things done.[109] Roosevelt was their man, quick to slash through the red tape, easy with a joke or salty yarn. For the first time in his life, Franklin was one of the boys, authentically virile—or, anyway, the men's choice over "Joe Syphilis Daniels,"[110] as they dubbed their secretary when he banned alcohol from the officer's mess on ships at sea.

But Daniels saw deeper into the stealthy, catlike aspects of Roosevelt's nature, observing that Franklin "always had about him what women would call glamour and charm—to the nth degree—one of the greatest things a politician can have," adding: "Roosevelt had it just like an actress."[111]

This last was a perceptive comparison. On their honeymoon, Franklin had tried out with Eleanor the feline role he now played masterfully with Daniels: that of an overwhelmingly loving creature, who loved the nation, deeply loved the sea, loved the navy and all its traditions, but was at the same time in business for himself. Upon taking office, Franklin designed a new flag with the insignia of the assistant secretary to be flown during his inspection tours. He increased the number of guns in his salute from fifteen to seventeen and took to wearing dramatic navy capes aboard ship. He spent much of his first year with Daniels lampooning the boss's latest landlubber's gaffe or sniggering at Washington dinner parties about what a funny-looking "hillbilly" he worked for, until finally Interior Secretary Franklin Lane stepped in: "You should be ashamed of yourself," he told Franklin. "Mr. Daniels is your superior and you should show him loyalty or you should resign your office."[112]

A judge of character as canny as Josephus Daniels knew that he was dealing with a supreme user of people. Franklin had a power of focus that was magical. In his hawklike gaze and beaming bright smile was such clear longing for his chief's goodwill, such pursuit of Mr. Daniels's advice and wisdom, such apparent loyalty and interdependence, that Daniels felt personally needed by Franklin. He would soon discover that it was he who had been depending on Franklin.

Woodrow Wilson was dazzled by this six-foot-two star of the sub-cabinet, "the handsomest young giant I have ever seen."[113] English political hostess Margot Asquith declared Eleanor's husband "the most desirable man" she had ever laid eyes on.[114] The Yale football coach, Walter Camp, selector of All-American teams, described the Franklin Roosevelt he trained in a cabinet calisthenics class as "a beautifully built man, with the long muscles of an athlete."[115] Roosevelt cousins who had written him off as "the man on the handkerchief box" could not have imagined "Cousin Sallie's boy" ever meriting acclaim for his masculine appeal, let alone as an Adonis.[116] Uncle Will, Auntie Bye's husband, Admiral William S. Cowles, had sent Franklin off to the Navy Department with more than a hint of the trouble ahead: "The girls will spoil you soon enough. I leave you to them."[117]

TEN YEARS EARLIER, ELEANOR HAD seen Franklin as a prince like her father. She had joined him in a matching royal pair. But the same traits that had appealed to a debutante—charm, confidence, intellectual curiosity—looked different to a thirty-year-old mother of three. Now she saw Franklin's nonchalance, his self-interest, his guile. For reasons she would not grasp until much later, surface lightheartedness and gaiety—the camouflage of her father's alcoholism—turned her stomach while also drawing her. "During all these years," recalled daughter Anna, "if [Franklin] would go out—which he did—with the men to play poker in the evening and come home with a breath on him, she died. She just couldn't stand it. She told him this."[118]

But alcohol was not the central source of their trouble. Unlike many of the Roosevelt men, Franklin was not an alcoholic, though he himself was the first to admit to the compulsions of politics. After yet another all-too-brief appearance at Campobello, he wrote to Eleanor on the dash back to Washington: "I do so wish the holiday had been longer and less interrupted while it lasted. I felt Tuesday as if I was really getting back to earth again—and I know it is hard for both of us to lead this kind of life, but it is a little like a drug habit: almost impossible to stop definitively."[119]

They had entered into lasting conflict over dishonesty. "She is addicted to a frankness that would blaze headlines across the nation," observed a later Washington columnist.[120] Her husband's first instinct was to tell the partial truth. Franklin was a bender of the facts; and he so wholly trusted in his own trickiness that he believed no one would catch on when, in his first national campaign, he lied to the people of Butte, Montana, that he had written the constitution of Haiti.[121] The night of his primary election for the U.S. Senate, he declared that he had carried a majority of rural precincts. In fact, he had won in only 22 of 61 counties. Tammany had beat him two to one upstate, four to one in their city strangleholds. "Never mind," he said to a friend, "we paved the way."[122] But Eleanor did mind.

Marital resentment can have the effect of turning people inward and selfish; Franklin and Eleanor turned outward. The more disappointed they were by each other, the more readily they took on the problems of a world that was suddenly—for them, almost mercifully—lurching toward war.

NINE

Pregnant yet again, she realized the time had come to hire a secretary.[1]

After tagging along on one more wearisome inspection trip to a Gulf Coast navy base, Eleanor took a name from Auntie Bye—a young lady whose parents Bye had known from N Street,[2] Minna and Carroll Mercer's daughter Lucy, age twenty-three. She came to the Roosevelt household in December 1913, well turned out in a stylish wardrobe from her previous Washington employer,[3] an influential interior decorator who had gone into mourning and given Lucy her civilian clothes.[4]

Eleanor was happy to employ the girl three mornings a week. She paid her $30 and treated her as a social equal, though Lucy was yet more: another Cinderella with a fatally flawed father and magical mother; Queen Victoria had pronounced Minna Leigh Tunis "the most beautiful of American women."[5] Her father, Carroll Mercer, scion of an old Maryland family, had served with Uncle Ted in the Rough Riders,[6] thereafter pursuing an Elliott Roosevelt–style sportsman's life, until financial reverses, alcoholism, and divorce spiraled him downward. By the time Lucy's parents parted in 1903, when Lucy was twelve, they had squandered a fortune.

Lucy stood almost as tall as Eleanor, with a rounder, full-breasted figure,[7] and, to go by one family memoir, "a hint of fire in her warm, dark eyes."[8] She served the household as a member of the family, moving smoothly through her tasks, upholding rules, perfecting systems, remaining cheery and flexible. When handling bills and letters, she would fan her paperwork around her on the floor and, in a twinkling, have everything in order.[9]

Franklin heralded her entrances and exits with his big round butterscotch voice: "Ah, the Lovely Lucy."[10] Anna remembered feeling happy when she was greeted by the amiable Miss Mercer.[11] The boys listened for the secretary's soothing, Southern-inflected voice. In a household that could be tense for days on end, Elliott welcomed an ally who was "gay, smiling, relaxed."[12] Not surprisingly, Lucy made a hit with snobbish Mama during one of Eleanor's many official trips with Franklin: "Miss Mercer is here, she is *so* sweet and attractive and adores you, Eleanor."[13]

BY THE FIRST OF AUGUST 1914, everyone knew the world was changing far faster than anyone could handle. By the fourth, an immense German army was crashing through neutral Belgium, aimed at Paris.

"A complete smash up is inevitable," reported Franklin. "These are history-making days. It will be the greatest war in the world's history."[14] He had the trick, already, of turning crisis and alarm into confidence and dash.

Eleanor was not part of the unstoppable conflagration; she passed the time on cool Campobello, expecting her baby on August 26. But Franklin was suddenly in the middle of surging events, as England, bound by "a scrap of paper," honored its old agreement to defend Belgium and declared war on Germany. Two days later, Austria came in against Russia, which by then had joined France and England. The Ottoman Turks lined up with Germany and the Central Powers, and the "war that will end war," per H. G. Wells's October 1914 study, began putting out lights all over Europe.

Eleanor could not follow Franklin at anything like the same speed. She did, however, put her own hopes for peace on hold to support her husband when he found himself blocked on the warpath by a noncombative boss at a slumbering Navy Department—to say nothing of a fleet with fewer than two hundred ships on active service.[15]

"To my astonishment on reaching the Dept. nobody seemed the least bit excited about the European crisis," Franklin reported to Eleanor on August 2. "Mr. Daniels feeling chiefly very sad that his faith in human nature and civilization and similar idealistic nonsense was receiving such a rude shock. So I started in alone to get things ready and prepare plans for what *ought* to be done by the Navy end of things."[16]

"I am not surprised at what you say about J. D. for one could expect little else," she tutted in return. "To understand the present gigantic conflict one must have at least a glimmering of understanding foreign nations . . . Life must be exciting for you and I can see you managing everything while J. D. wrings his hands in horror."[17]

He did have one powerful ally in war preparedness—Rear Admiral Bradley Allen Fiske, a walrus-mustached Spanish War veteran, who had been arguing since March for a bigger navy. Fiske viewed the pacifism of women like Eleanor as the enemy to American readiness, and, even more confusedly, blamed women's suffrage for "effeminizing" the country and blinding men like Secretary Daniels to the navy's dangerously slow mobilization.[18]

"We've got to get into this war," boomed Franklin to whomever would listen.

"I hope not," Daniels replied each time.[19]

As Franklin trumpeted preparedness up and down the corridors of the War, State, and Navy Building, Eleanor prepared to give birth. Good, reliable Blanche Spring arrived on Campobello on August 12. Franklin, by then, had made the peculiar decision to jump into a Democratic primary for U.S. senator from New York. In June, a boomlet had also been started with little real hope of making Franklin the Democratic candidate for governor.[20]

Sensing their moment for a bold upward move, Franklin and Louis Howe had fixed sights on the Senate primary, despite Roosevelt's oft-repeated aversion to this institution pledged to slow and stately deliberation. They had confidence that with the navy behind Franklin, Tammany would be a cinch to beat. They miscalculated. Expecting to face a stooge, they got James W. Gerard, the forty-seven-year-old New York Supreme Court justice who was Woodrow Wilson's now-unwelcome ambassador to the German Empire. Gerard's post kept him too busy to come home to campaign, but he won widespread admiration for his tireless efforts to get Americans out of Germany.[21]

In August, Franklin managed to squeeze in a flying visit to Campobello. When their big-city birthing veteran Dr. Albert Ely failed to appear on the 16th, Franklin sailed across the swift Narrows to Lubec, the easternmost point of the continental United States, bringing back Dr. Eben Bennet. After hours of labor with little progress—Eleanor all the while urging the doctor to go to his other patients—she delivered late on the 17th another better-than-ten-pound baby, the second Franklin Delano Roosevelt, Jr.[22]

Wasting no time, Franklin dashed back to New York for a six-week primary fight. Eleanor looked upon his sudden determination to become a senator with a cool eye. "It never occurred to me to be much excited," she admitted. "I carried on the children's lives and my own as calmly as could be."[23] It was a strange time for a senior official in Woodrow Wilson's Navy Department to run for an office in which he himself didn't think he belonged, and especially to be asking for Wilson's backing: Ellen Axson Wilson had died suddenly of Bright's disease mere days prior.

Gerard won the primary three-to-one (but lost to James Wadsworth in November), sending Roosevelt back to huddle with Louis Howe about turning a senatorial defeat into an executive's victory. FDR's heroic potential rested on his being *the* Chief, not *a* lawmaker. He had fallen short, but not of the office he felt he had been born to assume. His eye was still on the prize. "It would be wonderful," he told a friend, "to be a war President of the United States."[24]

WITH A HEALTHY NAMESAKE SETTLING in, all should have been well. But Eleanor and Franklin could not find their way forward as a couple. The war would expose their secret, first stumbled upon during their honeymoon: they could not make each other happy.

"Something locked me up & I can't unlock," as she came to characterize her upbringing's emotional legacy.[25] She yearned for closeness, and yet her own responses prevented it. She would never be kittenishly playful with him; he would never confront hard truth with her. They could scarcely ever relax with each other.

Things that once drew her to Franklin now pushed them apart. On Sundays, she disliked his skipping out to play golf at the high and mighty Chevy Chase Club while she worshipped with the children at stately old St. Thomas Parish on Dupont Circle. She welcomed the steady part of churchgoing for her young family, hoping to awaken her children to the Gospel message that one cannot live for oneself alone.[26] But St. Thomas's had its own snobbery and conceits; the Reverend C. Ernest Smith, its dogmatic rector, defined a Protestant as "a person who is opposed to the Roman Catholic Church."[27]

Franklin avoided worship outside his Hyde Park parish, partly because he loathed sermonizing, and partly due to his clannish attachment to St. James's, where he followed in his father's footsteps as vestryman and, later, senior warden. For the Hyde Park Roosevelts, being Episcopalian was outwardly a kind of horsemanship, clubby and pedigreed. Franklin had no need of membership in another congregation, nor would he have considered "transferring his letter" to a parish as preening or high society as St. Thomas's.[28] Rather, he made sardonic sport of seeing how casual the assistant secretary of the navy could be about attendance; and the more he got away with his games—one Sunday playing as many as forty-five holes of golf without anyone the wiser—the more his pleasure intensified.

Eleanor often felt alone during their travels as public official and wife. On their first morning in San Francisco, in 1915, set to open the Panama-Pacific International Exposition with Franklin K. Lane, Eleanor awakened early to the delivery of a huge bouquet at the door of their hotel room. She thought the flowers were from her husband and felt all the old tenderness—until she opened the tiny card and saw to her surprise the name of the *other* Franklin. This was the state of orange blossoms and sunshine, read Franklin Lane's note, and he wished her first impression to be of the strength and brilliance of California's beauty.[29]

Admiration helped; she was getting so little. Her Franklin could still make her feel that she was the most important person in the world: focusing suddenly on her with his hawklike eyes. Enticing her into a spin around the dance floor. Hurling her into a sudden playful romp at a picnic. Yet these gestures found no circuit to complete, leaving her conscious of something she could never fulfill, let alone enjoy. Instead, submission to her husband and his mother was her one method for keeping an uneasy peace. By caving to Sara's interference—by holding herself back from declaring, *This is my territory, clear out*—Eleanor perfectly fitted Franklin's desire for the distribution of power in the family.

Behind closed doors, Franklin now maintained his own liberty by keeping secrets *with* his mother. When Mama thought of renting her half of their double mansion on Sixty-Fifth Street,[30] Franklin withheld the information from Eleanor. In a sense, Mama and Franklin weren't holding back from Eleanor so much as they were playing up to each other. Franklin understood that sharing a secret heightened the part of his mother that drew identity and power from exclusivity. With that gleaming smile of complicity, Franklin could always take people prisoner through their little weaknesses.

Displaced to Campobello, Eleanor worried that she could lose him to one of Washington's "summer wives," the young stenographers who doted on bachelor husbands while "the Missus" (as Franklin referred to Eleanor) shuttled the children north until September. Franklin's letters were full of awkward omissions, and since by custom Eleanor and Mama had always shared his latest news aloud, Eleanor sweated the politics of their triangle, nervous when Franklin so obviously withheld information: "I have to invent," she grumbled, "and that is painful."[31]

Franklin never thanked Eleanor for managing his mother, much less the logistics of re-establishing a trio of children, their latest governess, assorted pets, a pair of maids, and up to fifty pieces of luggage in a two-stage annual getaway, from June in Hyde Park, to July and August on Campobello. Isabella Ferguson was perhaps the first to spot Eleanor's potential as a mobile administrator: "I never heard anything to equal your life—of calls & trains," she told Eleanor. "My dear you seem the embodiment of 20th Century activity."[32]

That was the trouble. Franklin was *creating* "the 20th Century." For the time being Eleanor was just . . . *activity*. Eleanor was preparing to be drawn into nursery conflicts. "I hate not being with you and seeing it all," she wrote during one of his more important naval assignments to Europe. Embarrassed, she added, "Isn't that horrid of me?"[33]

Eleanor's way involved a certain martyrdom. Her duty, as she committed herself to it daily, was to please Franklin—to be sure that her own faults did not disgrace him on inspection trips to navy installations in Florida and along the Louisiana Gulf Coast. Treated in Eleanor's lexicon as "feats of endurance," these heat-prostrating twenty-hour-a-day slogs gave her the chance to show Franklin that she was so strong she couldn't be hurt. Whether he noticed was another matter.

One night at a dance at the Chevy Chase Club, he hardly seemed concerned when she excused herself and went to find a cab. He had been conspicuously quick to his feet every time Lucy Mercer or her sister Violetta rose to go anywhere. Franklin seemed pleased to stay behind and did not get home until morning, returning to N Street with the Warren Robbinses. It was they who witnessed what happened next, passing it along to Cousin Alice, who could almost be heard licking her chops as she listened:

The three approached and Franklin opened the vestibule door:

"Whereupon Eleanor arose from the doormat, pale like a string bean raised in the cellar . . ."

Franklin said, "But, darling, what's happened? What are you doing here?"

"Oh," said Eleanor, "I forgot my key."

And Franklin said, "But couldn't you have gone to Mitchell Palmer's house, where there's a guard?"

"Oh, no, I've always been told never to bother people if you can possibly avoid it."

"You must have been hideously uncomfortable."

"Well, I wasn't *very* uncomfortable."[34]

Eleanor's self-effacement, stretched on the rack of usefulness, did not lead to a strengthening of character, much less a stronger marriage. It did, however, prepare her, better than was immediately obvious, for work in the war.

ON FEBRUARY 9, 1917, ELEANOR attended the annual meeting of Woman's Volunteer Aid in the upstairs ballroom at Maison Rauscher, social Washington's salon for catered receptions. The post-*Lusitania* death toll and sunken Allied vessels had reached breaking point. A thousand women had thronged to hear Mabel Boardman recruit volunteers for auxiliary work in the Red Cross should America enter the fighting.

President Wilson would shortly become the first commander in chief to declare women partners in one of the nation's wars, but the jobs women would fill were still indeterminate. Eleanor was typical of the *Social Register* turnout at Rauscher's. She could not drive, cook, or type, which ruled her out of the motor corps, kitchen corps, and clerical corps. When uniformed workers from each of these divisions reported on their activities, she and her friends were astonished to find, as Caroline Phillips observed afterward, how little they *could* do.[35] There would also be a uniformed refreshment corps—the ladies of Washington's calling system certainly knew how to pour hot liquid into cups—but no canteen service had yet been organized.

With Washington itself preparing to go on wartime footing, Eleanor would have broader duties as a subcabinet wife. The prospect of becoming one of the more prominent capital hostesses—not just another face at the dinner party, but a social leader expected to show the same resolve and élan as her saber-rattling husband—worried her. She liked noticing others; she dreaded being noticed. Even a train conductor calling her name for a telegram was enough to make her shrink from the hand delivering the message.

Her fear of social exposure had flared in private the previous autumn, when, just as their guests were about to arrive for a dinner party mainly made up of Franklin's faster Washington set, she burst into spontaneous tears while putting Elliott to bed. She and the children had only recently returned from Campobello, as a terrifying infantile paralysis epidemic had swept up the coast from New York, and Franklin had anxiously urged her to stay with the children on the island well into October. In Washington, Lucy Mercer had kept house for him.

Upon returning to N Street, Eleanor became conscious "that there was a sense of impending disaster hanging over all of us."[36] She referred to the looming conquests of Imperial Germany, but her children sensed otherwise. For years, Elliott would attribute her tearful party jitters to her usual shyness and social stress. But, as he came to realize, "Those were the early days of Father's involvement with Lucy. Mother was facing the breakup of the marriage, and she felt at the moment that she was powerless to do anything to prevent it from happening."[37] Elliott watched as his father appeared and asked what was wrong; his mother answering in a choked voice: "I'm afraid I cannot face all those people, Franklin."[38] Nonsense, he told her, and demanded that she pull herself together for their guests.

*   *   *

On April 2, 1917, at 8:30 p.m., in the great stilled chamber of the U.S. House of Representatives, Franklin made sure she had a seat among the hundreds of visitors packed into the gallery to hear a pale but calmly forceful President Wilson make his case for war.

Hardly daring to breathe, Eleanor listened to Wilson argue that the United States must cast its lot with the Allies and enter Europe's most terrible and disastrous war ever—not for revenge or conquest or as an assertion of power, but to champion the rights of mankind in the fight between autocracy and democracy. She joined the applause mounting from the floor as Wilson established that peace was impossible for the world's free societies while the autocratic power remained on earth. A stronger navy would be needed, and a new army of five hundred thousand conscripts; but the months ahead called for more than men and materials. The task required "everything that we are and everything that we have"—giving blood and guts and lives and fortunes to Germany's foes.

"The world," said Wilson, "must be made safe for democracy."[39]

Eleanor returned home "half-dazed by the sense of impending change." Anxious about what the war would mean for Hall and for Franklin, she grasped the subtext of what Wilson himself, resolved but heartsick, knew he had asked Congress to approve that momentous day—a "message of death for our young men."[40]

Franklin wasted no time trying to get into uniform, immediately lobbying his boss to go to sea as an officer. But when Josephus Daniels raised the question of commissioning Franklin for active duty, President Wilson stated: "Neither you nor I nor Franklin Roosevelt has the right to select the place of service to which our country has assigned us."[41] He would stay at his desk.

War was declared on April 6, 1917, and from then on, everyone in the government worked "twenty-five hours a day."[42] The calling system was put in mothballs,[43] replaced by nationwide knitting campaigns. Franklin had predicted correctly: from coast to coast, the women of America took up double-pointed needles as "Our First Line of Defense."[44]

Knitting brought women together, starting conversations. Suffragists took up "purling," "ribbing," and "casting off" as new forms of activism. Churches relaxed rules so that congregants could ply their needles during the sermon. Women took knitting bags to movie theaters. Old-guard masculine bastions like *Scribner's Magazine* tried to cast the trend as "a nation of women turning their backs on feminist movements, and setting themselves to that least exciting, most old-fashioned, most feminine of occupations, knitting—the knitting of millions of sweaters, of socks, of wristlets, of scarfs for the men who had so consistently frowned upon or pitied or derided them."[45]

Once started on a project for a soldier at the Front, many volunteers discovered they "couldn't put it down."[46] Eleanor loved the work: "I simply ate it up."[47] She spent one afternoon a week taking wool, needles, and knitting patterns to navy wives and picking up the completed socks, vests, and wool helmets. Two days a week she visited the wounded in the naval hospital. Whatever time she had left went to the Navy Red Cross, whose knitting service, under Mrs. Franklin D. Roosevelt, officially sent 8,976 articles of clothing to shore stations and men at sea.[48]

When she realized that many women of her acquaintance were waiting to be told what to do, Eleanor lent a hand to Isabel Anderson, the public-spirited Boston heiress married to diplomat Larz Anderson, who was then forming the District of Columbia chapter of the Red Cross Refreshment Corps. The fifty Washington ladies whom Anderson and Roosevelt recruited to provide food and drink for soldiers passing through Union Station joined seventy thousand women in canteen service nationwide.[49] By war's end, survivors of the Western Front would call the American Red Cross "the Greatest Mother in the World."[50]

Three early mornings a week, Eleanor left her children to nannies as she crept out of the house in her crisp blue Refreshment Corps uniform and reported for duty in the small tin-roofed canteen in the railroad yards.[51] A mile and a half north of Union Station, under the wide District sky, the yard spread over a sooty acreage of hazardous crisscrossing steel rails and shrieking car-wheels. In winter, Eleanor worked cold and drafty day shifts; but in summer, arriving to serve from six until midnight and often beyond, she would make her way down a steep embankment[52] into a shadowy world where low switch lights dotted the tracks, red and green signal lamps flared, and the headlights of panting engines gleamed through the dusk.

Train after rattling train toiled in, loaded with soldiers, lumbering over the switches, backing into the lighted shed, alongside which Eleanor and her three shift-mates worked the canteen. She fed wood by the cord into a menacing contraption known as an army field kitchen, then dropped sacks of coffee into the boilers over the fires, brewing 160 gallons at a go.

With as many as nine trains in the yards at once, and every man aboard to be offered coffee and jam sandwiches, crullers or buns, averaging two pieces of food per soldier, some two thousand sandwiches needed to be ready to go at any hour of any day. In the hot, dim hut, the women took turns slicing bread on a primitive cutting machine, then spread the open faces with jam, wrapped the finished sandwiches in paper, loaded them onto trays, and hurriedly fanned out over the rails, often just as the bell tolled, to hand up the ration with a murmured word of encouragement.

At first, railroad officials had objected to the women being on the tracks at all. What was the idea of their being there to "help" the men? It took the canteeners a full summer of earnest hard work to overcome the railroaders' prejudices[53] and for the commanding officer of the Refreshment Corps to get authorization from the War Department for a direct-line telephone connecting the troop train clerk and the hut. With this, they finally had correct, confidential information about the movements of troops, enabling the canteen to render twenty-four-hour service, furnishing food and mail for ten to fifteen thousand men each cycle, the daily numbers frequently reaching twenty thousand.

Squads of four volunteers worked each shift under paramilitary discipline imposed by officers ranked from lieutenant up to colonel.[54] Privates like Eleanor, working three or four shifts a week in Company A, learned to identify a captain such as Mary Sheridan, eldest daughter of the Civil War general, by the three discs on her epaulet, to obey orders instantly, and to jump to any task.[55] The three volunteers working the last shift remained on duty all night in emergency cases. The first morning shift went on duty at 6 a.m. The following winter, these icy risings occasioned James Roosevelt's complaint to his grandmother: "Do not you think that Mother should not go so early?"[56] But by then Private Roosevelt had a reputation to live up to: Col. Mrs. Mason Gulick and her staff knew they could rely at any hour on their "willing horse."[57]

Eleanor canvassed every train, large basket of sandwiches hooked over one arm, meanwhile holding open a huge canvas mail bag for the soldiers in the train windows to drop in their letters and postcards, or reaching up with a Gulliver-sized coffeepot to tip its spout into the tin cups in the outstretched hands.[58] When the trains pulled out of the station, her heart ached. The boys seemed so playful in their broad-brimmed campaign hats. Some scarcely knew where they were; many had little or no idea where they were going.[59] Certainly, no one had ever seen young American men shipping out in such multitudes, barracks bags slung at their shoulders. To Isabella Ferguson, Eleanor said it was "a liberal education in the American soldier."[60]

Full mobilization meant that for the first twelve months of Eleanor's service,[61] no fewer than 1,700,000 newly drilled doughboys passed through the Washington canteen, bound for Hoboken or Newport News. The draft of June 1917 (the nation's first since the Civil War) registered more than 10,000,000 men between the ages of twenty-one and thirty—25,000,000 over the next year and a half. There seemed no limit to it, almost as if the immigration that had shaped the city of her childhood had suddenly reversed action. By war's end, fully 2,500,000 members of the American Expeditionary Force would have flowed past Eleanor's chronically shorthanded hut to scatter across the sea.[62]

"The war," reflected Eleanor, "was my emancipation and my education."[63] It freed her to develop her natural capacity for organization. As wife of the assistant secretary of the navy she was pleasant, energetic, quick-learning: an amateur with potential. But the paramilitary, semiprofessional Red Cross brought out the systematic professional in her. Her accounting system for the canteen's shop, where soldiers lined up to buy tobacco products and candy bars, was a model of efficiency for the other volunteers; she was one of two officers who always left her accounting for the next shift in perfect condition. She was also singled out to oversee the working visits of renowned volunteers: "We had 6 trains this p.m. & Mrs. Woodrow Wilson & that is a burden I can better describe in words than on paper," she told Mama.[64]

In later years, those who had known "Private" Roosevelt in the railyards were amused at the illusion that the Mrs. Roosevelt of history seemed to "spring suddenly into usefulness." In reality, wrote one of her fellow canteeners, "she started her career of usefulness and efficiency years before, and added to it as time went on."[65]

THAT SPRING, AS WAR FEVER swept young male America, Grandmother Hall was upset that Eleanor's brother Hall intended to leave his young family to fight in Europe's clash of arms.

To Eleanor's dismay, Grandmother demanded of *her* why Hall did not "buy a substitute" to take his place in the draft. Eleanor had never heard of such a loophole, and during yet another of her thankless duty visits to Tivoli said sharply that no one would do such a thing. But in the New York City Civil War lottery, both her grandfathers had been able to afford the $300 fee to enter a substitute, and Grandmother Hall insisted that it was what a *gentleman* would do.

Grandmother dug in. So did Eleanor. The Selective Service regulations now clearly spelled out that "no person liable to military service shall hereafter be permitted to furnish a substitute for such service."[66] When workingmen were summoned to lay down their lives for their country, it was only right for men of privilege and property to answer the same call. Substitution overvalued the worth of the rich man and undervalued the contribution made by soldier or sailor.

This was, she later recalled, the outspoken beginning of her lifetime's fight to transcend tribalism. She had long stuck by Oak Lawn laws because Oak Lawn had given her all that she had had of childhood. Something, she was not yet sure what—perhaps the transparent absurdity of social exclusivity in wartime—was beginning to awaken her to the need for a middle way.[67]

Uncle Ted, meanwhile, had limped to Washington, bellicose and uninvited. When the partially blind, Amazon fever–ridden, fifty-eight-year-old former president made the rounds at State, War, and Navy, Josephus Daniels could not have been more relieved to hear him declare a preference "to lead the army rather than to command the fleet."[68]

Privately, Wilson viewed TR and his proposed division of Rough Doughboys "as just a spectacular feat to put himself before the public."[69] After receiving and hearing out Roosevelt at the White House, Wilson decided in favor of forming and training the army by new methods that shared the burdens of service more equally; and asked Secretary of War Newton Baker to let Colonel Roosevelt down easy, while wiring TR his own reasoning.

Eleanor was relieved but sorry to see Uncle Ted sidelined; she knew how important it was to him to bear the same risks as his boys. In the end, however, it was always the same. Despite his impassioned love of country, it was all about TR. Eleanor yearned for a cause that was greater than herself.[70]

ON JUNE 24, 1917, SHE fired Lucy Mercer. The official reason was that the war gave her fewer social obligations. In fact, the opposite was true. To maintain morale, diplomatic Washington kept its machinery whirring with the normal round of receptions, teas, and dinners.[71] "I wonder that you find any time for letters at all," wrote her brother, "with the distractions of family and the arduous linguistic labors of entertaining Japanese, Mexicans, and Hottentots."[72]

Jealousy brought her to let Lucy go. The more watchful Eleanor became, the more invisible was Lucy, and the more airtight the seal on Franklin's narratives. To Eleanor he adamantly accounted for every detail of his days, recording to the minute the timetable of his arrivals and departures, even including to and from the dentist's chair.

Occasionally, the times he gave Eleanor did not match those he more casually supplied his mother (off by as few as fifteen and as many as thirty-five minutes), but the women were not passing his letters back and forth, and if they had, what did it matter that Franklin claimed to Eleanor he had reached the dentist by 8:45 and to his mother insisted it was 10:10? Franklin's vehemence about the facts made it easier for everyone to pretend that the facts were true.

He cared that Eleanor believe him. Franklin chronicled places, people, and weather, pretending to share the pleasure of occasions, but in reality his gaslighting was a bid for Eleanor's trust. Good character had been the coin of his courtship and young manhood, on the flip side of which gleamed his ambition to be Number One. When he was not right with "Babs," he was not right with the world. But now he had fallen in love outside his marriage, and he was willing that first war-time summer to risk being wrong with Eleanor to test that love.

Five days after being fired from 1733 N Street, Lucy joined the Navy Department. Under a brand-new Daniels wartime program to create "the best clerical assistance the country can provide,"[73] eleven thousand women had been enrolled as yeomen. Fulfilling Wilson's progressive vision of equal partners in the nation's service, Josephus Daniels's "Yeomanettes" were the only women during the war who served in the United States Navy on the same footing as men of the same rank, receiving equal pay and allowances.[74] Lucy accepted one additional privilege. After being sworn in at the Navy Yard, Yeoman Third Class Mercer was assigned straightaway to the Office of the Assistant Secretary of the Navy.

ELEANOR HAD ALWAYS DONE MORE than her share of knitting, but now her needles bit like fangs, gobbling up whole skeins of wool. *Babs*. Franklin sounded as if he were calling a lost little lamb: *"Ba-a-a-bs!"* What a contrast to the relief with which he had greeted Miss Mercer's morning arrivals at N Street: "Ah, *the lovely Lucy!*"[75]

At the canteen, she accustomed herself to the heat in the little corrugated-tin shack with its cooking fires burning under the metal roof: "I've come to the conclusion that you only feel heat when idle."[76] Likewise, she was learning to use fatigue to concentrate her energy. The more worn down she got, the more basic her judgment about what really mattered.

Throughout this first full summer of her husband's offstage pairing, she knew only to protect herself from what she instinctively did not want to know. Whisperings had been heard, recalled one Washington insider, "on all sides."[77] Franklin's passion for Lucy, agreed another, was "known to everyone in Washington except Eleanor."[78]

That summer, she redoubled her patriotic efforts.[79] Joining the rest of the nation in wheatless and meatless meals so that scarce foodstuffs could supply the army's needs, she signed a pledge card from the Patriotic Economy League and made good on it by cutting back her daily menus. She allowed two courses for lunch, three for dinner, while excluding bacon, serving cornbread and meat but once a day, and halving the quantities of laundry soap used by her family of seven. She also made each of the servants sign a pledge card to do all within his or her power to economize, even if that meant that her upstairs maids Millie and Frances would now be on watch for "evidence of shortcoming in the others," ready to rat out offenders.

When the conservation section of the Food Administration picked Eleanor's "program" as a model for other large households, even including the servants spying on one another, the *New York Times* scheduled a reporter's visit to the exemplary Mrs. Roosevelt.

Meanwhile, her annual banishment to Campobello loomed, even though the children had whooping cough. Franklin's eagerness to pack her off was more galling than usual. His constant bugling about "Campo" as the paradise he himself would revel in, if only he could get away, grated. Each time he lamented how lonely summertime Washington would be without "Babs," she held herself in check, merely assuring him he would have *quite enough* to occupy himself.[80] Then she sent the barely recovered children ahead to Canada with their governesses and the cook, so that she could maintain her belt-tightening post, at least until the reporter's visit.

On that day, Franklin went to work as usual but punished Eleanor's Campo-resistance campaign by failing to come home for lunch, leaving her to face the *Times* on her own.

Eleanor had just surrendered herself to island exile when the food-conservation story appeared as "How to Save in Big Homes." The *Times* presented a laughable Mrs. Franklin D. Roosevelt as the most practical and effective of three outstanding women who were playing their conscientious part in making the world safe for democracy. Eleanor's strategy of having daily conferences with her servants contrasted with the sculptor Gertrude Vanderbilt Whitney's opening of her home in Newport to a series of patriotic classes on food conservation and the social activist Dorothy Whitney Straight's offer to do same for the summer colony at Southampton, Long Island.[81]

FRANKLIN SENT A BLAST OF sarcasm from the office: "All I can say is that your latest newspaper campaign is a corker and I am proud to be the husband of the Originator, Discoverer, and Inventor of the New Household Economy for Millionaires! . . . Honestly you have leaped into public fame, all Washington is talking of the Roosevelt plan."[82]

In the hush of Campobello, Eleanor's quotations seemed to shout. *Making the ten servants help me do my saving has not only been possible, but highly profitable.*[83] Anyone could tell that that wasn't *her* saying such a foolish thing, but she felt no less disgraced, because, as she took pains to explain to Franklin, "so much is not true and yet some of it I did say." Mortified, she denounced the reporter—"I do think it was horrid of that woman to use my name in that way"—and vowed never to let herself be caught out again. But that was cold comfort on a rocky Canadian island. "I'd like to crawl away," she admitted, "for shame."[84]

When homemakers around the country wrote in to the Navy Department with questions about Mrs. Roosevelt's economizing program, Franklin had Lucy forward the letters to Eleanor with answers that Franklin asked Lucy to dummy up and deliver to his wife for use in her replies.

"Why did you make her waste all that time answering those fool notes?" demanded Eleanor. "I tore them and the answers up and please tear any other results of my idiocy up at once." She scarcely drew breath before adding: "She tells me you are going off for Sunday and I hope you all had a pleasant trip but I'm so glad I'm here and not on the Potomac!"[85]

Franklin's letters circled around Lucy Mercer and Nigel Law, the twenty-four-year-old British third secretary, who was known to be fond of Lucy, and Cary T. Grayson, President Wilson's doctor, and his wife. Franklin did not seem to be reading her letters, Eleanor said, "for you never answer a question, and nothing I ask for appears!" *He* in person appeared least of all, excuses and alibis now his standard closing: "I do miss you so very much, but I am getting busier and busier and fear my hoped-for dash to Campobello next week for two days will not materialize."[86]

Each time he insisted that it was all on account of work that he was bearing up "all alone without you," or that it was *she* who was "a goosy girl to think or even pretend to think that I don't want you here *all* the summer," she decided it was best to say nothing.[87]

When a throat infection put Franklin in the hospital, Eleanor trekked back to Washington, a "burning fiery furnace" that month,[88] and nursed him for a week, returning to Campobello with his promise that he would come to the island on August 26. If he reneged, Eleanor planned to return at once to make good on the vow she left him with: "My threat," she warned, "was no idle one."[89]

If family lore can be counted upon in so private a struggle, she had threatened to leave him.[90] And yet further outings with Lucy followed, only now without Nigel Law, and, worst of all, Eleanor had to hear of these plans not from her husband but as a cheery fait accompli by letter from Lucy.

Eleanor found a pretext to put Miss Mercer in her place. She reimbursed Lucy for petty cash that she had spent for Eleanor's navy knitting program, and when Lucy returned Eleanor's check, as a friend might, Eleanor refused as her former employer to relent, sending back the check with a still stronger letter. This had the desired effect, flushing out Lucy as the willful troublemaker: "She is evidently quite cross with me!" relayed Eleanor to Franklin.[91]

Franklin was forced to action by this battle of wills between wife and mistress, and he settled the whole matter of Navy League knitting by going to Secretary Daniels and disbanding the program.

That same week, a curious thing happened in the department. After receiving a perfect performance grade and promotion to Yeomanette Second Class, Lucy was abruptly discharged by "Special Order of Secretary of the Navy," no explanation offered.

WHEN ELEANOR RETURNED FROM CAMPOBELLO that fall of 1917, Cousin Alice buttonholed her one afternoon at the Capitol Rotunda to ask point-blank if Franklin had "told" her—leaving the question deliberately unfinished.

Eleanor knew better than to trust Alice, who had wanted to divorce as early as 1912,[92] when her genial and popular husband, Nicholas Longworth, the Ohio Republican congressman, broke with her father over TR's Bull Moose abandonment of their party. More painfully, Longworth was a well-known adulterer, but when Oyster Bay ruled against divorce, and Longworth—House majority leader in

1923 and Speaker from 1925 to 1931—continued on a long career of dishonoring Alice, she retaliated in full measure, becoming the capital city's master of such modern arts as How to Implement a Whispering Campaign and When to Resort to the Highly Publicized Washington Scandal.

Eleanor remained guarded. Her voice rose as she replied that she did not believe in knowing "things which your husband did not wish you to know."[93] Then she excused herself and hurried away.

THE DAY BEFORE THEIR THIRTEENTH wedding anniversary, while making sandwiches for the soldiers, Eleanor sliced her finger to the bone. She bound up the wound and went right on working.[94] Anna reported to Granny: "Mother cut her finger badly yesterday in a bread machine down at the canteen, and Doctor Hardin came and sewed it up."[95] To Eleanor's surprise, the crisis passed without further complication. She could now depend upon "a certain confidence in myself and in my ability to meet emergencies and deal with them."[96]

In May, the Red Cross promoted her to captain[97] and asked her to go to London—sailing in ten days, if possible—to set up a canteen, a "little piece of America," which would serve some three thousand men daily.[98]

"It is a fearful temptation," confessed Eleanor to Mama, "because I feel I have the strength & probably the capacity for some kind of work & one can't help wanting to do the real thing instead of playing at it over here."[99]

She was finding herself envious of Cousin Ted's wife, the other Eleanor Roosevelt[100]—"Eleanor Theodore," as the tribe called the tall, golden-haired, charming, and capable Eleanor Alexander Roosevelt, to distinguish her from "Eleanor Franklin."[101] While Eleanor "T" broke the army rule against officers' wives by wrangling her way onto French soil as the first female manager of a Y.M.C.A. hotel ("doing more good than twenty men" by serving as "a mother and a sister to lonely soldiers"[102]), Eleanor remained in official Washington under "F's" wing, earning token recognition as co-head of the women's nursing auxiliary at the Navy Department.[103]

She yearned to break out. Coming home from a day shift, she was obliged to go from nurse and social worker to subcabinet wife and hostess with a brief pause as mother of three children getting ready for bed. Sometimes she reached her front door in uniform just as her guests were arriving in evening dress, and so learned the art of the quick change. From here on, a lifelong habit.

But these were not career moves. Her achievements were not professional. For the time being, she got things done by being Mrs. F. D. Roosevelt, and the more constrained she felt as a woman of rank and position upon whom responsibilities fell, the more jealous she became of Franklin's opportunities, especially because in Washington she sometimes made an impression as the wiser, better informed of the two. Ray Lyman Wilbur, the Stanford University president turned wartime food administrator (coiner of the slogan "Food Will Win the War"), met Franklin and Eleanor at a picnic dinner given in Rock Creek Park by the Franklin K. Lanes for the Herbert Hoovers. Wilbur would remember that he and his wife "were more impressed by Mrs. Roosevelt than by the Assistant Secretary of the Navy. She seemed to have an unusual grasp of what was going on in Europe, and I was struck with her comments and how they were similar to what I had already heard from Hoover."[104]

And yet when both received the call overseas, she could not give herself permission and Franklin could. On May 12, she closed the Red Cross question, saying, "I really won't go abroad,"[105] and in July, Franklin secretly boarded a destroyer escort to a troopship convoy, the first risky passage of an eight-week inspection mission beginning at U.S. naval bases in the Azores.

Two days after Franklin had sailed, Eleanor received the shocking news that her cousin Quentin Roosevelt, age twenty, a first lieutenant in the 95th American Aero Squadron, had been killed in aerial combat over German lines. He had died instantly, Eleanor wrote Isabella Ferguson, "by two bullet holes in the head so he did not suffer and it is a glorious way to die." Yet she knew what this loss would mean at Sagamore Hill.[106]

"I am so sorry for Aunt Edith and Uncle Ted," she told Mama.

"Think," she reminded Franklin, "if it were our John."[107]

Quentin, the grinning, best-loved youngest of Uncle Ted's brood, recalled people to the bright-eyed little rascal whom the country had loved to see climbing trees or shooting spitballs as leader of the so-called White House Gang. Grown stocky and determined ("We boys thought it was up to us to practice what Father preached"[108]), Quentin had gone to war as a golden youth attractively engaged to Miss Flora Payne Whitney, to whom TR now broke the news before making a public announcement.[109] Eleanor caught the noble spirit comingling national grief and personal sorrow when she reminded Mama: "I suppose we must all expect to bear what France & England have borne so long."[110]

For Uncle Ted, the loss would be overpowering. "To feel that one has inspired a boy to conduct that has resulted in his death, has a pretty serious side for a father," TR lamented; "and at the same time I would not have cared for my boys and they would not have cared for me if our relations had not been just along that line."[111]

Exactly two months later, Eleanor attended Uncle Douglas Robinson's funeral at Henderson, the old family seat nine miles up the mountain overlooking north-central New York's Mohawk Valley. The loyal brother-in-law who had given her father his last chance had become, by age sixty-three, a chronically enraged husband and an overworked downtown real estate executive and trust officer. He and Aunt Corinne had not made each other happy: Uncle Douglas had worshipped her, and she had kept a cool distance, always defended against his rage.[112] At work, the drain of men going to war had left Uncle Douglas fighting on alone for the survival of multiple firms and fortunes,[113] until one afternoon that September he had suffered a heart attack on the train home to Henderson. After the services, Eleanor comforted her own great comforter, Aunt Corinne, and was harshly lectured by Uncle Ted about Franklin facing the test of real war.

TR warned, as he had before, that Franklin was in danger of doing damage to his future. He *must* get to the Western Front in an AEF uniform, and it was *Eleanor's* duty to see that he *go all-in* before the fighting was stopped.

This incensed her. If anyone knew his duty, it was Franklin. He had stayed the course as a big-navy assistant secretary—longer, in point of fact, than Uncle Ted had done in the same job—and Franklin had carried out his duty on the express orders of the commander in chief.[114] Moreover, Franklin had taken 1913's "crab fleet" of super-annuated pre-dreadnaughts[115] and overseen a greater naval expansion than that of Uncle Ted's White Fleet, launching more than 157 new vessels—"incomparably the greatest navy in the world," Wilson had proclaimed.[116]

Enlisting for overseas duty in the army would be absurd—but entirely Franklin's decision. Indeed, during his inspection of the Naval Railway Battery at the Front, without any prompting, Franklin seemed to have wakened to Uncle Ted's position. He realized that *because* he was thirty-six and automatically exempted from the latest draft call, he felt all the surer that his rightful place was not as a "chair-warmer" behind a Washington desk,[117] but as a commissioned officer attached to the Naval Bombing Squadron ready for action near Sainte-Nazaire.

Eleanor had become ever more committed to Wilson's stand on peace, and instinctively felt she owed greater allegiance to the President and to the fight for the peacetime organization he had sketched in the last of his Fourteen Points: "A general association of nations," in which "great and small states alike" would come together as sovereign members of a common council to stop future local clashes from becoming global catastrophes.[118]

"Under new draft law please register me at Hyde Park," wired Franklin from France, the first Eleanor knew of his aim to get into the fighting.[119] On his voyage home aboard the USS *Leviathan*, virtually a hospital ship of Spanish flu cases, Franklin made sure through Secretary Daniels's office that Louis Howe got word to Mama to meet Franklin on arrival with a doctor and an ambulance. He had been brought low by double pneumonia.

No wire reached Eleanor; she had to be alerted by telephone by Lathrop Brown, Franklin's college roommate, now assistant to Interior Secretary Lane.[120] But she made it to the pier to board the ship with Mama and Dr. George Draper as soon as it docked.

Franklin did not seem to Eleanor as emaciated as the men with whom he was traveling, nor "so seriously ill as the doctors implied."[121] But she held her tongue as four navy orderlies under Dr. Draper's instructions ran the patient home in an ambulance, bearing him into Mama's half of the house, since their own side was still rented to the Thomas Lamonts. Three years before, after Franklin had undergone emergency surgery for appendicitis, Eleanor had been upset that Mama had beat her to the bedside, arriving with a new silk kimono for her boy. But now, no matter how sick Franklin was or which side of the house they were on, Eleanor was fully conditioned to surrendering her husband to his mother.

Grateful for this chance to reestablish simple usefulness as he lay sick and abed, Eleanor put away Franklin's things. Thinking to help him catch up on the mail, she looked among his letters. She knew her husband. He would have correspondence from English shoemakers on top of offers from stamp and coin companies, along with unpaid bills for his favorite silk pajamas, three new pairs of which she was not at all surprised to find in his luggage.[122]

THE LETTERS SHE ALSO FOUND that day have come down to history[123] as a packet,[124] or a bundle,[125] sometimes beribboned,[126] occasionally perfumed.[127] By one reckoning, there were enough communications to describe the whole as hefty.[128] Another account claimed just one single missive. Blanche Wiesen Cook, Eleanor's most comprehensive biographer, has pictured "a stack" of letters tied up in "the proverbial red ribbon."[129] In other contemporary versions, the ribbon is given the texture most often ascribed to Lucy Mercer's voice: velvet.[130] Yet another documentarian hangs the fate of the Roosevelt marriage on a knotted string.[131]

Whatever the fact, Eleanor never expected to open a suitcase and find Lucy Mercer's handwritten letters. How many lines she read, we do not know, nor what they told her beyond the appalling truth: Franklin had lost his heart to her social secretary.

Lucy, after all, was a perfect match for the man Franklin had become. By Eleanor's own later judgment, she herself had been a deeply insecure, often unresponsive, and overcritical spouse. Even beyond sex and coziness and lighthearted loving, Lucy gave Franklin the constant validation to which he felt entitled. Naturally, he would have preferred an uncritically loving Lucy, smiling at every request, curling to her tasks on the floor.[132]

"A lady to her fingertips," as Eleanor's own favorite son, Elliott, recalled. "Femininely gentle where Mother had something of a school-marm's air about her."[133] This last was particularly cruel. Eleanor's intellect *was* her gift, and with typically strong insight, she knew that Franklin's real secret was that he needed nobody.

Sara Delano Roosevelt had a morbid horror of divorce.[134] She would not allow the guilty party to set foot in her house; even the innocent party was questionable. The rupture of a marriage signified the "complete failure of a woman's life."[135] Divorce was thinkable only to the richest: Vanderbilts might divorce, or even Astors. But not Delanos; a courtroom revelation that Franklin was mixed up in such events—legal grounds in New York State required proof of adultery—was unthinkable.

"Every thought, every wish, every plan, of Sara's heart," explained a close friend, "had been thrown with single-minded zeal into the perfection" of the life she had made for and with her only son.[136]

Before anyone could do anything rash, Mama convened discussion, calmly facing Franklin and Eleanor in one of the narrow rooms of No. 47. She began by asking Eleanor what she intended to do about Franklin and Miss Mercer.[137]

Ever after, the family storytellers agreed that Eleanor offered to give Franklin "his freedom."[138]

"Don't be a goose," replied Franklin, reasserting authority: Girls were "goosey," men remained above the battle.

But, Eleanor later told a friend, "I was a goose."[139] By which she meant that she was adamant about one condition: that Franklin *think*. Since her discovery, she herself had not raged, nor asked for further detail, nor even sought the counsel of a friend; but she had reflected. Before undoing their bond, Eleanor insisted, he must carefully weigh the effects of his decision on the children.[140] If he still wanted to part ways after every consideration—including the annulment he would need, were he to marry the observant Roman Catholic Miss Mercer—Eleanor would bow out.

Mama would hear of no such thing. She knew perfectly well that if Franklin meant to divorce Eleanor, she, Sara, could not stop him, but neither would she blindly side with her son, nor would she use Lucy Mercer to cut Eleanor loose.

The fact was, Sara wanted her daughter-in-law to stay. Eleanor was tradition. She was the chaste, no-nonsense stanchion of Franklin's future, and if truth had been told, Eleanor's submissiveness had allowed and would go on allowing Sara to be the über-mother she wanted to be. Without this central virtue, which Sara's generation still called chastity, "even Joan of Arc," by one friend's account, "could not have passed into Sara Delano's good graces."[141]

Louis Howe shuttled between all parties, convincing Franklin that his political future depended upon a grand alliance with his wife and mother. As conditions were explored for what would be more Roosevelt coalition than traditional devotional marriage, Louis soothed Eleanor by acknowledging that she was not merely "still needed," but indispensable. No matter what had happened, she remained vital to Franklin's faith in the future.

Mama was also necessary. Still empress of the family purse, she could dictate steel-bladed terms: here, a vow to cut Franklin off without a penny if he went ahead and left Eleanor. She would see to it that none of her blue-chip stocks or substantial cash reserves came his way, and he would never inherit his beloved home on the Hudson. On this, her position was sweeping and final.

History, having no records of Franklin's thinking, cannot say which consideration made the difference. According to one of many renditions of Eleanor's discovery of his betrayal, Franklin was said to have been "unmasked for the first time in his life."[142] Yet, in point of fact, he no more exposed his true self now than in any other response to crisis over a lifetime of impenetrability to his wife, his closest associates, and political adversaries.

FDR never offered a word of insight into what Lucy Mercer meant to him. Franklin's cousin Daisy Suckley, a confidante of his later years, felt strongly that despite Lucy, Franklin's feelings for Eleanor were "deep & lasting." Their tragedy, maintained Daisy, stemmed from their inability to relax into each other.[143]

At some point, Franklin did manage to let Eleanor know that he

was sorry for hurting her.[144] That was something new, almost experimental. He also volunteered to give up Lucy for good. Contrary to
legend, Eleanor did not ask Franklin for this.[145] A wife's instinct may
have told her that he would go on seeing Lucy in public; official Washington intersected often enough with *Social Register* Washington that
such reunions would leave Franklin susceptible to relapse. Be that as it
may, Eleanor stipulated that if Franklin wished to remain married, he
must demonstrate that, even platonically, he still wanted *her* as his life
partner. She would not stay where she was not wanted. On that point
she was as clear as glass.[146]

For Franklin's part—to the end of his life—he would keep Lucy
Mercer concealed in a category by herself. Part old flame, part soul
mate, part tender of his heart, she would always be the woman he
loved, the Lovely Lucy, and he would arrange for her to reappear at
intervals during his years as president (mostly after her own marriage
to Winthrop Rutherfurd ended in widowhood) under the pseudonym
"Mrs. Paul Johnson." By the end, the risk to a well-insulated war president was as nothing compared to the life-altering damage that would
have been done in 1918.

"It seemed amazing," mused Cousin Alice. "It could have been
the end of Franklin."[147] To be caught cheating on his much-respected
wife—a Red Cross canteen captain—and found romancing Yeomanette Second Class Mercer would have been scandal and ruin for the
assistant secretary of the navy. Josephus Daniels would have had to
fire Roosevelt at once. Franklin would have gone no further in the
Democratic Party. Certainly, no candidate for president had ever
reached the White House as a divorced man remarried to a Roman
Catholic.

Franklin would never put so much of himself on the line for anyone ever again. Almost a quarter of a century later, Eleanor would
confide in a friend how hard it still was to accustom herself to Franklin's "lack of real attachment to people." She "could never conceive of
him doing a reckless thing because of personal attachment."[148] With
those to whom he drew closest after 1918, he would resort to the safer
pattern established with Mama and Eleanor, belonging no less to one
than to the other. Among his life's romances, Lucy remained unique

in this all-important regard: From September 1916 to September 1918 he had risked everything for her.

Franklin's attitude toward the Christian covenant of marriage seemed reverent but hardheaded. Fundamentally, he was his own judge, perfectly willing to give himself the benefit of the doubt.

Eleanor had the greater problem in doing herself justice at this crucial turning point. She was thirty-three, the mother of five surviving children. Young Franklin Roosevelt had been her rescuer. He had restored her belief in love and family and home. The sudden loss of that faith was deeply destabilizing, but she did not shirk from seeking to understand her part in their marriage's undoing. She sat with it. "I faced myself, my surroundings, my world, honestly for the first time."[149]

TEN

S HE STAYED WITH HIM. MERCIFULLY, at this shattering moment, she was called to nurse her husband and children through the Spanish influenza pandemic of 1918, then infecting more than one third of the population worldwide. An estimated 675,000 Americans would perish from Spanish flu. Washington would be hit especially hard, its army camps and naval stations circulating a second-generation pathogen among civilians.

Franklin, all five children, three servants—everyone in the new house on R Street except Eleanor—took to bed. As she attended her "galaxy of invalids," she saw little difference between day and night. Each afternoon, helped by cook and chauffeur, she shepherded supplies and food to the American Red Cross, as often as possible challenging regulations to carry the hampers into the hospital herself. She stayed as long as she dared, going from bed to bed to say a word of cheer to each of the fever-wracked government girls lying in the long rows. Back on R Street, she lamented that she could not "just" be a nurse: "I had to appear at stated times for meals, dressed like a lady, and with the manner of a lady who had nothing to do."[1]

THE FIRST WEEK OF NOVEMBER, as German delegates reached Allied lines with a flag of truce, and Woodrow Wilson in Washington received the first offers for an armistice, Franklin went to see the President to declare himself unable to wait another day before joining the fight. Too late, Wilson told him.[2]

Three days later, as Allied envoys gave armistice terms to the Germans in the Forest of Compiègne, Franklin reported to an old friend: "The consensus of opinion seems to be that the Boche is in a bad way and will take anything, but I am personally not so dead sure as some others. If the terms are turned down and the war continues, I think I shall get into the Navy without question."[3]

By dawn on the 11th, Germany had signed the document, and the guns that had desolated Flanders Fields and so much else in Europe fell silent at the eleventh hour of the eleventh day of the eleventh month. Nearly 11 million soldiers had lost their lives; 21 million more had been wounded. Civilian deaths numbered some 9 million additional souls, including 1.5 million Armenians massacred by the Ottoman government. The American Expeditionary Force (AEF) had led the Allies to victory with more than 3 million men, but sustained fewer than 326,000 casualties, including 179,625 battle deaths.[4] From this global conflagration the United States now emerged as the world's foremost industrial superpower, its principled leader, Woodrow Wilson, the guide to a new world order.

Armistice, wrote Eleanor, "brought relief and thankfulness . . . beyond description."[5] At one o'clock that afternoon, she packed herself into the overflowing galleries of the House of Representatives, while Franklin took his place on the floor alongside Secretary Daniels. She joined the surging ovation that greeted the grave but triumphant commander in chief. For Wilson, the war represented not so much a victory as a moral achievement that would now test American leadership of victors and vanquished alike. At the start of the year, he had presented his preliminary plan for the peace to Congress, but he had not yet formally offered this fourteen-point outline to his Allied colleagues, each of whom held his own nation's needs and interests foremost. Both Britain and France had reservations about Wilson's idea for postwar territorial settlements—"self-determination," or the right of all peoples to live on mutually agreed upon terms of freedom and security "whether they be strong or weak."[6]

For now, the liberation of France was real enough, and at Wilson's announcement of the evacuation of Alsace-Lorraine, an emotional current, such as Eleanor had never felt from a crowd, jumped the entire U.S. government to its feet in a roar.

IN FAMILY ALBUMS OF 1918 to 1920, Eleanor looks like a stowaway, tucked off to the side, head down, ashamed of "her" ordeal. Franklin, clenching his pipe in an iron jaw, stares straight ahead. At center, Mama blandly presides over a world in which the messiness of life is the merest of inconveniences: "A gentleman's hands may be *soiled*," she taught her grandsons, "but they are never 'dirty.' "[7] The Roosevelt Five—two big roughnecks, a small pair of lost boys, and a glowering blond schoolgirl—look ready to audition for the Hyde Park fall pageant.

On Sundays, Franklin now attended church with them: "a great sacrifice to please me," Eleanor acknowledged.[8] But she could not let his marital faithlessness go. They slept in different rooms, rose at different times, performed their separate functions with the children— she, daily studies, habits, prayers; he, nightly romps, kisses, larks. Eleanor tried to enjoy herself at Franklin's parties but dropped her enforced cheer once home. "Dined alone," reports her diary. "Franklin nervous and overwrought and I very stupid and trying. Result a dreadful fracas."[9]

She remained fearful of being a nuisance. In her letters, she steadfastly called him "honey,"[10] and went on penciling seating charts at which "E.R." and "F.D.R." bookended the table.[11] But she could not see past her suspicion that he no longer needed her; and for the moment, she was right. "He did not want to be bothered," James Roosevelt would write. "He cared more about his life than he did his wife."[12]

She could not stop working to prove that he did need her—at the Army-Navy Ball, for example, turned out at his side in a gown of king's blue net over silver cloth inlaid with rhinestones.[13] Yet she had never felt less appealing, or more useless, or more fed up with her place in the old order of things. Struggling with Mama, and Franklin's Delano aunts, Eleanor diarized: "They all in their serene assurance and absolute judgments on people and affairs going on in the world make me want to squirm and turn Bolshevik."[14]

At this moment of worldwide change and distress, Eleanor Roosevelt was neither feminist nor suffragist nor even anti-suffragist. She left the fight for the League of Nations to Franklin and turned away from Alice Hay Wadsworth's invitation to join the National Association Opposed to Woman Suffrage, a fiercely anti-Amendment organization whose staunchest officers included Franklin's mother.[15] New

York women had secured the state vote by referendum in 1917, but on Election Day 1918, when Franklin returned to Hyde Park to cast his midterm ballot, Eleanor stayed home with the children. For now, taking any stand was "outside my field of work."[16]

REGULATIONS DID NOT ALLOW SPOUSES overseas, but on December 24, 1918, one day after Sara Delano Roosevelt had paid him a call, Josephus Daniels signed special orders sending Eleanor with Franklin on his mission to dispose of all naval property in Europe.[17] The "missus" would look after his health—that was their story.[18] In reality, the voyage allowed them back into circulation on a forgive-and-forget basis.

Eleanor jumped into active duty as her husband's spur, merging Franklin with events and people that might help politically.[19] On board the *George Washington*, one of their fellow passengers recalled, "she used always to be telling [him], 'I met so-and-so. He's an interesting fellow. You should talk with him. *He's* interested in more than sailing.'"[20] Eleanor arranged for Franklin to drop the shuffleboard and socializing with his postgraduate partner in crime, Livy Davis, and join her in meeting the opposing Chinese delegations she had befriended—one from the north, one from the south, both on their way to Paris and the talks. Eleanor brought the sides together, gave them tea, conversed in French, and learned that they, too, had been waging war at home yet getting along at sea.[21]

On the sixth day of January, wireless radio brought news of personal loss and worldwide shock. Uncle Ted was gone. In his sleep at Sagamore Hill, a pulmonary embolism had struck, his valet counting the seconds between his last breaths. For many, it was unimaginable that so boisterous and swashbuckling a figure could have slipped away so gently.[22]

The highest function of the President of the United States, Theodore Roosevelt believed, was that of educator. He had himself learned in office, globalizing a self-contradictory democracy of fantastic wealth and cruelest poverty, then tilting some of the vast inequalities of industrial capitalism back toward the individual. Eleanor and Franklin had been two of his most devoted students, but neither could find the words to express the impact he had had on their lives. "The greatest man I ever knew," attempted Franklin.[23] "Another great figure off the stage," tried Eleanor.[24]

She took care to wire heartfelt messages to Aunt Edith, Aunt Corinne, and Auntie Bye, whose lives she knew would never be the same.

THE PRELIMINARY PEACE CONFERENCE WAS in full swing by the time they arrived. Journalists packed the hotel bars in record numbers, while the arrondissements of Paris recovered the million residents who had fled during the final bombardment. Delegates from each of the Allied and Central Powers, along with permanent officials and advisers, translators and telegraphists and subordinates, crowded into hotels which became embassies in miniature. The Germans, guarded behind a barbed wire–topped stockade fence at the Hôtel des Reservoirs, bitterly complained that they were being treated "like the inhabitants of a Negro village in an exposition."[25]

The Roosevelts left calling cards at the palace of the Prince and Princess Murat, the Wilsons' presidential residence near the Parc Monceau, and went to tea with Edith Wilson. Edith was enjoying a reprieve from the world press, newly portraying her as "the dazzling first lady of the planet"[26] rather than a Lady Macbeth with undue influence.[27] Paris had accorded the President—the first to go to Europe while in office—a massive, idolatrous welcome, his hands kissed by bandaged soldiers, his garments grabbed in worshipful delirium. Rome, Milan, and Turin each followed with geyser-like outpourings. Triumphant though his visit was, Wilson's great mistake of failing to include in his delegation any senator from either party would come back to haunt "the savior of the world" when he brought home his Covenant, the basic constitution for a League of Nations, which Wilson had embedded in the peace treaty.

Standing by her husband these peacemaking months abroad, Edith Wilson set precedent for the inclusion of first ladies in the statecraft of post-dynastic Europe.[28] Nonetheless, when Eleanor took lunch with the U.S. dignitaries' wives[29] and heard Mrs. Wilson criticized for letting the President's schedule preempt her visits to the wounded, she invited the first lady into her own project of calling on naval casualties at the hospital specializing in plastic surgery. Where Eleanor had barely been managing eye contact with men whose faces had been burned or blown off,[30] without flinching or a trace of pity, Mrs. Wilson warmly approached each bedside, found something to say to each man, and left a few flowers.

Eleanor turned in a more confident performance with the President of France. When called upon to converse in French with Raymond Poincaré—or at lunch with the chief of the French naval staff, Admiral Ferdinand de Bon, and his family—something genial came into her manner, her smile sparkled in her eyes, and she found the right words, even a touch of élan. Comfortable in the lifelong practice of outperforming her age group, she masterfully renewed friendships with French diplomats last seen in Washington. Bernard Baruch, advising Wilson on the economic sections of the Treaty of Versailles, welcomed Eleanor with roses.

"I never saw anything like Paris," she exclaimed to Mama. "It is full beyond belief and one sees many celebrities and all one's friends! People wander the streets unable to find a bed."[31]

Eleanor and Franklin shared a navy-assigned room at the Ritz and played no official part in the conclave. But to an old friend, the Franklin Roosevelts had never looked more in charge of things: "They seemed to be on top of the wave, young and full of vigor,"[32] dining out every night. This included the bereaved and war-wounded Oyster Bay cousins: Ted Jr., before surgery on his shattered knee, and Kermit and his wife Belle, a sophisticated Virginia Democrat, with both of whom they established an authentic friendship that would endure through the cousinly converging and diverging of the rest of their lives.[33]

After dinner, Franklin liked to go out with whatever stag group of diplomats were tearing around Paris. The war's permissiveness bled into the after-hours portion of the conference. "Vice is rampant," reported the novelist Elinor Glyn.[34] Hotel rooms could be openly entered by unmarried partners; two Canadian Red Cross nurses were hardly the only ones pretending to knock at and then stay overnight in "the wrong room."[35]

Eleanor greeted Franklin with icy suspicion the mornings after his carousing; but so far as his naval mission went, Franklin could afford to moonlight. His official legal adviser, Thomas J. Spellacy, could be counted upon to be up first thing, handling the settlement of contracts that Franklin had negotiated the previous afternoon. The navy's chief paymaster, Commander John M. Hancock, was overseeing base closings as Franklin's business aide.

Eleanor's principal hindrance in Paris was the same as it had been in Washington. She had energy, she had a famous name, and she wanted to put both in service of the postwar world; but she risked alienation however she behaved. In order to have authority of her own, she had to be serious. To keep her place at the side of her lighthearted husband, she had to soften her earnestness. And Franklin was nothing if not devoted to keeping Eleanor guessing.

In Paris, she knew he flirted, but assumed he formed no serious attachments. Of course, flirting was dangerous in a man who aroused the highest hopes in people. He appeared to have followed Henry Adams's exercises as carefully as Walter Camp's—"Discuss serious things lightly and light things seriously"[36]—which, as one Adams biographer noted, "naturally led him into the company of women."[37] Men and women alike had a powerful sense of being essential to Franklin, believing themselves to have been granted access to the real, hidden FDR of struggle and need—when they were really only seeing Franklin Roosevelt bouncing people back at themselves, generating heat.

For Eleanor, this was heat that itched in her hair. "I can forgive," she would often say in later years, "but I cannot forget."[38]

THE BLASTED LANDSCAPE OF NORTHERN France, still technically a war zone, barred women. Filth lay over everything. Rats the size of buck rabbits[39] occupied the "great sea of mud." Eleanor understood that these and other sights, revolting to men and women alike, "must be seen to be fully realized."[40] But the day before they left Paris to tour the trenches, a sharp pain in her side made Eleanor gasp. By evening, she was running a high fever.

Early the next morning, they drove north in the lead car of a three-vehicle convoy, Eleanor shivering with fever between Franklin and Livy Davis. Every bump in the road was a knife in her ribs, but she was determined to make good as Franklin's field partner.

Two American army officers, veterans of a British brigade on the Somme, traded the driving, and narrated the fighting, as they motored over the straight military roads, past flattened villages and the standing skeletons of smashed cathedrals.[41] The lone few sticks that had been Bourlon Wood sent the gravest shudder through Eleanor, especially the lime trees: the retreating Germans had cut down every limb that might bear fruit.[42]

Whenever the cars stopped in view of the trenches, Eleanor got out with the men and insisted on hiking the traverses to see for herself the cost in lives-per-feet-of-mud. When army commissary sandwiches of grayish French bread and beef paste were handed around in the cathedral square at St. Quentin, she made herself choke them down, though it hurt to chew. Painfully aware that men had starved here, she stole away by herself to bury the unfinished sandwich in the rubble of the cathedral.[43]

In London, the pain plunged deeper into her ribs with every breath.[44] Forced by a choking cough to drop her pretense and submit to a doctor's house call in their suite at the London Ritz, Eleanor was not surprised to learn that the inner lining of her chest and outer covering of her right lung were inflamed. Her cough was so deep and wracking, and she had lost so much weight, the doctor suspected tuberculosis, but diagnosed "pleurisy." Mrs. Roosevelt must be thoroughly examined once home. In the meantime, bed rest.

Eleanor pushed back, contending that she had her rounds to make: the theater, dining at the Admiralty, clothes to shop for Anna. All her life she would be "too busy to be sick."[45] In these enfeebled weeks, her immune system contained what proved to be a serious infection; but the still-undiagnosed bacteria lodged, dormant, in her lungs.[46]

Franklin took time from his closing-out duties to stay with Eleanor for a room-service lunch and dinner. Eleanor felt better and tried a dinner party, but when Franklin became fascinated by his dinner partner, Kathleen Bruce Scott, Eleanor sensed—her word—*difficulty*.[47] Lady Scott, widow of Captain Scott, the Antarctic explorer, was a political insider whom the polished Colonel Edward M. House, Wilson's most trusted adviser at the peace talks,[48] was using as go-between to the British Treasury. Kathleen Scott was also a well-known winner of hearts and confidences, and she was dazzled to meet Franklin. Her knack for sculpting statesmen's likenesses authorized her to afterward diarize: "He is very good looking."[49]

The old string-bean Eleanor of the Chevy Chase Club had gone home alone and made a welcome mat of herself. The Eleanor awakened by Flanders Fields, having already been forced to "face certain difficulties,"[50] neither blamed herself nor took offense. She made a conscious decision to adapt—"to accept the fact that a man must be what he is." At the same time, she finally put her foot down—after all, a woman also must be what she is—and "dragged F. home."[51]

Her temperature spiked again to 101. Over her protests, Franklin pronounced her too sick to go out, and refused to let her accompany him as he paid calls in London.[52] "A full day," reports Kathleen Scott's diary from that afternoon, "but the wonderfullest thing was a talk I had at the Pollens' with Franklin D. Roosevelt."[53]

"I hate to have him going off without me," grumbled Eleanor, after Franklin had left with Livy Davis for Brussels and a lunch with King Albert of Belgium, followed by marine base inspections in occupied Germany.[54] She awaited him in Paris.

She confided in her daily letter to Mama how surprised she was that "instead of becoming more independent I am growing into a really clinging vine." She missed the children, but she longed for Mama, and told her Lucy Mercer avenger: "I do hope we never have to separate again."[55] Sara replied in kind, reporting that in the latest episode of her rivalry with Cousin Susie Parish, Susie had said, "Eleanor is an angel." Mama had seen and raised her: "—an angel with a heart and a mind."[56]

And a husband nowhere to be found. Anxiously expecting Franklin to appear on February 8 for an eight o'clock dinner with Commander Hancock, Eleanor and the good paymaster called it quits at eleven. Eleanor then kept vigil in their room until she thought she would lose her mind imagining all the things that could have gone wrong. When Franklin at last sailed in, carrying a range of battlefield souvenirs, along with a collector's trove of old books from the Rhineland, she replied to his stories through a clenched jaw.[57]

The trip would prove to be the first of many accommodations in which they found that they could neither end old habits nor begin new ways. Their son James would describe the marriage as "an armed truce" that endured to the day Franklin died.[58] Their bond was more like the war itself: lines frozen, an unbreachable gap widening between what each wanted and what the other could give.

THE DEMOBILIZATION OF THE U.S. Navy abroad completed, they sailed home among the Wilsons' official party. The evening before they landed, fog thickened. Bells rang. Engines reversed, then halted.[59] A thousand yards from a jutting shore, the President's flagship was dead in the water. Eleanor dashed below to alert Franklin, already in full gallop to the bridge to help Captain McCauley. "I might have known," she said, "he would need no word from me."[60]

They were not far off Marblehead, reckoned Franklin, ordering the necessary adjustments. When the fog lifted on the morning of February 24, the *George Washington* was found to be headed for Thacher Island, off rocky Cape Ann, sixteen miles north of Marblehead. Had it not been for his piloting, the ship would likely have gone aground. "Even in a fog," observed Eleanor years later, "he could usually get into port."[61]

Franklin was struggling through a murkiness of his own.[62] As he walked the deck with his naval aide, Eleanor's cousin Sheffield Cowles, Franklin admitted, "If I'd followed what was best for me, I'd have resigned as Assistant Secretary and enlisted in the Navy and been an officer on a destroyer."[63] Cowles had noticed Roosevelt's self-doubt earlier in the voyage, when official protocol required him to address the crew and he had been "very bothered by it." Louis Howe had directed Franklin's Navy Yard speeches, helping to turn the clubman-who'd-rather-be-yachting into a fluent friend of labor. Perhaps in Louis's absence Franklin had gone slack. "He had no facility at all," recalled Cowles. "It was an agony for him to speak." Years later, when FDR expressed admiration for the freewheeling style of the young Texas Congressman Lyndon Johnson, he conceded, "That's the kind of uninhibited young pro I might have been as a young man—if I hadn't gone to Harvard."[64]

When the *George Washington* landed in Boston Harbor at eleven that morning,[65] half a million people turned out to cheer. Calvin Coolidge, the newly inaugurated governor of Massachusetts, welcomed home the triumphant president with a few limp sentiments typed on notecards. Duty done, he stood stock still, almost lifeless. Franklin would long remember how Coolidge then took a step toward Wilson. All at once sincere, direct, and effective, Coolidge declared that he would let his trust in "a League of Nations or some other kind of organization" join with the people's faith in Wilson's principles for peace—Massachusetts senior senator and League nemesis Henry Cabot Lodge be damned. "We are united behind you," proclaimed Coolidge, as fervently as "Silent Cal" had ever said such a thing in public life.[66]

The war would bring many new requirements to American politics; among them, a candid speaking style. Crucial to the record of any younger man campaigning for high office would be overseas battle service. And medals. Boston's moving picture houses that very day premiered not one but two films glorifying Uncle Ted and identifying his decorated sons as the nation's supreme warrior heroes.[67]

Six months earlier, when Franklin had considered running for governor of New York, he had buried the hatchet to become the Tammany candidate only to discover that Charlie Murphy's district captains planned to run him as "TR's son" who had "turned Democrat." They further intended to tell the voters that he had "returned from the front loaded with honors."[68] Franklin withdrew at once.

Returning from Europe with nothing on his chest but buttons, he might as well have sailed into political oblivion. For the first time since 1910, the future looked uncertain.

ELEVEN

Back in Washington, Eleanor dedicated herself to the shell-shocked and the dead.[1] Each day that spring, as the Republican-majority Senate went to war over Wilson's peace, Eleanor brought flowers across the Potomac to the military funerals at Arlington National Cemetery. If no mourners appeared, she stood as lone witness to the descending casket, ensuring that no soldier was buried alone. In time to come, Eleanor could not hear taps without thinking of these raw spring days and the disoriented young women gone from wives to widows before her eyes.[2]

In March, the American Red Cross asked her to inspect conditions at St. Elizabeth's, the government-run psychiatric hospital where the navy had established a unit to treat shell-shocked men returning from France. More than two thousand soldiers and sailors had been all but imprisoned there. Overcrowding; staff losses to the war; subsistence wages[3]—all meant that military patients were now penned in with the criminally insane[4] and tended to by orderlies hired from among prisoners at the District Jail.[5]

At the time of Eleanor's first visit, hundreds of paralytic inmates were chained to beds with soiled linens.[6] Semi-starved patients routinely attacked one another,[7] and every month or so, an inmate would kill a nurse or orderly; every few days, one escaped.[8] The army sent a detachment of three hundred soldiers to enforce the rules, but it was then found that sick men in the navy's shell-shock unit were being held under armed guard for minor infractions.[9] The list of abominations went on and on.

Eleanor bore her father within her, was thus terrified of mental wards—of insanity itself. As a female visitor she felt a double horror of being conspicuous, and paled at the thought of becoming unable to conceal her panic while locked in with the inmates.[10] The rows of hard, straight beds, their occupants staring from frightened eyes, seemed an invitation to give up and back out. But she had seen the trenches, knew what these men had refused to give in to; and so, with her first deliberate steps into the ward, she found her nerve—and a mantra: *You must do the thing you think you cannot do.*

At the far end of the room stood a young boy with fair hair, muttering to himself, repeating the nightly orders to take cover. Eleanor watched as the sun in the window "touched his hair and seemed almost like a halo around his head."[11] She followed his progress when revisiting the ward, and he became her reason for venturing ever more trustingly into St. Elizabeth's. In cases of "nervous disturbance," the newer term for shell-shock, doctors saw improvement by placing the patient "in a favorable environment to counteract the effects of the unfavorable one that had injured him."[12] Eleanor found she could be useful to these men by returning consistently to exude confidence and curiosity—just as Mrs. Wilson had.

She spoke in a new voice to her friend Franklin K. Lane. War work had gained her a measure of authority in Washington. After days of being sealed into the wards, Eleanor could now urge the secretary of the interior to launch an investigation to overhaul St. Elizabeth's. Lane, a reform presence in the administration, believed that the most unforgivable sin in governing was a lack of generosity. Although he had never visited the facility on the far side of the Anacostia Flats, he was certain that as a matter of policy the federal government should "want our soldiers and sailors to be more certain of our gratitude."[13] In June, when the House refused to increase the hospital's operating budget or to allocate funds for new equipment,[14] Lane asked the Senate for some $322,000 for improvements to laboratory and staff buildings.[15] When the upper house voted to increase the hospital's appropriation to $1 million,[16] Lane reviewed the upgrades, which included $20,000 for hydrotherapeutic baths for patients, and gave his approval.[17]

It was a coup for a "Gray Lady" in a federal hospital[18]—to extend herself to a friend in power and exert herself on behalf of those unprotected by a government in their debt. Eleanor next applied pressure to Secretary Daniels and Franklin to install bathrooms for women at the

Navy Department and to give a certain female doctor greater power at St. Elizabeth's. Both were done.[19]

Again and again she advocated for the patient, broaching issues beyond the strictly medical, sitting down with the sailor's wife or mother; one by one, man by man—her signature pace for the next twelve years, or until 1932, when numbers and needs would again explode beyond previously known limits. In the meantime, as Eleanor's activism evolved, she did not see herself reaching to solve social problems so much as engaging with individuals to unravel discontinuities between the old order and modernity.

IN HER TWO-MONTH ABSENCE, THE household had erupted with resentments among cook and maids, children and nurses. Two of the older staff had quit. Eleanor let the remaining objectors return to New York, and thereupon hired a new cook, kitchen maid, butler, and housemaid, all local to Washington, all African American. They arrived March 15 and went immediately to work. In her regular bulletin to Mama, Eleanor assumed her class's contempt for African Americans, sighing, "Well, all my servants are gone & all the darkies are here & heaven knows how it will all turn out!"[20] According to a family account, Sara was "horrified at the idea"[21] of what Eleanor portrayed as "a complete darky household."[22] In her autobiography, Eleanor would present her new cook, Nora Gibson, as a focus of empathy and emotional interest, even as she expressed her surprise at how comfortable she herself felt with a black household staff: "Though their eyes may mirror the tragedies of their race, they certainly have much to teach us in the enjoyment of the simple things of life and the dignity with which they meet their problems."[23]

Within months, however, when "their" problems became an individual matter. The new butler asked to be excused from serving a buffet luncheon because a relative had died suddenly of pleurisy. Eleanor once again adapted the Southern form of racial mockery to make her contempt sound more acceptable: "With darkies," she clucked, "one is always suspicious even of a death in the family,"[24] further implying that to be strict with "inferiors" was the better part of a matron's inherited acumen, since "their" laziness, dishonesty, or treachery had "always" aroused suspicion, whether among the enslaved African Americans who appeared as plantation "darkies" in Aunt Annie Gracie's sentimental Georgia tales or among the blackface caricatures misappropriated by the "Navy Yard Minstrels," which Eleanor and Franklin attended that December as guests of that avatar of Southern white supremacy Josephus Daniels.[25]

In mid-March, Josephus Daniels crossed the Atlantic for an Allied naval conference, leaving Franklin acting secretary and Eleanor to host two thousand guests at navy teas.[26] She welcomed countless more to garden parties, lawn fêtes, band concerts, and luncheons at R Street for Marine Corps officers and their wives.[27] Occasionally, Lucy Mercer appeared at Washington functions, including the debutante tea that the Franklin Lanes gave for their daughter.[28] Franklin Roosevelt was fortunately unable to attend. Eleanor diluted the inevitable encounter with her husband's mistress by volunteering to help receive guests. Beaming at everyone, including Lucy, she shook hands vaguely, and when the moment came, no one suspected.[29] Except for the very few friends with whom she shared it, Eleanor believed that Lucy Mercer was the secret that would die with her.

THE EVENING OF JUNE 2, 1919, a wave of anarchist bombings broke out in American cities. Crude hand-delivered devices detonated at the homes of eight judges and legislators in New York, Boston, Pittsburgh, and Cleveland. Near midnight, in Washington, a suitcase-toting anarchist hopped from a car on R Street Northwest, and advanced toward the brick town house in which United States Attorney General A. Mitchell Palmer and his wife and daughter were asleep. On the low front steps he lost his footing.

When the bomb went off, killing the anarchist, Eleanor and Franklin had just parked their car at its garage near R Street. They dashed home to find bloodied gore on their steps, the front door blown open. The Palmers' windows opposite had been blown out. Wood and glass hung shattered in the Roosevelts' window frames. Inside was eerily still.

Then eleven-year-old James appeared on the second-floor landing, sweaty and frightened, uncertain what had happened. Franklin was already taking the stairs three at a time, shouting "Jimmy!" He embraced his son so tightly that James never forgot "the ardor of it."[30]

Eleanor, remaining below, had already turned to the emergency: notifying the police; checking on the Palmers, who had narrowly escaped harm in the wreckage of their home; offering to drive the attorney general, a devout Quaker, to the hospital. In one version of the story, Eleanor called up to James, sharply ordering him back to bed. In another, she downgraded the blast to "just a little explosion."[31]

This instant metabolizing of an anarchist's bomb established a family legend of "Mother's self-control,"[32] which corroborated Eleanor's minimizing of hurt in crises that injured her children, such as when Elliott managed to get the embers of a Campobello picnic fire stuck under the strops of his temporary leg braces. Eleanor belittled the second-degree injury to Franklin as "only skin burns."[33] Another time, hearing that Jimmy had contracted a spectacular case of poison ivy, Eleanor hurried with great concern to his bedside, only to disparage him as "a very silly boy who should have known better."[34]

The children and others took her underestimation of hurt as a coping skill shading into indifference; on the contrary, she was an absorber of grief. She felt each new pain, but disciplined herself, like a field medic who looks graver and graver but does not snap. She didn't sink under it; she was able to absorb it and keep going.

A WEEK AFTER THE BOMBING, Spartan Eleanor reported to Isabella Ferguson: "This past year has rather got the better of me it has been so full of all kinds of things that I still have a breathless, hunted feeling about it though for the moment I am leading an idle if at times a somewhat trying life!"[35]

She was, just then, supervising the children at the Delano household at Fairhaven, signaling Franklin in Washington: "No word from you, and I am getting very anxious on account of the riots."[36]

Of the 2.3 million black draftees who had answered the call, as many as 400,000 African American soldiers, including 1,353 officers, had served among front-line French units or with the segregated American Expeditionary Force. Back on U.S. soil—having been denied by Wilson their rightful place in the victory parade down the

Champs Élysées—demobilized black veterans discovered that their service to the nation had only intensified white racial hostility.

Fighting men who had survived the world's first mass slaughter and been decorated with the Croix de Guerre were expected to come home and resume Jim Crow servility. Warned by black and white leaders alike to remember they lived in "the white man's country,"[37] they found, from Arizona to Upstate New York, that the least assertion of rights was met by swift reactionary reprisal. The lynching of African Americans increased from fifty-eight in 1918 to seventy-seven in 1919, the violence often triggered by white soldiers still in uniform. Among the nation's lynching victims were at least ten war veterans, some put into the noose while in uniform.[38]

In Washington on July 19, white servicemen, ignited by a minor sidewalk incident, went on a rampage, pulling black passengers from streetcars, and attempting, unsuccessfully, a lynching, afterward dispersing and reappearing throughout the night. As hostilities spread across the city,[39] the NAACP appealed to Josephus Daniels to take into custody sailors and marines who had participated in the initial assaults—a rapid response that could have averted further violence. Daniels, true to form, not only took no action but in abdicating his duty freed all able-bodied seamen to abandon theirs.

No surprise, then, that the next round of rioting began at the Washington Navy Yard, when white sailors filtered into the surrounding neighborhood to assault black residents coming home from church. By Monday morning, the attacks had escalated from bricks and stones to rifles and bullets, with randomly targeted shots now issuing from hit-and-run vehicles.

Before the "Red Summer" of 1919 cooled off, twenty-six cities across the United States had erupted into unprecedented levels of interracial bloodshed and arson claiming hundreds of lives, leaving thousands wounded and thousands more homeless. In Chicago and Texas, as in the nation's capital, when African Americans fought back, their courageous defense of lives and homes galvanized (and shocked) blacks, edified (and shocked) whites, thus offering, according to NAACP field secretary James Weldon Johnson, "the turning point in the psychology of the whole nation regarding the Negro problem."[40]

Eleanor waited another twenty-four hours without any word from Washington, then demanded to know why Franklin wouldn't respond. "I couldn't sleep at all last night thinking of all the things that might be the matter." On Thursday, July 24, he answered at last: "Luckily the trouble hasn't spread to R Street. . . . It has been a nasty episode and I only wish *quicker* action had been taken to stop it."[41]

Josephus Daniels had denied every request. President Wilson, home from the Peace Conference, viewed the rioting with "concern," but considered such incidents the problems of local officials, his full attention going to his Treaty fight with Congress, the most volatile national debate since the Civil War, with the peace of the world hanging in the balance.[42]

Fortunately, Secretary of War Newton D. Baker had also been mayor of Cleveland, and it was Baker, alone among federal officials, who fielded two thousand troops to back up the floundering District police. In his duty as assistant secretary of the navy, Roosevelt did nothing to stop or punish the lethal mayhem caused by naval personnel, revealing at worst a dangerous dereliction of duty and, scarcely better, the distancing jokey banter of upper-class bigotry: "With your experience in handling Africans in Arkansas," he reminded a Harvard classmate, "I think you had better come up here and take charge of the Police force."[43]

Resisting his wife's essential demand—Eleanor would rather be hurt by a letter's hard truth than comforted with a lazy lie—Franklin's report of July 24 breezed on: "There is little news, except the rain has continued and I hope will let up for a game of golf which I go to in an hour. Probably," he concluded lightly, "I will stay out and dine at Chevy." He judged the riots "to be about over, only one man killed last night."[44]

No year had ever divided her as 1919 had.

On August 14, the twenty-fifth anniversary of her father's death, Grandmother Hall died. Eleanor joined her three spade-jawed aunts and barely functioning uncles to lay Mary Livingston Ludlow Hall to rest in the family crypt behind the churchyard at St. Paul's, Tivoli. Reflecting on her guardian's life, Eleanor determined never to be dependent on her own children.[45] G'ma had voided herself, Eleanor believed, by endlessly indulging without ever truly helping hers to help themselves.

In October, Eleanor diarized: "I do not think I have ever felt so strangely as in the past year. Perhaps it is that I have never noticed little things before but all my self-confidence is gone and I am on edge though I never was better physically I feel sure."[46]

She was living in an "empty place between two eras," as Bruce Catton described the fractured spheres of 1919–1920.[47] Calmly receiving ever more bad news, she accepted the well-bred nihilism of the fall of the house of Hall: Aunt Pussie's unhappy life ended in tragedy as she tried to rescue her daughters from a Greenwich Village house fire that put all three to death.[48] Eleanor took the next train to New York—a blizzard had tied up the city—and arranged for the bodies to be taken up the Hudson for burial at Tivoli.

African American veterans were not the only targets in the new Red-Scare Washington of 1919. The Roosevelts' crusading neighbor, A. Mitchell Palmer, warned Congress that "on a certain day," the same "radical organizations" that blew up their street now planned to "rise up and destroy the government at one fell swoop." Making the most of wartime sedition laws and the thuggish loyalty of a twenty-four-year-old file clerk named J. Edgar Hoover, Wilson's attorney general turned public avenger,[49] launching an army of government agents to crush "dissenters" and "alien radicals," including socialists, women's rights activists, and immigrants, especially Italians and Eastern European Jews. The "Palmer-Hoover Raids," carried out under a new division of the Justice Department's Bureau of Investigation, claimed six hundred arrests and five hundred deportations by year's end. The number of "radically inclined" American citizens in Palmer's pogrom eventually came to as many as ten thousand before the hysteria burned itself out on the strangely uneventful May Day 1920. By then, however, Hoover had established his authority over the General Intelligence Division's surveillance, wiretapping, and filing systems, which already contained, like the bacilli of future outbreaks, sixty thousand names of known or suspected radicals.

The navy, meantime, was engaging in a more clandestine but no less vicious roundup, to prosecute homosexual behavior believed to be affecting the twenty-five-thousand-man Naval Training Station at Newport, Rhode Island. As acting secretary, Franklin supervised the sting operation, naming it "Section A," and officially attaching it to his own office. Using innocent new recruits as "operatives" in morally indefensible violations of civil liberties, he deputized two naval officers to draft as many as forty sailors to serve as decoys in what Roosevelt secretly assured Attorney General Palmer would be a "most searching and rigid investigation."[50] Whether gulled by the insidious fake science behind Palmer's crusades, or boyishly intrigued by the sting's police-blotter sordidness, Franklin let himself be snowed into imagining that the "enemies" of Woodrow Wilson's war-making agencies—homosexuals at the Newport YMCA, including one Episcopal parish priest—justified his own approval of action that was plainly wrong from the outset.

Just then, the Wilson government itself was rudderless. Outside the town of Pueblo, Colorado, on his railway stump tour for the League of Nations, the crusading president had collapsed in mental breakdown. Back in Washington, a stroke on October 2 left Wilson a shawled invalid, his left side paralyzed, his real condition undisclosed. For the next seventeen months in an immobilized White House, Edith Wilson redirected the flow of presidential business, becoming, as one historian noted, "the twenty-eighth-and-a-half president of the United States."[51]

Neither the Senate nor the American people were any closer to agreeing with Wilson's terms for peace. The new Republican-controlled Congress refused to put American foreign policy and military forces at the command of a world peacekeeping organization. The incapacitated Wilson, alternating between states of defiance and despair at the "selfishness" of the League's opponents, pressed for passage of Covenant and Treaty as he had signed them. He refused to budge, even for Edith, even when she pled with him on personal terms on the day of the Senate vote. "Better a thousand times to go down fighting," rasped the old professor, "than to dip your colors in dishonorable compromise." The Treaty of Versailles failed in the Senate by seven votes.

As 1920 BEGAN, FRANKLIN K. Lane, Wilson's fast-aging interior secretary, privately exclaimed: "The whole world is skew-jee, awry, distorted and altogether perverse. The president is broken in body and obstinate in spirit." With Prohibition starting the following day—the Eighteenth Amendment was expected to reduce crime and corruption, solve social problems, and improve health and hygiene—Lane added: "Drink, consoling friend of a perturbed world, is shut off; and all goes merry as a dance in hell!"[52]

Eleanor hoped Franklin would get out of government service so that they could "disappear" and she could "lead a hermit's life for a year with only my husband & children and real friends to think about."[53] But in June 1920, Franklin traveled to the first-ever Democratic National Convention held on the West Coast, his mission as a New York delegate to support the nomination of Governor Alfred E. Smith for president.

On the forty-fourth ballot of "that gigantic circus," as Edna Ferber described the San Francisco convention,[54] the delegates compromised on Ohio governor James M. Cox, a reformer whose political tenacity as a three-time Democratic gubernatorial winner in Republican Ohio made him the choice of the urban bosses. Party insiders eagerly sized up Franklin Roosevelt as a progressive internationalist who could attract independents as a vice presidential candidate: Progressives, even Bull Moosers who had hoped to vote for Theodore Roosevelt in 1920, might sign on with the "Democratic Roosevelt." As one Republican newspaper put it, "Fifth Cousin Franklin" had been chosen "to put the honey of a name on the trap of a ticket."[55]

Cox vowed a "March of Progress"—he would run a twenty-two-thousand-mile, thirty-six-state campaign, bannering his vision of an innovative postwar federal government—but needed a stronger connection to Wilson and Washington, and so immediately gave his approval to the handsome, energetic young insider with the name whose magic cut both ways. H. L. Mencken spoke for all who wanted no part of a "Roosevelt II," casting Franklin as a "pale and somewhat pathetic" sequel, "resembling the Rough Rider much as a wart resembles the Matterhorn."[56]

Eleanor heard the news by wire on faraway Campobello. "This certainly is a world of surprises," she remarked, adding later: "Not very many people could be found who were willing to run with Mr. Cox on a ticket whose main plank was to be the League of Nations."[57] Franklin's alliance with the first-ever divorced presidential nominee supplied just that touch of sardonic irony that Eleanor relished, considering how carefully the Roosevelts had avoided divorce for fear of its effect on presidential ambitions.

Glad for Franklin, Eleanor traveled to Hyde Park with the children for his formal notification reception, a grand outdoor gala organized by their Dutchess County neighbor Henry Morgenthau, Jr., then to Washington to give up the house as Franklin resigned as assistant secretary of the navy.

Sara supported her son's new quest as the next step toward his becoming "our future President," and sent him off from the crowd-trampled lawns at Springwood with her benediction: "All my love and interest goes to you, and as always is centered in you."[58] A news photograph, captioned "How Mother Felt About It,"[59] showed Sara and Franklin locked in an embrace that looked more like a mother's wartime parting from a son than the kickoff for a national political campaign. Between Eleanor and Franklin, cameras would catch moments of fun and games, and she still addressed him in letters as "Dearest, dear Honey,"[60] but nowhere in the documentary record is there a single instant so publicly demonstrative.

Eleanor regarded her husband's prospects coolly, as did Louis Howe, who felt certain that Ohio Senator Warren G. Harding, the banal Republican nominee promising "good government and good times," could become president with the help of the Massachusetts governor who had broken Boston's police strike, Calvin Coolidge. If women voters came around to the Republican interpretation of the League of Nations—as a "world super-government"[61] empowered to take their sons and brothers and fathers to fight more of Europe's wars—Harding's lazy, war-weary message ("Not Nostrums but Normalcy"[62]) would no doubt run ahead of Cox's coattails campaign.

Howe wired Eleanor asking for a photograph that the campaign could hand out to the newspapers. It was urgent, he told her. The *Chicago Tribune* was one of several outlets putting together a "Democratic Leaders and Their Wives" photogravure-style feature.

Louis insisted: "Is there one at the house here that I can have copied?"

"Are no pictures of me," she wired.[63]

Until now, Eleanor had not had any reason to supply personal photographs for publicity. After being humiliated in the *New York Times* fiasco acclaiming her wartime household thrift, she had harbored a deep distrust of the newspapers. This time, it was the *Chicago Tribune*: in the absence of a real photograph, the paper hung Eleanor's name over the society portrait of a tight-lipped young matron with an enormous silk bow on her head.[64] This "Mrs. Franklin D. Roosevelt" was replaced in other Sunday supplements by another, darker-haired woman; most likely Madeline Burke Hooker, wife of Maj. Harry S. Hooker, Franklin's former law partner, whom sitting beside Franklin at a Washington Senators baseball game the real Eleanor chatted up in the row behind.

She accompanied Franklin to visit with the Coxes at their home in Ohio, but went only once or twice to the campaign offices at Grand Central Palace in New York. There, she met Franklin's campaign manager—his former Navy Department secretary, Charles H. McCarthy—and got her first glimpse of Marguerite LeHand of Somerville, Massachusetts, McCarthy's newly rehired assistant from wartime merchant-shipping days.

When Franklin departed for the first eighteen-day, twenty-state rail epic, Eleanor returned with the children to the quiet of Campobello. Grace Coolidge, her counterpart as vice-presidential "nominette," allowed no appearances beyond waving to hometown folk.[65]

Then, on August 19, the voting population doubled overnight. With Tennessee's ratification of the Nineteenth Amendment, the 1920 election became the first in which, constitutionally, any American twenty-one or older could vote; in reality, poll taxes and other forms of suppression blocked African Americans and poor whites from voting in some states, while others, such as Alabama, kept white women at home on Election Day.

White women were nonetheless making history that summer as delegates to the national party conventions, rising for the first time to speak on the convention floor. Franklin was not about to have his wife sit on the sidelines. From Labor Day through Election Day, her every show of support would be good politics. He wrote Eleanor at once, and the sincerity of his need of her was all she needed to hear.

BOARDING THE *WESTBORO* FOR THE four-week swing across the country's middle, she found herself an alien—not just the only woman on the campaign special, but the wife of a candidate who treated life on the stump as a great lark: going without food, rest, exercise, or fresh air so that he could give more than a dozen speeches a day, in addition to frequent impromptu talks and press interviews, before bringing staff and newsmen together for a late-night poker game in a berth at the far end of the car.

"I really don't see," muttered Eleanor, "that I'm of the least use on this trip."[66]

In the Midwest, to her surprise and annoyance, tiny Louis Howe came aboard, peering out suspiciously from under his drooping newsboy cap. Four months shy of fifty—a full generation older than the youngest of Franklin's snappy, fedora-hatted war veterans[67]—Louis now shared Eleanor's harem position, that of "aging first wife,"[68] and did not like it.

Eleanor, in turn, could not see what Franklin saw in Howe, "nor why everyone thought him such a genius."[69] She resented Louis's unchallenged standing as steward of her husband's—therefore her own—destiny. Further, since she just then felt as certain of her judgment as she ever had, she hoped that the campaign's arduous schedule and expanding inner circle would break Howe's singular hold on her family's future.

In the tight spaces of the *Westboro*, it was clear who among the "Cuff Links Gang" made Franklin laugh, whom he could tease in the nightly card game, and which of the more hardboiled campaigners could roll with the nicknames that Franklin dealt out. "Ludwig" strained to keep up. Short-tempered from chronic insomnia, forever testy and controlling, Louis immediately challenged one of the typists, twice his size, to an onboard fistfight.

Just as quickly, he revealed himself opposed to Franklin's "playboy" approach to whistle-stop campaigning.[70] Each night, when the team's advance man, circulating up ahead in the next rail town, relayed via coded telegram crucial intelligence for the following day's message, Franklin paid scant attention. On major issues of the campaign he considered himself an exceptionally intuitive reader of the electorate, and preferred playing cards to incorporating tips on local sentiment about the economy or Prohibition into his stump speech. Howe trusted the coded reports and knew he could rely on Stephen Early, now an Associated Press reporter whom Howe had worked with in the Navy Department's press operation. When one of Early's wires told him that the League of Nations should be "paramount" in the next day's speech, Louis took a chance. While Franklin played on in the poker game, he knocked on Eleanor's stateroom door.

In her one interview at the campaign kickoff, she had expressed a simple, if now unpopular, faith that seeking a lasting peace in the League of Nations would be the carrying out of the greater moral purpose for which the U.S. had entered the war. "We fought for it, and we should adopt it," she had said, adding a kind of farewell to the passing era of Wilsonian internationalism: "If we don't adopt it, it will be useless."

Franklin had repeatedly popped into the Springwood library during the interview, asking her advice on questions of campaign correspondence. Each time, she had paused to give her clear, cool attention to the matter, discussing it, noticed the reporter, "as she saw it."[71] Eleanor would recall feeling "detached and objective," at finding herself in the spotlight, "as though I were looking at someone else's life. I cannot quite describe it, but it [was] as though you lived two lives, one of your own and the other which belonged to the circumstances that surrounded you."[72]

Knock by knock, Louis's stateroom consulting drew Eleanor into the strategic demands of news management in the new age of mass communications. Each night she would join Louis and Marvin McIntyre, former newspaperman and publicity consultant for the Navy Department, as they fed a rough draft of the next day's speeches to the hardworking Associated Press reporters: Kirke Simpson, a veteran of Uncle Ted's 1912 Bull Moose campaign, who two months earlier had filed a 5 a.m. scoop from the Republican Convention that had put the phrase "smoke-filled room" into the language of American politics;[73] and the AP's young star, Stanley Prenosil, whom Eleanor decided she could trust, as each night she contributed to the process by which Prenosil filed stories for the morning editions that accurately quoted Franklin's speech draft as off-the-cuff remarks.[74] Her fear of newspaper people was softened by these wry, tough team players who led dogs' lives to devote themselves to a highly competitive business. Her recognition that newspaper correspondents were no different from other human beings—"good and bad," grasped Eleanor[75]—brought her around to Howe and to his conviction that "no group of people has a higher standard of ethics."[76] It was up to her, she realized, to distinguish between corruptible hacks and newsmen with a lifelong allegiance to reporting the facts.

CHUGGING SOME 3,350 MILES WEST and east, fifteen states in seventeen days, returning by way of Illinois, Indiana, Michigan, and Ohio, Louis dropped his jealous reserve and Eleanor her righteous disdain.[77] Saratoga summer theater had been Louis's youthful passion; he remained a stage manager at heart, thrilled to be the dramatic engineer behind the scenes. With Louis's blocking and direction, Eleanor had a new part to play out front, following Franklin onto the *Westboro*'s rear platform to listen as if hearing for the first time remarks he had delivered at twelve stops already. When Franklin made an extended address—in a square near the railroad station, or in towns big enough for a proper auditorium—Eleanor mounted speakers' platforms as bare as gallows, uncomfortably aware that the eyes glued on the candidate were now tracing every line of her face and figure.

Timing Franklin's remarks, she served as stage hook. "It's becoming almost impossible to stop F. now when he begins to speak," reported Eleanor to Mama after another day of clocking the bantering, head-tossing asides and eyelid-shuddering ad-libs. "10 minutes is always 20, 30 is always 45 & the evening speeches are now about 2 hours! The men all get out and wave at him in front & when nothing succeeds, I yank his coattails!"[78]

When Franklin finally got down from the platform, women crowded around him. Personal magnetism, later called charisma, had played a significant role in Theodore Roosevelt's popularity, but not until the 1920 Republican nominee Warren G. Harding discovered that women found him alluring had electoral sex appeal been on anyone's mind. Louis Howe intuitively grasped that Franklin would remain catnip to female voters only by having a publicly working marriage. He made sure that when Eleanor moved off the platform she looked on adoringly as Franklin left the hall circled by women, while the newspapermen from the *Westboro* circled behind *her* to tease and mock.

"Of course, Franklin's looks bring all sorts of admiring comments," she noted coolly.[79]

It was the last presidential campaign to be conducted without full-fledged radio broadcasting,[80] so the advance relay of speeches could still keep the candidate ahead of the news cycle. In her compartment, reading wire news and local editorials with a fine comb, Eleanor thrilled to find printed in evening editions a word or phrase that she herself had supplied when, at all hours the night before, Louis Howe had knocked on her door to consult on the latest draft.

Where Josephus Daniels sent Franklin encouragement ("You are hitting the bullseye in every speech"[81]), Eleanor now knew that her husband's arguments had been weak on logic at Louisville and strong at Wheeling, and that after stirring the hearts of hatless men at four-corner crossings, he might give into glib tendencies before the next city crowd, overpromising with vague generalities. Earlier in the summer, Roosevelt had assured Californians, "The tariff as an issue in the campaign is a joke," forgetting that it was no joke to the 240,000-odd woolen mill operatives, their stockholders, and the millions of wool growers denied protection under democratic tariff law.[82]

Through 1921, the *St. Louis Times* routinely greeted Franklin's claims as "talk only, and Franklin D. Roosevelt talk at that—which is the cheapest in the market."[83] Whether Franklin was speaking to small groups or large, Eleanor could now spot the moment mid-sentence when he calculated whether he could get away with finishing with a whopper or whether a half-truth had to be customized.[84]

Cannily positioning himself as Uncle Ted's true political heir, he baited the Republicans into sending Theodore Roosevelt, Jr., to Sheridan, Wyoming. Greeted by the largest crowd ever assembled at a political gathering in northern Wyoming, including two hundred automobiles and a delegation of Rough Riders, a fired-up Cousin Ted denounced Franklin as a "maverick" who did "not have the brand of our family."

"It was meant meanly," admitted Cousin Alice. "All Franklin had to do was say, 'I wear no man's brand, not even the brand of my cousin Theodore Roosevelt, to whom I was devoted, for whom I once voted.' Instead of that, he took it seriously and was frightfully cross about it. It hurt, you see."[85]

Being called an unbossed individualist wasn't what hurt. Where TR Jr. hit Franklin and made it stick was on an accusation that Out West had become a far bigger campaign issue than the League of Nations; namely, the GOP demand for immediate discharge of some forty thousand useless clerks still in war bureaus on the government payroll. When Cousin Ted championed reallocating these wasteful salaries to assist war veterans, he got to Franklin because the argument—indirectly and very personally—exposed FDR's war record. TR, a twice-wounded and decorated combat hero, was calling out Franklin for choosing to spend the war behind his desk as a "useless clerk."[86]

Franklin answered the next day in Butte, Montana, the biggest city between Chicago and San Francisco, where brass bands played on downtown street corners and large, expectant crowds had gathered to hear a "forcible speaker with a message of interest." But Franklin proceeded to disgust Butte's rough-and-tumble individualists, first with nasty slaps at Harding, then by lavishing the greater part of his speech on the glorification of himself while condescending to his audience of bowler-hatted Rotarians and copper-boomtown entrepreneurs, whom he took to be "laboring men and women." Repeatedly congratulating himself for "permitting" officers and men to come to him personally with their grievances, he waited for applause not forthcoming for his tolerance with subordinates.

Butte's interest was flagging. Franklin tried to tune them up on the League of Nations rumor that Britain would have six votes to the U.S.'s one: "Now you all think we have but one vote in the League of Nations," he spieled. "That is a lie. I have two in my pocket." And with a magician's wink and a nod he added, "President Wilson slipped one over on Lloyd George . . ."

The crowd broke out into prolonged jeers, which visibly flustered Roosevelt, according to one reporter. For a moment, the Easterner seemed uncertain how to proceed; then he plowed ahead in full bluff: "You know I had something to do with the running of a couple of little republics. The facts are that I wrote Haiti's Constitution myself, and, if I do say it, I think it a pretty good constitution."

The U.S. had stolen the independence of Haitians, flung an army of occupation and enslavement upon them, established harsh censorship and a rampant spoils system, and wantonly exploited the small nation. The new constitution drawn up in the U.S.—the one for which Franklin claimed authorship—had been rammed down Haitian throats with bayonets. The new president was powerless, the occupying forces often overrode civil courts, and no Haitian outcry was allowed to reach the U.S.[87]

Even if Franklin's claim was half-true, why boast about participating in one of the most discreditable chapters in America's history as an imperial nation? Later, he tried explaining to reporters that by "two votes in his pocket" he had meant the votes of Haiti and Nicaragua, which he claimed the U.S. could control. Furthermore, he insisted, it was because of these pocketed votes that the entry of the U.S. into the League would not allow the European allied nations to ship American soldiers abroad to fight their battles.

The crowd greeted the end of his speech with derisive glee.[88] "Afterward," wrote Josephus Daniels's son Jonathan Daniels, "he always denied he had said that."[89]

WHEN THEY REACHED BUFFALO ON the return trip, Franklin dashed off to speak in Jamestown, giving Eleanor a chance for a Niagara Falls visit—her first. Louis took her.[90]

That morning, three workmen had been killed in an explosion at a chlorine-gas factory.[91] The war's demands for chemical industries had turned the continent into a developing source of hydroelectricity—a testing ground for America's future industrial superpowers. Just that month, the Army Corps of Engineers revealed its godlike plan to harness the falls for hydroelectric power and still preserve its magnificence.[92]

Eleanor, nearly six feet, and Louis, barely five inches over five feet,[93] appeared classically lopsided, but as Elliott would much later observe, "Louis and Mother made an extraordinarily well-matched couple."[94] Both regretted having never attended college. Both had borne the grief of losing a newborn son. Both had lived on in marriages that required doing without.

At Niagara, they took in everything together. Eleanor chided herself for having failed to register before now Louis's "rather extraordinary eyes."[95] Away from the campaign, the political operator subsided into a calm awareness that deeply impressed Eleanor; and the delight they shared in their afternoon at the Falls struck a tender chord. "It is more than likely," speculated Elliott in later years, "that he was the first suitor treating her as the dissatisfied, incomplete woman he knew her to be."[96]

In Albany, Louis had witnessed the unremitting intensity of Eleanor's need to be useful to a husband whose disregard of her abilities tormented her. Howe felt much the same insecurity about his own status as chief adviser to his "Beloved and Revered Future President."[97]

Now, as they were pulled uncomplainingly across a continent, Louis saw how toughness sustained Eleanor. No campaign hardship was too much, no whistle-stop pandering too grating, even when Franklin seemed to take his greatest pleasure in the magician's art of fooling his audience without cheating it. If enduring her husband's ascension to the highest levels of men's-world politics could satisfy her great need to be needed in order to feel secure in partnership, she would sleep with grit on her pillow every night and smile through soft-sell oratory to the end of the line.

Caring was not yet at the center of Franklin's political identity. He wanted proof of his artistry far more than he wanted to advance the public welfare. His one touchstone was his country; he did not yet understand "the people" as people; fine-tuning their response to his candidacy was for Franklin the triumph of craft he took greatest pleasure in.

For Eleanor, caring was the defining question of her existence.

Louis's understanding of this was enough for now, as Eleanor much later acknowledged: "He probably cared for me as a person, as much as he ever cared for anyone and more than anyone else has."[98]

On October 30, 1920, when the *Westboro* rattled in over the New York Central switches and Eleanor stepped out at Grand Central Terminal, she came home with her most important ally for crossing the unseen wilderness ahead.

COME ELECTION DAY, A COLD rain intensified the November chill. Without great hopes for a Democratic victory, Eleanor cast her first-ever ballot, for her husband. It had been a month since the embittered President Wilson had stated publicly that the election had become a national referendum on the League. Anti-Wilson animosity was "evident everywhere and deeply rooted," the Cox campaign reported from the field. "He hasn't a friend."[99]

The result of the vote was a Republican landslide. Harding-Coolidge carried the electoral college by 404 to 127, pocketing thirty-seven states, and running up 61 percent of the popular vote.[100] What was more, Republicans took control of the House, 303 to 131 seats, and the Senate, 70 to 26.

Franklin had believed himself loved and adored by heartland voters.[101] He was surprised to be buried in an avalanche. But the resounding overthrow of Wilsonism had a liberating effect, since it pardoned him, as Jonathan Daniels put it, from "a sort of duty to be great."[102]

Eleanor was also ready to let go—a little. For now she took comfort from "the feeling that at last we were going to have lives of our own and not always be subordinated to some higher duty."[103]

Mama closed her datebook on the 1920 election as if favorable weather conditions had prevailed: "Franklin rather relieved not to be elected Vice President."[104]

TWELVE

Back in the metropolis, down to the terrifying summer of 1921, she kept clearing a path. But to go where? As what?

"If I had to go out and earn my own living, I doubt if I'd even make a very good cleaning woman," judged Eleanor. "I have no talents, no experience, no training for anything."[1]

She tried cooking lessons, but what good was cooking to a lady with a cook? She sent James back to Groton, and Anna and Elliott to Granny at Hyde Park with a tutor, while she camped out at Sixty-Fifth Street, took a class in shorthand and typewriting, put the younger boys in East Side private schools, and brought them all together for weekends at Springwood with their busy father.

Cox's burial at the polls had been his running mate's ascension as a presumptive 1924 presidential candidate—certainly a likely New York governor with an unlimited future. Theodore Roosevelt, Jr., Franklin's tribe rival for the chief executive's mantle, had been seduced away to Harding's loose and easy Washington as assistant secretary of the navy, leaving the former assistant secretary to dominate the largest state in the union from the new first city of the Western Hemisphere.[2]

Eleanor was expected to rejoin weekly ladies' luncheons, reestablish her subscriptions, choose her charity boards.[3] The Bryson Day Nursery, for example, one of Mama's pet institutions, where for ten cents a day working women left their tots. Cousin Susie Parish had served as treasurer. "The Bryson" would be "the perfect opening," declared Mama, citing Eleanor's goodly ways and native decency toward such women—to say nothing of all the nice things she could do for Mrs. Auchincloss and Mrs. Bacon to help organize this year's rummage sale.[4]

"I don't know how she escaped it," remarked one friend.[5]

"Her first choice," another friend later divulged, "was still to enter into her husband's work."[6]

But except when volunteering for his more progressive social causes, nurturing Franklin's career always made her out to be staid and prudish. How was she to further her interests in things that mattered to both of them? In the arrogant, unregulated, and fearful America of the booming decade ahead, could she, by herself, commit to the out-of-fashion disciplines of international cooperation and world peace when Franklin was now, by his own boast, "one of the younger capitalists"?[7]

By day he headed the downtown office of Fidelity & Deposit, a Maryland-based surety and bonding company, the third largest in the country, with $500 million in annual risks. By night he flexed his muscles on the speaking circuit, spreading his essential animal joy and signature expression ("I love it!") across five state committees, countless charity boards, civic enrichment groups, political clubs, the Harvard Board of Overseers, and capital drives for the Boy Scouts of America, the Woodrow Wilson Memorial Foundation, Lighthouse for the Blind, and the Cathedral of St. John the Divine.

Eleanor wondered aloud if he ever again intended to spend an evening at home.[8] But it was her own intentions that remained unclear. She had no plan for her life, and no adult would have said a word had she stayed in bed every morning with a breakfast tray and done little more than give "Cook" the day's order. She might then reply to a few letters before attending her board meeting and making final arrangements for a lively dinner party at which she would serve pre-Prohibition champagne for Franklin's boss, a Delano-like coal industrialist turned *Baltimore Sun* owner, aviation explorer, and yachtsman; the flamboyant Van Lear Black thought Franklin Roosevelt the most attractive man he had ever met.

THE NEW YORK LEAGUE OF Women Voters came to her rescue. Chairwoman Narcissa Cox Vanderlip invited Eleanor to join the board and take charge of their committee on legislation. The position required following the twisty passage of congressional bills and obscure Albany measures in order to post League members on the pros and cons of legislation significant to women. She was restless to accept but worried that the League's lawyer, Elizabeth Fisher Read, a legal scholar and practicing attorney who served as consultant to Eleanor's committee, would resent her inexperience.[9] The alternative was the Bryson rummage sale.

Eleanor gave a firm no to the day care,[10] and when Mama responded by getting her invited to join a ladies' circle that had been "sewing for the poor" since the first Grant administration, Eleanor cunningly became a member.[11] She would never get Mama's approval for any step toward her own independence, but she knew when to cut her losses, and by attending the Monday Sewing Circle's monthly meeting, she released herself and her conscience from obligation to the woman she had spent fifteen years trying to please.

Her new mentor, a systematic legal thinker, had been trained at Smith College, Columbia University, and the law school of the University of Pennsylvania. Elizabeth "Lizzie" Read provided a weekly classroom for what Eleanor ever after described as "the intensive education of Eleanor Roosevelt." Far from condescending, Read treated Eleanor as a serious student of government, teaching her how to investigate baked-in problems that appeared to be beyond solution. Long past Eleanor's first crack at congressional reporting, Read's rigorous demands for weighing evidence and presenting precise documentation set standards for thoroughness and accuracy that remained professional benchmarks for life.[12]

Eleanor was thrilled when Lizzie invited her to East Eleventh Street for dinner with her life partner, the Barnard College journalism professor Esther Everett Lape. Their Village apartment, set in the leafy heart of American Bohemia, was a snug, scholarly place which the two intellectual powerhouses kept filled with cut flowers and "a kind of quiet gaiety that is more satisfactory," decided Eleanor, "than the very hilarious kind I sometimes have about me."[13]

Lizzie was short, practical, the calmer of the two. Esther was black-haired, with warm brown eyes, chic in her patterned-silk dresses and modish strings of pearls. She had a caring, critical nature that gave her "a kind of nervous power."[14] Together, they worked fiercely at co-editing the League's legislative review, *City-State-Nation*, and were forever bringing urgent freelance projects to fruition. For Eleanor they prepared stylish dinners, sipped champagne, and savored her superb accent when they read French poetry aloud with the salad and cheese.

Lizzie and Esther spotted and nurtured Eleanor's gift for action: her directness in taking the necessary steps to get done the things that others could only dither about.[15] Unlike the women who had raised her—"the kind," according to Edith Wharton, "who expect to be talked to collectively and to have their questions left unanswered"[16]— Eleanor was interested in activating information and seeking real answers. She reached for authority, imaginative engagement, commitment, responsibility: positions that had been conceded to women in the old social order, but only if they stayed home.

Validation from Lape and Read as "a woman who does things" helped Eleanor to see herself fitting into the rising tide of reformist energies.[17] Still just an Uptown visitor—a kind of Sunday painter—she could come and go without fuss or arrangements, her confidences secure. Esther adopted herself as the closer mentor for Eleanor. They were nearer in age, and Eleanor could take—indeed, was hungry for—Esther's bold, sharp judgments, the most constant being Eleanor's caretaking of others at a cost to her own needs. "She always believed that whatever was left on her doorstep was her responsibility," tut-tutted Esther. "Whatever came her way was hers to handle."[18]

Lizzie argued that it was important to learn to discriminate between those who needed help and could make use of it and those whose need could never be filled. As for whether it was nobler to satisfy personal obligations or to work in the interest of bettering humanity, Lizzie declared for personal commitment: "You could work fifty years for a cause and find your life too dreary and barren to be endured."[19]

Effectiveness—a pragmatic life of being effective—was the goal.

POWERFUL VOICES IN THE GREATER world of activist women briefly cut through the muddle of Eleanor's underemployment. As a delegate to the League of Women Voters' national convention in April, she scouted the talents of each speaker in Cleveland's Masonic Hall, taking care to report her observations to Franklin in sharp, snappy thumbnails: Carrie Chapman Catt, the League's white-haired leader, was "clear, cold reason"; Dorothy Kirchwey Brown, chair of the Child Welfare Committee: "Amusing, apt, graceful." Minnie Fisher

Cunningham, Texas suffragist, the League's first executive secretary, and all-round force of nature: "Emotional and idealistic, but she made nearly everyone cry!"[20]

Cunningham's core message, that in a democracy no citizen had the right to be a loafer, gave Eleanor permission to turn loose the drive she always seemed to have more of than anyone else.[21]

The selflessness and pure spirit of League leaders appealed deeply, as did the potent, world-remaking force of millions of new voters using their hard-won franchise to clean up corruption in politics, turn government away from war, and protect individual lives from the crushing excesses of industrial capitalism. When action needed taking on that scale, she had no use for stridency or self-pity—party and platform were the tools for transforming the system. Equality for women interested her, but winning elections interested her more. The message she really wanted to give women voters now that they had the ballot in their hands: *Vote Democratic*.

And so, with the old barriers that had confined women's political activities crashing down around her, she closed that night's letter to Franklin: "Much much love, dear, and I prefer doing my politics with you."[22]

The next day, she met Edna Fischel Gellhorn, former Junior Leaguer, tireless campaigner for women's suffrage, and the League's first vice president. Gellhorn would become a frequent and generous collaborator with Eleanor in a sisterhood of causes;[23] her daughter, Martha, the world-renowned war correspondent of the Second World War, and youngest son, Albert, an eminent oncologist, would both play critical roles in Eleanor's far future. At the moment, Edna Gellhorn ignited the convention by parading the hall, brandishing banners at the head of the St. Louis delegation, proclaiming the power of women in nearly every one of Missouri's 114 counties—a vital message, as the national membership rolls were lagging behind the League's more populist predecessor, the Women's Suffrage Association.

On the last day in the hall, Eleanor leapt to her feet to answer Carrie Chapman Catt's summons to each delegate to "come forward to stay the hand of men." President Harding had just proclaimed the American government's final rejection of the League of Nations, and

Catt, throwing her set speech away, spoke for fifteen minutes in a cold fury. She begged the spellbound audience of a thousand to act together, to act as women, to confront men directly, and to be silent no more.[24] "We have waited too long," she warned, "and we will get another war by waiting."[25]

Less than a month later, when Vassar professor Winifred Smith objected to the government's arrest and deportation of the Soviet representative in Washington,[26] Eleanor had her first chance to answer Minnie Cunningham's challenge.[27] Professor Smith's criticism of Washington's extreme Red Scare tactics had provoked Vice President Coolidge to charge that women's colleges were "filled with radicals," and that Professor Smith was "dangerous." On May 23, Eleanor brought the matter to the biggest women's political group in Dutchess County, the Women's City and County Club in Poughkeepsie, not far from the Vassar campus. At the club's regular meeting, Eleanor proposed a resolution condemning Coolidge's statement.[28] The members responded with a yes vote, censuring the vice president.

The press then pounced on Eleanor, gawking at the "strange coincidence" that she had incited her fellow political women to chastise her husband's recent rival.[29] "Foolish of me," she diarized, "ever to do anything of the kind."[30] Henceforth she would be armed against those who would use her to undermine Franklin's prospects.

But then, just as she was taking these first steps toward self-control, fate showed its claws at Campobello.

Before Eleanor retreated with the children and assorted governesses for the summer, Esther Lape and Elizabeth Read came for the weekend. Esther had spotted Eleanor's frustrated need to remain vital to her husband. As the women discussed League matters, reform politics, and world peace, Esther drew in Franklin, consulting him as the master strategist. On Sunday, he returned Eleanor's friends to the Hyde Park station, carrying their bags to the platform. "He was wearing one of those baggy brown suits," recalled Esther. "He looked so strong and healthy."[31]

Franklin was zooming everywhere that summer. Perhaps the only thing he put to rest was the myth that he was always Dr. Peabody's good boy. In Southampton, at Sheffield Cowles's wedding to the popular Margaret "Bobbie" Krech, he had shocked the Oyster Bay contingent, who remembered him at the reception, according to Edith Roosevelt's biographer, making an "uproarious" spectacle of himself as "a lusty womanizer and noisy celebrant."[32] Eleanor spun it that her husband had been "going on his nerves."[33]

On July 21, the Republican-run Senate Naval Affairs Subcommittee declared Roosevelt responsible for administering one of U.S. naval history's most disgraceful episodes: the use of raw recruits to entrap homosexual civilians. Prickly with indignation, Franklin demanded and was given until sundown to prepare a public rebuttal to the committee's 625-page majority report. But even as he and Stephen Early and his new assistant, Missy LeHand, raced through the summer swelter to examine six thousand pages of newly released testimony, the damning details were leaked, revealing to the world that Franklin Roosevelt had been censured for gross abuse of his high office.

"Lay Navy Scandal to F.D. Roosevelt," headlined the *New York Times*, although owner Adolph Ochs had recently attended Van Lear Black's stag testimonial at Delmonico's welcoming Roosevelt to Wall Street. The patriarchal paper limited the damage to a page-four story discreetly subheaded, "Details Are Unprintable," even as it saw fit to print on Page One the damning evidence of how eight ballplayers on the Chicago "Black Sox" conspired with a gambling syndicate to deliberately lose the 1919 World Series to Cincinnati for $100,000.[34]

Eleanor wrote from Campobello: "It must be dreadfully disagreeable for you, and I know it worries you though you wouldn't own it. But it has always seemed to me that the chance of just such attacks as this was a risk one had to take with our form of government and if one felt clear oneself, the rest did not really matter."[35]

But how could Franklin feel clear? The subcommittee had made public for the first time the findings of a naval court-martial. Not only were Roosevelt's actions unfortunate and ill-advised, agreed the committee's two Republicans and one Democrat, but "most reprehensible."[36] The details of their investigation clearly showed that after three days of conferring with his "Section A" officers Franklin, a subcabinet official and "man of unusual intelligence and attainments," knew per-

fectly well—indeed, had tried to cover up—that his own secret orders
for the sting operation had put young enlisted men in "a most deplorable, disgraceful, and unnatural" position.[37]

"One should not be ruffled by such things," Eleanor held; and
when the *New York Daily News* later that year asked for Franklin's
motto in less than thirty-five words, he replied: "Never remember an
injury or forget a favor."[38]

Franklin had been deeply injured. Partisanship could be blamed,
but he knew the truth. Committee member Henry W. Keyes, Republican of Vermont, had scapegoated him, and Franklin couldn't live with
it. He wanted vengeance. He set his hardening rage upon one scheme
after another, finally sitting down with Missy LeHand to dictate his
personal grievance to the senator. Finding himself sounding stuffy and
impotent, he never mailed the letter, but remained unappeasably furious; and for the next fifteen years, he held Keyes responsible for inten-
sifying his susceptibility to viral disease.[39]

Franklin later distanced himself from the devastating effect of
public disgrace by claiming that his depleted constitution could be
blamed on a career in which he never felt able to say no. Taking in-
ventory of how his own risk-seeking nature might have teetered and
toppled with the follies of the decade,[40] FDR reckoned that if disease
had not thrown him off the rails in 1921, "I would have been dead in
five years."

ONE COMMITMENT IN PARTICULAR HAD hampered his leaving for
Campobello. As president of the Boy Scout Foundation of Greater
New York, Franklin enthusiastically served as toastmaster for the
Lake Kanowahke Scout Camp jamboree at Bear Mountain. This
meant entertaining more than fifty Foundation supporters as they
steamed upriver on his friend Barron Collier's party boat, awash in
illegal gin. Duty done around the campfire, he hurried back to clear
his desk in the city, as Missy LeHand helped as best she could to get
him on his way to Van Lear Black's motor yacht, a decommissioned
141-foot naval patrol boat.

"I thought he looked quite tired when he left," reported Missy to
Eleanor, "so perhaps he will have a good rest."[41]

The voyage was supposed to be a pleasure cruise. In nasty weather Franklin had to take over from Black's captain to pilot *Sabalo* to safe anchorage beyond the daunting Bay of Fundy tides. Off Campobello, he took a party to fish for cod from *Sabalo*'s motor tender. Overheated, baiting hooks, promising great sport—ever eager to please—he slipped from the tender into the sea, chilling himself so severely that he felt his arms and legs turning to marble. All his life he had been energized by Welchpool Harbor's bracing temperatures. Never had the water seemed—his word, that day—"paralyzing."[42]

Landing in a blue haze on Campobello, Franklin took the children sailing on the adjacent Cobscook Bay, putting ashore to stamp out a forest fire, then swimming afterward in a kettle-hole pond, dipping into the bay, and trotting a mile home—a last harried lamp-rubbing of the Strenuous Life. This time, however, the teeth-gnashing genie failed to appear, leaving Franklin alone on the cottage porch, exhausted, spark-burned, pawing a handful of days-old mail. It was his first quiet moment to think about the tarnish he had put on the Navy Department. At the same time, a deep, uneasy chill had settled under his skin—a touch of lumbago, he thought. He could weigh up the consequences later, after a change of clothes, some dinner, bed.

First, the stairs.

IN THE MORNING, TRYING TO shave, he felt a distinct weakness in his right knee. Eleanor took his temperature—102 degrees—and sent to Lubec for the doctor. Louis Howe ("who, thank heavens, is here," she exclaimed[43]) had come to Campobello to draft a 1922 run for the U.S. Senate—only days after Franklin's censure by a subcommittee of that body. Leaving the men to strategize, Eleanor and Louis's wife, Grace, had concurrent plans with the children for a camping trip.

All that was now off, for by the time Dr. Bennet arrived and diagnosed an ordinary summer cold, Franklin's right leg would not support his weight. That night, the left knee buckled, and Eleanor moved into the window seat alongside his bed.

It was light when she woke. Franklin was struggling to get up. He tried to swing out of bed—his legs wouldn't move. All through the morning, one after another, from thumb to toes and back up to fingers, the muscles refused. The day appeared to have turned on him. All along until dinnertime, the afternoon refused to be the good old afternoon. Nightfall seemed a sinister business. By the time Eleanor returned with Franklin's supper tray, he could not hold a fork.[44]

Rarely seen in a father of five,[45] his symptoms were not unlike those of polio's more familiar victims: children, typically awakening one morning in high summer, stiffness at the back of their necks. Within hours, power would drain from their limbs. If they survived the ravages of the virus's acute phase, they grew into old-looking young people with bodies twisted like roots, then into childlike teenagers with pipe-cleaner legs. Many died at onset, choking down last frozen breaths.[46]

Still called "the baby malady" a quarter century after its first outbreak had taken the lives of eighteen small children in a Vermont village, infantile paralysis remained a mysterious and random killer. Little was known about why the virus struck one victim but not another; or why some forms were mild, lasting only two or three days; or why outbreaks remained disproportionately prevalent in rural communities. FDR's likeliest source of infection had come through contaminated drinking water at the Bear Mountain scout jamboree.[47] Depletion of his immune system, dating back through two decades of severe, chronic infections, ranging from sinusitis to typhoid fever, on top of the stress of overwork and the public crisis of the Senate inquisition, had likely rendered him that much more susceptible.

But polio had not yet been diagnosed, and for forty-eight hours on their fog-bound Canadian island, exactly halfway between the North Pole and the Equator, Eleanor held her breath.

LEAVE IT TO LOUIS TO recruit from Bar Harbor the first brain surgeon in America. Eighty-four-year-old William Williams Keen, Jr., had been one of six surgeons who for several hours on a yacht under sail off Cape Cod had riskily operated in secret to remove a tumor from President Grover Cleveland's mouth.[48] Now, nearly thirty years later, the white-bearded surgeon decided that Franklin was paralyzed because of a blood clot pressing into his lower spinal cord. Boldly, Dr. Keen declared that massaging Franklin's legs was vital to dissolve the clot.

For the next eleven mornings, as all muscles from Franklin's hips down blazed at the slightest touch, Eleanor doggedly followed the Keen massage regimen. She alternated sessions with Louis so that she would have time to spoon-feed Franklin while managing his food trays. He also had to be catheterized in these first weeks, and was having difficulty controlling his bowels as well. Eleanor learned to sterilize and insert a lubricated glass catheter, to move his hindquarters on and off bedpans, and, with Louis's help, to give him a bath.[49]

Before their eyes he transformed. Gone was the hyperactive charmer and larkish campaigner in the prime of life, replaced by an invalid pinned to a mattress suffering the powerlessness of pain without end.[50]

Until at last, the storm broke.

Franklin reckoned the date as August 25, 1921—"the 12th day after I was hit." Like a man overboard, treading water in a fast night sea, glimpsing the safety of shore: "I knew I would live."[51]

That day, Dr. Robert W. Lovett, leading orthopedic surgeon at the Harvard Medical School and the nation's foremost specialist in the treatment of infantile paralysis, arrived from Boston. He performed a lumbar puncture, which allowed him to diagnose definitively what Louis Howe and his uncle Fred Delano had both suspected—acute anterior poliomyelitis.

Eleanor asked the urgent question: Were any of the six children, including Louis's son Hartley, vulnerable? Lovett was confident that if they had shown no sign of outbreak after two weeks they had escaped.

As to Franklin's recovery, three possibilities hung in the balance: complete revitalization of the wasted limbs; partial healing with residual paralysis; or total paralysis with severe permanent disability. Which it would be, they had no way yet to know. When the infectious phase was over, probably within a matter of weeks, they could begin to think about transferring to a hospital.

Lovett lifted their hopes by judging the case mild. He cautioned, however, that some of the back and leg muscles could go either way— "toward recovery or turn into completely paralyzed muscles." Tactfully, he let Eleanor know that massaging the limbs in this acute stage was the greatest harm she could have done. "Let the children alone during that period," Lovett had recently warned his colleagues in Cambridge, "otherwise the disease becomes worse or is prolonged."[52]

Franklin's mother had been in Europe on a prewar-style Grand Tour when the virus struck. She returned to the double shock of having been kept in the dark and then welcomed home as if to a "party" that her bravely smiling, freshly shaven Franklin had "got up" for her. Sustaining his gallantry, she sat cheerily by his side and saw him through several of his meals, but lasted only another twenty-four hours before he had talked her into retreating to Fairhaven to attend a family wedding.

Sara noticed his legs. She had always been proud of Franklin's lean, shapely limbs—now so lifeless they had constantly to be repositioned by hand to keep up circulation. She told herself not to worry: already Franklin was improving "from the waist up," and in the happy atmosphere Eleanor had managed to create in the stricken household, her son would make a "hasty" recovery.[53]

The truth was, no one had any idea what was going to happen, or when. On the 31st, after another day of back muscles withering rather than strengthening, Franklin despaired of regaining control of his body. So far gone into torment was he that when Dr. Bennet rowed over from Lubec, Franklin implored him to instruct Eleanor to resume the now-forbidden massages. They were torture, no question, but they were *something*. Doing nothing—that was the horror.

Day upon day, the family kept vigil, the children sensing that their father was being tested as never before. Only later would he share his secret: he had lost his nerve, and in the rapid, darkening delirium that followed, Franklin Roosevelt's faith had been shaken. "I think," wrote Eleanor, "he felt he could ask God for guidance and receive it,"[54] and so, when none came, he felt his God forsaking him.[55]

ELEANOR AND LOUIS BECAME TWO tired and distressed people. Taking alternate night watches in the sickroom, they discovered that they were equally determined and united. They would not let him be beaten.

They had no precedent in the annals of American history. No president or vice president or even cabinet member had ever been raised up to high office paralyzed. Polio had just closed that door. Immediately, Louis and Eleanor pried it back open. In her autobiography, Eleanor would cast this new dawn as an electrifying movie moment; less *Sunrise at Campobello*, more silent-screen title-card: *Louis Howe Takes Charge.*

THEY BOTH DID. THE INFECTIOUS period over, Franklin safe for travel, Louis stage-managed and Eleanor enacted what appeared to be a moderately urgent seasonal transfer from an end-of-summer sickbed in the Canadian Maritimes to Manhattan's Presbyterian Hospital. So far as reporters were given to understand, Franklin had been ill with a severe cold, and though threatened by pneumonia remained as eligible as ever to return at full strength to life and work.[56]

Lowered headfirst down the front steps in a canvas sling, Franklin was belted to a homemade stretcher, his lifeless Frankenstein limbs covered by a blanket. As the children mumbled, "So long, Pa,"[57] he stuck out his chin and flash-grinned his way down across Campobello's rough ground and stony beach. Eleanor followed to the family pier, where the wind rose sharply, then boarded the tossing vessel behind her husband. "Don't worry, chicks," their father called out, "I'll be all right!"

John, the youngest—five-and-a-half—later stated the fact plain: "From then on, I had no parents."[58]

They crossed the two miles of spray-drenched seaway in an open dory, landing at the steep, slime-slippery sardine dock in Eastport. There, by ruse of a "mix-up," Louis decoyed a gang of reporters to another landing, while he and Eleanor had just time enough to load the deadweight of Franklin onto a luggage dray, cart him over cobblestoned streets, hustle him by further improvised stretcher to a private railcar, and lift him in through an open window.

Inside, now in view of reporters on the siding, Roosevelt appeared chipper after his bout of summer-holiday grippe. He smiled and smoked his pipe. Chatted with his wife, joshed Dr. Bennet. One of the family's Scotch terriers sat obediently at his side.

In fact, pillows propped him up. Eleanor swabbed the sweat from under his traveling fedora. Duffy clawed her to get the withheld treat.

. . . All perfectly concealing the unspeakable truth: Franklin Roosevelt was a rag doll. Louis Howe had staged the illusion so that anyone peering in would *want* to see the youngest vice-presidential nominee in more than half a century try to cheat "the old man's friend," as pneumonia was called. That this handsome statesman was unable to lift even his head made the effect uncanny.

Thanks to his newspapering expertise, Louis's tableau translated smoothly into print: FRANKLIN D. ROOSEVELT ON ROAD TO RECOVERY, read one headline, the accompanying front-page story picturing the former assistant secretary puffing commandingly on "his famous briar pipe."[59] Less than two months had elapsed since the *New York Times* had declared "unprintable" the details of Roosevelt's political disgrace at Newport. All was now forgotten in the page-one drama of so dynamic a national leader and family man attacked "below the knees"— almost as if, in this one special case, the virus had discreetly served him penance below the waist.

In years ahead, a quill cigarette holder, uptilted, clamped into the famous Roosevelt smile, would replace the briar pipe as FDR's trademark. For now, and over the nearly six-hundred-mile ordeal ahead, this casualty of a Boy Scout jamboree's infected water supply needed the equivalent of a Civil War bullet to bite on.

Met at Grand Central by his mother and a Hyde Park friend, Tom Lynch, he once again had to be belted in and stretchered through the window for transfer uptown in an ambulance. George Draper, the Harvard acquaintance and holistic orthopedist who in 1918 had brought Franklin ashore from the influenza-ridden troopship—the day Eleanor found the Lucy Mercer letters—had committed to taking charge of day-to-day treatment at the healing clinic he directed at Presbyterian Hospital.

Informing reporters about Roosevelt's prospects, Draper conceded that he could not tell how long his patient would be kept in hospital, but certified that his condition was already "much improved." Roosevelt was "regaining control of his legs." The reporters could "definitely" tell their readers that he would not be crippled. "No one need have any fear of permanent injury from this attack."[60]

A "slight attack," reported the *World* in all editions the next day.

And so began the subterfuge that would turn recovery into a guessing game down to the opening gavels in each of the 1924 and 1928 Democratic National Conventions.[61]

For Eleanor the question was not only whether Franklin would walk again. Would he realize that he needed her? Could she find a way in these next months and years to be useful to his recovery? And if she could not, would she still have first place in her husband's life in 1924—in 1928? Or would she—this time—be publicly replaced?

IV

STATE-WOMAN

I became a much more ardent citizen and feminist than anyone
about me in the intermediate years would have dreamed possible.

E.R.[1]

THIRTEEN

Beyond every hospital window loomed the unreal city.
To Mama, George Draper's notion of returning Franklin to convalescence on East Sixty-Fifth Street seemed pure recklessness. Crowding into a household of schoolchildren, trained nurses, and random visitors would open her son's weakened body to a long winter of germs. Yet Dr. Draper had expressly advised that the more of his normal activities Franklin could resume, the fewer reasons he would have for the extreme alienation sufferers felt when trying to adapt their new bodies to their old lives. Retreat to Hyde Park would be a "terrible waste."[1]

Sara, sixty-seven years old, had been overriding physicians all her life. On the one hand, she expected no less than the latest findings from Dr. Lovett's Harvard Infantile Paralysis Commission; on the other, she saw no reason not to trust her own common sense, since even the geniuses in Cambridge admitted that poliomyelitis "defies the ordinary laws of health and hygiene."[2]

Sara wanted her son home at the river. If Lovett and Draper could accomplish wonders, and those wonders kept her son in the city for a month or two, then Sara would countermove by keeping Hyde Park open for "our dear invalid,"[3] as she had done for his semi-invalided father thirty years before. She imagined that in the Springwood library with his books and stamps and ship models arrayed around him Franklin could write a history of his naval hero John Paul Jones.

As a boy, playing his mother to get what he wanted, talking at a remove from the truth, Franklin had learned to keep inconvenient facts concealed. Recovery from paralysis meant being at one or two removes from loved ones. The new Franklin had no intention of being shut away upriver—sailor-suited into his mother's clutches.[4] "I am not going to be conquered," he emphasized, "by a *childish* disease."[5]

The public would eventually be given to understand that Franklin had "formerly suffered from the disease."[6] But, as with asthma, Uncle Ted's "childish" disease, which remained ever ready to strike, polio's long-term effects would shape every moment of Franklin's future. No longer could he be Uncle Ted's step-by-step imitator in the ascent to power. Nor his mother's beloved invalid. He had the chance now to let go of who he thought he should be.

EVENINGS ON EAST SIXTY-FIFTH STREET, Eleanor and Louis kept house on the No. 49 side, drawing together like "conspirators," said several friends.[7] They were too busy with Franklin's lists of things to do—Louis pinch-hitting at Fidelity & Deposit, Eleanor proxying her husband's civic boards and social causes—to accommodate Sara's "magnificent martyrdom," as the children called the serial drama that frosted the side-by-side households whenever their dowager grandmother started sniffing out that, once again, her son was spurning her.

Together with Louis, Eleanor quietly prepared for Franklin's plan to come home on crutches and spend the winter working with trained physiotherapists. By spring, he hoped, his hips and legs would be strong enough to resume his Wall Street routine. While still on Campobello, he had accepted appointment as executive officer of the New York State Democratic Committee and pledged himself to political and civic duties regardless of disability. This had been their purpose in returning Franklin to New York, when they could have chosen Boston and Dr. Lovett's blue-ribbon clinic: Franklin's paycheck, his political life, his future—all awaited his command in Manhattan.[8]

The partners ghostwrote Franklin's political correspondence in advance of November's state and municipal elections. When Tammany Democrats made a clean sweep of city and county offices, picking up twenty-three seats in the state assembly,[9] each of these new allies received a letter of congratulations from Franklin D. Roosevelt. The bold, slanting signature—forged by Howe—gave no hint that the former vice-presidential candidate was now flattened to a hospital bed twenty-three of every twenty-four hours.

As for his best chances for sustaining long-term improvement,

Eleanor supposed that because his doctors were the world's experts, one must follow their slow, carefully scheduled system of "after treatment."[10] She kept her doubts to herself, knowing from her childhood that, for ill or for good, only the most terrible disabilities truly define their sufferer.

But even if Franklin did regain partial use of his legs, she presumed he would never again walk unaided. She worried that bias would shadow him, casting suspicion and fear over whatever good he could accomplish. Survivors of infantile paralysis were considered useless beings, faulted for the anguish of their families. The modernizing science and technology of the postwar era ensured that polio's severest cases—"cripples" a mild usage—would be immobilized in gargantuan iron lungs hidden away in grim hospital wards. Public health authorities, quick to declare "polios" responsible for annual economic loss to the nation of more than a billion dollars ($15.3 billion today), despaired of "estimating the silent burden which every family must bear that has one of these victims of infantile paralysis."[11]

Certainly, no such monster was going to campaign from coast to coast to become president, nor stand tall on the East Capitol steps with one hand on the family Bible to be sworn in as the chief executive of all the people. If a thousand-year miracle did bring Eleanor's husband to the White House, what would happen when the people discovered that no matter how well braced or how well attended, he could nonetheless lose his balance while reaching for a telephone and end up powerless on the Oval Office carpet?

"Do you really believe," she asked Louis in private, "that Franklin still has a political future?"[12]

Louis had bet his own family's prospects on it, turning down a boom-time oil-company job and a salary that would have meant security for Grace and the children so that he could carry on his mission of making Franklin Roosevelt president. When, in January, a Texas newspaper branded his boss "a cripple for the rest of his life,"[13] Louis made no concession to the almost universal assumption that FDR's political career was finished. He packed his wife and son off to a Poughkeepsie boardinghouse while their daughter attended Vassar College—he promised to visit weekends—and then went right back to circulating Franklin's ideas for revising the state party's nominating procedures in letter after letter.

Eleanor considered a future even in state politics "almost hopeless."[14] Yet few grasped as she did that Franklin always did exactly as he wanted. No matter what he was told, especially by experts with whom he appeared to agree, he did things his way. Discharged from the Presbyterian, he had himself transferred out under cloak of night. By installing an array of leather straps and rings over his bed, he strengthened the biceps and torso enough for him to arm-wrestle visitors. When his sons stood stiffly at his door, he read their shyness, stretched out his arms, and held them in his powerful embrace, grinning and covering their tears with chatter about how "grand" they looked. Then, against doctors' sickbed orders, he invited them to "hop in!"[15]

Eleanor and Louis encouraged visits from old friends like Arthur Willert and William Phillips, with figures of the Wilson age like Josephus Daniels, Colonel House, and Field Marshal Joffre, to each of whom Franklin relished demonstrating his latest recovery skill. He was weeks from sitting up to be pushed in a wheelchair—further still from the acrobatic finesse of crutchwork—but these visits, appearing in the next morning's papers, gave the impression of a life of power ongoing.[16]

Sara much later conceded that she understood perfectly well that Franklin had "no intention of conforming to my quiet ideas for his future existence."[17] But it was Eleanor—and Louis—who saw that the ordinary business of a daily life could never be her son's medium. When not in office, when not scheming or dominating or commanding, Franklin tended to reveal himself as the tedious hobbyist he had been since boyhood. Eleanor had come around on Franklin's books and stamps, and found herself thanking heaven for the many convalescent's hours hidden in the hull and rigging of every model sloop. But she also understood, more now than ever, that if he was to be Franklin Roosevelt, he had no alternative to high office. Without his greatness, he would be an incomplete man. He *had* to turn helplessness to power, just as Eleanor had to fight for their common breath, and Louis had to go on plotting a course for the White House, even though they all knew that a man who wanted to be president could not also be a "cripple."

THREE WEEKS AFTER COMING HOME, Franklin's fever returned. His vision blurred. Brushing aside serious concern, he took the setback as temporary, a fixable nuisance. When the pain behind his eyes did not go away, but worsened, and he could not read, they lived for a few frightening days with the possibility that he might lose his eyesight also. When his right knee then locked in a bent position, Mrs. Kathleen Lake, his first physiotherapist, had to be summoned from nursing a cold to unlock Franklin's leg by painfully stretching it on a plank laid over his bed frame.

That was only the start of the torture. To prevent the contracting cords of muscle from permanently torqueing his hips and feet to deformity, both legs were stretched straight, then encased in full-length plaster casts. Thick wooden wedges were then pounded in behind the plastered calves, like pegs into lobsters' claws.

Each morning, Eleanor noticed the way he worked his jaw as Nurse Lake drove the wedges in further. She stood by, hugging her sides tightly. Not since watching her father taken away to undergo the re-breaking and re-setting of his smashed leg had she been so seized by pity—or at such a loss for how to help or comfort or commiserate, since pity was the one emotion above all others that Franklin would not permit.

Franklin Junior, a pale, serious seven-year-old frightened by these latest threats, asked Eleanor how Pa could stand to face the pain every day. "He does, dear," was her answer. "He does."[18]

John, the youngest, a month shy of six, was asked in later years if the family had drawn closer because of his father's fight to regain his legs. The assumption that increased "togetherness" would have defined the Roosevelts' experience of recovery surprised him. After all, he lived on the fourth floor on his grandmother's side of the house. "I really wouldn't have noticed anything like that," he said. "We had our nurse and governess."[19]

At night, Eleanor slept on a cot in a corner of John's room, so that Nurse Edna Rockey could be on call in her room. Younger than Nurse

Lake, and attractive,[20] Edna Rockey had served in France as Eleanor would have wanted to: with a gas and shock team on a hospital train.[21] At Franklin's insistence—very much against orders—Nurse Rockey brought in oil to minister the one treatment that he claimed relieved his legs: a deep-tissue massage, notation of which would appear in the record of his case as "two minutes hard rubbing (Swedish!) on each leg & back massage."[22]

Asked by Nurse Lake how much massage was involved in these nightly sessions when she was not present, Franklin answered, "Oh, just a little to rub the oil in to build up the muscles!"[23]

Oil or no oil, Nurse Rockey's unduly high spirits, mingling with Franklin's happy shouts of laughter, got on Eleanor's nerves. But she nonetheless made room for the young nurse as a kind of resistance to her mother-in-law.

It troubled Eleanor that Franklin no longer called for her at night, or first thing in the morning, to weigh problems and solutions over his breakfast tray. Leroy Jones, his caregiver, now spent full days at his side, lifting and carrying him through every task he was unable to perform for himself: into and out of bed; on and off the toilet; to and from the table. For "brain work"—and a good deal more, as would soon be evident—he had Missy LeHand come in to take dictation.[24] There was one slot in the afternoon when Eleanor could have taken over basic nursing duties, but this only furthered her standing as a taskmaster, as Nurse Lake related to the doctors: "If only his wife could be persuaded that he does not need urging on all day and entertaining all evening, I think he would not be too tired and would do better physically."[25]

Eleanor's insistence had increased as the refrain echoed outside: "Poor Roosevelt, he's through. Too bad about Roosevelt, he's through. Too bad."[26]

To keep hope alive, Eleanor served at a New York State Democratic Party Women's Division lunch to raise funds to send a legion of women like herself to organize upstate counties—Wyoming, Livingston, Yates, and Seneca—the kind of "black Republican" strongholds where Al Smith had received exactly one vote.[27] But the luncheon group would be larger than any she had spoken to, and Nancy Cook, assistant to Harriet May Mills, head of the Women's Division, had asked her to anchor the roster of speakers, including Cook's boss.[28]

The invitation unsettled her. Recently Eleanor had overheard someone say, "Eleanor Roosevelt always pretends to know more than she does."[29] She was shocked and ashamed, but a part of her also ran quickly to a clear, almost objective awareness: "It was inevitable," she decided, "that I should be found out,"[30] later adding: "I have always known that one of my greatest faults was that I seized the main points and anything colorful about a subject and didn't really dig deep enough down to have my foundations firmly placed on facts."[31] Now was her chance to reset her foundations, but she dreaded being a disappointment.

Further, the state Democratic organization was poorly run and underfunded, and the Women's Division worst of all. For publicity they used a secondhand mimeograph from the Red Cross, and for an office the private dining rooms of the Democratic Club. To keep the lights on, the state chairman squeezed $100 from whichever volunteers showed up.[32]

On the appointed day, after a visit to the hairdresser, Eleanor stood stiffly before the women, her legs like water beneath her.[33] A hundred potential contributors, including her mother-in-law and several old friends from her Roser School days, sat peering at her. Mercifully, she had a message to deliver: Democratic women would have more influence among male party leaders if they paid their own way at the state convention that fall.

The words came haltingly, then all in a rush, and when the ordeal was over the affair had brought in $4,500 in cash and checks and another $7,000 pledged—about $160,000 in today's money. This was a surprise to her, but a true reflection of the influence that women's organizations had been building since their sudden growth during the war.[34] Afterward, she sought out her contact, and presented her with an Allenswood-style *petit cadeau*, a bouquet of Parma violets—the stronger-scented Mediterranean bloom.

Nancy Cook, all blushing cheeks and swelled blue eyes,[35] thanked her and applauded her. Eleanor's success with the older check-writing women had made Nan, an embattled younger assistant, look good to the suffragist generation in charge of the Women's Division. Eleanor, elated, wanted nothing more than to share in Nancy Cook's accomplishments. Here was a slangy, merry, contemporary for her rebellion against the old order. Eleanor surprised them both by asking Nan for the weekend in Hyde Park, the invitation soon followed by others to include Nan's life partner, Marion Dickerman.[36]

"Eleanor," she could already hear Sara say to the prospect of two Democratic party women for dinner at Springwood, "you know it is a bit hard to cater to a group of unknown numbers!"[37]

ORGANIZING DEMOCRATIC WOMEN FOR AL Smith, she started in Dutchess County and moved west, taking to the stump to decry Smith's opponent.

Louis Howe was helping with her voice. As usual, she sounded perfectly well modulated in private—"a lovely soft voice," said her friends[38]—while in public, she got more and more nervous, and the faster she spoke, the higher her voice pitched, spiraling into warbling falsetto. At which point she giggled.

"Why?" Louis Howe asked her after listening to one of her talks at the Women's Trade Union League.

"There wasn't any reason to laugh," agreed Eleanor.

"I know there wasn't," said Louis, trying to keep from laughing himself. "So why did you give that *silly* giggle?"

Justine Wise Polier, the future first woman justice in New York, recalled being present at the WTUL when Eleanor spoke that spring: "She was still very shy, and we younger people didn't quite understand her manner, or her way of talking, which seemed a bit remote."[39]

Louis taught her how to bring her presentation down to earth. Howe was a believer in what he wryly called "the unusualness of plain speaking."[40] In 1920, women voters had shown themselves immune to flowery talk and sentimentality, both standard to male candidates on the stump. "Women are businesslike," Howe had been informed. "They want facts, facts, and more facts."[41] To hold the interest of Republican women in far distant counties, Eleanor would have to "have something to say[42], say it, and sit down."

Chenango County, a Republican bastion representing Protestant religion, private property, and democratic traditions, had been knocked off balance by wartime collectivism, the women's vote of 1920, and strong third party showings. Speaking to an audience in Norwich, the county seat, Eleanor asserted that women by nature were progressives, and that it was impossible to be both a Republican and a progressive under the leadership of Governor Nathan Miller. "The women of this state have, I think, decided to go forward with the Democrats to better things, rather than remain with the Republicans, futilely digging among the war-destroyed ruins to build a pitiful imitation of our old industrial structure."[43]

She remained dismayed by her voice. In all likelihood, deafness in her right ear was playing a part, brought on by her attack of typhoid fever in 1912. By 1914, as she noted in her autobiography, she was "somewhat deaf." When her message began to bubble up with giggles, she could hear just enough to be horrified that she sounded exactly how men had expected women to sound when they let "them" into politics.

Joining forces with Nancy and Marion on the road, she canvassed porch-to-porch in rural districts, urging aproned housewives to come to meetings, assuring them their help was needed and that they would have meaningful assignments. Few who dared to sign up could then find the courage to turn up; and when Eleanor brought along the party's better-known speakers, they faced near-empty halls.[44]

"It is a discouraging job," she wrote to her activist friend and Dutchess County neighbor Elinor Morgenthau, "but it is always so much worse alone."[45]

In Oswego County, she and Nan went to see Mayor Fitzgibbons, who had once said that he would vote for a baboon if the animal was a nominated Democrat. They had written ahead telling him that they would come, but on the Fitzgibbons' porch, Mrs. Fitzgibbons said she was very sorry but he wasn't home. "Oh well," said Eleanor, "that doesn't matter, we'll just sit here and wait for him." She took out her knitting and sat there with Nan, waiting. Finally, the mayor, who had been in the house, could stand it no longer, and came out to talk.[46]

Fieldwork with Nan and Marion allowed her to combine her energy with work and work with friendship—friendships that ever-increasingly took the form, if not yet the fulfillment, of love affairs. "She was very much in need of more affection and devotion than was available to her," observed Esther Lape, "and these two women gave it to her."[47]

Marion Dickerman, a joiner, and Nancy Cook, a loner, were opposite types: Marion, tall, slim, prudish, often fussily overcorrect, was assistant principal of the Todhunter School, a private academy for girls on Manhattan's Upper East Side. Nan, stocky, affectionate, drily witty, was a chain-smoker with bulging blue eyes that flashed daggers. Her angular face had a swan's beauty that remained concealed by what Nan wanted the world to see as the smoldering hostility of a working-class girl from Massena, New York. She had gone to the World War as a nurse's assistant, but after fitting men with artificial limbs she had come home hoping to be a nurse or, at the least, a woodworker.

Politics had intervened. She threw in to help Marion make her name as the first woman to run for the New York legislature. Nan ran the campaign in Oswego against Assembly Speaker Thaddeus Sweet, much of which meant defending against dirty dealing: lights cut off in auditoriums as Marion spoke; car tires deflated or punctured;[48] and an opponent accusing Marion of inciting "the nationalization of women," whatever that meant, since better roads and a forty-eight-hour work-week were their campaign's straightforward issues. Politics activated Nan's inner crusader; she, like Eleanor, craved the satisfactions of working at a loved one's side day and night, and they came within seven thousand votes of beating the incumbent.

Eleanor's good-mannered attempts to accept Marion and Nan on equal terms did not last. She found Nan Cook irresistible and showered her with attention. Nan, as Eleanor first saw her, might finally seal a long-sought bond. Marion, ever the assistant headmistress, later contextualized Eleanor's feelings: "That was a difficult time for [her]. Franklin was back from hospital. She and Nan began to feel a definite attraction for each other."[49] Whether or not Eleanor yet thought of their intimacy on sexual terms, she had found a peer in Nan; Marion was six years younger. "Eleanor loved me," clarified Dickerman, "but not with the devotion that she had for Nan."[50]

*   *   *

THAT SEPTEMBER, AT THE DEMOCRATIC State Convention, women delegates flowed into Syracuse, a thousand strong. Eleanor led the Dutchess County delegation into the skydomed arena, as advance guards of four different women's groups arrived to support the re-election of Al Smith for governor and to fight for a female nominee for secretary of state. Three candidates had emerged from their committees: Marion Dickerman, Harriet May Mills (Nancy Cook's boss), and Eleanor Roosevelt.[51]

At a dinner the first night, attended by more than six hundred women at the Hotel Leavenworth, Eleanor raised more than $2,500 for campaign expenses as she sounded a theme she would echo to her recuperating husband: The women had not come to replace the men but to work as committed equals.[52]

Tammany boss "Silent Charlie" Murphy turned a deaf ear, refusing to allow women on the slate. The delegates showed no interest in taking a stand. Only Al Smith seemed to be listening. Voted out in the Republican landslide of 1920, he promised to fill appointments in his second administration with social reformers like Frances Perkins, Smith's 1919 appointee to the state's industrial commission, where she had become a proxy vote for the interests of working women and factory girls. Murphy had no such interests. It would take another two years for the aging Tammany chief to recognize that women were more than delegates, poll-watchers, and bell ringers.

Passed over for New York's secretary of state, Eleanor stalked the convention floor: arguing, cajoling, twisting delegates' arms for Smith, pausing only to consult Franklin by telephone at Hyde Park. All the while, William Randolph Hearst lurked in the background, awaiting Murphy's nod.[53] Rumors circulated that Murphy had made a deal with Hearst to be governor, Smith to be kicked upstairs to the U.S. Senate—or the other way around. A former deputy police commissioner had been sent to Smith's headquarters in the Onondaga Hotel to give him Murphy's orders. Smith remained defiant,[54] refusing to appear on any ticket with Hearst, even if it meant breaking with his chief and mentor.[55]

By Friday, with the delegates deadlocked, it seemed likely that Murphy would now produce a dark horse. "There were a great many people in that Convention who would have been delighted to see a new man come in," recalled Herbert Claiborne Pell. "It was the Roosevelts, Frank and Eleanor, who stood absolutely solid back of Smith. They would recognize no possibility of anyone else."[56]

Hearst finally withdrew; the press lord of San Simeon was finished in politics. Al Smith went on to reclaim the governorship in the biggest landslide in state history. Franklin appeared to be the figure to whom the most powerful new man in American politics owed everything.[57] Smith rewarded him with the chairmanship of the Taconic State Parkway Commission.[58]

Brother Hall wrote Eleanor: "What job is Smith going to give *you?*"[59]

SHE DIDN'T EXACTLY FIT INTO the system anymore, and neither did Franklin.

In October, he returned to Fidelity & Deposit with crutches under his arms and fourteen pounds of steel braces outside his suit pants. One misplaced crutch-tip on the slick marble lobby floor of 120 Broadway sent Franklin clattering down like a bag of golf clubs.

Loyally, Eleanor kept the visitors coming at home, the younger the better; and so asked Josephus Daniels's son Jonathan, a law student at Columbia, for Sunday supper and to bring his roommates. "Well, I conveyed the information," recalled Jonathan, "but Billy Carmichael was very much in love and that was the only night he could see his girl, and Lipford was somehow tied up, and Coles said to me, 'Jonathan, look, I'm on the make here now, and I haven't any time to spend with any has-beens.' "[60]

Painfully, Franklin learned to handle indignities, redirecting people's attention from flailing legs or a rolling hat by producing the more powerful distraction of laughter. He made his voice do the work of his legs, speaking more loudly, more urgently, more steadily, so that before visitors entered his room, they heard him. His vitality engaged them before they had even seen him. Face-to-face, all smiles and hands and beefy biceps, he landed his charm like a gleeful kiss. All the while, subtly but aggressively, he allowed no commiseration. He would never let anyone put him in that "other" category.

As the boom decade surged ahead, he indulged his sweet tooth for risk,[61] launching classic 1920s get-rich-quick schemes: helium-filled dirigible service between New York and Chicago; a coffee substitute; a German mark venture; live lobsters, stockpiled and released during surges in market price. None caught on. He tried another: oil wildcatting in Texas. And another: automatic vending machines.[62] Experimentation worked its own remedy. "Franklin had a restless mind," explained Eleanor. "It had to be busy with a number of things."[63]

He designed his own armless wheelchair ("a little kitchen chair on wheels"[64]) and tried every cure: cold-water exercises in Buzzards Bay; deep-heat lamp therapy; auto-suggestion ("Day by day, in every way, I am getting better and better"[65]); the Lovett Method, the Golthwaite Method, the Hibbs Method, the Chicago Method; even a compressed-air treatment invented by a Kansas City "aerotherapeutics" quack who placed his "air-bathers" in a Pullman-length tube of steel where their naked bodies received five to twenty pounds of pressure per square inch for twelve hours a day.[66]

Just before Christmas, jealous of the attention Eleanor now attracted whenever she gave a speech, Franklin asked to participate in the Women's Trade Union League's annual party at the Lexington Avenue headquarters that Eleanor had helped build. It was one of the happier Christmas seasons since the war. Everyone seemed to be getting ahead again, and Franklin assented to read *A Christmas Carol* to the unionists' children. When he got to the part about Mr. Fezziwig's annual ball, he sounded like a man who knew how it feels to look back from enchained old age to the times of youth. At the final passage, as he narrated the elation of Scrooge's awakening, he read with his own new joy. Some said that that night was the beginning of his return to public life.[67]

The real turning point had come in Vincent Astor's pool at Rhinebeck. When the heated water unwound his wasted muscles, he felt the sensation of motion. "The water put me where I am," he caroled to his mother's chauffeur, "and the water has to bring me back!"

THE POLIO VIRUS THAT HAD lodged in Roosevelt's spinal cord in August 1921 had *not* been transmitted by seawater. But, as the historian Michael Knox Beran has written, "Roosevelt's bitterness supplied him with the animus he needed to create a system of his own, one in which he would again be the center of the universe, the sun around which everything else revolved."[68]

Overnight in 1924, he discovered such a place, a world of radiance and warm water tucked away in a rolling hill country that felt far from everywhere. When Eleanor and Franklin and Missy arrived by train at the tiny spa town then known as Bullochville—population, 470—Franklin had the pool at the old Meriwether Inn completely to himself. He had heard from his friend George Foster Peabody about a partially cured New Yorker, Louis Joseph, who had treated his paralysis with hot baths at home—until swimming in a mineral-fed guest pool at a once-glamorous Georgia holiday resort, seventy-two miles southwest of Atlanta.

The water at the deserted inn rose to the vast swimming pool from mineral springs deep within Pine Mountain. Heated by volcanic fires to a steady ninety degrees, the water felt like blood heat, even in the coldest months of winter.[69] After three straight weeks of being lifted into and out of the pool by his valet, Irvin McDuffie, Franklin could feel life in his toes for the first time since Campobello. The effect on his legs was indescribable. Below the surface of the mineral-rich water he was—walking.

The sunny side of Franklin D. Roosevelt had found his legs—or, anyway, the *feeling* of fluidity so long as he could make his home in mineral water. In the happy days, weeks, and months ahead, Franklin could not get enough of the ramshackle spa. The easy neighborly feel of everyone. The warm Georgia sun flashing through stately pines. The complete liberation from the harsh, shaming model of Victorian hospital treatment. The genial, make-do, self-determined spirit he could bring to every activity. That first October at Warm Springs he made more gains than in all of the previous three years.

"This is really a discovery of a place," he told Eleanor after she had gone back north only a few days after arrival.[70]

For her, Bullochville, later renamed Warm Springs, *was* a pecu-

liar kind of "home." Her father and Uncle Ted's ancestral Southland
was now the nation's most rural and impoverished region. Bullochville
stood ten miles from the nearest paved road. The automobile detoured
anyone with money or leisure time to other destinations, leaving the
town to become, in one historian's view, an "anthropological museum
of Southern folkways"[71] where entrenched Jim Crow laws prevented
African Americans from free and equal citizenship. The acute poverty and primitive living depressed Eleanor, especially the daily ordeal
of neck-wringing and feather-plucking before a chicken could be put
into a pot on the stove.

Over the years she would occasionally remind people in Bulloch
County that her grandmother was a Bulloch,[72] but it didn't sound real,
possibly because for her it was unnerving to be so publicly and accept-
ably related to slaveholders. Warm Springs, even as it became the nation's best-known polio rehabilitation center, directly identified with
FDR and the vitality and longevity of his presidency, would nonetheless uphold Jim Crow laws, staunchly excluding black guests throughout the next two decades.

That first visit, Eleanor could not get over the cracks in the walls
of their guest cottage—she could look through them and see daylight.
She was grateful that Franklin could take so much joy and satisfaction
from his progress in the pool, but she could not see herself keeping
house here.[73] Bullochville unsettled her because she was afraid to connect to it and Franklin wasn't. She could not get back fast enough to
the modern side of the Mason-Dixon Line.[74]

FORTUNATELY, STATE PARTY POLITICS WERE catching up to her,
gradually becoming a twenty-four-hours-a-day, seven-days-a-week
mission. At last she was free to serve as she had wanted to serve when
she'd *needed* to lose herself in the war. By 1924, party leaders had put
her in charge of the Women's Division budget, which made her a
shrewd judge of the shadier side of local politics, learning how and
when to put campaign funds into play, spotting who could be trusted
to carry through a program and who was likely to forget about the
plan and abscond with the money.[75]

Asked to coordinate a strategy for turning Governor Smith's new

November, Eleanor ranged across the state with Elinor Morgenthau, making her appeals to long-neglected Democrats.

Her speeches had gotten better. People quieted faster, applauded more. Sometimes they laughed. Local newspapers recognized her as a gifted speechmaker,[76] counting her, with Democratic delegate Caroline O'Day, well-known for her beautiful speaking voice, as "two of the most prominent women in the state as speakers."[77]

The farther she traveled, the more confident she felt in her authority when people asked questions. Upstate or down, she kept herself on the jump, using the automobile as an organizer's tool and an information gatherer, since in small towns and crossroads villages a car always drew a little crowd.

The new gently curve-graded highways gave her a different sense of time. Whether 265 miles to Syracuse or 309 to Plattsburgh, she had the luxury as she drove of limiting her concern to the here and now. Once on the ground and moving on foot, she could bring her full attention to bear on the particular needs of particular individuals.

One by one, club by club, woman by woman, Eleanor overcame entrenched resistance in fifty-seven counties—all but five. Her main problem organizing Democratic women was that few had any loyalty to the party's agenda. Most cared passionately only about whichever issue had gotten them interested in voting. One of the reasons the state Democratic men refused the women serious consideration was that female organizers often had not gone beyond their own town or social circle to learn what women voters wanted. "Organization," said Eleanor, "is something to which [the men] are always ready to take off their hats."[78]

DAYS AFTER FRANKLIN FIRST SET off for warm waters,[79] his mother had just sat down to lunch at No. 47, when a maid heard a roaring sound in the chimney, followed by a hail of creosote in the firebox: ROOSEVELT HOME AFIRE; SERVANTS SOON QUENCH IT, headlined the New York *Daily News*.[80]

In Sara's early motherhood, fire at home had caused the shrieking, roasting death of her much beloved youngest sister. Laura Franklin Delano, eighteen, known as "Laura Franklin," had accidentally ignited the material of her nightgown. Suffocating in flame, she ran down the stairs at Algonac and out to the lawn where an uncle caught and wrapped her in a rug. Her nephew Franklin had been a six-month-old in skirts.

Home fire hazards were now his own most active fear. Recently, he had called everyone into his bedroom to see what he could "do."

The household gathered. When he was sure he had everyone's attention, he slithered face-first out of bed, dragging his massive torso and breadstick legs across the floor by his elbows. Eleanor understood that he "had to feel that he could get to something." During one grinding stretch, Franklin had gotten Louis Howe to look down at his bare feet: "See, I can wiggle my toe." A few months later, he called out, "Come and look!"

Balanced by wooden bars he floated full-length in a gym apparatus.

"See!" he shouted. "I can stand alone." Others choked up, but FDR never stopped beaming.[81]

Eleanor had been dry-eyed that time, but seeing Franklin Roosevelt as a creeping creature of the ground—this horror forced her to assimilate the metamorphosis of the magnificent, striding man she had married into what was a powerful animal—humping the floor, heaving across a room ahead of fire. This time she wept, walking quickly from the room.

Her eyes from then on automatically searched the nearest fire exit, assessed for potential harm public spaces and conveyances that Franklin inhabited. Access for the differently abled remained in the dark ages, but thanks to the good government of Al Smith and determination of Frances Perkins after the Triangle Shirtwaist catastrophe, legislation had mandated safety push-bars on the inside of fire exits. Eleanor's long service as accessory to Franklin's youthful egoism, immature deceptions, adult untruths—all would now gradually expire; replaced by a new mission to protect and preserve her partner and their partnership, which drew a parallel line with her own emergence into public life.

Franklin would have to find the road back himself. He had chosen to start at the remove of a coastal houseboat; but that apartness allowed Eleanor's old feelings of duty and loyalty to renew. "I do hope that he'll keep in political life," she told Frances Perkins. "I want to keep him interested in politics. This is what he cares for more than anything else. I don't want him forgotten."[82]

FRANKLIN'S EXTENDED CRUISES ABOARD FIRST one houseboat (*Winona II*), then another (*Larooco*), allowed him to live on the sunnier side of his miseries while enjoying overall good health, camaraderie with friends, and, according to Dr. Lovett, undiminished sexual function. In 1923, houseboating in America was "something new under the sun," as Isabel Anderson, Eleanor's fellow canteen organizer, wrote in her pioneering account of family adventures afloat. Bobbing along inland waterways or docking in riverside houseboat colonies was just unusual enough to match up with polio's erratic recovery rhythms and social apartness.

The $1,500 charter fee concerned Eleanor. "In view of the considerable cost of bringing up a family of five children, we have to consider carefully," she said.

"Well," Franklin replied balefully, and his bitterness shocked her: "I think I might as well do as much as possible in order to improve as much as I can, because I shouldn't be any greater burden than is necessary."

Missy knew firsthand the chaos of illness and the slow patience of recovery from having suffered rheumatic fever at age fifteen. Her spirit was as bright and mordant as his. She had deep blue eyes, a lovely, throaty voice, and her laugh was quick and kind. Her charm and intelligence and common-sense protectiveness made her his ideal companion; an auxiliary seagoing wife, pacing the flow of his shipmates and guests, often Harvard classmates and their wives, so that Franklin wouldn't overdo it.

The children, visiting, took their father's closeness with Missy "as a fact of life." Elliott registered the barest of mild surprise when he found Missy on Franklin's lap in the main stateroom. As for her wearing only a bathrobe, "it was no great shock to discover that Missy shared a familial life in all aspects with Father."[83]

Sara disliked the idea of her son and Miss LeHand, forty-one and twenty-three, remaining indefinitely afloat. This new intimacy of Franklin's worried her. In her experience, older men were especially vulnerable to the charms of their nurses and secretaries. During Franklin's father's ten years of invalidism, Sara became sensitive enough to the phenomenon that she instituted a house rule that no one particular nurse could be "kept on longer than a few days."[84] The connection back through Franklin's illness to her husband proved overwhelming to Sara; when Franklin returned from this first Florida float, his sideburns grown out into muttonchops like James Roosevelt's side-whiskers, Sara, dabbing at tears, begged him to shave them off.

Quietly, Eleanor had been smoothing the way for Missy. She was grateful to her for sacrificing her independence to help Franklin restart his life.[85] Opening the way to Franklin's access to a minute-by-minute companion proved a watershed to Eleanor. "Either you must learn to allow someone else to meet the need, without bitterness or envy, and accept it," she later wrote in *You Learn By Living*, "or somehow you must make yourself learn to meet it. If you refuse to accept the limitation in yourself, you will be unable to grow beyond this point."[86]

Eleanor's kindness and affection for Missy were counterstrikes to Sara's old jealousies. In February 1923, Missy was called ashore by the news that her father had died. She spent the next two weeks in Somerville, then returned to the *Larooco*. "I haven't told Mama that Missy is back," Eleanor loyally reported to Franklin, "because I think she has more peace of mind when she doesn't know such things." And when the scene shifted to Warm Springs, she told him, "I am so relieved that Missy can be in Georgia all the time."[87]

Franklin would return this loyalty the following year when he built the Stone Cottage at Val-Kill, presenting it, so far as his mother was concerned, as a "weekend house for Nancy and Marion." The 180-acre parcel on the old Bennett farm was, after all, *his*: when it had come up for sale in 1911, he had bought it. He proposed that Eleanor and Marion and Nan share a lifetime leasehold on the land, but become tri-owners of the cottage. It was generally considered a getaway that Eleanor might pull out of the hat of her "free time"—a wishful retreat for now, and in the long run a source for serenity in nature. It would become all that and more to Eleanor as she sought to get out from under her mother-in-law's roof.

The trouble had started during that first primitive winter of Franklin's recovery, when the household on East Sixty-Fifth Street had split into hostile factions as sixteen-year-old Anna was egged on by Sara to wage war on her mother and Louis Howe. "The most trying winter of my life," Eleanor called it.[88]

Howe's regular bedtime talk with FDR over the events of the day had provided the flashpoint, Eleanor having facilitated the daily check-in by giving Louis the bedroom nearest Franklin's, which was Anna's. Sara had then stepped in and whispered to her granddaughter that it was unfair that she should be banished to a tiny fourth-floor room when "that dirty little man," as Sara still called Louis, had the run of hers.[89]

Anna's response was harsh, as a teenager's might be. What angered her far more than Louis Howe taking over her bedroom was Louis Howe sending her harried and already neglectful mother out of the house and into a public life that, for now, only *he* could share with her. Speeches and fundraising for the women's division doubled the time Eleanor spent away from children. Anna, along with Elliott and James, blamed Louis Howe for "moving mother into the spotlight of public life."[90] Howe was the villain who had persuaded Eleanor she had a "higher destiny than merely being a mother," and now Anna could not count on her emotionally.[91] "She would be very loving and friendly, and then next moment when you'd think she still was loving and friendly, she'd be very critical, very demanding, very difficult to be with."[92]

"As if," reflected Anna, "some battle were going on inside herself."

Going silent was still Eleanor's one weapon. When Granny showered the children with a bright sugary love, or impressed on them the prestige of their Hudson Valley birthright, Eleanor tried to reclaim the upper hand with a cold, lowering silence. As her mother and aunts had done, she exercised authority by whisking herself away with an icy look and then, behind closed doors, prolonging her isolation—and, cruelly, theirs. A friend in later life once said that, much as she adored Eleanor, she was concerned that when the children misbehaved, their mother wouldn't speak to them for days, but if they went to their grandmother, she would reward them with a pony.[93]

This "very bad tendency"[94] only made it harder for her children to understand what had made her so mad.

"No dear," she would say, "I wasn't angry—only a little sad."

And that, as one close observer noted, "can drive a whole family around the bend, as hers was driven."[95]

Anna's feelings of neglect were compounded by her father's inability to respond to her frustrations with anything more than distemper of his own. Her status as favored child went up in smoke when she brought domestic complaints to the dinner table to which Franklin himself had just been carried. Overloaded, not yet able to function as a paraplegic parent, Franklin snapped at the child to whom he had always felt closest.

Eleanor later saw that she had failed to recognize that Anna was also struggling outside the household, trailing in her studies and socially isolated at her cliquish new Upper East Side school. Eleanor had hoped that the headmistress, Maria Bowen Chapin, would become Anna's "Marie Souvestre." When Eleanor remonstrated with Anna about the disappointing reports she was receiving from Miss Chapin, Anna's devil-may-care attitude provoked yet another parent-teenager spat, which boiled over into a poison-pen letter that Anna dashed off to a cousin, bitterly denouncing Louis Howe as the source of all evil. Eleanor discovered the letter, destroyed it, then tried in vain to hold Anna accountable for unkindness.

Sara, meanwhile, had been looking for an opening to reassert household control. Pointing to Eleanor's rooming arrangements, she persuaded Anna that her mother had deliberately displaced her in favor of Howe: "needling me to keep on hating this guy."[96] Then, one afternoon, upon entering the second-floor library, Anna found Howe sitting on a chair and her mother at his feet, eyes upturned as he stroked her hair with a hairbrush and murmured something quiet and close.[97] Anna felt the shock not just of intruding where "obviously I wasn't wanted,"[98] but of seeing and hearing her mother bestow fondness and affection "much more openly than she ever gave it to her own children."[99]

Sara then crossed a line, confiding to Anna that her mother had fallen in love with Louis.[100] By summer, Grace Howe would also suspect an affair between her husband and Eleanor. Whereas Grace confronted her husband directly, Sara used her apprehensions as slippery pretext to recruit Anna to spy on Eleanor.

Louis answered Grace's fears point by point, creating a brief, sometimes brutal history of their marriage's mutual disappointments. He turned at last to the painful truth: "I have said nothing of Eleanor for I know that in your heart you know there is not, nor ever *could* be anything to which you really could object—She has been dear and kind to Mary and Bub and you and she has done much to make what was a very hard place for me to be in endurable—Can you blame me if in my utter loneliness I have found her friendship a very pleasant thing."[101]

Anna remained on high alert, only gradually "getting onto the fact that, unless I chose differently, I could be used as a football by Granny in trying to influence Mother."[102]

That was exactly what happened in June 1924, upon Anna's graduation from Chapin, when Sara mandated that Anna, now eighteen, would debut in New York society that winter. This meant joining the debutante rounds during Tennis Week at Newport in August, all to be supervised by Cousin Susie and Uncle Henry Parish and the summer colony matrons who stirred gossip among the "cottagers" at Bailey's Beach.[103]

Anna set her jaw against Newport. Staying with family friends in Arizona in July, she made a last-ditch appeal to her mother for clemency, closing, "Gee! I wish Newport would blow up & bust."[104]

Eleanor could have put a stop to the whole business. It was the same trial by ball gown that *her* grandmother had enforced after all. Perhaps the memory of her own season of social self-consciousness made her think that her beautiful blond daughter would do better. In any case, she neither sided with Anna nor countermanded Granny's plans, and let Sara pick out which gowns Anna would wear to whose dance and by which young men she would be squired to what Bellevue Avenue ball.

Anna briefly considered bringing the case to her father, but realized she couldn't: "He would never give me the time of day." Besides, it was her mother—going along "100 percent with Granny"[105]—that had left her bewildered.

Just over a month later, in Newport, Cousin Susie took it upon herself to tell Anna about the affair that her father had had during World War I in Washington. Cousin Susie stressed how hard it had been on her mother; and Anna could feel the older woman's pleasure in imparting "the truth" about her father—much as Aunt Pussie had relished twisting the knife when she told seventeen-year-old Eleanor about the man Eleanor's father had been. But even though Anna could have gone to Eleanor for an explanation, "I couldn't talk to my mother about it," Anna recalled. "I didn't know who to talk to."[106]

"Poor Mother" was all Anna could say in Newport.

Six months later, when Sara for the second time had preempted Eleanor's fondest wish—to take Anna to Europe—Eleanor, having held her rage since hearing that Cousin Susie had interfered, settled for taking Anna aside and telling her the truth about Lucy Mercer. She said nothing of her mother-in-law, and Anna asked nothing: she knew how much tension existed between her mother and her grandmother.[107] But she was flattered and pleased to be trusted as an adult by the mother who had for so long deprived her of symmetry in their relations—who had been unable to trust her oldest daughter for fear that she would betray Eleanor to her father. But Anna gradually became her mother's "emotional partisan," and as a grown woman she decided that she could imagine what it would be like to have a houseful of young children and receive such news.[108]

At Springwood from now on, so long as Eleanor remained polite, compliant, aloof, things moved smoothly. But if she skimped or hurried distractedly through some household ritual, Mama would punish her with a cutting remark.[109] "Mama has done nothing but get in little slaps today. . . . Mama was awful last Sunday and made us feel each in turn that we'd like to chew her up."[110]

When she did have to be around Sara, she focused her attention inside herself. At one manorial Sunday lunch at Springwood, the family was joined by a Vassar undergraduate from one of the river families, Claudia Hatch.[111] Newly politicized, speaking on street corners for the common man and as a vocal supporter of FDR for governor ("He was as close to socialism as we could get"), Hatch found it mordantly funny that there could be a footman behind every chair in a progressive Democrat's house. "Nobody saw the joke except for Eleanor, who had this sardonic smile."[112]

Mama and the aunts and sewing circle ladies still supposed her to be a "temporary" politician; indeed, as she herself kept telling Franklin she was being until he returned. Sara's friend, the novelist Phyllis Bottome, observed Eleanor's "iron self-control"[113] whenever the older generation appeared, whether it was Uncle Rosy joking with Franklin over the hypocrisy of progressives like Marion and Nan making use of the Stone Cottage—"Hope your Parlor Socialists are not living too much on the fat of the land with you, against their principles!!"[114]—or Aunt Maude complaining all through a lunch about Eleanor's "failure to appeal to men—and then to fall for Louis Howe," whom Maude did not like any more than Sara did.[115]

Eleanor would go out of her way to meet official visitors at the Big House, and to be there when Franklin or the children returned home. But when the weekend was over and she had dropped the last one at the depot, she would go back to the house to say good-bye to Sara, then leave. Motoring the three miles east of Springwood, over Route 9 and beyond the Creek Road, she would spend a quiet evening in the cottage with Nan, making supper, and writing editorials and letters, in one of which she confessed to Franklin:

"The peace of it is divine."[116]

Val-Kill was built for Eleanor to get away from Sara. Yet, after saying good-bye—after jilting her mother-in-law to spend the night with Nan Cook—Eleanor felt guilty sneaking away.

Sara had the ability, one frequent visitor noticed, "not to be aware of what she did not want to know."[117] What she *did* allow about the Stone Cottage, as she relayed to Franklin in Warm Springs, was that "Eleanor is so happy over there that she looks well and plump, don't tell her so, it is very becoming, and I hope she will not grow thin."[118]

FOURTEEN

ON FEBRUARY 4, 1924, FRANKLIN drifted into St. Augustine and from the deck of his leaky houseboat saw flags flying at half-mast[1]—Woodrow Wilson had died of heart failure in Washington, a broken sixty-seven. "Poor Mr. Wilson lingered some time," reported Eleanor, filling in whatever Franklin could glean in Florida about his former chief's bleak final months on S Street.[2]

"The tributes to him everywhere have been fine," confirmed Eleanor. She had heard at dawn the guns in every fort around Greater New York honoring the commander in chief who had put nearly three million men under arms overseas.[3] In Washington, however, Senator Henry Cabot Lodge, the Covenant-killer himself, had presented a shockingly disingenuous farewell valentine from the Senate floor. "I must say if I had been Lodge, I would not have made his speech," remarked Eleanor, adding, "would you?"[4]

More than any other president of Eleanor's early political life, far more than the Bull Moose TR, the unwavering Wilson, fighting—and failing—to create a universal organization to stop all future wars before they started would shape the future Eleanor Roosevelt of world peace and human rights.

HIGHLY RANKED AMONG WOMEN ACTIVISTS, Eleanor was now giving speeches everywhere she alighted. As far west as Detroit, while preparing young Michigan women to vote, she admitted, contra Wilson *and* Lodge, "Our generation allowed dreadful things to happen, but the same things will happen in your generation, and you must be educated to meet these new problems."[5] She told her audience of three hundred twenty-one-year-olds that war would be their problem, too, because statesmen all too often missed their chance to keep the peace: "Somehow, they feel they might be looked upon as cowardly should they inaugurate such a movement." After all, she submitted, "It is born in every little boy to fight—to use his fists."

Women, therefore, must be the ones to use their heads. She advised "developing a world mind" to think globally, for it was up to the women to champion American participation in the International Court of Justice at The Hague—the nine-member tribunal in Holland which the League of Nations had set up so that countries could bring war-provoking disputes to arbitration before armies mobilized. Entrance into the World Court, she proposed, would be the first step the United States could take toward ensuring international peace.[6]

Between speeches, Eleanor worked weekends at the League of Women Voters, raised money for the Women's Trade Union League's new clubhouse, and dug in deeper on new findings for the Consumers' League. As legislative director of the bipartisan Women's City Club of New York, she stood up for child labor laws, workmen's compensation, and the adoption of an amendment to the Penal Law legalizing the distribution of birth control among married couples.[7]

Without aiming toward her own influence in the Democratic Party, she was able to deprive old-line party men of their suspicions about a meddlesome "squaw," as politicians' wives were known. The smiling, well-dressed woman who came knocking on their doors draped in foxes presented the old quality of refinement and distinction but now combined it with a crisp touch of professional detachment. Eleanor's clean, practical arguments for a literacy rate at least as high as that of Japan[8]—and for children released from factories to be sent to schools, and for mothers and babies made safe from preventable fatalities—put the men to shame for resisting such plainly worthy American ideals.

Guilty about her new life in politics, she assured Franklin that she was the merest of stand-ins, as everyone awaited the star's comeback. "I'm only being active till you can be again," she disclaimed. "It isn't such a great desire on my part to serve the world & I'll fall back into habits of sloth quite easily! Hurry up for as you know my ever-present sense of the uselessness of all things will overwhelm me sooner or later!" She closed: "My love to Missy, & to you."[9]

A life mainly apart revealed glimpses of benefit to both: "I could see they had a good understanding," observed the writer Gabrielle Forbush after a dinner with the Roosevelts. "It showed in the way FDR looked at her and she at him, as they said good-bye. He was really proud of her and said something in her praise as she went out." And when Sara pinned her stiff little smile on Eleanor's back, saying, "Yes, my daughter-in-law is *so* busy," Franklin pushed right in with an appreciative word for his wife.[10]

THAT JUNE, WHEN THE DEMOCRATS brought their convention to New York City for the first time in fifty-six years, the national party leader, Congressman Cordell Hull of Tennessee, hoped Eleanor would head the committee presenting the planks that women wanted in the party's platform. She accepted, immediately finding herself "up to my eyes in work" on the issue of child labor.[11]

She mustered with the state Democrats marching into Albany to boost Al Smith for president. The women had come to settle yet another question: Who would choose delegates for the two places that had been opened to women on New York's eight-member national group? Naturally, the Women's Division leaders felt entitled to make those picks themselves. But Boss Murphy had always chosen delegates to reward longtime trusted service to himself or the Tammany wigwam. He could see that female *votes* were good for business, but why should he let "political women" have greater say on his delegation? As he maneuvered to put a Tammany loyalist into the highest office in the land, Murphy wanted full command for this final triumph.

"I imagine it is just a question of what he dislikes most," Eleanor reported to Franklin, "giving me my way or having me give the papers a grand chance for a story by telling the whole story at the women's dinner." She added, "There's one thing I'm thankful for: I haven't a thing to lose, and for the moment, you haven't either."[12]

That night at the Division gala, Eleanor urged revolt; and for those still uncertain about challenging the established order, she spoke of her own over-willingness to please: "It is always[13] easier to compromise, always easier to let things go," she said, bringing the fights of Hyde Park to the Ten Eyck Hotel. "To many women, and I am one of them, it is extraordinarily difficult to care about anything enough to cause disagreement or unpleasant feelings, but I have come to the conclusion that this must be done for a time, until we can prove our strength and demand respect for our wishes."

The next day, she brought the fight to a fighter. Al Smith, brown derby tipped rakishly, cigar double-parked alongside the gold filling in his smiling mug, only looked and sounded like a *New York World* comics page character. When Smith fought for progressive causes, he fought as a reformer alongside reformers, not as a politician playing the angles. Eleanor had proven the women's power to expand their own budget and to raise their own funds. Smith needed the party to grow if he, the greatest social welfare reform governor in state history, was to take the White House without debts to Wall Street or big business. The Women's Division was carrying its own weight; the women had earned the right to choose their delegates. Murphy backed down.

ELEVEN DAYS LATER, AT HOME on East Seventeenth Street the morning of April 25, the Tammany chief awakened to an attack of acute indigestion and was dead in a matter of hours, age sixty-five. On hearing the first shocking reports, Franklin extolled Murphy as "a genius who kept harmony, and at the same time recognized that the world moves on."[14]

The rising urban world of the mid-1920s was changing the nation's rural self-image. Just over half of all Americans now populated the industrial cities. To many rural citizens, the biggest of them all—New York, with its nearly seven million melting pot souls by decade's end—appeared foreign, alien, anarchic. "It has become necessary that the United States cease to become an asylum," announced Representative Albert Johnson.

The Hoover-Palmer Raids of 1919 had persecuted individuals as "foreign aliens." As xenophobia and demonizing of American citizens now became a widespread social norm in the South and West, Congress opened debate on exclusionary new laws banning all Asians on the Pacific coast and turning the dead face of nativism against Atlantic arrivals from specific countries.[15] Eugenicists warned Republican majorities in the House and Senate that a continued flow of immigrants from Eastern Europe and Southern Italy would "pollute the American gene pool."[16] The Johnson-Reed Immigration Act, authored by the chairman of the House Committee on Immigration, proposed permanent quotas that would deliberately target whole populations of Jews, Italians, and Asians.

Franklin supported the effort through a column in the *Macon Telegraph* which he had taken over for a Georgia friend who had fallen ill. In one of nine columns, he argued that on the question of Japanese exclusion from the United States now before the 68th Congress, "it is necessary only to advance the true reason—the undesirability of mixing the blood of the two peoples. . . . Anyone who has traveled in the Far East knows that the mingling of Asiatic blood with European or American blood produces, in nine cases out of ten, the most unfortunate results."[17]

Less than a month later, President Coolidge signed the Immigration Act of 1924, running roughshod over almost two decades of goodwill and cooperation with the Japanese government. Only hours after signing, Coolidge publicly admitted that while he supported capping European immigration, he would have vetoed the bill if its only exclusionary provision had been the "unnecessary and deplorable" denial of the right of Japanese who had settled in the United States after 1907 to become naturalized US citizens.[18]

Official exclusion of "the un-American alien" translated to a ceiling on *total* immigration in any one year of 60,000, with a final cap set at 150,000 by 1927, bringing to an end the America that, as Eleanor rightly recognized, "had profited a thousandfold by what they have brought us, many of them representing the best brains of the countries from which they come."[19]

White supremacists, eugenicists, and leaders of the newly revived Ku Klux Klan all heralded the new legalized racism as a positive turning point in American civilization. Senator Lodge called it the most important measure Congress had ever passed, ominously predicting, "It reaches far into the future."[20]

Lodge was right: the measure made inevitable the war with Japan that had been brewing ever since President Theodore Roosevelt had mediated the Treaty of Portsmouth to end the Russo-Japanese War, ensuring that Japan's expansionist entry onto the world stage in 1904 would one day have to be settled to the satisfaction of American imperial interests in the Pacific. Twenty years later, America's exclusionary treatment of Japanese citizens triggered a national day of mourning in the Pacific empire of Japan, during which Admiral Yamamoto proclaimed that the insult to Japan's honor would be forgivable only in a very long time, if ever.

It would take just seventeen more years for the United States to be drawn into the fight that both empires, provoked by others, including China and Germany, had been spoiling for since Japan had become the first Asian power to defeat a European power, on TR's watch. Not surprisingly, Yamamoto would be the one to lead the attack that sank the American fleet at Pearl Harbor and roused a sleeping, isolationist America to the all-out war guaranteed by Senator Lodge and the Immigration Act of 1924.

AS ELEANOR TOOK THE STAGE at Town Hall to tell three thousand Democratic women, "Our first job is to show these strangers how we feel about our Governor," those "strangers" were burning crosses on dark hillsides across the Hudson[21] to show the delegates how they felt about Al Smith carrying out "the Pope's orders" to "make America Catholic."[22]

A reawakened Ku Klux Klan, playing on fears beyond those of its Southern racial terror network, had paid publicists to broaden its base through college fraternities, baseball leagues, glee clubs, and country fairs. This "Second" KKK claimed that as many as four million "100 percent" Americans had joined its "Protestant crusade" against the "foreign alien." The New Jersey Klan had recruited sixty thousand new members—more than in Alabama[23]—and gathered a third of its membership to denounce Al Smith as a "crossback" Catholic from "Jew" York.

While ignited crosses fanned prevailing fears of immigrants, Eleanor presided as chairman over the Democratic Women's Advisory Committee's two-day meeting on questions of child welfare, public health, the tariff, civil service reform, law enforcement, and other issues. The committee urged a dry plank in the Democratic platform.

None of it particularly mattered. The Democratic Convention known as the "Klanbake"—the first national debate of racial terror tactics by a political party—dragged on through sixteen straight days of bitterness, futile balloting, and vicious fighting.

At party headquarters, twenty blocks uptown from Madison Square Garden, Eleanor awaited the ruling from the Resolutions Committee. She had submitted the women's plank three days before. Each day she returned, and each day they kept her waiting outside without the least acknowledgment of the party's support for any of the women's provisions. The seriousness and timeliness of the child welfare issue could not have been clearer. The U.S. House Judiciary Committee had conducted hearings on proposed constitutional amendments in February and March, finding that millions of children in the workforce, from the Ohio onion fields to Manhattan sweatshops, had no legal or economic protection.

As Eleanor held her position outside the bolted door, the committee leaders inside deadlocked over a vote on the Klan. Men hoping to break the impasse hurried in, then emerged hours later more defeated than ever.

Shut out, Eleanor and the women decided to bring their appeal to William Jennings Bryan, whose sincere efforts for world peace Eleanor had taken to heart during the Wilson era. Bryan had remained a strong believer in expanding the federal government's power to improve and safeguard the lives of ordinary (mainly white) citizens by imposing better laws and protective regulations. Surely, he would give children in Ohio's onion fields a fair shake. But the Great Commoner rebuked Eleanor: If she wasn't satisfied with the proposed child-labor plank, "why not try another party?"

MURPHY'S DEATH HAD MEANWHILE FREED Franklin to take complete charge of the Smith interests on the convention floor.

But what to do after he had been transferred to a folding chair? Using crutches would seal him as a brave but incurable paraplegic. His solution was to get to Madison Square Garden early enough that when everyone else arrived, he would be found beside the placard of the New York delegation already working the room from his aisle seat. When the convention came to order, there was Franklin with the New Yorkers solidly behind him. Then he dispatched scouts and pickets around the floor, remaining seated throughout the day as couriers brought in reports from outside quarters. These revealed that Governor Smith's campaign was growing in momentum and gaining an eleventh-hour support.[24]

Those who had last seen Franklin in the 1920 campaign— as Cox's lanky, radiant running mate—were astonished to find the mellow and unhurried Franklin Roosevelt of 1924.[25] Those who remembered the impetuous, insubordinate assistant secretary of the navy were touched by his "extraordinary sweetness."[26]

"He keeps smiling all day long," reported the *Brooklyn Daily Eagle*, which proclaimed FDR "the brightest spot in the convention," adding: "It is generally believed that were Mr. Roosevelt in good physical condition he would be nominated in short order."[27]

He gave the famous "Happy Warrior" nominating speech that day at noon—eight crutch-borne steps to the podium, aided by Jimmy's rigid right arm. A misstep, a flailing fall, would have been the end of his public life. "I was afraid and I know he was, too," recalled Jimmy. "As we walked—struggled, really—down the aisle to the rear of the platform, he leaned heavily on my arm, gripping me so hard it hurt."

Once his hands found wood to grip at the rostrum, the world paused with him. Every face staring at him held its silence for a fraction of a second. In that moment, eyes shot upward as Roosevelt drew down from the Garden skylight the sun spears of a cloud break over the metropolis—then ignited a firestorm of sound and fury for Al Smith. As observed by Louis Howe's biographer, what appeared a miracle was closer to "an hour or so stolen from his sickness."[28]

Anna, sensing the depth of emotion for FDR from the delegates, whispered, "Jimmy, do you think Father may become president?"

"Unfortunately," said the son with bruises on his arms, "it's out of the question."[29]

HAIRNET IN PLACE, NEEDLES IN hand, Eleanor looked on from the gallery, overhung by tobacco smoke and the heavy summer heat. She knitted. "One might as well do something useful."[30] And smiled in solidarity with the women delegates sitting in tight formation through scores of ballots, to prove they were better "soldiers" than the men.

On the convention's fifth brutal day, the party debated the terror organization, but dared not go on record against it. The anti-KKK plank was defeated by four-fifths of a single vote; and in the end, Bryan, the party's champion of the common man—so long as the common man was white and Christian—stopped the Democrats from condemning Klan terrorism, establishing the bigoted Southern-bound Democratic Party in which, for the next twenty years, Eleanor would struggle with the politics of white Protestant supremacy. The party signaled inclusion and equality to a broader base, meanwhile subjecting African Americans to some of history's worst abominations in order to satisfy the Southern voting bloc's cultlike dependence on Jim Crow.

On Prohibition, the party's "wet" urban Democrats were challenged on moral grounds by rural "drys." Seventeen thousand white people—not an African American or Asian American in sight—overflowed the convention floor to watch the fight between McAdoo (Klan, dry, Big Oil, anti-immigrant, but also party leader of reform against liquor interests) and Smith (progressive, wet, anti-Klan, inclusive pluralistic society) descend to the level of personal feud, ending in a double knockout. Pundit Arthur Krock catalogued it as a "snarling, cursing, tedious, tenuous, suicidal, homicidal roughhouse."[31]

On the one hundredth ballot the convention deadlocked.[32] Three tallies later, the conservative Wall Street lawyer John W. Davis became the Democratic presidential nominee. In the November election, he carried the old Confederacy, plus Oklahoma; Republican Calvin Coolidge took all the rest going away.

IN THE WAKE OF JULY's chaos, a young Rockland County chairman named James Farley looked ahead to November. No one was taking the GOP to task for their scandals, he noticed—except for Eleanor Roosevelt. Only she had the sand to tie Smith's Republican opponent for governor—her own cousin, Theodore Roosevelt, Jr.—to the Harding administration's record of corruption.[33]

Enlisting Nan Cook for carpentry, Eleanor followed a Louis Howe design to outfit her Buick touring car with a huge brown papier-mâché teapot whose spout puffed out "steam." She liberated Anna from Sara's post-Newport debutante plans, bringing her along with Emily Smith, the governor's daughter, and a small band of Democratic women, as they embarked from a series of New York City rallies to lead a procession of cars that followed the Republican candidate wherever he went across New York State.

At more than a hundred rallies in towns where Cousin Ted had appeared the day before, the "Singing Teapot" would roll up to the gathering, dry ice steaming from its spout, until all at once the lid "boiled over with Republican corruption,"[34] and the speaker—Eleanor or Harriet May Mills or Florence Jaffray "Daisy" Harriman—would pop up over the rim to give a stump speech contrasting Governor Smith's "good government" accomplishments in Albany with the Republicans' secret $100 million leasing of naval oil at Teapot Dome Reserve in Wyoming.[35] If that failed to do the trick, Anna Roosevelt would then seed the crowd with miniature pasteboard teapots. OIL'S WELL! headlined the *New York Daily News*, MISS ROOSEVELT CHASES TEAPOT DOME BUBBLES.[36]

Isabella Selmes Ferguson, now remarried to Democratic Congressman John Greenway, turned to her husband and asked, "Do you think Eleanor has lost her mind?"[37]

Eleanor later regretted her opposition to her cousin. Yet she never saw the need to apologize for smearing Cousin Ted, even after all disclosures that might have connected him to the administration's malfeasance proved him innocent.

On Nov. 4, the "Coolidge or Chaos" slogan was answered with victory for the entire Republican ticket in New York State —all except Theodore Roosevelt, Jr., and with Ted's loss at the polls, Eleanor's role as the teapot's mastermind stirred a family tempest that would not be contained by the election itself.

Cousin Alice let it be known that she, too, would like to outfit a campaign car—with Lucy Mercer mounted on the hood.[38] It was the only time Lucy's name entered partisan combat: a reminder of how fortunate Franklin was to be on the sidelines.

So far, polio had immunized FDR. So had Eleanor. Among women who knew the Lucy story, or who might be told it over teacups, there was a great deal of respect for Eleanor, who was viewed as the hurt-but-rational wife, bravely keeping the family together.

But when Franklin became a candidate, all bets would be off. Infantile paralysis had a strange power to reactivate the basest fears.

To KNOW HER OWN MIND had been Eleanor's Souvestrian liberation. To have emotional needs, however, still remained unsafe in marriage and child-rearing, especially so in her mother-in-law's domain. Better to stay self-controlled, subordinate her desires to fulfill the demands of others, make known her true feelings only indirectly. In case of fury, best to turn to the wall, face it alone.

That first spring at Val-Kill, she slept dormitory-style with Marion and Nan, a singleton alongside a twin-bed couple. In the trio's one big room at Stone Cottage, Eleanor the people-pleaser and go-between couldn't help stirring excitements and resentments as she turned in both directions, testing her primacy, as a child does with parents. As Anna understood it, "Mother never recovered from the traumatic childhood. She had to have people to whom she was first in the world."[39]

Almost forty years on from Half-Way Nirvana, Eleanor had another chance to put herself back together with a carpentered Mom-and-Dad. One day, when Marion got mad about being the target for another of Eleanor's cold rages, their confrontation plunged Elliott Roosevelt's daughter into a new world of emotional accountability. Eleanor's attempt to respond revealed her almost total inexperience, at forty-one, when challenged in a relationship of equals. There would be no hiding out in Big House submissiveness in the Stone Cottage's one big room. She tried reaching for honesty: "It is new for me to have anyone know when I have 'moods' much less have it make any real difference." Then she retreated to the safety of the wall: "If you'll try not to take them too seriously, I'll try not to let myself have them."[40]

As Nan and Marion gave Eleanor a child-sized home in which to workshop a more authentic version of herself, her anger less often reached its wall-facing levels when she rejoined Franklin and the children for family meals under Springwood's roof. Still looking glum in her side-place at Sara's dinner table, Eleanor found ways to be truthful yet no less loyal to her mother-in-law, although she was notably less successful in new adulthood with that other scepter-wielding surrogate, Susan Ludlow Parish.

Cousin Susie, at sixty, a spoiled, willful hypochondriac, liked to claim that she had brought up Eleanor.[41] As others in the family were all too well aware, Susie "felt that she deserved a rating just a notch higher to the affections extended by Eleanor to her mother-in-law."[42] In this matronly triangle, the least sign that Eleanor was drawing closer to Sara cued Cousin Susie to beckon Eleanor to her invalid's bedside at Manhattan, Newport, or West Orange. At the rare family occasion that brought them all together, Susie looked for any opportunity to take the upper hand, especially the rare revelation that Sara had adopted some newfangled notion of these modern times:

"Sallie," Susie would say, "I really didn't think that you would quite fall for that idea."

"Why Susie, dear," returned Sara, quickly and brightly, "I can well understand how that *does* puzzle you, because you don't seem to have a grasp of that subject, and after all, it *is* somewhat involved."

It was only a matter of time before Eleanor, hooked once more, came hurrying to Susie's rescue. "Now, Mama," she would say in her classroom voice, "that was a rather complicated subject, and you know, Mama, Franklin told you much about it only yesterday! Would anyone care for more coffee?"[43]

COTTAGE LIFE COMBINED PURPOSE WITH pleasure in ways that had never been available to the fading dowagers of Old New York and Old Hudson Valley. The Women's Division of the Democratic Party had given Eleanor a job and a voice of her own; now Val-Kill drew politics and life into a unified whole. As she shifted her interests away from the small world of upcountry Episcopal patricians and toward a wider network of working professionals, often Catholic or Jewish, frequently same-sex life partners, she began the third phase of her transformation from Republican President's Niece to Democratic Official's Wife to Party Politician in her own right.

Besides, she had fun. Dressing the part of the New Woman, she and her friends pulled on tweed knickerbockers, men's shirts, and short neckties to visit Eleanor's beloved Auntie Bye in the old world of Avon, Connecticut. "Alas and alack!" exclaimed her aunt after the Val-Kill trio had departed. "Since politics have become [Eleanor's]

choice of interest all her charm has disappeared, and the fact is emphasized by the companions she chooses to bring with her."

But Bye's holding of Nan Cook against Eleanor was less reactionary
than a mixture of old-fashioned class snobbery and extended-family
wear and tear. For Eleanor, the Val-Kill experiment was a big change
relative to the Big House at Hyde Park; it freed her from the old and
opened her to the new, while not quite vaulting her day-to-day standards and practices all that far beyond those of the more progressive
of her Avon or Oyster Bay cousins. Asked her opinion of the decade's
hot new music, Eleanor replied carefully and almost matronly: "I do
not live the kind of life that is brought in contact with what you mean
by jazz. The children play what they call jazz music on the Victrola
which sounds to me rather attractive."[44]

The important thing was her own trio, and the freedom and joy
she felt when Nan and Marion let her occupy a primary place between
them, and with each separately. With Marion, she could comment on
the old bridal form of monogramming linens and towels, letting the
EMN initials of their first names render all three of them "the bride";
while Nan loyally gratified Eleanor's sense of marital injury, supporting her feelings at moments of conspicuous neglect.

Eleanor energized Nan and Marion, however unconscious she
was of her effect. By becoming the intermediary, by taking active
part in Nancy's feelings for Marion, and the other way around, the
geometry of the relationship was transformed and made dynamic.
Her power, however, did not reach full strength until she could feel
the charge of helping *them* get what *they* needed. Nancy wanted to
make furniture in wood; Marion wanted to teach girls in a finishing
school. Eleanor connected herself to both by the most direct current
at her disposal.

Little by little, she built up a reserve fund—an endowment—to
buy the Todhunter School for Marion. In homage to Marie Souvestre,
Eleanor would teach American history there two days a week, gradually taking on greater administrative duties until she, too, was an assistant head.

At the same time, out of her family money, she built and equipped
the furniture factory at Val-Kill, a two-story stucco building to house a

cottage industry in furniture-making to be overseen by the three Stone Cottagers. Nan would run the day-to-day operations.[45]

She revered Nan's talent, her "inventive genius," Eleanor called it.[46] Building a furniture factory was Eleanor's way of doing for Nan what Eleanor would have done for her if Nan could have been "the one & only great love" of her life. She needed to show Nan that despite her own ever-more-public service, she cared about the work and the privacy Nan loved so much.[47] She needed the factory to justify—on a larger scale than the cottage could—what she had "done" to Sara by moving out of the Big House. If a woodworking shop in the back of the cottage could attain larger purpose and meaning by serving Franklin's political ends at the national level, then at that scale it would also alleviate "the guilt she felt over the fact that she had built her own cottage," said Anna, "and had done so because she wanted to get away from Granny."[48]

FRANKLIN BOUGHT WARM SPRINGS IN the spring of 1926, paying $200,000—more than two-thirds of his assets. His law partner Basil O'Connor pronounced the place an overpriced money pit. Seeing another risky scheme, Eleanor confronted Franklin with the fundamentals: "I know you love creative work, my only feeling is that Georgia is somewhat distant for you to keep in touch with what is really a big undertaking. One cannot, it seems to me, have *vital* interests in widely divided places, but that may be because I'm old and rather overwhelmed by what there is to do in one place, and it wearies me to think of even undertaking to make new ties. Don't be discouraged by me; I have great confidence in your extraordinary interest and enthusiasm. It is just that I couldn't do it."[49]

She doubted there would be enough left over for the children's educations, and added: "Don't let yourself in for too much money, and don't make Mama put in much for if she lost it, she'd never get over it! I think you ought to ask her down to stay for a week. She's dying to go and hurt at not being asked. I'll bring her if you want and Missy could move out while she stayed. I'm trying to be decent but I'm so conscious of having been nasty that I'm uncomfortable every minute!"

They lived now at the center of small-scale cottage colonies, a thousand miles apart—Eleanor, at Val-Kill, as a locally minded furniture factory owner and part-time city schoolteacher; Franklin, at Warm Springs, as a resort builder and rehabilitation pioneer, "Doc" Roosevelt, whose state-of-the-art hydrotherapeutic center gave fountain-of-youth hope to guests determined to regain motion in their legs.

Gradually, they built their partnership around independent versions of themselves. For seven years, they had been redefining their marriage: coming to terms with unhappiness. Now, starting from their separate needs—Eleanor's, to be wanted for herself alone; Franklin's, to be his own man on his own two feet—they were creating new happiness. In both camps, everyone worked *with*—not for—the Roosevelts. Their valued associates were people who had had it hard. Even Missy LeHand, whom many thought to be a Roosevelt peer, had been raised by a working-class single mother.

Each had a resolutely devoted cornerman—Louis Howe, master strategist, in the shadows when Franklin won, right out front when he lost; Malvina "Tommy" Thompson, Eleanor's sharp-edged executive secretary, the choke-point in years to come, cutting off the stream of demands and requests so that Eleanor could function. Both Louis and Tommy knew pain, sorrow, bitterness—the things that Franklin and Eleanor could not publicly acknowledge. Almost all had had alcoholic fathers, and in some cases, the abuse had been violent.

When Franklin returned to Hyde Park on brief visits, he, too, sneaked away from his mother's house to come over to Val-Kill and slip into the pool. Eleanor was all too conscious of her mother-in-law's feelings about her living in the Stone Cottage—the "love nest," Franklin called it, or "the honeymoon cottage." Mama, alone now in the Big House, had her seasonal patterns, migrating to Fairhaven, Campobello, East Sixty-Fifth Street, and the capitals of Europe, but Eleanor felt responsible for leaving her alone along the river.

"I've reached a state of such constant self-control that sometimes I'm afraid of what will happen if ever it breaks!"[50]

Her children vexed her no less. Instead of fewer problems as they grew older, it seemed their problems only become greater; and as Eleanor got older, she realized that there was little that she could do.[51] She decided that the best place for her as a mother was as an uncritical presence in the background. All she could do with the boys was to have them know that her love was unchangeable. "Life does about as much disciplining as poor human nature can stand."[52]

When Anna announced her engagement to Curtis Bean Dall, a socially conventional securities salesman for Lehman Brothers, Eleanor suppressed her misgivings, believing it was her duty as a parent to let Anna make her own choice.[53] "Eleanor [did] not feel she could stop her," recalled Esther Lape.[54]

She had asked Esther and Lizzie Read up to Hyde Park to have a look at the young man, who was nine years older than Anna and lived for Class of 1920 reunions at Princeton football games. "He's already an old man," said Lizzie. But it wasn't just a raccoon coat and receding hairline that made Dall seem old for Anna. As Esther noted, it was Anna herself "who was very young, so much so that it seemed appropriate for her to romp around doing gymnastic things."[55]

Sara, meanwhile, championed Dall every step of the way—as much for the suitability of the match for Anna, as for Curt's potential to Sara.

Sara had two trustees looking after her finances, her brother Warren and, of course, Franklin; their names appeared on the stamp of each of her securities. Now, in one stroke, SDR made Curt their peer by granting her grandson-in-law equal fiduciary responsibility for the growth and preservation of her capital and estates. As June 5, 1926, approached, she named Curtis Bean Dall her third trustee, revealing his true caste function: he was Anna's husband, but he *worked for Granny*.

Dall's star shone so brightly with the dowager, compared to the disapproval from every other member of the family (James deliberately tripped Curt while ice skating), Curt would afterward wonder if Granny's royal seal might not have caused a counterreaction in Eleanor.[56] Where Franklin was blandly welcoming, Eleanor gritted her teeth and kept her distance. "She didn't try to do what other mothers would have done," observed Esther Lape, "combatting the engagement indirectly by making other things more attractive. Eleanor never thought she could lead children's lives for them."[57]

Anna would later say that she got married not out of love but because she wanted out—"to get out from the ambivalence I found here between Granny and Mother and Father."[58] But, as time would prove, Dall was Anna's vote for the power of Granny.

On the eve of the wedding, when Eleanor asked Anna if there was anything about the intimacies of marriage Anna would like to ask her about, she got a firm *no*. Next morning, the bride went up the aisle on her brother James's arm. As she approached the chancel in the Hyde Park parish church, her father stepped forward on Elliott's arm. Deep circles under his eyes hinted at the effort sustained to bring him vertically to this moment. Always an observer of the proper form, he passed Anna in her veil along to Curt in his cutaway and the Reverend Dr. Peabody in his robes.

Granny held the reception at Springwood and gave the couple their first apartment in an elegant new building at 39 East Seventy-Ninth Street. Eleanor, horrified at the full-circle completeness of Sara's take-over, was stunned to discover that Granny, anticipating her reaction, had sworn Anna and Curt to secrecy about the "wedding present."

"I am so angry at her for offering something to a child of mine without speaking to me," E thundered to F, "& for telling her not to tell me that it is all I can do to be decent." Reflecting on the last five years, she offered an astounding insight to the man with whom she shared a failed marriage, a dead child, and a crippling disease: "Sometimes I think constant irritation is worse for one than real tragedy."[59]

For once, Eleanor blasted Sara, who of course wilted into sweetness and puddles, bellow-blubbering that if Eleanor felt like that then she would take it all back and "the children" could fend for themselves.

An apology arrived in precisely three days, though it was worth waiting a quarter century just to hear Mama say, "I did not think I *could* be nasty *or* mean, & I fear I had too good an opinion of myself— Also I love you dear too much to ever want to hurt you."[60]

Mama, by then, had reinstated the apartment, and Eleanor had insisted on offering to help Anna and Curt move in when they sailed home from their honeymoon in the British Isles. When Anna got pregnant by the first of the year, expecting to deliver in March (she would be just shy of twenty-one), Eleanor's story circled back again when she made the case to Anna for a home delivery, which in Manhattan in

1927 was like suggesting a covered wagon for a journey west. Eleanor explained how comforted she had been, pregnant and motherless at twenty-one, to have Blanche Spring at her side. She very much wanted to give Anna *her* hand to hold when labor pains struck, and at last, shedding decades of reserve, came straight out with it.[61]

To her surprise, Anna agreed to the plan. Eleanor sensed she was happy—both about coming home from East Seventy-Ninth Street and about giving birth. "I confess to dreading it," Eleanor confided in Isabella Greenway, "more than I ever dreaded it for myself."[62]

On March 25, 1927, Anna, pulling hard at her mother's hand, gave birth to a baby girl, Anna Eleanor Roosevelt, third of the name.

THE PLAN FOR FRANKLIN IN '28, was to deliver the nominating address for Al Smith at the Democratic National Convention in Texas. "I'm telling everyone you are going to Houston without crutches," said Eleanor, "so mind you stick at it!"[63] Otherwise, he intended to stay at Warm Springs, and make the final push to walk without any sticks, not even a cane.

Helena Mahoney, director and head nurse, made it her business to remind civilians that there were no magic elixirs on order at Warm Springs. Just the individual patient's daily routine, early bedtime, and the four fundamentals: bathing in the springwater, sunbaths, massage, and walking (with braces, crutches, canes, or on parallel bars). "Doc" Roosevelt, and his daily verbal massaging of every guest's hopes and fears, was the magic that thawed frozen people.

Franklin had reached the physical limits of his progress in 1923. Left powerless below the waist, he had turned himself into a man of iron. He and Helena Mahoney had together developed a method for walking that balanced him on braced legs between Helena's rigidly held arm and a cane onto which he placed most of his weight. By hitching his torso first one way then the other, he could lift his legs as she shifted his weight. It wasn't actual walking but looked close enough. It gave him confidence that if he stuck with the regimen long enough, he could go and give the speech without crutches.[64]

On a Saturday in June before Houston, during lunch at Hyde Park, the Democratic National Committee's Belle Moskowitz telephoned. FDR would not roll himself out to the phone. Then word came that Smith himself was on the line. After a long conversation, Franklin returned.

"What was it?" asked Mama.

"Oh, Al Smith."

"What did he want?" said Eleanor.

"Same old thing. He wants me to be the candidate for Governor. It's ridiculous."

Eleanor knew Franklin needed administrative training. If he was ever to be president of the United States, experience as chief executive of the Empire State would be as critical as his apprenticeship at the Navy Department had been. Nevertheless, she remained deliberately aloof from his political thinking.

Louis opposed a run for governor in 1928. He was already preparing for a straight shot at the White House in 1932. He did not want FDR's exposure to two gubernatorial elections in the meantime to change that plan one iota. Everyone in the Warm Springs circle, especially Missy, who had by now had serious health issues of her own, said no, he should wait.

In the June heat of Houston, the Democrats renewed their declarations of confidence in the idea of world peace, the League of Nations, and the World Court of Justice. On the third day, FDR rose, "pale with years of struggle against paralysis," his body "nervous and yet self-controlled," and proceeded forward, swinging his hips, balanced by a cane in one fist and the arm of Elliott under talon grasp by the other. . . .

And so, he walked back into the center of the ring, ten steps from chair to speaker's platform, and took the podium.

Beads of sweat popped from his big, smiling face. In his audience, throats constricted, tears watered men's eyes.[65] From every corner of Sam Houston Hall, Roosevelt unleashed a "roaring, formless gigantic voice"—"a volcano of sound" that bulged and shook the walls and roof. FDR received the benediction of the delegates as a man "softened and cleansed and illumined with pain."[66]

AFTER HOUSTON, ELEANOR WAS PUT in charge of women's activities for the Smith campaign, becoming one of the two most powerful women leaders in America.[67]

The 1928 campaign —Democratic governor Al Smith versus Republican secretary of commerce Herbert Hoover—shaped up as the "most embittering and primitive electoral contest of our times."[68] Temptations of liquor, hypocrisy of politicians and law-enforcement, religious prejudice, the role of Tammany Hall—all formerly local concerns—were now hot-button presidential campaign issues pitting a "wet" Catholic against an anti-liquor Quaker with an uncertain position on Prohibition.[69]

In the North, archbishops convened huge gatherings of Catholic women, urging them to vote.[70] In the South, as Franklin reported from Warm Springs, "floods of scurrilous and disgusting" religious bigotry appeared in campaign literature supporting the Republicans.[71] It was an ignorant assumption everywhere that if Al Smith became president, the Pope would set up shop in a wing of the White House.

Conservative newspapers nationwide praised Franklin when he spoke out against the "campaign of bigotry" being waged against Smith, but took care to absolve the Republican Party leadership of any taint of participation. All of which meant that it was up to Eleanor to appeal to fair-minded Democratic women that Smith's Roman Catholic faith would play no part in his conduct of the presidency.

In all regions of the country, county clerks were reporting the greatest women's registration in history.[72] For the first time in the eight years since enfranchisement, eligible women voters—28 million strong, a larger bloc than the nation's farmers, and the largest potential female vote in any country in the world—were expected to choose the next President.[73]

Eleanor had begun supervising women's pre-convention activities in April 1928. The Smith offices saw endless streams of women—thousands, by one count—"laughing, chatting, drawing off their gloves, powdering their noses, tucking locks of hair up under their hats," according to one reporter. The task of organizing these "serious women, with enthusiastic lights in their eyes"[74] to join the campaign in forty-eight states and four territories was so vast that the modesty of Eleanor's office, as well as of the energy that dynamized her executive habits, surprised people.

Every day, from eight in the morning to midnight, she worked without limit, a far-sighted, highly intelligent, and loyal boss.[75] She avoided power struggles between party leaders and the DNC, while coordinating activities with hundreds of Democratic women, sending and answering mail, setting up and staffing committees, dispatching women leaders to regional headquarters, and giving luncheons, teas, and dinners at East Sixty-Fifth Street for visiting business and professional women.[76] "Mrs. Roosevelt can do at least six different things at one time without getting her wires crossed," marveled one coworker.[77]

She reported to one of the most politically influential women in the United States. Belle Lindner Israels Moskowitz, a behind-the-scenes power in state politics and the only woman among the Democratic National Committee's executive leaders, presided over every particle of the Smith for President campaign from the desk adjoining Eleanor's at headquarters.

Born in Harlem to East Prussian Jews, Moskowitz at fifty-one had served as a settlement worker, labor mediator, social reformer, organizer of women for Smith for Governor in 1918, publicity director for every Smith campaign, and trusted adviser in Albany. Smith knew she was a woman of striking individuality; and he was that rarity in American politics, the man who considered women intellectual equals. He listened to Moskowitz: her preparations were assured and logical; her plans translated into success at the polls.

Eleanor came to dislike Belle's haughtiness, her from on high judgments, the superior smiles of satisfaction when she got her way in the man's world. But, for getting things done—good things, the right things—and passing the credit along to her boss, there was no one like Belle Moskowitz. Hourly, daily, week after week, from the desk alongside, Eleanor learned the feminine politics of staying out of the limelight to maintain the "independence" of the powerful man's success.[78]

Their difference lay in how Moskowitz treated her female colleagues; no one at headquarters felt they could ever do enough to meet Belle's exacting high standards. Eleanor, by contrast, became known as the colleague you worked *with*, not *for*.[79] No unfair top-down decisions. Never a sharp word. She gave clear, definite answers to complicated questions and her instructions and orders were always explicit.

She did not interfere in an assistant's work, or dictate to subordinates. "Working together is her idea of working," said one.

Unrewarded activity has a striking authority. Eleanor's immense energy did not expect specific rewards, as she proudly said deprecatingly to Franklin: "I'm just doing what Mrs. Moskowitz asks me to do and asking no questions, the most perfect little machine you ever saw."[80]

After Smith won the party's nomination for president, Eleanor had hoped to join the children and Franklin on Campobello, but the DNC needed her to direct women's activities from New York headquarters. The first thing she did was enlist a group of prominent women to be her shock troops, from Alabama to South Dakota, and from Boston to Lexington, Kentucky. She sent Molly Dewson, a retired social worker, to St. Louis to command the Southern campaign, which was rife with feuds. To drum up newspaper features, June Hamilton Rhodes. To speak across the West, former governor Nellie Tayloe Ross of Wyoming. To appeal to new voters, she recruited Rosamond Pinchot,[81] a stage sensation and niece of Eleanor's friends Pennsylvania governor Gifford Pinchot and Cornelia Bryce Pinchot.[82] Rosamond, one of thousands of young women whom Smith's candidacy propelled into the arena, became the first in a series of protégées who embodied Eleanor's own society-to-politics crossover.[83]

On October 1, the afternoon before the nominations were made at the state convention at Rochester, the delegates held off. With no other candidate close to FDR in stature, they awaited word from Governor Smith.

Smith was awaiting word from Warm Springs. With John J. Raskob, the Wall Street banker turned Democratic National Committee chairman, he grilled Eleanor. Did she think his running for governor would injure his health? What about FDR's financial obligations to Warm Springs? Would Roosevelt accept the party's nomination, run for governor, and carry Smith's home state in the November presidential election if he were relieved of all financial anxieties? Eleanor said she was sure he would not accept on that basis.

Were there any other reasons that might keep him from running?

No? Well, then, would she please telephone him? They had been trying all day. Eleanor had come to enjoy the way Al Smith embodied the
freewheeling new politics of the twenties. He was not just the Happy
Warrior; he was joyful in his takedowns, he got charmingly mad, and
it rubbed off on Eleanor, licensing her to stop being afraid of her own
aggression.

She was about to betray her husband, after all. She was asking
Franklin to sacrifice his one dream (walking again) for his one other
dream (becoming president). If only it were that simple, Franklin
could cut himself away from the most important undertaking of his
life at Warm Springs; he could go against Louis Howe's dead certainty
that he should sit this one out and run for president in '32; he could
go against Missy's every protective instinct. And still not win. In 1928,
Republicans held the cards in New York State; victory for a Democrat
running his first statewide race was anything but assured.

Yet if he won, Eleanor would betray herself by doing little more for
the well-being of her fellow citizens than receiving visitors alongside
her husband, pouring tea for the wives of Albany pols, and ensuring
that official dinners were appetizing for all. Such would be the expectations of "the govenor's lady" in 1929.

Eleanor knew what she was doing. Franklin had avoided the politicians that day so that he could poll the one whose vote he valued most
but was too proud to ask for.

THE OPERATOR PUT THROUGH A call. Franklin was making a speech
at a local function in a nearby town and refused it. Eleanor, guessing
that he and Missy were driving back to the Meriwether Inn, interposed
a wire: "Franklin you will have to answer the telephone."[84]

Finally, he did. He took the second call in the lobby of the old fire-
trap, standing on braces just outside the phone booth because he was
too bulky to fit in. The phone stretched to his ear. Gleefully he told
Eleanor how all day he had avoided every politician calling from up
north and would not have answered unless it was she. Eleanor replied
that those politicians up north, Mr. Smith and Mr. Raskob, had begged
her to call. She was with them now, as well as with Herbert Lehman,
a New York banker who volunteered to join Franklin on the ticket

as lieutenant governor. She had a train to catch to the city—to open school next morning—and was leaving Franklin on the line with Governor Smith. . . .

Even so, it took Smith, Raskob, and Lehman a total of three calls. Each time, Franklin admitted that they had him pinned and he would take his party's offer, whereupon Missy, at Warm Springs, looked her man dead in the eye and said, "Don't you dare!"[85] By midnight, Franklin finally put it on the delegates—he would follow *their* wishes.

At one in the morning, the convention roared its approval. Eleanor's train was by then far down the tracks. When she reached Grand Central and heard that her husband had agreed to the nomination, she wept.[86] "I don't want Franklin to be Governor," she confided to a friend on the Smith campaign. "It will spoil our lives. He doesn't want to be Governor. What shall we do? I want to stay in New York and do my school, and Franklin has his [rehabilitation] work outlined for him."[87]

Her wire went to Warm Springs that night: REGRET THAT YOU HAD TO ACCEPT BUT KNOW THAT YOU FELT IT OBLIGATORY.

WHEN FRANKLIN SHOULDERED THE GUBERNATORIAL nomination, he was understood by the public to be ambulatory. "Everybody knew how Franklin Roosevelt had been seriously ill for several years of infantile paralysis. Only lately," reported the *Boston Globe*, "he had walked with comfort. Still he uses a cane."[88]

The *New York Times* regretted that the Democratic Party had endangered the recovery of a devoted public servant. Had the delegates only waited two more years and nominated Roosevelt for governor in 1930, "then all of us independents and Republicans would have been delighted to vote for him, but this year, as you see, the thing is sorrowfully impossible for us."[89]

Eleanor, of course, was blamed by other women for overreaching. "All American wives, undoubtedly, asked themselves," said the *Boston Globe*, "'Why did his wife let him? Won't it be expending too much of the strength she has helped him build up? Why did she not put her foot down? At least, why did she not in some manner interfere?'"[90]

Eleanor firmly rejected the idea, as contrary to all her principles. "I never interfere. I would not," she explained. "It would seem to me I would have no more right to say Mr. Roosevelt could or could not run, than he would to tell me I could not teach. It is a terrible thing," she said, "to interfere with other people's lives. We all have the right to our own decisions: we all must live our own lives, no matter to whom we are related."[91]

On Franklin's campaign for governor, Frances Perkins noticed Eleanor's newfound ability to "go about among people in a natural, simple, cordial way." She gave the impression of doing everything easily. She seemed unrushed, never flustered, never hurried, never harassed,[92] even though she was delivering as many speeches as her husband, "if not more," marveled the *New York Times*.[93] As chair of the Women's Advisory Committee, meanwhile, she spent an equivalent number of days on the stump for Al Smith. Upstate, she carried Smith's message of popular government and advanced social legislation—workmen's compensation, ballot reform, wages-and-hours laws—often enough to be rumored to be Catholic.[94]

In Jamestown, New York, hailed as one of the most prominent women in Democratic politics, she spoke to a lunch meeting of Upstate Democrats.[95] Afterward she convened a smaller group of party leaders at a lakeside house to discuss plans for the campaign. She did not come, she said, to lecture or to harangue. She asked everyone in the room to consider that the fundamental issues of the presidential campaign were the same as "the three great processes that have to do with human progress. They are: think, feel, and act.

"So far, we are still in the thinking process of the campaign. Before we begin to feel we must increase our knowledge so that we might look at the issues and judge them in a nationwide way, not think about ourselves but the whole country and all peoples. With increased knowledge we will set our imaginations to work so that we will understand and feel that which we know."[96]

She spoke of Hoover from her own recollections of him, serving as a food administrator in the Wilson administration, leading the women of the nation at the time they needed to be led. Then, of course, the wonderful work in Europe. Feeding the people who needed to be fed. But she had always wondered, why had the Great Humanitarian never gone "any further back of what he had done?

"He never learned the reason why the government had come to that state where we had to feed Europe. He never thought out a solution to the problem."

She contrasted Hoover's "one-track mind," his shallow indirection, with Smith's broad-minded, direct approach to problems such as responding to the national crime wave by introducing new housing legislation. "He saw that no citizen growing up in a crowded condition could develop normally and be good."

Smith, declared Eleanor, "goes back to the roots of things."[97]

FRANKLIN RAN AS A REFORM Democrat, attacking intolerance, telling upstate audiences that he hoped that he would not receive one vote "because my opponent, Mr. Ottinger, is a man who believes in a different church of God." He hoped "God would have mercy on the miserable soul of anyone who cast a ballot for intolerance in this campaign."[98]

FDR outpolled Ottinger in the Brooklyn neighborhoods where Jewish voters produced the greatest majority ever for a Democrat—against the first Jewish candidate for governor in New York. Statewide, from four million votes cast, Franklin won by just over twenty-five thousand—a close-enough margin in the closest gubernatorial contest in New York history, people had to ask: What made the difference?

"Roosevelt luck" would become a trope of FDR's victories, as "Roosevelt weather" came to mark a magical thinking about Franklin's smiling blue-sky destiny. No one could ignore Eleanor's influence, but few realized they were getting two for the price of one. It was easier to recognize that lucky Franklin Roosevelt was superstitious: he loathed Friday the thirteenth; never sat down to thirteen at dinner; and made other travel plans if a crucial trip fell on a loaded Friday.[99] With three Fridays-the-13ths—never to occur again in his lifetime—1928 was in some ways his luckiest year.

Polio had left Franklin's superstition intact but conquered his ambivalence. Eleanor noticed that once he had made a decision now, he put it aside, and went ahead with the rest of his work. It was the ideal temperament for governing in crisis. "He grasps what it means in human suffering," she observed, "but he has a saving sense of humor and of fun, and he knows that even if you are going to the guillotine, it helps to go with a smile!"[100]

Before polio, he had smiled "from the teeth out."[101] Now, in public, his "Christian Science smile" masked the strain in his eyes.[102] Louis Howe had discovered a goose-quill cigarette holder at Bertram's pipe maker in Washington,[103] and Franklin recognized its utility as more than a jaunty prop. He needed to smile through clenched teeth, and the holder enabled him to lift his chin and throw his head back, signaling a confidence and hope that recast him in the world's imagination as a figure of Atlas-like strength. The big brave man who "bears the weight of his country on a smile."[104]

Under Smith's defeat, Roosevelt's gubernatorial victory seemed the only positive comfort Democrats could find in the wake of the Hoover cyclone. Every political commentator with a typewriter had already picked Roosevelt as the next Democratic presidential candidate, "health permitting."

Eleanor was crushed. She had felt strongly that Smith's election would mean something critical to the nation and the future. "But whether Franklin spends two years in Albany or not matters comparatively little. It will have pleasant and unpleasant sides for him," she predicted to Elinor Morgenthau, "& the good to the State is problematical. Crowds, newspapers, etc. mean so little, it does not even stir me but I know it does others."[105]

On the first of January 1929, Franklin was inaugurated, standing tall, his left hand on the family Bible. They moved into the Executive Mansion, Governor and Mrs. Roosevelt. "Frankly," she told a reporter, "I don't exactly know what is before me, or what living in the executive mansion entails. But I expect to solve problems as they come along. That has always been my way—and things always get done."[106]

FIFTEEN

At a quarter past midnight, November 9, 1932, when the flash from Palo Alto, California, hit Democratic headquarters at New York City's Hotel Biltmore—HOOVER CONCEDES DEFEAT—Eleanor knew that the worst had come true. Her husband was to be the next President of the United States.

In his first scripted statement, FDR paid tribute to "the two people in the United States more than anybody else who are responsible for this great victory"[1]—Louis Howe and James Farley. Eleanor went unacknowledged.

She gave her own press conference under glaring lights near the Roosevelts' Biltmore suite. Striding into a mob of reporters and popping flash pans, she held her carriage erect and her head high. "I had learned from watching her," wrote Lorena Hickok, the Associated Press reporter covering Eleanor, "that she walked that way when she was in trouble or unhappy."[2]

During fast rounds of shouted questions, Eleanor for one instant glanced pointedly aside to Hickok: "The expression in her eyes was miserable."[3]

After the scrum, another reporter, John Boettiger, Eleanor's young friend from the *Chicago Tribune*, made his way to her side. "I wish I knew," he said in a low voice that startled her, "what you are really thinking and feeling."

Eleanor held her tongue, later admitting, "I was probably more deeply troubled than even John Boettiger realized."[4]

Five months earlier, on June 30, the day of the nominating speeches at the Chicago convention, Eleanor had been huddled with Franklin and his mother around a radio and telephones in the governor's mansion on Eagle Street. She sent a woeful letter to Nan

Anna Rebecca Hall
Roosevelt, one of
the most beautiful
and socially
ambitious women
of Gilded Age New
York, made Eleanor
feel unwanted.

Elliott Bulloch
Roosevelt,
the charming
younger brother
of Theodore
Roosevelt, was
Eleanor's hero.

3.

Cruelly called "Granny" by her mother, Eleanor was "Little Nell" or
"Father's Little Golden Hair" to her smitten dad.

4.

May 1887: Anna and Elliott,
with three-year-old Eleanor,
were sailing for Europe
aboard the *Britannic* (at
right), when a collision
with the *Celtic* killed five
passengers, injured scores
of others, and came close to
sinking both ships.

When Elliott Roosevelt's addictions killed him at thirty-four, Eleanor visualized
the quietly commanding person she would one day create for herself to help
manage the recovery of the nation under Franklin.

Elliott Jr., Eleanor's younger brother (at left), succumbed to diphtheria
at age three—the same infection that had killed their mother
five months earlier, leaving Eleanor and her youngest brother,
Gracie Hall, not yet two, to be raised by Grandmother Hall.

Grandmother Hall (Mary Livingston Ludlow Hall, at left) and Aunt
Tissie (Elizabeth Livingston Hall Mortimer, at right), photographed
circa 1915 with Eleanor (standing) and her daughter Anna.

President Theodore Roosevelt at Sagamore Hill, the family home on Cove
Neck, Oyster Bay, New York, 1905. Uncle Ted so wholly approved of
his favorite niece that he took his daughter Alice to task for "gallivanting
with Society and for not knowing more people like Eleanor."

9.

Auntie Corinne (Corinne Roosevelt Robinson), Eleanor's father's younger sister and defender during the worst of his binges, demonstrated an unwavering confidence and faith in Eleanor.

10.

Cousin Franklin (Franklin Delano Roosevelt, fifth cousin) at about the time he asked Eleanor to dance at Auntie Corinne's young people's holiday house party.

Eleanor (middle of back row) at Allenswood School,
Wimbledon Park, Southwest London, 1900.

12.

Eleanor in new suit,
1900, while remaining
for the summer with
Aunt Tissie and the
Mortimer family, St.
Moritz, Switzerland.

13.

Aunt Pussie (Edith
Ludlow Hall
Morgan) took it
upon herself to shame
Eleanor, at sixteen,
with the horrific facts of
her father's final days.

14.

Eleanor,
photographed
by Franklin,
on honeymoon,
Papadopoli
Gardens, Venice,
June 26, 1905.

15.

In Venice, Franklin
suffered the first of
four honeymoon
outbreaks of hives,
in addition to
nightmares and a
perilous sleepwalking
episode.

16.

Eleanor with Baby
Anna, Hyde Park,
1906.

17.

With America's entry into the First World War, knitting became a new form of activism for American women.

18.

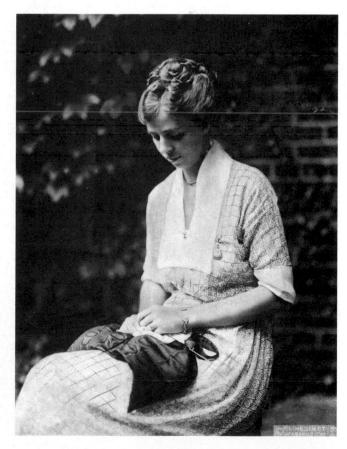

Under Eleanor's leadership, 1917–1918, the official knitting service of the Navy Red Cross sent 8,976 articles of clothing to shore stations and men at sea.

Lucy Page Mercer, Eleanor's social secretary, 1913, before Franklin and Lucy became intimates during the summer of 1917.

20.

Franklin's mother, Sara Delano Roosevelt, anchored the family (photographed at Campobello, summer 1919) in the prolonged aftermath of the Lucy Mercer affair.

Louis Howe, serving as Franklin's secretary and principal political adviser, was jealous of anyone who came too close to his boss, including, at first, Eleanor.

Joining Franklin's unsuccessful 1920 whistle-stop campaign for vice president, Eleanor forged an alliance with Howe that became the rock and steel of FDR's later rise to power.

23.

Warm Springs, Georgia, 1924: three years after polio struck, three months before beginning one of the bravest political comebacks in American history. "None of us took him very seriously," recalled Al Smith adviser Joseph Proskauer.

24.

Eleanor, a new voice in Democratic state politics, New York, 1924.

Eleanor dressed the part of the New Woman as she and her fellow activists Nancy Cook (second from left) and Marion Dickerman (right) pulled on knickerbockers to organize the 114 counties of New York State.

The camera all too often made Eleanor look ugly. State Trooper Earl Miller showed her how to have her picture taken as the dynamic woman she had become.

Election Night, November 8, 1932: Franklin, now President-elect Roosevelt, shows Eleanor incumbent President Herbert Hoover's concession telegram.

Cook in Chicago, revealing that she felt buried alive at the prospect of becoming the President's wife. After all she had contributed— campaigns, committees, articles, investigative reports, speeches, radio broadcasts— she could not accept that it would now be her business to pour tea, never to speak so much as a word of politics. The week after the November election, for example, Eleanor was expected to be toastmaster at the National Consumers League dinner at the Hotel Astor.[5] Was she to drop it? She did not know how to handle this and was sincerely considering taking action. It might not happen right away, she said, but after FDR was elected, she hoped a new life could open to her with Earl Miller, the New York State Trooper who understood her difficulties and deep aspirations as Franklin did not, as her sons could not. . . .

Nan showed the letter to Marion. Both knew that this was the fiery side of Eleanor's icy silences. They agreed they had to bring this to someone; and so, on the triumphant night of July 1, they showed Eleanor's cri de coeur to Louis Howe. "His pale face darkened as he read it," narrated the Roosevelt historian Kenneth Davis, "his lips drew into a thin line, and when he had finished he ripped the letter into shreds, tiny shreds, and dropped these into a wastebasket."

"You are not to breathe a word of this to anyone, understand?" said Louis. "Not to *anyone*."[6]

For the rest of the presidential campaign, Lorena Hickok, assigned to FDR's national campaign, allowed every Eleanor story she filed—"Wife of Nominee Ignores Campaign of Husband"[7]—"Back to Her School Job"[8]—"Poetry, Not Politics, Holds Thoughts of Mrs. Roosevelt, Driving Back Home"[9]—to pass first under Louis Howe's editorial eyeshade.[10]

THAT WAS JUNE 1932. COVERING the Smith presidential campaign in 1928, Hick could not have imagined joining herself to any such inside job, much less risking professional suicide for Mrs. Franklin D. Roosevelt. It was bad enough for a reporter of Hick's stature to be assigned the woman's beat.

Yet the more she had studiously avoided Mrs. Roosevelt as a subject, the more smitten she was by Eleanor. For the first time in two decades, a colleague found reason to warn Hick about getting too close to her sources.[11]

The hardboiled reporter could admire the professionalized Eleanor as "an outstanding civic and welfare leader"[12] who personally maintained Spartan standards of modesty and austerity. Yet it was the very stuff of women's pages—ER's $10 dresses and lunches at drugstore soda fountains—that caught at Hick. One day she noticed that Eleanor kept her long, thick hair contained within the fine black strands of an elasticized hairnet. To Hick's horror, the net crimped just enough of Eleanor's forehead to vary the shape of her face.[13] Of all the reporter's scribbled impressions of Eleanor's looks ("very plain"), clothing ("unbecoming"), and commanding presence as mistress of the Executive Mansion in Albany ("a very great lady"), none told better how tightly contained Eleanor had kept herself—before Hick—than did the picture of a black hairnet gathered in the center of her forehead.

The day after Smith lost the 1928 election to Herbert Hoover, Eleanor invited Hick to East Sixty-Fifth Street. Hick went, of course, to interview Mrs. FDR, the Women's Division generalissima, but the occasion seemed not to call for pad and pencil. Hick was flattered to find an elegant silver tea service laid out. There were cakes. No one else was expected. Eleanor poured as for a dear friend, smiling and chatting. To Hick's further surprise, Eleanor had turned herself out elegantly. She even relaxed while being interviewed. "But," sighed Hick, "the hairnet was still there."[14]

On the governor's annual visits to state prisons, hospitals, and high-cost but run-down welfare institutions, Franklin and Eleanor would arrive in an open touring car with a motorcycle escort. Steep entrance staircases and long interior corridors kept FDR outside, shaking hands, inviting the superintendent to take a drive, finishing up with a press conference. Eleanor went in with a deputy to inspect the kitchen and its rows of shined-up cooking utensils, large carving tables swept clean, stove spotless.

"What are the inmates getting to eat," Franklin asked her as they drove away from one prison.

She named the lunch foods on the menu the dietician had shown her.

"Didn't you look into the pots in the stove?"

She had not: she had copied the menus for the whole day.

"Eleanor, don't you think that when the wife of the governor appears, the menus are going to be better than usual?"[15]

After that, she double-checked to be sure that (a) the visit coincided with meal preparation, and (b) the food on the stove corresponded to the mimeographed offerings. She let nothing get by her. At state hospitals, she pulled covers off beds, examined mattresses, checked the laundry in the basement. Were linens and clothing looked after? What happened in the wards at night? Were they treated like caged animals?

In state prisons, FDR trained her to start with the basics and move toward more complex issues. Was the paint peeling? Were there enough beds? How crowded was each tier? Were the men free to smoke? When religious services, library books, or trades classes were offered, did inmates feel free to accept, or were they forced by jungle law to treat any kindness or prison privilege as unforgivable weakness?

AS BOOM CYCLED AROUND TO bust in October 1929, President Hoover kept his foot on the gas pedal of prosperity, declaring that "any lack of confidence in the economic future and the basic strength of business in the United States is simply foolish."[16] Six weeks later, robust Christmas shopping seemed to verify that things were back to normal. The White House then announced in March that the worst effects of the economic slump would be corrected by the end of April. On Thursday evening, May 1, 1930, in a speech to the Chamber of Commerce of the United States, Hoover declared, "We have now passed the worst."[17]

The next morning, as after each of Hoover's fatuous assurances, the stock market bucked and plunged yet again. Franklin sensed his moment to step in as Democratic rival-in-chief. The next day he asserted, "We have not yet turned the corner."

"It will be interesting," mused the *Baltimore Sun*, "to paste these two prophecies in your hat and see which is right."[18]

Hoover made his forecast accurate by faking employment statistics so that the economy more "scientifically" agreed with the Great Engineer's predictions. Short intervals of good news occasionally followed his empty prophecies—automobile sales spiked briefly, railroad loadings were up. But as unemployment hurtled from 16 percent in 1931 to almost 24 percent in 1932, FDR deduced that without bold federal relief, the soup-kitchen lines that Eleanor served several nights a week would only lengthen. Down-and-outers now waited to eat from the latest loads of garbage dumped by municipal trucks at West Ninety-Sixth Street, then drifted into tar-paper Hoovervilles in Central Park, nowhere else to turn.

FDR took advice from a range of experts and economists, including Eleanor's network of women reformers in welfare and labor: Frances Perkins, Florence Kelley, Pauline Goldmark, but especially Molly Dewson, the first female political boss in U.S. history, admiringly known in FDR's camp as the "Little General."

Acting on his faith in the state's "social duty" to the unemployed, Franklin wrung $20 million in relief funds from the Republican-controlled legislature to establish a New York template for large-scale public works offering unskilled jobs.

Eleanor tested the principle, which she had first floated in Wilson's segregated Washington, that public officials at home in public residences should set an example of the conditions under which people should work in hard times. Framing her own corner of the labor movement, she proposed a union for domestic workers to the Philadelphia Council on Household Occupations: "Perhaps you will be shocked," she told her audience, "but I believe in trade unions. If you want a responsible group of people to deal with, you have got to have unions of household workers that could establish a definite scale of working hours, wages, and vacation time."[19] She called on every woman in her audience to try each household task, find out what it took to do it right, and then answer honestly whether or not, just because she *was* a woman, she felt primed to care for a household.[20] "Writer" and "lecturer" would in time become her entries on questionnaires, but she later insisted that she had felt "very proud" to enter herself as homemaker.

"When one adds up what it means to a nation," she wrote, "one must concede that the well-run home and the well-brought-up children are more important even than a well-run business. More people are affected by the occupation of a housewife and mother than are ever touched by any single business, no matter how large it may be."[21] The problem of housing was central, she believed, to solving the problem of poverty. "Out of bad housing come inhabitants of prisons, sanitariums, insane asylums, and homes for delinquent children."[22]

The financial crisis fell hard on shelter. As a director of the City Housing Corporation, a private New York company that in 1924 financed America's first experiment with a planned residential Garden City, Eleanor attempted to promote in northwest Queens a community of well-designed accommodations at minimum cost for working people. Plans included Jewish residents but excluded African Americans and other minorities. Now, as the Depression forced foreclosures on mortgages that had gone into default, she joined the side of Sunnyside Gardens residents fighting back against the owner.

As a member of the more broadminded Rockefeller-funded Housing Association of the City of New York, Eleanor championed better low-cost lodging among the poor and the aging. She inspected tenement neighborhoods, making recommendations for upgrades, and fought to see improvements enacted with or without Franklin's gubernatorial endorsement.[23] In their new working partnership, she felt empowered by the squaring of their strengths: "I knew about social conditions, perhaps more than he did. But he knew about government and how you could use government to improve things."

On many things about which "most men would have asked their wives what they thought," observed Frances Perkins, "he didn't." And yet, Eleanor felt between herself and Franklin an unalterable "understanding of teamwork."[24]

Their adjustments to Franklin's physical challenges were now neatly systematized by his life as governor. At forty-six, Eleanor was just realizing how much she wanted to resume her own life as a physical being. In an age of nervousness, she developed the ability to relax body and mind and let go completely. When a lecturer passing through Albany taught a class of ladies how to relax, Eleanor prided herself on becoming "the only one who really learned what he was talking about."[25]

The method proved ideal for the kind of fatigue that would come over her in the middle of a day of inspections. All she needed was an unused room or office where she could stretch herself flat on the floor, feet uncrossed, hands relaxed at her sides, and let her mind go completely blank. Then, the trick was to imagine herself resting so heavily on the floor that she would "get the feeling that you were going right through the floor." Ten minutes of this updated Souvestrian technique restored energy more fully, she insisted, than a full hour in bed.[26]

Tips on wellness, rest, and budgeting went both ways between herself and "Doc" Roosevelt of Warm Springs. Anna, now ER and FDR's go-between, urged Eleanor to spend a little money on her clothes—improvements intended to polish up the governor's summer inspection visits. Hick noted the difference a printed-silk dress made in setting off Eleanor's still-slender figure, and, even more, in restoring her mobility. The open car browned her face, a slow summer sundown softening her features. As evening gathered, her whole temperament seemed to hum electrically.

Fortunately, on Franklin's orders, a new companion had come into Eleanor's life—a man so wholly involved in daily exercise and healthful living, she seemed to have forgotten about wearing a hairnet.

TWELVE YEARS YOUNGER THAN ELEANOR, Corporal Earl Miller, New York State Trooper, accompanied her on official trips from Eagle Street.

Reassigned from FDR to ER once she refused limousines and insisted upon driving herself everywhere, Earl became Eleanor's friend and guide as she declassed herself. She had long been seeking opportunities to transcend the more exasperating of her class's condescension and social restrictions. Earl, a former circus acrobat and Golden Gloves contender, was well acquainted with the "corrugated side of life,"[27] as Harry Houdini called the loose interconnection of circus, vaudeville, stunt magic, burlesque, striptease, and bawdy nightclub acts. Now, as Eleanor's bodyguard, he introduced her to prole joys— guns, cars, tourist cabins, vernacular speech. He belly-laughed at her sardonic observations and helped her to realize the universality of her plain sense of humor and wry, optimistic fatalism.

Her straight-woman dignity was always ripe for teasing, especially since she still rebelled against having her picture taken. Now when she froze in front of the camera, Earl would make comedy of getting her to relax, coaxing her to smile "just for one picture," then clowning behind the Kodak until she broke out the characteristic Roosevelt smile.[28]

Animated by Earl, Eleanor for the first time enjoyed being a standout; and in the home movie they costarred in, she took delight in the preening pirate who kidnaps her, sweeping a happily gagged and blindfolded Eleanor into his arms with a seductive glint in his eye.

With or without a camera, he called her "Lady," or "the Lady," and made no bones about being the kind of familiar who manhandles m'lady. He was all about having fun with the body, which was exactly what Nancy and Marion held against him. He was direct and blunt, with a Roman wrestler's physique. On seeing Earl shirtless, clad only in swimming singlet, one could well believe he could stop a bullet.

As the governor's bodyguard for three years, Earl had been FDR's sole security when at Hyde Park. He took up special vigil during the hours preceding an execution at Sing Sing prison, when the governor more than once received importuning visits from a family member or business associate of the condemned. Earl did Eleanor a similar service, unofficially and for which she was intensely grateful, after once again receiving an emergency warning from Tivoli, where a monstrous Uncle Vallie lived on in crude alcoholic poverty,[29] his binges now involving underage farm boys with a tubercular mother.[30] Eleanor may have wanted the state police to raid Oak Lawn, but as so often in Vallie's rap-beating history he was protected, this time by the Volstead Act. Private intervention a necessity, Earl drove down from the governor's mansion, taking Vallie by surprise in the middle of the night, muscling him into restraints,[31] and delivering him to the local lockup.[32]

Eleanor came to adore and depend on this handsome younger man, whom she could shower with affection while involving herself in his every thorny romantic and financial problem. She took great zest from Earl's acceptance of the privileged place she wanted him to have in her life, and at first gave him monthly spending money and the key to her Eleventh Street apartment (as she did to her increasingly far-gone brother Hall); Earl, in return, brought his life into hers, carrying along the current favorite from among his dancers and young comers—"for her, daughters by proxy,"[33] as Joe Lash later deduced; just as Earl "took the place of a son in many ways," said Eleanor, "even though he was somewhat older than my boys."[34]

Naturally, rumors followed, especially after Eleanor's attempts to keep private her getaways with Earl and various of his girlfriends to a far-north Adirondacks hideaway at Chazy Lake. The more Eleanor kept the press in suspense, the more people gossiped, as they did about Missy LeHand and FDR, seen to be "boyishly happy" in Missy's company. Most nights they worked together at Albany until late, Missy "curled up before the fire on the floor like a kitten."[35]

Earl made a career of dismissing the talk: "You don't go to bed with someone you call Mrs. Roosevelt"[36] was always copy. He fattened on the privileges of being Eleanor's current one and only, and had no intention of sacrificing those privileges for ordinary coupledom with one of his girlfriends, even if the down payment on a bungalow was all taken care of by "the Lady."

In September 1932, after an experimental affair with Missy Le-Hand left Missy furious and sad, Earl changed his mind, marrying seventeen-year-old Ruth Bellinger, a second cousin of his first wife— for the express purpose, he later claimed, of stopping the talk about himself and the wife of the Democratic nominee for President. The wedding was public enough: the reporters who had been covering the governor's office were all wedding guests. The day was hosted by Eleanor, attended by the candidate as "an interlude from politics,"[37] and all but celebrated in bold type at Val-Kill, with Mama and Louis Howe attending, Elliott as best man, Anna as maid of honor, and Anna's daughter, Sistie, as flower girl.[38] For a wedding present, the Roosevelts gave Earl and Ruth a parcel of land at Hyde Park.

FDR safely elected, Earl had the marriage annulled on the grounds that Ruth was underage.[39] In 1941, he again married lovelessly— Simone von Haver, a waitress at the Van Eyck Hotel who, despite Eleanor's practical warnings, ended up falling in love with Earl in Pensacola, Florida, as he prepared to go off to war. Their wedding, sponsored by ER, took place without fanfare, the marriage no more successful, and the divorce a good deal more toxic, as Simone claimed to reporters that Earl's relationship with Eleanor was adulterous.

This time, the split made public a yet more peculiar truth: Eleanor had twice shepherded a younger intimate into hollow vows on false pretenses, when what Earl had wanted was to go on serving "Mrs. Roosevelt"—and himself. Pathetically, Earl went on claiming that his marriages had "never been successful in killing the gossip."[40] In truth, Earl and "the Lady" remained paired. Earl became a great convenience within the family, who then did not have to examine Mother's relationship with women. And Eleanor could escape her schedule, put her "White House feet" up in Earl's little place outside Albany, and darn socks and sew for him while he worked on his hedge or cut the grass.[41]

Throughout the Depression and war years, as Eleanor could steal such moments from the very public White House and the more private side of a presidential partnership that stayed tolerant of adultery, she blocked and staged with Earl a conventionally gendered relationship in yet another auxiliary home. Although her radio earnings amounted to found money, she burned through $20,000 buying, furnishing, and maintaining the small home in Loudonville, ten minutes north of Albany, which Earl essentially kept for her.

Meanwhile, back at Val-Kill, Nan Cook and Marion Dickerman had long thought that Earl took advantage. They strongly objected to the State Trooper's too-familiar tone when advising—*telling*—Eleanor what to do.[42] Adorable Earl could be a bit of a dunce, went the Val-Kill line; and more than Nan and Marion thought him "absolutely gorgeous, a stallion, and stupid."[43] Now, except for Tommy and Eleanor's children, they believed him underhanded.

"I was never fooled about his affairs," owned Eleanor. "I had a deep respect and affection for him and I believe he had for me. I have no doubt that [her own letters to Earl] could be misconstrued, but considering the fact that he is at least fourteen or fifteen years younger [in fact, twelve], any gossip about improper relations seems ridiculous. I think it may be hard for people to believe that any one gives anything without quid pro quo but that is the case occasionally."[44]

Earl's girlfriends and Earl's marriages, above all else, safeguarded for Earl the status and for Eleanor the pleasure and for them both the security of the place Eleanor never stopped making for a lost son or missing father. A select few of Earl's women Eleanor annexed as friends, notably the dancer Mayris "Tiny" Chaney.

ELEANOR UNDERSTOOD HICK AS SHE had understood Earl—"another person like you," she explained to her newest one and only, "in whose soul there is no peace."[45]

Earl, for all the Sam Browne shine he brought to guarding the house of privilege, always drifted back to a demimonde of nightclub dancers and tough guys. Hick, by contrast, was done with the past. Born on March 7, 1893, in East Troy, Wisconsin, she was the eldest daughter in a family dominated by her father's abusive drinking and chronic unemployment. Her mother made ends meet sewing dresses, but Anna Waite Hickok died of a stroke when Hick was thirteen, and her father, who had been inflicting beatings throughout childhood, raped Hick when she was fourteen. Addison J. Hickok surprised no one when he put his daughter's pets to death. He later committed suicide. When Hick was asked to contribute to her father's funeral expenses, she answered: "Send him to the glue factory."[46]

Leaving two younger sisters in East Troy, she worked in a boardinghouse and on a farm until she was taken in by her mother's cousin in Battle Creek, Michigan,[47] finishing high school there. After a year of college, she got herself a seven-dollar-a-week job on a Battle Creek newspaper—assigned, she later recalled, "to meet all trains."[48]

One of them took her out of town—to New York City—in February 1918. For the next six months she covered city politics for the *New York Tribune*, taking from her first interview at Tammany Hall the lesson every fresh-faced reporter learns: stick to the questions. A glance at her notes afterward revealed that she had learned precisely nothing from or about "Silent" Charlie Murphy, while he "knew all about me."[49]

She lived every day for its deadline, a practice of turning bitterness to productivity: "There's no other work that requires such devotion. It's no game for physical weaklings. You go without sleep, without food. You have to completely forget your own self."[50]

She became the Associated Press's star, its highest paid female reporter, covering such national sensations as the kidnapping of the Lindbergh baby and the Walker-Seabury hearings that helped propel FDR to the Democratic nomination. Her fellow news hawks thought her the quintessential shoe-leather beat reporter, "soft-hearted and hard-boiled,"[51] her whole body "rippling with merriment" on a Prohibition story about drunk sewer rats; the tears flowing as she smashed out copy about Charles and Anne Morrow Lindbergh's infant son. Colleagues noticed her beautiful legs, a peaches-and-cream complexion, arresting blue eyes;[52] they recognized her as something different and special in a newspaperwoman—"quite a gal," they told each other, and meant, in part, her audaciousness, but, still more, her excellence, her eye, her humanity.[53] High school classmates had named Lorena Alice Hickok most likely to become a famous suffragist.[54] For Eleanor, she was a midlife Nelly Post, a rule-breaker, and very quickly much more.

WITHIN A MONTH OF EARL's marriage in 1932, Eleanor was in full pursuit of romance. On the campaign train through the Southwest, she sprung Hick from the reporters' pack, bringing her along to see Isabella Greenway. In Nebraska she teased Hick into following her into an eight-foot-high cornfield row and out the other end through a barbed-wire fence. Eleanor glided coolly through stalks and soft-iron strands into the adjacent pasture, leaving Hick puffing and panting, shawled in corn tassels, plucking rusty barbs from her silk stockings.

She brought Hick aboard a plane that Eastern Air Transport had put at her disposal for a night flight. The pilot roared over incandescent Broadway, dipping at Columbus Circle, then turning northeast—out over the dark of Long Island. At 6,500 feet, the cold night city sparkled in the windows, and the smoke rising from factory chimneys over the Jersey meadowlands reminded Eleanor of the Doré Bible illustrations from her upriver childhood. "What a lot can happen," she remarked to Hick, "in the short space of one's life."[55]

Eleanor encouraged her new sidekick to follow along as she attended Missy LeHand's mother's funeral in Potsdam, near the Canadian border, then pulled Hick onto a side trip along the St. Lawrence River to the site of a New Deal power project that would connect the

Atlantic Ocean with the Great Lakes. The streets there showed no sign that the country was engaged in a momentously important presidential contest. "Franklin is going to be dreadfully disappointed if he loses this election," she told Hick. "For a while he won't know what to do with himself."[56]

After dinner with friends of Eleanor's, they boarded their night train to New York. One lower berth was free. Eleanor spread herself along the long, narrow couch opposite.

Over Hick's protests she insisted, "I'm longer than you are." Adding with a smile: "And not quite so broad."

They talked through the night, Eleanor revealing to Hick Franklin's admiring warnings ("Better watch out for that Hickok woman. She's smart") and Tommy's benediction (Eleanor's telling response: "So I decided you must be all right"). She told the story of her Ugly Duckling childhood, her mother's death and her father's disintegration, touching lightly on Grandmother Hall, her drunken uncles and screwball aunts. Hick asked if she might write "some of that" in her next article about "Mrs. Roosevelt."

"If you like," said Eleanor. "I trust you."[57]

BETWEEN THE ELECTION AND THE inauguration, Eleanor had earned $60,000 (more than a million dollars today) from writing, speaking, broadcasting, and endorsing, and given the lion's share to women's charities; and in alternate weeks to the Salvation Army and the Henry Street Settlement, for its visiting nurses, as well as to the Catholic organization that helped women, the Children's Aid.

These earnings triggered a national referendum on what a president's wife ought and ought not to do. She was denounced for taking $3,300 for a radio talk—about $64,000 today—and giving it to a relief organization to aid the unemployed. She had offers from an airplane manufacturer representing thousands of dollars that could be turned over to the needy. One New Jersey editorialist, recalling that the public had loved Grace Coolidge for "not wishing to be more than the mistress of the White House," asserted that "most folk" still believed that presidents' wives, "like little girls at home, should be seen and not heard." One concession was granted for Eleanor: "She is by birth an

Oyster Bay Roosevelt, rather than a Hyde Park Roosevelt, and hence incorrigibly dynamic."[58]

People excoriated her for speaking on controversial topics, bitterly complaining of her "lack of dignity." Prohibition organizations slammed her when she suggested in one of her radio talks that Prohibition had failed the very citizens it had been designed to protect, among them, "the average girl of today."[59]

In her own youth, recalled Eleanor, liquor was never available to young women; because of alcoholism in her own family, she had rejected the glass of sherry she had been taught to drink socially. Now Prohibition was bringing gin and whiskey and grain alcohol into the social lives of young people in the sort of pocket hip-flask once found on camping trips. Today's youth needed to learn not only what to drink but how to "stick to the proper quantity."[60]

Christian church people hissed and howled. They had expected piety from a Christian president-elect's wife. Many of them did not accept that a young woman "must" carry any liquor at all. Norman Vincent Peale, speaking before four hundred wildly applauding, table-pounding members of the Women's Christian Temperance Union at a Prohibition lunch at the Hotel Commodore, demanded, "In the name of Heaven how can she stand up and say that every girl early in life must find out how much rum she can hold? Her knowledge of the United States does not go west of the Hudson River, and yet here is this statement by this child of the rich who doesn't know anything about American life."[61]

Cruel jokes ranging from the tasteless to the gross became a fixture of Republican strongholds, from congressional cloakrooms to Cousin Alice's sitting room to country clubs that named certain golf course holes guarded by tilted sand traps "Eleanor's Teeth."[62] Leaders of the automobile business repaired to their club lounges, where, one shocked son of a Detroit auto executive recalled, "the most fun they had was telling jokes about Eleanor Roosevelt."[63] And not just the club*men* abhorred her. The flesh of a certain kind of club woman "*crawled* at the sound of the words 'Eleanor Roosevelt,'" as Philip Roth later characterized "Mrs. Edward H. Maulsby of Greenley Road, New Canaan, Connecticut."[64]

From New England, where country people "think she better stay home and mind her own business and look after her husband and her family,"[65] to the Midwest, to the South, where the *Nashville Tennessean* lauded her for "displaying courage, energy, intelligence and other qualities which Americans like,"[66] profound distrust and disagreement prevailed about who and what Eleanor would be in the White House.

A feminist college professor proposed Eleanor for secretary of education ("because she represents a new approach to living"),[67] while the diarist Arthur Inman took her measure as "a typical society clubwoman type" who "advises everybody about everything and tries to set worthy examples to be followed."[68] In the strongly held opinion of Scribner's editor Maxwell Perkins, who had met Eleanor, FDR's election had ensured "a woman President" since "poor easy-going Franklin is ridden with both whip and spur."[69]

Nancy Astor, an American serving as a member of the British Parliament, joined the debate: "Perhaps many of you do not realize what an asset it will be to have as first lady of the land a woman who really knows about social problems, thinks about them, cares about them, and dares to talk about them."[70]

Editorials condemned her "aggressive personality"[71] and accused her of using her husband's victory as a screen behind which she now plotted to achieve her own ambitions. "Mrs. Roosevelt would do well to remember the people did not elect her president," tutted one editorial. "A little more retirement would be well on her part."[72]

She countered by appearing on a radio program to speak on the inoffensive topic, "Keeping Your Husband Happy."

"The people of the United States have set themselves a certain standard for their President's wife," she reasoned, "and I think in so far as that standard does not clash too strongly with her private life she should be careful not to offend."[73]

She took care to pitch her voice lower and to shut down the slide-whistle glissando-giggle that seemed to cause greatest offense. Personal criticisms occasionally annoyed or hurt her, but she disciplined herself to the same indifference with which her first political guru, Auntie Bye, had taught her to turn from purely partisan attacks by depending on her own conscience.

The trick was to look herself straight in the eye. "If you are honest," said Eleanor, "you will always be your own most severe critic."[74]

FDR's TRIUMPH, BANNERED IN HEADLINES on Wednesday morning, November 9, 1932, piled up a record-sized landslide in forty-two of forty-eight states, carrying twenty-three Democratic governors (out of twenty-seven) into office across the country, and securing complete control of the Senate and House of Representatives by safe majorities. Hoover picked up fewer electors—59—than Al Smith received in 1928. Roosevelt and Garner won with 472—the greatest Democratic victory since the Civil War.

The Roosevelts would be arriving in the White House at the hour of the most momentous crisis since the guns had fired at Fort Sumter. Who one was and what one believed was just then less important than what one *did*, and on that playing field, Eleanor comported herself in public by the old rules of conduct. Aunt Corinne, who died a few days short of FDR's inaugural, had attended a reception in Eleanor's honor earlier in February at the Waldorf Astoria, and acclaimed her niece's keen mind, great heart, and stout courage.

In private, meanwhile, Eleanor was pursuing Lorena Hickok by new rules. The night before the election, a campaign reporter had asked if she could ride in the car, even in the rumble seat, that Hick and Mrs. Roosevelt were driving to New York after hours. Eleanor, in her headlong urge to act out the drama that she and Hick had commenced—to prove that Hick would have the exclusive privileges of *her* one and only—lied to the other reporter, rebuffing her twice. Her dismissal was brutish, final, and unfair, and it was Hick who remonstrated sharply: "You aren't going to be able to do that sort of thing after tomorrow." She pointed out that her competitor, while from a news organization with less investment in coverage than the AP, had just as much right to expect a fair shake from Mrs. Roosevelt.

As Inauguration Day drew closer, Eleanor confided more and more to Hick about her dread of becoming mistress of the White House. Hick boiled down Eleanor's anxiety to "three big worries": her husband, her children, her own future. In each case the fear was about measuring up. Would Franklin ever be able to do enough for the desperate, discouraged souls counting on him? Would her four grown sons and daughter fall for the usual spoiling of a president's children, only to be turned to scorn and contempt when they made mistakes? So much was expected of them. And from herself.

Eleanor remembered exactly what a superb job Aunt Edith had done as White House hostess, presiding for seven years with tact and dignity. She scarcely left the White House for other than seasonal migrations, and when she did, it was news.

She doubted that she was capable of doing such a job. Or so she wanted it to appear to Hick, who had about as much interest as Eleanor did in the endless invitations, dull formal dinners, and fights over rank and prestige at the horseshoe-shaped table for state dinners.

Eleanor had already made a strange offer to Franklin, proposing to take care of his personal mail in the White House. He had shut that down at once. Sorry—Missy's job. He had offered nothing for his wife in the administration, leaving Eleanor to "work out my own salvation."[75]

"I'm afraid it may be a little difficult," said Eleanor to Hick. "I know what Washington is like. I've lived there."[76]

The most difficult thing Eleanor had sustained in the final three years of Wilson's Washington was Lucy Mercer. Now Eleanor was carrying forward, not just a love affair, but a grand passion; and not in the home of the assistant secretary of the navy, but, soon, in the most visible, the most famous see-through household in the country. With a high-profile newspaper reporter.[77]

Would any president's wife, before or after Eleanor, conduct a love affair during her husband's presidency? The important thing was to handle it so well that no one would notice. She would be under stress, she would need to air her feelings, but it would not ripple through her relationships. She would not make it a challenge to Franklin. It would not compromise her with her children, or with Tommy. And she would never put a foot wrong in public.

In Washington, she rebuffed her cousin Warren Robbins, State Department protocol officer, and his suggestions on how Eleanor must arrive as first lady designate to finish up business with the Hoovers. Instead, she walked—plain old Eleanor with spiffed-up Hick—down wide Connecticut Avenue, from the Mayflower to Lafayette Square, and across the two-way, everyday traffic of Pennsylvania Avenue to the White House Northwest Gate.

Early the next morning, the two slipped out the Mayflower's apartment entrance on De Sales Street and stole away by taxi to Eleanor's sacred grove in Rock Creek Cemetery. She wanted Hick to see Saint-Gaudens's shrine to Clover Adams and know that this was where she had renewed her courage during the shock of Franklin's affair. She showed her R Street, too, and, that night, her copy of Franklin's Inaugural speech, as if tempting Hick to file a story about what Franklin planned to say to the despairing country. Nothing less, at that moment, than the biggest scoop in the Western Hemisphere.

INAUGURATION MORNING DAWNED LEADEN AND blustery—"a dark dour day, in one of the darkest, dourest hours in the nation's history," reported the columnist Damon Runyon, on loan from Lindy's to democracy's defining moment.[78]

Overnight, the New York Stock Exchange and the Chicago Board of Trade had suspended operations. The Federal Reserve Bank of New York had lost $36 million in gold. Banks in twenty-three states toppled, one after another, as panic and hoarding dominoed every lintel, pediment, and capital still standing—an unseen terror unprecedented in peacetime history. "One has a feeling of going it blindly," observed Eleanor, "because we're in a tremendous stream, and none of us knows where we're going to land."[79]

"They simply do not know what will happen to their banking situation," recorded Harold Nicolson. "The whole country seems very close to a smash."[80]

In February, Hoover had twice tried to get Roosevelt to shoulder his bank failures. When the Federal Reserve Board recommended that the President order a National Bank Holiday, Hoover could see nothing but a trap.[81] Now he fumbled the traditional Inaugural-eve dinner for the incoming president, still more awkwardly making a last-ditch appeal to collaborate on overseas gold shipments and bank withdrawals.

At eleven on Inaugural morning, when the Roosevelts' open car pulled up under the White House portico, and the Hoovers surrendered the front entrance an inch at a time, Eleanor broad-jumped from her place to smooth things over.

Every eye turned to see the resentful Mr. Hoover offer a boneless handshake to the first lady designate. Then, climbing into the backseat, the one-term thirty-first president gave his successor a terse word, a grudging hand, and that was the last of it. "President Reject,"[82] as *Time* had dubbed the embittered Hoover, checked out then and there, riding the rest of the way motionless.

The president-elect, smiling triumphant, appeared the master of the moment. Franklin Roosevelt flooded the dark day as if he were made of light, a big bold electrified sign on a hillside heralding the American notion that *Things Can Be Fixed*. He himself could not be made afraid.

So annoyed were Republicans by the new leader's courage and spirit, some had been rumoring through the week that Roosevelt was suffering "elation," a "common after-result of infantile paralysis."[83]

On the drive to the Capitol, Eleanor asked her predecessor what she would miss about life in the Mansion. White-haired Lou Hoover, who had made the President's house monarchical by placing marine buglers on the stairs, replied that it was "the feeling of being taken care of" that she would miss most of all—the never needing to make travel arrangements. . . .

Eleanor, who had been making her own travel arrangements since the age of fifteen, vowed then and there that she would never allow herself to become dependent on White House pampering.[84]

The crowd was massed twelve-deep on the curb as Eleanor and Lou Hoover rode past. The iron-colored sky would brighten for a moment; staring faces would pop in the shifting light—a woman with a child pushing to the front, a man snatching off his hat—but altogether they seemed to be waiting.

At the Capitol, high up on the Dome, a pair of flags flew like wings. Eleanor attended the swearing-in ceremonies for Vice President Garner in the old Senate Chamber, then descended the ramp from the Capitol doors to take her place among the official party on the Inaugural platform over the East Front steps. Chief Justice Charles Evans

Hughes greeted her with doffed black skullcap. The outgoing president arrived, joined his wife. High dignitaries sat densely packed. The stage was set.

Franklin entered on James's arm, the two of them silk-hatted and swaying like penguins as they descended to the rostrum. The bare, lofty Corinthian columns of the East Portico rose on either side of the garlanded platform. Franklin handed off his hat and for a moment stood bareheaded in a bitter breeze hinting of snow. Then, balanced by his left hand on the three-hundred-year-old family Bible opened at the thirteenth chapter, First Corinthians, Franklin raised his right hand and repeated the oath after Chief Justice Hughes.

The President turned to face the crowd of thousands gathered on the Capitol Plaza. He allowed a single gleaming smile, then mirrored the serious faces of the people as he delivered his message. It was time, said President Roosevelt, to face conditions boldly and honestly. He affirmed his own stark commitment to "speak the truth, the whole truth." With steel bracing his legs and hips, he upheld the nation's powers of survival and revival by remembering its fortitude and hope in dark hours past.

He chopped out his words like tomahawk throws. "Let me assert my firm belief that the only thing we have to fear is fear itself."

Eleanor glanced at the crowds, sensing again that "they would do anything—if only someone would tell them what to do."[85] And for a moment she took in their doubt like a mouthful of seawater—then felt calm newly ascendant when Franklin announced his intention to ask Congress "for the one remaining instrument to meet the crisis—broad executive power to wage a war against the emergency, as great as the power that would be given to me if we were in fact invaded by a foreign foe."[86]

All the waiting was over. The roar of purpose that greeted this suggestion—the biggest applause of the speech—renewed her faith in her husband's power to reach through numbing despair to join people to his own self-assurance as it built through confidence and nerve to outright daring. "I always felt safe," said Eleanor of the years just ahead, "when Franklin was in the White House."[87]

*　*　*

Upon entering 1600 Pennsylvania Avenue by the front door, Eleanor drew off her gloves, revealing the ring Hick had given her: a breath-catching sapphire encircled by diamonds.

She did not know where to conduct their interview for the AP, which marked the first time that the wife of a president in office would speak for publication. Her second-floor sitting room was the only place she could call her own, and for now there were only packing crates on which to sit.

She had taken Mrs. Hoover's bedroom in the southwest corner and would furnish it with Val-Kill pieces and some easy chairs and a sofa by the fireplace.[88] For her actual bedroom, she chose Mrs. Hoover's dressing room, and for a bed would install a three-quarters daybed, also from the Val-Kill workshop. Her desk would stand in between sitting-room windows that looked onto the South Lawn and a hundred years of serial presidential plantings.

Bared by winter, a vast American elm started by John Quincy Adams held the Washington Monument in its vaselike branches. It struck her that she was really going to live here.

She was glad to help Hick with an exclusive. At least she had that much clout. That week, Sara Delano Roosevelt, mother of the thirty-second President of the United States, was featured in the red-bordered international proscenium of *Time* magazine. The story treated Eleanor as a minor nuisance, while extolling Sara's exceptional closeness with her son. It was a lesson from an American success primer: when the son becomes terribly important, the mother gets the credit, stands proudly at her boy's side, and the wife can find her own place to sit.

Time could mount her at the farthest point in the old family triangle, but the AP interview catapulted Eleanor into a future she would barely be able to catch up to in an unimaginable dozen years, let alone the next four. Starting on packing boxes in Mrs. Roosevelt's second-floor sitting room, they ended in the bathroom—the only place, Eleanor and Lorena claimed, they could find privacy for a serious press interview. "Hardly the kind of thing one would do with an ordinary reporter," objected one backstairs account, "or even with an adult friend."[89]

THE THREE-HOUR INAUGURAL PARADE MARCHED past the presidential reviewing stand like a snow globe of the giddy world now gone bust. Eleanor sat beside Franklin—"looking small, dark, and unpretentious," noted literary critic Edmund Wilson, "her little round black hat tilted fashionably over one ear."[90]

When the presidential party left the reviewing stand by its rear door, Sara went ahead at Franklin's right side, James still on duty at his left. Eleanor trailed. Small yellow crocuses were blooming in the flower bed.[91]

FDR and Mama entered the Mansion together. Eleanor brushed aside old feelings and got to work. She was expecting a thousand for tea. When three thousand showed up, the First Lady herself moved to one of the side tables and began to serve the guests, confounding the White House butler. "The help didn't know what to do," recalled Alonzo Fields. "She was really in our way."[92]

Among the crowd were "cave-dwelling" Washingtonians, Hooverites like Agnes Meyer and her husband, Eugene Meyer, who in just under three months' time would buy a small local newspaper at a bankruptcy auction after stepping down as chairman of the Federal Reserve Bank. Agnes, repelled by Roosevelt's inaugural address ("bold but colorless and empty") with its "tactless" lording of "inaction" over Hoover, was yet more disgusted by the new Roosevelt wife. The *Washington Post* could have had no better critic at that afternoon's White House reception ("undignified and shabby") than Agnes Meyer, noting for her diary the strange sound made in Washington ears by Eleanor Roosevelt's closing remark—a startling admonition to every person eating cake in the East Room: "Now your party is over."[93]

MRS. ROOSEVELT

I know your town.

E.R.[1]

SIXTEEN

Downstairs, neither Eleanor nor Mrs. Nesbitt, the Hyde Park bake-shop neighbor she had recruited as White House cook, could work up any charm for cockroaches. No matter how they scrubbed it, the old wood just wouldn't clean. The White House kitchen with its worm-eaten wooden drains and rusty dumbwaiter wasn't even sanitary; its electric wiring was dangerous. They poked around, opening doors, expecting hinges to fall off and things to fly out, but it was no use. Eleanor would eat anything Mrs. Nesbitt cooked and say it was delicious—but nothing good could ever come from this kitchen, not even Mrs. Nesbitt's famously awful Christmas fruitcakes, until *Public Works Project No. 634* began its makeover, two years hence.

Even then, nothing could appear on the President's table without rumors flying that Eleanor was taking revenge for Lucy Mercer with a fruitcake. In reality, as the Depression reached its peak, Eleanor collaborated on flavorless menus with the inexperienced Henrietta Nesbitt, not as a vengeful wife striking back at her straying husband, but as the nation's social leader, deliberately demoting the place of food as a way of reinforcing the country's priorities in its time of economic trials.

Upstairs, Eleanor confided to Hick: "My dearest, I cannot go to bed tonight without a word to you."[1] She had marked her engagement book that day with single-word reminders: *Capitol, parade, tea*. For the 6:30 p.m. slot, she had inserted the one event of Inauguration Day that qualified as a recorded memory: "Said good-bye to Hick."

"I felt a little as though a part of me was leaving tonight," she admitted. "You have grown so much to be a part of my life that it is empty without you even though I'm busy every minute." These were "strange days & very odd to me but I'll remember the joys & try to plan pleasant things & count the days between our times together!"

Cousin Alice had swept in that night for the family dinner. Leader of the Oyster Bay branch soon to be labeled the "Out of Season" Roo-sevelts, Alice took her first shot cleanly: "Well, Eleanor," she said, "I wonder how you're going to be able to handle this." Elliott overheard and kept tabs as Alice renewed the conversation once or twice through the rest of the dinner, each time leaving Eleanor, from her son's per-spective, "on the verge of openly crying right there at the dinner party."[2]

Getting into bed, Eleanor kissed Hick's picture good night and re-peated the kiss the next morning.[3] That first of more than four thou-sand nights in the White House,[4] she went to sleep with Lorena in her thoughts, repeating to herself their nightly endearment, *Je t'aime et je t'adore*.[5]

The next day was Sunday, and she had to arrange to get Franklin Jr. and John back to college. Besides the fact that their father was going to close all the banks on Monday, Eleanor didn't have enough cash on hand for their train tickets.

"Franklin, what do I do?" she asked. "The boys have to get back. . . ."

She would go on calling him Franklin; to her ear "Mr. President" was pretentious; too stuffy, in any case, for everyday use.[6]

"I wouldn't worry about it too much," he replied, "we'll manage to get their tickets somehow."[7]

And that was when it first occurred to her, "If you lived in the White House you would be trusted to pay—you didn't need cash on the spot."[8]

TWO MORNINGS AFTER THE INAUGURAL came grim news. Chicago Mayor Anton Cermak, fighting for his life in a Miami hospital, had succumbed to the bullet wound he sustained in the failed assassination attempt on the president-elect on February 15. FDR had just finished speaking from his open car to a welcoming rally of fifty thousand in Bay Front Park, when from twenty-five feet away in the warm night the firing began.[9]

Giuseppe Zangara, an Italian anarchist, stood on a bench, holding out a .38 revolver. His first shot missed FDR and struck the Chicago mayor as they were shaking hands. A woman in the crowd had just got up on the bench for a better view when she saw Zangara shooting.

"Don't do that!" said Lillian Cross, grabbing the man's arm, and pushing it up in the air as the weapon scattered fire, wounding three others besides Cermak but leaving Franklin untouched.

Mayor Cermak had been instrumental in securing FDR's nomination in Chicago the previous June. But it was Lillian Cross of Miami who sat in a place of honor at the Inauguration in Washington, her trip sponsored by a New York newspaper.[10] Eleanor invited Lillian to a White House tea, and FDR broached the imponderable truth on everyone's mind: "How much greater and sadder a tragedy was averted by your unselfish courage and quick thinking of course no one can estimate."[11]

But tragedies nonetheless dominated the administration's first days. Radio reports of Mayor Cermak's death came on the heels of the mysterious end of Montana Senator Thomas J. Walsh. FDR's pick for attorney general had died Thursday, March 2, on the train from Miami to Washington as the seventy-three-year-old lawmaker hurried to his own swearing-in after marrying Mina Nieves Perez Chaumont de Truffin, young widow of a rich Cuban, in a clandestine wedding in Havana. By March 6, ER was accompanying the President and a stunned cabinet to the Capitol for a funeral.

As Walsh lay in state in the Senate chamber, conspiracy theories abounded about his having been poisoned in Cuba, the victim of a Republican plot to forestall a federal investigation of the aluminum industry.[12] Any threat to corporate power appeared designed to tar the Roosevelt administration, since FDR's first presidential arrows—closing the markets, declaring a bank holiday—had been aimed over the heads of the six hundred corporations holding two-thirds of all industrial wealth in the nation and toward the heart of the mere twenty banks and banking houses controlling the availability of American capital. FDR's advisers were calling this crisis of capitalism "a cruel hoax" on the individual citizen; FDR himself told off one economist: "People aren't cattle, you know."[13]

The would-be rich, never tired of not being rich enough, blamed Bolsheviks and a shadowy ring-kissing papal underworld. Phony allegations claimed that Zangara's target in Miami had been Cermak all along, the mayor's ties to organized crime to blame.[14] Outgoing president Herbert Hoover, a newly inexhaustible bogeyman for extremist rumor, had supposedly paid off FDR's failed assassin in gold hoarded by vengeful Republicans. Meanwhile, during these ugly days of the banking crisis, as more and more financial institutions closed their doors, ordinary citizens trying to withdraw savings jammed the streets, adding to the calamity swirling around the administration's unruffled center.

Eleanor had made nonchalant statements to reporters and friends ("These, after all, are things which everyone in public life expects and must be taken calmly"[15]), but whenever she traveled with FDR, she quietly began carrying a tear gas pen in her pocketbook. Once she took it out to demonstrate to Hick how she would protect the President: "I could stand with my back to him and fire it," she announced. Hick didn't have the heart to tell her that it would never work—not with "that crowded pocketbook of hers!"[16]

"Hick darling," wrote Eleanor the night after Senator Walsh's funeral, "how good it was to hear your voice. It was inadequate to try to tell you what it meant. Jimmy was near and I could not say, *je t'aime et je t'adore* as I long to do, but always remember that I am saying it."

The following day, when Lorena turned forty, on March 7, Eleanor swore that *next* year she would be with her on her birthday. It had become their theme: the struggle for a better future in which both would shed their responsibilities so that each might have the other all to herself. "I *will* be with you," vowed Eleanor. "Oh! I want to put my arms around you, I ache to hold you close." Now soothing herself: "Your ring is a great comfort. I look at it and think she does love me, or I wouldn't be wearing it."[17]

It was a terrifying spring and summer.

Eleanor and Franklin's prevailing nature was to turn bad to better—to do what had to be done to save the country. But what if they couldn't? People had expected blood to run in the streets if Hoover remained in office. Someone set on being president in FDR's generation did not expect to take over such devastation. A president of the United States expected success, world power. America was going to fill in all the empty spaces of the land, master all seven seas. By industry.

By canal-building. By armored naval presence. America was going to remake the world.

Equally idealistic, if on different terms, Eleanor had not fully accepted Franklin's semi-authoritarian politics as a necessary distortion to achieve the ends of good governance in a time of crisis. And yet both now crossed the Rubicon of belonging, not just by suspending membership in the class of their upbringing, but by consciously rejecting the pinching, propertied fears of educated and influential people who in the first years of the Depression were actively afraid of a Bolshevik-style workers revolution leading to a Communist takeover of the government.

"I am an old man and have probably not long to live," Woodrow Wilson's close adviser Colonel House had told Eleanor's friend Caroline Drayton Phillips one year before, "but I am looking forward to having my throat cut and my pocket picked if Hoover is re-elected."[18]

The country, "dying by inches,"[19] hung on. As FDR set course for the New Deal, more than a million unemployed men searched for work. Some 250,000 "boxcar boys and girls" rode the rails seeking a better life;[20] while homeless women—140,000 wandering the nation's roads; 22,000 in New York alone—focused Eleanor's earliest attempts to put domestic violence, malnutrition, starvation, dysentery, and pellagra onto the national agenda. Higher up the social ladder, a new kind of discrimination was forcing women out of work: if their husbands had jobs, married women were let go from schools, government, and privately run businesses. Since FDR had taken office, the total number of working women had risen, but a popular backlash now ordered all women to stand down: "Don't steal a job from a man."

In the blur of the administration's first hundred days, Eleanor worked to be sure that at least one emergency relief camp would welcome women by summer. In May, when her former fellow social worker, Harry Hopkins , took charge of the Federal Emergency Relief Administration (FERA), he promised that "needy women shall be given equal consideration with needy men,"[21] and in June provided federal funds to open Camp Tera, high above the western bank of the Hudson, midway between New York and Hyde Park.

FERA had been established to channel $500 million in federal money to state and local programs in construction and public works. One of the problems, Hopkins admitted, was how to create full-time, full-paid jobs for women. So far, most federal projects were either heavy construction work, not considered sustainable for women, or little more than poorly managed "leaf-raking" cleanup teams in local parks.[22] "We have found almost a complete lack of imagination on work projects for women," said the relief administrator. "On the fingers of one hand I can count the states where there has been imagination."[23] FERA needed specific, practical project ideas; and since Hopkins, true to the New Deal's "do it quickly" ethos, was ready to put at least a quarter of a million and as many as 400,000 women to work in less than thirty days, there was no time to waste—or to plan.

Drawing upon her network of female experts, Eleanor assembled them on short notice, and on November 22, 1933, opened a White House Conference on the Emergency Needs of Women, convening more than fifty leaders from across the nation, including Secretary of Labor Frances Perkins, Congresswomen Isabella Greenway (AZ), Caroline O'Day (NY), Edith Nourse Rogers (MA), Mary T. Norton (NJ), Mabel Broadman of the American Red Cross, Ethel Swope of the American Nurses Association, and Mrs. August Belmont (National Women's Party).

The conference, beginning at noon in the East Room, delivered ideas: canning centers, sewing rooms, housekeeping agencies, emergency nursery schools, musical programs, and historical research.[24] Rose Schneiderman, the formidable head of the Women's Trade Union League, proposed farm camps for unemployed women in the sewing trades. The result was that for the next five years of women's work relief, ER served as White House go-between, as adviser and sponsor and critic, but above all as friend to jobless women.

On November 22, 1933, an editorial cartoon appeared in the *Dallas Morning News*, depicting a "forgotten woman" walking the roadway alone to a far distant town that holds the promise of jobs. But only one of many motorists—a car marked "Mrs. F. R."—cares enough to pull over, stop the car, and give the woman a lift.[25]

* * *

Anna had fallen in love with the *Chicago Tribune* reporter John Boettiger. Deeply attached after ten months in secret, Anna finally confronted Curtis Dall with her true feelings. Curt, doggedly pursuing his course, most recently as chairman of the executive committee of the Distillers and Brewers Corporation of America, had not noticed any change in his wife, and so was struggling just "to realize anything like this could really happen."[26] Eleanor, though previously no great fan of Curt, felt sorry for her conventional son-in-law. Franklin tried to smooth the waters from the second-floor sitting room in the White House, bringing in Curt for a reassuring word, scheduling a session with Anna, and candidly (for once) letting Eleanor know he was "not very keen" on John Boettiger, but promised to be fair.[27]

Eleanor had jumped right in with Boettiger, rallying to the notion that this handsome, idealistic man had the temperament to restore the life that Anna was missing. He was over six feet tall, with broad shoulders, as Eleanor noted approvingly.[28] She encouraged the secret romance and shielded it throughout its first twenty-four days aboard Franklin's coast-to-coast whistle-stop campaign round-tripper, through election and inauguration, and even at Thanksgiving, telling white lies to FDR to cover up that Anna was with her true love.

At their first Christmas in the White House, which shaped up as the nicest day John had ever had, he blushingly took Eleanor aside and whispered in her ear what a day he was having. *He would never*—the words as warm as his breath—*forget it.*[29]

Eleanor was no less candid about her competitiveness, making no bones about how John had become "one of the people for whom I have a very special and personal feeling" and teasing Anna with that affection: "She and John always maintained they had known each other before John knew me," Anna later said.[30] Eleanor also teamed up with Anna, taking on the room-for-two editorship of *Babies Just Babies*, a slick new moneymaker for the publishing empire of health fanatic and physical culture pioneer Bernarr Macfadden.[31] Boettiger, hoping to avoid embarrassment now that he was on the inside, had resigned from the *Chicago Tribune* and gone to work in Washington for Will H. Hays, lobbyist for the Motion Picture Producers and Distributors of America.

Romantically, the three always lunched at the Algonquin as "their" spot.[32] John, nothing if not an embellisher, went Earl Miller one better with his Eleanor nickname, "Lovely Lady," or "L. L.," and she relished the exalted place he had made for her in his letters: "So you see how happy I am," confided John to Eleanor, the day after their first Christmas, "but really the greatest of my joys is in sharing your love, and in giving you my love without stint."

As for Anna, Boettiger felt possessed of the anxious conviction that they were capable of a kind of mind-meld: "Our subconscious thoughts speed back and forth, and while we don't have the black and white facts of what goes on, we FEEL each other's thoughts." Naturally, Eleanor "above all people understands US."[33]

By July 1934, Anna was divorced from Dall,[34] and in November 1934, John was divorced from his wife, Alice, with whom he had helped raise a daughter, now thirteen, and a son, now ten, both from Alice Behrendt's previous marriage.[35] When Anna and John revealed their intention to be married in 1935, Steve Early, the former newsman, took action. Learning from a number of Boettiger's newspaper colleagues that they knew him to be emotionally unstable, indeed mentally disordered, the President's press secretary brought these findings to Anna. Also, a small pistol.[36] "You may need this sometime," said Early as he presented the weapon. "I'd like you to have it."[37]

ALL UNBEKNOWNST TO ELEANOR, so she could still innocently exclaim to Hick, "Oh, if people didn't have to be unhappy!"[38] This, just as, late one afternoon in May 1933, Louis Howe asked her if she would drive him out along the Potomac to a spot in Virginia where a second army of "forgotten man" veterans, demanding early payment of a one-time bonus promised by Congress in 1924, had pitched camp.

Although General Douglas MacArthur would now mobilize almost three hundred thousand recruits for the ambitious start of the Civilian Conservation Corps, many had poisonous memories of July 28, the previous year, when MacArthur had massed his regular army infantry on the Ellipse and sent more than two hundred mounted cavalrymen (led by Major George Patton), five tanks, and a battalion of gas-masked foot soldiers (led by Major Dwight D. Eisenhower), to roll over twenty thousand jobless World War I veterans.

A pelting spring downpour had just drenched this second bonus army's encampment at Fort Hunt. Eleanor had already shaken more than a thousand hands that day, assorted White House visitors—teachers, classes of recent graduates, nurses—spent two hours signing her name to pictures and cards; had lunch for the President and guests, and tea for an ex-senator, his family, and guests; and in between, given a speech at the DC Federation of Women's Clubs. Aunt Tissie and her lovely daughter Mara had stayed overnight. And now Louis had parked the big Lincoln convertible roadster that he was either too weak or too tired to handle, got into the backseat, laid himself down in the honeysuckle-scented air, and announced that he was going to sleep. He directed Eleanor to go and talk to the men—get their gripes. Whatever she did, be sure to say the President had sent her.

Eleanor waded through ankle-deep mud to where men stood in chow lines. She asked how they were getting along, and as word of her arrival spread, the veterans in the mess tent gave three cheers for Mrs. Roosevelt.

"I'm afraid," she said, "I am unable to talk to you about that one thing you want most to know about."

Forbidden politics, she assured them that they would get fair consideration from her husband. Then, on the spur of the moment, she reminisced about how her own antiwar beliefs had been formed while visiting the trenches in 1919. The men answered with songs from the Front, and Eleanor asked, "How many of you know 'A Long, Long Trail'?" Everyone did, and she sang it with them, but felt guilty because, as she reported to Hick, "they were nice to me,"[39] and the most she could do in return was parrot the President's offer of dollar-a-day positions in the MacArthur-led Civilian Conservation Corps.

For the time being, it was enough. One two-time Bonus veteran would let the country know: "Hoover sent the army, Roosevelt sent his wife."[40]

ANNA'S SEPARATION THAT SPRING EMBITTERED those who believed the President's family should set higher standards for the whole country.[41] Elliott, meantime, had all but abandoned Betty Donner, and their four-month-old son, William.

Betty, a favorite of Eleanor's, felt she must now return the family pearls that Eleanor had presented her before marrying Elliott. From the dog collar Sara had given Eleanor to wear as a bride, ER had been re-stringing the pearls for each of her daughters-in-law. Starting with Betsey Cushing, James's bride, in 1932, she had been cutting into the collar, row by row. To Betsey she gave a perfectly matched string of the pearls. Then one to Betty Donner, which Eleanor now insisted she keep; and if Elliott now divorced Betty and married this Ruth Chandler Googins of Fort Worth, Eleanor would present the bride with another strand from the family collar. In 1937, Ethel du Pont would receive her string on marrying Franklin Jr., and the following year, the remaining pearls would be strung for Anne Clark of Boston.[42] Thus would Eleanor link all her daughters-in-law back to Mama. So much for subverting tradition.

As the Hearst press licked its chops for "the first White House divorce," Franklin's mother took her cue to remark to a family friend asking about Anna and Elliott: "But of course they have had no bringing up."[43]

Sara, meanwhile, had extended Curtis Dall's legroom in the family. She retained him as one of the three trustees of her finances,[44] putting herself in position to enjoy the advantage with Anna and Curt's children, Sisty and Buzzie—the great-grandchildren to whom she read aloud the Sunday comics page, letting them snuggle into her as if she were the satin puff covering her bed. On the subject of divorce, Sara threw the challenge not to Franklin but to Eleanor: "Why don't you tell [them] that that is wrong?"[45]

"Because I am not quite sure that in certain circumstances it *is* wrong," she replied.

Eleanor later argued with herself that she and Franklin had had the advantage of being protected by the older generation's very strict dos and don'ts about marriage. As parents, by contrast, they had most often withheld judgment, hoping to embolden their grown children to think for themselves, to decide for themselves. Neither Eleanor nor Franklin had spoken directly with their children about sex, and certainly not about sex in marriage, leaving Eleanor to wonder, as the younger generation's marriages began to fracture, if their laissez-faire approach had been compatible with the daily efforts of loving another.

Elliott had met Betty at the summer parties at Northeast Harbor. When the girl he was in love with suddenly accepted someone else's marriage proposal, Elliott just as impetuously put the question to Betty. Her father, a steel magnate, hoped to be made ambassador to the Court of St. James's; her mother had social ambitions. Betty was fragile, destabilized by her brother's suicide in a sanitarium. She herself would suffer deep depressions in the years ahead,[46] beginning with a postpartum siege after the birth of William.[47]

All too soon, however, Elliott had given up on Betty and quit his job in a New York advertising firm. Four days after the Inauguration, he left wife and baby at the White House for Eleanor to look after, piled into a Plymouth roadster, and headed west with a friend, not planning to stop until they had crossed the Mississippi and found jobs. Filled with dread for Betty and especially for four-month-old William, now called Bill, Eleanor watched Elliott drive out the White House gate with $15 in his pocket.

"I wish I felt surer of Elliott," she wrote.[48]

Her guilt overflowed. "I guess I was a pretty unwise teacher as to how to go about living," she owned in her nightly accounting to Hick. "Too late to do anything now, however, and I'm rather disgusted with myself. I feel soiled."[49]

Filling her pockets with the same stones a few days later: "My zest in life is rather gone for the time being. If anyone looks at me, I want to weep. I get like this sometimes. It makes me feel like a dead weight and my mind goes round and round like a squirrel in a cage. I want to run, and I can't, and I despise myself. I can't get away from thinking about myself. Even though I know I'm a fool, I can't help it! You are my rock, and I shall be so glad to see you Saturday night. I need you very much as a refuge just now."[50]

Someone had to go and talk cold sense to Elliott. But the first lady of the land did not just drop her obligations to escort home her wayward son who had now met some girl at a rodeo and livestock show. Eleanor got Franklin to telephone Elliott in Texas. The call backfired.

"I don't know whether you were the one who had Father call me up in Fort Worth," Elliott wrote, storming her in response. "It was a very unfortunate mistake—You know that for years I have had little or no respect for his advice. I have felt that he had no right to offer it to any of his children. Someday he may realize what you have done for him in at least holding the family so that it has presented a united front. . . . He is hard and cold and his affection is superficial—He has sacrificed everything and everybody to his consuming ambition."[51]

Elliott had graduated from Groton, then failed the entrance exam to Harvard. He had long had a vested interest in denying his father's formidability. He saw FDR as a great illusionist, and it was his mother who made the illusion stick. If his mother had dropped out—there went the Roosevelt illusion. In a certain light, there was something frightening about FDR, and he had seen it:

"I have no feeling anymore about Father. I perform my 'lip service' and keep up the 'family tradition' with the public because I feel that that is the duty I owe the public of this country. Further than that to hell with it. How he felt justified in advising me concerning my matrimonial difficulties is beyond me. Why, he even came through with some statement about it being a wise thing for me to compromise in marriage. When I stated that two people who really loved each other had no need for compromise he blew up and stated that my marriage was similar to his running of the government, that compromise was necessary in this world to succeed in anything. Such a pompous, asinine comparison proves to me the smallness of the man's mind. . . .

"Betty is a brick," continued Elliott, "and will make someone a fine wife someday. I admire her, and hold no rancor or ill feeling. We weren't suited, and I took the step. If the publicity harms any of the family I am sorry from the bottom of my heart, but Father's popularity is such just now, that it will not hurt him especially in my humble opinion."[52]

Eleanor drew a line before leaving Washington, announcing that she would accept no public or political engagements. It was a personal trip to visit her son in Los Angeles. She gave no hint of urgency.

But there was no mistaking yet another break between the generations, as for the first time all across the rooftops of America, people could look up and see the wife of the President of the United States speeding over their town. Asked what she would do while making her historic hop, she answered, "I shall read. I shall write. I shall knit."[53]

The day before going aloft, she welcomed one of the passing generation to the White House—an eighty-year-old Kentucky widow who had written to her. Pattie Willis South, former owner of the Crab Orchard Springs Hotel in Nicholasville, Kentucky, had wished all her life to eat one meal in the White House—"if it be only bread and milk," she told Mrs. Roosevelt, who greeted her on the front steps of the North Portico and welcomed her in as her lunch guest.[54]

TO THE SOUTHWEST, SHE FLEW. Across the Mississippi, the great green flatlands giving way to drought-stunted desert. Homing beacons flashed from refueling airfields as they chased the twilight to Arizona.

As the "flying wife of a flying president," she was invaluable to an untried aviation industry now serving fewer than three thousand customers annually in a nation of 130 million. Eleanor's calming, friendly interest in air travel, combined with the familiar Roosevelt smile flashing from the open hatch of a Ford Tri-Motor, "should be worth millions in advertising!"[55] enthused one industry monthly.

In March, Eleanor had returned to Washington from New York by air, the "First White House Lady to Travel in Plane."[56] For the honor, she withstood the cabin's stink of uncirculated disinfectant without herself being nauseated. Eleanor's whole history of seasickness had no future chapter in the air; and in April she put this to the test, departing the White House immediately following dinner for a night flight over the city in a Curtiss Condor with Amelia Earhart. Takeoff and landing for the "first lady of the land and first lady of the air"[57] were handled by Eastern Air Transport Company pilots, but Amelia took over, and high over the Potomac briefly turned Eleanor loose at the controls.[58]

Flight had been a bruising business. But "it does mark an epoch, doesn't it," Eleanor was said to have mused, "when a girl in evening dress and slippers can pilot a plane at night."[59]

She would have liked to become a pilot herself. She went so far as to pass a physical test for the license. But, as she explained at year's end to the female master of the new medium, "My husband convinced me that it was a waste of time to learn when I could not afford to buy a plane."[60]

Now America opened beneath her, and on she went. Will Rogers, the Oklahoma cowboy whose folk virtues and droll political wit had made him the nation's highest paid star of film, radio, stage, and syndication, marveled: "Out at every stop, standing for photographers by the hour, being interviewed, talking over the radio, no sleep. And yet they say she never shows one sign of weariness or annoyance of any kind. No maid, no secretary—just the First Lady of the Land on a paid ticket on a regular passenger flight."[61]

"The country has made the thrilling discovery that Anna Eleanor Roosevelt is an individual," trumpeted Amon G. Carter, the Texas newspaper publisher who accompanied ER on one leg of the journey,[62] returning home to declare Eleanor's "new qualities of excellence" a "revelation to the Nation" and the President's wife "the most satisfying and heart-lifting figure in the Roosevelt Era."[63]

The corrugated-aluminum-skinned "Tin Goose," America's first dependable commercial airliner, landed at Tucson and taxied in on one engine, juddering along the runway on three fat rubber wheels. Uniformed ground officials at the open hatch door doffed their hats as Mrs. Roosevelt stepped out into the sunlight, one vast continent-spanning smile.

With twenty-four hours in Tucson, she stayed in one of Isabella Greenway's pink adobe guesthouses. Doubly deafened from engine noise and her bad ear, she took Elliott and his dark, attractive, nimble-witted new fiancée, Ruth Chandler Googins, to her sitting room after dinner and asked them to tell her everything. She had made the journey, she said, to try to understand their point of view. Elliott recognized his mother's "stern determination to live . . . without condemning," and would later appreciate how difficult it had been for ER "to be tolerant of the conduct of [his] generation."[64]

Her worry for Betty and William aside, she felt worse for Elliott's older brother than for Elliott himself. Jimmy would more than once cross paths with male elders who cut him dead until the elder discovered that he was not Elliott, "the boy who disgraced the family." The offended made clear they didn't blame Elliott for getting a divorce;

his offense was "having been brought up to certain gentlemanly standards, only to show very poor taste."[65]

"I'm afraid that expresses my own feeling," confessed Eleanor to Hick, "but I hate to have people feel that way. Perhaps they don't in the West. How I am going to hate having Anna criticized in the same way!"[66]

When Elliott and Ruth left her at midnight, Eleanor was certain Ruth cared about her son and had more stability and sense than he had. She sized up her next daughter-in-law as the belle of a small town "with affairs back of her," and guessed that Ruth would run the finances and manage Elliott. "She might even become a habit and have the wisdom to weather the storms."[67]

Until Elliott was divorced, the couple agreed not to meet or communicate directly. Eleanor stated all the reasons, even after grant of decree, for continued delay, but asked nothing. "I cannot live Elliott's life for him," she would be overheard saying on returning home.[68] For the time being, they had gone over issues about finances, business, and drinking. Elliott had promised he would not run up bills on the family name then run away, in the Uncle Vallie manner.

She left him $250, said she trusted him to do what was right and wise, and returned to the airfield, flying on to Burbank[69]—a rash of lights glowing in black countryside.

Then they were coming down into a vast glittering light-bed, gliding in over clear yellow lines of light that stretched all the way to the Pacific, dropping now over the green-dotted runway, and down with a bump. Then taxiing, tilted, tail down into a ten-thousand-thronged circle of sodium light, cameras, faces.

Next evening, at one of her stops in Los Angeles, friends of her brother took Eleanor aside "to talk over the tragedy of Hall's life." After, she explained to Hick, "I am impotent to do a thing, for he is another of life's undisciplined souls."[70]

BACK IN WASHINGTON, THE FIRST lady resumed the radical activity of having a lover all to herself and of being loved for herself alone. With a hectic day, of course, "and no plans possible on account of Congress," she cleaned up mail, had a press conference, "and now I'm going to bed pretty weary after talking to everyone and trying to seem interested, when I was not much."[71]

Each day closer to their next reunion was a day marked off on her White House calendar. And if, at some official event, something personal and stirring broke through the formality, such as Arturo Toscanini conducting the New York Philharmonic Symphony at Constitution Hall, it made her, she confessed to Hick, "want you even more than I do as a rule."[72]

Alone in New York, Hick was toughing out a "stormier time"; crying herself to sleep, doubting her judgment.[73] Separation, for Hick, fomented unending anxiety: "At times life becomes just one long dreary ache for you."[74] Her old bitterness spilled out: "Why is it that as soon as I get to care about or depend upon anyone or anything that it must always be taken away from me?"[75] Apologies ran right over grievances: "Oh, I'm bad, my dear, but I love you so."[76] She had so little to go on: "I've been trying today to bring back your face. Most clearly I remember your eyes, with a kind of teasing smile in them, and the feeling of that soft spot just northeast of the corner of your mouth against my lips."[77]

Eleanor felt herself fortunate to have fallen in love with a woman both serious and playful. Lorena's first lover, Ella Morse, had called her "Hickey Doodles," but Eleanor stuck proudly to "Hick"—a workhorse nickname, a woman of the real world, a no-nonsense investigator. Hick resolved their initial crisis by sacrificing her newspaper career at its peak to report instead on the conditions of Americans suffering the effects of the Great Depression. To join the New Deal, she signed on as chief field investigator for Harry Hopkins, joining a team of writer-investigators assigned by the Federal Emergency Relief Administration (FERA) to deliver detailed on-the-ground reports from the nation's poorest corners.

From the road, Hick took over where Louis Howe and Earl Miller had left off, helping Eleanor to forge the new identity of the first lady, locally informed nationwide. Hick would be the invisible force behind Eleanor's press conferences for women, overcoming her initial resistance by citing FDR's recognition of how a single issue such as Prohibition's repeal could be better controlled from the women's side.

She helped Eleanor become her kind of president's wife, sharp, tough, skeptical of received wisdom. Eleanor was now the author of three books; serious articles in high-circulation magazines; and a monthly column, "Passing Thoughts of Mrs. Roosevelt," for *Women's National Democratic News*. Then, in 1935, Hick's reporter's intuition and critical ear catalyzed Eleanor's break into big-time syndication.

That August, Will Rogers, world-famous entertainer and avatar of the common man, died in an airplane crash at the age of fifty-five. With more than forty million readers, Rogers's daily and weekly columns for the McNaught Syndicate had demonstrated the power of a single voice to live in readers' hearts and influence public opinion. V. V. McNitt, manager of McNaught, briefly hoped he had found a replacement when no less a star monologist than Alice Roosevelt Longworth debuted in seventy-five newspapers with "What Alice Thinks." Not to be outdone, rival United Feature Syndicate approached Eleanor to go up against Cousin Alice, trying her out for a month of practice columns.

"The writing is easy so far," Eleanor told Hick in December 1935, "they just want one incident out of the day & so far I've had no trouble."[78]

Hick had been struck by the consistency of Eleanor's nightly letters from the White House, the middle paragraphs never failing to bridge the more personal notes of opening and closing with a purposeful accounting of her day. She was sure that if Eleanor wrote her five hundred words a day as if to a friend with whom she enjoyed keeping up to date, newspaper readers couldn't help but feel that she was their friend. Even from the nation's most exalted household, she could naturally write a letter to them, confident that these were matters of mutual interest.

Cousin Alice, meanwhile, had faltered almost at once. Her opinions, brittle and narrow, made little sense outside Washington. She knew politicians' weaknesses and with passionate zest exposed them— Harding wasn't a bad man, he was just a slob; Coolidge had been weaned on a pickle; Hoover was less exciting than the Hoover vacuum cleaner: of course, *it* was electric. Even her husband, House Speaker Nicholas Longworth: he would rather be tight than be President.

This was the kind of hyperinsider acumen the press loved. But for the same reason that Alice had no trouble speaking her mind, but felt incapable of making a speech, "What Alice Thinks" revealed that if she were not defying, dominating, zinging, or bullying—above all, getting away with it again—she soured. Alice, as she aged, wanted to keep people where they were; herself especially. By 1935, she ever more sharply needed to contrast herself with the "*oh, so good*"[79] Franklin D. Roosevelts, though in fact she never attacked Eleanor on serious political grounds and seemed uninterested in shaping opinion against her cousin's causes. She damned Eleanor for goodness only when the damning allowed her once again to be bad. The mischief of her Eleanor impersonation, a full-on performance, done for friends, never failed to bring her back as Princess Alice—Alice, the irrepressible—Foxy Alice the First Daughter who forced her father to throw up his hands and snap, "I can either run the country or I can attend to Alice, but I cannot possibly do both." It remained the one truly successful role of her lifetime.

Eleanor wanted to expand her relationship with people, especially people with whom the president's wife would not ordinarily be in touch, but when United Feature Syndicate launched "My Day" in fifty newspapers on December 31, 1935, it was not expected to last beyond the administration.[80] Tommy Thompson also had her doubts, since they were already doing "two days work in one,"[81] but both women loved solving the day's problem together, whether aboard a lurching destroyer, in the backseat of a roadster, or holed up in a distant hotel, Eleanor at her knitting, Tommy at her typewriter, their dictation routine fixed at exactly an hour, so their copy was a model for saying what Eleanor wanted to say. There were no grace notes or obvious influences. "My Day" was not writing for effect, or to be remembered; it was to get something done. Six days a week, she and Tommy turned out a hundred lines in two columns, earning $1,000 a month.

All this airing of her thoughts, first to Tommy, then to as many as four million readers,[82] led to an increase in her performance. Wherever she went the rest of her day, Eleanor was suddenly that much more real—Pygmalion's statue transformed. Hick and Tommy hadn't just sculpted a more beautiful woman from the statuesque Eleanor of 1932, they had empowered a fluid first lady.

For that was Eleanor's first great innovation: self-guided movement. Never before had a president's wife set out on her own to assess
social and economic conditions in distant states or overseas to American "possessions" like Puerto Rico. Never before had a first lady visited
a foreign country unaccompanied by the President, as Eleanor did the
first summer, driving Hick through eastern Quebec.

Most Americans still expected the President's wife to stay home
and take care of her husband and the house—not to go up in airplanes,
or down a bobsled run at the Lake Placid Winter Olympics, or inside a prison or Masonic Temple. No one minded a cheerleader for the
health of children's eyes and teeth.[83] Gradually, fewer minded that the
wife of the President was driving alone by night through villages and
four-corners hamlets and stopping for gas on the outskirts of town.
She made it plausible—and safer—for a woman to travel alone, to
drive her own car.[84]

"Did anyone ever tell you," said one filling-station attendant peering in her window, "that you look just like Mrs. Roosevelt?"

"Oh, lots of times," she replied, smiling, and drove off.[85]

Reporters loved to clock her mileage: 38,000 miles in 1933, 42,000
in 1934, 35,000 in 1935,[86] 42,000 in 1936, 43,000 in 1937.[87] Keeping close
to her fellow citizens, staying on the jump, disappearing into the land.
Louis Howe would produce a map before the start of her trips and
point out places on her itinerary: "Now in this town you will find the
sentiment is thus and so, or in that county you will find that the people
think a certain way on a certain subject."[88] She went on instinct, confident that Louis Howe's grassroots information network was all the
advance she needed.

Cousin Alice, playing identity politics, claimed that New Deal Eleanor was "doing on a tremendous scale what the lady of the manor did
in other days when she looked after the tenantry." At the same time,
she praised Eleanor for being "here, there, and everywhere, gracious,
friendly, interested, always with something to say," and, aware that
times were changing, suggested that any woman now becoming the
President's wife "ought to screen well and have a good radio voice."[89]

Mrs. Longworth was right. Radio, the most intimate of the new
mass media, furnished homes and imaginations with a personal Mrs.

Roosevelt. It also magnified the flaws in Eleanor's broadcasting voice, which still ranged several octaves, shrilling so high, or clipping along so quickly, that some listeners shuddered to hear it.[90]

"Now, I must remember," she would tell herself in the car on the way to a radio program: "*Slow and low*."[91]

In newsreel images, she had no trouble establishing stamina, so long a battleground in the "usefulness" of women in professions. Week after week, the tall silver screens of neighborhood movie houses catalogued each threshold moment of her tireless travels: boarding and disembarking from gangways, cabins, coaches, and cabs, waving with a genteel hand, eyes lost to her big toothy smile.

From her first refusal of Lou Hoover's White House limousine, she walked everywhere. "She goes her way, very serenely," observed one reporter making a close account of her early days as first lady. "She performs her public duties with an unstudied graciousness, even, I venture, interest. But she lives her own life. She is no slave to her position. She couldn't be enslaved by anything."[92]

To maintain independence insofar as possible, she declined Secret Service protection at every possible turn. They insisted she carry a pistol whenever she drove her car by herself. Eleanor applied for and received a pistol permit in 1933,[93] and on her birthday that October, Earl gave her a .22 Smith & Wesson Outdoorsman revolver. She looked entirely natural handling a gun. "I ought to be," she later remarked, "for my father could hold his own even in the West in those early days when my uncle Theodore Roosevelt had a ranch in the Dakotas."[94] Earl taught her how to load the pistol, hold it, lift it, and sight down her arm, so that when she squeezed the trigger she could, with practice, place the shot. Mainly, she left it locked and unloaded in the glove box of her car.

On newspaper editorial pages, the most snickered-at buck teeth in America were replacing Uncle Ted's tombstone teeth as the staple of political caricaturists. Even on Washington's rising National Cathedral, stonecutters would later crown one parapet with a Mrs. Roosevelt gargoyle, the creature's overbite so grotesquely extended that its slab-like teeth projected rainwater away from the roof.

*   *   *

RETURNING TO THE NATION'S CAPITAL from Tocquevillian travels, she reported the country to FDR, sometimes in person-by-person detail, often on subjects upon which no modern president had been briefed.

"Franklin, we must do something about those sharecroppers," she announced after one trip to Alabama and Georgia. "Wallace and Tugwell brag about their farm program, but I tell you, Franklin, the beneficiaries are *not* the men who do the work but only those who own the property."[95]

Back from a tour of New England states and Pennsylvania, she had investigated wages, which differed from industry to industry, region to region. "They are awful, Franklin. Simply awful. Why, people can't live on them and raise a family as they should."[96]

After a trip to North Carolina, she said, "Franklin, it's really true that the public schools for the Negroes are inferior to those for the whites—inferior in libraries, inferior in faculties, inferior in facilities."[97]

When he was wrong on matters affecting particular communities, she told him. "He had few around him except Eleanor who told him he was wrong," said Justice William O. Douglas. "She was his antenna, and I noticed he usually followed her advice."[98] Whether the issue was economic, racial, or religious, "FDR had complete faith in her judgment and ability to observe," said Jim Farley.[99] The President took pride in announcing to the cabinet,[100] "My Missus says they have typhoid fever in that district," or "My Missus says the people are leaving the dust bowl in droves because they haven't any chance there," or "My Missus says that people are working for wages way below the minimum set by NRA in the town she visited last week."[101]

Lou Hoover had become a familiar sight on downtown streets and at the wheel of her own car. But never before had a president's wife so regularly informed her husband and key figures of his administration. She gathered data and intelligence on behalf of African Americans, Southern tenant farmers, subsistence homesteaders, even the all-but-forgotten people of the territories. She traveled so much that a *Washington Post* headline announced, FIRST LADY SPENDS NIGHT IN WHITE HOUSE. That June 1934, a schoolteacher in Madison, Wisconsin, asked her class whose footprints Robinson Crusoe had found on the desert island? The answer came tentatively: "Mrs. Roosevelt's?"[102]

What made Eleanor different from her predecessors was not just the reach or breadth of her travels but the dignity and respect she conferred upon immigrant communities cut off and marginalized by the Immigrant Act of 1924. West Virginia coal miners brought into the mainstream for the first time by the New Deal and the Democratic Party had never seen a woman who proxied to the government for so many millions of workers. Why, this president's helpmate might even find her way into one of those brand-new institutions formed by the New Deal, the industrial union. Or, as one miner said to another in the prophetic cartoon of June 1934: "For gosh sakes, here comes Mrs. Roosevelt."

The joke was as much a dividend of the *New Yorker* magazine's well-established war between the sexes, as a play on a political crisis so extreme as to plunge even a first lady into a male-only underground. Since she had not yet gone down into a mine as of June 1934, the *New Yorker* seemed almost to have caught her in the act of projecting herself into places she didn't belong.

"In strange and subtle ways, it was indicated to me that I should feel somewhat ashamed of that cartoon," wrote Eleanor, "and there certainly was something the matter with a woman who wanted to see so much and to know so much!"[103]

FROM THE SPOT IN THE hollow where she was talking with a group of miners, she could see a little girl struggling to carry something. She had been watching her come along the road and was not surprised when the child stopped to look at her.

"Why, you are Mrs. Roosevelt. My mama say she is happy if you come to her house."

She walked upslope with the girl, picking their way through stagnant, sulfur-tinted puddles, and when they got to the house, which was black with coal dust on the outside, a Polish woman was sitting inside at the table. The kitchen was clean.

"Mama," said the girl, "this is Mrs. Roosevelt."

The woman jumped up and threw her arms around her, kissing

her on both cheeks. Her husband was clearing more than $1 a week after deductions for rent and the company store, and when they came back to the kitchen, she proved as much by proudly asking Mrs. Roosevelt if she would eat with them.

She had to say no—she had just had breakfast.

But the miner's wife wouldn't let her leave without eating something, so they sat down and had a piece of bread together.

Six months later, when she came back, she knew the moment she crossed the threshold for another visit that something had happened. It was dark. The floor was spread with rags on which multiple people had spent the night. After a few minutes the old man came out from one of the back rooms and said, "Mrs. Roosevelt, you have come. I have wanted to ask you something for a long time."

And he told his story. The mine had closed down; strikes, anti-union violence, coal companies going bankrupt—by now, some two hundred thousand miners were permanently out of work. When the WPA began road, sewer, and water projects, the old man was given work for a time, and then suddenly let go: he was not a U.S. citizen, so he could not work for the WPA.

"Mrs. Roosevelt, I vote. I vote often," he begged. "Why I no citizen? They tell me I no citizen."

His children had been born in America; they were citizens, but he was not. For more than thirty-five years he had worked in the mines and played his part in transforming the hilly farm country of the 1890s into the explosive, unequaled coal producer of World War I, reaching almost 4.4 million tons annually by 1921.[104]

This was his country. He had aided the national war machine and furthered the wealth of the United States and had the right, Mrs. Roosevelt believed, to receive in return for his labor at least a minimum of security and happiness. Yet there was nobody in the community to help him find out what his rights were, or what he should do. Just as it had been nobody's business, when he first arrived in West Virginia, to see to it that he learned English and took civics classes at night to prepare for citizenship.

When Eleanor looked at the stove and saw the scraps being prepared for dinner, she understood that the woman would not now be able to ask Mrs. Roosevelt to dinner. These, she realized, were the moments when morale broke down.

It brought home to her "how important it was that in every community there should be someone to whom people could turn, who were in doubt as to what were their rights under the law, when they couldn't understand what was happening to them. I wish we had one in every place throughout the country," she told the Chicago Civil Liberties Committee,[105] "one group of people who really care when things go wrong and do something when there is an infringement of the individual's rights."

But since there was no one like that, she made it her business.

ON AUGUST 18, 1933, AT the request of FDR and Clarence Pickett of the American Friends Service Committee, which for two years had been carrying on charitable work among West Virginia miners, she set off with Hick to make a fact-finding visit to the West Virginia coal fields, slipping into a Morgantown hotel at midnight. "So secret was her arrival that only one man on the police force, Chief Smith, knew about it."[106]

At Scotts Run, one of the most concentrated mine districts in the country, twenty-five mines were packed along a four-mile front. Eleven of them were still operating, most under union agreements, but were only able to give their men two or three days of work each week, at between $3 and $4 a day. Eleanor left her car and hiked the rough wooded hills to make a house-to-house canvass, taking note of conditions in the towns of the union and non-union mines and questioning miners as to the advantages of working under union agreement. One miner's wife clasped her hand and said, weeping, "I know your husband is doing all he can but please, please tell him to hurry. Things have been so terrible."[107]

All along the red mine-slag roads from Scotts Run, she found women trekking the ten miles to Morgantown to work as domestics or to beg on doorsteps for old clothing to keep their children warm. Men sold mountain berries and sassafras roots door to door. The previous winter, families had lived on boiled wheat. Red Cross flour had warded off actual starvation. It was, she thought, the worst poverty she had ever seen.[108]

She presented her findings to Franklin and to General Hugh S. Johnson, National Recovery Administration (NRA) executive head. "It was believed," reported the *Pittsburgh Press*, "that she had communicated with him as to the actual conditions of operations and among the miners."[109]

She and Louis Howe decided that moving some four hundred out-of-work miners from Scotts Run to new tracts of land would alleviate their problems and put a check on any possibility of a Communist revolution. Within a week of her visit, FDR, Louis, and she had agreed that the federal government should secretly buy a farm property once owned by a colonial landowner—the Arthur Farm, spreading over more than a thousand acres, fifteen miles up the mountain from Morgantown in Preston County. By October 12, 1933, Harold Ickes, secretary of the interior, had announced that the farm had been bought as a homestead demonstration project for unemployed miners, sawmill hands, and farmers. Each family would receive a house costing about $2,000, sitting on two to four acres for farming, and the community's central institution of self-governance would take the New England town meeting as its model. A Val-Kill-like factory would provide supplementary income.

Within another month, surveyors had shot the lines of the Arthur farm, and Louis Howe ordered the first fifty prefabricated Hodgson houses to be shipped to Arthurdale. Franklin declared that he wanted five-acre lots to allow people to have a cow. The work of building the community had begun, as had ER's partisanship for building experimental communities within the system.

SEVENTEEN

By July 15, 1934, homesteaders had moved into forty-three of the first fifty homes at Arthurdale. Another 150 were out for contractors' bids. The average unit cost of the first houses and outbuildings had come to $4,880—above the initial $2,000 estimate, but well below the $10,000 reported in the *Saturday Evening Post*.

The Hodgson prefab houses had turned up one problem after another. Poorly insulated and lightly built for icy Preston County winters, their ten- by forty-foot dimensions failed to line up with the cinder-block foundations the miners had already dug. Pre-set brick fireplaces missed the cottage walls by as much as eight feet.

Eleanor had been the troubleshooter since mid-November 1933, when she and Eric Gugler, a New York architect, arrived to correct the problems with the houses. Eleanor asked Nancy Cook to plan the household interiors and worked with Gugler to extend the walls to include the fireplaces, which of course drove up costs, as did each home's separate well, electric pump, and septic system, not to mention a special grease trap, indoor plumbing, and the supplementary furnaces when the original woodburning fireplaces proved inadequate to the harsh winters. Few rural communities knew such conveniences, Eleanor was paying for some out of her own pocket, and the final cost for each house reached as much as $8,550.

Beyond the individual farms, more than 440 acres were worked collectively, plowed, planted, and harvested for Arthurdale's produce co-op. Adding to the social and farming experiment, the progressive educator Elsie Ripley Clapp,[1] an associate of John Dewey, was hired to plan the community's school. Clapp believed it could serve a central role in restoring community life and promoting the ideal of self-realization as an expression of civic responsibility. But the students would have to wait for books, desks, and chairs, even for school buildings, none of which were ready when school opened that fall of 1934.[2]

Arthurdaleans, meanwhile, would not have any African American neighbors. Despite Eleanor's arguments, West Virginia's entrenched prejudice and Jim Crow laws, heightened by Depression violence, prevailed. Arthurdale, like Warm Springs, remained whites-only. Back in Washington, congressional Republicans wasted no time heaping contempt on the project as "Eleanor's baby."

Trouble came when Republican leaders in Congress examined the costs of subsistence homesteads. Reedsville was pronounced "a dismal failure."[3] The *Morgantown Post* added up what the government had spent in nine years. Exclusive of loans it came to $14,000 for each of the 165 homestead units of three acres each. Inclusive of $677,754 in government loans, each of the 165 homestead units came to $18,100. *Time* magazine tutted, "The average American farm is of 174 acres valued at $5,518, according to the 1940 census."[4]

Critics had a field day. Senator Arthur H. Vandenberg, a vocal member of the Republican minority, had championed the New Deal's public works programs, welcoming the Civilian Conservation Corps's reforestation teams—two and a half million men—to his state's depleted timberland and abused farmlands. With Arthurdale, the Michigan senator attacked furniture building as a big-government threat to nearly seventy employers in his hometown, Grand Rapids, long touted as "The Furniture Capital of the World."[5] Vandenberg further framed Arthurdale's cottage industries as a form of collectivism distinct from the New Deal. "Social responsibility and socialism are entirely different things," sniffed the senator from "Furniture City."[6]

Forced to account for unprecedented activities, Eleanor gave Congress an itemized account of $36,000 in radio earnings—almost half as much as the presidential salary of $75,000—donated to the Friends Service Committee between May 14 and December 31, 1934. One half year's salary she had given to Elsie Clapp, teacher: $3,500 for incorporation of Reedsville Cooperative; $111 for handicraft; $6,000 for Logan County West Virginia; health work, $6,000; scholarships for girls at Kentucky and West Virginia educational camps, $500; general work of Friends Committee, $3,000. Total $19,111.60. The 60 cents was for tax on checks.[7]

*   *   *

SHE WAS FIFTY, THE YEAR that she would cycle into menopause.[8] Grandmother Hall, Cousin Susie, and generations of Ludlow women had lived by the idea that as soon as they were no longer vessels for children, their feminine value diminished. A woman of Eleanor's age and class was supposed to throw a veil of mystery over "the change of life" and resume homemaking and local charity work without a thought to exploring her own interests. "If she really cares about her home," countered Eleanor, "that caring will take her far and wide."[9]

Her birthday morning had produced October's brightest blue weather, but she stayed indoors with an article she was readying for publication with Hick's help. For the first time since they had fallen in love, Eleanor felt secure enough to expose her careless punctuation, slapdash facts, and ingrained tendency to do anything but take herself seriously. "I will try to do better work as long as it matters to you!" she assured Hick, admitting that on the one hand, "I care so little at times," while on the other, "I realize if one does anything, one should do it as well as one can."[10]

A similar ambivalence had found voice that week in Washington, when Minna Miller Edison, wife of the famous inventor, attended a conference on relief administration. In the course of making a plea to her fellow delegates to remember the needs of the elderly, Mrs. Edison had started women talking when she asserted that the wife of a great man could lead a more useful life "ministering to him and making life flow more smoothly for his work than if she had sought a career of her own."[11]

Eleanor had stopped trying to do it all for Franklin fifteen years before. "Stamina," explained one friend, "enabled her to continue to serve him, her household, and at the same time to lead a life of her own."[12] Now she exceeded her husband in popularity among women. Two voters in every three approved of the way Mrs. Roosevelt had "occupied the place of First Lady since her husband's election."[13]

She now took very quiet satisfaction from demonstrating to official Washington that she could do the impossible better than any of them. Starting on the first day of the New Year, she was responsible for hosting—with the President, of course—five official receptions each social season: the diplomatic (abstemious and weight-watching); judicial (light-drinking, nibbling); congressional (big business around the punch bowls); departmental (long, slow lines); and the army and navy (chowing down).[14]

Eleanor welcomed groups no one had ever imagined being received in the President's house. She had conducted a surprise visit to see for herself conditions described as "barbaric" at the National Training School for Girls, a reform school north of Georgetown, where a huge brick building along Little Falls Road looked like a haunted house.

Inside, she found poorly lighted hallways, chilled and rat-infested rooms. The "students," mostly African American, ages fourteen to eighteen, were kept like prisoners in spite of ample grounds and beautiful views. "Never have I seen an institution called a school which had so little claim to that name," she said.[15] Other first ladies had briefly visited, but Eleanor was the first to make the girls *her* guests.

At four o'clock in the afternoon of May 16, 1934, nearly fifty young women arrived at the White House. They wore silk print dresses, arranged by Eleanor with WPA funding; and each shook hands with the first lady, who led the girls on a tour, served lemonade, ice cream, and cake, then sent them on to Mount Vernon. The event was hailed in the black community's newspapers as a powerful symbol of the progressive sentiments of the Roosevelt administration, while *Time* attacked the girls as thrice-convicted "diseased prostitutes," opening the way for editorials to suggest that President Roosevelt was not a victim of infantile paralysis but of *syphilitic* paralysis and was therefore mentally disturbed.[16]

Conservatives and Southerners, for whom all this was "unthinkable," wanted the girls severely chastised, since "Mrs. Roosevelt's appeal, as released through the press, made no mention of the need of converting these girls to a sense of shame and a resolve to mend their ways, so that they would need no institutional incarceration for venereal disease treatments. Rather, her entire appeal centered on the need for better material comforts and institutional advantages for the girls."[17]

All too briefly, she did reform the reformatory. With Eleanor's intervention, cottages were built, gas replaced coal stoves, the girl's private rooms were heated and given electric lights, bars were removed from windows. Classrooms were set up for housekeeping, business, and "beauty culture" training.

When she next visited the school, "The change is so remarkable I would not have known it to be the same place."[18] Sadly, the improvements instigated by ER had cost $100,000 and became a pretext to slash spending. Conditions would deteriorate and the school would ultimately succumb to a combination of congressional interference, mismanagement, and complaints from neighbors.

LOUIS HOWE HAD JUST BEGUN planning FDR's 1936 re-election campaign, when he fell ill that spring of 1934. Unable to resign from his official job as the president's secretary or his unofficial role as adorer in chief, "Colonel" Howe became the latest sideshow ghost of the Lincoln Bedroom[19]— "the least seen and least understood secretary to the President that Washington has ever known."[20]

Louis's pitiful helplessness about anything except power and politics drove Eleanor mad as she supervised his nursing. Franklin, true to form, stayed clear until she shifted Louis to the naval hospital in Bethesda,[21] and then it was safe to have himself wheeled into the patient's room, calling out a mock Act-One-Scene-One greeting: "Ludwig! You've just got to get back to the White House and get in the show!"[22]

Even more than the banishment of Lucy Mercer, or Missy's ascension to the position of unofficially accredited junior wife, Louis's long fade made it painfully clear that Eleanor would not be called in to fill the breach. By September 1934, she was striking out again on her own—serving as stump speaker and finance chairman on behalf of the congressional candidacy of her longtime friend and Val-Kill partner, the veteran social welfare leader Caroline O'Day.

O'Day, sixty-five, never before in elective politics, had a geographically and demographically challenging race for New York's representative-at-large. Before leaving the White House and boarding the *Midnight*, Eleanor called a press conference to make clear that she was leaving her official duties as first lady completely behind. As "plain Anna Eleanor Roosevelt," she then delivered five out-and-out political speeches in Buffalo, Rochester, Syracuse, Albany, and Manhattan[23] to carry her appeal for O'Day the length of the state she had mastered for Franklin.[24]

Nothing she had done in her first tradition-shattering term had so angered Republican women. "She can no more cease being First Lady than she can cease breathing," declared one GOP matron, who quickly begged reporters for anonymity.[25] Insisting that it was "obviously impossible"[26] for Mrs. Roosevelt to break the rules this way, they flooded the press with the kind of venom that allowed the wise and knowing of Washington to predict that his wife's work would ruin the President. With so much covering fire, O'Day's Republican opponent in the three-woman race, Natalie Couch, a New York lawyer, could shade the first lady's move "questionable,"[27] but the strength of Roosevelt support statewide helped O'Day win the election as a strong pacifist and champion of immigration reform.

ELEANOR ALWAYS WANTED THINGS TO happen faster.

As FDR went on skirting anti-lynching legislation, and the Democratic Party ducked any issue that confronted African American disenfranchisement, segregation, or economic inequality, it became Eleanor's duty to respond to questions of discrimination in New Deal relief programs.

Eleanor had not recognized the depth of institutional racism in the New Deal until, in 1934, she urged the Subsistence Homesteads Division to admit African Americans to Arthurdale. Her intervention failed, as had her every appeal to FDR to take charge of the country's terror crisis and champion anti-lynching legislation. Joining the DC chapter of the National Association for the Advancement of Colored People (NAACP), she had made common cause with the national executive secretary, Walter White, the one determined crusader for racial justice in New Deal Washington. She now invited White, Clarence Pickett of the American Friends Service, and the presidents of six African American universities to the White House to discuss the Arthurdale situation.[28]

At eight in the evening on Friday, January 26, 1934, Eleanor opened the problem of race in the homesteads to the group. One of the educators, Robert Russa Moton, a Virginia-born son of former slaves and the president of the Tuskegee Institute, had been the keynote speaker at the dedication of the Lincoln Memorial, where he had been kept apart from the other speakers and made to sit alone. Five years later, Moton, a lifelong advocate of accommodation in race relations, made a deal with Herbert Hoover, Coolidge's secretary of commerce, then receiving highest praise for his handling of the Great Mississippi Flood of 1927, which had unhoused more than half a million blacks. Tens of thousands suffered various forms of re-enslavement at gunpoint in Hoover's tent cities. When Moton was chosen to head the Red Cross's investigation of the atrocities in the refugee camps, Hoover promised Moton that he and his people would play a significant and historic role in a Hoover administration if Moton would conceal the scandal. Moton, good to his word, hushed up the horrific findings. Hoover took the traditional Republican black vote in 1928, but as soon as the Great Engineer had claimed his prize, he refused even to acknowledge Moton. Blacks turned on Hoover in 1932, and because Franklin had been the political beneficiary, Dr. Moton was now able to vent his frustration directly with the President, who came in from another meeting in the Oval Office and joined what had become a historic and unprecedented tutorial on racial discrimination.

The meeting broke up after midnight, having "set before all of us," wrote Clarence Pickett, "a new standard for understanding and cooperation in the field of race."[29]

The group had by no means solved the homestead issue, but FDR might have been pleased with Eleanor's handling of it. After all, as Pickett recorded, "no one could have entered more fully into the nature of the problem or have expressed more intelligently a desire to find a way to help than did Mrs. Roosevelt."[30]

The President had the independence of the Philippine Islands on his mind that week, as well as the carping of congressmen unsatisfied on matters of patronage, and a budget director refusing to allow FDR's relief program more than $500 million for public works.[31] FDR and his aides tolerated Eleanor's intercessions, even when "my Missus" next pressured National Recovery administrator Donald Richberg to investigate the race-based wage differentials implemented by Southern industries and then asked navy secretary Claude Swanson why blacks were confined to mess hall assignments.[32]

Eleanor's agenda accommodated segregation while championing equal opportunity. It was fine for the President's wife to urge *states* to address the inequities in "separate but equal" public school funding— the farther from Washington and Dixie the better. FDR's Virginia-born press secretary scarcely noticed the African American press extolling Eleanor's sincerity and strength of character. By January 1934, she was receiving thousands of letters describing racial violence, poverty, and homelessness intensified by racial discrimination, all petitioning the President's wife for assistance. Eleanor frequently forwarded the hardest cases to Harry Hopkins and his assistant Aubrey Williams, to whom she had already sent a list of suggestions of ways to include African Americans more fully within Federal Emergency Relief Administration (FERA) programs.

Franklin was fine with that. White supremacists still dominated every committee of the House and Senate, but he was not concerned with them—some were good New Dealers, and he was candidly dependent on all of them as the firmest constituency of the Democratic Party.

Walter White had meanwhile been bombarding the President with telegrams, letters, and interview requests, all of which had been turned down. "I realize perfectly that he has an obsession on the lynching question," wrote Eleanor to press secretary Stephen Early, "and I do not doubt that he had been a great nuisance . . . both now and in previous administrations. However, reading the papers in the last few weeks, does not give you the feeling that the filibuster on the lynching bill did any good to the situation and if I were colored, I think I should have about the same obsession that he has."[33]

She then tried to defend White's recent protests, which had gotten him arrested in the Senate restaurant. "It is worse with Walter White because he is almost white," she explained to Early, a white Southerner who had helped stall lynching legislation for fear of losing the Dixiecrat wing of Roosevelt's congressional coalition. "If you ever talked to him, and knew him, I think you would feel as I do. He really is a very fine person with the sorrows of his people close to his heart."[34]

The filibuster began on April 26. On May 7, Eleanor got FDR to agree to meet White to hear his side of the argument, in the hope that the President would intervene and break the filibuster. They met on the South Porch of the White House on a Sunday afternoon—White, Eleanor, the President's mother—and, finally, Franklin, who returned late from sailing the Potomac, and so expended most of their time with boating yarns. When Eleanor finally got in a word about the filibuster, the first thing the President did, defensively, was to explain to White his own predicament, giving one reason after another why he couldn't support the bill. When White countered with detailed arguments, FDR lost patience: "*Somebody's been priming you,*" he growled. "*Was it my wife?*"

Franklin pouted. "Well," he said, turning to his mother, "at least I know you'll be on my side," at which the older woman gave a crisp toss of her head, saying she agreed with Mr. White.

"If I come out for the anti-lynching bill now," resumed the President, "they will block every bill I ask Congress to pass to keep America from collapsing. I just can't take the risk."[35]

In October, Claude Neal, an African American farm worker in Florida, was arrested for the rape and murder of Lola Cannady, a white woman. He was abducted from the jail where he was being held, and the leaders of the lynch mob notified the press that justice would be served at the Cannady farm. Hundreds of people turned out to watch the lynching. Neal was taken to a secret location, brutally tortured, castrated, and killed. His mutilated body was hung outside the county courthouse. Sheriffs buried Neal, but a large crowd gathered demanding to see the body, and a riot broke out. Nearly two hundred African Americans were attacked and injured during the riot. The National Guard was eventually brought in to control the mob. The lynching and subsequent riot attracted massive news coverage, and many Americans were outraged and disgusted.

In December, on a national radio hookup, FDR was finally moved to put the power of the presidency against lynching—but only because, when two victims were dragged out of the San Jose jail, they were white. Twice more, in 1937 and 1940, when the House passed anti-lynching laws, FDR offered no presidential sponsorship, remaining silent as the bills moved to certain death in the Senate. Eleanor, alone in the gallery, stern and silent, sat in protest through hours of filibuster by the Southern wing of their party.

Thurgood Marshall, then a young lawyer arguing civil rights cases across the South for the NAACP, would later hold the President responsible for "most of the grim difficulty in changing racial patterns in America. . . . You cannot name one thing he ever did to solve the antilynching problem. He was threatened by Senator Tom Connally of Texas about what the Southerners would do if Roosevelt backed an antilynching bill. So Roosevelt never said one word in favor of it. He was not the great friend of Negroes that some people think. Now Eleanor Roosevelt did a lot; but her husband didn't do a damn thing."[36]

Marshall would come uncomfortably close to this side of Roosevelt in 1941 when Attorney General Francis Biddle brought him onto a phone call with the President to discuss the NAACP's involvement in a race case in Virginia. At Biddle's instruction, Marshall picked up an extension phone, only to hear President Roosevelt thunder: "I warned you not to call me again about any of Eleanor's niggers. Call me one more time and *you* are fired."[37]

"The president only said 'nigger' once," recalled Marshall, "but once was enough for me."[38]

AS THE PRESIDENT TORPEDOED THE London Economic Conference of 1933 and remained indifferent to France's fascism-friendly occupation of the Ruhr, Eleanor began reconciling herself to the compromises by which every democratic leader disappoints people. Still, Franklin's martini-stirring hubris exasperated her. Inside his sitting room on the second floor with Betsey, James's pretty wife, on one side, and Missy, laughing at his latest jest on the other, Franklin was about twenty; down in the Oval Office, arm-twisting one of the filibustering Southern Democrats in the Senate, just a few years older, to judge from the crafty thrill he took from the slow manipulation of his Deep South political bosses.[39]

Mordecai Johnson, president of Howard University, was the first African American leader to denounce the American system of racial terror by drawing the then historically incomplete comparison to Nazi persecution. Under the headline U.S. WORSE THAN HITLER, Johnson asserted in February: "Not one thing done to the Jews in Germany by Hitler can be compared to the treatment which colored people receive in the United States."[40]

Nazi propaganda called America the "Land of the Lynchers,"[41] citing government-sanctioned terror and violence against African Americans, entire Native tribes, Asians, Filipinos, and other non-"Nordic" groups as "proof" that "Nordic" America was as intolerant of its "racial inferiors" as "Aryan" Germany.

In tropical June heat, Thomas Mann, author of *Buddenbrooks*, *The Magic Mountain*, and *Death in Venice*, came for dinner at the White House, noting in his diary for June 29, 1935: "Black boys and butlers." He sketched the President "in a wheelchair," "rather ordinary food," "a lad in a white dinner jacket," and FDR's "energy and self-satisfaction." After a "too-long movie," Roosevelt took the German Nobel Laureate to see the marine watercolors in his study. When Eleanor gave the signal to disband, she lightly trilled, "*Auf Wiedersehen*."[42] Perhaps she was saying good night to the Germany of Goethe and Faust and Wagner and Lohengrin and Franklin's boyhood summer idylls: the Germany, indeed, of Thomas Mann.

The Fatherland's embrace of authoritarian rule had cleared the way for Berlin to menace all of Europe. Hitler had crushed parliamentary democracy, then swallowed the Saar, industrial key to a war-making Reich. German business and German youth alike had hailed rearmament and universal military service. Fourteen years of the Versailles Treaty's messy humiliations had prepared the most conservative German to fear chaos, demonize Communism, and embrace the crisp ruthlessness of a Teutonic savior promising redemption of past losses through his glittering vision of the thousand-year Reich to come.

Mussolini, a strongman ringmaster in the Nazi tent, had mobilized Italy, massed troops on the Ethiopian border, and on October 2, 1935, invaded Emperor Haile Selassie's Abyssinia, throwing Europe into war panic. Clearly, East Africa—colonial cradle of the First World War—was just one aim of these conquests. Where would the dictators strike next? What was behind their brutal aggression?

With such authorities as the Third Reich's foremost anti-Semite,

Julius Streicher, announcing, "One thing is certain—when this is all over, the Italian people will realize Jews are at the bottom of it,"[43] Europe's freedom-loving peoples turned to the mighty pillars of the International Court of Justice at The Hague in Holland. Better-known as the World Court, this was the nine-member tribunal that the League of Nations had set up in 1920 so that countries could bring war-provoking disputes to arbitration before armies mobilized. Each time Eleanor had urged Franklin as president to champion American membership in the World Court, he had eluded her with the grin with which he disguised his real plans.

Announcing that he would lead a drive to win Senate ratification of a treaty for American participation on the World Court, FDR became the fourth president to urge U.S. accession, which, though mainly symbolic, nonetheless gave the United States an opportunity, as FDR put it to the Congress, "once more to throw its weight into the scale in favor of peace."[44]

And so, on Wednesday, January 16, 1935, as the Senate opened debate on the protocol for American adherence to the court, the President sent up from the White House a message asking for ratification, giving FDR a chance to emphasize for his old League of Nations foes, "The sovereignty of the United States will be in no way diminished or jeopardized by such action."[45]

The Senate proved sharply divided on whether the time had come for America to step up to fulfill its international obligations. A vote was scheduled for Tuesday, January 29. With battle lines so closely drawn, the White House was willing to apply direct pressure, sending for every Democratic and Independent senator to appear at the President's desk so that the chief executive could arm-twist each man personally.

"Banking everything on the Court getting through this week,"[46] Esther Lape wired Eleanor on January 15, 1935. But, that Friday, instead of calling for a vote, Senate Majority Leader Joseph T. Robinson agreed to adjourn for the weekend.

Nearly two-thirds of the nation now owned radio sets, which funneled into people's living rooms the scheduled rants of populist demagogues like Senator Huey Long, sputtering from Baton Rouge about "the lyin' newspapers" and blaming Morgan, Rockefeller, Mellon, and Baruch for taking "eighty-five percent of the vittles off the table." Father Charles Coughlin, a Roman Catholic parish priest in Detroit, had an even greater knack for tapping into resentment against Wall Street. Rallying his flock at Madison Square Garden in May 1935, the "radio priest" launched a furious attack on the press and was hailed by twenty thousand wildly cheering believers as "President Coughlin"—"Our Next President." To reporters in the press gallery, the crowd shook its fists and chanted, "Throw them out! Throw them out!"[47]

That Sunday evening on NBC Red Network, Coughlin warned Congress not to "tie the Gordian knot of the World Court around the neck of the American people."[48] He kept deliberately vague the threat of a "secretive government" created by his usual targets: plutocrats, international bankers, and Communists (code for rich Jews), who would use "their own international court" to "dominate the armies and navies of the world."[49] Denouncing as unfair the decisions that Americans would receive from the World Court, Coughlin urged his listeners to send their senators protest telegrams immediately—"tomorrow may be too late."

Eleanor's speech, a fifteen-minute call to enlightened internationalism, marked the first time she had broadcast "as a citizen and as a woman" into the live hot center of a national debate.

Speaking in her clipped, unruffled voice to "ladies and gentlemen and friends," she came right to the point: "We do not want to get into any other war. Nor," she firmly reminded, "did we want to get into the World War." But modern times and modern technology were shrinking the world, its nations growing ever more interdependent, and the United States in its new role as the world's creditor nation had an obligation to maintain its own higher standard of living. On the familiar commonsense appeal that George Washington had recommended against entangling alliances, she recalled that by partnering with France, Washington had helped America win its war for independence.

She spoke directly to her listeners, and out of the sincere surprise of having heard that "you people who are listening to me tonight by your radios have no interest in the World Court." She said how sad that made her feel, "for I love my country and all its people, and I have a particular interest in the women and the young people. I feel when you have thought of this question in the light of today and of the future you will feel a deep interest in it too."

She outlined the need for nations contending in an age of mass slaughter to develop a body of international law that would enable them to settle disputes in court instead. She grappled with the fear of an international tribunal's jurisdiction, explaining that the U.S. would join under an optional clause that allowed no question concerning U.S. interests to be submitted to the Court without the people's consent. And she remembered the World War herself. She recalled how she had "looked on the acres of cemeteries in other countries where lie our boys and the boys of other nations." She paused and said plainly: "These dead are the result of war."

"We cannot escape being a part of the world," she concluded, making a special plea to the women of her generation who remembered the horror of war, and to Democrats, and to all women of America." She begged of them all, "if you want to see the influence of your country on the side of peace," to let their senators in Congress know.[50]

Overnight, telegraph offices did torrential business. Western Union added extra lines into Washington, operators working double shifts to funnel protest and outrage to Capitol Hill.

On Monday morning, with the Senate still recessed, tens of thousands of telegrams—eventually numbering some forty thousand—flooded Senate offices,[51] for and against ratification.[52] A Hearst newspapers crusade brought in another wave of "Stay out of it!" telegrams, followed by a mostly isolationist tide of lobbying for and against the measure, as well as various amendments that delayed the vote. In the Senate cloakroom, opponents of the resolution grumbled about the influence of Sunday night's radio speeches, bitterly criticizing Mrs. Roosevelt for "mixing up in this fight."[53]

On Wednesday came the vote, passage requiring a two-thirds majority. The measure needed no Republican allies to win: sixty-nine Democrats numbered ten more than two-thirds. But when the votes were taken, the Senate rejected the Court by a margin of seven votes—to volatile applause in the packed galleries. Counting up the thirty-six senators, including twenty Democrats, who had placed themselves on record against the principle of law before war, FDR grumbled about the apologizing they would be doing if they ever got to heaven, since undoubtedly God hated war as much as Franklin thought God did.[54] Senator Borah, a longtime "bitter-ender" opponent declared it the most important decision since the World War, and Interior Secretary Ickes conceded "a major defeat of the Administration."[55]

Eleanor remarked, "It is discouraging that Mr. Hearst and Father Coughlin can influence the country in the way that they do, but that is that."

FDR HAD MADE AN UNSAVORY deal with William Randolph Hearst to win the nomination in 1932—the price, Franklin had said, that reformers had to pay if they wished to wield power.[56] Hearst then quarreled violently with the New Deal, turned his newspapers viciously on FDR, and now in the spring of 1936 was looking for the Republican to run against a weakened President Roosevelt.[57]

The Supreme Court had handed the administration one constitutional defeat after another, often by one-vote margins, on New Deal pillars such as the Railroad Retirement Act of 1934, portions of the National Industrial Recovery Act, the Agricultural Adjustment Act, and the Bituminous Coal Conservation Act of 1935. The big question for the 1936 election was whether or not the voters would go along with the conservative Hughes court and reject Roosevelt as the creator of constitutional shortcuts. A straw vote on the New Deal taken by the *Literary Digest*, which had been correctly predicting presidential elections for a quarter of a century, claimed that a majority of those polled stood against the administration's programs." Eleanor responded at once with a flurry of speaking engagements. After one, she came in to find that the White House switchboard had an urgent call for her from Bethesda. Louis Howe had died in his sleep at the naval hospital. It was April 18, 1936.

The real Louis had been gone for months.[58] Random sightings had continued on the second-floor corridor, and in his final days, Eleanor had begun to miss the things she had most resented about Louis. "Even when I complained," she eulogized to Hick, "I loved him."[59] Howe had offered to make Eleanor president, insisting in 1933 that as soon as

Franklin was through, he could get her elected. She just as firmly held that she had no interest. She understood that for Louis the whole show was his "power to create personages, more than [his interest] in a person, tho' I think he probably cared more for me as a person, as much as he cared for anyone, and more than anyone else ever has!" She added her usual tartness: "Sheer need on his part I imagine!"[60]

The last thing Eleanor had been able to fix for him was a telephone cord long enough to reach inside his oxygen tent.

Funeral rites in the East Room were followed by a twenty-one-hour burial journey, starting from Union Station on a cold rainy midnight. Just before the train left Washington, Eleanor visited the baggage car where the body lay and inspected the arrangements she'd been making—her final chance to be *his* Louis Howe.

She gave her approval to the undertaker from Gawler's, signed the papers, then handed along jurisdiction of the dark bronze casket to the Fall River, Massachusetts, funeral director. The innumerable little arrangements struck her as pitiful, and it depressed her to think of how often she had done this very thing.

"I hope I get put in the ground in the least expensive of coffins," she told Hick. "It all seems so unimportant when 'you' no longer exist."[61]

In the stillness of the President's car, she rode with Franklin through the chill Northeast spring night, reflecting on her discovery, as she had packed up Louis's things, that by the end of his life, he had framed and placed in his room more photographs of her—Eleanor—than comparable images of Franklin or Grace.[62]

Crowds had gathered to greet the train in Providence and Taunton and at the Fall River station. Some twenty-five thousand more onlookers silently lined the route to Oak Grove Cemetery, where they laid Louis McHenry Howe to rest under leaden skies and a budding mulberry tree.

Homeward, musing again on mortality, Eleanor decided that she would probably outlive Franklin. "I rather hope that I will be the one to go, before I go through this again."[63]

As FDR LAUNCHED HIS REELECTION campaign with a tour of Arkansas, Texas, and Indiana, Eleanor suggested that Eddie Peabody, the "King of the Banjo," and a regular at White House musicales, become a traveling member of the President's entourage. It was the sort of thing Louis Howe had given her an instinct about; she envisioned Peabody playing Southern banjo airs as a prelude to presidential platform appearances. But Franklin bristled at the notion of his campaign becoming a kind of old-time medicine show, ripe for Republican recasting as "Dr. Roosevelt selling New Deal tonic."[64]

Eleanor pressed her plan, Franklin decided against it, and someone leaked the story to the conservative press, which, on the one hand, portrayed ER as the administration's "No. 1 brain truster," and on the other, as a target of contempt for FDR's "official family," who upon hearing that the banjo act had been nixed heaved a collective sigh of relief that for once the President had put his foot down. Steve Early allowed himself to be anonymously sourced accenting the misogyny typical of the time: "Sometimes I think the Constitution should require that the President be a bachelor."[65]

Whether it was Franklin's male secretariat gathered around his bed and breakfast tray in the morning, or his mother joining whoever made up the family circle for cocktails in the West Sitting Hall, Eleanor always found herself back where she started. "I realize more and more," she confided to Hick, "that FDR's a great man, and he is nice, but as a person, I'm a stranger, and I don't want to be anything else!"[66]

One evening, Eleanor forthrightly told Sara that it would *not* break her heart if Franklin was not reelected. She then left to see about dinner, whereupon Granny turned to her eldest grandson, raised her voice for effect, and caroled to James: "Do you think Mother will do anything to defeat Father? Is that why she stays in politics, just to hurt his chances of reelection?"

"Now I ask you," rumbled Eleanor to Hick, offstage, in a letter that night, "after all these years?"[67]

When it came to direct threats to global peace—in 1935, Fascist atrocities in Ethiopia; in 1936, the Nationalist rebellion in Spain, as well as armed conflicts in the Far East and in South America—Eleanor remained unwilling to temper her own reactions to her husband's politically minded inaction. Now that countries around the world were once again "armed camps," she contended in *Why Wars Must Cease,* joining ten of the nation's foremost women to declare 1914–1918 a war of extermination,[68] "many peace time industries have taken on potential value" since "there has never been a war," argued Eleanor, "where private profit has not been made out of the dead bodies of men. If our country is to survive, our people must turn to love, not as a doctrine, but as a way of living."[69]

The Democratic-controlled 74th and 75th Congresses had harnessed the American heartland's most embittered beliefs about World War I to enact isolationist legislation eliminating the United States from Europe's wars. Each time the President signed another of the Neutrality Acts—1935 (banning munitions exports to belligerents, restricting American travel), 1936 (prohibiting loans to belligerents), 1937 (extending limitations to civil wars), 1939 (outlawing goods and passengers on U.S. ships to belligerent ports)—FDR applauded keeping the country out of what one senator called "the poisonous European mess."[70]

In private, Franklin abominated neutrality's constraint on executive power, while in public having to answer every European warning of authoritarian encroachment with renewed pledges that the United States would remain "at peace with all the world."[71] When the Spanish Civil War broke out in July 1936 and the administration maintained strict neutrality, Eleanor's frustration mounted. "Franklin knew quite well he wanted the democratic government to be successful, but he also knew he could not get Congress to go along with him. To justify his action, or lack of action, he explained to me, when I complained, that the League of Nations had asked us to remain neutral. But he was simply trying to salve his own conscience. It was one of the many times I felt akin to a hair shirt."[72]

Before the Republicans nominated Kansas governor Alf Landon that same summer, Jim Farley overconfidently claimed that the election was "in the bag."[73] Then the seamlessness of the Republican convention in Cleveland and the popularity of the Landon-Knox ticket in the West and the East challenged the Roosevelt strategists.

With a fight shaping up, anxiety grew about what effect Eleanor's "flamboyant career" would have on FDR's chances in what political reporter Joseph Mitchell—later the highly regarded *New Yorker* magazine staff writer—was now calling "the most momentous political contest in the history of the nation."[74]

Of the 60 million female citizens counted in the US Census of 1930, 36 million were of voting age,[75] many just now coming out from under Old Country assumptions. Eleanor did for women what the union movement did for labor. She pervaded. She was not just a consort or a surrogate but, more alarming to Republicans, a "woman of unequaled influence," reported *Time*, "superlative in her own personal right."[76] The less she responded to her critics and enemies, the more she mobilized friends, making them angry enough to go and vote—and not necessarily the way their husbands had told them to.

Her wholehearted participation at interracial gatherings strengthened her position as an admired ally of African Americans, while her often-unexpected visits to black colleges, CCC camps, churches, and WPA housing projects drew praise from the leading voices of the black press: "In our day there has never been a mistress of the White House so energetic, so brave, and so fired with enthusiasm of service to the common people,"[77] all of which served to consolidate the President's strength among black voters and panicking their Southern oppressors.

The idea that, "Negroes almost worshipped Eleanor Roosevelt," as one historian told it,[78] inflamed Southern politicians like Georgia governor Eugene Talmadge, who seized the opportunity to attack FDR through his wife, publishing photos several times through the campaign of Eleanor accompanied by African American ROTC students at Howard, captioned "Nigger Lover Eleanor."[79]

Every day that Franklin's second-term candidacy was a topic of conversation, Eleanor was accused of neglecting her husband and their children, wasting taxpayers' money, dying of cancer, fostering Communists, having a nervous breakdown, looking for another man to marry.[80] She was hated above all for the truth of her criticisms and the effectiveness of soothing the sharpest of them with a smile. Finding that government subcontractors had designed an entire $8 million Resettlement Administration project with laundry tubs and coal bins in the same room, she tutted, "A woman would have seen that right away, because she's the one who does the washing." Beaming, she added: "It simply proves what I always say, that a man should have a woman at his elbow when he's planning these things."[81]

Rumors circulated in many Southern states about "Eleanor Clubs" supposedly forming to activate African American female servants in white homes. The *Richmond Times-Dispatch* reported that domestic workers were preparing to evacuate kitchens all across the state.[82] In one version of the rumor, Eleanor herself had organized the members of the "clubs," each of whom had sworn to resign on the spot if their white employers spoke against the President or his wife. Many variations went the rounds: the Eleanor of Southern imagination had urged blacks to "show more backbone," and therefore domestics had allegedly planned to engage in a sidewalk terror campaign to slam older whites into the gutter.[83] The club slogan was believed to be "All Negroes out of the kitchen by Christmas,"[84] its members expecting to be received at the front door and addressed as "Miss" or "Mrs." Reports from Texas, Mississippi, North Carolina, Alabama, and Florida prompted FDR to order investigations by the Secret Service and FBI, and though no evidence was ever found to support such claims, they were repeated so frequently that "Eleanor Clubs" became treated as fact.[85]

When the Republicans milked her many speeches and articles and broadcasts for opposition research, it was hard for them to choose just which disaster would provide the best dirt to fling at FDR—her career as a major radio performer; product sponsor; political writer; or, as Joseph Mitchell judged her, "the equal of Columbia University president Dr. Nicholas Murray Butler as a newspaper oracle."[86] In public remarks following the controversial trial and conviction of German immigrant Bruno Hauptmann for the kidnapping and death of the infant son of aviator Charles Lindbergh, she questioned whether or not circumstantial evidence was safe ground for a conviction resulting in a death sentence, provoking uncertainty about the president's views on capital punishment.[87] Her speeches to college students sounded subversive: "Study history realistically"—"Do not always believe your country is right"—"You'll love your country just as much, the same as you love your parents, although you might not always believe them to be right."[88]

On June 27, when FDR accepted his party's nomination under the open sky at Franklin Field, Philadelphia, he reached out on the platform to shake hands with the poet Edwin Markham,[89] his crutches jammed, and he toppled forward. With the Secret Service working to get him back into position, he comforted Markham, who wept at what had happened, and then went out before a hundred thousand Democrats, took his place at the microphones, and gave a dazzling speech.

"This generation of Americans has a rendezvous with destiny," began FDR, his voice "never more confident, never more commanding, never warmer in its sympathy," according to veteran White House reporter Raymond Clapper. Roosevelt played on his audience with all his skills, asserting that theirs was "a war for the survival of democracy," and he was enlisted for the duration.[90]

In November FDR defeated Alf Landon, carrying forty-six out of forty-eight states, winning re-election by the largest margin in history.

LAND, WATER, AND ELECTRIC POWER were now in better supply for many. Factories began to run again at full blast. Banks performed soundly. Keels were laid down for two new 35,000-ton battleships— the first built in two decades and the first to be armored against air attack.[91]

But hard times were not over. The Supreme Court had dismantled New Deal farm policy by striking down the Agricultural Adjustment Act of 1933; further rulings showed that the justices appeared ready to invalidate Social Security, the Tennessee Valley Authority (TVA), and the National Labor Relations Act, calling into question the very foundations of the President's power to mobilize the country.

"I see one-third of a nation ill-housed, ill-clad, ill-nourished," declared FDR in his 1937 inaugural address, reminding the Court and the United States: "The test of our progress is not whether we add more to the abundance of those who have much; it is whether we provide enough for those who have too little."[92]

Emboldened by the scale of his electoral victory, the President then opened the second administration by announcing a one-third cut in relief spending and his promise to balance the budget.

This vexed Eleanor. She knew that recovery, according to Keynesian economics, was a function of government planning and spending. From the austerity of balancing her own checkbook she could also see what was going to happen to the staff and programs at an emergency agency like the Works Progress Administration (WPA) when, for instance, the $1.5 billion earmarked for relief in 1938 was slashed to $750 million, or as little as $500 million. "I do hope," she told her readers, "that we make our economies without making people suffer who are in need of help. There are wise and unwise economies as every housewife knows and figuratively speaking the women of the country should be watching their husbands to see that the national budget is balanced wisely."[93]

But on "this budget balancing business," she learned as she went and left others to try pinning her down as an aristocratic Democrat, a democratic aristocrat, a Red, a reactionary, a renegade Republican, a New Deal humanitarian—and those were the nicer things people called her.[94]

As her second term began, people understood her as an urban liberal Democrat, foe of slumlords, friend of labor, advocate for the voiceless. She was trusted by the Washington African American community. Yet events of these next two years would force ER to challenge her beliefs about herself, the world she was leading, and the world she had been raised in.

On April 24, 1937, the *Afro-American*, "a distinguished newspaper—foremost for forty-three years" in Baltimore, with distribution in Washington, Philadelphia, and New York, ran an editorial "with painful regret," calling attention to "a serious error made by [ER] in the May *Ladies Home Journal* when twice she uses the epithet 'd——y' to designate members of the colored race. The error becomes grievously regrettable when one realizes the broad grasp that the First Lady has on public sentiment and the interpretation that is bound to come from her lack of thoughtful respect for a group that had come to believe in her with such profound admiration."[95]

The appalled editors of the African American press had every reason to take Mrs. Roosevelt at face value as not just a friend—but *the* friend—of racial equality. "What are we to believe?" George B. Murphy, Jr., managing editor, asked ER directly. "The fact that this reference appeared in print means that it was read several times after it was written, during revision and proof-reading. In light of your wide and democratic contacts throughout the country, it hardly seems possible to us that you were unaware of the fact that no self-respecting colored American tolerates, or condones the terms 'nigger' or 'darky' through which the white South makes known its contempt for colored citizens—regardless of their cultural status.

"Will you please, then, tell us, as one of the small group of white Americans whom we have so far been able to respect and admire, how this harm came about, and what you, as an American gentlewoman, would care to do to correct it."[96]

Tommy, not Eleanor, offered an explanation:

"In writing her autobiography, Mrs. Roosevelt was quoting her great aunt, who was born in Georgia and lived on a plantation, and who had great affection for the colored people. When Mrs. Roosevelt referred to them as darkies it was a term of affection. She was talking of that period and quoting her great aunt, and the word had been used in all the early stories as they were told to Mrs. Roosevelt."[97]

But, in point of fact, ER used no quotation marks. She simply deployed the old language in her own autobiography, specifically to identify one person, namely, her father's coachman.

Of course no one mentioned the odd fact that the Roosevelts had been the original translators of their own Roswell plantation tales. Well before Joel Chandler Harris popularized the Br'er Rabbit stories in the *Uncle Remus* books, Eleanor's great-uncle, Robert Barnhill Roosevelt, had collaborated with her grandmother, taking the tales by dictation from Mittie, then confecting them for *Harper's* magazine, where, as Theodore sternly noted, "they fell flat."[98]

Tommy concluded the explanation to Murphy with: "Mrs. Roosevelt had not the slightest intention of hurting anyone's feelings and will change this word in the book, now that it has been brought to her attention."[99]

"It is not a mere question of social propriety," the *Afro-American* insisted. "It is a far more serious question when the very First Lady of the land openly sets her approval on the very spirit of humiliating racial tactics which the South has used to keep colored citizens down economically, culturally and socially. In this stage in this serious matter let's be generous and say the First Lady did not mean this epithet as an affront, or that she is ignorant of its serious consequences. Then at least she is due American colored citizens an immediate apology, else she has done us a greater wrong than any good she has ever done."[100]

But she delayed her apology. When speaking or writing to white Southerners, Eleanor never hesitated to say that because of her Georgia ancestry she had "always had an understanding of the problems facing Southern white people on interracial questions." She forthrightly stated that she "quite understood the Southern point of view" and was "familiar with the old plantation life."[101]

As for the African American point of view, "from my earliest childhood I had literary contacts with Negroes," she explained to *Ebony* magazine readers in 1953, "but no personal contacts with them." She recalled "reading about Negroes" when Aunt Gracie "would read to us from the Br'er Rabbit books and tell us about life on the plantation. This was my very first introduction to Negroes in any way. It was a rather happy way to meet the people with whom I was later to make many friends because all the stories our aunt told us were about delightful people."[102]

Eleanor did not reply when the members of the DuBois Circle, also in Baltimore, Maryland, wrote on May 7 to say that they were amazed to read such a word in Mrs. R's prose, presumed it was unintentional, but wished to remind her that use of such a term was "an affront to 12,000,000 Americans."[103] A White House secretary, presumably Tommy, wrote in pencil "usual explanation/will make correction in book." Tommy also gave the usual explanation to E. Birdie Smith, managing editor of the *California News* ("The Greatest Weekly West of the Rockies/Covers California Like the Sunshine") in Los Angeles, where Mrs. Roosevelt had "received a great deal of criticism from prominent Negroes and from church and social organizations in our city."[104]

To a Tuskegee graduate who wrote her an outraged letter asking how "the paragon of American womanhood" could "use the hated and humiliating 'darky,'" Eleanor did respond herself, explaining that it had been used by her Georgia great-aunt as a term of affection: "I have always considered it in that light. I am sorry if it hurt you. What do you prefer?"

BY SEPTEMBER 1937, WITH VAL-KILL in turmoil and her relationship with Nancy Cook and Marion Dickerman coming apart, Eleanor and Lorena Hickok had been drifting in different directions. "I've tried hard[105] to be perfectly acquiescent this summer," Hick told her. "I think the feeling that I had to do most of the trying just got me down and completely discouraged. And I've hated the thought so of seeing you—or trying to see you—when you didn't want to see me. Perhaps I was right. I may have been wrong. I don't know any of the answers."

They flirted with ways of showing the world without telling a single person that Mrs. Roosevelt was in love. Hick liked making a mock-horror memory of Eleanor's long tickling fingers the night they shared the cabin in the auto camp. Eleanor was powerfully drawn to "all the little things, tones in your voice, the feel of your hair, gestures . . ."[106] On ER's special plane to Puerto Rico, they played the Groucho Marx game of ditching decorum and goosing the dowager for a giggle, Hick playfully swatting the first lady's bottom in front of the press gals, Eleanor maintaining perfect aplomb.

Each wrote nightly; intimacy in bed, or its geographic opposite, duty in the field, was the unambiguous text of their letters. Going to work for the New Deal leveled their playing field: Eleanor as the President's field scout for Southern Appalachia, Hick as Harry Hopkins's chief investigator among a team of crack reporters (including the nomadic Martha Gellhorn), traveling the country, section by section, reporting on the effectiveness of local relief administrations as well as the physical and mental condition of those receiving help from the Federal Emergency Relief Administration (FERA).

Eleanor was a believer in Nature as the great revealer of character. It was a form particular to her class and generation: shipwrecked Edwardians faced with survival, the butler becomes the leader, the aristocratic family his desert-island servants. Her first motoring trip with Hick had been a lovers' idyll on Canada's Gaspé Peninsula—tourist cabins with laughable bedsprings, quoits to pitch out back, canoes turtled under the pines. Their second outing, a real camping trip to

Yosemite National Park, proved to be a light comedy of errors, full of exactly the sort of trading-places reversals the nature satire was supposed to stir up. Hick, the wisecracking ace reporter, panicked when she read Eleanor's written instructions to the Yosemite guides: "Miss Hickok will require a quiet, gentle horse, since she has not ridden for some time. . . ." Hick had never ridden, much less in the High Sierras, much less on steep mountain trails eleven thousand feet above sea level.

"How," she growled to Eleanor, "could you do this to me?"

Said the "reluctant" first lady, always struggling to get back on the horse after her husband's career had thrown her again: "Oh, you'll manage."[107]

Sitting tall in the saddle of her huge palomino, Eleanor, formerly the fearful, shamed rider, became a daring and accomplished high-country horsewoman. Four days on an old brown mare taught Hick how to roll a cigarette in the saddle and to fall gently off the horse when she decided they both needed a roll in the river.

Hick, the type to scarcely get a breath on her way to the bar, panted pathetically all through their high-altitude holiday but never dropped out of the game. Eleanor elatedly climbed to still higher peaks, followed by admiring young guides, forever banishing her honeymoon nightmare of Franklin and Kitty Gandy roped together on the spires of the Faloria.

The sexual reserve that had constrained Eleanor's earlier life had been loosened by months of affection from and for Hick—but only up to a point. Eleanor had originally seen herself as the one locked up; and Hick did indeed turn a key in Eleanor, allowing her a far easier give-and-take than she had yet managed in any of her relationships. But Eleanor naturally became the more dominant and extroverted partner as she more and more confidently grew in public. Hick, the former Front-Page star, was the lover suppressing a "rich nature" to "keep down" all that she yearned to give.[108]

Their strong sexual attraction was not as clear to others. History would view them ambiguously as lovers, yet the record they left of their erotic pleasure and lovers' joy makes unmistakably clear that the relationship wasn't sexuality on the one side and good works on the other. Hick was no predator, Eleanor no closeted do-gooder. Neither were they schoolgirls with soon-to-be-outgrown crushes. Behind cabin doors or under the stars, all barriers fallen, all hairnets burned, all acts of love being equal, passion *was* spent. They were sexual intimates. Eleanor Roosevelt and Lorena Hickok is not a story of unfulfilled sexuality or of sexuality unveiled or of a cheated woman's revenge on her husband. The story is of intimacy—left incomplete. The question is why their bond, having deepened during their first infatuated eighteen months, no longer came first. Did Eleanor *want* to be close?

"I know you often have a feeling for me which for one reason or another I may not return in kind but I feel I love you just the same," Eleanor tried explaining in May 1935. "So often we entirely satisfy each other that I feel there is a fundamental basis on which our relationship stands."[109]

But even as she reassured Hick, she was growing beyond the daily churn of their secret attachment. There had come a moment of shocked recognition that suggested a turning point. Hick's report from New Orleans pictured the steep economic decline of "the whole white collar class" in Louisiana. Set against the desperation of unemployed reporters, reduced to begging, Hick described the bulk of cases—some 85 percent of the whole—on which the agency needed to spend time and resources. These were African American, and Hick had no doubt that "thousands of those Negroes are living much better on relief than they ever did while they were working." Hick wondered, "If we were not carrying so many Negroes, if perhaps we couldn't solve the white-collar problem to some extent by giving more adequate relief." She recognized that if such engineering were ordered from Washington, "we'd undoubtedly be up against a charge of racial discrimination."[110]

Eleanor realized that Hick was proposing to drop African Americans from New Orleans' relief rolls so that white recipients could be given the whole sum of available monies. Blacks were so catastrophically poor anyway, pronounced Hick, they "really could manage to subsist without it."[111]

THAT WINTER, ELEANOR SCALED BACK her responses to Hick's needs and demands. She took care to manage expectations about how free she could make herself. Then, feeling guilty that she'd retreated, she committed to a Long Island weekend alone with Hick in a friend's cottage. In the next special delivery—it never failed—Franklin Jr. jumped her with a letter threatening to quit college if his parents (i.e., Eleanor, since no one expected the President's involvement) didn't make "more effort to understand him."[112] In the meantime, he was rowing for Harvard at Annapolis, so would Mother please just come watch him on the 25th?

She hated having to postpone "our weekend," Eleanor told Hick, offering alternate dates. "Let me know what you can manage," she added, "& please don't be upset."[113]

Hick was ever afraid of losing the relationship for which she had given up her career. She turned her investigative eye upon rivals for ER's devotion, surreptitiously gathering information, suffering every comparison, the pettiness of being mean diminishing the high-heartedness that had drawn Eleanor to her in the first place. Disappointment was no good either—it just made Eleanor cloak herself in silence.

"What a nuisance hearts are," tried Eleanor, "& yet without them life would hardly be worthwhile!" She added: "Well I've talked & knitted all evening so now I must get to work on the mail. A world of love & I wish I could put my arms around you."[114] As Hick had long since detected, Eleanor's answer to Hick's feelings of neglect was always to flee, "the next task the uppermost thing in her mind."[115]

CERTAIN NEW DEAL PROGRAMS HAD begun to have dramatic modernizing effects on the isolation and poverty of the South. Highway expansion conducted by the Works Progress Administration had more than doubled the total mileage of new or improved roads throughout Dixie. Around every curve in Alabama in 1938 seemed to be another sign announcing, WPA-men at work.

But after five and a half years of unprecedented federal spending, "The South's unbalance is a major concern" contended the President, "not merely of the South but of the whole nation." FDR convened a body of scholars and writers to investigate economic and social conditions in the region. Their ensuing publication, *A Report on the Economic Conditions of the South*, detailed the region's desperate poverty.

It also declared that the region was "the nation's number one economic problem" because of low industrial and farm wages, low family incomes, and few public services.

The report was nearing completion when Roosevelt was visited by Joseph Gelders and Lucy Randolph Mason, two of the South's most determined reformers. Gelders, an organizer for the International Labor Defense, was a Birmingham native who worked tirelessly to eliminate poverty and racism, and Mason, who hailed from a well-to-do Virginia family, was the public-relations representative for the Congress of Industrial Organizations (CIO) in the South. Gelders had long envisioned a region-wide conference to address the repression of civil liberties in Southern cities, and in Mason and Roosevelt he found a receptive audience. Roosevelt saw in a conference the opportunity to publicize the grim findings of the report and possibly rally more Southern support behind the New Deal. Eleanor widened its scope, suggesting that the conference address all of the problems afflicting the South, including segregation, limited educational opportunities, and low wages.

The Southern Conference for Human Welfare held its inaugural meeting on November 20, 1938, in Birmingham's Municipal Auditorium. Labor's new gains in organizing both blacks and whites in the cities and rural areas combined with bolder demands from African American churches to draw in labor leaders, industrialists, government officials, farmers and sharecroppers, civic leaders, ministers, politicians, economists, and students—to create the largest liberal gathering the South had seen—neither race relations rally nor labor meeting, but rather a citizens' forum to consider constitutional rights, women and children in industry, prison reform, youth problems, and race.

The conference was billed as "the South's answer" to the national emergency council report that "their section" was the nation's foremost economic problem—a trope that Eleanor assailed from the moment she stood to address a mixed-race audience of more than seven thousand, including three thousand delegates.

The three-man Birmingham City Commission, governing body of the city known to progressives as "the little Hitlers," afterward denounced it as a "left wing movement financed in whole or in part by Communists" and demanded a congressional investigation, asking the House Un-American Activities Committee to determine to what extent federal funds were made available or pledged, what part the deputy Works Progress administrator Aubrey Williams had played in organizing the conference, and to what extent prominent Southerners were bribed to attend.

Out of the SCHW would come resolutions for federal legislation to abolish the poll tax; a movement supporting a federal antilynching law and "full citizenship for all persons regardless of race"; demands for equal pay for black and white teachers; a plan for a voting rights campaign. . . .

The conference subdivided into sections—on Race Relations, on Southern Youth, etc.—and in the youth section, "the discussion of the Anti-Lynching Bill reached its most dramatic heights. It precipitated a heated discussion between Congressman Patrick of Alabama and Mrs. Eleanor Roosevelt, and in an inept answer by the Congressman to Mrs. Roosevelt's question why he opposed the Anti-Lynching Bill if he objected to lynching."[116]

On the second day, Eleanor spoke about the poll tax at an integrated workshop, then joined the full body of delegates at the Municipal Auditorium, which overnight had been surrounded with police wagons.

Then, New Deal administrators, white and black leaders from thirteen Southern states, labor organizers, university presidents and professors, newspaper publishers and editors, Southern liberals, Senator John H. Bankhead, coauthor of the Bankhead-Jones Farm Tenant Bill, and Associate Justice Hugo Black of the Supreme Court, who had maintained strict silence as he tried to live down revelations he had been a member of the Ku Klux Klan, moved on into the building, deliberately violating the city ordinance that made integrated meetings illegal.

The stout, jug-eared rookie public safety commissioner of Birmingham gave the order in his bullfrog voice: "White and Negro are not to segregate together." And with that malapropism, Bull Connor nullified the agenda set by the President of the United States and made race the medium of the Southern Conference for Human Welfare.

* * *

THEOPHILUS EUGENE "BULL" CONNOR PEGGED a cord from the lawn outside the auditorium and through its front doors, running up its central aisle to the stage, bisecting the seating so that at least two thousand African Americans ended up segregated from five thousand whites for Eleanor's speech that evening.

Eleanor, meanwhile, had found a seat in the area set aside for blacks. Quickly, police marched up the center aisle to inform her she was in violation of the city statute. She folded up her chair. Rather than submit to the humiliating ordinance and take herself to the whites-only section, she deliberately placed her seat in the aisle. When she un-folded it and sat down, she was sitting squarely astride Bull Connor's police line. She refused to move, and Connor and his men dared not touch the first lady of the United States.

Likewise, Eleanor dared not make more of violating the ordi-nance. The President's wife could not afford to put the President in an awkward position, as she spelled out when declining to be drawn into reporters' questions after her evening speech. Asked, "What do you think of the segregation here tonight?" she answered, "I do not believe that is a question for me to answer. In the section of the coun-try from which I come, it is a procedure that is not followed. But I would not presume to try to tell the people of Alabama what they should do."[117]

The Birmingham-raised historian Diane McWhorter observes that in context of the more personal firestorm of Bull Connor's responses to the Civil Rights social revolution twenty-seven years later, Eleanor's cool action in the Municipal Auditorium would be understood as "a gutsy moral stand." But in November 1938, most white Southerners saw a low-level drama, "the wife of the President of the United States browbeaten by a crude radio personality,"[118] starring their strongman Bull Connor in his national debut.

The next day, the conference voted to condemn the South's Jim Crow laws and never to meet again in the future in cities with seg-regation ordinances. For Eleanor, the risk of being arrested was im-personal. But she took very personally the jeopardy in which she was placing her friend and New Deal colleague Mary McLeod Bethune,

exposing the highest ranking African American woman in government to confinement in Bull Connor's Black Marias.

Bethune's response to Eleanor—unexpected forgiveness—set the
stage for events the following year, when the world-famous contralto
Marian Anderson, sponsored by Howard University, was denied the
chance to give an Easter Sunday concert in Constitution Hall, the only
venue in Washington large enough for the diva's usual audience. The
powerful private organization that governed the facility—the Daughters of the American Revolution—cited their policy of limiting the use
of the hall to white artists. That was enough to set off alarms at Howard and in the press, which the DAR only magnified by defending its
policy, touching a nerve throughout the capital city and beyond.

With Birmingham's implacable defense of its segregation ordinances still at the front of her thoughts, Eleanor examined her own
conscience as a member of the DAR, telling her readers, "I have been
debating in my mind for some time a question which I have had to debate with myself once or twice before in my life. The question is, if you
belong to an organization and disapprove of an action which is typical
of a policy, should you resign or is it better to work for a changed point
of view within the organization?"[119]

In the past, when such an organization invited her to work actively,
she usually stayed in until she had at least made a fight and had been
defeated. Even then, upon accepting defeat, Eleanor invariably decided that she had been wrong to have let herself get that far ahead of
the thinking of the majority. But, with the wired-shut DAR, there was
no telling if there even was a minority position; and, in any case, no active work could be done by the first lady with the organization's "Generals," who considered the President's wife much too liberal anyway.[120]

To remain a member would imply approval of the DAR's racist
treatment of a great artist whom Eleanor had invited to sing at the
White House three years before, and to whom Eleanor was now
scheduled to present at the NAACP's annual convention its highest
honor, the Spingarn Medal.

And so, on February 27, Eleanor announced to her readers that she
had resigned membership in a patriotic organization whose unjust actions she deplored. Privately she told the president of the DAR, whose

name she had not revealed in her column: "You had an opportunity to lead in an enlightened way and it seems to me that your organization has failed."[121]

The first lady's resignation—supported by 67 percent of Gallup's respondents, 33 percent opposed[122]—turned an episode of local bigotry involving a provincial ladies' organization into an international news story that brought Eleanor further smears from Southern reactionaries alongside such awakenings of conscience from Northern whites as that which she received from old Dr. Peabody, still headmaster at Groton School, who shook his fist both at the DAR and at "the prejudice, I might say cruelty, with which we have dealt with the negro people. Your courage in taking this definite stand called for my admiration."[123]

Walter White collaborated with Anderson's business manager, the famed entertainment impresario Sol Hurok, to propose that the diva present her program at an outdoor concert, free and open to all, on the steps of the Lincoln Memorial, which fell under the mantel of Harold Ickes, whose first official act as FDR's irascible secretary of the interior had been to abolish the department's segregated lunchrooms, followed by further decrees to desegregate facilities in National Parks across the country. With the President's express approval, and Eleanor's behind-the-scenes advancement, Ickes arranged for the concert and presided himself as Anderson stood on the chilly steps of the memorial, overwhelmed by the vast crowd of more than seventy-five thousand, which stretched as far back as the Washington Monument—the "first civil rights rally," as it would come to be called.

Legend to the contrary, Eleanor was not present to hear Anderson break the anticipatory hush of the audience with a proudly determined rendition of the national anthem, or the grave, supremely controlled "America" that followed. The spiritual "Nobody Knows the Trouble I've Seen" had a transfiguring effect, re-forming what had made Anderson vulnerable and her audience ashamed into a new, electrifying surge of hope. She had decided that it would be inflammatory for her to attend—her presence might incite haters. But she nonetheless opened up and magnified the day, having muscled those radio stations on which she herself broadcast to carry the concert live. Without those recordings, history itself might have been deaf to "freedom's concert."

Birmingham 1938 had pegged the boundary in Eleanor's public life. After the Southern Conference she could not go back to the white world of official Washington and to business as usual. She now had to ask her readers why they swore vengeance upon Adolf Hitler but suppressed Marian Anderson. . . .

It would take a little longer for her to kiss Dr. Bethune on the cheek without self-consciousness. But she could no longer task Tommy to placate the editor of the *Afro-American* with some well-intended nonsense about how much Mrs. Roosevelt's family had loved the servants it had enslaved. In Birmingham, in 1938, by defying the local statute and standing up and placing herself, as if for the first time, as the national intermediary, she had found her way to address the internal split running, as tautly as Bull Connor's pegged cord, from the stage of the Municipal Auditorium, back up through the central aisle, out the main doors, all the way north to the big, now more inclusive spaces between Washington and Lincoln's monuments.

EIGHTEEN

A CAR WITH ILLINOIS LICENSE plates passed her twice, followed her into a gas station, then pulled up alongside and parked.

Happily, two young couples tumbled out to shake her hand. Said one of the women, "You look much nicer than your pictures."[1]

This had been happening since 1933. In Abingdon, Virginia—the town of her father's painful exile—throngs of well-wishers had lined the streets, overhung with flags, and a band was leading Mrs. Roosevelt's open-car processional up the packed main street on its way to the Mountain Music Festival,[2] when the astonished voice of a little girl piped up: "Why, she ain't so bad lookin'!"

Eleanor laughed and didn't think about it again, until the same startled recognition began to repeat in other places, as people meeting her found themselves astonished that the Eleanor before them was far more lovely than the homely Mrs. Roosevelt of pictures.

"Your pictures libel you, Mrs. Roosevelt!" they called out to her.[3]

As she drove or walked on, thrilled whispers followed the encounter.

"I never realized Eleanor Roosevelt was so beautiful."[4]

"Even if her teeth were not right and the set of her face a little off," one woman told her diary, "there was an extraordinary radiant quality about her."[5]

"You never told me she has such blue eyes," took up the husband of a reporter.[6]

One columnist gushed about her limbs: "I feel that I just have to say this, especially as I don't think I have ever read it anywhere before. Honestly, Mrs. Roosevelt has beautiful legs and quite trim ankles and small slender feet!"[7] Another noticed that for so tall a woman, "she has a peculiar undulating walk."[8] Still others were amazed by the elegance of her wardrobe and the fluidity that rolled through all her movements, all angularity of her long arms and legs "erased by the soft, flowing lines of her clothes and the relaxed manner in which she moves."[9]

Her height increased in the enchantment, gaining at least an inch in the telling, then another in diaries, and still another in the vast literature of the Roosevelt years. In real life she was an inch under six feet.[10] Ernest Hemingway, a solid six himself, and no fan of adverbs, proclaimed Eleanor "enormously" tall. Esther "Eppie" Lederer, the advice columnist Ann Landers, was amazed when she met Eleanor: "I mean, she's huge."[11]

Foreign visitors in the late-1930s were astounded to open a magazine or attend a Broadway musical and find the first lady of the land portrayed in so casual a manner. Her New Deal travels in the first administration so rapidly and completely transformed people's image of her that by 1936, a common mystery probed in stories about Eleanor was how her "real" beauty had made people "forget her ugliness."[12] Some saw her gift of engaging with people's hopes and dreams as an expanding expression of her Christian faith. Others argued that she hadn't been ugly in the first place—only an "ugly duckling" beside her beautiful, swanlike husband. "Her ugliness may have been an asset," diarized one young actress: "The vain silly side that is so noticeable in all of us pretty women is completely absent in her." Life itself had "given her a richness that makes one forget her ugliness," concluded her protégée Rosamond Pinchot.[13] The writer Brendan Gill countered that it wasn't a matter of having to forget: "the ugliness simply wasn't there."[14]

New confidence in her own powers was the most common explanation.[15] "She exuded strength, drive, curiosity," commented one reporter, "and combined them with the ability to decide and to act. She had an exuberant belief that progress was there to be achieved, if only one worked hard enough."[16]

"Her secret is vitality," said one observer of her free-range encounters. "It is all most tangible. It reaches out to you, it takes possession of you."[17] People felt it in the steadiness of her hand—the handshake firm, the hand itself surprisingly soft in one's grasp.[18] "She has a handclasp that means something," they said in Wisconsin, "a handclasp into which she injects a fine impersonal warmth, a vitality." A man in the Bronx, Victor Rodriguez, once shook her hand, and decades later could "still feel her warmth in my palm."[19] Another New Yorker, a speakeasy owner, gave the credit for "changing the country back into the United States" not to FDR but to Mrs. Roosevelt. "She was the genius of that family." Because of her, recalled "Broadway Tony" Soma, "we are adventurous today."[20]

"It wasn't the handshake," expanded one Democratic party leader. "One of Mrs. Roosevelt's special traits was that of looking at a person straight in the eye. It was a human spark in her eyes—the recognition of nobility of each individual, black, white, red, yellow, young, old, men, women—that established a bond which was a very personal experience for all who met her, even fleetingly."[21]

Her stride "rapid and lengthy," as the Secret Service described it,[22] she swept into places like Muncie, Indiana, her manner unruffled and unhurried as she met with the press in her hotel room upon arrival. Later, upon discovering that two reporters from the high school paper had been made to wait in the lobby, she gave the girls an "exclusive" for the *Munsonian*, which captivated the old pros from the wire services, who never quite believed that anyone could have that much goodwill.

For some townsfolk, her enormous corsages and sentimental jewelry touched a sympathetic chord, as did her slim hands, the fingers tapered like those of a glove model, her "perfect filbert-shaped" fingernails the pride of her official portrait painter.[23] Others were charmed by the crinkles that appeared under her eyes when the 4-H Club presented her with a large white goose for a pat on the head[24] or the high schoolers offered her an invitation to speak at their graduation[25] or the Boys Club boys sang "How Do You Do, Mrs. Roosevelt" as she nodded her head in time to the music. When they launched into the Caisson Song, with its swinging "Over hill, over dale" opening lines, they faltered a bit, but she urged them on with an eye-crinkling smile, topping the applause at the end with her benediction, "That's swell, that's really fine singing."[26]

Afterward, the men handed her copies of a Portland newspaper carrying her picture on the front page, the caption nominating her for vice president. The women, who only that morning at breakfast had been appalled to learn that Mrs. Roosevelt had already finished her Christmas shopping in October,[27] were surprised and comforted by her easy laughter and neighborly way of chatting on street corners. By four o'clock in the afternoon, when they found her dispatching her daily column from their local Western Union office, they wondered when she had found the time to write such a thing, and asked, "Anything in it about Muncie?"

"Yes," she replied, and they beamed.

SOON AFTER COMING TO POWER in 1933, Adolf Hitler had been confronted by an American correspondent about racial policy.

Germany's strange new chancellor was a figure out of the Inquisition: black forelock, lifeless eyes, death-white face. Having first saluted the United States for criminalizing marriage between whites and blacks, Hitler now modeled Nazi Germany's crusade for "racial purity" on American eugenics laws, inflicting the first of more than 350,000 compulsory sterilizations on the children of German mothers and French West Africans serving in France's military occupation of the Rhineland after World War I.[28]

The failed beer-hall bum of the 1920s, ever increasingly normalized as an apostle of hate during Germany's severe economic hardship, had so glamorized and harmonized *Judenhass* (literally, *Jewhatred*) with fears and hidden pleasures at all levels of German society that he could look right through the American reporter to state the banal fact: the same "feeling" would sweep the United States in a few years.

As if on cue in August 1938, the *Nation* declared, "Anti-Semitism is growing in the United States. As tangible as a heavy fog, it is spreading through the new areas of our social life and carrying with it the threat of unspeakable future ills." The editors admitted both their reluctance to raise the issue and their certainty of its truth as well as its amorphousness: "Like a fog, too, this prejudice is hard to fight, hard even to get hold of and analyze. You know it is there, but you are at a loss to describe its exact shape or substance or dimensions."[29]

A month earlier, at the Évian-les-Bains conference called by FDR to consider the possibilities for the resettlement of Jewish refugees in agricultural countries, thirty-two nations proclaimed themselves un-willing to make room for large numbers of Jews, fulfilling Hitler's sinister calculation that Germany was not alone in *Judenhass*.[30]

By 1939, 5 to 10 percent of the U.S. population were haters of Jews, and another 45 percent "mildly so."[31] Nearly half of the general public thought of the Jewish people not as a religious group but as a nationality, like the Poles, the Swedes, and the Italians.[32] Elmo Roper, Jr., Gallup's rival in sampling public opinion,[33] found that 53 percent of Americans felt that Jews were "different" and "needed social and economic restrictions." To the question *Do you think Jews have too much power in the United States?* more than a third and sometimes more than one-half answered yes, the number of anti-Jewish respondents increasing from 42 percent in 1939 to 58 percent in June 1945.[34]

On the West Coast, the Immigration Act of 1924 had blocked two generations of resident Japanese from U.S. citizenship. Yet by 1935, when only 126,947 people of Japanese extraction were living in the United States, the California Joint Immigration Committee bellowed, "There are 500,000 armed Japanese in the United States." Another harebrained hate group, the Japanese Exclusion League, echoed, "They breed like rabbits! Their birth rate is between three and four times that of our own race!"[35]

The high priests of radio, led by FDR's archenemy Charles E. Coughlin, condemned American involvement in another European meat grinder, claiming that international Jews and Communists were dictating "Rosenfeld" foreign policy for their own profit.[36] The leader of the German-American Bund, announcing a campaign "to rid this country of Jews," told a rally in Queens that because of the "Jew Deal,"[37] American politics had seen a rise, from 4 to 60 percent, in the number of Jews holding government positions. In fact, 15 percent of FDR's top executive appointments were Jewish,[38] in an era when Jews represented 3 percent of the general population.

Roosevelt took a stand against discrimination in January 1939. He overrode the fainthearted Treasury Secretary Morgenthau and *New York Times* publisher Arthur Hays Sulzberger (both feared an uptick in hate) to appoint his old friend and adviser Felix Frankfurter, the venerated Harvard Law School professor, to serve in the vacancy left by the death of Supreme Court Justice Benjamin Cardozo. But, as historian Leonard Dinnerstein wrote, "one's fingers and toes" could do the job of counting the number of Jews in policymaking positions in the Departments of State, War, Navy, and Commerce, the Federal Reserve Board, the Federal Trade Commission, the U.S. Tariff Commission, and the Board of Tax Appeals. Moreover, of FDR's 192 judicial appointments, only 7 went to Jews (52 to Catholics), almost the same number as those of his three Republican predecessors.

Earl Miller, blunt and boastful, typified a kind of bigotry that revealed itself closer to the Roosevelts. Protective of his attachment to the first family, Earl liked to show off his access, and loved to bring strangers to Eleanor's Eleventh Street apartment, where he took childlike pride in sleeping in Eleanor's bed; in being indulged by Eleanor and handled by Tommy, in keeping with the game of belonging. Ex-lovers rarely play this role so brazenly; it would have been embarrassing if Earl had been Eleanor's lover, as there proved to be another side to him, discovered by Charlotte Kraus, a recently arrived twenty-eight-year-old Austrian émigré, singing in Miami nightclubs when Earl met her in March 1939 and offered her a lift north to New York City.

Kraus had gratefully accepted, but after the luxuries of Miami, the extreme poverty of rural Georgia, viewed from the interior of Earl's 1939 Cadillac, had upset her. When she asked who the people were, living in tarpaper shacks, Earl, terse and uncomfortable, answered, "Negroes. They work on farms around here. They're all right, don't worry about them. That's the way they want to live."

Farther along, in a roadside restaurant for dinner, Kraus asked the waitress for sweet unsalted European butter. Earl scowled. "Only Jews eat sweet butter," he told Kraus.[39]

Appalled, she challenged him: "And what if Jews eat sweet butter? Is that something to be ashamed of? Do you consider Jews inferior?"

Casually, Earl answered, "Yes. I think Hitler is right in many respects. The Nordic race *is* superior."[40]

As Kraus probed deeper, she discovered that without any reservation or conscience, Earl Miller held the basic beliefs of "Nordic" eugenicists, Nazi propagandists, "blood and soil" white supremacists, and America Firsters.

When the Nazis had entered Austria a year earlier, on March 12, 1938, Kraus had fled her homeland, emigrating to America. Her father, appalled, had demanded, "Who do you think is waiting for you in America—The President?" Now here she was, the guest of a favored friend of the first lady of the United States. Four months after that, Charlotte Kraus would be the guest of President and Mrs. Roosevelt at Hyde Park, singing for the King and Queen of England at a hot-dog picnic during the royal visit.

ELEANOR HAD GONE FROM SHRUGGING off the doomed snobbery of her marginalized Hall aunts, to joining her mother-in-law in harsh anti-Semitic social superiority, to upholding institutional restrictions as a creator of the Todhunter School's limited enrollment policy for Jewish applicants, to canceling a speech in Lancaster, Pennsylvania, when she learned that the club at which she was to speak barred membership on the basis of religion. But not until 1937, the same year she endorsed the creation of a community for Jewish refugees in Palestine, and two years before resigning in protest when her friend Elinor Morgenthau was blackballed from membership in the Colony Club of New York.

In 1932, as Lake Placid, New York, hosted the Winter Olympics, and Jewish groups protested the use of state funds to build an Olympic bobsled track on land controlled by the harshly discriminatory Lake Placid Club, Eleanor had ridden past the club's exclusionary signs (no Jews or dogs allowed) to get a morning's use of the club's toboggan chute before experimenting with the Winter Games bobsled run. It would take her to the far end of the 1930s to abandon ideas about "Jewish" traits and "Jewish" energy that would have made Lake Placid clubmen cheer.

While helping Franklin, for example, disentangle himself as governor-elect from Robert Moses and Belle Moskowitz, the stars of the previous administration, she couldn't resist putting Moses and Moskowitz in their place with a grudging, if admiring, "Gosh, the race has nerves of iron and tentacles of steel!"[41] The Jews as a "race" was a conception Eleanor would continue to use, up through her support for the partitioning of British Palestine—to the shock of the Roosevelts' friend and partisan *New York Post* publisher Dorothy Schiff.[42] Up to Hitler's first annexation demands in 1938, ER would all too readily identify "certain mannerisms or traits of character which rub us the wrong way" in Jews "who have been successful and who have the advantages of education and culture."[43]

Elinor Morgenthau occasionally suspected that Eleanor was deliberately not inviting her places because Eleanor knew that Elinor wouldn't fit in.[44] As her father's daughter, Eleanor knew very well what it felt like to try to fit in when people judged her based on her father's monstrousness.[45] Still, she responded with surprise to her friend's discomfort: "I am sorry dear, that you felt hurt, and your letter made me feel badly, but I've been pretty busy and I can only hope that I will see you often when we both get back in August."[46]

Eleanor took care to protect Elinor when Marion Dickerman and Nancy Cook guarded their inside track at Val-Kill, sometimes so jealously that Elinor felt pushed away. Elinor, brittle, had long suspected Marion and Nancy capable of some degree of anti-Jewish suspicion. She nursed feelings of neglect, frequently imagining friendship's small gaps as major breaks, which Eleanor was quick to sense but slow to reset.

"I didn't say half of what I wanted to when we were talking the other day," she wrote Elinor. "I've grown to love you and to feel that you and Henry were not only 'our' but 'my' real true friends and tho' I can't take away the feeling you have it makes me unhappy to feel that it is worrying you and I want to put my arms about you and keep away all the disagreeable things which have made you feel this way."[47]

With Hick, Eleanor offered the more hardboiled response: "If one is to have a healthy relationship, it must be on some kind of equal basis. You simply cannot be so easily hurt. Life is too short to cope with it." Another time, reproaching Hick for protesting a change in plans: "I know you feel badly & are tired, but I'd give an awful lot if you weren't so sensitive. You are worse than Elinor Morgenthau & haven't her reason!"[48]

Publicly, Eleanor had begun to explore in speeches and articles, as a matter of personal and national housekeeping, the questions raised by Nazi pogroms: What turned religious intolerance into hatred?

How did hatred boil over into violence? "Take ourselves here in the United States," she invited *Liberty* magazine's readers in December 1938. "Many of us might say that among the vast majority of less well-educated and less well-born Jews, and even among those who have been successful and who have the advantages of education and culture, there are certain mannerisms or traits of character which rub us the wrong way. But that is not what leads to hate and persecution, for we feel that same way about other nationals and we have no desire to wipe out any of them because we are still sure of our equality in [economic] competition."

Eleanor kept a file of facts for use in speeches and articles,[49] including notes on Jewish contributions to American wars, from which she could recite or conclude: "They are wiser than we are, they succeed where we fail." She listed admirable attributes: "Perhaps we need their brains and appreciation of the cultural things in life, perhaps we need their quick response to the ethical value of a situation and their sense of responsibility in giving and their imaginative powers."

When Eleanor joined H. G. Wells in *Liberty* to debate on racial and religious intolerance, she identified a lack of confidence as the crucial factor in groups or nations that persecuted Jews. Those countries that felt financially competitive and militarily able to defend themselves felt no need to attack Jews whose success only added to the nation's strength. "It is the secret fear," ventured Eleanor, "that the Jewish people are stronger or more able than those who still wield superior physical power over them which brings about oppression."[50] The same tended to be true, she proposed, for an economically enfeebled region such as the American South, where any sign of African Americans becoming better educated and financially independent ensured that lower-income whites would go to extreme lengths to keep blacks powerless.

The same was true for FDR and herself. Because her husband felt supremely confident on a world scale, he did not hold his wife's direct challenges to his administration against her. He could find strength in her contribution to their own political alliance when she made it her personal responsibility to help the "forgotten man" of FDR's campaign promise. Nor did he intrude as president upon her daily connection to a widespread reading public. Franklin never said a word for or against anything Eleanor wrote for publication. His staff frequently became hysterical: "Mr. President, this can't go on, you've got to ask her to stop."

"This is serious," Steve Early would warn, "this will ruin you."

But FDR never caved. "It will blow over," he would say. "They'll forget it."[51]

Once, when Eleanor asked, point-blank, how he felt about her contrary stance on the latest antilynching bill, Franklin looked her in the eye. "You go right ahead and stand for whatever you feel is right," he told her. "Besides, I can always say that I can't do a thing with you."[52]

For sixty-five years the U.S. Congress, having abolished local government in the federal city in 1874, had ruled over local municipal affairs through a presidentially appointed three-member Board of Commissioners.

At St. Elizabeth's after the war, Eleanor had learned the full range of congressional oversight applied by the district commissioners to shell-shocked and other "convalescents." From the White House in 1932, she had continued to probe conditions in Washington's long-term welfare facilities and penal institutions, and had brought to light abuses to impoverished women, the indigent elderly, and children of the state. Yet Eleanor was not invited to testify before any congressional subcommittee—no president's wife ever had been. The country's foremost female lay figure was not given a voice in a subcommittee investigating welfare institutions in the nation's capital for another three years, when at last Eleanor strode into the old House Office Building, entered the marble caucus room, and took the witness chair opposite Representative Thomas D'Alesandro, Jr., father of the future Speaker of the House, Nancy Pelosi.

As late as 1936 most of the press still viewed what Mrs. Roosevelt did as "breezing about."[53] Joseph Mitchell, filing a three-part series to the *World-Telegram* in May 1935, was one of the few reporters outside the White House pool who recognized Eleanor as "one of the most expert investigators in a nation of investigators."[54]

But when it came to Washington's penal institutions—the District

Jail, the Workhouse and Reformatory at Occoquan, and the Industrial Home School for "backward, truant, and delinquent" boys[55]—the notion of inspections by a first lady was utterly foreign. Inspections by anybody, for that matter, rarely happened at all. The district commissioners more often looked the other way, appointing a committee to look into matters only if the local press began to circulate rumors about daily inmate escapes, interpersonal violence, or corrupt management.[56]

Eleanor went ahead and made her own appointments and drove herself to the Blue Plains Home for the Aged and Infirm, the Home for Impoverished Women, the Children's Receiving Home, and the Industrial Home school for boys. Received cordially and shown around by the head of the facility, she would stubbornly go off tour, poking around until she saw with her own eyes that an overcrowded prison camp populated almost entirely by African American boys served meal after meal of stone-cold, inedible food.

No matter how often she inspected the District of Columbia's welfare and penal institutions, bringing her report directly back to the White House, she never failed to be shocked how one horror or another would almost always emerge in an utterly mundane way.[57]

Driving with her brother Hall out North Capitol Street one morning in January 1937, the mere sight of the District Jail's caged windows started her imagining what nights must be like inside, "with all that closely packed humanity thinking no very happy thoughts."[58]

The superintendent, Thomas M. Rives, led the tall Roosevelts through the tight high-ceilinged corridor that ran the length of the jail, until they reached the prisoners' mess hall, a narrow birdcage with tall barred windows in the South Wing. Down the middle of this room ran a mess table—a single, uninterrupted surface composed of bench-style picnic tables laid end-to-end so that everything happening along this narrow alleyway could be seen at a glance.

Mrs. Roosevelt's practiced eye took it all in, her nose meanwhile telling her that the room was as clean as it could be, "considering its construction." As to ventilation, however—perhaps that needed some updating. A certain odor did seem to linger with especial heaviness, but perhaps, as she remarked to Superintendent Rives, that "could be ameliorated by the use of modern ventilation fans."

The official party was about to move on, when Eleanor's attention was caught by something—a peaked white muslin tarp covering something large beyond the far end of the mess table. At her request, the covering was removed, and there stood the electric chair.

Superintendent Rives conceded that this was "one of the extremely undesirable features" of a brown-brick jail whose double-tall spaces had been designed in 1872 to accommodate gallows—not the 2,200 volts required for modern electrocution.[59] The way the facility was now wired, the mess hall was the only room with outlets sufficient to the current needed to put a condemned man to death.

The electric chair was not among the utensils Franklin had trained Eleanor to look into at the cafeterias of New York's state-run institutions. She had once inspected a prison in which *stocks* were still used in the mess hall. That was in Georgia, the Atlanta Penitentiary's farm colony for "trusted" prisoners.[60] This was the District of Columbia; this was 1937.[61] Nazi Germany had by now established no fewer than nine concentration camps to systematically torture and break tens of thousands of political enemies. The District Jail, by contrast, housed a daily average of some 507 inmates, five of whom awaited execution,[62] but about 64 percent of whom were "inebriates" jailed for little more than vagrancy and intoxication.[63]

It took but a moment for the hard truth to reach through Eleanor's nostrils. Here in the capital of the United States, the death penalty could only be administered in a stark wooden chair next to a table where mostly homeless men, suffering chronic malnutrition and alcoholism, ate their cereal. The ninety barbaric seconds needed for temperatures inside a condemned man's head to reach 140 degrees meant that when his fellow prisoners filed in for breakfast, no modern fan system was breezing away the leftover stink of charred flesh, scorched hair, or evacuated bowels.

The sobered-up survivors had a choice: eat their food through the haze of the "hot squat," as they called it—or eat nothing at all.

* * *

THE YEAR 1939 WAS ELEANOR'S second watershed in the White House: the year she became a world figure, a newsmaker with a place of her own in national debates,[64] and, according to *Time* magazine, the "foremost female political force" on the planet.[65]

As the newsreel and radio epoch went with the men to war, the wives of the great were scarcely seen and even more remotely heard. Stalin's wife had died of typhus. There was no Frau Hitler. Signora Mussolini, a farmer's daughter depicted as the exemplar Fascist housewife and mother, was universally ignored. Madame De Gaulle, a tough conservative Catholic, had no life of her own politically. Madame Chiang Kai-shek, wife of China's Nationalist leader and member of the formidable Soong family, was in a class by herself as the face of modern China.[66]

The nearest woman of photographic significance was Elizabeth the Queen Consort, an acknowledged female presence beaming from cars, while the unrecognized, unelected wife of the British prime minister remained invisible. The "strong-willed," "stern," and "not very feminine" (jibed her peers)[67] Clementine Churchill set a brave example as a fire watcher risking life and limb during nightly rooftop anti-aircraft combat with the Luftwaffe. The very survival of England would depend on the civilian volunteering of a million British women. But no one heard phrases attributed to Lady Churchill, shaken as they might have been by her fighting view of the "horrible world" of Christmas 1941: "Europe overrun by the Nazi hogs, & the Far East by yellow Japanese lice."[68]

On the front page or over the airwaves, Eleanor's opinion mattered.[69] With isolationists and internationalists fighting bitterly over the U.S. role in Hitler's war, the news day began and ended on the question of what America stood for. Eleanor's speeches championed the defense of freedom as a network of action, requiring thought and participation from each individual in an expanding, all-inclusive community.

"In a democracy, no one else does our thinking for us," she told the students at Hunter College. "Youth must accept responsibility for doing its own thinking."[70]

28

The first lady of the state of New York, photographed in her bedroom at the Governor's Mansion, Albany, November 11, 1932, three days after Franklin defeated Hoover for the presidency.

29.

Lorena Hickok, the star AP reporter with whom Eleanor began a secret and sexually intimate relationship as she became first lady of the United States.

30.

Eleanor broke with—and also upheld—many White House traditions. In 1933, she brought women and women's issues into Washington's daily news cycle.

31.

Through her syndicated newspaper column Eleanor connected with four million readers every morning.

LECTURE BY
MRS. FRANKLIN D. ROOSEVELT

Subject- "Relationship of the Individual to
the Community"

MEMORIAL HALL
Tuesday Eve., November 15, 1938

Admission $1.00   at 8:30 o'clock

Presented by the Women's Organization of Bryden Road Temple

32.

Replying to hate mail about her coast-to-coast lecture tours: "I have never tried to tell other people what they should think, or feel, or do. I have simply tried to show from my own experience and my impressions the things which might be effective or interesting or even helpful to other people."

33.

Eleanor's embrace of FDR's relationship with Marguerite "Missy" LeHand (center) paralleled her own emotional liberation from her husband.

34.

Eleanor visits the Winn
family in a new Public
Works Administration
model house in the
poorest section of
Christiansted, St. Croix,
U. S. Virgin Islands,
March 12, 1934.

35.

Nancy Cook and
Eleanor show
support for the
National Recovery
Administration code
for shorter work
hours and higher
wages at the Val-Kill
Furniture Workshop,
July 1933.

Eleanor resigned from the Daughters of the American Revolution when the organization refused to allow Marian Anderson to sing in Constitution Hall, but she was unable to attend the April 9, 1939, concert on the steps of the Lincoln Memorial.

On February 9, 1940, Eleanor testified (another first for a first lady) before the congressional subcommittee of Thomas D'Alesandro, Jr., father of the future speaker of the House Nancy Pelosi.

38.

Eleanor met Joseph P. Lash in 1939 when he was a radical
student organizer testifying before Congress. Lash later
became Eleanor's official biographer.

39.

Eleanor flew to the Democratic National Convention in
Chicago and, with a few notes in her handbag, brought a
hall of defiant delegates to heel with her "no ordinary time"
speech, July 18, 1940.

40.

Sara Delano Roosevelt was unhappy to have no official rank or place at White House state dinners; to keep the peace, Eleanor often yielded her high place at the president's table.

41.

Eleanor's brother Hall, photographed with FDR in 1931, drank himself to death in September 1941. Eleanor never felt able to be the loving surrogate he needed.

42.

Three months before the attack on Pearl Harbor, Eleanor began work with
New York mayor Fiorello La Guardia as codirector of the Office of Civilian
Defense, the first official governmental position held by a first lady.

43.

Entertaining soldiers on White House Lawn, June 12, 1942.

44.

ER with Lieutenant General Millard F. Harmon (left) and Admiral William F. Halsey in the South Pacific, September 15, 1943.

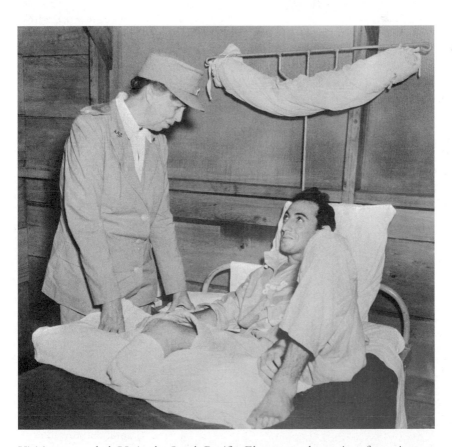

45.

Visiting wounded GIs in the South Pacific, Eleanor made a point of meeting as many American soldiers as she could, including Japanese-American servicemen.

46.

Greeted by Japanese-American internees at the Gila River
"Relocation Center," accompanied by Dillon S. Myer, director of
the War Relocation Authority, Arizona, April 23, 1943.

47.

FDR's funeral
procession, from Union
Station to the White
House, April 14, 1945.

Eleanor, flanked by Anna and Elliott, Truman in the shadows, at
FDR's burial in the Rose Garden, Hyde Park, April 15, 1945.

ER walking Franklin's famous Scottie, Fala, at Val-Kill, 1946.

50.

Advising President Truman, April 12, 1946.

51.

ER greets (at left) Vyacheslav M. Molotov, Soviet foreign minister, and (center) Andrei A. Gromyko, Soviet delegate to the United Nations, before the opening of the UN General Assembly, October 23, 1946, New York City World's Fair building.

The NAACP leadership, (from left) Dr. James McClendon,
Walter White, Roy Wilkins, and Thurgood Marshall. Eleanor
joined the organization's national board in 1945.

Opening the 1947 session of the United Nations General
Assembly at Flushing Meadows, New York.

54.

Dr. David Gurewitsch,
the love of Eleanor's
later life, 1947.

55.

David and Eleanor,
Israel, 1952, at the start
of their trip to Iran,
Pakistan, and India.

56.

Eleanor (photographed
in 1957) wearing the
necklace strung with the
claws of the tiger her
father shot in India, south
of Hyderabad, in 1881.

Adlai E. Stevenson was Eleanor's kind of man in private, because he needed her, but as Democratic nominee for president in 1952 and again in 1956, Stevenson's strengths became weaknesses that disappointed her.

Eleanor preparing to address the Democratic National Convention, Los Angeles, July 13, 1960.

59.

ER and her *Prospects of Mankind* producers broadcast from
the White House, March 1, 1961, as President John F.
Kennedy announced the start of the Peace Corps.

60.

Four presidents, John F. Kennedy, Lyndon B. Johnson, Harry S. Truman,
Dwight D. Eisenhower—and three First Ladies—attended Eleanor Roosevelt's
burial in the Rose Garden, Hyde Park, November 10, 1962.

"Apathy must be combatted," she continued at Colby College. "Better to try to tear things to pieces than not try to do anything!"[71]

Standing before the younger members at the Women's City Club in Washington, she suddenly said, "I'm so tired of programs of study I don't know what to do." She remembered being her audience's age in 1910 and attending umpteen lectures and demonstrations about first aid, then the new thing: "I was always sitting at somebody's house listening to somebody talk about what somebody else did." Now, in January 1939, after the head of the junior club had asked her for suggestions for a program of study, she rebelled. "Go out as discoverers in your own country," she urged. "One hour of going to see things with your own eyes is more worthwhile than twenty hours of talking about things."[72]

In Chicago, she reminded the Civil Liberties Committee, "In many other forms of government the importance of the individual has disappeared. The individual lives for the state. Here, in our democracy, the government still exists for the individual. But that does not mean that we do not have to watch, or that we do not have to examine ourselves to be sure that we preserve, for all our people, the civil liberties which are the basis of our democracy."[73]

THE WAGNER-ROGERS BILL, JOINTLY MOUNTED by New York Democratic senator Robert F. Wagner and Massachusetts Republican representative Edith Nourse Rogers, proposed to allow special entry to twenty thousand German and Austrian Jewish children. On February 13, 1939, Eleanor urged its immediate passage, the first time she had given her full public support to pending legislation.[74] She wired Franklin, asking if she could tell Sumner Welles—the page at their wedding, now undersecretary of state—that they both approved congressional acceptance of the bill. FDR, cruising in the Caribbean aboard the USS *Houston*, wrote back,[75] "*You* may, but it's better that *I* don't for the time being."

In May 1939, Secretary of State Cordell Hull advised FDR to reject the German liner SS *St. Louis*. Carrying 937 German Jewish refugees from Hamburg, the ship managed to land twenty-two passengers in

Cuba. The rest were blocked under the 1924 immigration laws, despite negotiation with American Jewish groups, pressure from the U.S. government, and public protest. After being resettled in the United Kingdom and Western European countries, as many as 254 former *St. Louis* passengers were killed in the Holocaust.[76]

The American people wanted as little to do with Hitler's victims as possible. A Gallup poll revealed in March 1939 that 83 percent of Americans opposed loosening the immigration quota to let in a larger number of Jewish refugees, fearing that breaking the established limits for countries like Germany, Austria, and Poland, would invite still more "undesirables," the latter synonymous with Communist agitators and Nazi spies.

Eleanor made it her mission to save as many Jewish European children as she could, establishing with the NAACP and civil rights lawyer Louis S. Weiss the U.S. Committee for the Care of European Children; opening doors and finding places for children escaping Spain's civil war; evacuating children from England, often with the intercession of Clarence Pickett's American Friends Service; and always pressing the State Department to increase a thousand to five thousand, and five thousand to fifteen thousand.[77]

FDR had one aim above all others: to move the woefully unprepared United States off neutrality and into war preparation. Meanwhile, he preferred to keep the refugee issue away from Congress, where he could only lose the support of the Southern Democrats he needed to arm England and kick-start domestic manufacture of war materials.[78]

American anti-Semitism had broad support from the Southern Democrats. Jews were seen as midwives to integration and racial reform. On immigration, the whole Southern bloc voted unanimously against any increase in the quotas, but eventually would vote, to the member, unanimously, for Lend-Lease and its funds for food, oil, and war matériel for the Allies.

At Évian, America had been viewed as the "interpreter of the conscience of humanity." But over these next five years, on the few decisions FDR allowed himself to be drawn into concerning the plight of

European Jews, he sided with his State Department crony Breckinridge Long, with whom he shared an uncanny grasp of the narrow
xenophobic viewpoint of most Americans.

"Franklin, you know he's a Fascist," insisted Eleanor.

A luncheon guest recalled that this made FDR "really cross." He
said, "I've told you, Eleanor, you must not say that."

She said, "Well, maybe I shouldn't say it, but he is."[79]

Long, a former ambassador to Italy and aficionado of Mussolini's
dictatorship, had returned in September 1939 by FDR's appointment
as assistant secretary of state, in charge of the Visa Division. From this
stronghold, he became the most bureaucratically powerful xenophobe
and anti-Semite in America, delaying and then effectively stopping
imperiled Jews from leaving Europe by ordering his consular officers
to "put every obstacle in the way to postpone and postpone and postpone the granting of visas."[80]

After the *Kristallnacht* pogrom in November 1938 left 800 innocents slaughtered, 20,000 German and Austrian Jews arrested, and
more than a thousand synagogues destroyed, some 300,000 panicked
refugees put their names on the waiting list for an American immigration visa. The quota allowed a maximum of 27,370 people born in
Germany to immigrate to the United States each year, which meant
that by 1939 the list was more than a decade long. Breckinridge Long
filled the German quota for the first time that year, and he almost filled
it again in 1940. But in every other year of Long's dominance over the
Special War Problems Division, of which the Visa Division was a part,
he worked to "keep America for Americans"[81]—justification enough,
he believed, for delaying and denying visas that would have saved as
many as 200,000 lives.

Eleanor's new intimate, Joseph Lash, the outspoken former leader
of the Student League for International Democracy, a socialist youth
organization, brought two leaders of the Austrian anti-Fascist underground to dinner at Eleanor's Village apartment on June 24, 1940. Karl
Boromäus Frank and Joseph Buttinger were organizing an American
rescue committee on behalf of the thousands of intellectuals, political
leaders, writers, and artists, many of them Jews, caught in the death

trap of Occupied France. For months, as Hitler subjugated country after country, anti-Nazi and anti-Fascist leaders had been taking refuge in France. Now, Frank and Buttinger explained, showing Eleanor a list of names, the craven agreement of Marshal Pétain's rump government in Vichy to "surrender on demand" any Germans named by the Nazis, meant that the Gestapo was hunting high-value targets hiding underground in France. Could Mrs. Roosevelt help bypass the State Department's quotas for the heroes on Frank and Buttinger's list?

She telephoned FDR at once, asking what could be done. Irritated that she did not take for granted that he was already doing all that possibly could be done, Franklin then raised all the obstacles: an immigrant-phobic Congress; filled quotas; Cuba and other Latin American countries resistant to U.S. efforts. FDR went on: "Can't locate people in France. Spain won't admit even American refugees—." Eleanor interrupted to remind him that he had always said the United States could bribe the Spanish and Portuguese governments.

"He kept bringing up the difficulties, while Mrs. R. tenaciously kept pointing out the possibilities," recorded Joe Lash.

Ringing off with the President, she agreed to take Frank and Buttinger's lists and have them sent to the consular offices in Europe. She shook her head in wonder at her own inability to understand what had happened to America, traditional land of asylum, flaunting an insolent, self-pitying unwillingness to admit political refugees.[82]

Karl Frank would eventually credit Eleanor's persistence for the State Department's expediting of emergency visitors' visas to political refugees.[83] Through Eleanor the first two hundred names went to Karl Frank; he recruited a Harvard-educated journalist named Varian Fry, who returned to Marseille in August with the list and $3,000 taped to his leg to conduct a daring rescue operation that saved the most imperiled of Europe's artistic elite. Among these were Hannah Arendt, André Breton, Marc Chagall, Marcel Duchamp, Max Ernst, Arthur Koestler, and Heinrich Mann—as many as four thousand in the end.

The arrival, a month later, in Norfolk, Virginia, of a Portuguese cargo ship brought the issue of Breckinridge Long's cruel restrictions to a head.[84] Three hundred and seventeen passengers had chartered the *Quanza* to flee Europe, and after a thirteen-day voyage, 196 of them, including 66 American citizens, disembarked in New York Harbor, including the French movie star Marcel Dalio and his wife, Madeleine LeBeau, a year from becoming the tear-streaked face of French defiance, singing "La Marseillaise" in *Casablanca*. The other 121 voyagers, "lowly refugees," according to the *New York Times*, were turned away. "They were all Jewish. They all had money," stated Long in his diary. The *Quanza* sailed for Veracruz, where the Mexican government allowed in thirty-five passengers. But after various Caribbean ports denied admittance to the remaining eighty-six refugees, and the ship was about to turn back for Portugal and certain doom in Hitler's Europe, the captain put into Norfolk for fuel, landing at Sewell's Point coal pier.

By then, word of the refugees still on board had reached Eleanor in Hyde Park. She telephoned Breckinridge Long and, as he told it, "expressed her interest in the children and a few other categories." She then appealed to FDR. He endorsed Eleanor's plan to enlist the authority of the President's Advisory Committee on Political Refugees, whose representative, Patrick Murphy Malin, used his powers to allow all of the refugees ashore while lawyers went to work to extend their temporary entry.

Long, meanwhile, "remonstrated violently" when Malin reported these efforts from Norfolk. When Long reached the President at the White House the next day, as FDR had instructed him to do, Long felt certain that FDR "did not want to talk to me on the subject, and I inferred—and it now seems correctly so—that he would leave the matter entirely in my hands."[85]

FDR's skill was the handling of human beings. He could get people to do what he wanted them to do by making them feel free to do as their own best judgment dictated,[86] which he then happily betrayed if another point of view served his larger purpose. By working no less stealthily with Malin and the PAC, Eleanor managed to override Long and arrange for everyone still onboard the *Quanza* to be admitted under temporary visas. None was ever asked to leave.

To her surprise, Irving Berlin's *Music Box Revue of 1938–1939* celebrated her among the communicators of the new mass media: "*Walter Lippmann*: politics. *Walter Winchell*: broadway. *Dorothy Dix*:

love. *Louella Parsons*: movies. *Cholly Knickerbocker*: society. *Dorothy Thompson*: foreign. *B. C. Forbes*: finance. *Mrs. Roosevelt*: everything."[87]

Joseph Goebbels, another shrewd ventriloquist of new world media, exploited pent-up German rage by throwing Mrs. Roosevelt's column back at her. On February 3, 1939, Eleanor's defense of France's legal right to buy airplanes from an American manufacturer offered Hitler's propaganda chief the boilerplate he needed to transfer racial terror, inhumanity to immigrant families, and indifference to workplace discrimination back where it had come from.

Speaking through the Berlin *Lokal-Anzeiger*, Goebbels advised President Roosevelt's wife to "keep her pen away from things of which she is ignorant," listing the topics suitable for a "militant" writer: lynching, child labor, public morals, and "twelve million unemployed."

"It is not good for a nation," said Goebbels, "if not only the husband but also the wife enters the political china shop."[88]

Eleanor trounced the Nazi Megaphone in a single retort: "I thought their whole attitude was that women didn't count."[89]

Her column more and more allowed her to write as the most accessible woman, a citizen linking to other citizens on subjects that connected people to their government. Writing in opposition to Robert Moses's proposed Battery Bridge construction in New York City that spring, she argued for the preservation of "the few beautiful spots that still remain to us on an overcrowded island. After all, lower Manhattan at Battery Park is one of the gateways through which many of us leave and enter our country. These moments are important moments in our lives and the irritation of an eyesore perpetrated in the name of progress will be bad for the souls of many Americans."[90] On July 17, Secretary of War Harry Wooding shelved Moses's scheme, declaring the bridge over New York Harbor a prospective threat to national security.[91]

Her column brought popular attitudes to policymakers and the experience of politics to the people. During the state visit of King George VI and Queen Elizabeth that summer, her daily reporting gave the whole country a seat at the (picnic) table.

Franklin had planned the visit as a public-relations kindling of the Anglo-American friendship, which he hoped would soften isolationist hearts when England's hour of need struck. He well knew that Congress had already hardened itself, invoking the Neutrality Act of 1937—born of bitterness at England's defaulting on its First World War debt. This time, the Republican Congress would demand munitions transactions in cold cash. Britain, in turn, would fancy herself forced by uncouth bullies to humiliate herself before the world as the bankrupt empire she was.

Their Britannic Majesties had come to win over the people of the United States, but George VI and Queen Elizabeth had a tough job, in part because the abdication of his brother to marry Wallis Simpson the previous year had trivialized the monarchy. But the Windsors were also popular. Upon the royal couple's arrival at Union Station on June 7, much of official Washington promptly lost its head; or, as one headline put it, PRESIDENT'S WIFE STAYS HERSELF.[92] Eleanor, "one of the least flustered of all people in Washington this week," brought calm to a tense and sweltering capital that had been harassing the first lady over her plan to serve hot dogs to royalty at a picnic, and begging her mother-in-law to "stop Eleanor" from "imperiling the dignity of our country."[93]

Sara would take full credit for being first in history to entertain British rulers in a private house in America, but there was no question who was hosting Their Britannic Majesties. Franklin and Eleanor treated the King and Queen of England as a nice young couple they were having to Hyde Park for the weekend; and when Franklin bade a tired George VI good night with a breezy "Young man, you need to get to bed," the king later wondered why his own people didn't treat him that way.

If the idea of royalty meeting American royalty and eating the food of Coney Island failed to add to the interlocking propaganda pushing the Anglo-American friendship, the crash of plates at the state dinner hosted by Sara on Saturday evening saved that day. Sara wanted it kept "a deep, dark family secret," but Eleanor overrode her, and with Franklin's permission told the world through her readers that nothing that befell them as hostesses or hosts could be more painful or trying than what had happened that Sunday to the President's mother.

Too many pieces of Limoges had been placed on one side of Sara's center-supported serving table. In the middle of dinner for the king and queen, the table tipped over. Hard-paste porcelain saucers, bowls, and various sized plates smashed by the dozens, sustaining a level of noise so extreme that for a minute, wrote Eleanor, "no one could think."[94]

Into a mortified silence, Eleanor's sister-in-law, Betty, widow of Franklin's half brother Rosy, loudly grumbled, "I do hope that wasn't *my* china."

Sara laughed off the smashup.[95] Following suit, "Their Majesties remained completely calm and undisturbed," reported Eleanor, almost as if conscious of comforting her readers when they continued the story.

A lifetime later, in a small village in Israel, when a boy sent to prepare lemonade for Mrs. Roosevelt and a group of children rushed back with a pitcher that slipped, crashing to the floor, everyone but Mrs. Roosevelt froze, staring at the spilled drink and broken glass. Calling for a towel, she comforted the crying boy; and, as she mopped up the mess, told him about the many smashed glasses when the King and Queen of England had visited *her*.[96] "You mustn't worry, son," she said, "it happens everywhere."

During the royal visit, a tacit armistice on international issues had been more or less observed by politicians if not by a press swept up in the sentiment of the Anglo-American friendship. Conservative Republicans in the New York delegation praised King George and Queen Elizabeth as "a gracious and democratic couple," but warned that the visiting monarchs had not changed "one single vote in the determination of the American people to keep out of Europe's wars."[97]

FDR knew that a vast majority of Americans would not go to war to save England.[98] But he also knew what he was doing, and that Sunday night at ten past eleven, he and Eleanor saw their young weekend guests off to their train.

Hundreds of villagers thronged the Hyde Park station to say a final farewell. For ten minutes the hosts and the visitors, still in their elegant dinner clothes, exchanged parting words alongside the red-brick depot. A raucous cry went up as Their Majesties boarded the observation platform on the blue-and-silver royal train. The Americans accorded the parting couple a fervent rendition of "Auld Lang Syne."

The locomotive pulled away for Canada, and the last choruses of friendship's anthem followed king and queen into the summer dark. "One thought of the clouds that hung over them and the worries they were going to face," wrote Eleanor, "and we turned away and left the scene with a heavy heart."[99]

THE CLOUDS BROKE BEFORE SUMMER's end. On August 23, when Vyacheslav Molotov and Joachim von Ribbentrop, foreign ministers of the Soviet Union and Nazi Germany, signed a ten-year "nonaggression" pact in Moscow, Stalin and Hitler looked as if they would control the shores of Europe. Tyranny stretched from the Atlantic port of Brest to Vladivostok, Soviet gateway on Asia. Not even the Mongols had managed so complete a chokehold on freedom.

Some saw the Nazi-Soviet pact as a way of containing Stalin; others as final proof of Hitler's ultimate wickedness. What, after all, was the Soviet dictator saying—that, in the end, if handled properly, everything could become a purely financial matter? He could even buy Hitler, which was as much as to say, he had struck a bargain with the Devil.

Three days after news of the pact, Eleanor, at Val-Kill, spoke to the President in Washington. "Like all women who like to keep the daily happenings on as even a keel as possible, I casually inquired the hour of his arrival next Monday night, only to be told firmly that he would not arrive in any case until Tuesday morning and he might not arrive for months to come."

Franklin's tone implied that arrivals and departures were of no importance now. In fact, nothing personal or individual counted because perhaps the fate of all civilization hung once again in the balance. What did it matter whether they ate or slept or did any of the things which they had thought important yesterday?

"My heart sank," recorded Eleanor, "for that was the old 1914 psychology. It is rather horrible to have a past experience of this kind to check against the present."[100]

* * *

TEN MINUTES BEFORE NOON ON the sunny calm morning of August 31, 1939, high tide crested the James River, wafting up the creosote smell of the new ship's cradle of timbers and steel. Eleanor took her place at the bow, anxious as always to do her part without a hitch. She fully understood that she represented one of the most seagoing presidents in U.S. history and a botched christening could very well doom *America*, the largest, roomiest, costliest, safest, fastest, most state-of-the-art merchant vessel yet built in the United States, combining the best of technology, art, and style to represent the nation's idea of itself as builders of a global vessel that would return the U.S. merchant fleet to a dominant position on the oceans of the world. The launching, declared FDR, "is one of the most important events to take place in the world this year."[101]

And so, before thirty thousand onlookers, three radio networks broadcasting live, and a bank of newsreel cameras, Eleanor waited for the first whistle before stepping forward, calling out, "I christen thee *America*!" and swinging a bottle of Ohio champagne toward the prow.

At five the next morning—September 1, 1939—Franklin awakened her with the call she knew would come eventually. "Babs," he said, hoarsely, "it's happened. Germany has invaded Poland."[102]

The Luftwaffe was dropping bombs on women and children in Polish cities. Later in the day, Hitler would order the extermination of the mentally ill. Now he was going to address the Reichstag, and Franklin tasked Eleanor with listening to the speech. When she snapped on the radio set, she heard Hitler explaining that the Nazis would not depend on Italy—indeed, would not "call in any outside help for this struggle."[103] Germany intended to enslave the free world all on its own.

The day before, Eleanor had reached home from Newport News, Virginia, and a brief visit with Franklin at the White House, in time for the 7:45 arrival of her dinner guests in Hyde Park. A letter from Germany awaited her—from her Allenswood roommate, Carola von Schaeffer-Bernstein, begging Eleanor not to fall in with the world's "easy" and "harsh" judgment, but to sympathize with Nazi Germany, which was "misunderstood," and not to hate her personally.

As Eleanor listened to Hitler on the radio, Carola's letter kept coming to mind. She wanted to ask her old roommate the same questions she was posing as a columnist: "How could you feel kindly toward a man who tells you that German minorities have been brutally treated, first in Czechoslovakia and then in Danzig, but that Germany could never be accused of unfairness to a minority?"[104]

Eleanor had heard directly from survivors escaping to the United States that this same man was imprisoning and savagely torturing and killing German "minorities"—not only Jews, but Catholics, Jehovah's Witnesses, liberal Protestants, German Communists, and homosexuals.

Eleanor emphasized to her readers on September 2 that she felt no bitterness against the German people.[105] She hoped "almost against hope that the qualities of the individual Germans whom so many of us have known and respected and loved will make it impossible for them to carry out harsh and unjust demands."[106] Meanwhile, she felt sorry for them. "But for the man who has taken this responsibility upon his shoulders I can feel little pity. It is hard to see how he can sleep at night and think of the people in many nations whom he may send to their deaths."[107]

As the Nazi war machine went on gobbling up Europe's helpless nations, Charles A. Lindbergh broadcast to Americans, declaring that another European conflict posed an even greater threat to Western civilization than the first. Hitler, argued the aviator, was no Genghis Khan or Xerxes "marching against our western nations," but merely the instigator of "a quarrel arising from the errors of the last war."[108] When Lindbergh boosted the Luftwaffe's superior readiness for air combat, but held that Hitler would prove no threat to the continental United States, the war-wary majority of the country gratefully sided with Lindy. Eleanor listened and heard a believer in the German Wehrmacht.

"Mrs. Roosevelt Says He Has Nazi Tendencies," reported the Hazleton, Pennsylvania, *Plain Speaker*, counterpointing ER's opinion with that of General Hugh S. Johnson, the former NRA chief. Johnson took issue with "pro-war pundits" mistaking Lindbergh's "pro-American" opinions as "pro-Nazi," no columnist more "emotionally biased" than "the first lady of the land herself." Eleanor's suspicions about Lindbergh were "exactly the kind of stuff," fumed Johnson, "that got us into the war in 1917."[109]

CAN AMERICA STAY OUT OF war? asked every editorial page in the country.

"I not only sincerely hope so," began FDR, reluctantly backstepping to keep the White House aligned with the isolationist sentiments of the vast majority of the nation, "but I believe we can and that every effort will be made by the administration so to do."[110]

Eleanor's greatness lay in moving forward with a certain calm grimness. As storm clouds gathered over the Atlantic world, she was firm: We can't turn away from this; it would be so much nicer if we could. We must face this, and we can't get it done overnight. We have to be patient, resolved, as we rise each morning to a more threatening world.

She waited until September 6 to reply to Carola von Schaeffer-Bernstein. She could not understand, she said, how "people of spirit" could "countenance the kind of horrors which seem to have come on in Germany, not only where the Jews are concerned, but as in the case of the Catholics and some of the liberal Germans."[111]

Then, inexplicably reversing herself, Eleanor returned to the kind of class assumptions which she and Carola had brought to Mademoiselle Souvestre's study in 1905. "I realize quite well that there may be a need for curtailing the ascendency of the Jewish people," she wrote, agreeing with her Nazi-sympathizing friend, "but it seems to me it might have been done in a more humane way by a ruler who had intelligence and decency."

This was among the strangest of her several strange statements about the Jews and Germany—and not far from FDR while meeting Churchill at the ten-day Casablanca Conference in January 1943, advising French military leaders to adopt a plan that would allow Jews the right to engage in medicine and law in North Africa, but in numbers that "would not permit them to overcrowd the professions." As the minutes recorded it: "The President stated that his plan would further eliminate the specific and understandable complaint which the

Germans bore towards the Jews in Germany, namely, that while they represented a small part of the population, over fifty percent of the lawyers, doctors, school teachers, college professors, etc. in Germany were Jews."[112]

Eleanor's similar affirmation of Germany's "need" to restrict or winnow "the Jewish people" offered no awareness that, whatever construction could be put on it, the "curtailing" of an ethnic group by a modern industrial state could never be the action of a "decent" or "intelligent" leader, nor could mass extermination, however unimaginable in 1939, be "done" in any humane way.

TEXAS CONGRESSMAN MARTIN DIES—A FORMER New Deal partisan, now "a cornpone Hitler,"[113] per *New Yorker* humorist S. J. Perelman—had by 1939 turned the House Un-American Activities Committee into a character-assassination machine.

In an October raid throwing back to A. Mitchell Palmer's harassing "red hunts" in the last war, Dies's agents illegally searched and seized records already turned over by the American League for Peace and Democracy, a coalition of pacifist and left-wing organizations including the American Communist Party. Inflaming the fears of a highly gullible radio and newspaper audience, Dies fed an all-too-willing press with the latest "red list" of 563 government employees, including clerks, stenographers, and an office cleaner, none of whom were Communists, but all of whom happened still to be on the League's mostly out-of-date mailing list.

As Dies's witch hunt reached peak intensity—"I don't believe a lot of the testimony myself," the chairman cynically admitted[114]— Eleanor joined the Herald Tribune Forum, a program tightly constructed for radio broadcast about underground enemies, entitled, *American Democracy Fights Back*. Thirty thousand clubwomen had applied for three thousand places in the Waldorf Astoria ballroom, and Eleanor opened the second part of the program on October 24 with a ten-minute talk, "Humanistic Democracy—The American Ideal," in which she warned that "in suppressing alien-controlled groups," such as Communists, "we also suppress some of our own freedom."[115]

On November 30, 1939, the House Un-American Activities Committee (HUAC), subpoenaed members of a student group called the American Youth Congress (AYC) to testify to their "loyalty" to the United States. Tipped off about HUAC's summonses by her new friend Joe Lash, Eleanor consulted Franklin, who OKed her unannounced presence at the hearing to see whether witnesses were treated fairly.

At the noontime break, still waiting to testify, the student leaders demanded that the Dies committee be dissolved. Eleanor invited them back to lunch at the White House. When she learned they had nowhere to sleep that night, she invited all ten of them to stay through the week, to dine with the President, and to discuss freely the Soviet invasion of Finland.

Listening to Joe Lash's testimony was the beginning for Eleanor of a long, lasting friendship. As so often, she fell immediately and deeply. But unlike any of the other Ones and Onlys—even Earl Miller—ER chose him. Joe was her special promising young man. Finding him outside her ordinary world reinforced it. He released her from the automaton quality she had found in motherhood, and made her feel larger, just as her contacts with the working class enlarged him. The fact that Joe was on the front lines of this edition of America's serial red scare—and, later, in harm's way in the South Pacific—suddenly brought into focus that her relationship with her sons, disadvantaged by so many years of unreconstructed dysfunction, had become all too perfunctory.

And as Joe fell secretly in love with Trude Wenzel Pratt, still married, unhappily and with children, Eleanor acted as the forbidden couple's adviser and fairy godmother, invisibly but influentially, as she preferred it, urging them to find their own bliss.

A lifetime of finding herself powerful when entering an ascendant couple's drama as their go-between, as she had from her own parents up through her daughter's second, seemingly more passionate marriage to John Boettiger in the mid-thirties, assured her of her place with Joe and Trude. Meanwhile, Joe and his young people gave her another kind of hope for the future.

The plan for the American Youth Congress Citizenship Institute, held in Washington from February 9 to 11, 1940, was to bring young men and women to the nation's capital to learn how government worked and to lobby for federal jobs and student aid programs. The administration had a strong desire to prevent conservatives on Capitol Hill from cutting New Deal social programs and offered cooperation to the AYC. Eleanor saw to it that scores of young delegates were housed with New Dealers around Washington, or at the Riding Hall at Fort Meyer, or even, for a night, on the floor in the White House.

At an introductory meeting, she had agreed with the AYC leaders in their sympathy for Spain—and for China and Czechoslovakia. "But," she told the students, who refused to brand the Soviet invasion of Finland an act of aggression, "I also have sympathy for Finland."[116] Whether she agreed with everything that was said was not the point, she insisted. What mattered was that all participants in the institute feel free to state openly what they had on their minds and in their hearts.[117] She spent the afternoon listening with increasing admiration for their candor as, one after another, young activists rose and told of the difficult position in which they found themselves as world events shifted.[118] It was in this democratic spirit of youth speaking its mind that Eleanor persuaded Franklin to meet with the delegates, even if the only place spacious enough for such a meeting was the South Lawn.

It was a critical moment for FDR: the Congress distrusted the President; the Democratic Party had turned insubordinate to his wishes; his political career itself was in doubt. He had no wish to meet with a group for whom the Soviet invasion of Finland was a sacred cow. It annoyed FDR that these student leaders refused to criticize Stalin or his brutal tactics. They would not be budged—or charmed.[119]

At the appointed hour on February 11, Eleanor followed Franklin out onto the South Portico and stood behind her husband, wishing that Joe Lash's comrades had better manners.[120] The young activists had paraded up Constitution Avenue, filing onto the White House lawn with their signs and banners: JOBS NOT GUNS, said one. SCHOOLS NOT BATTLESHIPS, read another. THE YANKS ARE NOT COMING, declared a third. Jack McMichael, a Southern clergyman and chairman of the Youth Congress, had made a moving appeal to the President to keep up his fight against poverty and prejudice, begging the administration not to abandon New Deal reforms for war preparedness.

FDR waved, vaguely noting the protest signs. "He doesn't like the smell of the Albatross that his wife has hung around his neck," said one observer to another.[121]

Discarding his prepared speech, he tried out a tired-sounding argument meant to defend the false starts and second attempts at various social justice programs. He scolded the young people about "handouts" and warned against accommodating politics to popular sentiment— the rebuke extending beyond the activists to include Eleanor, who loyally maintained her post behind him.

Harsh words for the Soviet Union drew hisses from the activists. A final, flippant presidential send-off admonished the young people to "keep your ideals high, keep both feet on the ground, and keep everlastingly at it."[122]

On radio, Fulton Lewis, Jr., reported that most of the "main horde" of Youth Congress members who had "swarmed the south lawn" had "Polish or Russian" names. Lewis insisted that radical youth had done more in three days to prove the Dies committee charges than Congressman Dies had struggled to do in two years. Only the "unflagging Mrs. Roosevelt" could still believe that subversive Communist organizations had any place in America or on the President's appointment calendar.[123]

The activists stood clumped together, "too disheartened to applaud, too wet to boo," remembered one. Woody Guthrie was there among them, and later wrote a song, "Why Do You Stand There in the Rain?"

IN APRIL, MRS. ROOSEVELT FAILED to appear for a scheduled speech. The audience waited. Finally, a message reached Denver saying she couldn't be there. The next day's papers revealed the story: Eleanor's nephew—Hall's son, Daniel—flying to Mexico and back with a friend, had been killed at the controls when their small plane crashed in a storm outside Mexico City.[124] Danny was twenty-one.

She had a high threshold for bad news. To Eleanor, there was nothing strange about further grim reports—the blows had been falling all her life. The hurt could always be modified with immediate action.

As a kind of family coroner, she worked closely with doctors, notified lawyers, dispatched the press, consoled survivors, discreetly probed causes, brought home bodies. A twenty-two-year-old Delano cousin who had committed suicide on the Parana River in the Argentine territory of the Chaco. A Roosevelt cousin who had drowned when his dinghy capsized in Oyster Bay. Another, gone AWOL in 1944, tried for desertion. Yet another dead in a fall from the fifth-floor bedroom window of a brownstone. In the White House family, she attended the funeral of her maid's son against the rules of segregated Washington. When the wife of White House doorman John Mays died suddenly, ER made sure members of the staff stayed with him at his home until she could get there herself.

"It is not one's activities which are really important in this life," she decided. "When you lay down the things you do, day by day, someone else always takes them up. The really important thing is what you are as a person, what your character and your presence have meant to those you lived with, and what influence you have had on the atmosphere of your home or your environment—regardless of whether this was a restricted one, or a broad one which touched many lives and large numbers of people. That is what lives afterwards in the memories and in the hearts of those who knew and loved you. As you influenced these people, so your influence will spread, through their contacts and their activities."[125]

BEFORE DAWN ON MAY 10, 1940, Nazi blitzkrieg swept into the Low Countries, bringing total war to Western Europe. For the third time, Hitler described his conquests as acts of "protective custody,"[126] this time *after* German warplanes had bombed Brussels and Rotterdam and thundered into France. In England, Neville Chamberlain's misguided appeasement policy collapsed. The chief of the British naval staff strode into No. 10 Downing Street and remarked, "Well, it has started at last."

It was all happening overnight.[127] As Americans sat beside their radios, German panzer divisions rolled up the vaunted French Army, sending two million French soldiers to prison camps. The Third Republic was wound up in a matter of days, the encircling Nazi war machine swallowing Paris like a boa constrictor. Winston Churchill, called back from political wilderness to Whitehall, rose in the House of Commons and spurted out "blood, toil, tears, and sweat."

Discussing the "European situation" with Franklin on May 14, Eleanor saw that he was greatly worried.[128] He had it on good intelligence that the Allies' position was virtually hopeless, as was America's ability to come to the rescue; even war matériel would take as long as six months to get overseas. England was in imminent danger. Should an invasion come, the British government would either escape to Canada or fight on until overwhelmed. If the Nazis triumphed over the United Kingdom, they would control the British Navy, and therefore Africa and South America, ultimately, putting the United States in grave danger.

In June, one observer—not her husband—noticed that Eleanor looked "tired, drained, and unhappy."[129] She now realized that there was going to be no negotiating with an amoral Germany. Should Hitler achieve the impossible and invade the American continent, she suspected that far too many Americans of the Charles Lindbergh school could be attracted and subjugated, "by the amazing success of the Nazi system."[130] Hitler's political and racial creeds would "threaten our very civilization," she had told the African American scholar Ralph J. Bunche during an interview at the White House on May 15. "It is entirely possible," said Eleanor to Bunche, "we might be destroyed by them."[131]

She and Franklin spoke once more in early June about the world to come if Hitler should achieve world conquest.

"Well, there would be one thing anyway," said Franklin, meeting Eleanor's realism halfway. "We'd both be dead."[132]

IN THE MONTHS BEFORE THE 1940 Democratic Convention, Franklin said frequently that he had little interest in a third term. He was not thrilled at the prospect of breaking a mighty tradition of the Republic, but if he decided he had to run, it would be the plain determined judgment of an experienced politician.

Eleanor was ready to get on with life after the presidency. She told Anna that if her father didn't leave the White House in 1941, *she* would. The prospect of another four years of dividing herself between what she wanted to do and what she had to do held no appeal. She judged herself to have lived "very impersonally" in these recent years. "It was almost as though I had erected someone outside myself who was the president's wife. I was lost somewhere deep down inside myself."[133] She liked to be with the very few people she really cared about and longed to do the things that mattered to her, and to finish them by herself. In the White House, everything was always left unfinished.

Franklin urged others with presidential ambitions to seek the nomination—Hopkins (until his health worsened), Farley (until his frustration with FDR got the better of him)—but he never quite took himself out of the running. For all his protests and wishful plans to retire to Hyde Park and the now completed Top Cottage, Eleanor knew he feared that the New Deal would be pulped as soon as he was gone. After the failure to pack the Court, after the elections of '38, Franklin was something of a political has-been—until the war came along.

POLAND, NORWAY, DENMARK, HOLLAND, BELGIUM, Luxembourg, and France. By September, all had bowed to the expanding Third Reich. Hitler's army had very rapidly slaughtered at least a quarter-million souls in seven nations. A shocked world had reason to believe that the "world's greatest military machine" might be unstoppable. In the American press, "Der Fuehrer" commanded front-page illustrations as a melodrama villain, painted in dark Disney-lush pen-and-wash portraits. An Ohio newspaper posed the anxious question: "Hitler, the Conqueror?"[134] It all but assured a single answer: Roosevelt, the President.

When he lost only ten states on Election Day 1940—an astoundingly small number for an unprecedented third term—FDR felt the juices flowing again. He wasn't quite the old FDR, but 80 percent of FDR was 100 percent more than anyone else.

As this new assertion of her husband's power took shape under U.S. neutrality laws, ER could find no public role to play in partnership with the commander in chief. After the fall of France, Eleanor had offered to go to Europe to supervise the relocation of war victims, but FDR and the Secret Service had declared the risk of the President's wife being captured by the Nazis insupportable.

Eleanor's fear that the war would get in the way of domestic progress had briefly lifted when she saw Harry Hopkins back in the White House the night Germany invaded Western Europe. "I knew that he had never been interested in military affairs and that he'd stick with me no matter what happened."[135]

Malvina Thompson noticed Eleanor's uncertainty mixing with the boredom of repetition. "She has wanted desperately to be given something really concrete and worthwhile to do in this emergency and no one has found anything for her. They are all afraid of political implications, etc.," Tommy reported to Anna. "Outside of making two radio speeches for the Red Cross, she has not been asked to do anything. She works like Hell all the time and we are busier than ever, but I know you can understand that she wants to feel she is doing something worthwhile and it makes me mad, because she has so much organizing and executive ability she could do a swell job on anything she undertook."[136]

As the President shifted from social policy toward the worldwide massing of arms, barely objecting when Congress voted to end the CCC, the WPA, and the NYA (National Youth Administration), Eleanor quietly sank into a profound discouragement. FDR turned to Harry Hopkins, who defected from being the brightest knight in Eleanor's court to live full-time under FDR's roof, and in the best guest room in the White House—the big suite in the southwest corner of the second floor, formerly Lincoln's study, comprised of one large bedroom (with a four-poster bed), a small sitting room, and a bath.

"Harry and Missy are thicker than the well-known thieves at the moment," tattled Tommy to Anna; "he has gone completely over to the other side of the house. If your father does not eat with your mother and any guests, Harry eats with him and Missy, and it makes me mad and ready to smack him because your mother was so darn faithful about going to see him when he was sick, agreeing to take Diana if anything happened to him, etc. It seems to me if he had a lick of sense or appreciation, he would make it a real point to spend time with your mother. I can well understand your father not wanting to have his meals with a lot of more or less strange people but it would not hurt Harry Hopkins."[137]

IT HAD NOT ESCAPED ELEANOR's eye that the world's greatest depression could be solved by the world's greatest war.

Having witnessed how TVA electrification and WPA construction had provided the infrastructure that allowed poor rural communities to leap forward in material progress and social change, Eleanor, teamed up with Florence Kerr, WPA assistant administrator for women's and professional projects, pinned her hopes on a new Social Defense Administration. They would ready an unprepared, undernourished, unfit, unskilled America to fight two of the most unyielding war machines the world had ever seen.

During the early months of 1941, amid the debate about supplying military aid to foreign allies while remaining officially neutral, Eleanor and Florence proposed what they called "an American plan" that would recruit virtually every American woman to undertake war-related and socially beneficial tasks. Women, most of them volunteers, were to assist with conservation, feed those in need, set up day-care centers. They would give workers, minorities, and the poor a direct stake in the war's outcome and democracy's future.

How, after all, could the army expect to field the half a million more soldiers it needed by January 1942 when young men by the hundreds were failing their military physicals?[138] How would industry meet the President's request for fifty thousand warplanes within the next twelve months without training women and African American men for the jobs workers had left behind after enlisting? How would local communities keep up morale for a "democratic way of life" if citizens left out of a decade of reforms were still stuck in substandard housing, suffering malnutrition, dying from disease, struggling to find work, and seeing their vote stolen and civil liberties trampled by a whites-only government and justice system? The ER/Kerr plan would attempt to showcase American democracy as the best possible system for all peoples, taking inspiration in Lady Stella Reading's British Women's Voluntary Service, and ultimately finding expression in FDR's executive order establishing the Office of Civilian Defense.

In the meantime, Eleanor took her case for "social defense" to the heartland. It was June 1941, and admirers in St. Paul, Minnesota, mobbed her at the airfield, while an isolationist group, Mothers of Minnesota, picketed her speech, mustering thirty women to march in grim silence, carrying signs: MY DAY NOT YOUR DAY—MOTHERS PROTEST ROOSEVELT'S WAR.

Inside the auditorium, a crowd of some eleven thousand filled the hall, including hundreds of participants in a two-day regional conference of Democratic women. Four young men in the gallery booed Eleanor when she stepped to the microphone to start her speech. She regarded them with a thoughtful smile. She was now, after all, the mother of four young men of military age, and Elliott and Jimmy had already enlisted. Many of the Mothers of Minnesota had meanwhile left their placards outside so that they could come in to hear Mrs. Roosevelt.

She kept herself under tight restraint. It was these individuals before her, forming an eleven-thousand-headed creature of popular opinion, who had persuaded the isolationists in Congress to stop Franklin from defending *their* interests, not just across the Atlantic, but in the Western Pacific.

The Japanese would need the rubber and cordage and metals of the Philippines—were Americans so naïve as to let them take it? When imperial forces tried to seize the Southeast Asian oil fields long in the hands of the British and the Dutch, why wouldn't the colonial powers hold "their" oil? Why should Americans fight any less for *their* westernmost territory? Did anyone besides Franklin, with his stamps and cockeyed theories of improving the Pacific through controlled "crossbreeding," even know where Guam was—or that Guamanians were American citizens by birth?

After eleven years of depression, another U.S. territory, the Hawaiian Islands, still eighteen years from statehood, might as well have been a foreign country to Eleanor's audience. To families in the Upper Midwest, for whom the grit of the Dust Bowl had barely been swept from under the stove, it made no sense that their sons were once again in danger of being taken away.

Franklin presented the war to isolationists as a new kind of fight, "not only in its methods and weapons but also in its geography." The struggle would be global, fought on or in "every continent, every sea, every air lane in the world." Defending American security and American ideals would be a matter of defending freedom wherever in the world freedom was under attack. Nazis and Fascists were "gangsters," a threat as immediate as any that the Midwest had just lived through under the reign of crime boss Al Capone.

When a member of the audience asked about "going to war under foreign entanglements," Eleanor reframed and clarified: "Is [that] when your country is in danger? Is it your conception that it is only to be defended when attacked on our own shores?"

She mocked Hitler's protests of innocence. "That gentleman," she sarcastically called him. If isolationists couldn't see the threat to America in his subjugation of Austria, Czechoslovakia, Poland, Denmark, Norway, Belgium, Holland, or France, she asked only that each auditor recognize that Hitler would never be stopped without force of arms. The time would soon come when American citizens would have to defend themselves if they wished to remain free.

As for her husband, Eleanor declared: "No president—I don't care who he may be—wants to send his people to war. No president takes that responsibility without consulting his people," she emphasized, to strong applause.

Then she framed her case for preparedness around a simple vision of national defense: "When force is abroad in the world, and when it is successful, we must have equal force—or submit to domination."

She urged women, as well as men, to clarify in their own thinking what they would defend. She had carefully considered the question herself "because I know this country of ours fairly well, and I know there are many things which are not perfect." She contrasted the founding ideals of life, liberty, and the pursuit of happiness with the "many people in this country today who, because of race or religion or economic conditions, have neither liberty nor the opportunity to pursue happiness."

The constitutionally enshrined tradition of civilian control of the military would,[139] she believed, shape the particular character of this war: "This is a war of people—a war of morale—a war of citizens."[140] Or, as FDR would express it in his invasion prayer of June 6, 1944, the combatants were citizen soldiers, "men lately drawn from the ways of peace."

THE GERMANS LAUNCHED OPERATION BARBAROSSA from Poland on June 22, 1941, invading Russia through an Eastern Front stretching from the Arctic Ocean south to the Black Sea. Stalin, believing himself immunized by the Molotov-Ribbentrop pact, had disregarded repeated warnings of a German invasion, and by midsummer the Soviet Union looked as if it might collapse. The Third Reich's Eastern Campaign had overrun the Red Army, the Luftwaffe had disposed of some seven thousand Soviet planes, and the Germans were closing in on Moscow.

Nazi racial policy had pronounced the majority of the Russian population "sub-human," marking for slaughter, deportation, or enslavement tens of millions of Slavs and Jews.[141] As the Soviet High Command dithered, uncertain how to defend the capital, Nazi propaganda informed the Soviet people they had been freed from one brutal tyrant by the "military genius" of another. Western analysts, meanwhile, saw an inevitable end—the only question was how soon.[142] There seemed a real chance that Stalin would lose the war by Christmas. If so, the Soviets' latest ally, Britain, would go next. And after that—Manhattan?

On the first day of Germany's invasion, Missy LeHand checked herself into a private hospital on Eye Street. Franklin's closest companion had fallen ill on June 4, suffering from a blood clot in her lungs, which, combined with a rapid, irregular heart rate, clouded her brain and left her vulnerable to further clots, stroke, or heart failure. "She's been taking opiates & had a heart attack & then her mind went, as it does," explained Eleanor to Anna, referring to an earlier breakdown Missy had endured in Warm Springs.[143]

Missy convalesced in her rooms on the third floor of the White House, under the care of a navy doctor, various specialists, and a round of private nurses. On her first day of recovery, Franklin checked in on her at eleven-thirty in the morning and again at five-

forty that afternoon, in between keeping office appointments with
War Secretary Stimson, special envoy Myron Charles Taylor, and
labor leader Daniel J. Tobin, and lunch at his desk with seventy-
nine-year-old Supreme Court chief justice Charles Evans Hughes.
Just before four in the afternoon a familiar old face appeared in the
West Wing under the alias "Mrs. Paul Johnson." Lucy Mercer had
come from Aiken, South Carolina, and accompanied the President
back to his second-floor White House study, where for several hours
they could be alone.

BEFORE LEAVING FOR CAMPOBELLO IN June 1941, Sara said to the
rector of her parish, "I must take care of myself. I can't let anything
happen to me now because I must not add any burden to the many he
is carrying now."[144]

Joe Lash on June 4: "Mrs. James is ill. May have had a stroke. Mrs.
R said she and Pres never get on. Would start to quarrel half an hour
after they were together and Pres always felt as if she were trying to
influence him. But though there was no companionship between the
two, he would be very much affected by her death. Every year Pres
would urge his mother to go up to Campo early, 'before it gets too hot'
etc, so that he could be at Hyde Park more. She would say he was trying to get rid of her and then he would soothe her feelings."[145]

Upon Sara's return to Hyde Park in September, FDR had recently
returned to Washington, planning on a real visit later in the month.
One night the following week, he obeyed an instinct—but also a signal
from Eleanor—to go to his mother at once.[146] He took the next train
home and found her dying. Just before noon on September 7, after
an anxious twenty-four-hour vigil, Sara died in bed, Franklin holding
her hand at the end.

Minutes after she was gone, a massive oak, the largest tree on the
place, crashed suddenly to the ground. Franklin in his wheelchair led
the way outside, awestruck by the colossal uprooting. "There was no
storm, no wind, no lightning," tallied Secret Service agent Mike Reilly.
The soil at Springwood was sandy loam underlain by slate, not ideal
for the branching roots of a great tree, but on a clear Indian summer
morning, Hudson River geology still did not account for the sudden

end of Hyde Park's mightiest oak.[147] "It was never the true explanation to a lot of us," said Reilly.[148]

At Sara's funeral, the pews at St. James's were restricted to unavoidable relatives and families who worked at Springwood.[149] Franklin wanted his bereavement as private as possible. Even on a regular parish Sunday he detested getting into the pew and settling down to pray "with everybody looking at me." During his mother's service, he never left the automobile that had brought him. A choir of eight voices sang her favorite hymn, "O Love That Will Not Let Me Go." Other men carried Mama's mahogany coffin to her open grave in the churchyard. Franklin stood by the car.[150] He would draw no closer.[151]

Within herself, Eleanor noticed an edge of numbness. She kept "being appalled at myself because I couldn't feel any grief or sense of loss, and that seemed terrible after thirty-six years of fairly close association."[152] Franklin, she could see, had already begun to forget all that was ever disagreeable in his relationship to his mother.

His one great emotional contact in life was gone. "Nothing was ever quite the same again," reflected Eleanor. "By December we were in the war, and Franklin never had any time; he had too much to do."[153]

FROM AN EARLY AGE, HER brother had predicted his own death at fifty. Hall drank himself to death exactly on schedule.[154] Eleanor loved him dearly, but she had been thwarted in the past ten years by helplessness, watching the waste of Hall's life play itself out into his final alcoholic hours, through which she sat by him at Walter Reed Hospital.[155] Until his death she never gave up hope that somehow, some day, he would be all right.

Hall's daughter Eleanor later said: "He loved her more than anyone and knew he had disappointed her because he drank so heavily. He tried in a way to protect her from himself, from his great drinking bouts. He knew what trouble she'd had as a little girl (the father and her uncles), but he just couldn't help himself."[156]

Watching terminal alcoholism close over her brother, Eleanor wrote: "It's such an unattractive death. He's mahogany color, all distended, out of his head most of the time & his speech is almost impossible to understand. He moves insistently & involuntarily so you try to hold him quiet & it is really most distressing."[157] At the end, Hall was downing a quart of gin per day, with Eleanor herself smuggling the bottles to him.

In the stillness of five-thirty one morning at Walter Reed, her brother succumbed to cirrhosis of the liver, leaving five surviving children. It was September 25, 1939.[158] She drove at once from the hospital to the White House and went to her husband's bedroom with the news.

Franklin in his wheelchair struggled to her side and put his arm around her. "Sit down," he said—almost a whisper. She sank beside him, and he hugged and kissed her, and held her head on his chest.[159]

WAR PREPARATIONS HAD BEEN LISTLESS in May when Eleanor turned down a job at the brand-new Office of Civilian Defense (OCD) created by FDR to mobilize the home front for war. The agency's first administrator seemed a likely choice—New York mayor Fiorello La Guardia, named by FDR as the "whirlwind" most likely to sell to large numbers of Americans still resistant to "Europe's war" that it was America's war, too. La Guardia's mistake was thinking that FDR had charged him with protecting the civilian population, when in fact the President had created OCD as a transformational agency. La Guardia, a politically independent social reformer and natural born first responder, running the nation's biggest metropolis, saw it as more ambulances to chase, bigger blazes to extinguish.

Eleanor caught FDR's idea of morale-building. She still hoped to enact the programs that she and Florence Kelley had envisioned for the Social Defense Administration: civilian volunteers to be trained to work in nursery schools, housing projects, jobs.[160] Eleanor saw OCD going beyond gas-mask distribution to creating a stronger country from the ground up. So, when La Guardia realized that he needed a codirector for the agency's "war service" functions, such as childcare, health, housing, and transportation, he offered the job to Eleanor. Her brother still clung to life at the naval hospital in Bethesda. "I could not," she noted, "have been very useful to him for the first week."[161]

The morning after returning from Hall's burial, she strode

headlong from the White House up Connecticut Avenue to the Dupont Circle Flat Iron Building. On the tenth floor, she took her new post alongside Elinor Morgenthau, the two of them at twin desks with twin vases, twin telephones, and twin clocks. Between them, these two 1920s peace workers now had six sons of military age. Eleanor became the first first lady to hold an official, if unsalaried, job at a government agency. As leader of the remarkably uncoordinated and ineptly titled Community and Volunteer Participation Service of the Physical Fitness Division, she kept so tirelessly to her immediate tasks of recruiting and hiring that her critics said Mrs. Roosevelt might even be seen around Washington now for a week at a time.[162]

Even more incredible to the Washington press corps was that no fewer than sixty-two "coordinators of physical fitness" were established in regional offices to coach horseshoe pitching, Ping-Pong, and folk dances.[163] Eleanor herself, much to her critics' delight, had brought a portable phonograph from the White House, and a little before noon in fine weather, she would clap her way down the office hallways to roust everybody out onto the rooftop, where she would put on a record. "We would all gallop around and fling ourselves about and then were permitted to return to our offices," recalled Gilbert Harrison, a young recruit of ER's in charge of the youth program.[164]

One night when Harrison had joined the family dinner, John Boettiger, newly re-enlisted as a lieutenant colonel in the army, got to talking about the war, speaking as if it was understood by all that the Japanese were an inferior race. Neither Eleanor nor Anna nor anyone else challenged Boettiger as he went on, until all at once Harrison cut him off with a clean "How much does that differ from what the Nazis say?" Boettiger stood down, and Eleanor flashed her OCD protégé a broad smile.[165]

IN NOVEMBER, SHE ASKED ATTORNEY General Francis Biddle what the Justice Department planned to do about Japanese Americans on the West Coast. FBI Director Hoover seemed to have a list of suspected Japanese agents believed capable of threatening national security. Would the attorney general guarantee the rights of resident

Japanese Americans? After all, an independent consultant had filed a report to the President on November 7, concluding that no Japanese "problem" existed on the West Coast and no armed uprising would follow the outbreak of war. "The Japanese," noted Curtis B. Munson, a Chicago businessman sent by FDR to investigate the "Japanese question" on the West Coast, "are more in danger from the whites than the other way around."

Among the Issei (first generation Japanese settlers) and Nisei (their grown children), Munson found an eagerness to demonstrate loyalty and a low risk for sabotage, as "their easily recognized physical appearance" would make it "hard for them to get near anything to blow up if it is guarded."[166] As for what emergency steps to take: "We do not want to throw a lot of American citizens into a concentration camp of course, and especially as the almost unanimous verdict is that in case of war they will be quiet, very quiet . . . because in addition to being quite contented with the American Way of life, they know they are 'in a spot.' "[167] Munson nonetheless broached his dismay at the number of bridges, dams, harbors, and power stations vulnerable to attack, and when Franklin passed the report on to Secretary of War Henry Stimson he highlighted the "guarding of key points."[168]

The month before, as so often happened in her working life, Eleanor began educating herself from the grassroots up about the effects of discrimination. In October, when the influential bilingual daily, *Rafu Shimpo*, sent its twenty-six-year-old American-born editor to Washington to ask about the fate of Japanese Americans in case of war, Eleanor met with Togo Tanaka and promised her assistance. At a press conference she praised the patriotism of the Nisei, who by then were joining the U.S. Army in large numbers. "The Issei may be aliens technically, but in reality they are Americans and America has a place for all loyal persons regardless of race or citizenship."[169]

On December 4, 1941, broadcasting on her *Town Hall Meeting of the Air*, Eleanor assured listeners that "no law-abiding aliens of any nationality" would be discriminated against by the government.[170]

"I hope," she said, "we shall never see concentration camps in this country, though I know we need to put certain people in places where they can do no harm. But I trust we shall not be so hysterical that we come to fear people who may actually be more devoted to liberty than many of us whose ancestors came here earlier than theirs did."[171]

Two days afterward, the eminent federal jurist and close friend of the Roosevelts Judge Jerome Frank found in Eleanor's promise to "aliens of good record" a moment of truth: "If ever any Americans go to a concentration camp, American democracy will go with them."[172]

Then, on Sunday, December 7, the world stood upside down.

ELEANOR LEARNED FROM ONE OF the White House ushers. She had been giving a Sunday luncheon for more than thirty guests and had not heard until mid-afternoon. At 6:45 that evening, December 7, 1941, she was the first to speak to the nation.[173] FDR would address a joint session of Congress the next day at noon.[174] Eleanor had already thrown away the script for her regular Sunday evening *Over Our Coffee Cups* radio address. Instead of canceling, she went on air and plainly presented the situation as both a global fight and a serious personal moment uniting all American citizens. She sketched the key players, depicted the steps so far taken, and quickly came to the entry point in the conflict for herself and those in the ranks of "We, the people."

For months, she recounted, everyone had sensed and resisted the looming upheaval. People had carried on their daily routines, muddling through questions of how and when or even if to prepare. But now the American people had met their enemy. "There is no more uncertainty," established Eleanor. "We know what we have to face and we know that we are ready to face it."

For many, this broadcast was the first inkling that the all-out attack on Pearl Harbor, inconceivable as it was by itself, was part of a much larger campaign of aggression unfolding across the International Dateline. Eleanor described bombings affecting "our citizens" on the big island of Hawaii, on Guam, Midway, Wake, and the Howland Islands. In the Philippines, the biggest concentration of U.S. warplanes anywhere in the world had been destroyed by a swarm of Imperial Japanese bombers. Densely populated Manila was lost, the island of Luzon overrun and occupied by relentless Japanese ground forces, leaving sixteen million Filipinos—U.S. nationals—dispossessed.

Eleanor brought the vastness of Japanese conquest to human scale by zooming in on "one of our transports loaded with lumber on its way to Hawaii" which had been sunk without warning. Then she stepped aside from Map Room talk to say "just a word to the women in the country tonight."

Like many of those listening and planning, she had sons already seeing action. One of hers—*a boy*, she stated starkly, referring to Franklin Jr.—was at sea on a destroyer. Two of her children and their families were in the danger zone on the Pacific coast. "You cannot escape anxiety," she sympathized, "you cannot escape the clutch of fear at your heart. And yet, I hope that the certainty of what we have to meet will make you rise above these fears."

"I have faith in you," she asserted. "I feel as though I was standing upon a rock, and that rock is my faith in my fellow citizens."

Her voice, so arduously disciplined into *slow and low* delivery, had never been steadier.

"Whatever is asked of us, I am sure we can accomplish it. We are the free and unconquerable people of the United States of America."[175]

THAT NIGHT, THE GREAT WHITE dome of the United States Capitol loomed black over Washington, its lights and surmounting lantern colonnade snuffed until war's end. Treasury Secretary Henry Morgenthau doubled protection around the White House, arming the guards with tommy guns and deploying steel-helmeted riflemen, bayonets gleaming, every hundred feet along the old iron fence.[176]

Radio reports of enemy airplane carriers spotted off the West Coast had brought home the previously absurd notion that militarist Japan had the capacity to bomb America's undefended coastline. The President, strained and pale but deadly calm, was preparing for a world in which Japanese forces reached Chicago.[177]

Eleanor's putative boss, still in Washington after the cabinet meeting that afternoon, was on the job that night. FDR had wanted a home defense administrator "who would attract public attention as a good ballyhoo artist," and who, as speechmaker, would "make people realize what the effect of a German victory would be."[178] Mayor La Guardia was now tearing up and down the wide avenues of the nation's capital, blaring from a police cruiser, "Calm! Calm! Calm!"[179]

For Eleanor the crisis was a federal opportunity to establish clear
state-by-state lines of gubernatorial authority. From the strategy of
hamlet-to-continent cooperation,[180] she began the process of instilling
new habits in as many citizens as possible.

At her staff meeting on Dupont Circle the next morning, she dispatched OCD regional directors to urge governors to authorize local
defense councils, from Alaska to the Pacific Northwest on down the
length of California, to put their ground plans into action immediately.
Everyone must cover their windows to prevent enemy aircraft from
spotting lighted targets.

Director La Guardia, meanwhile, was doing things his way. Since
August the "Little Flower," as he was affectionately known by New
Yorkers, had been personally handing out plum civilian defense assignments to mayoral friends around the country.[181] Having thus
established his own chain of authority, he was now set to elbow governors off Page One.

Eleanor asked an aide to install blackout curtains in the White
House, then struggled back through a vast traffic jam of rubberneck-
ers and army trucks to accompany Franklin and a large presidential
party to the Capitol. There, a special police force the size of a small
blue lake awaited their arrival. In every direction on the chilled Capitol Plaza huddled a vast unspeaking crowd. No one cheered, no cat-
calls from the back—a sound like rain washed over the President's car
as more than fifteen thousand onlookers clapped in grave solidarity.[182]

In the House chamber at half past twelve, the conjoined branches
of government came to attention for the President as he entered on
the arm of his oldest son, resplendent in marine captain's dress uniform. Eleanor had seated herself in the gallery with Edith Wilson, and
was distinctly conscious, as if foregrounding a vast *tableau vivant* with
President Wilson's widow, that she had lived through all this before.

"The day when President Wilson addressed the Congress to announce our entry into World War I," remembered Eleanor. "Now the
President of the United States was my husband, and for the second
time in my life I heard a president tell the Congress that this nation
was engaged in a war."[183]

It took but thirty-three minutes for House and Senate to pass a joint congressional resolution empowering the President to take the nation to war against the island empire in the Pacific. Democracy's lone dissenter was once more the ashen-faced, red-eyed Representative Jeannette Rankin of Montana.

After a final briefing to her OCD staff, Eleanor dashed for the airfield, gave a press conference, and by 0800 was aloft.[184]

AGITATOR

The spurring was not always wanted or welcome.

E.R.[1]

NINETEEN

T HE NIGHT AFTER PEARL HARBOR, a fleet of thirty Japanese planes crossed the California coastline west of San Jose, flying inland. The waning moon, still more than three-quarters full, offset the statewide blackout, making San Francisco's industrial rooftops crystal bright. Circling the port town, the enemy aircraft split into two squadrons, flying north and south—too high to be caught by searchlights but triggering air-raid warnings.

On the westbound night flight from Washington, the pilot handed Eleanor a wire report: San Francisco was under air attack.[1] She woke up Mayor La Guardia, who abruptly ordered their route changed—they would bypass Los Angeles and fly directly to the "target zone."

When their plane descended to refuel in Nashville, Eleanor telephoned the White House to find that the enemy raiders had flown back to their offshore carrier without bombing San Francisco.[2] The army, however, had failed to inform local officials, and a rumor-fueled frenzy had surged up the coast, broadcast by the police radio system. Banner headlines in War Extra editions of San Francisco newspapers chased the story in every direction: NAVY HUNTS JAPS OFF PACIFIC COAST . . .

War hysteria was in full cry when they landed for scheduled meetings in Los Angeles. To Eleanor, the Burbank airfield appeared deserted; to La Guardia, dangerously undefended. Consulting with public officials downtown, Eleanor emphasized that she had not flown west to deliver alarmist warnings. She had come seeking insight on how best to assist local defense councils in protecting all citizens in these early stages of the military crisis: "I came to find out from you what are the most helpful things we in Washington can do to help you. Tell me what you found lacking and what you want."[3]

Mayor La Guardia wanted to militarize coastal cities with a rapid buildup of guns.⁴ Before Pearl Harbor, the mayor had lent his authority to an FBI initiative to put military sidearms such as the Smith & Wesson six-shot service revolver into the hands of auxiliary police forces made up of OCD volunteers. Together with J. Edgar Hoover, La Guardia had estimated that keeping the peace after air raids and defending against a coastal invasion would require arming civilian volunteers with a quarter of a million handguns.⁵

Fixated on any plausible rumor of aerial attack or coastal invasion, La Guardia focused entirely on the protective category of OCD's mission, leaving Eleanor to establish the health, recreational, and social activities that the home front would require, to say nothing of providing low-cost housing, recreation centers, even additional sewers.

The mayor did not support Eleanor's proposal for mandatory national service for women or appear much interested in what community sewing groups could do if they turned their needles to sandbags and parachutes. Even so obvious a wartime need as nursery and day-care centers for young mothers pulling long shifts in defense work escaped the OCD director. La Guardia decided to follow the English model of fitting women for emergency nursing positions and air-raid assistance; and so, he commanded New York's fashion world to come up with cheesecake uniforms decorated with stylish insignia—costumes, really. Eleanor urged La Guardia to decide what women volunteers were going to *do* before spending another nickel on what they would wear.

Eleanor's plan for defense stewardship on the West Coast sent her to city, county, and state defense council offices from San Diego to Sacramento to register, train, and put volunteers into the field. Mainly, she listened, soliciting ideas particular to each community, then linking leaders in a naturally developing coalition as she made her way.

The mayor followed a separate itinerary, chasing alarms, meeting the press, and frantically waving his hands as he wrung high drama from every "red warning" that signified enemy planes overhead.

"The situation is serious, very serious," bawled La Guardia to San Francisco. "This is no time for speculation as to what is going to happen. It is happening now. It has happened here."⁶

La Guardia thrilled to the changeover. He no longer had to warn

Americans to be ready to defend their cities "*if* anything hits us."[7] The months of quasi-military preparation of warning systems, practice blackouts, and fire precautions had at last become "real," and this former member of the House Military Affairs Committee had no interest in discussions. Before his train had even stopped at San Francisco, the mayor had jumped off, blaring, "I don't want any blah-blah meeting, I want to see your police and fire chiefs first!"[8]

Eleanor spoke in one broadcast after another about the supreme un-drama of preparing one's house for effective blackouts: Don't be alarmed when you hear the air-raid siren. And don't be silly enough to be caught by surprise. Be ready. Don't say, "Nothing can happen to us." Pray that it doesn't, but be prepared if it does.

La Guardia spread fear: "We are not as well prepared at this moment as those of us who know would like us to be." Eleanor conveyed a steely belief in the system, urging trust in authorities and alert reporting of suspicious activity: "But don't try to be the FBI yourself."[9]

Nine days had passed since Pearl Harbor. Federal agents had raided homes and businesses, kicking in doors and forcing at gunpoint the removal and automatic deportation of more than a thousand Japanese Americans deemed a threat to national security, including Buddhist and Shinto ministers, Japanese-language schoolteachers, and instructors in *jukendo*, the art of Japanese sword fighting. The U.S. Navy had seized all Japanese American fishing boats.

Californians wanted to punish any Japanese, including U.S. residents and U.S. citizens. "Lock up the Japs!" overnight became the rallying cry up and down the coast.

ELEANOR'S CHALLENGE, UNLIKE THAT OF any first lady before, was to offer answers in coastal communities where the shock and fury was only rising as Japan went on winning and conquering in the Pacific. In addition to seizing British and Dutch-held Southeast Asian oil fields, Nippon imperial forces bombed U.S. air and naval bases around Manila, plundered Malaya, and occupied Guam, beheading, raping, and torturing Guamanians, and those were only the barely speakable horrors that Japanese soldiers inflicted on Americans.

The "dastardly, inhuman attack" that left thousands of soldiers and civilians slaughtered on U.S. soil now stoked decades of local racial resentment into a hatred so profound that every law-abiding citizen of Japanese ancestry was suddenly under suspicion not just for being a spy or saboteur but for not being human at all.[10]

At every stop, Eleanor passed along the assurances she had received earlier in December from the Departments of State and Justice that there was "absolutely no reason" why any law-abiding foreign-born person need have any feeling of anxiety in the United States.[11] She pressed local audiences: "Give American born Japanese, and even Japanese nationals who lived in this country for years, who have children and grandchildren and who have bought defense bonds—give them every consideration."[12]

After visiting a poultry farm, she used her conversation with five American-born Japanese teenagers to remind Californians that these loyal citizens were serving in the U.S. Army and responding to the U.S. Department of Agriculture's demands for a massive increase in pullets so that many more billions of eggs could be dried and shipped to Nazi-encircled England.[13] What she didn't or couldn't say was that the government had warned that Japanese American poultry farmers who didn't maintain egg production would be treated as wartime saboteurs.

"Let's be honest," she said to her readers, after returning to the White House on December 15, the 150th anniversary of the Bill of Rights:

"There is a chance now for great hysteria against minority groups— loyal American-born Japanese and Germans." She acknowledged that covert spying by Axis agents from Germany, Italy, and Japan had been "very active in this country during the past few years, just as the Communists have been." Gradually, the FBI and the Secret Service had been rounding up these infiltrators. But, she emphasized, "the great mass of our people, stemming from these various national ties, must not feel that they have suddenly ceased to be Americans.[14]

"This," ventured Eleanor, would be "the greatest test this country has ever met." It would prove to a world in chaos whether democracy in the United States could offer a pattern to other pluralistic countries in a postwar Europe, Asia, Central and South America.

"If we cannot meet the challenge of really believing in the Bill of Rights," said Eleanor, "and make it a reality for all loyal American citizens, regardless of race, creed or color; if we cannot keep in check anti-Semitism, anti-racial feelings as well as anti-religious feelings, then we shall have removed from the world, the one real hope for the future on which all humanity must now rely."

ELEANOR HATED TO SEE THE People's House twisted by wartime fears into the President's fortress. Members of the public were barred; only men in uniform now admitted to the state floor as Saturday-morning sightseers. Gone were the inclusive openness and informality of the neighborly President and Mrs. Roosevelt of 1937: shaking hands with 16,650 members of the public, offering tea to as many as 22,353, receiving another 4,346 for dinner, giving the freedom of the house to 319 overnight guests.[15] Some of those last had slept in reproduction American beds supplied by the furniture factory at Val-Kill, which had given the Roosevelt White House a general air of small-town ease and visitors a sense of belonging.[16]

Now Eleanor and the wartime skeleton staff were fingerprinted, the kitchen crew assigned gas masks, all hands required on deck for air raid drills. Ushers stood mainly idle, since the comings and goings of wartime officials were kept under wraps, and a machine gun nest defended the roof. At night, blackout curtains pinned shut the stately windows of the old presidential mansion. "It could hardly be deader," remarked columnist Drew Pearson, "if it had been bombed."[17]

Democracy's endless struggle between openness and security seemed personified in Eleanor and Franklin's tense wartime balance of civil defense and civil liberties. As niece and wife of two American Presidents shot at by close-range assassins, Eleanor was the first to say, "A man must be protected while he is the President of the United States."[18]

Washington was in the grip of wartime paranoia. Congressman Dies had just issued his latest warning to Nazi sympathizers on government payrolls. Dies had already submitted a list of nearly three thousand "known Communists" holding "key positions"[19] in the administration, or on the federal payroll, including Alger Hiss, Harry

Dexter White, Harold Glasser. It was time, declared Dies, for a long-overdue purge.

WHILE ELEANOR WAS ON THE West Coast, Hitler had made Franklin's job a lot simpler. On December 11, the German dictator declared war on America, a pointless act since this handed the neutral United States unrestricted entry into "Europe's war" and personally freed the President from having to keep his word about sending armies overseas. Defeating Germany before it got any stronger (by swallowing England, for instance) meant that FDR would now not have to overreach in the Pacific; he could build up the required airpower, manpower, and firepower before lunging to satisfy the American thirst for vengeance in the Far East.

Hitler had made it personal, too. Unable to conquer Soviet Russia and needing to distract the Reichstag and the German people from the costly failure of Operation Barbarossa, the führer now blamed Roosevelt for starting the war. Raging in front of Germany's impotent lawmakers, Hitler attacked the American President and his lazy wife and corruptible, gallivanting sons. He paused to sneer at Eleanor: "Ours is a world of work and not one of deceit and racketeering."[20]

Hitler knew his people. Rank-and-file Germans loved to feel superior to those they imagined to be decadent princes. In reality, all four Roosevelt sons had waived desk jobs and string-pulling: Elliott, first of the family to volunteer, had taken the riskiest assignment he could with an army air force bomber squadron in England. Jimmy, executive officer of Merritt "Red Mike" Edson's 1st Marine Raider Battalion, a seaborne special-force commando unit, was bound for jungle fighting in Guadalcanal. Franklin Jr., aboard his destroyer *Mayrant*, was seeing action in the North Atlantic. John, an ensign stationed at the naval air station in San Diego, would also get sea duty on a destroyer. Even forty-one-year-old John Boettiger could easily have remained exempt as the President's son-in-law. A navy enlistee in the earlier war, Boettiger was unable to remain comfortable in a civilian newspaper job when his brothers-in-law were exposing themselves to the most hazardous combat conditions, and would soon join the army.

Eleanor wished they had all not felt forced into such extreme fighting assignments by the double standard to which press and public held accountable the strapping, sometimes feckless sons of the first family. As Christmas 1941 approached, she felt she had only Joe Lash. "I've grown to feel closer and closer to you, & depend on you greatly & it's a great pleasure & a source of real contentment to be with you," she told him, admitting, as she had to Franklin long ago: "I know I grow greedy, for instead of just being thankful for the time I have with you, I always want more!"[21] Looking ahead to the coming year, she was "sure of one thing," Eleanor told Joe: "the knowledge that you love me will bring me happiness no matter what else may come."[22]

THREE DAYS BEFORE CHRISTMAS, CHECKING in with Franklin during his usual breakfast in bed, Eleanor learned that an important visitor was arriving at the White House early that evening for a three-week stay.[23] They would be twenty for dinner, at an hour still unknown. She would need to change some of her Christmas plans and lay in a large supply of French champagne, sherry, Scotch whisky, and ninety-year-old brandy.

"Oh," remembered Franklin, blandly adding to Eleanor's lengthening list of assignments the better-known names of the British prime minister's entourage, including Lord Beaverbrook, "Of course you'll see to it that under the Christmas tree everybody has presents."

Furious, but smoothly playing her supporting role in a White House now on war footing, she struck a withering note before moving on: "You should have told me. Why didn't you tell me?"[24]

Churchill had invited himself, was one reason. The prime minister had originally expected to stay at the British Embassy, anticipating that war-planning with the President might get "stiff."[25] Eleanor had been in Seattle when the meeting was set, and "Naval Person," as Churchill code-named himself in telegrams to Franklin, had already begun bravely dodging his way across heavy North Atlantic seas in a thick double-breasted sea overcoat and navy cap.

Franklin signaled his confidence and resolve to Churchill by coming out to meet his plane on the tarmac, locking his legs into their braces and pushing down hard on his cane when the DC-3 from Hampton Roads landed at the Anacostia Flats Naval Air Station across the Potomac from the new National Airport. Eleanor greeted the two heads of state and Harry Hopkins at the elevator door on the second floor at the White House. She had "thought of everything that could make our stay agreeable," recorded Churchill.[26]

The famously demanding houseguest had met his match in the legendarily thoughtful hostess. "Mrs. Roosevelt runs the best theatrical boarding house in Washington," the critic Alexander Woollcott advised Ethel Barrymore. But even Woollcott, who once moved into the White House long enough to welcome Eleanor home from *her* travels, never stayed longer than two weeks.

With her champion three-week houseguest from England, Eleanor was her usual wonderful and only somewhat critical hostess, later admitting that she had been "frightened" by Churchill's boozing. From the tumbler of sherry served the moment he awoke, through eighteen-hour days of valets keeping the prime minister's glass freshly charged with scotch and soda, Churchill's exacting requirements about French champagne were followed by his appalling filibustering about the need to maintain "the superiority of the Anglo-Saxon race."[27]

Churchill even managed to suffer a mild heart attack, kept secret by his personal physician; for how would it look to a world at war if the British prime minister was injured trying to open a sticky window in the Rose Room? Had the story been in the next morning's news, the world would have seen "a cripple" and an invalid with a heart condition working together to face the Axis Powers. If Churchill had succumbed then and there, it is likely that the popular idea of Eleanor as an indifferent homemaker would have been blamed for the sudden, shocking end of what was later recorded as the most intimate wartime alliance in history.

Eleanor made exceptions for everything the prime minister, his entourage, and her husband threw at her. "We may be called upon to forgive much in the coming months," she told her radio listeners, "but that should not be so difficult if we keep in mind our own failings and our own mistakes. We have a hard task and a costly one to perform, and when it is over we will have an even harder task to deal justly and mercifully and to lay the foundations for a new world order."[28]

To Anna, she explained, "I like Mr. Churchill, he's loveable & emotional & very human, but I don't want him to write the peace or carry it out."[29]

In Eleanor's ears, Churchill's war often sounded as much like a racial war as Hitler's. The meeting, of course, was for Franklin to put forth his Grand Strategy to Churchill, especially his decision to pour American might into a "Germany First" policy, but though the prime minister agreed, he also preferred to come at it from the periphery—from North Africa. What was to the American view peripheral was to Churchill essential. When the Far East came under discussion, the prime minister declared himself shocked by the President's admiring view of China as a postwar power to equal the British Empire.[30] For Roosevelt, China meant "four hundred million people who are going to count in the world of tomorrow," observed Churchill's doctor, Sir Charles Wilson. "But Winston thinks only of the color of their skins."

To Eleanor, their guest's unashamedly patronizing view of colonial peoples offset his steely understanding of the depths of Nazi aggression, which would be crucial to Allied leadership. There was nothing to do about Mr. Churchill at this momentous hour except to hold out for a postcolonial world in which he would be out of power.

On this, she and Franklin were in agreement. When Roosevelt and Churchill had met in secret off Newfoundland to sign the Atlantic Charter that summer, the President had made clear his disdain for British imperialism. Churchill had become "apoplectic" when his grandly cherished ally observed, "I can't believe that we can fight a war against Fascist slavery, and at the same time not work to free people all over the world from a backward colonial policy."[31]

Toward the end of the White House visit, FDR and Churchill discussed the choice of a name for the new Anglo-American-Soviet alliance. They had not yet found the right one, when FDR, having his breakfast in bed thought of something. At once he summoned his valet and had himself wheeled over to Churchill's room, where the prime minister was taking another of his working baths.

"How about *United Nations*," Roosevelt called through the door.

Churchill answered without hesitation: "That should do it."[32]

For now, however—much to Eleanor's chagrin—Franklin seemed to share ever more freely in their guest's unreconstructed sense of white racial superiority. His mother was gone; and with her the shadow history of the Delanos' commercial ventures in China. The entire Pacific Rim was now in play, and Hitler had relieved the President of his promise to American mothers to keep their sons out of Europe's war. FDR played his accustomed role of champion of colonial peoples, but felt somehow freer to indulge in officers-club rants about having "never liked the Burmese," wishfully urging Winston to "put the whole bunch of them into a frying pan with a wall around it and let them stew in their own juice."[33]

THE NIGHT BEFORE CHRISTMAS, CHURCHILL spoke from the Blue Room balcony to a crowd assembled on the South Lawn. A crescent moon hung overhead as the prime minister put aside his "might is right" rhetoric, replacing it with warmer imagery of local Christmastide revels among cottage dwelling people.

It was the first Christmas Eve without her mother-in-law, and Eleanor had been dreading it for Franklin. She felt her own lingering sadness at her brother's absence from the holiday, which also lacked Missy LeHand's comforting presence and cheery, knowing ways: her calming effect on Franklin.

Missy's breakdown kept her in Warm Springs. Before Christmas, she had tried to end her life by choking to death on a chicken bone. "There's an easier way," said her friend Mabel Irwin, whose husband was the Warm Springs medical director, "but maybe she couldn't take the easier way."[34] In a strange irony, when FDR had choked on a chicken bone just before the 1932 convention, the dislodging of the obstruction from the candidate's windpipe pivoted the history of the twentieth century.[35] Missy may have known all too well how little the freeing of a chicken bone from *her* throat was going to change the history that "F.D." was now going to make with or without her.

When Eleanor asked Franklin during cocktails in the Red Room whether he had telephoned to wish Missy a Merry Christmas, he admitted that he had not and did not plan to try. She took this disconnect in stride; the old story: she could see Franklin as he was, but that did not stop her from advocating for the man Missy needed him to be, or, afterward, discussing with Joe Lash her never-ending shock that whereas she *had* to have contact with the people she loved, *needing* to be refreshed and strengthened by her closest relationships, Franklin "seemed to have no bond to people, not even his children."[36]

He did acknowledge their new circumstances in one way that Christmas Eve. FDR declined to take up his traditional reading of *A Christmas Carol*, as if Scrooge's hauntings would add one too many ghosts to the President's ever more complicated relationship to past, present, and future. How could anyone bear to hear Dickens's final blessing when the lucky ones among the millions of young men now enlisting in the biggest war in human history would come home as Tiny Tims, if they came home at all.

On Christmas morning, they took Winston, almost as if he had become their great big child, for services at Washington's Foundry Methodist Church. Christmas itself "was a very sad day for me,"[37] admitted Eleanor. None of the Roosevelt boys had been able to get leave. Anna and John remained in Seattle, and Eleanor sorely missed the room-pounding energy of the grandchildren. She was grateful to her friend Mayris Chaney for coming to Christmas dinner, but still wished, as so often before, that she could take things lightly, could be more like FDR—"could be less personal"[38]—or, like their houseguest, could splash through a White House Christmas and an address to Congress like a boy in a tub full of toy boats.

Upon returning from her West Coast trip, she had initiated conversations with FDR about Japanese Americans and their rights as citizens, urging the President to make a clear move toward an official antidiscrimination policy. FDR agreed—or so Eleanor thought—and suggested that the time had also come for the United States to compel England to give self-governing status to India. Further, it was time, said the President, "to get more equal rights for Negroes here." Afterward, Eleanor told Tommy how surprised she was by FDR's inclination to move on these problems.

All through the early days of 1942, Eleanor appealed to the nation's conscience: "I think almost the biggest obligation we have today is to prove that in a time of stress we can still live up to our beliefs and maintain the civil liberties we have established as the rights of human beings everywhere."[39]

In January, the attorney general of California, Earl Warren, declared his support for imprisoning Japanese Americans. "I have come to the conclusion that the Japanese situation as it exists in this state today may well be the Achilles heel of the entire civilian defense effort. Unless something is done it may bring about a repetition of Pearl Harbor."[40]

Walter Lippmann toured the West Coast and interviewed Warren, then reported the likelihood of an all-out raid by Japanese air units combined with fifth-column saboteurs on the ground. Lippman's February 12 syndicated column changed the debate by framing it as a federal military matter, therefore inarguable by civilians. It began to seem logical that loyal Japanese American families needed to be isolated for their own protection.[41]

Westbrook Pegler, the reactionary Hearst columnist, took his cue to thunder: "The Japanese should be under guard to the last man and woman, and to hell with habeas corpus until the danger is over."[42] The attorneys general of Western states, consulted by the army, favored incarceration: Troy Smith of the state of Washington and Charles A. Sprague of Oregon both recommended martial law; Bert Miller of Idaho wanted "all Japanese be put in concentration camps for the remainder of the war." And in case anyone had missed his real point: "We want to keep this a white man's country."[43]

U.S. Attorney General Biddle remained opposed, declaring that the Department of Justice would have nothing to do with the unconstitutional rounding up and incarceration of citizens. Only enemy aliens could be removed under existing laws. The President, however, could proclaim the entire West Coast a militarized zone and then place it under martial law. Or the army could legally evacuate all people in a specified territory if such mass removal was deemed essential from a military point of view. But, held Biddle, American citizens of Japanese origin could not be "singled out of an area and evacuated with other Japanese."[44]

And yet, of course, they were. Senator Lodge had been dead right. The Immigration Act of 1924, which had banned Japanese from entering the U.S., established for the whole country what the Chinese Exclusion Act of 1882 had done for the West Coast—a normalization

of racial fears that would allow two generations of government officials to systematize atrocities of the kind that American armies were
sent overseas to fight.

"There is no blinking at the fact that our people, our territory, and
our interests are in grave danger," FDR had told Congress the day
after Pearl Harbor. Nothing had changed his mind about the country's safety coming first. In the War Department, Secretary Henry L.
Stimson acknowledged that a "tragedy" was in the making,[45] but with
the backing of Assistant Secretary John J. McCloy, a staunch believer
in the imprisonment if "reasonably undertaken and humanely conducted,"[46] Stimson persuaded the President of the "military necessity
of a wholesale evacuation."

General John L. DeWitt, commanding general of the Western Defense Command and the Fourth Army, sent his recommendation to
the War Department on February 14: remove the Japanese from "sensitive areas" and restrict their right to enter, remain in, or leave such
areas. His message to Congress was clear: "A jap is a jap. It makes no
difference whether he is theoretically an American citizen, he is still a
Japanese."[47]

THE SECOND WORLD WAR HAD looked like a war *against* racism. But
on February 19, 1942, the President went ahead and ordered every
person of Japanese ancestry on the West Coast be driven out of his or
her home, stripped of businesses, yanked from schools and colleges,
blocked from bank accounts, ganged into trucks, and herded to "assembly centers." The ripe horse stalls at the Santa Anita racetrack
served as one three-month detention facility for parents and their small
children. The prisoners were then transported under armed guard to
one of ten hastily constructed concentration camps, called "relocation
centers," from California to Arkansas.

Executive Order 9066 removed from as many as 120,000 persons
their constitutional rights to basic freedoms and to equal justice under
the law. More than 70,000 were natural-born American citizens; altogether, they represented almost 90 percent of Japanese Americans in
the United States,[48] although as Eleanor would painfully come to acknowledge in 1943, the victims did not have to be of Japanese ancestry

to be hauled off without charges or trials. In the actual carrying out of the President's order on "Evacuation Day," they simply had to be "Oriental looking people"[49] to be flushed from their homes.

This most inhumane and un-American decision appalled Eleanor. Yet she loyally defended the administration in public; in private, her government and her husband embarrassed her. Imprisoning American citizens in concentration camps diminished Franklin in her eyes, but also raised the ghost of their marriage's oldest question: What did she expect? Her husband had been raised by a mother brought up in Southeast Asia, who, when Franklin had been quarantined with scarlet fever at Groton School, adopted as an endearment—"my little *reconcentrado*"—a term applied by one of her neighbors, explained Sara, "to groups of starving Cubans."[50]

In intent, Roosevelt's camps were like those of the Spanish in Cuba in 1897. Unlike many concentration camps in the twentieth century, the idea was to keep the Cuban civilians alive and protected until the Spanish were victorious. At least 30 percent perished from lack of proper food, sanitary conditions, and medicines.

With East Asia as his next battleground, Roosevelt privately revealed his own "racial arrogancies." As president, FDR believed that it was vital to the world order to keep China within Western influence. He envisioned putting a stop to Japanese conquest by repopulating the Pacific Rim with certain choice "cross-breedings" that he believed would create a "stock" less aggressive than the Japanese. Dutch-Javanese "crossings," for example, were "good," as were Javanese-Chinese. Chinese-Malaysian was a "bad mixture," the Japanese-European "cross" worst of all, and the Chinese-European "not at all bad."[51]

British Embassy ministers and foreign correspondents hardly knew what to make of a president so casually asserting such claims by "burbling away in his hare-brained fashion,"[52] according to one; "bagatellising," said another.[53]

In 1942, FDR set a Smithsonian scientist to work on a private study of the effect of racial crossing. The Czech anthropologist Dr. Alex Hrdlicka, founder and forty-year curator of the Division of Physical Anthropology, fielded the President's questions about Japanese "racial characteristics"—nefariousness, for example, and trickiness, and ruthlessness—and was only too eager to reinforce FDR's notion that the development of the Japanese cranium accounted for these traits.

Hrdlicka's specialty, embedded in the larger field of eugenics and "scientific" racism, was the study of racial anatomy, physiology and pathology.[54] His conclusion that the shape of the skull held the keys to intelligence and behavior provided additional confirmation of "superior race" legislation, such as Virginia's 1924 Eugenical Sterilization Act, signed into law just as Franklin was publishing his first "race mixing" column in Georgia's *Macon Telegraph*, and later becoming the model sterilization law for other states and for Nazi Germany.

The Smithsonian was the authority informing—corrupting—the war president's differing ways of handling Atlantic and Pacific theaters, as well as, most shamefully, his Executive Order 9066. Public opinion was also on FDR's side.[55] As many as 59 percent of Americans viewed as necessary the President's precautionary bypassing of constitutional rights.[56] Protest came from such Socialists as Norman Thomas (imprisoning California's Japanese Americans, he said, was "like burning down Chicago to get rid of gangsters"[57]) and academics like Monroe Deutsch, provost of the University of California, who wired dissent to Justice Felix Frankfurter, arguing that the evacuation struck "an unprecedented blow at all our American principles."[58] Frankfurter, meanwhile, praised John J. McCloy at the War Department for handling "a delicate matter with both wisdom and appropriate hard-headedness."[59]

As for Roosevelt himself, "I do not think he was much concerned with the gravity or implications of this step," reflected Attorney General Francis Biddle. "He was never theoretical about things. What must be done to defend the country must be done."[60]

Eleanor's bewilderment at her husband's abandonment of basic American rights and freedoms took the form of private objection. She made her opposition known to Attorney General Biddle and scanned her mail for any signs of distress coming from what one of ER's young associates at OCD tried calling "humane concentration camps."[61]

The President, meanwhile, had appointed Milton Eisenhower, younger brother of assistant army chief of staff General Dwight Eisenhower, to carry out Executive Order 9066. Deeply troubled by the assignment, Eisenhower put aside his opposition to the President's order, and, as first director of the War Relocation Authority, declared himself "determined to carry it out as effectively and humanely as possible."[62]

Eleanor walked roughly the same tightrope when she announced in March: "I am very happy to see that there is established a War Relocation Authority, which will have charge of the program for relocation and employment of persons who must be moved out of military areas. Unfortunately, in a war, many innocent people must suffer hardships to safeguard the nation. One feels that a program which provides work is certainly better than having nothing to do."[63]

Clarence Pickett's American Friends Service had volunteered to help run the camps, and Eleanor hoped that the Quakers would make a life of wrongful imprisonment somehow more bearable. But for families and individuals stripped of everything except that which they could carry, nothing softened the barbed-wire fences, the blocks of ramshackle barracks, stone-cold in winter, furnace-hot in summer, whole families confined to single rooms, each gritty year piled on top of the bleaker year before, at a cost to the 120,000 victims of more than $400 million (about $7 billion today) and to the already overburdened wartime taxpayers of $350 million.

Eleanor found herself shocked by the scale of Franklin's mistake, and as time went on, and the future invasion of the American mainland failed to materialize, she remained aghast at the nonexistence of any case of spying or sabotage brought against any Japanese American in the United States. Strangest of all, California's top law enforcer— the next governor of the state and the future chief justice of the United States—took this absence of evidence as "the most ominous sign of our whole situation."

It was the Salem witch trials echoing across the continent and back again. Asked at a congressional hearing on February 21 how the California authorities knew which among the state's Japanese Americans could be trusted as loyal, Warren explained that with the "Caucasian race," they could "arrive at some fairly sound conclusions," but Japanese were, and here Warren unpacked all the stereotypes: inscrutable, clannish, sneaky, impossible to tell one from another.[64]

As letters reached Eleanor from among the imprisoned, she gave as much individual help as she could to smooth opportunities for jobs, college, the military. When she discovered that frozen bank accounts were causing unnecessary hardship to thousands of Issei farmers and small businesses, she notified Henry Morgenthau, arguing that these farmers were irreplaceable, since they produced 75 percent of the country's winter vegetables. She asked that the Treasury Department permit them to withdraw at least $100 per month, and Morgenthau agreed to relax the orders and release funds for living expenses.[65]

There was nothing new about Eleanor disagreeing sharply with the President. His repeated caving to Southern lawmakers on any form of anti-lynching legislation had deeply shaken her, as did FDR's unwillingness to make any straightforward statement or offer any program to integrate the armed services, which was the same story as lynching: "He must not irritate the Southern leaders," she told Joe Lash, "as he feels he needs their votes for essential war bills."[66] Incarceration of Japanese Americans now put a lasting wedge between them as Eleanor's primary role in Franklin's wartime presidency became that of a self-appointed agitator.

The Smith Act in 1940 had begun the process in earnest. When FDR signed legislation requiring the nation's three-and-a-half-million resident aliens to register and be fingerprinted at post offices throughout the country, lamely expressing his hope that no "loyal" aliens would be subject to harassment because of fingerprinting, Eleanor, appalled, had spoken up: "Something curious is happening to us in this country, and I think it is time we stopped and took stock of ourselves. Are we going to be swept away from our traditional attitude toward civil liberties by hysteria about 'Fifth Columnists'?"[67]

This time, the administration's use of government to destroy both individual lives and a whole subpopulation of the United States left Eleanor aghast at her husband. Franklin firmly believed that the U.S. was embedded with Nazi sympathizers who, in the event of a German invasion, would upend the country through Fifth Column activity. But if he was willing, throughout the war years, to detain eleven thousand Germans and more than three thousand Italians, why hadn't Franklin ordered Attorney General Biddle to throw the Germans into camps?

The Germans were the ones blaring their traitorous Bund rallies from Madison Square Garden. Why were the Italians dropped from the official list of enemy aliens as early as Columbus Day 1943—when FDR personally opposed letting anyone out of his concentration camps to return home before the end of the war? ("I don't care about the Italians," FDR told Biddle. "They are a lot of opera singers."[68]) And for what? One of the war's bravest and most highly decorated army units, the 442nd Regimental Combat Team, had been made from the second-generation sons of Japanese immigrants. Their valor and sacrifices to save their fellow soldiers would mock the senselessness of Franklin's Executive Order 9066.

IN THE WHITE-HOT SUMMER OF 1943, rioting broke out in the Poston and Manzanar relocation camps. The war still on, there was no new advantage to admitting to one of the biggest mistakes ever made by the government of the United States. But FDR wanted to know what was going on in the camps, and Eleanor agreed to go and see.

Meanwhile, she had heard from women of New Zealand and Australia that their strained and anxious countries, through which had passed hordes of U.S. servicemen, would welcome a transpacific visit similar to her transatlantic tour to England in 1942. The idea of another journey to see war work done by women made sense to her, especially if she could also report on the needs of American soldiers, whom she knew from Joe Lash felt neglected in their Pacific backwaters. In one 1943 panel, a hardboiled sergeant, having just dressed down a raw recruit, warns, "Now don't go writing letters to Mrs. Roosevelt."[69]

Letters and rumors swirled around her plans for the South Pacific, one source advising Vice President Wallace, "She [does] not want to go. She was ordered to go. The Negro situation was too hot."[70] In June, when racial tensions erupted into violence in California, in between riots in Mobile, Alabama, and Detroit, Michigan, Eleanor told reporters blaming young Latinos that the situation in Los Angeles had been provoked by "elements which had little to do with youth."[71] In her column, she described the rioting among white servicemen, police, and Latinos in Los Angeles as "a racial protest . . . a problem with roots going a long way back," pointing out that "we do not always face these problems as we should,"[72] the *Los Angeles Times* headlined, "Mrs. Roosevelt Blindly Stirs Race Discord," while accusing her of communist sympathies in an accompanying editorial.

Vile "Eleanor stories" proliferated,[73] especially in the South. In Virginia, the belief that "when white men go to the Army, the Negro men will have all the white women," gave way to reports that "a Negro made the remark that he had his white girl 'picked out' just as soon as the Negroes take over," while in Georgia an African American allegedly boasted, "Aren't we going to have a time with these white women, when all these white men go off to war!"[74]

Among GIs in the South Pacific Eleanor was already the subject of constant field rumors, such as the one that had begun appearing in her mail early that summer: Was it true that Mrs. Roosevelt denounced marines who had contracted venereal disease in the Pacific? Had she really condemned them to six months quarantine on an offshore island?[75]

These stories did her no harm, she reflected. "The people who spread [them] are evidently too stupid to realize that my only concern would be that such a story would hurt the men themselves. If our boys think that here at home the wife of the President, or any other woman, says or writes such arrant nonsense, they must be made extremely unhappy by it."[76]

Eleanor had seen the Pacific war's earliest casualties in West Coast hospitals. The wounded from her son Jimmy's outfit—the 2nd Marine Raider group at Guadalcanal—had taught her that if she wanted to understand how men like her own sons had suffered she must visit the scene of the first major Allied offensive against the Japanese, "the Rock," as Marines had dubbed volcanic Guadalcanal. She would only worsen it by making uninformed visits. The Guadalcanal survivors she had met in California had been in no mood for bromides or deference. Japan had seized the island to control sea lanes to the United States and as a transit airfield to Australia and New Zealand; the stakes could not have been higher for either side.

On July 10, she received an additional V-mail incentive to get to Guadalcanal. "You know I would be desolate if Rover came to this part of the world and left without seeing me," wrote Joe Lash from a Quonset hut stationed on the island. Joe was then serving on Guadalcanal for eighteen months as a weather forecaster with flying status. Eleanor's feelings of responsibility for the circumstances of his banishment had made her hypersensitive to his needs, even when they amounted to nothing more than ordinary GI gripes, loneliness chief among them. "I am entirely amenable to any arrangement that can be made."[77]

She pleaded with her husband to send her as far as possible into the war zone. Seeing the Western Front of the last world war with her own eyes had helped her grasp the nature of shell shock before going into the wards at St. Elizabeth's. To know at all what it meant to repel a suicide attack—to be even moderately useful as she went on visiting men in field hospitals—she would need to get as close as she could to the islands where dug-in defenders were still fighting to the last inch.

ON JULY 13, 1943, FDR confided in Belle Willard Roosevelt, spouse of Eleanor's cousin Kermit, in whose struggles with depression and drinking Franklin had tried to help: "I am having a hell of a time with Eleanor. She is determined to go to the Pacific War Zone and I say she can't—the Army would never sanction such a trip. She wants to go to Australia, which would be a good thing, but she says once there, that she will wangle her way to the front, and I am not going to let her go unless I have it in writing, because she is quite capable of getting there. At the moment, it is a stalemate."[78]

In the end, having rejected Eleanor's earlier request to visit the Soviet Union and China, FDR saw the South Pacific as a good trade for them both, Eleanor took additional leverage from offering to pay her own travel expenses, and more when she persuaded the chairman of the Red Cross to allow her to inspect the organization's installations in the Pacific. Franklin had to cave then. He offered Eleanor letters of transit on the condition that she vow not to meddle with the running of the war. He who *was* running the war, in grand alliance with the leaders of the United Nations, never stopped using Eleanor's high profile and extended reach for advantage or just to make other aristocratic women visiting at Hyde Park feel less guilty by comparison to such an exasperating pot-stirrer, since what else could Zita of Austria-Hungary think of Eleanor, when the former empress asked the President if his wife wouldn't be exhausted by such a trip, and Franklin replied, "No, but she will tire everybody else"?[79]

She kept her trip—especially her hope that it would include a jungle visit with Joe Lash—secret from everyone but Tommy, with whom she left her best jewelry and instructions for its distribution should she fail to return. "Your mother is so pleased with herself," reported Tommy to Anna. "She has lost twenty-five pounds and looks very slim and young, and it has not made her face look drawn. She looks very well and seems to be in good spirits."[80] The White House reporters had not heard even a rumor when the AP's Edith Asbury spotted what she thought was the mark of a vaccination. Asbury asked about it, and Eleanor slowly replied, "Oh, I was picking raspberries and scratched my arm."[81]

Uncertainty about her itinerary kept her guessing to the last minute, even about packing—until she realized that two blue-gray Red Cross uniforms and a typewriter would be just about all she needed for her five-week, thirty-thousand-mile journey.[82]

When at last she departed from San Francisco on August 17, she strongly doubted that she was doing the right thing by making a kite-tail of island arrivals—all leading to fleet headquarters east of Australia. It was reassuring that "Mother" had won by a landslide when GIs at a San Pedro training camp voted to find out for whom American soldiers stood ready to fight. And that Eleanor was cited for "combining all the best attributes of a mother, grandmother, and First Lady of the Land."[83] But it did nothing to improve her confidence to find herself ranked after the boys' wives, daughters, and sisters, and before Mrs. MacArthur; Queen Elizabeth; Queen Wilhelmina; Madame Chiang Kai-shek; and Hollywood's "Oomph Girl," Ann Sheridan, "because she typifies the type of girl we left behind us."

The farther she flew—Oahu to Christmas Island to Tongareva, Bora-Bora, Aitutaki, Samoa, and Fiji—the longer the soldiers at mid-Pacific and South Pacific American outposts had gone without seeing a woman. Each time Eleanor's plane descended upon another airfield slashed over coral, she felt apprehension knowing that every dogface peering from a jungle tent had heard that a female VIP was expected and had laid bets on which film star or pinup girl was going to step out onto the tarmac: legs first (Betty Grable); in a thin summer dress mildewed and falling apart in the humidity (Ann Sheridan); or full-lipped and decked out in a Hawaiian tablecloth (Dorothy Lamour).[84]

Instead, here was smiling Mrs. FDR, necklaced in native beads, wryly tying a grass skirt to the waist of her Red Cross uniform.[85] She would afterward recall the men looking at her as if she were "some astronomical phenomenon."[86] As had been true in civilian life, action became her. "In person," said a medic, "she was better looking than the pictures showed."

MOST OF WAR, EVEN IN the Solomon Islands, was preparing for war: stringing barbed wire, getting supplies through the jungle, cutting brush, sending out patrols. *Sweat saves blood*, went the Marine Corps expression.[87] Eleanor was nothing if not the personification of daily toil.

Following her sons' advice not to take every meal with the brass, she ate one meal with the noncommissioned officers and another with the enlisted men, and the only way to pull off this last was to be up at five when the men got breakfast.

Island-hopping from base to base, one crimson dawn after another, Eleanor absorbed the central trauma of the Pacific war's benumbed, blood-soaked fighters. Young marines, in particular, caught in the bitterest horrors of the endless island-after-island meat grinder, were shocked to discover a frenzied brutality in themselves, despite their steely Corps training. For some, it was an ironclad faith in their own goodness that was most bitterly tested. One such marine survivor, Corporal Eugene B. Sledge, justified their disturbing mirroring with a suicidal enemy: "We had to be just as dedicated to America as they were to their emperor."[88]

LANDING AT FLEET ADMIRAL WILLIAM F. "Bull" Halsey's headquarters on Noumea, New Caledonia, on August 26, Eleanor presented her letters from the President.

The admiral had dreaded her coming no less than she had dreaded arriving.[89] Halsey had crossed paths with Eleanor a number of times over the years and had admired her but classed her as a do-gooder. When she arrived at Noumea, he hated having to wrench his attention from the New Georgia campaign, nearing its climax, much less "put on a necktie" to honor the President's wife with appropriate hospitality.

"Bull" Halsey could find "no excuse for her entering my area and monopolizing planes, crews, and fuel that were needed for military purposes."[90] He told Eleanor that he could not promise to allow her to visit Guadalcanal and said that the decision would be made after she completed her trip to Australia and New Zealand. "He sounded so doubtful," she told Tommy, "that I am discouraged & really sorry that I came."[91]

She was particularly upset about Joe Lash. He had been "terribly keyed up" by the prospect of her visit, promising to "keep myself shaven and in a clean set of [khakis] on all the days you mention, so that not only shall I be presentable on a moment's notice, but so that you will bring back a good report to Trude. After the glowing accounts you have written about her radiance and beauty, I can't afford to have you bring a sad tale about a decaying, sallow-looking G.I."[92]

She settled for making a package for Joe and writing him. "I'm sorry," she told Tommy, "as seeing all these masses of boys who seem pleased just to see me as a stranger makes me realize it might have meant something to Joe." She added, "I simply will never face another hospital at home & while I'll write the column I don't think I'll bother to talk of anything but the Red Cross when I come home. I'm going to feel ashamed to have been so nearby & yet not to have gone there & want to forget about it as soon as possible."[93]

BACK ON NEW CALEDONIA ON September 14—Australia and New Zealand had been flag-waving successes—Eleanor still did not know whether Guadalcanal was off limits. Pessimistically, she guessed she would be starting homeward the following morning. Admiral Halsey had assigned her to Wicky-Wacky Lodge, his safest billet, where he could keep a cordon of MPs stationed around the place the whole time she was there. The first night he gave a small reception and dinner for her, and early next morning started Eleanor on her rounds.

"Here," recalled Halsey, "is what she did in 12 hours: She inspected two Navy hospitals, took a boat to an officers' rest home and had lunch there, returned and inspected an Army hospital, reviewed the 2d Marine Raider Battalion—her son, Jimmy, had been its executive officer—made a speech at a service club, attended a reception, and was guest of honor at a dinner given by Gen. Harmon."[94]

During the course of her transpacific trip, she visited the men on seventeen islands and saw more than four hundred thousand soldiers, always reminding them that they were very much on the President's mind and that he had asked her to tell them that every day when he went down to the map room in the White House, "He notes on the maps where you are and what you are doing."

On the hospital wards, she took the hand of each soldier, looked him in the face, asked his name and where he was from. "May I phone your mother when I get home?" she would ask. "With your permission, I will write and tell your parents that you're all right."[95]

She lingered with each prematurely aged boy, getting to know him a little—enough, anyway, so that, as one doctor said, "She was Mother personified," speaking to patients as if the world was still a gracious place, while also saying *I know you can handle this*.

After observing Eleanor on the hospital wards, speaking to the men of their hometowns, Halsey acknowledged, "It was a sight I shall never forget." When she left, said one doctor, "there was moisture in every eye," and the ward sounded with men blowing their noses, loudly swearing at "the cold" they had recently picked up.[96] Halsey further admitted, "I was ashamed of my surliness. She alone accomplished more good than any other person or any group of civilians who had passed through my area."[97]

Her last evening on New Caledonia, Halsey announced that Mrs. Roosevelt was to be ready the next morning to leave under strictest secrecy for the big hospitals on Efate, which the Japanese had never bombed and Halsey hoped would remain under their radar. Providing all went well, Eleanor could expect to continue up to Henderson Field on Guadalcanal the following day.

Up at 3:45 and off at 5:00, she landed at 9:20, her official tours of three Guadalcanal hospitals, a recreation field, and a cemetery occupied her through a long, hot morning. Shortly after 2:00, a note reached her in a briefing tent announcing that Sgt. Lash was waiting for her outside, and all her weariness turned instantly to excitement as she hurried out to hug and kiss Joe. He noticed she was weary. Nonetheless, she visited his weather forecasting station and his corner of the tent where she could see that he was using the moccasins and reading lamp she had sent.[98] They returned to the mess hall and sat happily talking until a big yellow Pacific moon came up—perfect air raid conditions, so that Joe had to report back to his unit, leaving Eleanor to relive "every minute" they had had together.[99]

"How I hated to see you leave last night," she told him. "When the war is over I hope I never have to be long away from you. It was so wonderful to be with you, the whole trip now seems to me worthwhile. It is bad to be so personal, but I care first for those few people I love deeply and then for the rest of the world I fear."[100]

DAWN ON D-DAY, JUNE 6, 1944, brought the largest amphibious invasion force in history across the chop of the English Channel. Ahead of the great armada stood Hitler's Fortress Europe, concrete bunkers, land mines, and machine-gun nests defending the Normandy coast. Roosevelt and Churchill, sea rovers and gamblers both, prayed that the Allied invasion of northern France would establish the long-awaited second front and turn the tide of war.

Six months later, on December 16, 1944, the day of Hitler's Ardennes Counteroffensive and the start of the Battle of the Bulge, Eleanor's widowed Aunt Tissie died of a heart attack at 1105 Park Avenue: without illness or pain, wired Eleanor to Aunt Maude in Ireland.

Four days later, when Eleanor returned to New York to attend Tissie's funeral, she finally had time to read a document sent by the former New York Supreme Court judge Joseph M. Proskauer, approved by FDR and endorsed by some thirteen hundred prominent Americans, calling for an international charter intended to serve as a postwar guarantee of individual liberties.[101] This "Declaration of Human Rights," identified six points, including the "recognition of the individual human being as the cornerstone of our culture and civilization" and the establishment of the new postwar world "on the basis of the dignity and inviolability of the person." The document also demanded a "recognition of the fact that bigotry and persecution by a barbarous nation is a matter of international concern because it eventually throws upon the peace loving nations the burden of relief and redress." It demanded policies for repatriation and rehabilitation, as well as "an international machinery" to provide new homes for "those who wander the earth unable or unwilling to return to the scenes of unforgettable horror from which they fled."

"All the points seem to me to be excellent," Eleanor told her readers, "but to make them worth the paper on which they are written will require some really concentrated work, not only on the part of those who signed the document, but on the part of many other people in this nation and throughout the world."[102]

On the eve of America's fourth wartime Christmas, FDR delivered his Yule message to a crowd, fifteen thousand strong, gathered around the national community Christmas tree on the South Lawn: "We cannot say when our victory will come. Our enemies still fight fanatically. They still have reserves of men and military power. But, they themselves know that they and their evil works are doomed. We may hasten the day of that doom if we here at home continue to do our full share."[103]

THREE MONTHS PASSED. FDR WEAKENED dramatically.

He took Anna with him to the Crimea conference on the reorganization of postwar Europe. His achievement at Yalta— persuading an increasingly fragile Big Three to agree to do, as one observer put it, "most of the things we failed to do in 1919"[104]—had been hailed by one London newspaper as "a landmark of human history."[105] Even Herbert Hoover pronounced the Yalta agreement "a strong foundation on which to rebuild the world."[106] When the President reported to Congress after returning to Washington, Eleanor registered shock from the visitors' gallery to see Franklin let himself be wheeled into the House chamber. She was not surprised to hear him mask his real condition by appearing to ask for, and warmly receiving, his audience's indulgence for "an unusual posture of sitting down during the presentation of what I want to say."[107] That was vintage FDR deflection, the candid toss off: just too beat from his fourteen-thousand-mile journey to "carry about ten pounds of steel around on the bottom of my legs."

But it was the first time in his career that he had exposed his dependence on leg braces. His slowed voice, the words thickened and subdued, signaled a slide into invalidism. If his command confidence had not continued supreme—"It's a long, tough road to Tokyo!"[108]— Eleanor might have taken the seated speech as a sign that he was dying.

Into the first month of the fourth term, she noticed that his eyes were dulling to a sun-bleached glaze. Her responses to his drop-off in strength puzzled others. To Anna it seemed that there was no clear sign that her mother was permitting herself to be aware of the dramatic decline.[109]

Yet as so often for Eleanor with FDR, her courage had to be invisible. From the paralysis of 1921 had come their essential compact: Franklin D. Roosevelt would never be an invalid, even when seriously ill. Also, their mystique as a couple: Roosevelts didn't scare. Eleanor wasn't denying her husband's deterioration, only keeping up her end of it.

THE BIGGEST WAR IN HUMAN history made forty years of March Seventeenths just another remembrance. With the U.S. Ninth Army now sixty miles west of Berlin, and the Red Army ready to converge from the East, Franklin could confidently predict the fall of Berlin and Allied victory in Europe. He spoke of traveling together again when he made peace visits to England, Holland, and France and of traveling with Eleanor. He wanted her at his side when he opened the United Nations in San Francisco on April 25.

They were alike in recognizing that a new international organization was vital to the United States' chances for a peaceful world. Roosevelt on his own would have a hard time persuading other nations, particularly Britain, the Soviet Union, and China, to feel secure in a world dominated by a single superpower. Franklin must also avoid the brittle inflexibility of Woodrow Wilson with the Treaty of Versailles, the League of Nations, and the U.S. Congress. At the same time, neither Franklin nor Eleanor could completely ignore his thinning, pale condition.

Once Franklin had recovered from his deep post-Yalta weariness to see the Pacific fighting to its finish, the work of moderating a hard and bitter peace would begin. Roosevelt could leave the balance of the fourth term to the vice president, and Eleanor would happily see him home to Hyde Park to watch the ships on the river from Top Cottage, as he had promised Daisy Suckley he would.

Eleanor's own clear-sightedness had long-since resigned her to the outside. "He might have been happier with a wife who was completely uncritical," she decided. "That I was never able to be, and he had to find it in other people."[110] Nevertheless, she had consciously kept up her spurring and goading—"agitating," as she called it. Even when their marriage had been stunted by decades of drought and dysfunction, and her political contributions happened not to be timely or welcome, she had never stopped trying to be useful—therefore, loving. "I was one of those," she said, tracing an edge, but with no regret, "who served his purposes."[111]

In April, Franklin decided to go down to Warm Springs, where he had always rebounded before. Eleanor was relieved that Cousin Daisy and Laura "Aunt Polly" Delano would go along and see that he got his rest. "I knew that they would not bother him as I should by discussing questions of state." She kissed Franklin good-bye, sent him on his way,[112] and at the other end Warm Springs welcomed him with open arms. The stationmaster, who had witnessed almost a quarter century of Roosevelt homecomings, observed that the President now being lifted as "absolutely dead weight" from coach to car was "the worst-looking man I ever saw who was still alive. Just like a sitting-up dead man."[113]

FDR's doctors still hoped that complete rest and weight gain would bring him back. Lieutenant Commander Howard G. Bruenn, the diligent navy cardiologist assigned by Rear Admiral Ross T. McIntire to monitor the case daily in the Little White House, argued that the President could be saved "if measures were adopted to rescue him from certain mental strains and emotional influences." He meant freeing FDR from the stress of his wife's daily prodding to take action on whichever crisis seemed that morning to matter most.[114]

For Eleanor not to call, however, would have been to permit the world to know that the man upon whom the world was depending for strength and hope was failing. Which was exactly what the President's secretary William Hassett was seeing at Warm Springs: "He is slipping away from us and no earthly power can keep him here."[115]

Eleanor went on phoning, interrupting, intruding from Washington. On one call she urged Franklin to send arms to a needy band of freedom fighters in Yugoslavia. Bruenn clocked that discussion at forty-five minutes and afterward recorded a rise in his patient's blood pressure of fifty points.

In Washington on the morning of April 12, 1945, Eleanor announced to reporters at her weekly press conference that she planned to accompany her husband to San Francisco for the founding of the United Nations later that month. Nothing since the start of the New Deal had given her so much excitement.

She had a busy few days ahead: dinner with the American Friends Service Committee, a tea for New York Democrats, a visit to a handicapped children's clinic. She spent the rest of the morning at the White House with Charles Taussig, an adviser to the UN delegation, and despite Aunt Polly calling from Warm Springs to say that Franklin had fainted, Eleanor followed Rear Admiral McIntire's advice and went on to her afternoon speaking engagement to minimize suspicion.

In Warm Springs, signing official documents at his worktable in the living room, Franklin had just turned back to Lucy Rutherfurd and Daisy and the business of sitting for a portrait by Lucy's friend from Locust Valley, the exiled Russian painter Elizabeth Shoumatoff. Lunch was about to be served, at 2 p.m. Franklin, fumbling with age-freckled hands, seemed to be looking for something. He tried to smile. His massive forehead furrowed. A quivering hand came to his temple. "I have a terrific pain," he said, "in the back of my head."[116]

It was after three at the Sulgrave Club when Eleanor gave a quick start.[117] She was wanted on the telephone. Steve Early, audibly upset, asked her to come home at once. Eleanor did not ask why: "I knew down in my heart that something dreadful had happened."[118]

Upstairs at the White House, Early and Admiral McIntire came to her sitting room and told her the President had slipped away.[119] Cause of death: extensive and acute cerebral hemorrhage. His doctors had applied continual resuscitative measures. He died at 3:35 p.m. Central War Time.

Eleanor's first thought was of Vice President Truman and then of her children.[120] She sent a cable message to the Pentagon for transmittal to her sons overseas: "Pa slept [*sic*] away this afternoon. He did his job to the end as he would want you to do." She signed it, "all our love."[121]

Twenty-five minutes later, Eleanor stepped forward when Harry Truman was shown into her sitting room. She put her hand on the new president's shoulder, and said, "Harry, the President is dead."

Truman, ashen-faced, replied, "Is there anything I can do for you?"

Eleanor's answer passed immediately into legend: "Is there anything *we* can do for *you?*" she returned, "For you're the one in trouble now."[122]

THEN SHE WAS ALOFT, FLYING to Georgia. Upon reaching Warm Springs before midnight, she learned that Lucy Mercer had been with her husband at the moment of his death; indeed, had been his houseguest the last three days of Franklin's life.

Her effort to control her shock and anger was visible to Aunt Polly and Daisy as Eleanor rose, walked to the bedroom where Franklin's body lay, and closed the door behind her. Five minutes later, she emerged, dry-eyed.

The next day—the first Friday the 13th that Franklin had not had to fear—was the one that Eleanor remembered as being "long and heartbreaking."

Two words filled front pages: ROOSEVELT DEAD!

Everywhere she looked, people were stopped in their tracks, blank, bewildered, speechless, openly weeping, as if a parent had just died. The country hardly knew how to carry on. For many, the President's death would be the greatest personal blow of the war. That the fighting continued without the President—the payoff battle for Berlin in the offing—left many feeling abandoned, panicky, afraid.[123]

Eleanor kept her feelings to herself. She had been shaken to learn that Anna had served as her father's hostess for innumerable secret visits with Lucy over the final years at the White House. There had been additional rendezvous at Bernard Baruch's South Carolina estate and at Warm Springs at Thanksgiving 1944. Each time, the elaborate security net around the wartime president had to be lifted like a curtain, then dropped back into place after Lucy had driven over.

It wasn't Anna's fault, and Eleanor knew it. Still, it hurt that Franklin had so easily drawn their daughter away from her. Franklin could always take people away from her, spreading among his inner circle a fog of airy, careless tricks and ruses. At his dying moment, he did just that.

THE DARK GREEN FUNERAL TRAIN bearing the president's mortal remains swayed out of Warm Springs on Friday, rolling north. In every station and depot, a guard of honor stood at attention, as for the next twelve hours, all along the line, people came to the tracks in ones and twos and throngs of thousands; some singing hymns, others looking on, haggard and drained, faces glazed with tears. Their grief surprised her: Eleanor had not envisaged that the nation would be inconsolable. "I never realized," she said later, "the full scope of the devotion to him until he died."[124]

When the *Ferdinand Magellan* pulled into Washington's Union Station Saturday morning, President Truman with Henry Wallace and Harry Hopkins, the entire cabinet and Supreme Court, all boarded the funeral train and stood solemnly waiting to pay their respects. General George Marshall, impeccable, unstinting, had arranged for the President's flag-draped coffin to be carried on a black army caisson drawn by six white horses, flanked by riderless mount and two-column motorcycle escort, leading a massive military procession to the White House.[125] Marshall's helmeted troops presented fixed bayonets six feet apart along the entire route of the cortege.

FDR had raised the American presidency to its highest powers. Two of the most selfless and tolerant leaders in American history— General George Marshall and First Lady Eleanor Roosevelt—would now ensure that, although FDR had died within grasp of the unconditional surrender he had fatefully demanded at Casablanca, his state funeral at the White House and burial in Hyde Park would honor every American fighting on to "total victory." Just as crucially, the fallen commander in chief "now personifies, as no one else could," wrote E. B. White, "all the American dead—those whose absence we shall soon attempt to justify."[126]

It was a beautiful April day. Gunfire still sounded across Europe, the South Pacific boiled in blood, and a stillness like no other spread over the bright marble and Quonset-hutted capital city that FDR had built during an unmatched four terms as president. As many as half a million people pressed in shoulder-to-shoulder under the giant trees on broad Constitution Avenue.[127] Among these hushed and hatless throngs, a whispered exchange or chirping bird overhead made the only sound until the creaking of the caisson was heard. Then quiet sobs broke out here and there as the big oaken wheels rolled past.

Eleanor, outwardly composed, rode with Elliott and Anna in the car immediately following the casket, appearing in bereavement "almost impersonal," she reflected, "perhaps because much further back I had had to face certain difficulties until I decided to accept the fact that a man must be what he is, life must be lived as it is . . . and you cannot live at all if you do not learn to adapt yourself to your life as it happens to be."[128]

Morning at Hyde Park on April 15 dawned cloudless and cold. Apple blossoms had begun to bleach the riverfront. Twenty-five years before, on a hot clear July day, Franklin had started his career in national politics by telling his neighbors from the front steps, "Anything I have ever done has come from the soil here."[129] Now the world's neighbor was going back to it.[130]

The burial service jammed hundreds inside the tall hemlock hedge surrounding the quarter-acre rose garden. A few minutes before ten, a lone gun in a nearby field fired the first round of a twenty-one-gun presidential salute. Muffled drums, prayers, hymns, a bomber flying overhead—forty-five minutes later, a detail fell out from among six hundred scarlet-caped West Point cadets and fired the final three-volley tribute to their supreme commander. Then, taps sounded on the still air, and eight enlisted men from all branches of the armed forces bore the bared casket to the grave.

After the flag was folded and presented to Eleanor, and the mourners had begun to file out, Elliott glanced at his mother as she went to the side of Franklin's elderly Aunt Betty. When everyone but the gardener and work crew had gone, the strain that Katherine Marshall, in Washington, and Elliott, here in Hyde Park, had seen etched into Eleanor's face smoothed out.[131]

Head bowed, smoky black veil pushed back, she watched over the grave as it filled. Franklin had chosen a spot at the center of his mother's rose beds and left detailed instructions for the plain white marble bier that would bear his name and dates—and Eleanor's. It was his wish, she now understood from the blank spaces of the stone itself, that their resting place was to be the same.

If Franklin left more specific plans for entombment, as family lore said he did, Eleanor did not confront until later her husband's curious, perhaps fanciful request to be buried in a cut-lid coffin with the head-section left open to the warm brown earth. The notion baffled and appalled her, in part because she herself felt something close to revulsion at the thought. From oldest childhood terrors, she retained a visceral dread of fresh-dug soil, whole clumps of earth embedded with stones, the sound-smothering weight imprisoning her.[132] FDR welcomed the sanctity of soil. He liked, as he once told her, "to be where things are growing."[133] Only later would Eleanor come to accept a friend's more biodiverse view that Franklin "wanted to get back into circulation as quickly as possible, and what better way than for his molecules to be incorporated immediately into his own rose garden?"[134]

Until the last shovelful of earth had been smoothed down, she stood straight and dry-eyed, her gaze fixed on the soil. A reporter could not help glimpsing that she wore at her throat the small fleur-de-lis—her young husband's wedding gift.[135]

WITHIN AN HOUR, SHE RECEIVED the mourners, thanking each, then boarded the Trumans' special train to Washington. She intended to waste no time packing up the White House. "I never did like to be where I no longer belonged," she remarked to Joe Lash.[136] She insisted that President and Mrs. Truman and their grown daughter, Margaret, encamped in Blair House, have full run of the Mansion as quickly as possible.[137]

On the 16th, she briefed Bess Truman on the workings of the President's house ("I liked her," she told Hick[138]) and invited the Missourians to lunch, taking up her seating duties one last time.

"Mr. President, you let me sit on your right," she began.

Then, in a gesture that brought a wash of quickly handkerchiefed tears to Marine Colonel Jimmy Roosevelt's eyes, she installed her successor in the place that for twelve years had been hers.

Weary, she could not rest. The tasks—the mail bags—calling for her attention numbered in the hundreds and thousands. For the first time in a decade of meeting her daily deadline, she went five days without filing so much as a semicolon to United Feature Syndicate. Nor did she read any of the scores of black-bordered editorials paying tribute to the glory of FDR and, on the whole, misjudging his replacement.

H. L. Mencken, Bad Boy of Baltimore, could take a bitter pride in having had a President Roosevelt to growl at for almost half the forty-six years of his newspaper career. Harry Truman seemed a "third-rate Middle Western politician on the order of Harding" by comparison to FDR. As for Eleanor, "It was she, not he, who really invented the New Deal." Nor could Mencken resist using "the most influential female ever recorded in American history" to re-size her husband and to consign ER to a widow's weedy oblivion: "She is alarmingly homely, she has lost her job, and she is growing old. . . . Tomorrow she will begin to fade, and by this time next year she may be wholly out of the picture."[139]

Catching her breath long enough to sketch her plans to the members of the News Conference Association, she poured them tea in the state dining room and remarked that from now on she would be seeking interviews rather than granting them. She discussed using the Washington Square apartment as her headquarters as she carried out Franklin's wishes. Then, thanking each of the newspeople as they filed out, she shook their hands and later sent each a personal note of sympathy or congratulations or remembrance, as if it were they who must be consoled upon losing a partner and the house they had lived in for twelve years.[140]

By Thursday night, April 19, the second floor stood barren of personal belongings. The next morning, army quartermaster's trucks loaded with barrels and crates would rumble off the grounds, bearing Franklin's Tut-like collections to the presidential library he had established just to the east of the Rose Garden at Hyde Park.

When Eleanor gathered for the last time with family and intimates at the west end of the long corridor, they had to send for an ashtray from the state rooms. "The eyes of John and Anna, Jimmy and Romelle, Elliott and Fay, and Anne, John's wife, were like burnt holes in a blanket," observed Belle Willard Roosevelt. Kermit's widow was struck by the "gift all Roosevelts I have ever known share—the ability to maintain a light touch in sorrow. It's a very moving approach to death: keeps those we love with us from the moment they die."[141]

Into the dining room, Eleanor said without thinking, "Belle, sit on Franklin's right . . ." Heads swiveled, and she cried out: "Children, do you think I'll ever learn not to say that?"[142]

After supper, they used Eleanor's barren sitting room to hear a tribute to ER on the radio. On the gallows-like floor, they listened to the newspaperwomen's memories, which of course were all in the past tense. Surprisingly quickly it became impossible to hear yet another paean beginning "Mrs. Roosevelt was . . ."

The children hung on in grim fascination until finally Anna rose and approached her mother, solemnly intoning, "Darling, if you will stretch out on the bed, I will look for a lily. This is beautiful, but it is the end—there is nothing else left but to bury you, which obviously should be done promptly. . . ."

To Hick, of course, Eleanor wrote her valedictory: "Nearly all that I can do is done. The upstairs looks desolate & I will be glad to leave tomorrow. It is empty & without purpose to be here now."[143]

Out her sitting room window the 1826 John Quincy Adams elm still held the Washington Monument in its vase-like branches. The obelisk flashed its red snake-eyed warning lights, and the view to the south stood open to frame Jefferson's new temple on the Tidal Basin.

Night after night she had poured herself out from this spot, penning and sending to points across the globe literally scores of thousands of notes, cables, cards, and letters answering some particular need or trouble, however small or large, beginning with her own locked heart and the first turning of its key: *Hick my dearest, I cannot go to bed tonight without a word to you* . . .

She who had opened the gates to many never before welcome in official Washington had made a point never to slam a door in the Mansion.[144] Now, whole slabs of national history fell in behind Franklin's death, shutting away "those of us who laid in his shadow." And now, she reminded Hick, it was up to them "to start again under our own momentum & wonder what we can achieve."[145]

TWENTY

Sunup at Val-Kill. The wind had blown all night, let go at dawn, leaving one star shining above the moon's thinnest sliver. With the new morning came a cup of hot water and lemon, a cold shower, new strength, and new thoughts.[1] She was a phoenix without the dramatics of the pyre. Her screened-in sleeping porch recharged her, gave her a feeling of "taking in."[2] In the cold night air she went to bed and got up at daybreak ready to start again.

One morning, driving over from Val-Kill, she came across a magnificent cock pheasant strutting across the road. Fala barked at it from the passenger seat, but the bird was imperturbable. "He looks at us," thought Eleanor, "as though he were saying *Look at me; I am one of the most beautiful creatures you have ever seen*." Then she wondered about the pheasant's mate, reflecting, "I haven't seen the hen as yet, but I am sure she must be a particularly modest one. She must have had to admire her husband so often."[3]

In his will, Franklin had left the Big House and a portion of its surrounding acres to the federal government to serve as a museum, a short walk away from his presidential library. If Eleanor or the children wished to live in the Big House during their lifetimes, they could elect to do so. Three years earlier, after his mother's funeral, Franklin had sprung on Eleanor that the time had come for her to take over Mama's room. But, naturally, she could not, and she had told him so, confiding to Anna: "Of course I know I've got to live there more, but only when he is there & I am afraid he hasn't realized that & isn't going to like it or understand."[4]

The place was hopelessly antiquated, overstuffed, redolent of old books, the tang of woodsmoke lingering in leather, beeswax, and dust. Eleanor was ready to let it go, but she put the question to each of the children, writing to the boys who were still at war. "All five really would have liked the idea of living there," Elliott later recounted, "but not one of us could possibly have afforded to keep it up."[5]

Yet each son believed *he* was the one to assume, if not the house itself, then the power of the house.

It fell to Eleanor to leave every room a kind of blueprint of what it had been—the Boyhood Bedroom, Mama's Snuggery—while dividing up the tangibles among her daughter and son-in-law, grown sons and daughters-in-law.[6] "How I hate *things*!" she fumed to Joe Lash.[7]

ON MAY 8, V-E DAY, the flash of victory in Europe left Eleanor sad that Franklin could not have broadcast the triumph. But her titanic task had to be done by June 15, and she did not pause to celebrate with the rest of the free world. Besides, she told Aunt Maude, "I won't feel any lifting of the burden, I imagine, till the Japs are through. They seem to want to fight till the bitter end!"[8]

The defeat of Nazi Germany, however, did allow her to pause to alert her readers to the threat of a similar enemy within. On April 16, the day after Franklin's burial, Edward R. Murrow had broadcast over American radio the first eyewitness account of a Nazi concentration camp—Buchenwald—without ever once describing the victims of the camp's atrocities as Jews.[9] *Time* and *Life* magazines did the same in their first reporting from Dachau, opened on April 29, identifying the camp's 32,000 survivors only by their nationality or political party, while depicting Dachau's "skeleton stacks" of dehumanized bodies as "men of all nations . . . prime opponents of Naziism. . . the very earliest Hitler haters."[10]

"Are we learning nothing from the horrible pictures of the concentration camps which have been appearing in our papers day after day?" protested Eleanor in her column on April 30. "Are our memories so short that we do not recall how in Germany this unparalleled barbarism started by discrimination directed against the Jewish people? It has ended in brutality and cruelty meted out to all people, even to our own boys who have been taken prisoner."[11]

Most reporters, indeed, most U.S. army generals, could not at first comprehend camps where vast gas chambers and crematoria had been expressly built for the mass murder of European Jews. Americans would not learn of the full mechanized extent of the Nazi plan for the "Final Solution" until well after the Soviet liberation of the largest of the killing centers, Auschwitz-Birkenau, in which more than 1.1 million people had perished, including nearly one million Jews.

Eleanor was among the first to connect these dots and to put the unspeakable truth into morning newspapers from Augusta to Albuquerque a week before the war's end: "This bestiality could not exist if the Germans had not allowed themselves to believe in a master race which could do anything it wished to all other human beings not of their particular racial strain."[12]

Even as Nazi horrors shocked the world, Eleanor insisted that there was nothing, "given certain kinds of leadership, which could prevent our falling a prey to this same kind of insanity." She warned: "The idea of superiority of one race over another must not continue within our own country, nor must it grow up in our dealings with the rest of the world." It was not enough to defeat Nazi Germany "if we at home do not take every step—both through our government and as individuals—to see not only that fairness exists in all employment practices, but that throughout our nation all people are equal citizens. Where the theory of a master race is accepted," stated Eleanor, "there is danger to all progress in civilization."[13]

THE NEWS OF THE FIRST use of an atomic weapon reached her on August 7. If it were to end the war, she had no objection to President Truman's targeting the Japanese city of Hiroshima with a bomb equal to the force of fifteen thousand tons of TNT. If the horrific blast, repeated three days later over the city of Nagasaki, would forestall the planned U.S. attack on the heavily defended Japanese home island, save a million more American GIs, and hasten a complete surrender, then Eleanor seconded President Truman's decisions and could feel "only pity and a deep desire to aid those who suffered through no fault of their own."[14]

"This discovery," she told her readers, emphasizing collective responsibility as the first reports began to sink in, "must spell the end of war."[15]

On V-J Day, August 15, 1945, Imperial Japan surrendered, bringing the war to an end. Men tended to look at the victory, women at the cost. More than sixty million dead the world over, including for the first time in human history the mechanized extermination of a people: the six million European Jews of the Holocaust.

All told, her life's two world wars—so far—had claimed more than a hundred million people.[16] Franklin had hoped that out of the failure of the peace of 1918 would now come a "universal organization"; Eleanor felt strongly that a "United Nations" would serve the postcolonial world far better than an Anglo-American peacekeeping force.[17] Women, she also believed, "might have a better chance to bring about the understanding necessary to prevent future wars if they could serve in sufficient numbers in these international bodies."

For months after leaving the White House she would fend off continual suggestions that she seek the highest offices in the land. "I do not think we have yet reached a point," she answered for 1948, "where the electorate is ready for a woman Vice President who might possibly become President."[18] In the meantime, Eleanor wanted more women elected and appointed to offices that directly affected policy. For herself, she intended to lead a "private and inconspicuous existence" in her freer, unbound old age.[19] She turned away myriad committee chairmanships, and so far as serving the public in elective office, she told anyone asking that her husband had been the whole show.[20]

A reporter nonetheless waylaid her one morning outside her building on Washington Square. "The story is over," she insisted, hurrying away into the metropolis, a fully private citizen for the first time since before what was now to be called World War I.

On Sunday, December 30, 1945, the U.S. delegation sailed for England and the start of American participation in the universal, or, anyway, fifty-one-member United Nations Organization (UNO) that had eluded President Wilson and which FDR, imagining this second postwar world, had hoped would give "all peace-loving nations" a chance to put "an end to the beginning of all wars."[21]

RMS *Queen Elizabeth* waited on the tide at Pier 90, as the nation's diplomatic stars stepped from limousines into the floodlighted glare to deliver weighty parting statements before a swarm of reporters and newsreel cameras.

Debonair Edward Stettinius, the former secretary of state, boarded the gangway "like a prize-fighter entering the ring."[22] Now first U.S. representative to the UNO and acting chairman of the delegation, Stettinius and his retinue were followed by the jug-eared Texas Democrat Senator Tom Connally, chairman of the powerful Foreign Relations Committee. Next came Michigan Republican Arthur Vandenberg, the Senate's former leading isolationist, new champion of bipartisan internationalism; and Vandenberg's senior consultant, drafter of the preamble to the UNO's charter, and master secret-keeper of the darker side of U.S. foreign affairs, sourpuss John Foster Dulles.

Brilliant young Alger Hiss had come along as the State Department's principal officer in charge of the delegation, followed by trusted advisers Abe Fortas, the future Supreme Court justice, and Ralph Bunche, that rare bird, an African American in the State Department.[23]

Eleanor arrived in a taxi. She strode unnoticed along the pier, lugging her own bag, briefcase, and typewriter. She boarded "all alone," noted Bunche in his pocket diary.[24] Carrying a fur scarf over one arm and toting the heavy briefcase up the gangway, she seemed to S. J. Woolf, a reporter from old Albany days, "like a mature Edith Wharton heroine capable of meeting modern problems." The New York illustrator was struck by the way Eleanor kept transforming through life, remarking that she was now "a Gibson girl transplanted into the atomic age and unafraid of it."[25]

In fact, she was petrified. Making her way to her stateroom, heavy-hearted at the thought of working day by day without Tommy's help and companionship, Eleanor felt "rather lost and quite uncertain about what lay ahead." She sensed that among her fellow delegates she was "not very welcome."[26]

When President Truman had called Eleanor earlier that month to ask her to serve at the first meeting of the United Nations General Assembly in London in January, she had declined. Franklin Jr., home on leave between naval postings, had stopped in at his mother's Washington Square apartment, and would remember Eleanor telling the

President, "Oh, no! It would be impossible. I'm totally inadequate to this."[27]

Truman's most recent Big Three meeting in Potsdam made any view of Eleanor's "inexperience" ridiculous. So far as Churchill and Stalin were concerned, there could not have been a replacement more un-ready than Franklin Roosevelt's unfortunate successor. Truman knew no one in the American foreign policy establishment or scientific community, an acute nightmare when it came to the vastly destructive new weapon that Roosevelt had kept secret from everyone, including his wife and his vice president.

Truman urged Eleanor to reconsider, as did Tommy, and the matter was left open. But as much as she wanted the job and believed the newly chartered UNO to be the one hope for a world already chafing at the peace, she felt gripped by "fear and trembling" that she would fail.

The humbling consequences of warfare with nuclear weapons gave a solemn responsibility to the first UNO delegates: "We have learned how to destroy ourselves," Eleanor would write in the days at sea. "Mankind can be wiped off the face of the earth by the action of any comparatively small group of people. So it would seem that if we care to survive we must progress in our social and economic develop-ment far more rapidly than we have done in the past."[28]

This time, she said, the people had been scared badly enough to realize that if they did not do something to prevent the outbreak of World War III, "there might be a morning when we would not wake up."[29]

She had worried the decision for several days, consulting with El-liott, now her principal adviser. Truman, meanwhile, had requested a poll of senators on ER's candidacy. Majority Leader Alben Barkley found that Republican John Foster Dulles deemed Mrs. Roosevelt "too independent," while Democrat William Fulbright saw her inexperi-ence sending the wrong message about the UNO.

Alger Hiss had taken the list of delegation nominees to the Senate Foreign Relations Committee, whose members reacted with stag-night hostility: "Oh . . . *Eleanor*!"[30] Senator Vandenberg judged Eleanor un-qualified and protested her appointment directly to President Truman. John Foster Dulles did the same. Both gave ER credit for being sincere, as had many of the editorials that affirmed Truman's choice. Dulles questioned her loyalty, saying he didn't trust FDR's widow to take orders from President Truman. "He felt the world was coming to an end when he heard I was joining the delegation," remarked Eleanor.[31]

But when the Senate voted on December 22, promptly confirming ER's appointment, only one senator voted against her, Democrat Theodore G. Bilbo, possibly the most obscene white supremacist in the twentieth-century Senate, which as always gave the gentleman from Mississippi ample opportunity to fatuously disqualify Mrs. Roosevelt on grounds that she "endorsed intermarriage" and "forced our Southern girls to use the stools and toilets of damn syphilitic nigger women."[32]

Another wrinkle was that Soviet power had not been a prime UN issue when the London session was set up to establish the General Assembly's bylaws and to preview the workings of the Security Council. It would not become apparent that the Security Council was going to be polarized until Stalin refused to relinquish occupied territory in Iran, triggering the first showdown of the Cold War. Rising East-West hostilities would begin to fray relations between the United States and the USSR while the delegates were in session, and Truman would need the gold standard of the Roosevelt name in London, which in turn would stabilize his chances for reelection in 1948. He would benefit as well from Eleanor's steady demeanor to regulate the delegation. Truman never wavered from his belief in Eleanor, feeling in his craw that she would reflect greatness on postwar America. "Your country needs you," the President had implored her. "Indeed, this troubled world needs you."[33]

Preparing for the London winter, she had gone to a Russian-émigré doctor, a friend of Trude Lash's, for a checkup. He told her she was tough, the healthiest human being he had examined in a long time. Two months later, when Tommy Thompson went to the same doctor after a severe gallbladder attack, he told her after an exam that she, too, was tough—a workhorse, "but that I am a 'little horse,'" explained Tommy to Anna, "[and,] while your mother is tough, she is 'a big horse.'"

"Not very complimentary," decided Tommy, "but descriptive. He is a psychologist as well as an 'internal doctor,' and added that your mother gets exhilaration out of what she does; that I have more detail etc., which is not exhilarating."[34]

IN HER CABIN, A PILE of State Department position papers had been spread on a table. She had no idea who had left them—they were marked "SECRET"—but she knew her duty when she saw it.

Unfortunately, they were useless; she could barely understand certain passages as prose intended to convey meaning. Each paper succeeded only at *disinforming* the reader. Nevertheless, she kept at it; by the time the outbound *Queen Elizabeth* had cleared the harbor, the tugboats, and the Narrows, only to creep along for hours, horns blowing and bells clanking through a dense fog off Sandy Hook, day had broken. The State Department had no more policies to keep from Eleanor Roosevelt, but neither did she know the United States position on anything at all.

She spent the first few days at sea "much alone" and doubted that she could be a meaningful member of the delegation. "I was really frightened. I knew what people thought of Franklin, and what they thought of me, and what they expected of me, and I knew that I didn't know what to do or how to do it."[35]

Each morning and evening, when she took her walk on deck, additional position papers were left in her cabin. Fortunately, Hiss was now holding compulsory State Department briefings in the lounge. These began on the first day and continued across the North Atlantic, Eleanor attending each one, often as the sole delegate present. The team's expert advisers were surprised to have even one truly conscientious delegate, and came to admire her readiness to listen to the support staff's arguments,[36] against which she sharpened her own questions.[37]

Ralph Bunche, the delegation and staff's only African American, concluded that ER, its only woman, was the one member of the contingent trying to grasp the fine points of each position so that she could hold herself accountable to U.S. policy. Bunche, "always conscious of the handicap of race," recognized that his own approach to the all-white delegation was similar to Eleanor's.[38] Neither would rest until she or he carried twice the load of their white male counterparts. "I knew that if I failed to be a useful member," reckoned Eleanor, "it would not be considered merely that I as an individual had failed, but that all women had failed, and there would be little chance for others to serve in the near future."[39]

A FEW DAYS OUT TO sea, Senator Vandenberg stopped her in the passageway to her cabin. "Mrs. Roosevelt," he said, "we would like to know if you would serve on Committee Three?"

Eleanor immediately wondered who "we" might be. Committee assignments had already been made in Washington. And if so—if Alger Hiss had formalized the final decisions in consultation with the delegation's State Department advisers, the secretary of state, and the President—why had Vandenberg and the others kept Eleanor out of the loop, conferring only among themselves?

She imagined them puzzling over the General Assembly's six committees—Politics and Security; Economic and Financial; Human, Social, and Cultural; Administrative and Budgetary; Legal; Trusteeship—and deciding, "Ah, here's the safe spot for her— Committee 3, the *human, social, and cultural* group. Can't do much harm there!"[40]

She felt slighted at not having been consulted,[41] and resented Vandenberg overriding Hiss and taking it upon himself to decide who would serve where. Yet Arthur Vandenberg was fast becoming one of the chief architects of postwar international leadership and bipartisan cooperation. Eleanor agreed to serve on Committee 3, asking only that she be given as much information as possible about its mission.

In the weeks ahead, she learned to consult the delegation's principal adviser, Durward V. Sandifer, who at San Francisco had served as secretary general and the U.S. delegation's chief technical expert. She had not expected to have any help at all, and couldn't believe her good fortune in being assigned a thoughtful, modest, and highly trained international lawyer and foreign service official. Before the end of the London session, Eleanor would adopt "Sandy" as her confidential adviser and primary ally, and Sandy's wife, Irene, and daughter, Muriel as close new friends. "It was a case with Sandy and Mrs. Roosevelt," said Alger Hiss, who was responsible for the matchup, "of love at first sight."[42]

By the time the delegation landed in England and settled into a London routine between rooms at Claridge's and meetings at King Albert Hall, the Committee 3 objectives and guidelines from the President and State Department remained a will-o'-the-wisp. Eleanor had no more use for "secret" position papers, and even less helpful was Truman's new secretary of state, the former New Dealer and federal-city power broker James Byrnes, who did not reach London until mid-January. Eleanor greeted his arrival with grave concern: "Secretary Byrnes seems to me to be afraid to decide on what he thinks is right and stand on it." The U.S. contingent, after all, was in a position to lead: "But we don't. We shift to conciliate and trail either Great Britain or Russia." Simply put: "Secretary Byrnes is afraid of his own delegation."[43]

And so, Eleanor and Sandifer were on their own to develop a policy on a problem that no one had realized would create the greatest political heat of the session. The "safe" Committee 3 had put Eleanor in charge of the fate of a million desolate souls left displaced by the war.

IN LONDON AT CLARIDGE'S, SHE could hardly get from one place to another without a crowd forming. The widow of England's "best friend" who had shown her own loyalty with her war visit in 1942, she was by far the most sought-after member of the delegation—the one American who, by Great Britain's standards, had scope and humanity. What mattered in London in 1946 was her dedicated plainness. The British saw in her a thrifty, practical woman, hard at her work, getting things done, wearing clothes no better than she had to, and without the American taste for splash. No one in England had bought a new suit for four or five years.

As the widow in chief, she struck a note with a nation that had lost 400,000 men. The pain and disillusion of victory had just sunk in. Crudely calculated, America had lost three persons per thousand; Britain, ten persons per thousand. The top brass, especially General Eisenhower, had been heroes to the British; the average Yank, however, was "overpaid, oversexed, and over here." People in England were feeling chewed up and spat out by America. A small group called the Married Women's Association, dedicated to economic equality be-

tween spouses, represented six English women whose American soldier husbands had turned their backs on them and on their children.
The women were seeking divorce or reconciliation—they also needed
money to defend suits in U.S. courts—and hoped Eleanor would in-
tercede for them from London.[44]

On January 10, a group of about five hundred GIs, protesting the
delay at being sent home, held a meeting outside the Grosvenor Square
headquarters of the U.S. commanding general, London area. A couple
dozen of the men broke away and hurried off to Claridge's to enlist
Mrs. Roosevelt's support.

In her suite, Eleanor received a call from the desk—the men had
sent up their names. She invited them upstairs, then a few moments
later heard what sounded like an enormous number of Halloween visitors in the corridor. She opened the door, beaming delightedly.

"How do you do?" she said. "I am glad to see you all."

"We came here, Mrs. Roosevelt," replied Sergeant J. T. Trevers of
Dallas, Texas, "because we want you to help us."

"Come in," said Eleanor, "and tell me all about it, boys."[45]

SHE HAD DISCOVERED IN A memo that displaced political dissidents
were likely to be killed as war criminals if they went home. As many
as a million such refugees, including a large portion of women and
children, were struggling to survive, much less restart useful, productive lives, in camps in the American, British, and French zones of Germany.

The largest national group of "DPs" were Poles; some were Yu-
goslavs and other Eastern Europeans; many were Balts, from Latvia,
Lithuania, and Estonia, now annexed by the Soviet Union. The war
had driven them from their homes. Fleeing invasions or persecutions
and myriad forms of brutality, they had fallen into the hands of the
Nazis, who enslaved them in camps. Now, after two years of care
sponsored by the United Nations Relief and Rehabilitation Administration (UNRRA), these hundreds of thousands of anti-Communists
or Catholics or Jews feared execution if they returned to their Russian-
occupied homelands.

The Soviet position on refugee resettlement was brutal: displaced persons must go home. Any refugee who did not want to return to his or her country of origin was a traitor to his or her country and should be forced to repatriate and accept whatever punishment they had coming to them. Or, as an alternative, be tossed out of the camps to fend for themselves.

Eleanor replied to these delusions in committee discussion, asserting that the Soviet view "fails to consider the facts of political change in countries of origin which have created fears in the minds of the million persons, who remain, of such a nature that they choose miserable life in camps in preference to the risks of repatriation."[46]

Backed by Sandifer, Eleanor established the position that refugees were not traitors or "Fascists," as the Russians labeled them. As individuals, they should be guaranteed political sanctuary and the right to choose whether or not they would return to their homeland.

The Russians opposed this resolution in committee, putting forth a proposed restriction against returning "war criminals disguised as refugees" to their countries of origin.

The U.S. insisted that you couldn't compel uprooted people to go back where they came from if they didn't want to.

And there the matter rested. But when it became clear that the head of the Soviet delegation, Andrei Vyshinsky, the Great Prosecutor, legal mastermind of Stalin's Great Purge, was going to challenge the committee's recommendations and present the Soviet case at the final plenary himself, the members of her delegation acknowledged that Mrs. Roosevelt did not necessarily *have* to defend the U.S. position. She might not be up to dealing with the villain of the Soviet show trials of the 1930s.

The men sent up trial balloons alerting one another that someone had to step up to take on Vyshinsky. Then, quietly, John Foster Dulles asked Mrs. Roosevelt to say a few words. Dulles, Vandenberg, and a State Department counselor and former New Dealer, Benjamin V. Cohen, were impressed by Eleanor's ability to meet Soviet stubbornness as a businesslike lady. She was luminous, plainly clear, with an invincible firmness of her own. She never had to say what she had to say twice.

She had gotten a first taste of Soviet intractability in 1942, during

Vyacheslav M. Molotov's visit to the United States, when the USSR's foreign minister had asked President Roosevelt for a separate meeting with ER to talk about social issues facing both countries. Although she saw Molotov frequently and sometimes sat next to him at dinners, she learned it was impossible to penetrate his guard. Molotov was so hard-headed that Western diplomats called him "Stone-ass."

In the last session of the General Assembly, the UN's modernistic gold-on-blue insignia—a gilt projection of the globe embraced by olive branches—hung spotlighted above a multi-tiered dais. Amid this Fascist architecture, the vice foreign commissar of the Soviet Union presented his sovereign case for restricting the political activities of displaced persons, accompanied by shocked tossings of his white head.

Clear and forceful in her opposition, Eleanor punched back hard against the proposed restrictions, which Vyshinsky claimed were critical to preventing "Fascist collaborators" from circulating a "call to treason" in refugee camps. If restrictions were not also adopted against "propaganda" in refugee camps, the United Nations and her members would be endangered.

"The restrictions are restrictive to human rights and human freedoms," said Eleanor, to loud applause that ripped through the cavernous Methodist Church Central Hall. She argued that the proposal before the assembly provided adequately for the return of war criminals. Refugees, however, were not criminals. Many remained in the camps temporarily because they disagreed with their home governments. They must be allowed to live where they liked.

"Are we so weak in the United Nations," she asked, "that we should forbid human beings to say what they see and hear, what they think and believe? They may even say things against the United States, but I still think it's their right to say them."

Vyshinsky returned to the rostrum to reply that "unlimited freedom as advocated by Mrs. Roosevelt does not exist in any country." He said it was "indispensable to limit the will and actions of man; otherwise man could kill or steal. This is true also of nations and governments. It is impossible to have unlimited freedom, for freedom is limited by life itself. Otherwise there would be no society or society of states."

Realizing that Vyshinsky often talked for over two hours, Eleanor purposely kept herself down to under fifteen minutes, and let her voice quaver with indignation. Vyshinsky tried tactics of his own. His speech rambled, he flung around abusive accusations. He made it sound as if the Soviet Union were the victim. He went over the same arguments endlessly, bristling with oaths and imprecations against the American government.

"Mr. Vyshinsky," she said, "we here in the United Nations are trying to develop ideas which will be broader in outlook, which will consider first the rights of man, which will consider what makes man *more free*. Not governments, Mr. Vyshinsky, *but man*."

Sandifer seemed pleased as he leaned in and whispered, "The Russians won't like that."

Vyshinsky had turned bright red, but, for a change, had no comeback.[47]

The General Assembly rejected all three Russian proposals and voted unanimously for an investigation of the refugee problem. "Mrs. FDR" was declared the winner on front pages around the world. Eleanor refused a victory lap—"Well, *the West* won," she insisted, meanwhile privately arranging to fly the next morning into the heart of Germany to see the camps for herself.

The vote had gone until a late hour, and when adjournment was finally announced, Eleanor made her way over to her opponent. She did not want to leave with bad feeling between them. "I hope the day will come, sir," she told Vyshinsky, "when you and I are on the same side of a dispute, for I admire your fighting qualities."

He shot back, "And I, yours."[48]

BOUND FOR BERLIN AT DAWN, the U.S. Army plane flew over the bomb-cratered world of rubble that had been Middle Europe. Without of course having killed anyone, Eleanor felt she knew what it was to be a mass murderer. If one took responsibility for a vast amount of destruction, whether done with a nuclear bomb in a matter of seconds, or "when precision bombing had done the best it knew how to do," the result was down there in the rubble.[49]

Landing in Frankfurt, she visited the refugee camps for Jews at

Zilcheim. A woman kneeling in the camp's muddy road threw her arms around Eleanor's legs, murmuring, "Israel!" Again and again: "Israel!"

It was Eleanor's first real understanding "what that small land meant to so many people."

It rattled her to see the freed camp prisoners, having survived the unimaginable, living on in deprivation. Yet somehow they faced the future resolutely. One of them struck her deeply: a boy who couldn't remember his name, knew not where he had lived or who his parents were or what had happened to them. The boy, who looked no more than nine but happened to be twelve, had a younger brother to take care of, as Eleanor had had at that age. And he sang for her "A Song of Freedom," after which no one listening could speak.

In Frankfurt, Eleanor found her Allenswood friend Carola von Schaeffer-Bernstein, strangely unchanged by the war, a bit more worn, dressed plainly, and reserved toward Eleanor. Her family's house had not been bombed. Her husband had survived, as had her daughters, but one of her sons, in the German Army, had been killed. They said nothing of that—they avoided the whole subject of the war—until Eleanor got up to go, remarking on the tragedy of Germany as a whole.

"It was everybody's fault," answered Carola, quickly. "We are all to blame. None of us has lived up to the teachings of Christ."

Eleanor said, "You've always been a very religious person. How is it possible that one can be so devoted to the principles of the church yet not protest the mistreatment of the Jews?"

"Sometimes it is wiser not to look over the hill," came the answer.[50] Eleanor never saw or heard from Carola again.

Back in London, the UN General Assembly, representing all fifty-one member states, elected its first president, Paul-Henri Spaak, Belgium's foreign minister. His investiture coincided with a celebration of his birthday, and when asked what he most wanted for a present, Spaak instantly replied, "Mrs. Roosevelt."[51]

Unofficially she was told that she would be reappointed to the Human Rights Commission for a term of four years. The next meeting would be in New York City in January 1947 and the July meeting in Geneva.

Speaking to reporters, having not answered any personal questions since Franklin's death, she realized that for the first time in her life, she was able to say exactly what she wanted. "For your information," she marveled, "it is wonderful to feel free."[52]

Before flying home, Dulles approached, vinegar faced: "I feel I must tell you that when you were appointed I thought it terrible, and now I think your work here has been fine."[53]

Senator Vandenberg was expansive, even comparative: "Mrs. Roosevelt did a finer job than any of us in cementing American international relations, at the same time protecting the interests of the United States."[54] Added the great Moose of Michigan,[55] "I want to take back everything I ever said about her, and, believe me, it's been plenty."[56]

Upon returning from London Eleanor got an attack of the shingles. Franklin Jr. worried that she was working "too strenuously and too continuously," pleaded with her to take time from her labors with the UNO and give *herself* some of her own time, "instead of giving it all to others." He thought she needed some rest.[57] Steve Early agreed with Franklin. "All of us know the importance of the work you are doing," wrote Early. "But, to all of us, you and your welfare comes first. And, as the President used to say: 'Let first things come first.'"[58]

Stalin had waited until early February 1946—fewer than six months since the Japanese surrendered—to declare capitalism implacably hostile to communism. Even as he denied to Churchill's face the first British diplomatic descriptions of an iron curtain coming down in Eastern Europe, scorning such reports as "fairy tales," the Soviet dictator commanded his people to build up the USSR's military and industrial might as a defense against "accidents."

A month later, at President Truman's invitation, Churchill came to Westminster College in Fulton, Missouri. By then, in the American mind, the USSR had shifted shape. The gritty wartime ally that had sacrificed more than eleven million soldiers and as many as twenty million civilians[59] now appeared in popular opinion as "fierce, aggressive, and fanatic."[60] On March 5, 1946, Churchill delivered his "iron curtain" address on the future of East-West relations, proposing that a permanent peace depended on the creation of a union of the English-speaking peoples against the Russians.

Eleanor, by then home from London and fully engaged in the U.S. struggle to establish a working relationship with the Russians through the UN, was disturbed by Churchill's anti-Soviet belligerency. She also felt partly responsible; she had not warned President Truman, since she had heard Churchill make similar proposals to Franklin and had seen Franklin ignore them entirely. As early as May 1945, with Franklin gone less than a month and the war in Germany barely won, Churchill predicted that most of Eastern Europe would be absorbed by the Soviets.

Then, in London in January, Churchill told Eleanor that in his view Russian policies offered little chance for a successful peace, and that he was going to make a proposal for an Anglo-American counter-alliance, which he couched in the old phrasings of a "fraternal association," a "special relationship between the British Commonwealth and Empire and the United States."[61] When Eleanor told British foreign secretary Ernest Bevin that Churchill should not make such a speech, Bevin assured her that the embassy in Washington would not allow it. Every foreign service officer was well aware of Great Britain's twenty-year treaty of collaboration and mutual assistance with Soviet Russia, which Bevin viewed as potentially stretching now to fifty years.[62]

She had offered to go to see the President when he appointed her, but he had not had time. It was typical of Truman's loyalty that he would have requested Churchill's speech; he thought Franklin and Winston had been such close allies that whatever Churchill was going to say would align with FDR's program. In truth, the two leaders had also had the most violent arguments—disagreements about the conduct of the war. Eleanor had seen their telegrams burning up the wires.[63] She should have insisted on a full and frank talk with the President, but ultimately she made a point of not admitting her influence. If a president must understand what he is doing and make it his own,[64] so must a former first lady.

In May, cheerfully settled into her new routine at 29 Washington Square West, she vowed: "I really am going to do much less, and after the 30th of this month, I plan to stay in Hyde Park and not make any engagements which take me away from home." She told Steve Early: "I never had the proper appreciation of shingles before!"[65]

WORLDMAKER

*The greatest thing I have learned
is how good it is to come home again.*

E.R.[1]

TWENTY-ONE

A FEW MORNINGS BEFORE LEAVING for Geneva and the second session of the Commission on Human Rights in November 1947, Eleanor glimpsed a bluebird flying over the brook. "There is always a little excitement," she reflected, "about going off to a new job."[1]

At sixty-three, she did not tire easily. Her feet occasionally bothered her—"my White House feet," she called them, after an X-ray showed that years of standing and handshaking at receptions had permanently altered the bones of her instep. She nonetheless felt better when on the go, and it was clearly her turn to spread her wings. "But," she conceded, "as I grow older, I find that I regret the things I leave behind."[2] Her walks in the woods with Fala. Thanksgiving at Val-Kill. November's mauve-colored sunsets west of the river. Her deep satisfaction in piling up Christmas presents all through the year, laying up treasure for what was now a three-hundred-person Christmas list.[3] "All these are hard to leave," she reflected. "Only the sense of something tangible accomplished, that may be of value in the future, will seem to me to make this trip worthwhile."

Geneva would be the Commission's first step toward establishing something never before undertaken by the nations of the world: a declaration of standards by which essential and pre-existing rights of individuals could be agreed upon as universal. Eighteen United Nations member states had been chosen to serve on the Commission. Eleanor, politician in her own right and widow wreathed in the prestige of the fallen world-war leader, was voted chairman by acclamation at the Commission's first plenary session earlier that year.

When a preliminary commission to draft a declaration had begun work over teacups in Eleanor's apartment in January, the scale of their task appeared daunting. Whole continental populations lay shattered, subject to famine and disease.[4] The full dimensions of the Holocaust had begun to emerge as the remaining leadership of Nazi Germany came to trial in the Nuremberg tribunals. An atomic-age peace appeared increasingly dubious. How long, after all, could the United States keep the secret to itself? As Eleanor saw it, so long as the U.S. alone possessed the bomb, the American people would be subject to "fear of a power which we possess but are not sure that we can control." Inevitably, this would now expand to encompass "fear of what others may do with that power if, before long, they have it too."[5]

By June, she had enlarged the drafting committee to eight members to accommodate Soviet complaints of underrepresentation, and had deferred to the majority's wish to draft, in addition to the rights enumerated in the Declaration, a Covenant that would function as its treaty, obliging signatory nations to grant, protect, and enforce through their own laws the universal rights specified by the Declaration. ER's position on giving priority to the drafting of the Declaration, rather than bogging down in the technicalities and nation-by-nation ratification of a Covenant, set the Commission on the fast track she believed it needed to gain public support. She was also mindful to consult with Senate leadership, after congressional suspicion of UN treaties had escalated the previous summer.

On June 22, India had filed a complaint citing the Union of South Africa for new violations in a long history of discrimination, which in less than a year would only intensify as the Afrikaner National Party made official the state-sanctioned system of segregationist policies against non-white citizens, the majority indigenous Africans. India's case against South African apartheid, stirringly argued in the General Assembly by representative Vijaya Lakshmi, terrified the U.S. delegation, whose members could all too easily imagine what would happen if a similar complaint was filed against the United States. Arthur Vandenberg, for one, admitted that he saw little difference between "Indians in South Africa and negroes in Alabama."[6] Tom Connally and John Foster Dulles joined Vandenberg in a plan to kill the Indian complaint, first by shunting it from UN jurisdiction to the International Court of Justice, then by burying it under the bureaucracy of multiple UN committees. Eleanor expressed concern that both methods would undermine UN credibility. She also recognized that India's complaint could establish precedent for an "oppressed" minority to "get its case before the United Nations in spite of its own government's [policies]."[7] But she went along with Connally and the team in agreeing that India had violated the UN Charter's clause protecting member states from intrusions into issues of "domestic jurisdiction."

The UN Charter, however, had also imposed upon each member state an obligation to refrain from policies based in race discrimination, and by that measure the postwar United States was failing even more deplorably than the Western nations now beginning to shed themselves of their colonial possessions and pasts.

"Negro veterans," reported NAACP leader Walter White to Eleanor in September 1946, "have been done to death or mutilated with savagery equaled only at Buchenwald." And with "no visible action in the form of arrests and convictions," explained White, the waking nightmare of the African American community was that the South's lynch mobs had been given a "green light to substitute the law of the jungle for the democratic process."[8]

In 1946—the second year in which the United States prosecuted Nazi war crimes at Nuremberg while condoning in four Southern states a terror campaign so brutal it involved the lynching, burning, dismemberment, blinding, and butchery of African American veterans and women—the UN's promise of an international bill of human rights convinced black advocacy groups, especially the powerful NAACP, that a moment of truth had arrived to right the centuries-old wrongs of slavery and Jim Crow.

Civil rights, promised by the Constitution and the justice system of the United States, had only yielded bitter disappointment. But now, human rights, secured by an international organization pledging to honor social, political, religious, and economic rights, appeared to offer to African Americans the sword and shield of full equality and justice.

On October 23, 1947, the NAACP petitioned to bring before the United Nations Secretariat renowned scholar W. E. B. DuBois's 155-page appeal to the world community for redress of violations of the rights of African Americans, including accounts of lynchings inhuman beyond imagination, the horrors of America's "color caste system," the economic disparity of whites and blacks, and the restricted legal rights of African Americans and other racial minorities seeking justice in the American legal system. But Eleanor could not show public support for her fellow NAACP board members.

"As an individual I should like to be present," she told Walter White, "but as a member of the delegation I feel that until this subject comes before us in the proper way, in a report of the Human Rights Commission or otherwise, I should not seem to be lining myself up in any particular way on any subject." She closed with the truth: "It isn't as though everyone did not know where I stand," then added, less truthfully, more diplomatically, "It is just a matter of proper procedure."[9]

It was much more than that, as she would soon discover in Geneva. A meticulously documented and horrifically detailed report on the systematic oppression of thirteen million African Americans would expose Eleanor's flank to the Soviet delegation.

"But how about your treatment of Negroes in your country?" she would repeatedly be asked. "How about your Ku Klux Klan lynchings?"

"I had no answer," she conceded. "What do you say, standing before a committee of a World Organization, when you are asked about the Ku Klux Klan?"[10]

SHE EXPECTED TO REACH SWITZERLAND in twenty-four hours, with a day to rest up before going into action with the Soviets. Her personal physician, Dr. David Gurewitsch, was flying with her—was in fact under *her* care—and when the elegant, triple-tailed TWA Constellation descended to refuel at Newfoundland, Eleanor dreaded to hear that mechanical trouble would hold them at Gander. Even for a well person, the Geneva flight was exhausting, and her doctor was a sick man.

In New York, a spot had been found indicating tuberculosis on David's lungs. Eleanor had offered Val-Kill for his recuperation, but as David's marriage reached the point of separation, he decided to close his practice, fly to Switzerland, and submit to the classic year-long tuberculosis regimen in a high-valley climate. He would have gone immediately upon diagnosis but was afraid to fly.[11] This was the same Russian-émigré doctor, part psychologist, part internist, who had seen Eleanor before London and Tommy Thompson after her gallbladder attack, calling them each "horses," the one "little" the other "big." Still not sure how to take it, Tommy explained to Hick that Dr. Gurewitsch's loss of nerve was Mrs. Roosevelt's opportunity: "He could not bear to take the trip alone, so Mrs. R volunteered to 'mother' him."[12]

Eleanor had telephoned the State Department herself. She despised special favors, but wanted to make the flight easier for David, and asked the acting secretary-general if he could get the doctor on her flight. Richard Sears Winslow could.[13] Everything from passport renewal to Swiss customs could be expedited. "Of course, going with her," remarked Tommy, "everything was greased for him."[14]

But Eleanor did more than trade on prestige to smooth David's passage. She stamped him as authentic and held out the grail of belonging in a new world of possibility.

She had met Dr. Gurewitsch at a White House musicale in 1940. He was eighteen years her junior—a tall, handsome, Swiss-born neurologist with debonair Middle-European manners. David's wife, a Scottish aristocrat, Jean Penelope Balfour, known as Nemone,[15] was the star that afternoon, enchanting the Roosevelts and their guests with a powerful presentation of ancient Scottish carols, Irish folk songs, and airs by Bach.[16] Nemone's success (and the troubles in the Gurewitsch marriage) would eventually render this first meeting less memorable to David and Eleanor than the more personal scene, four years later, when David made his entrance into Eleanor's life in wartime Manhattan.

Summoned to pay a house call on his patient Trude Pratt (coincidentally, David's Latin tutor when he had prepared for medical school in Germany), he had hurried to Trude's apartment, only to wait outside her door when no one answered. Just as he turned to leave, the door was opened by the first lady. Mrs. Roosevelt had come to help during the shortage of civilian nurses, and together they set to taking care of their friend. After FDR's death the following year, when Eleanor moved back to the Washington Square apartment and needed a physician, she telephoned David, asking if he would take her on and promising him that she was perfectly healthy and wouldn't take up too much of his time.

By then, David had been in New York eight years, having come from residency as a neurologist in Jerusalem to be a research fellow at Mount Sinai Hospital. In 1939, he had found a spot at New York's prestigious Columbia-Presbyterian Medical Center with the physical therapy service of the Neurological Institute, one of the first nongovernmental hospitals for the treatment of nervous diseases. David had an instinct for the new specialty of physical therapy and rehabilitation, which during one of the country's worst polio outbreaks in 1943 had led him to hot-bath treatments for children infected with the polio virus at the New York State Reconstruction Home at West Haverstraw.[17]

On his thirty-five-bed ward at Knickerbocker Hospital, he was known for listening to the patient, paying meticulous attention to the details of the patient's story, and remaining systematically focused on helping the patient. To a polio sufferer—most often, a young child with fearful parents—he gave not just the latest in treatment but a deeply comforting sense of being taken care of properly.

To women, David showed a sweet and gentle side. He was shy, essentially lonely, and sometimes morbidly self-doubting. As a lifelong outsider, he often felt unwelcome and underappreciated; if slighted, he all too easily took offense, deciding that he had been "too nice," then overreacting with sudden frustrated executions of will and command.

The discovery of the tubercular spot on his lung, which had also clarified his indecision about marital separation, left David fragile, needy, and wide open when he boarded the flight for Geneva. Someone had brought a transistor radio on the plane, tuned to the Palestine partition vote at the UNO, on which Eleanor had used all her energy and influence. One by one the votes were being counted as they awaited takeoff from Idlewild. In another twenty-four hours, the Jewish people would have a country to call their own, and Arno David Gurewitsch, a Jewish émigré born in Zurich to a recently widowed Russian mother, was startled to find—unbelieving to find—that Eleanor Roosevelt needed him.

* * *

THE CONSTELLATION TOOK OFF FROM Gander, the morning of the second day, making its expected eastbound hop. But when the aircraft nosed down over the western fringe of Ireland, landing at Shannon Airport, a thick fog overhung Ireland and Great Britain. Eleanor found herself imploring anyone who would listen as they disembarked for refueling: "We simply must go on."

For weeks she had been telling her eight-person team that they had to keep a tight schedule to make it home by Christmas. And now she—the chairman of the preparatory Commission on Human Rights—wouldn't even get to Geneva for the opening session on Monday.[18] More urgently, David was stranded another night.[19]

For passengers held in Shannon, overnight arrangements were rustic, the airline billeting them in a partitioned Quonset hut. The rooms had no heat, and the temperature had fallen well below freezing.[20] As always, Eleanor had packed the minimum. Having envisioned no hotel stops on the way, she had no nightgown to change into, "so I slept," she diarized, "in my panties and brassiere!"[21]

In the morning, the window revealed nothing of Ireland but the fog itself. "Fog is nice, if you know a place and are with someone you like," she once wrote. "It shuts you in and gives you a close & intimate feeling." She'd added, "But you don't want to meet a new place in a fog any more than you want to be intimate with a new acquaintance."[22]

Intimate is exactly what the fog let them be. She and Dr. Gurewitsch fascinated each other. She learned that this handsome, worldly man still struggled with old feelings of deprivation, inadequacy, and unworthiness. His philosopher father had died in a Swiss lake two months before David was born. He had regarded his brother, Vladimir, though only a year older, as his surrogate father. His mother had taken the two boys back to her family in Vitebsk when David was two years old, having remained in Zurich until then. She went to London and studied medicine, and after five years, when David was seven, in July 1925, Maria Gurewitsch took her boys to Berlin, settled, and began her practice. His mother had expected a genius; he felt he had failed her.

The publication of *Mein Kampf* alerted Maria Gurewitsch; she took David to Palestine to join a kibbutz. Eleanor listened to him describe how he and his wife were equally headstrong in their dedication to highly specialized fields, unable to trade off priorities about work and family. Nemone, the dominant parent of their only child, was wholly bent on developing her talent as a vocal artist; and whereas she could be sharply outspoken on certain marital issues, she fell dead silent on others, alternating between intense engagement and withdrawals that David chalked up to depression. He himself kept his more aggressive energies, even his sarcasm, concealed by a tightly controlled passivity, and therefore was easily triggered to frustration, anger, and self-loathing. The force David and Nemone exerted on each other was so charged that, for David, the almost equal poles of attraction and repulsion he felt from and for his wife kept him in a constant state of flux and fixation, swirling around the ever-unfillable hole of feeling unloved.[23]

Add to these currents a mother whose nullifying message to David remained curiously unyielding to his new world in postwar America. No matter that David had survived Nazism and the war to become a doctor and start a family, producing a grandchild—nothing he could do would ever matter as much to Maria Gurewitsch as her husband's drowning in a Swiss lake soon after finding answers to philosophical questions about man and God.

For Eleanor, here again was the dream of loving selflessly. Her satisfaction in seeing to David's needs during their layover, followed by her delight each time he returned (by phone or letter) to consult with her on his doctors and all the particulars of his old-fashioned sanitarium treatment—all this put her at her most self-assured with this man with whom she had felt an instant and permanent belonging. She had never begun any other serious, lasting relationship so predisposed to make her own claim to happiness.

Martha Gellhorn, Eleanor's friend and future girlfriend of David's, would warn him: "Mrs. R's problem is a craving to be loved."[24] Yet, for a change, Eleanor did not crave; did not doubt happiness itself. David was emotionally that much more needy in his life at age forty-five than Eleanor at sixty-three. The fog stranded them a third night.

At the first streak of clear sky they were up and away. In Geneva, Swiss officials had meanwhile been arguing about who would shake her hand first.[25] When Eleanor deplaned, the canton's president,

Louis Casaï, stepped up, and Eleanor's smile glowed through a snow shower,[26] making Casaï's pretty little welcoming speech even prettier,[27] and her French was flawless and heartfelt as she returned the compliments, saying how very happy she was to be here in the clean, tidy town by Lac Léman.

The skies cleared as night fell. She went to bed at midnight and could see the waxing crescent moon hanging "as though it were detached."[28] A few stars twinkled above the lake, dropping slowly into the cold glitter of lights on the farther shore, and she watched these sharp reflections before bed.

The next morning, even the Russians couldn't spoil her mood, and on her first day of the Commission's meetings at the monumental Palais des Nations chambers, site of the failed League of Nations, she peered inside the entrance. Doors swept upward to lofty ceilings over symmetrical acres of polished marble. As she went in to begin her long task of establishing the mechanisms by which fundamental freedoms could be safeguarded throughout the world, she whispered to a State Department adviser, "I'd love to slide on those floors."[29]

"DR. GUREWITSCH" GRADUALLY BECAME "DAVID." His voice, husky, low, Euro-accented, gave her joy; she started the day happier when she heard it, "brokenhearted" when she missed it.[30] His letters tantalized her. Guarded, penned in a small, tight hand, they addressed her over and over in the same deferential form used by everyone from the Queen of England to mob boss Frank Costello to people in the street. She begged him to call her Eleanor but went on being "Mrs. Roosevelt"; not even "Mrs. R.," the compromise Tommy and Joe Lash had managed.

He dared not respond at the level she wanted, and even flat on his back in the Schatzalp Sanatorium in Davos, wrapped in blankets and sunning himself on his individual balcony, David was setting the pace, not Eleanor.

In Geneva she was having greater success pushing her colleagues to wrap up the Commission's drafting phase and get home by Christmas. David, no matter how hard she insisted that he return with her and continue his convalescence in the Stone Cottage at Val-Kill, insisted

upon remaining at the high-altitude resort where he had been a TB
patient years before.

"I shall miss you," wrote Eleanor before[31] leaving Geneva. "May
your strength grow and with it our friendship. I'm grateful that you
wanted to come across with me for it gave us a chance we might never
have had otherwise. My thoughts turn to you often."

David—a worrier[32]—worried, meanwhile couching his anxiety in
a menu of courtesies. "Don't ever worry about being a nuisance," Eleanor said soothingly in reply. "I've always liked you and been DRAWN
to you since we first met and the trip just made me sure that we could
be friends." Despite what might appear to be outward confidence, she
still carried her "old insecurity when it comes to close relationships and
that is probably what makes you feel shy. I've really taken you into my
heart, however, so there need never be a question of bother again. You
can know that anything I can do [for you] will always be a pleasure for
me and being with you is a joy."[33]

A week before Christmas the draft Declaration was voted in by the
Commission, thirteen to four, and despite Eleanor's ear telling her that
the language was too formal, she was pleased to be able to report her
satisfaction to David—and to send him, among other presents, a shawl
in which she had found comfort for many years.

Outside the Palais entrance, Citroën limousines carried away exhausted delegates. Eleanor, looking surprisingly fresh, walked out
with her colleague James Hendrick and the Russian representative Alexander Bogomolov and his wife, pausing where the corridor opened
onto the soaring entrance hall.

"Now you can take your slide," urged Hendrick.[34]

And with that, she launched herself onto the marble.

TWENTY-TWO

T HE UNITED STATES HAD REACHED its zenith—out front of all other nations, the richest and mightiest in the world.

The U.S. contributed the lion's share to securing the North Atlantic community against aggression and to the Marshall Plan's rebuilding of all of Europe. Just as it anchored its fellow member nations in the North Atlantic Treaty Organization, a full-scale peacetime military alliance, mutually ensuring the defense of the Western Hemisphere, the United States also sent a missile higher than ever before (250 miles), prompting Eleanor to comment, "Anyone who really thinks about war is thinking about annihilation."[1]

Dread of premature extinction would filter through global thinking for the rest of Eleanor's life. "Fears breed fears," she noted in 1947 (much as she had in 1937), "and if we who are at present the strongest nation in the world have fear, we will breed it in other people."[2]

The peace that Franklin had not lived to see had succeeded in reducing suspicion to a single new enemy. The still-non-nuclear Soviet Union, represented by Vyshinsky in ER's confrontations with the Soviets in London, now did to smaller nations and vulnerable populations what it had been doing to individuals in secret throughout Stalin's murderous regime.

She herself remained consistently committed to influence—not to holding power. When wily Clare Boothe Luce flushed out Truman in July 1948, advising a switch in vice-presidential nominees, Truman agreed that Mrs. Roosevelt would be all right with him as a running mate. Eleanor for the umpteenth time declared that she had no intention whatsoever of running for any public office.[3]

As an elected or appointed official, she would have felt that any office was a demotion or a constraint. Now free to speak her mind, she was uniquely influential because her audience was listening. Through her column she could give her opinion on matters six days a week. Firmly, unscoldingly, she was there each day to remind people that a powerful America was supposed to be above racism, had a responsibility to find ways to give basic decencies to the poor. In a postwar nation where women were now supposed to go back to the kitchen and have lots of children, she voiced a radical domesticity.

"Never forget," she told a visiting graduate student at Val-Kill one day, "human rights are too important to be left to governments." Too important—and too easily abused or turned to disinformation and propaganda by authoritarian regimes. Eleanor pointed out to Richard N. Gardner, a future ambassador to Italy and Spain, the critical role that the non-governmental organizations were playing in implanting human rights in the UN Charter.[4]

She was concerned with individual people living their lives.

She felt individual pain, and it energized her. She saw the world dissolving back into individual lives, the individual welfare of people, their connectedness to one another, and to the organizations that served their likes and dislikes. "Few seem capable of realizing," she had written thirteen years earlier, "that the real reason that home is important is that it is so closely tied, by a million strings, to the rest of the world."[5]

ON JUNE 19, 1949, WHILE speaking at Fordham University, the New York archbishop laid into U. S. Congressman Graham Barden's bill for federal aid to education, arguing that if the North Carolina Democrat aimed to provide $300 million annually for public schools, then Catholic parochial schools, paid for by U.S. taxpayers, had every right to claim their share. Cardinal Spellman declared the legislation "un-American" and himself opposed to a public-supported and exclusively state-controlled school system, which he termed "tyrannical totalitarianism," while attacking Barden as a "new apostle of bigotry," and charging the congressman with "venting his venom upon children" and "conducting a craven crusade of religious prejudice."[6]

"The philosophy behind the Barden bill, whether its author or defenders intended so or not, is that the only truly American school is the public tax-supported school," asserted Spellman. "This is not true."[7]

Protestant groups flared at this Catholic attempt to "raid the public treasury."[8] A Methodist bishop charged the New York Diocese with "putting its hands in the public treasury" and Spellman with calling anyone who disagreed with him a bigot.[9]

From her own bully pulpit, Eleanor insisted that public funds should be used solely for public education: "The controversy brought about by the request made by Cardinal Spellman forces upon the citizens of the country the kind of decision that is going to be very difficult to make."[10]

She pointed out that it was possible to believe in the right of any human being to worship in whatever church he or she chose, and, at the same time, to wish to see federally supported public schools kept entirely separate from any denominational influence. The inability of any one religious group to dominate the country's public schools had contributed to a community of tolerance among all groups.

Spellman took her position as pretext for a personal assault, sending ER a letter questioning her fairness: "Why do you repeatedly plead causes that are anti-Catholic?"

Eleanor denied the charge, although in truth she saw in American Catholicism a social conservatism of the most startling kind. In 1951, an Irish minister of health was driven out of office by the bishops because his suggestions for subsidized health for the poor were seen as undermining the family.

Eleanor had first known Spellman as a vigorous opponent (with his fellow Massachusetts Irishman Joseph P. Kennedy) of Father Coughlin. She had approved of FDR's appointment of the new cardinal as the President's special wartime envoy in Europe, Africa, and the Middle East. Yet she was not surprised when Spellman supported Richard Nixon in the 1960 presidential election, rejecting his friend Joe Kennedy's son because of JFK's stand against federal aid for parochial schools, the very issue that had ignited Spellman's feud with Eleanor eleven years earlier.

She criticized Spellman for calling her "an unworthy American mother," knowing full well that Spellman had actually said that the stand Mrs. Roosevelt took in her column was "unworthy of an American mother." But Eleanor had correctly interpreted Spellman's letter as a condemnation of her children's divorces issued by the one authority in the Catholic hierarchy whom rich and powerful Catholics knew to be the most likely procurer of a marriage annulment.[11] One could infer that Spellman wanted people to believe that "her children might have been better [to their spouses] if they had had proper moral and religious education."[12]

The cardinal had New York's newspapers in his pocket. He had sent his letter to the major dailies before Eleanor had time to receive it, and reaction came swiftly. The Church was incredulous. Several cardinals flew to Rome to protest Cardinal Spellman's treatment of the former first lady. Governor Lehman objected in a forthright letter.

To Eleanor, Spellman's fatuous hypocrisies rankled—his claims to be the simple priest of the people ("Frankly, I prefer the Vargas girl to the Venus de Milo,"[13] Spellman had once boasted), when he was leader of the richest diocese in Mother Church. But what made her effective was her self-discipline. She could go to the edge with Spellman and stop there. She could now see underneath American politics' hard high-gloss surfaces to the cracks and flaws in many of the players. If Spellman's behavior toward Eleanor could be chalked up to "little more than a moment of peevish aggression," argued the writer and Catholic observer Wilfrid Sheed, it also suggested a subtext "of either unhappiness or well-earned indigestion."[14]

Spellman was, in truth, a sexually active closeted pederast.[15] Eleanor saw in his increasingly arch-conservative postwar politics a deeply reactionary intolerance—intolerance of, among other things, homosexuality. With his Red-baiting, fear-mongering, and "little mincing ways," as Jacqueline Kennedy noted,[16] Spellman epitomized, according to one observer of the period, the "self-loathing, closeted, evil queen, working with his good friend, the closeted gay McCarthy henchman Roy Cohn, to undermine liberalism in America during the 1950s' communist and homosexual witch hunts."[17]

No politician was more talented at twisting the truth than "Tailgunner Joe," the Roman Catholic senator from Wisconsin, Joe McCarthy—and none twisted the country more in the postwar era, starting with his fellow Catholics. "McCarthyism," observed one Protestant theologian, "was a special Roman Catholic temptation."[18] As early as 1951, Eleanor came out strongly against McCarthy and his anti-Communist witch hunt, later defending the *Nation* against McCarthyite censorship and coming to the aid of numerous entertainers who came under attack. As she said in 1950: "We are trying to prevent the establishment of a gestapo in our midst, and the curtailment of the right of free speech." Hollywood producers were "chicken-hearted about speaking up for the freedom of their industry."[19]

One friend of Eleanor's in particular had been badly hurt. Josh White, country bluesman and social activist, a favorite of FDR's, had performed repeatedly at the White House and at the third Inaugural, joining the Roosevelts at Thanksgivings and Christmases. But from 1947 on, White had been ensnared by anti-Communist hysteria; and in 1950, against Eleanor's advice, he voluntarily appeared before the House Un-American Activities Committee (HUAC), defending his right to earn a living as an African American folksinger with anti-segregationist views. Blacklisted—barred from radio, movies, television, and recording; unwelcome, even at folk festivals—White had left the United States for England, his career in limbo. By way of doing whatever she could to help, Eleanor had hired Josh's younger brother, William, as Val-Kill manager and chauffeur; and she took pride in serving as godparent to Josh White, Jr., now eight years old.[20]

On August 18, at Val-Kill, she had a sudden phone call from Spellman. The cardinal "happened to be in the neighborhood" and would like to drop by and pay his respects. Eleanor took mischievous pleasure in inviting His Eminence to tea.[21] He was well south of Hyde Park that morning, dedicating a chapel in Peekskill, New York, but if Spellman was willing to drive out of his way to continue his charm offensive, Eleanor decided to use the visit to enlist the cardinal's help.

When her guest arrived, jolly and chatty, without saying a word about their disagreement, Eleanor was jolly and chatty right back. Over the teacups, she raised the matter of Josh White and asked the cardinal's help. As she later explained to Justine Wise Polier, she would "at least try to get help for one person."[22] In these days of McCarthyism at its most toxic, Eleanor believed more strongly than ever that the country "had to be concerned with the individual,"[23] but it would take another decade and the country's first Roman Catholic President to break White's blacklisting.

IN AUGUST 1949, THE SOVIET Union covertly tested its first atomic bomb, stunning the United States, up to that point the world's sole nuclear power.

Eleanor entreated both the U.S. and the USSR to resist the natural instinct toward retaliatory buildup that would lead to an arms race.

A month later, the victory of Mao Zedong's Communist revolution on mainland China raised the question of whether it would be advantageous to both the United States and China to remain friends. China needed U.S. technicians to help with their development and certain types of machinery that could be obtained more easily from the U.S. than from the Soviet Union. Eleanor questioned whether Mao meant to prevent the counterrevolution threatened by Chiang Kai-shek and other more conservative forces in China by holding the loyalty of the Chinese people through lifestyle improvements. "The question, of course," wrote Eleanor, "must be raised as to how much Russia will supply [to] meet in part or in whole the needs of the Chinese people. [The USSR] is not yet fully meeting her own needs, nor, so far as one can discover, are her own satellites in Europe able to ship to her in sufficient quantities such things as she cannot produce or cannot as yet produce in great enough quantities.

"There is an enormous job of organization still to be done in the Soviet Union," she warned. "Transportation alone would be a development requiring many years, and without it there is no chance of reaching the remote parts of her own country. This is true to a far greater extent in China, and one wonders how long and how much can be put into purely military operations by the Chinese leader who must also promise his people many reforms."[24]

Eleven years later, while interviewing Bertrand Russell on British defense policy,[25] Eleanor locked horns with the philosopher when he proposed that the United States and the Soviet Union sign a declaration before arms negotiations stating that all-out nuclear war would be a greater disaster than all-out victory of either side. Eleanor, however, would have none of it. "Now *that* I would *not* be willing to sign," she said, adding that she doubted that Russell could get such a document signed by the people of the United States.

"I was horrified," he later recalled, "to hear Mrs. Roosevelt enunciate the belief that it would be better, and that she would prefer, to have the human race destroyed than to have it succumb to Communism. I came away thinking that I could not have heard aright."

But, upon reading ER's remarks in the next morning's papers, Russell had to face the fact that Eleanor really had expressed the popular "Better dead than Red" view,[26] revealing herself kin to the Sagamore Hill Roosevelts, with a surer sense of the country than her detractors admitted.

As Uncle Ted had gone from being the most progressive of conservatives to being the most conservative of progressives, Eleanor now arced from her image as the most unrealistic of liberals to becoming the most liberal of realists. As the historian Allida Black writes, postwar Eleanor "hid behind her traditional image to shape policy."[27]

HER SMILE WAS NOW EASY where for so long it had been merely dutiful. In the first decade of widowhood, she attained a far greater degree of authentic joy, and in so many respects a better life. She never thereafter had to wonder if people were thinking that Franklin had put her up to this.

She could be her passionate, adoring, uncritical self—the girl who found bliss dancing for her father and receiving his unfettered adoration in return. She raised the stakes with the small circle of her most beloved by showing the Lashes and David and Tommy unlimited affection, now also expecting it in return. "She made a great fetish of this," recalled Anna, with mixed feelings, for as she saw Eleanor deliberately opening herself to what at first seemed a more reciprocal relationship she well remembered how closed and acrid Mother had been in the family during Anna's childhood.[28]

On July 31, 1948, Lucy Mercer Rutherfurd died of leukemia. She had been seeing her sister through a depression, when Violetta took her own life, with a revolver Lucy kept in a bedside drawer, never dreaming her sister knew how to fire it. A friend believed the shock brought on Lucy's final illness.[29]

Two months later, Aunt Edith died at Sagamore Hill. In Eleanor's last letter to her, she had been glad to have an almost official opportunity to write her condolences for Cousin Ted—a tribute to Brigadier General Theodore Roosevelt's heroic death on July 12 after leading his first-wave battalion up Utah beach.[30]

The 1948 General Assembly met in Paris at the end of September, and the entire U.S. delegation prepared for the meetings, complete with jealousy among the delegates, condescending attitudes toward Eleanor by the career diplomats, and her old feeling of inadequacy when working among professionals. The difference from 1946, however, was that she was not on the job now as "a woman"—but as herself.

Nervous and apprehensive about her speech on September 28 at the Sorbonne—the heart of French studies and intellectual life— Eleanor checked over every word with her State Department advisers, including delegation leader George C. Marshall. She arrived to find the amphitheater packed by a jubilant crowd.

The audience listened with mounting excitement to introductions by the rector of the university, Rene Casin, and Paul Ramadier, former prime minister of France, then settled in to hear the widow of the great president speak—in French, no less—on "The Struggle for the Rights of Man."

ER spoke of the challenge to preserve individual liberty in a democratic society against the totalitarian model of empowering the state at the citizen's expense. She recalled her discussion two years earlier in London, when Vyshinsky had told her there was no such thing as freedom for the individual in the world. She attacked the Soviets, charging Russia with ruthless suppression of human rights at home and interference in other countries' concerns. "We in the democracies believe in a kind of international respect and action which is reciprocal. We do not think Russia should treat us differently from the way they wish to be treated. It is this interference in other countries that especially stirs up antagonism against the Soviet government."[31]

Her Canadian adviser, John Humphrey, was shocked to hear "a speech obviously written by someone in the State Department." He didn't blame the Americans for talking back to the Soviets, but "disliked their using Mrs. Roosevelt in these polemics. For she had become a symbol which should have been kept above the Cold War—a symbol around which reasonable men and women everywhere might have rallied."

But confidence in the UN's power had wavered from the start, just as news of a UN Human Rights Commission convening in New York in 1946 had left even those hailing its potential doubting its practicality. "Commissions cannot create human rights," argued the essayist E. B. White. "So far, the peace proposals do not include popular representation in the [UN] council and the assembly, and the people [of the U.S. and other countries], therefore, assume no personal responsibility for anything, and therefore will gain no personal rights."[32]

"Where," asked White, "do human rights arise, anyway? In the sun, in the moon, in the daily paper, in the conscientious heart?"[33]

Twelve years later, she reframed the question: "Where, after all, do universal human rights begin? In small places, close to home— so close and so small that they cannot be seen on any maps of the world. Yet they are the world of the individual person; the neighborhood he lives in; the school or college he attends; the factory, farm or office where he works. Such are the places where every man, woman and child seeks equal justice, equal opportunity, equal dignity without discrimination. Unless these rights have meaning there, they have little meaning anywhere. Without concerned citizen action to uphold them close to home, we shall look in vain for progress in the larger world."[34]

BY DECEMBER 9, 1948, EVERYBODY in the UN looked exhausted. The session had gone on too long. Its length depressed people and adversely affected the UN's standing in the world.

Eleanor worked six-and-a-half days a week, eighteen to twenty hours a day. The last lap would end with the vote in the plenary session on December 10. The Arabs and the Soviets would probably balk— the Arabs for religious reasons, the Soviets for politics. And she knew there would be trouble at home. Americans wanted security. They wanted control of atomic energy. They wanted peace. Some of them wanted formal evidence of international cooperation—treaties, agreements, pacts—but only on their terms and, as in 1919, without subordinating national sovereignty. Whether the American people would accept a document from the high councils of an international body was in doubt as the Declaration came to a vote.

She did not have to leave Paris to know that Americans were living in fear, acting with suspicion, appalled at the prospect of further atomic test explosions opening up holes in the floor of the sea, or incinerating deserts with heat equal to the interior temperature of stars. Many intelligent people had been shopping for something—anything—that might guarantee them peace.[35]

On December 10, Garry Davis, a former U.S. flier who in May had renounced his U.S. citizenship and rendered himself stateless to promote world citizenship, gave a rally at the Velodrome d'Hiver. Twelve thousand attended—many more than had ever been attracted to a UN General Assembly meeting.[36] People had lost confidence in the UN. If the Third World War was going to be fought with hydrogen bombs, went the thinking, and the Fourth with bones and stones, then the nation state system was pointed in one direction only—to mutual destruction—and Davis, a brave man, sick of violence, was simply the human face of what an enormous number of people felt.

Eleanor, meanwhile, radiated practicality. If Davis was the adolescent, saying, *We can do this overnight*, Eleanor was the grownup, forced to take the adult line that it would take longer. Garry Davis, the self-proclaimed first World Citizen, showed distress when ER advised him in a motherly way to go home and work in his own community before tackling the world.

AT LAST, AT 3 A.M. on December 10, 1948, at the Palais de Chaillot, after thirty-two straight months of the committee's work, forty-eight nations cast their votes for the Declaration. Two were absent and eight abstained: South Africa, Saudi Arabia, Yugoslavia, and the Soviet bloc, which opposed it on the grounds that the Declaration did not condemn Fascism. No votes were cast against it, and the United Nations General Assembly adopted the Universal Declaration of Human Rights.

Moments later, Eleanor walked into the General Assembly, quietly dressed, wearing no makeup, briskly taking the podium. The entire Assembly got to its feet. Her fellow delegates then accorded her something that had never been given before and would never be given again in the United Nations: an ovation for a single delegate by all nations.

AFTER TRUMAN'S COME-FROM-BEHIND UPSET OF Dewey in November, the tide had gone out fast on the administration's domestic agenda. From universal health insurance, to education, to the antidiscrimination policies of the Fair Employment Practices Commission (FEPC), few Fair Deal proposals escaped the new congressional conservative coalition that joined Southern Democrats to a majority of Republicans to crush Truman's ambitious attempt to modernize New Deal liberalism.

Amid the general shift away from pioneering liberalism toward self-conscious conservatism, there stood Mrs. Roosevelt. Just when her fellow citizens wanted a holiday from war and began to feel prosperous enough to take one without apology, she wanted to buckle down and make sure nothing like World War II would ever happen again. The world must not forget.

"The lid was off," Philip Roth would write of this moment. "Americans were to start over again, en masse, everyone in it together. If that wasn't sufficiently inspiring—the miraculous conclusion of this towering event, the clock of history reset and a whole people's aims limited no longer by the past—there was the neighborhood, the communal determination that we, the children, should escape poverty, ignorance, disease, social injury and intimidation—escape, above all, insignificance. You must not come to nothing! Make something of yourselves!"[37]

Eleanor was the custodian of basic human impulses that could not be tacked onto a party platform. She was the elderly relative who recalled you to your basic principles: Everyone, as a member of society, deserves to eat, to have decent health care, safe shelter, a public park. In the new postwar prosperity, Eleanor Roosevelt reminded her fellow citizens that they owed a debt to those on whom the world had landed hard—a debt that went beyond politics.

More than a professional politician, she herself was now a globalist. From her three months in Paris with the General Assembly, she had emerged as the world's foremost champion of human rights. The Universal Declaration of Human Rights had established, according to one of the foremost scholars in the field, a platform for global transformation that authorized all people to live in "humane" societies.[38]

She could now reach out and seek to make a difference anywhere—supporting India under Gandhi's leadership as it won independence from Britain; threatening to resign if Truman failed to recognize Israel as a sovereign Jewish homeland; meeting with Chilean protestors and rebels, victims of the atomic bomb, and, with characteristic evenhandedness, displaced Palestinians. Her constituency was the people of the world, and this made her all the more formidable at home, arousing puzzlement and fear. Was she a communist? A Civil Rights agitator?

As the years went on, Western diplomats would wobble over the Declaration's inclusion of health, education, decent living standards, and economic security. No one could agree how to codify economic and social rights that depended upon government intervention into the legally binding obligations of international treaties. In ways that weakened its practical usage, the Declaration reflected the Rooseveltian belief in government as the guarantor of individual liberty. As FDR had said in his 1944 call for a "Second Bill of Rights": "We have come to a clear realization of the fact that true individual freedom cannot exist without economic security and independence. . . . People who are hungry and out of a job are the stuff of which dictatorships are made."[39]

Eleanor had assured the General Assembly on the eve of voting for adoption that her government wholeheartedly supported economic, social, and cultural rights. Her committee, however, had not meant to "imply an obligation on governments to assure the enjoyment of these rights by direct governmental action."[40] But as time would tell and scholars came to see, "that was how all the states and civilian actors saw economic and social rights, and that is how her own husband's presidential administration viewed such rights."[41] Any requirement that the state make provisions so that the people could attain their individual rights to economic well-being was not likely to become law in the United States Congress, even if at the level of the State Department—and as foundation to the 1975 Helsinki Accords—the Declaration's articles had a lasting influence. For nearly seventy years thereafter, every administration would support human rights as a necessary commitment of American foreign policy.

SHE WAS EVEN NURSING HER doctor. At the zenith of her postwar power, Eleanor had fallen in love, but as Esther Lape perceived, David "never really reciprocated Mrs. R's feeling." Lape's impression was "that he was delighted to be taken by her on trips, and to be involved in a lot of things he would never otherwise have been near, but that he was selfish and thoughtless in many things."[42]

The uncomfortable truth about David Gurewitsch was not just how unloving she allowed him to be, but how willing Eleanor was to settle for being needed. Their exchange of lovers' photographs, placed on each other's bedside nightstand, speaks for itself:

David gave Eleanor himself in profile, the exemplar of the dark, handsome Mitteleuropa male in his magnificent prime. But Eleanor had to spring for its equally glamorous gold frame, which she also took the trouble to engrave. After Eleanor was gone, David would discreetly remove this emotionally ambiguous object from its place of honor at her bedside. Still later, he would confess to a writer he hired to help publish his photographs of Eleanor that it was the one thing he "stole" from among Eleanor's possessions.[43]

Eleanor gave David a framed and signed photograph for his bedside—a formal portrait of herself at sixteen, tender, clear, her upswept gold-spun hair and searching melancholy eyes the very image of an orphaned Edwardian princess. She had inscribed it in her shaky older woman's hand: "FOR DAVID—*From the girl you never knew.*"

FOR DAVID SHE POURED OUT her every wish to be loved. She thirsted for the revelation she had been in search of her whole life, the surprise that she could feel loved. Yet as never before, she risked making herself vulnerable, opening herself to a man whom she knew to be aloof and distant. "Above all others," she told him, "you are the one to whom my heart is tied."[44]

David was dazzled by ER's prestige. He did not dare to respond at the level she wanted, and it tore at him; but, not to worry, he was setting the pace not she, the prime proof of which was his curious insistence upon "Mrs. Roosevelt" as the only form of address he would allow her[45]—and her steadfast resignation to the pain it would cause her in the years ahead. "I want you to feel at home with me as you would with a member of your family and I can't achieve it! Something wrong with me!" she lamented in February 1956, after they had known each other for almost a decade. "I'd love to hear you call me by my first name but you can't. Perhaps it is my age! I do love you and you are always in my thoughts and if that bothers you I could hide it. I'm good at that."[46]

It was strange—willful. He would not relent and call her Eleanor. She blamed her own neediness: "I love you dearly David," she repeated, "but try to remember to tell me that *you* want to be loved by me now and then because I don't want to be a duty or a bother!"[47]

The more tender she was in her wish, the more assertive he became in his refusal. A punctilious executor of the most minor detail, he would croon "Mrs. Roosevelt" as he kissed her hand in the Continental manner that so irritated her children. (He was, noted a younger woman just after meeting David at seventy, "an inveterate hand rubber and toucher . . . almost holding onto you so you don't escape until he finishes talking."[48]) He insisted upon "Mrs. Roosevelt," almost as a form of commanding respect for himself instead. To those accustomed to hearing statesmen and politicians call one another by rank and honorific—"Mr. President," or "Colonel Howe"—David's insistence carried a touch of bluff, as if beneath his hard exterior he felt the weakness of his position with her, the unmanning awkwardness of unrequitedness, and was conflicted, or afraid, or just not strong enough to say *Eleanor*, lest he arouse unrealistic hopes—a doctor's worst fear—or, yet more dangerous, something real.

Adlai Stevenson, sixteen years younger, had never been able to call her Eleanor. They had met in Washington several times, but their friendship dated from the 1946 UN conference in London, when Stevenson had met the boat on which the delegates were arriving. Eleanor jumped off and said, "You probably know more about this than anyone here and I know less. Won't you come to dinner tomorrow night?" She then surprised—and flattered—Stevenson by including him, despite the slightness of their acquaintance, in a frank discussion of family problems, including her infuriated disappointment when a daughter-in-law, whom ER had asked to comment on a recent "My Day" column, pronounced it "Communist."[49] In this instantly trusting friendship with Stevenson, the issue of "Eleanor" v. "Mrs. Roosevelt" had not mattered. She and Adlai cared equally and tenderly for each other, perhaps because their working relationship—not without its problems over assertiveness—nonetheless had not yet faltered from its essential Good Aunt/Brilliant Nephew professionalism and symmetry.

David was different. "He was very attached to her," recalled a close colleague and friend. He knew that she was making more difference to him than he was to her, and he cultivated his status: "He felt she elevated him into a place he wouldn't have been without her. David was a self-promoter. He dressed well: bespoke suits, the finest shirts, the finest ties. He had that European air about him. He looked in the mirror."[50]

In certain ways, the transactional nature of David's presentation as Eleanor's personal physician was not unlike that of Thomas Louis Stix, her radio and television agent, who found that in granting exclusive rights to Mrs. Roosevelt's singularly prestigious image, he himself was given validation of a wished-for superiority. "She was special," said Stix. "And when you told people you represented Mrs. Roosevelt, you were special too."[51]

What drew Eleanor to David was the painstaking nature of this classically handsome man's lack of trust in himself. Right from the start, his loss of nerve about flying to Geneva had invited Eleanor not only to be his companion but to switch roles with her "sick doctor." She, the "failed" parent, fearful of harming her children, was almost effortlessly able to succeed at mothering this lovely, gentle man.

Well beyond their initial reversal in the fogged-in Shannon Airport, David's focus on his insecurity and chronic discouragements put Eleanor at the center of his life and career. Alert to the needs of his wife, Nemone, his daughter, Grania, and his cherished mother, he included Eleanor in this innermost feminine circle of his caring and protection, giving her for safekeeping the secrets and lies of his marriage and the affairs that overlapped it. His serial appeals for her support were catnip, as he often enlisted Eleanor in bearding his rendezvous.

"I got 3 rooms in the Dolder in Zurich," he wrote in his curiously passionless way. "Dolder is a big hotel. All the main rooms face a golf course. Very big. Each with a balcony. 3 rooms—for myself, Tommy and Mrs. R. I walk out to balcony just to look at the view and at that moment on the very next balcony to mine, somebody walks out and the person who walks out is my girlfriend. I know nothing about it and there is a connecting door between the two rooms. Mrs. R. on the other side. That lady had a husband with whom she was staying in that room. It took some maneuvering.[52]

"I had met the lady in the sanitarium. She had left the sanitarium and returned to London. Married to a concert pianist. He was giving a concert in Zurich. . . ."

Gurewitsch was having an affair with the tall, elegant Griselda Gould, recently married wife of Hungarian pianist Louis Kentner, who, with world-renowned violinist Yehudi Menuhin, was giving the first performance of William Walton's violin sonata in Zurich.[53] So David had brought Eleanor to Switzerland and into a nest of intrigue in the Grand Hotel Dolder, its black gabled roofs surmounted by witch-hat spires overlooking the wide blue mirror of the lake. "There was nothing that escaped her," he later remarked.[54]

Nothing—except David himself. On their trip to Pakistan and India in 1952, he again challenged her with a beautiful younger woman—in fact, by his own account, one of the most beautiful women he had ever seen.[55]

For six years Eleanor had felt "rather like a harassed commuter," hurrying back and forth across the Atlantic. When the General Assembly was finished in Paris in 1952, the end of her duties as a delegate, plus the ensuing election of Republican Dwight D. Eisenhower as president, meant that she was at last free to travel for its own sake. "It had been a good many years since I was a little girl reading anything I could find that told me about the world, but the fascination of faraway lands had not waned."[56]

Invited by Prime Minister Nehru (as he sat on the floor at Val-Kill talking to students) to the newly independent India, Eleanor was determined to go, and while there, to do no harm politically. Both Pakistan and India, having established their separate spheres of freedom, now took strong exception to being told how to handle their new sets of problems. They did not care for arrogant, meddlesome Americans telling them what to do, particularly since several billion dollars in U.S. aid was still required for the process of establishing full independence.

The State Department became anxious about Eleanor's travel plans. Starting from Paris, she and David had intended to go home the long way around (much as her father had done from India), flying from Paris to the Middle East—first Lebanon, Syria, and Jordan—then to Israel, then on to Pakistan, and India, and so on, around the world. But the United States minister in Beirut advised Eleanor that it would be "politically most unwise if not impossible" for David to enter Lebanon or other Arab countries.[57] In Washington, the State Department was also "troubled about a Jew going to an Arab country," Tommy, typically candid, told Anna. "Yesterday I was asked whether he is a U.S. citizen or not, and I am quite sure he is so I said yes. I asked Trude [Lash] and she is sure also."[58]

The State Department was afraid that David, traveling with Mrs. Roosevelt, would go with her into a country like Syria, get arrested himself, and then, not being "evacuable," touch off an international crisis. "So I gather," said Tommy, "they settled that by having him go straight to Israel."[59]

Going on to Pakistan and India, Eleanor had the impression that she and David would have to tread very gently, with great care against giving offense in word or action.[60] They were accompanied on the trip by still another young woman, Maureen Corr, Eleanor's new fresh-faced Irish-American assistant, as much a representative of the clean-cut, sardonic new youth of the 1960s as Tommy had modeled the hardboiled golden-hearted dame of the thirties. Eleanor had urged Tommy to stay home, sit this trip out. "These hops from one place to another are rugged," agreed Tommy, "and I think perhaps it is wise for me not to attempt them. However, it is a little deflating to be told that I am too old, and that she (Mrs. R.) is taking someone much younger. Conceit."[61]

David's life had been in flux; as had his relationship to Eleanor, remaining some amorphous combination of surrogate son, companion, Rooseveltian pioneer-of-rehab-medicine, and fellow outsider. His plan to accompany Eleanor now that he and his wife, Nemone, had made final plans to divorce, seemed to indicate some kind of new start. In any case, David was freer than he had been. Without the cover of his dramas with Nemone, however, his myriad quirks only became the more pronounced. By appearing shy, or by hiding behind his camera lens, he camouflaged his passive aggression. Sometimes, he spent entire social occasions, even in his own home, taking pictures. On the journey over the Khyber Pass, Eleanor made a great point of asking their driver's permission to stop so that "my physician," as she referred to David, could take some pictures.

For Eleanor, the Khyber Pass evoked her father, his 1881 hunting expedition, and a promise Elliott had made to Eleanor in 1894.[62] With David, all was well and good on the twenty-two-mile-long pass from Peshawar to the Afghan border, until they came to a place where it looked as if his picture-taking might be getting him into trouble.[63]

Midway across the pass, they had stopped on the side of the road to look at the houses in a tribal village, each heavily fortressed by high walls with gun slits and its own mud watchtower. Eleanor was fascinated by this image of neighbor defended against neighbor. Inside each compound, as they would discover, living areas were formally divided between men's and women's quarters. David had followed his eye to one or another of these and climbed higher for a better camera angle from which to take a picture. As Eleanor recalled the moment, "Suddenly a guard appeared and leveled his rifle at him."[64]

Eleanor learned that the sentry thought David was trying to spy on the women in a nearby house. The man was vehemently sure that David's camera was a pair of binoculars. Eleanor left the matter untouched, vaguely indicating that by the time this was settled, *her* curiosity to see the inside of one of these houses had become the driving force.

"Mrs. Roosevelt never lets anybody feel embarrassed in her presence," a profile writer had tried explaining years earlier. "You can do something wrong, but nobody will notice it, because Mrs. Roosevelt covers it up."[65] With David, it was more complicated. He was habituated by boyhood in Weimar Berlin to being one step from becoming a victim. This allowed Eleanor to take charge in ways that Franklin had denied her; with David she could enact the healing relationship, but this time with love, as she had been unable to do with her father and with Franklin.

In New Delhi, at Jawaharlal Nehru's official reception for Mrs. Roosevelt in the gardens behind the prime minister's residence, David was dazzled by the turbaned maharajahs, ladies in their brightest saris, beribboned military officers—a thousand guests from the A-lists of the world.

After chatting briefly with the minister of health, David took refuge behind his Leica, circulating through the party taking pictures, interrupted now and then by the factotum who had been assigned by the Indian Foreign Office to introduce Mrs. Roosevelt's consort formally to very important guests.

One of these was a maharajah resplendent in the gold braid and stars of a major general's uniform. He seemed to think that David was coming to Jaipur. David replied that he was sorry, but he and Mrs. Roosevelt had just spent two hours trying to make travel plans. The country was so enormous, Mrs. Roosevelt could not be everywhere. Alas, they had decided that they could not come to Jaipur.

The maharajah explained that he and his office had arranged a full schedule, many fetes, and entertainments. The most important was the Elephant Festival, held on the Hindu celebration day of Holi, a two-day rite of spring, when celebrants drenched one another with bright colored powders and water. It had been hoped that David and Mrs. Roosevelt would ride the biggest elephant at the head of the magnificent procession. . . .

David's foreign office guide just then touched his elbow, saying, "May I introduce you to Her Highness the Maharani of Jaipur?"

Gayatri Devi was among the most striking women of her generation. She was thirty-three, tall, elegant, with jet-black hair and a light in her eye.[66]

He blurted, "The Maharani of where?"

She was to become one of India's most powerful women, winning a seat in the Indian Parliament by a landslide. As a maharani, she was the third of Man Singh II's three consort-wives, all of whom lived with

the maharajah in his resplendent Rambagh Palace at the center of Ra-
jasthan's capital city.

"Of Jaipur," the factotum answered.

Without another word, David turned on his heels and said to Man
Singh II, "Your Highness, we are coming to Jaipur."[67]

FOR MRS. ROOSEVELT, DAVID LATER conceded, "going to see a beautiful maharani would not be *her* reason for going to Jaipur." He added,
"but if I wanted to go there, if she could give me pleasure, of course
she would do it."[68]

Eleanor had gamely agreed to play her part in the plan, though
from David's eagerness for the visit she might already have blushed
many shades of festival colors. Gayatri Devi never forgot Eleanor Roosevelt arriving at Rambagh Palace "scarlet-cheeked and puzzled, but
otherwise unharmed."[69]

The damage had been done. "Of course, she's very beautiful," said
Mrs. Roosevelt to David, as soon as they had a moment in private.

Upon their arrival at Rambagh, it was honeymooning at the English country houses with Franklin all over again. For the niece of
Theodore Roosevelt there must be a tiger hunt. Eleanor declined, pre-
ferring instead to see a museum exhibition. David, however, sprang to
join the maharani and set off with her to the Dravyavati River, where
a slain goat baited the far riverbank. When the tigers appeared, David
and his hostess were hidden on the near side. Both fired their rifles.
She hit the mark.

For Eleanor, brought out to admire the kill as the poor creature
hung from bearer's poles, David's tiger hunt with the Maharani of Jaipur was Franklin roped to Kitty Gandy, bursting back into the mountain inn to tell their tales. Then, as now, there was more to come.

The next day, Eleanor, David, and Maureen were invited to ride
on one of the maharajah's elephants at the head of a ceremonial procession as part of the city-wide celebration of Holi. Servants demonstrated how they must climb a ladder, then maneuver into the box on
top of the beast, who would then rise and lumber into position for the
ride through the city. Eleanor was thrilled, Maureen also excited, as
was David.

But, as they made final preparations to go aloft, something changed. Perhaps David had learned something about the festival, which signified the blossoming of love—"a day to meet others, play and laugh, forget and forgive, and repair broken relationships."[70]

Whatever it was, Dr. Gurewitsch was all at once concerned, very concerned, about Mrs. Roosevelt's "dignity and status." It was up to him, he decided, to protect her, and he all but forbade her to climb the ladder.

Eleanor Roosevelt had all her life been happiest when she discovered something she could do that she had been told she could not do. But when David Gurewitsch gave doctor's orders, she listened to him.

In the palace forecourt, she merely frowned, lowered her head by inches, and stood by, a little stooped and listing leftward, to watch as David and Maureen were lifted high up in the air on the back of the maharajah's magnificent elephant. Left alone, she scolded herself, furious "that I let myself be kept from trying," only later "chastising" David, as he told it, the grievance now his, since he had only been doing his duty.[71]

Whatever it was that made David give the order and Eleanor to obey it, both left Rambagh Palace in states of intense annoyance and frustration, which tinted the rest of their journey. As always, Eleanor remembered every detail and would not forget, or, this time, forgive.

David remained closed on the episode. Later he struggled to put his feelings into words, dodging first into ponderous quotations about dignity from George Santayana, until he pointedly faced the truth that Eleanor Roosevelt "did not need me to safeguard her 'dignity.'"[72] Still, as that later-day philosopher would so famously remind a new generation of spouses suffering their malignant narcissist partner's predations, "Nobody can make you feel inferior without your consent."

Eleanor was not yet ready to take her own advice, nor of course was David. At Hyderabad several days later she abruptly canceled the remainder of the trip, sending cables to Dean Acheson at the State Department, but then changed her mind and continued on to scheduled events in Allahabad, Benares, and Calcutta. "Part of her strong reaction," Maureen Corr revealed in later years to Joe Lash, "was that, in Hyderabad, David not only went off on the town, but there were girls involved."[73]

Before all that, however, she had one appointment of her own in India, a final rendezvous that she had not expected would ever come to pass.

"INDIAN FEVER" WAS THE EXCUSE that her father would use to the end of his shortened life. Although initiated into self-medication by his family's dependence on mercury-based stimulants, Elliott entered full-blown addiction after an elephant hunt on his 1881 India odyssey, from which he returned bearing a single trophy: the teeth from the Bengal tiger he killed and now mounted as a magnificent necklace that he planned to present to his mother. But then, finding himself in delightful courtship with the "second-most beautiful" of Old New York's belles and so brief, intense a reprieve from his darker mercurial self, he married Anna Hall, shortly to become Eleanor's mother in the stunning fog of 1883. The tiger's teeth had by then become a talisman of their courtship's not-yet-exposed underbelly, and Eleanor wore it still. Its crescent of amber-colored fangs gave an exotic flair to her UN dinners.

Elliott's one other respite had been the Taj Mahal—world symbol of wonder, symmetry, and love's true beauty. He had been deathly sickened by "Indian fever" by the time the column of the hunt's bearers, beaters, and stooped-over mahogany-colored men under big boxy medicine chests reached the city of Agra. Yet through his delirium he found hidden within the perfect forms of the Taj a kind of coded intervention from which he took a recognition of his own doom and his responsibility to save himself.

Surrounded by the beauty and squalor and vast colonial corruption of the British Raj at its Edwardian heights, Elliott had been upset by the Empire's injustices, even as he indulged on verandahs far from India's worst misery. "How easy," he diarized, "for the smallest portion [of the population] to sit down in quiet luxury of mind and body—to say to the other far larger part—lo, the poor savages. Is what *we* call right, right all the world over and for all time?"[74]

Only at the Taj Mahal had he somehow regained his spirit and balance, vowing afterward to do better, to redeem his promise as the family's "good" boy, to make his father, Theodore, and mother, Mittie, proud, of the man he would make himself once and for all—a pledge that collapsed into shame when Elliott returned home with an un-specified infection, likely a sexually transmitted disease. He continued the same cycle of pledge-making and -breaking first with Eleanor's mother, then with ten-year-old Eleanor, telling her that the Taj was the one place he wanted to be at her side.[75] By visiting the Taj together, they could be fused, spirits eternally symmetrical, Nell/Little Nell. He had vowed to take her someday.

As Eleanor remembered of her father's broken promise: "We were not to have a life together, and I suppose," she wrote at the time of her trip with David, "I have always felt, because I loved him so deeply, that I missed a part of my life that was promised me as a child."[76]

THEY HAD JUST LEFT AKBAR'S fort in late afternoon languor[77] when Eleanor realized that if they were going to get their glimpse of the Taj Mahal at sunset, as they had planned, they had better go very soon. David needed to check for his mail back at the hotel, and once they arrived there and saw how many letters awaited them both, they lost themselves in mail time.

Suddenly it was six thirty, and they were dashing for the Taj, which they entered through the walled garden as the coming night tinged the sky mauve. Before them lay the long series of oblong pools in which the tomb and its tall, dark cypresses were reflected. "I held my breath," wrote Eleanor, "unable to speak in the face of so much beauty."[78] She did not want to talk or to say the expected things about the Taj's per-fection. This first time, she wanted to sit at a distance and respond with repose, much as she had done in Rock Creek Cemetery, sitting before Henry Adams's monument to the grief of love's loss.

Eleanor knew well the story of how a Mughal emperor, builder of many beautiful palaces and tombs, had erected this most perfect tomb of all for his lovely wife, lost to death in childbirth, so that he could keep his promise to her that he would make her name live forever. But Shah Jahan unwittingly discovered a darker side of real love's purity when, in the painstaking process of making Mumtaz Mahal live forever in perfect white marble forms, he bankrupted himself, and then died before he could undertake the final curious project that had preoccupied him to the end of *his* short life, a matching tomb on the other side of the river, to be constructed entirely of black marble.

The idea of an exact mirror-image tomb for himself, a Black Taj connected by a river-spanning bridge to the Taj Mahal, fascinated Eleanor. "It was mind-boggling to us both,"[79] recalled William Levy, another close companion of these later years who filled in the smaller cracks as they opened in Eleanor's normalizing of David's neglect.

That night, when she and David returned to see the Taj by moonlight, Eleanor had reached the point in her life where helping those she loved was finally reversing its charge. David had sparked the turnaround on their first journey—overnight in Shannon Airport barracks—where Eleanor had taken it upon herself to read to him and bring him food, hiking back and forth a mile each way from sleeping quarters to airport dining room. Her version of "help," he later acknowledged, was overpowering.[80]

Now, drinking in the whiteness of the moonlit Taj, she and David could neither go further with their own romance nor force themselves to quit and get on with their lives. They looked at Mumtaz Mahal's perfectly symmetrical mausoleum from every side. Finally, Eleanor broke away and sat by herself on a stone bench halfway down the reflecting pool, as her father had long ago hoped that some day she would.

And there it was, mirrored in the pool—the image of a Black Taj. The perfect whiteness of Mumtaz Mahal's tomb, cast into darkness by the angle of the moon, hung upside down in silhouette on the still surface of the water.

TWENTY-THREE

I N THESE YEARS OF FRIENDS dying off, she seemed possessed of mystical substance.

American schoolchildren thought of her as a living saint. Her lamp of goodness did not illuminate her own presence, as a saint's would, but drove the bad back into the darkness and drew the good around it. Across the world, this torch for independence and freedom would in time retrofit her into the pantheon of humanity's demigods—Mohandas Gandhi, Nelson Mandela, the Dalai Lama.

America had never offered its greatest respect to older people. But Eleanor Roosevelt was now the Old Person With Most Authority. Truman kept on but was a gabby old uncle who came down from the attic now and then. Eisenhower faded markedly. To the very end, Eleanor remained standing among the towering handful who molded the course of world opinion.

Women of her daughter's generation took her as their hero, a bulwark in a cheapening world. "You are something so rare," Jacqueline Kennedy told her, "and so good for all women of my age to have to emulate—a great lady."[1] Her rivalrous friend Martha Gellhorn also knew her as "something so rare that there's no name for it, more than a saint, a saint who took on all the experiences of everyday life, an absolutely unfrightened self-less woman whose heart never went wrong."[2]

With young men—especially active Hollywood Democrats like Paul Newman and Warren Beatty, or political newcomers she took under her wing—she had a double standard. Her assistant Maureen Corr chided her for cutting slack to a young friend like Allard Lowenstein while drawing up short on her sons over minor household issues. "By now, Maureen," said Eleanor with a sparkle in her eye, "you ought to know me well enough to know that I like young men."[3]

She had met Lowenstein in 1948, at the annual Ethical Culture Encampment for Citizenship outside New York, and trusted him at once. At first glance this hyper-energetic son of immigrant Lithuanian Jews, educated at the Ethical Culture School and graduated from Horace Mann at sixteen with varsity letters in wrestling and football, appeared to be a kind of postwar Super Joe Lash. It was a different political culture now, and Lowenstein was the proof of it. In Lash's day, it was the rare New York Jew who started his career as a campus politician in North Carolina by championing the election of an African American to Chapel Hill's student council.[4] The difference showed even more strongly as time went on: where Lash in later years had become a commentator not a participant, Lowenstein remained an unrelenting activist, hailed by one commentator as "a restless samurai of American liberalism, moving from cause to job to campaign."[5]

After Lowenstein had protested against Fascism in Spain and racism in South Africa; written a book that ER hoped would become a movie starring Warren Beatty; stirred up reform Democratic politics in Manhattan; served as a lawyer on civil rights cases in Mississippi; organized and campaigned for Eugene McCarthy, Jerry Brown, and Edward Kennedy; served in Congress and as the only white board member of Martin Luther King, Jr.'s Southern Christian Leadership Conference and as an ambassador to the Human Rights Commission of the UN, Eleanor had looked her protégé sternly in the eye.

"Well, Allard," she said, summing up five decades of political wisdom, "you must remember you can't flush all the toilets."[6]

Duty to human beings and their rights; absorption with the United Nations; a willingness to take the next step on racial injustice; affection for Israel[7]—she herself found room for every cause. Far into the 1950s, Eleanor carried into the public sphere a whole new set of issues that had stubbornly remained outside ordinary discussion—the undiscovered poor, the unfortunate, the badly treated, the children of the world. She raised the question of how people of goodwill should respond in the coming decades to a whole range of matters—civil rights, racial justice and equality, working women. UNICEF's special projects to meet children's needs would, she hoped, prove their value and change the world picture where children were concerned.

She wanted people to adapt their local perspective and see themselves as part of something whole. To understand local conflicts all over the globe—between Armenians and Turks, Cypriots and Greeks, Swedes and Danes, Koreans and Japanese—the binary East-West equations of Cold War thinking would not be enough. "We are going to be near many people whom we have not had to know in the past. It is not going to be possible just to tolerate our neighbors. We are going to like them or they are not going to like us. Our neighbors are going to include people whose skins are yellow, brown, red, black, and white. Their religions will be more varied than the color of their skins and our liking must come from understanding. Regardless of race or religion, human beings have certain things in common and we must discover that quickly."[8]

People wondered how she kept doing it: the astounding travel metrics, the relentless pace, the global appearances as unofficial ombudsman for human rights. She was as self-effacing as ever about achievements, but proud of her endurance. When United Airlines named her a member of its new 100,000 Mile Club in 1953, she listed the honor in *Who's Who*, right after the Women's City and Cosmopolitan social clubs.[9]

They rarely asked why she did it. Or, *why now*, when she had earned her rest as an avatar of universal concern? When she could stop economizing on the people closest to her, and give herself and her family back the weeks and months that jet travel appeared to be stealing from her.

She insisted otherwise: "When one isn't happy, it is hard not to live at high speed."[10] Asked if she ever got lonely or depressed, she answered, "I can never remember being lonely, but if I feel depressed I go to work."[11] Work had always been her antidote for depression. Loneliness, she maintained, was a state of mind or of the soul and therefore untreatable, simply "the lot of all human beings."[12]

One April afternoon in 1953, during tea with a visitor, Eleanor excused herself to take a telephone call, returning noticeably sad. "Tommy—Malvina Thompson—is dying," she told her visitor, a young Episcopal priest, William Turner Levy. Tommy had been hospitalized for a few days, was not conscious or likely to become so, but the doctors had promised to telephone so that Eleanor could be with

Tommy at the end. "I'm not going out or seeing anyone," she explained to Levy, "but, as you are a clergyman, I didn't mind seeing you."[13]

On Sunday, April 12, eight years to the day after Franklin's death, Tommy died—also of a brain hemorrhage. Eleanor had been making final arrangements for that morning's annual wreath-laying ceremony at the President's grave when she received word, raced from Hyde Park to the hospital, reaching Tommy's bedside just before the final moments. "When she died," Eleanor later reflected, "I learned for the first time what being alone was like."[14]

Strands of the Episcopal faith of her earlier years remained to sustain her, less through the church itself than the humility and work ethic of prayers she wrote out and kept in handbags and desk drawers. "There is much we cannot understand," she wrote in 1960, "but we know that, without some help far beyond our own strength, we could never meet the needs of the world in which we live."[15]

ON SEPTEMBER 1, 1953, SHE moved from the Sheraton into East Sixty-Second Street, a garden duplex in a red-brick town house. Esther Lape had found the place while she and David were in Europe, and Eleanor knew at once that she was "going to like it much better than the hotel."[16] She now lived a short walk from David's apartment and his examination room, though as always Eleanor was the healing hand and David's the life being saved—or, at any rate, the postwar lifestyle David was making for himself, as a pioneering rehabilitation specialist and "thinking woman's Casanova."[17]

Eleanor had just taken the opportunity of David's failing love affair[18] with Martha Gellhorn to talk him out of moving his whole life and practice to Cuernavaca, where Martha had taken herself out of circulation to raise an adopted son. Like ER, Gellhorn was a nomad; fearless, consumed by wanderlust, thriving as a world-renowned war correspondent—the only woman to land on the Normandy beaches on D-Day—on what she called "the general chaos of war."[19]

Eleanor had felt protective toward Martha in the mid-1930s; upon hearing of the young war correspondent's entangled love affairs, she took it upon herself to write Martha's mother, Edna Fischel Gellhorn—Eleanor's women's-rights colleague of the twenties—that

Martha should not be allowed to "get sorry for herself and become just another useless, pretty, broken butterfly. She has too much charm and real ability for that."[20]

Now, in the Gurewitsch era, she gave Martha advice directly: a married man might not be the best choice for her. Gellhorn, a woman of many seductions and conquests—including Ernest Hemingway, to whom she was married from 1940 to 1945—much restless hunting, and few sustaining satisfactions, viewed David and herself as "the happy pairing of a 'sex maniac and a demi-frigide.'"[21]

Responding to Eleanor from Cuernavaca, Martha wrote, "David must not be one of the unhappy ones. He has everything he wants just now except me."[22] But, even as it took all of Eleanor's powers to talk David out of moving his life and work to Mexico to bid for Martha, Gellhorn had already, as Eleanor foresaw, moved on; and later in 1952, while David and Eleanor were in Paris, Martha broke it off and moved to England to pursue another man whom, briefly, she married.[23]

Whenever David's attention fell away, as it did during the Gellhorn dramas, Eleanor recharged it by *taking* charge. She had poise, assurance, and popularity far beyond her White House days,[24] and until now had used power and influence sparingly. But, if David needed a booking on the Cunard line at peak season, it was done. If he preferred having Nemone and Grania travel separately, Eleanor arranged that, too. Every door opened for Dr. Gurewitsch. Eleanor never allowed the awkwardness of unrequitedness to linger.

IN THE NEW COLD WAR thinking of East and West, the good strong Russian Army, ennobled as a wartime ally by sacrifice and resilience, now must be demonized as the "fierce, aggressive, and fanatic" forces of an evil Communist state.[25] It had only taken a year. In August 1946, ER had noticed the about-face: "When we were fighting the war together, even the American press frequently emphasized some of the similarities that exist between us. Now, however, it is always the differences that are exploited."[26]

The Cold War fantasy of Soviet Russia using an advantage in military might to stage a world Communist revolution had newly awakened the West's urge to rearm. Eisenhower's two terms would jump the U.S. nuclear arsenal from a thousand to twenty-two thousand nuclear weapons. Rearmament added to fears that the Korean War would become a general war, and as Eleanor observed, "Each war is greater in destructive ability. The people of the world have got to take and make the United Nations their instrument for peace."[27]

But the U.S. abandoned the idea of a unified Korea as a way of containing Soviet advancement, leaving the field to inertia and increasingly vague negotiations. Fears that Europe needed Germany among its defenses would open the way to German rearmament, which would heighten tensions with the Soviets, which would encourage Russia to cooperate better with the Allies, but England, France, and the U.S. remained anxious about Soviet infiltration and the chaos that would follow.

Eleanor understood that the postwar world was going to be smaller, tighter, closely connected by international air travel. Largely invisible to Americans, the biggest geopolitical change in her UN awareness was happening across emerging, newly independent Third World countries. Meanwhile, the necessity of negotiating with the Soviets was becoming one of her main themes. "This was the period of the Cold War but she was not a Cold Warrior," recalled Henry Kissinger. "She was open-minded on negotiating with the Russians, but she was not starry-eyed and she did not think talk was its own justification; she wanted to see some concrete results, and she was not apologetic about having an American point of view." The future Secretary of State added: "But all of this wrapped in a person who exuded humanity."[28]

"NEW YORK IS LONELY WITHOUT you," she wrote to David in September 1954, "but you know I always want you wherever I am."[29]

Martha Gellhorn had long thought of her as "the loneliest human being I ever knew in my life; and so used to bad treatment." She had wept for Eleanor, been shaken with anger for her; she had never liked FDR, "nor trusted him as a man, because of how he treated her." As Gellhorn knew all too well, "There is nothing good in sacrifices."[30]

As the smiling white-haired matriarch of the Democratic Party, she had added a dimension of humanity and omnipresence to the Truman administration, as she had tried to make the party a universal party—far more inclusive than Franklin's coalition party of Northern poor, Mid-

western agriculture, and Southern well-to-do. In Congress, the powerful Texan House Speaker Sam Rayburn would become the Additional
President under Eisenhower. From the White House to the Congress,
the discovery that the Democratic Party could rise again to unexpected
authority—Rayburn, LBJ, JFK—had yet to arrive. Mrs. Roosevelt,
meantime, was the queen who would authenticate the long-lost prince.

From the beginning of the 1952 campaign, ER had been Adlai Stevenson's champion. She felt needed by Stevenson—more than she had
by FDR, and though experienced enough to know what his trouble
was, she remained nonetheless fond and devoted. Politically, he was
too conservative for the postwar Democratic Party: too fair-weather a
friend to labor; too dismissive of Truman; too eager to dissociate himself from the grass roots of the New Deal.

All that could be smoothed over. It was Stevenson's wood-painted-
to-look-like-iron camouflage that voters soon saw through. He simply
couldn't find a way to be at ease with people. Venturing into public,
he was affable when he should have been rancorous, vain when the
occasion called for modesty. Tightly dependent on prepared speeches
and scripted appearances, he insisted on reading from pages at whistle-
stops, and even while barnstorming in rural states, had little instinct
for the flesh-pressing of retail politics. Once during the 1956 presidential primaries, outside a Florida supermarket, a little girl in a starched
white dress had suddenly stepped out of a crowd and handed Governor Stevenson a stuffed alligator. What he should have said, an aide
later suggested, was "I've always wanted one of these to go on the
mantelpiece at Libertyville." What a politician would never say was
what Stevenson did say: "For Christ's sake, what's this?"[31]

Genuinely intelligent, humanistic, Stevenson was best when in
opposition. He would even resort to a technique of creating his own
resistance by declaring his intention to do something, so that others,
especially women, would then tell him he could not do that.

Nine months after losing the 1952 presidential election to Eisenhower, Stevenson spoke to Eleanor about his willingness to step aside
for Lyndon Johnson or Stuart Symington or whoever could do a better
job of leading the party. Of course, Adlai wanted nothing more than
a second chance, and after ER gave him a good scolding, reminding

him that it was hard enough to win when one had the will to win and impossible when one did not, Stevenson resumed running for president—by testing Eleanor's faith in him.

Riding in a limousine in New York on their way to Harlem for a speaking engagement, they stopped at a red light. Teenagers and younger children recognized Mrs. Roosevelt, and maybe Stevenson, too, and crowded around the car, trapping it. As hands entered at the window, Stevenson recoiled, imploring Eleanor: "What should I say to these people?"[32]

She realized then and there that if he did not know, there was nothing she could tell him. A Roosevelt could shake five thousand hands. FDR could have seized the filthiest voter and made him think he smelled like a rose. There was an animal quality lacking in Stevenson. ER knew that those kids weren't asking for economic programs or the finer points of the Constitution from an Illinois governor with an excellent civil rights record. She had seen this before in another failed Democratic presidential hopeful: Al Smith had had no real feeling for the common people either. When Smith campaigned in an open car and could see factory workers crowding to the windows to greet him, he would grouse about how they should get back to work.

Stevenson was afraid of losing control, fearful of unintended consequences. At a dinner party at Val-Kill, when talk turned to the inadequacy of current leaders in an age of brinksmanship, Eleanor wondered aloud which had the grit to deal with a Stalin or a Churchill. She herself volunteered Tito, then added that Stevenson might be such a leader "after he developed more self-confidence."[33] FDR's former adviser and speechwriter Sam Rosenman disagreed, doubting Stevenson's drive. But it was more than stamina: Stevenson's gut feeling for ordinary people remained open to question. Rosenman explained that Stevenson had been asked by Cardinal Spellman to speak to the assorted local and national politicians who celebrated at an annual dinner named for Al Smith. The Illinois governor had already turned them down once. This year Stevenson had an invitation from the Woodrow Wilson Foundation to speak on the same night as the Al Smith Dinner, and he was on the fence about which to accept.

"You have to make up your mind," advised Rosenman, "whether you want to be a statesman or a politician."[34]

In July 1956, at the International Amphitheatre on Chicago's South Side, Eleanor once again rallied the liberal forces of labor for Stevenson, while former president Truman, bidding this time for the nomination of New York governor Averell Harriman, undercut Stevenson by questioning whether the former nominee really was fit to be president after all.

"Perhaps you can tell me," Eleanor addressed Truman after his bombshell had shaken the party, "the process of reasoning by which you reached the conclusion that Governor Stevenson is not prepared to take over the presidency." Coolly adding: "Especially in the light of your own experience in that regard."

"Oh I didn't mean that," said Truman. "I didn't mean to imply he isn't competent to be President."

"Well, if you didn't mean that, then just what were you trying to do?"

"I was trying to stir things up," claimed Truman. "Put some life and fight in this convention. It had no punch, no drive. There was no fighting."

"Fighting!" said Eleanor. "With whom? Democrats?"

"Certainly not between us. Don't worry, Mrs. Roosevelt, you'll see. In the end you and I will be together."

Countered Mrs. R.: "But will the Democratic Party be together? That is what counts, and not you and I. It doesn't matter whether you and I are together or not. But it matters a great deal, at least to me, whether when you get through the Democratic Party is together."

Silence. The old Missouri machine politician changed the subject.[35]

This time, Stevenson won the nomination on the first ballot and in the November rematch with President Eisenhower managed to eke out but 73 electoral votes to Ike's 457.

BACK TO VAL-KILL FOR THANKSGIVING and the first Christmas she could not send Hyde Park fir trees to her friends in the city because the part of the estate on which Franklin and later Elliott had grown Christmas trees had been sold.[36]

In her gray early life she had seemed old; in her sunny, smiling old age she had youth. She went from the childhood humiliation of being called "Granny" to being embraced by her own loving grandchildren as "Grandmere," and in late life as the national grandmother. On her seventieth birthday, the *Washington Post* published a congratulatory cartoon. In the Herblock drawing, a mother is pointing out the Statue of Liberty to her very small son. "Sure, I know who that is, mom," says the son. "That's Mrs. Roosevelt."

Five years later, the Democrats were about to set another tone of change. In the 1958 midterm election, they had taken thirteen Republican seats in the Senate, as well as both seats for the new state of Alaska, adding another in Hawaii in 1959—for the biggest swing in the history of the Senate. William F. Buckley, Jr., founder of *National Review* and spokesman for the conservative position in American politics, carped that the "liberal creed"— "more spending, more federal power, more appeasement abroad"— had become increasingly hollow, "save an intricate but ineffective methodological structure: Academic Freedom, Dissent, Democracy, the United Nations, Mrs. Roosevelt."[37]

"Here's to you, Mrs. Roosevelt," the singer-songwriter Paul Simon wrote and sang, before changing the name and mood of his new song to fit the soundtrack of the 1960s breakout movie *The Graduate*. Whether nostalgic or upbeat or reaching for something deeper, "Mrs. Robinson" would speak to a nation losing its authority and a younger generation angry with elders unable to own their part in the decline. Simon would leave tucked in his plaintive and surprisingly dead-on appeal to Mrs. Roosevelt: *"We'd like to help you learn to help yourself."*[38]

THE YEAR 1959 MARKED THREE decades in which Eleanor had spent no more than ten days in a row in any one apartment or house, or even in any one town or city.[39] She decided that she was "getting rather old to travel," at least on lecture tours, since she could reach only a few thousand people from lecterns, but on TV—well, TV was the future, and by 1958 she would endorse a brand of margarine, hoping to raise the consciousness of millions to world hunger and the need for Americans to share their abundance.[40] She herself took the commercial's $35,000 proceeds, bought a half share in a town house on East Seventy-Fourth Street, and from the age of seventy-five on, lived under the same roof with the man she loved—and with that man's wife.

Edna Perkel, born in New York City in 1924, had graduated from

New York University and NYU's Institute of Fine Arts to become an art dealer in old masters at a distinguished firm on upper Madison Avenue. When she met David in 1956, introduced by friends in the art world, he was twenty-two years older than she, divorced, the father of a teenage girl, and dating a high-profile fashion model. Edna stood five feet two inches. She was poised, deeply private, and radiated self-assurance so imperturbably, her boldness was its own charm.

In their earliest encounters, David switched from excessive shyness to excessive interest, and back again. Thrown together in Toronto by art world events, he went all out, beguiling Edna, sharing his life story over several days, requiring her close attention, but showing little responsiveness or curiosity in her. A Continental hand kisser at the start and end of each day, he seemed to want to be comforted, and, above all, accepted. He never once mentioned Eleanor Roosevelt. But on the return flight to New York, he brought all this curious courting of Edna to a moment of truth.

Raising his hand to eye level, he parted thumb and forefinger an assessing inch. That was the likelihood, David abruptly told Edna, of their getting married.[41]

The strangeness did not end there. Edna had organized a rare exhibition of contemporary British artists, which would preview in a gala charity event at her own E. and A. Silberman Galleries on October 11. In a taxi from the airport, David thrilled her by asking to attend her big night. He then took it all back by asking to bring someone—"a lady."[42] Edna now hardly cared if she ever saw this cad again, but David gravely promised to telephone Edna as soon as he knew if this unnamed lady could come on the eleventh.

Thus was Eleanor set up to share her birthday night. David had planned theater tickets to celebrate her seventy-second, and so, on the eleventh they went to Broadway as planned, afterward joining the crowd at Edna's gallery, still in their elegant theater finery, David wearing Eleanor's favorite flower, a small yellow rose, in the lapel of his dinner jacket.

Thus was the solid success of Edna's gala toppled. The buzzing room hushed as the crowd recognized Eleanor, deferentially pulling back. Edna came forward, David made introductions, then encouraged Edna to give Mrs. Roosevelt a tour of the exhibit. Both women stiffly obliged, conducting themselves picture to picture with elaborate courtesy, as David followed and other guests joined in a semicircle, everyone straining to hear the soft-spoken, increasingly mortified Edna describe works by Francis Bacon, Henry Moore, Graham Sutherland, and many others. Eleanor, bent low, strained and silent, followed her host with her left—her good—ear forward. David had forgotten to alert Edna to Mrs. Roosevelt's partial deafness.

An air of grim inevitability settled over Eleanor as she carried on her usual communications with David by letter and notes. Behind the scenes, he brought discussion of his feelings to her. She shared his misgivings. When David impulsively planned to propose to Edna during a patient's wedding in Paris, Eleanor held her tongue, acquiescing into denial, roundly hoping for David's happiness, as David lingered with indecision, afraid of hurting Eleanor.

When the real news finally came—in a telegram handed to Eleanor as she was about to leave on a trip with Maureen Corr—her face fell, ashen. David planned to marry on Edna's birthday, February 23—in two weeks' time. Eleanor managed to keep moving, but it was too final. David broke through the nightmare with a well-timed phone call; she felt the better for hearing his voice. By day's end she revived enough to offer her blessings and—of course—to make the arrangements. Within a day, the idea had hatched: She would give David his wedding at her apartment on East Sixty-Second Street.

After a couple more days she sent her love to Edna. She was prepared to do anything David wished. "Wouldn't you like a buffet lunch?"[43]

In Manhattan, February 23, 1958, was another winter Sunday. The sky was gray and grim, Eleanor pale, her living room filled with flowers. She had been effusive toward Edna in the days leading up to the day itself, but now Eleanor distanced herself, remaining formally pleasant but no longer fervent.

The ceremony in the living room, performed by a rabbi and friend of David's from prewar Berlin, proved to be "one of her most difficult moments," Maureen Corr later told Joe Lash. "She carried it off with style, having the reception in her apartment, but afterwards she was spent, completely, and looked terrible."[44]

"How did she carry it out," mused her old friend Esther Lape in later years. "By being absolutely fanatical in her devotion to Edna for whom she didn't care at all."[45]

Or, in other words, by doing as she had always done to adjust. This time, the difference was, she did it in her way in her own home. To the end of her life, Eleanor lived in the city of her birth, in a small household in the midst of the great metropolis, with David, who remained her doctor and the person she cared for more than any other, and Edna, vice president of a leading New York art gallery, who was now the doctor's wife.

They moved in together before Christmas 1959, and on New Year's Day 1960, Eleanor, seventy-five, and David, fifty-eight, and Edna, thirty-six, invited friends and family to 55 East Seventy-Fourth Street. Eleanor called the occasion by its pretty name—an "at-home."[46]

"I love my apt & when I get the 2nd floor it will be perfect," she told Anna. "Just now we are a little cramped everywhere except in the living room! That is a lovely room I think & I hope you will like it. I am very content and happy here."[47]

Right up to the Second World War, she had stayed on surprisingly good terms with the nineteenth century. Now she lived in the world of aluminum Christmas trees and the beginnings of a new revolution in popular music. "I know very little about 'rock and roll,'" she admitted to a young man in the record business. "I have seen some of my own young people do it rather conservatively. I would say if the photographs which I have seen are any sample of the way it is usually done, then I must frankly say that ... I have found that stirring up pure emotion with very little reason behind it is never a very good thing for young or old."[48]

In her bedroom, the walls were hung, as at Val-Kill, with her pantheon of photographs: she paid such careful attention to keeping vividly before her the sustaining figures of her life that she made city-and-country doubles of each picture. Her sitting room, furnished with unmatched pieces from the attics of great-aunts and grandmothers, was a surprise to visitors who expected a sleeker, more international setting for the First Lady of the World. Her things had an Edwardian air of safety-be-damned. One startled observer noticed that even the lamps "came from the nightmare era between gas and electricity."[49]

As always, there was her day. Between sunrise and sunset, to paraphrase Benjamin Harrison's remark about her uncle Theodore Roosevelt, she wanted to put the whole world right. Chairing a commission of inquiry into attacks on civil rights workers; campaigning for New York's reform Democrats; touring Israel, meeting with Israeli leaders; filing her column's daily allotment of eight hundred words; finishing her latest book; maintaining the mail and personal correspondence; buying little gifts for friends.

Three years earlier, musing on how death might come anyplace to anyone, she had marveled "how difficult it is for most of us to realize that actually at any moment life may come to an end."[50]

ELEANOR CELEBRATED THE BEGINNING OF her fourth quarter century with a new venture. On October 11, 1959, her seventy-fifth birthday, she launched *Prospects of Mankind*, a monthly TV program, taped at Brandeis University in Waltham, Massachusetts, and broadcast on Boston's WGBH-TV, the cradle of public television, soon to be famous for another tall, cultivated woman with a flutey voice, simplifying fancy French cookery. Eleanor's broadcast brought new and recognizable faces to complicated current events, as politicians such as Adlai Stevenson; Nelson Rockefeller; and the junior senator from Massachusetts, John F. Kennedy, joined in roundtable discussions of foreign and domestic affairs with Cold War experts, visiting heads of state, and academic stars such as Harvard's young Government Department star, Zbigniew K. Brzezinski, or their director of Defense Studies, Henry A. Kissinger. Executive producer Henry Morgenthau III, younger son of Elinor and Henry, recruited a young director, Paul R. Noble, and associate producer, Diana Tead Michaelis, who, along with Dr. Beatrice Braude, a linguist wrongfully blacklisted by the State Department during the McCarthy era, formed the team that twice a month came to East Seventy-Fourth Street to prepare Eleanor for the next program.[51] But she preferred to commute to Boston, since despite the pleasures of having a home with David and Edna, settling down had never been her intention.

"I am about to exercise the prerogatives of a woman and change my mind," she announced on June 15.

She had long been insisting that she would not endorse anyone for the presidential ticket until the Democrats met July 11 in Los Angeles. She had also maintained that in 1960 Stevenson would make a good secretary of state but should not again seek the presidency, explaining: "There's a feeling in this country against any candidate who has been twice defeated."[52]

After that statement, she had not been for any particular candidate, although tea-leaf readers added up her approving estimates of the Minnesota senator Hubert H. Humphrey as the national party's only real liberal democrat. She then distilled them all to: "He comes closest to having the spark of greatness needed in the White House,"[53] which certainly sounded like a full-on endorsement of the former mayor of Minneapolis.

Of the favorite for the 1960 nomination, Senator John F. Kennedy, she had most recently told reporters: "I would hesitate to place the difficult decisions that the next president will have to make with someone who understands what courage is and admires it, but has not quite the independence to have it."[54]

She was not the first party leader to cast shade on Joseph P. Kennedy's son. When someone asked Truman whether Senator Kennedy's allegiance to the Catholic Church alarmed him, the former president replied, "It's not the Pope I'm worried about, it's the Pop."[55] Everyone knew what that meant. A certain kind of Wall Streeter hated Joseph P. Kennedy for being the poacher turned gamekeeper at the SEC. A certain kind of internationalist remembered that he had been more than willing to cede England to the Nazis. For all Joe Kennedy's polishing of the apple as FDR's ambassador to the Court of St. James's, Kennedy had a malodorous reputation. Anyone connected to the liquor interests of the 1920s had touched pitch and been defiled. That was where distrust of Kennedy had started for a great many people besides Eleanor. Here was someone tied up with Capone. Liquor was dirt, corruption, and murder.

As a party leader, Eleanor also revealed her suspicions of the influence Joe Kennedy was having on his son, who embodied a new politics of image. In a line worthy of Theodore Sorensen, John F. Kennedy's speech writer and researcher for the Pulitzer Prize–winning *Profiles in Courage*, she referred to Senator Kennedy's absence on the vote to censure McCarthy, saying: "I wish young Kennedy would show less profile and more courage."[56]

Kennedy had a reputation among his Senate colleagues for asking the tough question. But on McCarthy he was silent. "McCarthy's methods, to me, look like Hitler's," ER had declared.[57] But in the Senate, few members found the courage to stand up against McCarthy's onslaught of false charges. Even when he threatened fellow senators with unprovable accusations of treason, or waved guilt-by-association lists of Communists "infiltrating" the government's most trusted institutions, only Margaret Chase Smith, William Fulbright, Brien McMahon, and Millard Tydings had directly objected. All were penalized. Tydings of Maryland, the bravest of them, paid with his seat. And since "Tailgunner Joe" was having no trouble destroying the careers of politicians considered "a little too liberal," Kennedy was not about to test the willingness of Massachusetts's famously parochial voters to stand behind him if he dared challenge the nationally popular, headline-grabbing, anti-Communist demagogue. When the Senate at long last took steps to curb and censure McCarthy in 1954, JFK remained conspicuously absent from the vote, claiming recovery from surgery. In private, the Kennedy household still loyally welcomed McCarthy as an ally of JFK's father, a political mentor of his brother Bob, and a casual suitor of his sister Patricia—his insidious influence on the nation and democracy itself unchallenged.

Fundamentally, Eleanor felt that Jack Kennedy did not care, which scared her off. She did feel that FDR cared. It might be a shallow kind of caring, but within certain inauthentic men there was a base of genuine caring. But Jack Kennedy, she felt, was inauthentic all the way through.

Now, without explaining her switch, except to say that the failures of Eisenhower's Cold War leadership had made maturity and experience essentials for the next president, she proposed that the national convention nominate a Stevenson-Kennedy presidential ticket.

Almost as soon as she had spoken, Stevenson said he was not a candidate, and Kennedy said he would not take second place.

*   *   *

Two MONTHS EARLIER, DORE SCHARY had assembled 3,150 extras to recreate the climactic moment of FDR's political comeback at the 1924 Democratic Convention—Franklin's ten fateful steps to the podium to nominate Al Smith.[58] Principal photography for the movie version of *Sunrise at Campobello*, Schary's Broadway hit about FDR's return to national life after polio, commenced at the Shrine Auditorium in Los Angeles.

It was no coincidence that at the Memorial Sports Arena, thirty years after Eleanor had stepped onto the national stage, she became politically formidable just by evoking earlier innocence, simplicity, and idealism. She had learned how to exploit her standing out of the seemingly safer, brighter older era, and to use it to connect with a new third of the nation, this time ill-tempered, ill-prepared, and ill-served by the Cold War's "military-industrial complex" which Eisenhower himself had built up.

Accompanied to the arena by her old friend, dancer Mayris Chaney, Eleanor entered the hall impressively, and gave her seconding speech for Stevenson's nomination. The applause was "warm and emotional," reported election chronicler Theodore H. White, and it "came from the heart."

Norman Mailer, the novelist turned reporter, listened to Eleanor explain in "firm, sad tones" why she could not support Kennedy and wondered if "she were not now satisfying the last passion of them all, which was to become physically attractive, for she was better-looking than she had ever been as she spurned the possibilities of a young suitor."[59]

Mailer meant JFK, but the young suitors on whose possibilities she had staked her political and personal life as a widow were Adlai and David. Of the men in her life, Stevenson—the man whose brilliance should have made him president but couldn't—was now most like her father late in his life, the Elliott of Abingdon, the man who should have been her leader and protector if he hadn't first drunk himself to death. Her almost ostentatious willingness to dream her father alive had become the same brazen high-mindedness in which she had costumed her aspirations for Stevenson, draping him in cape and epaulets. But it was now all revealed as a mask to her more tenacious realism, her inner toughness.

On July 13, the convention nominated JFK for president. Eleanor left the arena in a hurry,[60] beelining for the new international airport in Los Angeles, trying to get back to New York as quickly as possible. All the energy she had invested, canceled out by Stevenson's inability to make up his mind, bolstered her own resolve to finish her unfinished business in New York politics. It was the last time she let Stevenson upset her.[61]

Kennedy attempted to reach her by telephone, paging her at the airport, but she declined the call.[62] Back in New York, she took a call from Nannine Joseph, her literary agent: Mrs. Roosevelt's speech had been the highlight of the convention.

"Didn't do much good, did it?" replied Eleanor.[63]

ON AUGUST 14, KENNEDY CAME to Val-Kill for her endorsement—to concede her place. But ER felt sure that she could see a "cold and calculating person" behind the bright white smile in the young tan face.[64] William Walton, in charge of New York for Kennedy, played a role in arranging the meeting at Val-Kill, and later conceded: "Jack honestly didn't like her particularly."[65]

At about noon that Friday morning, Eleanor had just finished talking with fifty Democratic women leaders from the Hyde Park congressional district about the campaign activities of their candidate for Congress, writer Gore Vidal. Just as the women were about to leave, the phone rang in the cottage. It was her son John calling from Calais, Maine, near Campobello, where he and Anne were on vacation. Their daughter Sally had been injured in a fall from a horse at summer camp and now lay unconscious in a Utica, New York, hospital, where doctors were working to bring her back. John gave Eleanor a few directions on things he needed her to do, which she carried out promptly. In less than half an hour the word came back that all efforts to save Sally had been useless. "This beautiful, alive, lovely child was dead," wrote Eleanor.[66]

Eleanor's response asserted the master personality she had developed. Like a doctor undismayed by the worst, she behaved completely without fear when it fell to her to call her granddaughter Nina, Sally's sister, to tell her the news.[67]

Kennedy offered his condolences, and, of course, insisted they cancel their meeting. Eleanor said, "No, come ahead, but you understand I won't meet you at the airport, as I will be in mourning."

And so, Kennedy drove up to the cottage in Hyde Park and knocked on the back door. Clean-cut, sharply handsome, he carried himself with an air of forthrightness absent from their last meeting. Kennedy had grown through his commitment to the abnormal task of running for president of the United States. Eleanor had seen this before, and was pleased; Joe Kennedy's second son had mastered the art of trusting his own experience. Senator Kennedy now spoke in a voice unlike any other.

They had lunch head to head at a small table next to one of the packed bookcases near the fireplace. Eleanor wore the unbecoming hairnet. She was seventy-six, and not scared of it; and tired and grieved. She certainly didn't want to look like mutton dressed as lamb, and maybe especially because David was there that day, with his camera—and of course his young wife, closer in age to the candidate than either Eleanor or David.[68] It had the effect, overall, of heightening her own seriousness and, somehow, the magnificence of Jack Kennedy.

He had understood that Eleanor had a price for her support: secretary of state for Adlai Stevenson. But as they spoke privately, she insisted that all presidents should be completely free of encumbrances when choosing their own cabinets. No chief executive should be committed in advance on any office.

Unexpected similarities emerged as the meeting went on. Both had the skill of being nearly impersonal and withdrawn one moment, wholly present and focused the next. Both brought to politics the skill Eleanor had learned from Franklin: a disinterested pragmatism. Did a policy work? Was it the most effective means to solve the problem? Like Franklin, they had both learned to let the small things go, and even a few big ones: the burn would cool. JFK was already better known for his charm and wit than ER had ever been for either, but life in the twentieth century had taught both a crisp, sardonic, almost fatalistic style of humor.

In this unexpected likeness, they shared a temperament—a grimly accepting sense of the human condition that for Kennedy derived from his generation of GIs and the stoic strategies they had used to ward off the horrors of war. Asked to account for how he had become a hero of the Pacific war, Kennedy had once answered, "It was involuntary. They sunk my boat." For Eleanor, it had been losses in peacetime: Sally Roosevelt's death had cast yet another shadow over Hyde Park the day before.

Some of Kennedy's men believed that he "went away absolutely smitten by this woman," and that Eleanor "really wove her web around him." William Walton considered the meeting "a real peacemaking, and very important to him politically too. The reform movement began to come to him then, though they were still very slow."

Converted by the candidate's practical intelligence and candor, Eleanor proceeded to campaign for Kennedy coast to coast. "She would speak any place we wanted her to," recalled Walton. "I would meet her in a car and take her; and she would want to sit down for just two minutes before we went in, asking who was there? what were they like? what was the tenor of what we wanted?—with great power of concentration. She wouldn't even look at you; she'd just absorb it and say, 'Yes.' In you'd go, and she'd do it."[69]

On September 26, Eleanor joined seventy million of her fellow Americans watching the Kennedy-Nixon presidential debate, which she recognized as a milestone in television history—"the first time campaigning had been conducted on this level." She shared with the readership of ninety newspapers her deep distrust of Richard Nixon.[70]

And, finally, on November 6, two days before balloting began, a crisp and radiant Kennedy wound up his campaign with a marathon day of New York City speeches, a torchlight parade from the Biltmore Hotel up Broadway to Columbus Circle, and a massive nationally televised rally at the New York Coliseum.

At political rallies that election season, the writer John O'Hara had noticed that the orators now intoned "John—F—Kennedy," as they had once chanted "Franklin—D—Roosevelt."[71] In the same breath, O'Hara observed that "a Roosevelt can still get his name in the paper, but the magic has been passed on to the name Kennedy."[72]

Everywhere JFK went, crowds surged, women fainted, police struggled to keep eddying mobs from crushing bystanders. Up to eight feet deep along the parade route, thousands braved drenching rains for a glimpse of the hatless Massachusetts senator and his Texas running mate in the tall white hat.

Kennedy had pounded hard at his theme in fifteen speeches that day ("This country is going to move in the Sixties"), and Johnson, speaking first in the Coliseum, told ten thousand party faithful that he and Kennedy shared a deep desire for "government that cared." When, at last, the young man from Boston appeared inside the super-charged hall, his entrance causing "nothing short of bedlam," a beaming, waving Eleanor stood at his side.[73]

The instant the speech was over, as had been the campaign's contrivance since the spring primaries,[74] the band stirringly struck up FDR's Depression-defying theme song, "Happy Days Are Here Again."

HER AUDIENCES WERE NOW COMMUNITIES. "Arthurdale" had become whichever auditorium—or television studio—she next found herself in. David and Edna, living upstairs, were also an audience, as Nan and Marion had been at Val-Kill.

After a few months in the new routine of commuting to Boston and Brandeis, the *Prospects* producers noticed that she was slowing down. In a meeting, or on the set, waiting for the TV people to do their jobs, she would let her eyes shut for the flash of sleep required to get by. Paul Noble recognized that her mind seemed to wander in the middle of a thought. "I got the feeling she wasn't weary physically—if you started walking someplace, she beat everybody there. It was an attention problem."[75]

One solution was to have a co-anchor who could keep the conversation moving. Another, since Eleanor now wore a hearing aid, was feeding the sound of the discussion into her ear. "In the control room, if we ever felt she wasn't engaged, we'd just boost up the sound a little." A third, since ER was at her best first thing in the morning, was bringing breakfast to East Seventy-Fourth Street and making most of the month's big decisions about guests, topic, and script emphasis over Danish pastries. But about a year into this routine, in April 1960, Eleanor asked the *Prospects* team to discontinue the selection from the Peter Pan Bakery because Dr. Gurewitsch wanted her to cut back on sweets.[76]

* * *

THAT WAS WHEN SHE RETURNED home to East Seventy-Fourth Street one day and rang up to the Gurewitsches—Edna answered.

"Is David taking a nap?" asked Eleanor.

"No . . ." came the uncertain reply.

"Do you have any guests?" pursued Eleanor.

"No," said Edna, slightly maddened as always by Mrs. Roosevelt's mystifying indirection. "What is it?"

"Well, you see, dear, I've just been hit by a car, and I wonder if it's convenient for you if I come upstairs."[77]

She had been on her way to the hairdresser before a charity meeting in Greenwich Village. As she stepped off the curb on Eighth Street, outside of her hairdresser François's place, a young man backed his station wagon into her, knocking her down. "It was entirely my fault," she was still insisting minutes later. "I am old enough to look both ways when crossing a street."[78] She had by then factored in the trouble this young man was going to have—a young male African American at the wheel of an enormous car—explaining that it was not his fault, he hadn't knocked down Eleanor Roosevelt.

She urged the driver to go on his way, and he did. By the time she got home, the pain was severe and her leg was bleeding. She had a party of twenty-five schoolchildren waiting for her at the house and she attended to them first, then went up to the Gurewitsches, where David taped up her leg and gave her crutches. He strongly urged her to rest, but that night she went out through the pouring rain to give a speech at a fundraiser at the Waldorf Astoria. When she returned home, the Gurewitsches were anxiously waiting up for her.

Triumphant, she called out: "You see, you wanted me not to go. When they saw the condition I was in at the dinner, they raised more money!"[79]

Soon afterward, still not feeling her best, she checked in at a new local clinic upriver from Val-Kill, where she received, among other standard diagnostics, a blood test.

THE RIP VAN WINKLE CLINIC in Hudson, New York, was reporting mild aplastic anemia, also known as bone marrow failure.

David took up the results with some confusion. His patient was a famously fit seventy-five-year-old, so much so she had declared herself "too busy to be sick." Until now, Eleanor Roosevelt's health, as the whole world knew, really had been bulletproof. She never had so much as a headache, and had a hard time catching even a cold. Now, suddenly, a low white blood cell count? The bone marrow looked suspicious for an early stage of leukemia. Was that the underlying trouble? If so, how should it be treated? If not, then what?

David's medical specialty was physical rehabilitation. He worked alone in his East Side practice, in addition to his pioneering treatments for polio patients at various institutions, and his affiliation to the Medical Center at Columbia-Presbyterian, headquarters of the New York medical establishment high over the Hudson on Washington Heights.

There, he consulted several specialists about the Rip Van Winkle Clinic's findings, each of whom struggled for a diagnosis, while treating ER with steroids and transfusions, plus tests for leukemia, and, just to be safe, two of the three drugs known to cure most known strains of tuberculosis, about both of which the Columbia experts had suspicions. But all of this did little for Eleanor except return her to Washington Heights for more and more tests as she felt worse and worse from allergic reactions to the transfusions. David did not push the expensive option of biopsy. As he left it, according to one oversight investigator of later years, "sooner or later, her marrow would break down completely and internal hemorrhaging would result."[80]

Anna's third husband, Dr. James Halsted, happened to have established a first-in-the-nation group medical practice outside Boston.[81] Eleanor had cheerfully submitted to testing at the Rip Van Winkle Clinic, upriver from Val-Kill, because, coincidentally, she felt that "from a social point of view it was a good development in medical practice to have a clinic with lots of doctors together."

But when David telephoned the Halsteds that April to consult with Jim, he was concerned about the clinic's original diagnosis, and, recalled Halsted, David was frankly upset: "He thought she was going to die and that it might be really leukemia."

Halsted followed classic protocol, immediately suggesting that David recuse himself and "get a good internist to take charge," later adding that though David had "always been her doctor, everybody

knew that he was expert in physical medicine & rehabilitation problems, but that wasn't hematology."[82]

DAVID HANDLED IT BADLY. HE went directly to Mrs. Roosevelt—he
still could not bring himself to use her given name. He told her that
Jim and Anna didn't think that he, David, could take proper care of
her. They wanted him to get another doctor to be in charge now. He
bewailed the insulting truth that Anna and Jim—for that matter, all
Mrs. Roosevelt's children—didn't trust him with her case.

After all that had sunk in, she said, at last, "Well, David, if you
don't want to take care of me, I won't have *any doctor*."[83]

She consigned to his care her deepest fear. Five years before, on
June 17, 1955, she had attended the burial of Louis's widow, Grace
Hartley Howe, in gloomy Oak Grove Cemetery, a Victorian memorial park of monuments in the north end of Fall River, Massachusetts,
which had brought her back to the rich nineteenth-century culture
of death that she had grown up in. That Sunday, she had gone into
the city for the funeral of her friend John Golden, who had recently
suffered from ill health, so that, as with Grace Howe, Eleanor felt sure
that death was merciful for John, as it had been for Grace.

"After forty," she wrote, "we all live in borrowed time & there
should really be no cause for grief in the passing of one's contemporaries. Just a few more holes in this life to warn us to be prepared! I've
tidied up much in the house this year but this summer I must see that
all the papers I can get rid of are destroyed & the rest properly filed!"[84]

And so, on June 21, she brought to David the typed instructions for
her burial. Once she had his countersignature, she would leave for her
executors several instructions to follow after her death:

*I want Dr. David Gurewitsch or any doctor in charge to open veins to
be sure I am dead.*[85]

There were no guidelines for where her memorial service should
take place, no mention of her grave, or of sharing the ground and the
white marble bier in Mama's garden with Franklin. She gave orders
for a plain pine coffin and specified a blanket of fir boughs, but the
focus was more on how it would work on the *inside*, where she wanted

to be left free of embalming fluids, and resting on "plain pillows" and covered by a "sheet with cloth, and tied in."

From that day on, she placed herself wholly in David's hands. She never forgave Jim Halsted for challenging David's authority, the tension so extreme on her side that when Halsted was seated next to her at a family lunch, she whispered loudly to David, not caring if she was heard: "I *won't* be seated next to Jim!" and, pulling back sharply, "I don't want him ever to touch me!"[86]

Their inverted doctor-patient relationship would test the practical limits of David's abilities as a physician. As her health deteriorated, they would each feel forced by the other to make irreversibly complicated decisions.

FEW EXPECTED HER TO ATTEND President Kennedy's inauguration on January 20, 1961. Unannounced, she arrived in Washington on a train from New York, carrying her own bag through the falling snow. Having forgotten to pack a heavy winter coat, she arrived at a pre-Inaugural party that night in Georgetown, a warm sparkle in her eye after her brisk walk across the city. The party's hostess had expected a hundred souls to brave the weather, but no one came, and yet there stood Eleanor. "I'll never forget," said Mathilde Krim, "she was covered with plastic bags."[87]

At the Capitol East Front the next morning, she was among no fewer than eight former and future first ladies: Edith Wilson, ER, Bess Truman, Mamie Eisenhower, Jacqueline Kennedy, Lady Bird Johnson, Pat Nixon, and Betty Ford. Eleanor had refused JFK's invitation to sit on the platform and instead watched from a bench out front where she could hear and stay warm under an army blanket.

The Kennedys brought an updated Strenuous Life glamour to Washington. "Vigor" was the new word for fifty-mile hikes on the C&O Canal led by the attorney general and Supreme Court Justice William O. Douglas. Official Washington itself was now a bulked-up cityscape of monumentally scaled buildings with views of other enormous buildings. The big-sky dawn of modern government that radiated so brightly on her youthful visits to Uncle Ted's White House—growing through Wilson's federal expansions and Jim Crow contractions—reaching full scale in the twenty-year (1932–1952) Democratic creation of the military-industrial complex, over so much of which FDR had presided, was now a federal megalopolis connected by hotline to NORAD silos in the Nebraska wheat fields. All Uncle Ted had available to run an empire was a few men sitting in offices and a telegraph key.

She herself had done so much to change Americans' relationship to their government, to their nation's capital. Yet she now worried that she had overshadowed her children to the point where they had no place here to contribute. Indeed, her sons appeared diminished to the men now in charge.

James's divorces and corrupt business practices were one thing; Elliott's excess of corruption, another. John's drunkenness, still another. But Franklin Jr. had played a major role on the ground in JFK's West Virginia primary. "My son reminded the voters there of my husband and created a whole new image for Kennedy," said Eleanor. "Don't forget, there is still a picture of my husband in nearly every miner's cabin in the state."[88]

Kennedy had never been interested in sentimental choices, and recognized his debt to Franklin Jr., but after his defense secretary, Robert McNamara, rejected Roosevelt as unreliable and unqualified, Kennedy appointed him undersecretary of commerce.[89]

Eleanor worried, as she had when Franklin became a war leader, that President Kennedy was going to turn his back on domestic needs. She knew he studied foreign policy issues thoroughly and suspected he would spend his time as president with the national security establishment, which now contained the same government departments and agencies that would grow impatient with JFK in his disillusioned view of a president's actual control over events.

She aired her concerns with one questioner in 1962, saying "I don't ever think we're doing enough in Civil Rights."[90] After the Freedom Riders summer, she praised the administration for "using the Attorney General's office much more than ever before to get things done. The more we can hasten desegregation, the better it will be."[91]

The New Frontier was heralded as a great renewal of liberalism's

pragmatic experimentation, but Kennedy tended to be more traditional than ER. And ER's opening remark when they reached the
Kennedys' private quarters rang this truth:

"Where, Mr. President, is Mrs. Kennedy's desk?"

Kennedy had appointed Eleanor as chairman of the President's
Commission on the Status of Women, and under her guidance, the
commission identified the issues that soon became the agenda of the
women's movement. The final report laid out the blueprint for action.
Commissions modeled on the national one were soon created in every
state. Federal equal-pay legislation got its final boost as a result of the
commission's work. Fairer treatment of women employed in federal
and local government saw early success.

As on AAUN (American Association for the United Nations)
and on *Prospects* she worked with a new generation of bright young
women driven to validate themselves through professional achievement. Marrying the right young man might be a good thing to do,
but not the only thing to do. Women went to law school and medical
school in ever increasing numbers. Eleanor was not a career model.
There was no career as Eleanor Roosevelt; she was an individual not
to be repeated, and as time went by she stood more and more alone on
her pedestal.

ON MAY 17, 1961, AN ill-fated, American-sponsored invasion of
Cuba by a brigade of poorly supported Cubans handed President John
F. Kennedy a singular defeat at the Bay of Pigs. A month later, Fidel
Castro used a peasants' rally in Havana to send Kennedy a televised
message.

The young American president, in office only three months, had
taken personal responsibility for authorizing the botched invasion,
and was anxious to find a way to persuade the Cuban prime minister
to release the 1,180 captured Cubans now being held prisoner. At the
triumphal rally, after declaring that "the invaders have to pay for the
damage they have done," Castro announced that he would accept five
hundred heavy-duty tractors from the United States in exchange for
the prisoners. He then selected ten prisoners to form a "commission"
and sent them to the United States to negotiate for the machinery.

Where in the world was President Kennedy supposed to find that many tractors? And what did Castro mean—"heavy-duty"?

The day after the prisoners' arrival, the telephone rang during breakfast at Val-Kill. It was President Kennedy, calling to enlist Mrs. Roosevelt to form a private agency to work with the delegation for the release of all the prisoners. The President knew Mrs. Roosevelt would respond to the plight of the men as a humanitarian mission, and he knew she would make what had turned into a bad smell better.

Within a week, the Tractors for Freedom Committee had been established. ER headed up a fundraising campaign of $3.5 million, with help from Dr. Milton Eisenhower, brother of the former president and president of Johns Hopkins University, and Walter Reuther, president of the United Auto Workers Union.

One of the first people she called was Cardinal Spellman. Shortly, a $5,000 pledge was received at committee headquarters in Detroit, followed by a $25,000 donation from John "Jake the Barber" Factor. Soon, however, the terms of settlement changed when Havana demanded $28 million in cash; ransom—or extortion—Castro insisted on calling "indemnification."

"Ridiculous," said Eleanor. "I don't believe the United States can be intimidated by Cuba. If [the U.S.] wishes to do a humanitarian thing, it should do it."

Castro wanted Mrs. Roosevelt or Eisenhower to come to Cuba to work out the details, but instead, on June 13, 1961, the committee sent a four-man team of farm machinery experts to Havana.

Castro greeted their offer of light farming tractors with disdain. He insisted on five hundred heavy-duty machines. He increased the ransom but now offered fewer prisoners, withholding three Spanish priests, sixteen prisoners accused of crimes under the Batista regime, three invasion leaders, two invaders accused of killing militiamen, eight who died "accidentally" in transit to Havana, and as many as seventy captured in civilian clothes.

Eleanor, sensing Soviet influence, coolly remarked that five hundred heavy tractors would be capable of harrowing all of Cuba in three days. She added that the committee's team of experts had decided that the heavy-duty tractors Castro was demanding could be used in such quantity only in Siberia or central China. She further directed the committee's executive secretary to announce that so far as "indemnification" was concerned, Americans would not pay $28 million or $28—the United States would not be blackmailed.

Ten days after the farm-machinery team had landed in Havana, the Tractors for Freedom Committee disbanded, declaring that Castro had "made impossible a realization of our humanitarian goals."[92] Two weeks later all unopened mail contributions were returned to their senders.

HER HAPPIEST DAYS NOW INVOLVED winning fights. It was almost a secret—greater than keeping flowers fresh in the water of the toilet bowl—that she allowed things to get personal and that she was pursuing a killer agenda with Carmine De Sapio.

Wearing signature smoky glasses (for an eye condition) and the dark suit and tie and white dress shirt of a General Motors executive, Carmine De Sapio had appeared in 1955 on the cover of *Time* as the latest Tammany chieftain with dreams of controlling the White House. De Sapio was more acutely, if condescendingly, viewed by the city's leading conservative, William F. Buckley, Jr., as a "charming southern Italian who very much wanted to be respectable."[93]

In 1954, when Franklin Jr. ran for governor, De Sapio had told him to wait his turn. When Franklin ignored De Sapio's warning and tossed his hat in the ring, De Sapio unleashed the deadly power of the Wigwam, sabotaging Franklin Jr.'s campaign, ensuring his defeat in "a town," observed *New York Post* editor James Wechsler, "where Roosevelt is practically a religious name."[94]

To Uncle David, Eleanor reported: "F Jr. was defeated because they put a *very good* Jew against him. Ordinarily he has the Jewish vote but much of it had to vote for a good Jew. Then De Sapio & Buckley in Manhattan & the Bronx cut him in the Italian & Irish votes."[95]

Now, seven years later, as Democratic reformers established a precinct-level organization aimed at eliminating De Sapio, the seventy-seven-year-old Eleanor was ready.

Leading the 1961 reform movement, Senator Herbert Lehman persuaded Mayor Robert Wagner to break with De Sapio to run for a third term on a "Beat the Bosses" platform. Eleanor threw in with Lehman and Tom Finletter to encourage James Lanigan, a veteran of the Stevenson campaigns, to run against the Tammany boss in his Greenwich Village stronghold.

Eleanor went head-to-head with De Sapio on the famous *La Grande Famiglia* radio show, the dominant Italian-language voice in the Northeast.[96] No broadcast could have been more central to hundreds of thousands of WOV families, and yet, when Eleanor met the sinister boss on air at the WOV-AM studio on lower Fifth Avenue, she easily campaigned in her Allenswood-Rivington Street Italian, while De Sapio could speak only English and plainly did not care about community problems as she did.[97]

As the September primary election approached, De Sapio grew desperate. Tammany had not lost a race in lower Manhattan since 1939, but the Reformers held off the boss's last-ditch effort to mobilize the Puerto Rican and African American vote. Wagner crushed the machine candidate Arthur Levitt, and Lanigan beat De Sapio by 6,165 votes to 4,745.

More than thirty years after first tangling with the Wigwam, Eleanor had wasted Tammany with a wave of her hand. The admiring novelist Gore Vidal, having lost his race as the 1960 Democratic congressional candidate for Dutchess County, celebrated the kill with Eleanor in Hyde Park. Sitting out on the lawn, the party matriarch turned to him and gleefully summed up: "I told Carmine that if he didn't back Frank Jr., I'd get him —and I did it, didn't I?"[98]

ON THE LAST *PROSPECTS OF MANKIND* program, in May 1962, Henry Morgenthau III would recall noticing, "Some of the fabled energy had evaporated."[99]

With the rise of the curtain on Camelot, astronauts going suborbital, polio on its way to eradication, and the Beatles just over the horizon, the poetry wing of the counterculture dreamed of her. In December 1960, a clean-cut young poet with thick black glasses recorded a dream in which he discovers that he and Eleanor Roosevelt are neighbors in furnished rooms on the Bowery, the poet upstairs, Mrs. Roosevelt in the basement. Waiting outside her door, he announces, "I just want one minute to tell you something." She agrees: "One minute," first asking the young man to say hello to her grandchildren as she busies herself inside her place. When at last she returns, she is deaf as a park statue, big as the Colossus of Rhodes. The poet is desperate to be seen. "I have remembered you and your work," he says, choking back tears, "and I want to say I love you: what you have stood for and done, and my name is Allen Ginsberg."[100]

The fate of the Cuban prisoners had hung in the balance for six months—until January 3, 1962, when Cuban families in Florida launched a nationwide fundraising drive to ransom their sons and brothers. The Castro regime responded with a mass trial for treason; starting on April 8, a five-man military tribunal deliberated four days, then found 1,179 prisoners guilty and sentenced them to thirty-year prison terms. But the tribunal also set ransoms for each prisoner, ranging from $25,000 up to $500,000—totaling $62 million. . . . Less than a week later, 60 wounded and ailing prisoners arrived in Florida, ransomed on credit for $2.5 million, and expecting their comrades in arms still in prison to be freed within three months.

Finally, at Kennedy's request, James B. Donovan, the Wall Street lawyer and international negotiator who had swapped Soviet spy Colonel Rudolf Abel for American U2 pilot Francis Gary Powers, reopened negotiations with Castro—a process that spanned several months and seemed to have reached final-stage negotiations on October 20.

Two days later, the United States discovered Soviet missiles and bombers in Cuba, Kennedy blockaded Cuba, and the brinksmanship that would send the world as near to destruction as it had ever been began to unfold.

ENVOI

S HE HAD OUTLASTED TYRANTS. Now the end was in sight. The fevers of July returned harshly in August, night sweats, chills, but she had no fear of them.

David had given his word that she would not die in the hospital. The prospect of ailing and growing increasingly weak at home, in private, did not trouble her. There, after all, she could hear the happy sound of a small child—David and Edna's now thirteen-month-old daughter, Maria. She went out and bought a crib for Maria to use at Val-Kill.

Her own crib-mate from the birth of Val-Kill, Nancy Cook, had died just days before, survived by Marion Dickerman, life partners to the end. Edith Benham Helm, from ER's White House secretariat and the Wilson years, also slipped away that month, joining Edith Wilson, gone the previous December at the age of eighty-nine; and in this same season of a generation's passing, Molly Dewson, first female political boss, the "Little General."

Then the first of September brought word that Eleanor's old schoolgirl crush Nelly Post had died as Mrs. Montague Charles Eliot, 8th Earl of St. Germans, buried by her sons on Gibraltar.[1] By strange coincidence one of her life's other most-important unsung figures was soon to join that season's departed: Lillian Cross, who in Miami, the winter of '33, three weeks before FDR's first inauguration, had grabbed the shooting arm of Giuseppe Zangara, averting the assassination of the president-elect and much else in the twentieth century. She would be buried on the eleventh of November.

ON SEPTEMBER 5, THE WEDNESDAY after Labor Day, Eleanor had a visitor from St. Paul's Tivoli,[2] the rustic parish behind which she had buried every Hall in the crumbling family sepulcher,[3] most recently her brother. She now wanted to have the vault torn down[4] and the bodies buried properly. The local undertaker had found out it was Mrs. Roosevelt and the price had gone up by several thousand.[5]

But that was not why she had urged the rector of St. Paul's, the

Reverend James Elliott Lindsley, and his wife, to come for lunch at Val-Kill. Aunt Maude's husband, her beloved uncle David Gray, and Maureen Corr were also at the table, Maureen ladling out the house chile con carne, a family recipe. Unobtrusively, Eleanor was served a hamburger for the iron.

She was not interested in the meat or its nutrients. She seemed, recalled Lindsley, eager to talk about death. She thought out loud to her seventy-ninth birthday, coming up quickly in October. "What more do I have to live for?" she said.

"You might be ready to die," said the rector, and many years later he sighed deeply as he recalled, "Others were not ready to let her die."[6]

Archbishop McIntyre of Los Angeles had attacked her for certain remarks she had made on Edward R. Murrow's CBS radio program, *This I Believe*, telling listeners that she had no rigid views of the nature of immortality or after-death states. She said, "I don't know whether I believe in a future life," and suggested that in these matters, especially, it did no harm to think for ourselves. "I think I am pretty much of a fatalist. You have to accept whatever comes, and the only important thing is that you meet it with courage and with the best that you have to give."

To this, the archbishop responded by accusing Mrs. Roosevelt of "assuming the role of an agnostic and a fatalist," as if she were guilty of a double crime against the doctrine of the immortality of the soul. The archbishop then made an astonishing leap, declaring her unfit to chair the UN's Commission on Human Rights. How could Mrs. Roosevelt fashion a bill of human rights: "Does this mean an agnostic or an atheistic world?"[7]

Later, looking back on it, the Reverend Lindsley "was sorry he did not let her talk and say *why* she felt she wanted to die."[8]

At their lunch at Val-Kill, Eleanor told the Lindsleys about her most recent hospitalization. She launched a prolonged discussion about death, and said several times, "I am not afraid to die." She said she believed that nature conditioned people her age, schooling their bodies for whatever was to come; and she said that her work was done.[9]

WEAKER AND WEAKER, SHE MADE an appearance on a truck in Greenwich Village, just one block away from her old place on

Washington Square, campaigning for Ed Koch for assemblyman. Seventy-eight years old and terminally ill, Mrs. Roosevelt climbed up the ladder and began to speak. As soon as people noticed her, a great crowd gathered. A yellow cab came along, and the driver impatiently honked his horn. Several people hushed him. "Don't you tell me to shut up," the cabbie shouted. "I have a fare here in my cab and he's in a hurry." Someone told him that the person speaking was Mrs. Roosevelt. "*Eleanor* Roosevelt?" He got out of his cab and, letting his fare sit there, listened attentively until she finished her speech.[10]

Every day she struggled out from East Seventy-Fourth Street to run her errands, but her breathing shortened, and shaking chills would stop her in her tracks. She tried attending a reception for the U.S. delegation to the Seventeenth General Assembly, but her fever spiked, driving her home and into bed.

More urgently than ever, David pursued a diagnosis. "A doctor's role is to preserve life and not to prolong dying," he had often said. With Eleanor, however, the need to explain the cause of her illness, foremost to himself clinically, so that all paths to cure could be found and tried, overrode other considerations as he now consulted with specialists at Memorial Sloan Kettering Cancer Center, an infectious disease specialist, and with several internists at Columbia-Presbyterian, including Alfred Gellhorn, Martha's youngest brother, who got Eleanor to submit to a battery of tests up on Morningside Heights, none revealing for clinical diagnosis.

On September 23, she made cause with young John Lindsay on the subject of radiation. As members of a television-show panel Eleanor and the handsome New York congressman called on President Kennedy to let the American people know about the dangers of radioactivity in the field of medicine and fallout from nuclear tests. "The President has got to make a speech to the people and ask them to listen," implored Eleanor.[11]

Three days later, she could not keep it up. Her fever was taking over earlier each morning, more powerfully than before, and she was passing blood in her stool. Clearly, this was more than aplastic anemia and David made arrangements for admission to

Columbia-Presbyterian. Eleanor filed "My Day" to Harry Gilburt at United Feature Syndicate, meeting her deadline as always, and Jimmy, per David's instructions, came to help prepare his mother for the hospital.

But she would not go, she did not want to. She staged a strike, sending Jimmy up to the Gurewitsches with her terms: absolute refusal. If treated, she must be treated at home. David broke off his urgent telephoning, his erect posture stiffening, the German in his accent breaching its Anglicized cosmopolitan coverings.

Ordering Jimmy and Edna to wait outside on the stairway, David faced down his patient. The exchange was terse: David vehement, Eleanor embittered.[12] Silence followed. Finally David told her that if she did not go to the hospital, he would have to come down to her bedside *nineteen times* during the night ahead.

She announced that her housekeeper could pack her bag.

That was that. Her surrender was for David's sake alone. Her anger remained, implacable, pointing the finger. Her embarrassment, however, at having drawn the house to a sword's-point standstill was so great that on her first night back three weeks later, she would urgently ask David to tell Edna that she intended to "behave better."

She went quietly to Columbia-Presbyterian—her fourth hospitalization. But now she put her foot down: no visitors, no unnecessary tests, no more teams of experts arguing how to save their famous patient, no more pitying looks. Just as when she first became an orphan, later lost her second child in infancy, still later became her husband's partner in poliomyelitis, and more recently as the President's widow, she could not bear to be pitied. She responded by sympathizing with the person offering sympathy.

Letting herself be hospitalized "for David's sake" appeared possibly to be paying off this time. Aplastic anemia was heard of no more, and a new chest X-ray showed atypical results, which meant the doctors had no choice but to consider the possibility that David was right: tuberculosis would explain a lot of things.

Eleanor tried to dial back their anxieties by letting them treat her like a sick old woman. ("I tried to be good and do what I was told, hoping to get out as quickly as possible."[13]) She was, in fact, paler than ever, covered with bruises, an oxygen tank giving her some relief from shortness of breath.

From yet another huddle of the Columbia team came the theory that the cause of the fever was tuberculosis—according to David a re-activation of Eleanor's old infection, misdiagnosed by a British doctor as pleurisy after her visit to the Front in 1919, and now reacquired, possibly during one of her hospitalizations, although the doctors con-sidered prednisone the more likely source, since prolonged treatment with corticosteroids runs the risk of reactivating healed tuberculosis, which it did in Eleanor's case, but with a further twist.[14] On predni-sone, she had become reinfected with an untreatable form of tubercu-losis.[15]

The Columbia team now began a protocol to rule out "miliary" tuberculosis, a rare form that might explain the severity and per-sistence of ER's fevers. Because the latest X-ray showed no sign of TB spreading to the lungs, the team had no way to rule out tuberculosis in the bone marrow itself except by attempting a relatively dangerous biopsy. For this, David approached a prominent New York surgeon, Edmund Goodman, who agreed to perform the procedure as well as to obey David's one additional request: the surgeon was not to follow the usual protocol and visit the patient before the operation. Goodman found this unfathomable but took the biopsy as directed; and when he followed his own ritual of tiptoeing into the recovery room the next morning to check for bleeding around the incision, Eleanor stirred, of-fered an apology, and told Goodman that she disapproved of his being barred from seeing her before the procedure. She was sorry, he later recalled Eleanor saying, "to meet me at this stage in her life, as she had no desire to live in failing health."[16]

For the time being, the bone-marrow biopsy only started the clock on another long waiting period for answers—four to six weeks for a culture—and raised difficult questions about Eleanor's treatment. For if a bone-marrow biopsy had been performed as early as the Rip Van Winkle warning in April 1960—or even in August 1962—Eleanor would have had to undergo a painful procedure, but with those results, she and David—or an oncologist, if David had been wiser about recusal—could have been far more sure of what was causing the trouble and how to treat it.

But David, a recovered tuberculosis patient, saw himself standing alone with the disease. "It was left for me to make that diagnosis 40 days ago," he would tell Joe Lash as things continued downhill far into October. "Others should have made it. The dirty linen will come out," he vowed, casting a shadow over the Columbia-Presbyterian Medical Center that would last for years.[17]

NOW HER SUFFERING BEGAN IN earnest.

Chronic illness and rehabilitation, which had so often taken the place of love's transactions—sorrow, depression, extreme self-abnegation—brought back her time-honored response to disease. Turning to the wall, she would now live by will alone.

Waiting forty days for a lab culture was absurd. Every medical and personal account of Eleanor Roosevelt circa October 11, 1962, unmistakably describes a dying woman.

She had spent her whole life discovering the strength of her character. She could have given up so many times before. Now she had the guts to go home, to die in peace. But David wouldn't let her.

Neither would he recuse himself. "He saw himself as a savior, which is probably why he was such a good physio-therapist," commented a colleague at Columbia-Presbyterian. "He made her story a metaphor for his existence. He loved the story that the common-sense GP made the diagnosis when the big professor experts at the university missed it. That was his story, and when he was later telling his romantic tales about how he tried to save Mrs. Roosevelt and the doctors killed her, he was selective in the evidence and denying of the truth."[18]

Accordingly, even now, a biopsy would have moved things along. But the Columbia team, at David's pressing insistence, treated Eleanor "empirically," starting her on an anti-tuberculosis drug therapy with *two* of the three antimicrobial drugs then used to fight the disease in all its known forms.[19] It was another peculiar choice, and not good medicine, nor the most responsible treatment, since its efficacy depended on being taken in a consistent and prolonged manner, and Eleanor had already begun hiding pills by the dozen under her lip and further back in her mouth, then disposing of them when she was left alone.

Five days after the two medications were started, the fever returned. By October 12, Eleanor was on fire—105 degrees. "Patient very miserable with temperature rising," recorded a nurse on October 10.[20]

The third drug of the newly standard anti-tuberculosis regimen, P-aminosalicylic acid, known as PASA (1949),[21] could have been added to the streptomycin (1943) and isoniazid (1952),[22] and should have been, according to doctors reviewing records of the case in later years.[23] Certainly, that should have been enough to release Eleanor to go home.

She spent six more days in the hospital without any improvement and no answers. David brought his patient home in a small ambulance, and was appalled to find photographers and reporters waiting on East Seventy-Fourth Street. Anna had tipped them off. Eleanor still out of sight inside the vehicle, David made his appeal quietly and carefully: "Mrs. Roosevelt has been so good to you all her life," he said to photographers around the front door of Number 55. "Won't you let her come home without taking any pictures?" To which Anna shouted, "They're only doing their job."

The AP wire photo circled the globe showing Mrs. Roosevelt being carried inside on a stretcher, her face bloated and hair a fright.

But she was home, and her only regret was that she had forgotten to say a word of thanks to the stretcher-bearers. As for David, she held back until they were upstairs in the quiet of her apartment. "I *told* you to ask them to take only two pictures. Then they would have gone away."

ELEANOR'S "BUG," AS SHE CALLED it, remained a mystery to medical science for the next seven days. Then, on October 26, the bone-marrow culture began reproducing itself.

At last, David had his results. He now had a curable disease to treat: *M. tuberculosis.* "It shows we're on the right track," he told the press.[24]

Her children were stony. The "prolonged suffering," they told Joe Lash, "was exactly the way our mother did not want to go."[25]

But from everything David knew about Mrs. Roosevelt—as, impossibly, he still called her—he was certain that she would turn every ounce of her legendary will to fighting the disease as soon as he told her what it was. After all, *she* had helped *him* find the strength for a TB cure! She had walked a mile and back just to bring him soup through the fog at Shannon.

David brought home his "cheering" news to East Seventy-Fourth Street and rushed up the stairs to Eleanor.

Her chances to survive, he told her, had just increased "five-thousand percent."

She did not seem to understand: *He was going to save her*. David bent to speak into her ear: "We can cure you!"

"No, David," she said, firmly. "I want to die."[26]

ON NOVEMBER 6, HER BLOOD pressure plummeted. Two days earlier she had suffered what appeared to be a stroke, and had not recognized anyone since Adlai Stevenson had briefly left the Cuban Missile Crisis to come to her sickbed.[27]

Confined there, she was hardly recognizable to a world that had just survived its near-extinction.

Then it was Election Day again, and a story buried on page four of the *Miami News* indicated how serious her illness really was. It had finally come down to *this*: "Mrs. Roosevelt Can't Vote, Even As Absentee."[28] No one had thought to request an absentee ballot, or guessed she would do anything but vote as usual in Hyde Park on Election Day.

"I find myself praying," said Anna, "that whatever is the very best for her happens and happens quickly."[29]

HER SUFFERING ENDED AT 6:15 p.m., Wednesday, November 7, 1962—thirty years to the day after her husband's election to the first of his four terms as President. Anna was with her, as were Franklin Jr. and John. Elliott came on from Miami, and Jimmy flew from the West Coast. By most accounts her heart failed at the end, "beneath the burden of her illness." In one sense, her medical condition was understood to be the burden of being Eleanor Roosevelt; in another, of being David Gurewitsch's patient. One twenty-first-century bioethicist examining Eleanor's end-of-life care in a case study published in the

American Journal of Medicine, concluded that while most ethical standards for care of the dying were violated by ER's physicians in their desperate attempts to save her, "Gurewitsch's own retrospective angst over Roosevelt's treatment, coupled with ancient precedents proscribing futile or maleficent interventions (or both), along with an already growing awareness of the importance of respect for patients' wishes in the 1960s, suggest that even by 1962 standards, her end-of-life care was misguided. Nevertheless, one wonders whether a present-day personal physician of a patient as prominent as Roosevelt would have behaved differently."[30]

In November 1962, some of the children believed that a mistake had been made in their mother's diagnosis and final treatment. An autopsy became inevitable, which at least solved the problem of honoring the main point in Eleanor's instructions for burial: *I want Dr. David Gurewitsch or any doctor in charge to open veins to be sure I am dead.*

During the night of November 7, David and three other doctors, including Alfred Gellhorn, performed the procedure, discovering that "a remarkable amount" of tuberculosis bacteria had spread throughout her body, and that, unlike most patients, Eleanor had been unable to produce the cells and proteins to fight off the infection, in part due to prednisone treatment.

The autopsy also revealed an unexpected finding. Laboratory results showed that ER's strain of tuberculosis was resistant to the two drugs she had received—in fact to all known anti-tuberculosis therapies. She had probably come into contact with someone with an active, drug-resistant form of the disease. "On prednisone," summed up the findings, "which made her susceptible, she had become reinfected with an untreatable form of tuberculosis."[31]

By daybreak no one was more relieved by this finding than David, who told Joe Lash that "an enormous sense of relaxation" had come over him. "Nothing," he said, "could have been done to save her."[32] Years later Gurewitsch would reflect for Joe Lash upon the suffering he and his colleagues had inflicted upon their patient with their endless tests and ineffectual treatments. After their interview, Lash observed: "[David] had not done well by Mrs. R. toward the end. She had told him that if her illness flared up again and fatally that she did not want to linger on and expected him to save her from the protracted, helpless, dragging out of suffering. But he could not do it. When the time came, his duty as a doctor prevented him."[33]

For months after Eleanor's death, David repeatedly sought out physicians with whom he could talk about the case. One of them was Dr. Helen Gavin, who had been Elizabeth Read's physician, and lived with Esther Lape in Connecticut after Read died in 1943. Gavin had been a pioneer in tuberculosis treatment at Bellevue Hospital, and David would come to Salt Meadow, the house Gavin now shared with Lape, and sit on the floor at her feet, going over each step of Eleanor's treatment.

One medical truth stood out as Gavin listened to Gurewitsch. "Hardest luck for a doctor that his patient should have a form of TB nobody had ever heard of," said Gavin. "He will never get over not having diagnosed TB of the bone marrow earlier."[34]

Her funeral was on a grim chilly day, the 11th of November. Some years earlier, she had advised Lorena Hickok not to let anyone "hold memorial meetings for me." She found such services "cruel to those who really love you & miss you," and they "meant nothing to the others except an obligation fulfilled." Certainly, they "could mean nothing to the spirit in another sphere, if it is there at all!"[35]

In any case, she would consent to burial rites and wanted Charlie Curnan, her groundskeeper and driver, and Les Entrup, of the Hyde Park Luncheonette, to be her only pallbearers.[36] As for anyone else attending, "I'd like to be remembered happily, if that is possible," she proposed. "If that can't be, then I'd rather be forgotten."[37]

UNDER SILVERY WHITE SKIES, THE President of the United States, and the vice president, two ex-presidents, three first ladies (present, past, and future), the chief justice of the United States and an associate justice, the senior senator from Tennessee, the governor of New York, president of the General Assembly and representatives of several nations at the United Nations, the mayor of New York, and three past cabinet members formed what looked like a state occasion as they gathered into St. James's off the Albany Post Road. Behind the gaunt parish church a small flat gravestone marked the one loss like no other in Eleanor's life of too many burials—that of her son: *Franklin D. Roosevelt, March 18—Nov. 1, 1909.*

She may have wanted to go unmemorialized, but seating in the narrow church and for the burial afterward proved, First Lady Jacqueline Kennedy observed, "as complicated as an Inauguration."[38] Twinned memorial services would follow, one in Washington at the National Cathedral, the other at the Cathedral Church of St. John the Divine on Morningside Heights.

In the tight pews, Eleanor's four big sons rose above the other mourners to sing the first two hymns, "Abide with Me," and "Rock of Ages."[39] Anna had organized everything. "You made us all feel as if we were private people," the first lady later told her, "and could share your sadness—and be with your family as people and not as Presidents and Governors and Chief Justices—all the long parade of titles and black limousines that could have turned it into a state occasion—and the private feeling would have been lost."[40]

Mrs. Kennedy reached back to 1945, to one of America's most painful and magnificent transfers of power: "You gave us something," Jackie told Anna, echoing the just-widowed Eleanor's baton-passing to Harry Truman, "when we were the ones who should have been giving to you."[41]

The final hymn, No. 172, "Now the Day is Over," had been written for schoolchildren in the England of Queen Victoria, whose tiny childlike coffin Eleanor as a young woman had seen borne past. The hymn's author likened death to the close of a child's day of joyful play, cares at last put aside to release the spirit. Three years earlier, after a day in Jerusalem, Eleanor had recorded a similar exaltation.

She and David Gurewitsch had gone down into an excavation of the tombs of the Great Sanhedrin, the seventy-one rabbis appointed to sit as a tribunal in the ancient City of David. Coming back up into the sunlight of an April day in 1959, Eleanor decided that the nicest thing about the rabbis' crypts was that the land around them was being turned into a playground for children and that trees were planted there and that the view out over the valley was beautiful. People's desire for permanent graves buried deep under rock had seemed to her foolish:

"I would rather be out in the open," she ventured, "with the sky above me where my earthly remains can disappear rapidly. For my spirit, I am sure, will enjoy the soft rains and the sunshine and the white snow in winter and the fact that children can play happily in the garden."[42]

Yet now she would take her expected place in her federal family gravesite, just south of Franklin and the white bier whose precise dimensions he had measured, drawn, and directed to be set, east to west, alongside the graves—just as he had done with the heraldic apparatus for their wedding day.[43]

Shortly after 3 p.m., a gentle rain began to fall as the burial party entered the garden through an arch in the hemlock.[44] The plain silver walnut casket was lowered silently, covered by evergreen branches. Now the rector of St. James's consigned Eleanor's remains to the earth, pronouncing the whole world "one family orphaned" upon her loss.[45]

A West Point bugler played taps, the clear bitter notes of remembrance accumulating, until presently a bright light shone all around, drawing the eyes of the mourners to a cloud break over the river.[46] Sun rays converged upon the garden in which she had joined her husband. *Qui Plantavit Curabit*, after all: Sara had planted it, Franklin and Eleanor had tended it; together they had grown America. Now, on the snow-white stone, Eleanor settled the plain account of Franklin Delano Roosevelt, 1882–1945, and Anna Eleanor Roosevelt, 1884–1962.

The cloud break closed and a cold rain fell. Out beyond the hemlock hedge, below the ice pond and the fields, the river flowed back to the city of her birth.

ACKNOWLEDGMENTS

I met her once. She was my mother's boss, gliding over a jumble of cables and electronic equipment in the TV studio constructed on the stage of Brandeis University's Slosberg Music Center in Waltham, Massachusetts. I was four, and like practically everyone else, I asked Mrs. Roosevelt for something.

This was 1961. As the seer of the country, mobile trustee of an atomic age superpower, and world-circling investigator with an unusual range of sympathies, Eleanor Roosevelt had on her mind the most pressing needs of democracies old and new. Yet as airtime approached for another installment of *Prospects of Mankind*, her monthly educational program for WGBH-TV, here was one more request: Diana Michaelis's little boy wanted something.

Mrs. R. glided to a full stop. Time itself stopped as the white-haired lady leaned down and looked into my eyes. I believe I breathed out two words: *Juicy Fruit*.

She responded merrily, her eyes blue as gas jets, the big toothy smile luminous. I have no recollection of anything she said; I was held close by an intensely noticing gaze, which was so full of goodwill, it seemed to brim out of her eyes as light. I had never seen that: *actual goodness flowing out of a human being* and only long afterward realized how fortunate I was to have felt it full in the face at four.

By chance, forty years later, while starting research for a biography of the cartoonist Charles M. Schulz, I came close to that source again, this time in a basement beneath 200 Madison Avenue, coincidentally the site of Sara Delano Roosevelt's vanished town house, now the offices of United Media, formerly United Feature Syndicate. I had been granted access to examine cartons of correspondence marked Schulz/Peanuts/1950, the first year of the blockbuster comic strip, but was surprised and delighted to find—in alphabetically stored banker's boxes to the left of Schulz/Peanuts—extralong proof sheets of a newspaper column designated on the compositor's line: Roosevelt-MY DAY.

I took out a galley, drawn by a description of starlight from a sleeping porch. Another proof revealed that the columnist kept a pistol in her New York apartment. Yet another produced a recipe for "Some Mores a la Girl Scout," which I transcribed on the spot ("You toast the marshmallow slowly . . .") for my wife and kids. When a fourth galley brought to light the courageous public service of an Irish-born relative, George Hall of Flatbush, who happened to have been the first mayor of Brooklyn, I wondered if maybe there were *two* Eleanor Roosevelts, the way there had been another Winston Churchill. . . .

But, no, here in a 1943 column was the Mrs. Franklin D. Roosevelt of history, discussing her goals for Allied war policy in the same direct voice in which, six days a week, she shared a practical but continuously imaginative stream of consciousness about her friends, relatives, children, grandchildren, pets, friends, flower beds, luncheons and suppers, improvised desserts, and ceaseless visitors from all walks of life and around the world.

It was the same outflow of energy I had glimpsed at four. Well, of course this was *the* Mrs. Roosevelt. True to form, she had composed every "My Day" herself, always in the day itself, sometimes in less than an hour; and she never took a sick day or vacation: by the end, more than eight thousand pieces of writing. Only her husband's death as president and commander in chief had obliged her to put a crimp in the daily posting between friends—for four days. After FDR and World War II, the word count increased and the material became more consciously that of an international stateswoman, yet "My Day" went on appearing in the same women's or comics pages that now carried the small doings of an unloved roundheaded kid and a dog who would one day run for president.

Twenty minutes after promising myself "just one more galley," I had not lifted the lid on Charlie Brown and Snoopy. I was squatting like a fire starter over a nest of dry-leaf tinder, gently blowing on the glowing ember I hated to see go black.

AFTER BURNING A DECADE, I have incurred five outstanding debts.

The first is to Melanie Jackson, upon whose loyalty, confidence, and inspiring comradeship I depended more than ever before. Melanie turned aside thunderbolts to protect and support this work. I was especially lucky with *Eleanor* to have the full strength of her insight at home and advocacy abroad. Melanie's faultless radar for the needs of writers, editors, designers, translators, and readers exemplifies an ideal—a kind of UN agency of books in the global marketplace that publishing has become.

My second obligation is to the late Alice Mayhew of Simon & Schuster. Thanks to the strong support of past publisher David Rosenthal, *Eleanor* found its natural home with Alice. She warned me from the start that she would be tenacious, skeptical, prodding, fiercely realistic. But even Alice's legendary loyalty and gifts for narrative were sorely tested by my tendency to overcomplicate and Eleanor's to leave life unresolved. Fortunately, Alice was true to her word, pulling for the manuscript, chapter by chapter, year upon year; too many in the end.

Working right up to Christmas Eve with pages strewn around a hospital bed, she completed her last good fight with my defective prose. A little over a heartbreaking month later Alice was gone.

Young Eleanor Hillyer Parker bridged the decade of *Eleanor*, starting as a skillful summer intern still in high school; returning after an outstanding college career to serve as a whip-smart reader of early chapters; finally lending sustained editorial support, including an uncommon talent for omitting needless words. To Ellie Parker goes my third debt of thanks for all too often being the one hope upon which I relied for the future of book and country.

Luckily, Eleanor Roosevelt believed in protecting and guaranteeing individual freedom. Nothing could have forged a greater trust with her future biographers, scholars, and historians than the counterintuitive measure of making her personal and professional papers available for all to study. And yet, biographer beware. In the stacks of the Franklin D. Roosevelt Presidential Library and Museum in Hyde Park, New York, Eleanor's papers rise across 889.62 cubic feet—more than a million documents—their content traversing no fewer than nine ages of world history, from the Victorian era to the space age. And that's only the beginning—*President* Roosevelt also kept a few letters and other odds and ends you will need to see. Eleanor's paternal family of Oyster Bay Roosevelts and the 26th President also require looking into, as do the marginalized Livingston-Ludlow Halls of her mother's upbringing. Meanwhile, the roll call of significant Eleanor papers continues in no fewer than forty states from coast to coast; in Washington, DC, a single State Department file containing records of ER's achievements in human rights mounts to 198 archival boxes.

Bob Clarke, past supervisory archivist of the FDR Presidential Library, was my earliest high-altitude guide in Hyde Park, helping me to see exactly why a single volume life of Eleanor was needed. Veteran archivist Virginia H. Lewick also brought an impeccable clarity and needle-sharp precision to my research room inquiries. I am no less grateful to FDRL's present supervisory archivist, Kirsten Strigel Carter, and to her superb team, including Matthew C. Hanson; Sarah L. Navins; Patrick F. Fahy; and, in earlier years, Mark Renovitch; Sarah Malcolm; and Alycia Vivona.

Chris Brick, project director and editor of the incomparable Eleanor Roosevelt Papers Project (ERPP) at George Washington University, warmly welcomed me to the grown-ups' table of ER studies while keeping it as fun as the TV trays. I owe enormous thanks to ERPP's founder, the Eleanor Roosevelt authority Dr. Allida M. Black, for putting a click away the entire run of "My Day," among numerous other raw materials from broadcasting and print media never before accessible, let alone searchable.

I salute a number of master archivists—that rare, vanishing breed—particularly Wallace Finley Dailey, formerly of the Houghton Library at Harvard University; Jeffrey Flannery of the Library of Congress Manuscript Division; and the late Nicholas B. Scheetz, past manuscripts librarian in the Joseph Mark Lauinger Memorial Library at Georgetown University. This dream team of deeply knowledgeable and kindly pros shared their own insightful mapping of vast fields of Roosevelt timber, always with patience, a touch of hardheaded skepticism, and charitable good humor.

Special thanks to my admired comrade Timothy Dickinson, whose tutelary spirit, many kind prompts, and matchless storehouse of twentieth-century intelligence and literary grace crucially illuminated this portrait in its earliest stages.

I am also grateful to those kind partisans, professional and civilian, who helped me access previously unknown or unused material archives across the country. Brilliant Robert Nedelkoff served this book as field tactician, generously offering time and a rare talent for finding new or seldom-consulted sources, especially at the National Archives and Records Administration's presidential libraries, including the Herbert Hoover library; the John F. Kennedy library; and, Robert's home turf, the Richard Nixon library. At Texas Christian University's Mary Couts Burnett Library, Roger Rainwater, head of special collections, was uncommonly kind about a little-known reporter's reporter, Grace Halsell, and her eye-opening collection of papers from a brief stint as Dr. David Gurewitsch's ghost writer. Tara L. Key, Butler Library data sleuth and Antietam guitar slinger, generously read and reported on George Bye's letters. Lorna Prescott, a seasoned researcher, looked into the Helene M. Crooks Collection at Colby College.

I benefited especially from the independent thinking, loyalty, and rare ingenuity of Christopher Massie as he provided analysis of primary sources in the Houghton Library at Harvard, the Seeley G. Mudd Manuscript Library at Princeton, and newly opened sources at the New York Public Library's Manuscripts and Archives Division, especially the Arthur M. Schlesinger, Jr. Papers. Elizabeth Walker tirelessly and diligently consulted and interpreted archives for me in the early stages of documentation for a massive cast of principal characters. Emma Peabody brought her thoughtful eye to a summer's sleuthing in the Columbia Oral History Program.

My thanks to three friends for their generous support of this work: Joan Bingham, editor and book champion, for an early and important window-opening visit to Franklin and Mama's house in Hyde Park; Virginia Smyers Buxton, past rare-book librarian and bibliographer at Harvard's Widener Library, for indispensable material from the Arthur and Elizabeth Schlesinger Library on the History of Women in America and Boston's Francis A. Countway Library of

Medicine; and Joanne Turnbull, award-winning translator, and her husband, Nikolai Formozov, who parsed Eleanor's reports from the USSR of Nikita Khrushchev.

I could not have got very far without first immersing myself in Joseph P. Lash's voluminous Roosevelt scholarship, especially his personal interviews with every Eleanor player still alive, circa 1966–1971; or in Blanche Wiesen Cook's three-volume life and times. Anyone who attempts to cover Eleanor Roosevelt from cradle to grave owes a significant debt to Blanche Wiesen Cook, whose personal and political firepower led the way to a more complete ER. Looking into the same material from which others had fled, Cook rightly declared that omitting the Eleanor who had loved Lorena Hickok "simply cannot be done"—Eleanor Roosevelt, of all people, had to be faced for real.

To that end, I have benefited from the lives of a handful of women whose hearts and minds and work made them through the years "my Eleanors": Verinda Brown, Elizabeth Glascock Taylor, Caroline Speer Fisher, Abigail Friedman, Carrie Pointer, Mary Parkman Peabody, Ruth Agoos Villalovos, Caroline Kennedy Schlossberg, Emily Gloria Wilson, Marion Walton Putnam, Flora Miller Biddle, Barbara Freedman Berg, Sandra Nichols, Ellen Sulzberger Straus, Chris Prouty Rosenfeld, Ethel Skakel Kennedy, Mildred Faulkner Armstrong, Sally Fisher Carpenter, Judith Freed, Louisa Clark Spencer, Rose Burgunder Styron, Mabel Hobart Cabot, Betsy James Wyeth, Kristyne Loughran Bini, and Amie Bishop.

In a culture of 21st-century niches and silos, it's hard to conceive of, let alone accurately portray, FDR's personal power on the planetary scale it occupied for more than fifty years, from 1932 to 1982. To grasp the mana of Franklin Delano Roosevelt, I am in debt to Geoffrey C. Ward, who mastered FDR as no other biographer; William vanden Heuvel, generous with advice and tolerant of a newcomer's ignorance; Jed Willard, ingenious director of global engagement at the FDR Foundation at Harvard's Adams House; and the late Alan Brinkley, whose books were an indispensable guide to the history of liberalism and the use of government as the foundation of individual freedom.

Among Eleanorites, Gore Vidal and Henry Morgenthau III welcomed me backstage and into the wings before bowing out themselves. Among living Roosevelts, Eleanor Seagraves may be as close as one can come in the 21st century to her grandmother; I am very grateful for the privilege of interviewing and corresponding with the remarkable Ellie Seagraves.

My maternal grandparents, a young Amherst-and-Smith couple when they joined the Settlement movement in 1914, later worked with Eleanor Roosevelt in metropolitan New York's expanding world of higher education, as my mother did, still later, in the pioneering days of public television. I have a special obligation to Ordway Tead and Clara Murphy's South End Settlement House correspondence and Diana Tead Michaelis's personal and professional papers; and to her colleagues on *Prospects of Mankind*, especially Henry Morgenthau III, Virginia Kassel, Dr. Beatrice Braude, but none more generous or enduring than the brilliant Paul Noble.

This book also drew inspiration from those among my parents' Cambridge and Washington generation who directly and indirectly passed along their experience of the living Eleanor and Franklin Roosevelt and the world they made: Wilton S. Dillon; Elizabeth L. Eisenstein; Eliot and Joan Elisofon; Edith U. Fierst; John Kenneth and Kitty Galbraith; C. A. Gopalan; Stephen Graubard; Gilbert A. Harrison and Anne Blaine McCormick Harrison; Gerald and Nina Holton; Frances Humphrey Howard; Heyward and Sheila Isham; E. J. Kahn, Jr. and Eleanor Munro; Philip M. and Hannah Greeley Kaiser; Joseph and Polly Kraft; John L. and Katheryne Straub Loughran; Langdon P. Marvin, Jr.; Gjon Mili; Eugene and Chris Rosenfeld; James H. Rowe; Walter Ruth; Arthur M. Schlesinger, Jr.; Marian Cannon Schlesinger; Lisa Sergio; John Everly "Jack" Skuce; Robert Snyder; and Dorothy and Norman Zinberg. Special thanks to the late Page Huidekoper Wilson for her insights about our embassy in London during the successive ambassadorships of Robert W. Bingham and Joseph P. Kennedy; and to Ronnie Dugger, my spirit guide to iconoclastic American politics, for introducing me to Maury Maverick's Texas. Patricia Blake prepared me for the work of decades, long ago teaching me how and when to use a dictionary.

For interviews and for fresh material and perspective on ER's life and its people, I thank: Anna V. Bain; Clara Y. Bingham; Arifa Boehler; Rosanne Cash; Maureen Corr; Mary Costa; Peter Davis; Edna Gurewitsch; Ray Lamontagne; Albert Maysles; Frederick Eberstadt; Charles Elliott; Stacey Goodman; Rick Hamlin; Annette Hunter; Stephen B. Ives, Jr.; Lowell Johnston; Tom Lowenstein and Jennifer Littlefield; Robin B. MacDonald; Jane Plimpton Plakias; Alex Shoumatoff; Arne J. Steinberg; James W. Symington; and Julie Symington. Special thanks to members of the Collegiate School Class of '62 who vividly remembered Mrs. Roosevelt as their commencement speaker; and to Doug Stern of United Media, a kind man running "an East Coast syndicate."

For making letters and other informative material available, and for connecting me to the people, places, and continuing energy of Eleanor's political life, my thanks to: Nanci Aydelotte; Jonathan Bumas; Sam Campbell; Lorig Charkoudian; Bridget Colman; Jay and Cindy Cook; Patsy Costello; Linda Semans Donovan; Kathleen Durham; Marian Wright Edelman; Charlotte M. Fisher; Randy Florke; Leymah Gbowee; Judy Wiener Goodhue; Barbara Green; Andy and Jennifer Hammerstein; Joan Morgenthau Hirschhorn; Cy Irving; Caroline Rose Kaplan; Summer Rose Kennedy; Wilson Kidde; Barbara Landreth; Lilah Larson; Sandra Leoncavallo; Sean Patrick Maloney; Stuart Marwell; Selby McPhee; the late Phoebe Goodhue Millkin; the late Robert Morgenthau; Diana Nyad; Samantha Power; Richard and Heidi Rieger; Susie Rodriquez; Susan Schneck Sawyers; Ileene Smith; Borden W. Stevenson; Robbyn Swan; the late Robert Wood Tate; Katrina vanden Heuvel; Peter Vynhal; Liz Watson; Elizabeth Weinstock; Putnam County schoolteacher Christine Zeolla; and the exemplar of an Eleanor-inspired gender-barrier-breaking public servant, the late Joanne H. Alter, commissioner of the Metropolitan Sanitary District of Greater Chicago.

Acknowledgment must be made of a working trip to the 2010 Obama White House with Peter W. Kaplan and Klara Glowczewska of Condé Nast; with special thanks, indeed, to First Lady Michelle Obama and her staff for a Map Room interview and Blue Room meet-and-greet that added depth and clarity to the stereopticon view of the President's house that appears in these pages.

On the Woods Road north of Tivoli, New York, I was twice given the key to the house of Eleanor's youth. Strangely, in the seventy years since Uncle Vallie vacated Oak Lawn, the place had had just one other owner: a group of ten Estonian fishing families who came up from Brooklyn on fair-weather weekends. Fortunately, they had never spent a dime on improvements; benign neglect produced a kind of preservationist's miracle: in 2010, every original floorboard, newel post, and wallpaper remained. Special thanks to owners Rob and Sonia Iannucci; and to the talented preservationist Huntley Gill, associate of Guardia Architects; and to the Rev. Canon James Elliott Lindsley, for a clear-eyed view into the closed world of Clermont and its river families.

Dr. Deborah S. Gardner, resident scholar at Roosevelt House Public Policy Institute at Hunter College, made no less meaningful another important Roosevelt landscape: the double town house at 17–19 East Sixty-Fifth Street; Hunter's president Jennifer Raab was also supportive. Professor Ellen Condliffe Lagemann opened her Bard College classroom in Sullivan County's Woodbourne Correctional Facility to Eleanor's *Autobiography*; heartfelt thanks to the Bard Prison Initiative and Ellen's students.

Sandra Nichols returned from the world's villages to bring Val-Kill to life. Flora Fraser, more prescient than ever, gave concise grandmotherly advice, inspiring the confidence she correctly predicted would be indispensable for Eleanor's life. Eleanor Bingham Miller remembered Eleanor Roosevelt's visits to Glenview, Kentucky, as well as three dangerous North Atlantic crossings her grandfather Ambassador Robert Worth Bingham made to plead with FDR to stop Hitler. Tom Beller, shaman of neighborhoods, arranged a visit through the kindness of Gary Sernovitz and Molly Pulda to Eleanor's fourth-floor-rear hideout on 20 East Eleventh Street. Dr. Seth Lederman opened doors in New York City's medical community. For informative emails following Dr. Barron H. Lerner's talk during grand rounds at the Columbia University Medical Center ("Did Eleanor Roosevelt Die of a Medical Error?"), I am grateful to Dr. Timothy C. Wang (chief, Division of Digestive and Liver Diseases), and Dr. John N. Loeb (professor emeritus of medicine, College of Physicians and Surgeons of Columbia University); for interviews, I thank Dr. Jay I. Meltzer (clinical professor of medicine, emeritus, College of Physicians and Surgeons of Columbia University) and Dr. Barron H. Lerner (professor of medicine and sociomedical sciences, New York-Presbyterian Hospital) whose ground-breaking work, "Charting the Death of Eleanor Roosevelt" (2012), sparked my research in the FDR Library's primary sources.

My old friend Dr. Michael F. Gilson, cardiologist at Rhode Island Hospital, helped me understand Eleanor's Roosevelt grandfather's final illness. Robert L. Peabody and his colleague William Haddad provided impeccable legal counsel; Bob, boon companion of decades, acquainted me over the years with FDR's Groton School family, which happened also to be Bob's family circle. Ever-expanding thanks to Flora Miller Biddle, from whom has flowed a lifetime of inspiration, no less in this century than the last, and no less for *Eleanor* than for *Mushroom*; this time, sharing insights from the world of her mother, who came of age under the same Whartonian customs, migrations, and tragedies Eleanor survived with her Hall aunts.

I am grateful to the following biographers, historians, and scholars for their generosity in consulting on their subjects or mine: Jonathan Alter (FDR), A. Scott Berg (Max Perkins; Alice Roosevelt Longworth; Sam Goldwyn; Katharine Hepburn; Charles Lindbergh; Woodrow Wilson; Thurgood Marshall); Michael Beschloss (FDR, Joseph P. Kennedy; JFK; Khrushchev), Emily Bingham (Stephen Foster), Jane Brown (Dorothy Elmhirst), Katherine Bucknell (Christopher Isherwood), Robert Caro (Joseph P. Lash), Ron Chernow (FDR & ER), Kathleen Dalton (Theodore Roosevelt; Mary Margaret McBride), Nigel Hamilton (FDR), James Kaplan (Frank Sinatra), Caroline Kennedy (ER at Hiroshima; Bill of Rights), Maxwell T. Kennedy (WW II's Pacific theater), Michael Korda (Eisenhower; Avedon), Kristie Miller (Isabella Greenway), Patricia O'Toole (TR), Susan Quinn (Lorena Hickok), Cynthia Eagle Russett (Rev. William Turner Levy), Stephen C. Schlesinger (Edward Stettinius; Arthur Vandenberg; creation of the United Nations), Michael Shnayerson (Harry Belafonte), Sally Bedell Smith (William Paley; JFK; Bill and Hillary Clinton), Sam Tanenhaus (Whittaker Chambers; William F. Buckley, Jr.), Evan Thomas (Eisenhower; Nixon), Susan Ware (Molly Dewson), Steve Weinberg (Armand Hammer), Ted Widmer (Lincoln, JFK).

I owe thanks to the Westchester Library System and to the professionals and volunteers throughout who contribute to its rapid circulation. Two branches in particular served this book: Mount Vernon, which never discarded its rare Roosevelt-era holdings; and Bedford Free, at which Ann Cloonan and her team, especially the long-serving Carol Best, never failed to make welcome a reader of strange old "holds."

In an age of uncertainty and exhaustion, I have not been without brave friends or admired colleagues: John Abbott, Max Abelson, Joel Achenbach, Fred Adair, Renata Adler, Kurt Anderson, Carl Anthony, Adam Begley, Katherine Beitner, Christopher Benfey, Gioia Bini, Andrew Blauner, Carol Bundy, the late Chris Busa, Nancy Butkus, Michael Cannell, Murray Carpenter, William Cohan, Joe Conason, Richard Corman, Tim Duggan, Peter Emerson, John Farr, Rick Finkelstein, Paul Friedland, Deb Futter, Michael Gately, Joy Harris, Randy and Perry Howze, Robert Hubbell and Jill Bickett, Walter Isaacson, Mitchell Ivers, Donald Jurney, Charles Kaiser, Kathleen Klech, Anne Kreamer, Philip Kunhardt, Julie List, Liz Logan, William Ivey Long, Bevis Longstreth, Jennifer Maguire, Bob Massie, Philip McFarland, Susan Morrison, Mary Murphy, Lucy Nathanson, Adam Platt, Rich Read, Stephen Reily, David Remnick, Lillian Ross, Penelope Rowlands, Max Rudin, Paul Rudnick, Betsy Schaper, Susan Scheftel, Eric Schlosser, John Burnham Schwartz, Charles Scribner III, John Seabrook, Charlotte Sheedy, Roger Smith, Terry Steiner, Catherine Steiner-Adair, Richard Stengel, Daniel Stephens, Cyndi Stivers, Alexandra Styron, Doug Stumpf, Anne Tate, Griff Thomas, Glyn Vincent, Barbara Wasserman, Nicholas Fox Weber, Katharine Weber, Lizzie Widdicombe, Susan Furlow Widdicombe, and Laura Yorke.

Everlasting appreciation to my editors Jane Amsterdam, Lisa Chase, and Anne Fadiman.

Thanks to the pros: Thomas R. Rietano and the Nelson/Rietano Group; Nicholas Tarrant and the Ball Baker Leake team, especially Cindy Fong and Kari Aaman-Streeter; Duff Pacifico; John Dignan; Thomas W. Nash; William Rosenfeld; John Gerson; Mark Banschick; Kevin Kindlin; James Stellar; Liliana and Breddy Alfaro; Mandeep Sandhu and the Solutions Group team of tech wizards; Susan Armstrong-Magidson and Ross Mill Farm. Special thanks to Michelle Press of Getty Images, Andy Franklin of NBC News, and Peter London of HarperCollins.

To my community at SPF—Shawn Malon; Michael Alfinito; Thomas Northey; Stephen Sullivan; and, most especially, Melissa M. Romagnoli—love and gratitude.

I benefited from the care and judgment of Lisa Chase's reading of an early version of the manuscript; Elizabeth Bogner improved a later version. I have Susanna Styron and Elizabeth Hauge Sword to thank for their confidence and for coming to my support and advocating for my cause.

I am grateful to Nancy Roosevelt Ireland, literary executor of her grandmother's estate, for abiding kindness and for permission to quote from the writings of Eleanor Roosevelt.

At Simon & Schuster, I am fortunate to be published by Jonathan Karp and his incomparable team. Bob Bender adopted the orphaned *Eleanor* and made significant improvements in every aspect of the book. My thanks to Johanna Li, Bob's deputy; and to Team Eleanor: Julia Prosser, Brianna Scharfenberg, and Elise Ringo; art director Jackie Seow; designer Carly Loman; production editor, Lisa Healy; and copy editors Rick Willett and Nate Knaebel. To each of Alice Mayhew's talented deputies—Jonathan Cox, Stuart Roberts, Amar Deol, and especially Maria Mendez—there's almost no describing how great and important each of you was to Alice's shelves of symphonic liberalism.

Hers, alas, was not the book's only loss. I mourn Laurie Schneider Adams, Patricia Blake, and James Chace, whose close readings would have improved this work. The historian Robert K. Massie, my teacher in college, died before I could make good on our final *Catherine*-for-*Eleanor* exchange. Bob—a good friend and wonderful writer both—showed what could be done with spider silk when webbed correctly, day after day, in a quiet corner of the barn. Deborah Karl, daughter, agent, wife, mother, friend, and homeschooler of life writers, warmly shared lessons from Irvington, including the Golden Spike Theory of Biography: laying track from the ends to the middle.

In each of the past three decades, I have been inspired by the high standards and comprehending hearts of Betsy James Wyeth and Andrew Wyeth; I am saddened that Betsy, who inspired and safeguarded the freedom and integrity of my biography of Andy's father, is gone from the world and the work that she loved.

Sally Fisher Carpenter has been—and thank heavens remains—an essential friend and an accelerant in my writing life for forty years. Dr. Charles C. J. Carpenter, world-recognized infectious disease specialist and professor emeritus of medicine at Brown University, generously consulted on Eleanor's end-of-life treatment and its protocols but did not live to see how helpful he was to this work. The same must be said for Eugenie Hess Voorhees, Mary "Mimi" Havemeyer Beman, Capt. Mike B. Edwards (USN Ret.), B. H. Friedman, and David Halberstam.

Above all, I grieve the loss of my father during these years. Tender thanks to my caring Bishop stepsiblings and their families, to my brother, Peter, and to my beloved stepmother, Caroline Mallory Michaelis, a Tidewater granddaughter of FDR's US Navy, for her devotion through every hour of Dad's long enduring.

I am ever increasingly grateful for the emotional support of several beloved lifelong friends who stepped up during this project, especially Peter Harper Alson, Peter Ryerson Fisher, Jackson Friedman, and Max Kennedy. For fifty years Julie Agoos has weathered all, lifting worries and inspiring better work through her ferocious brilliance and constancy.

For being in my corner, I thank Christopher Bartle, Joan Bingham, Martin Bourke, Katherine Bucknell, Libby Cameron, Sarah Chace, Mars Child, Katherine Goguen, David D. Irving and Murr Lebey, Macculloch M. Irving, Charlie Kaplan, Peter Walker Kaplan, Rob Kaplan, Andrew S. Karsch, Jay Kernis, Jacqueline Kinghan, Ellen Lagemann, Mary Landa, Lucinda Lang, Margaret Lenzner and the late Terry Lenzner, Sally Munro Murray, Steve Ney, Liz Hillyer and Steve Parker, Bob and Laura Peabody, Tom and Margaret Rietano, Keith Runyon, Walter Sadowski and Laurie Donovan, Matt and Betsy Salinger, Nancylee Schlegel, Susan Schorin, Leslie Spencer, Loulou Spencer, Rosalind Roth Steiner, Jay and Bonnie Stockwell, Ditto Tawil, Helga Testorff, Griff Thomas, J. Robinson West, Jamie Wyeth and the late Phyllis Mills Wyeth. Special thanks to Matthew Rogers, for his enthusiastic faith in the book; and Ted Widmer, to whom I must also pay tribute as an inspiriting historian, writer, and friend, but especially, echoing Sherm Feller on a clear summer night, as "a great American."

My fourth debt is to A. Scott Berg, who inspired with his writing and his books the kind of work that, more prolific though I might have been, became my life. Scott's friendship has also been a lifeline, sustained by encouragement, vigilance, and love. During production of this book, he very kindly pitched in to suggest dozens of detailed improvements and corrections informed by decades of scholarship in twentieth-century lives adjacent to Eleanor's. I am indebted to Scott for his masterful reading of the manuscript, as I am ever thankful to Kevin McCormick for his dedication to excellence.

My fifth and final debt is to Nancy Steiner, my beautiful wife, and to the late Peter W. Kaplan, my cornerman in big-city journalism and my Pally for good. In 2009, each in their respective ways made it possible to remarry, to sign a contract for Untitled Biography of Eleanor Roosevelt, and to feel with a full heart that happy days were here again. When Peter died, a piece of the work went with him; what remains I lovingly dedicate to Nan, the book's first auditor and complete reader and my greatest champion.

Nan in these *Eleanor* years also knitted together the robust, loving extended blended family of Steiner, Fraiman, Adair, Smith, Michaelis, Bingham, and Finnerty. I thank Nan, above all, and Clara, no less. To both these tolerant, generous women, my deepest thanks. The same to Clara and to Joe Finnerty, in loco parentis during my longer absences from the family; and to my stepdaughters, Kate Fraiman, for seeing text and writer through more than one computer meltdown, and Anne Fraiman, for coming to the rescue in meltdowns, period.

I complete my task with a father's pride in Jamie, Henry, and Diana. I can never make the crossing Michael Michaelis made—Weimar Berlin to wartime London to postwar Boston—but I can gratefully thank my sons, Jamie and

Henry, for lifting burdens from my shoulders as you became men yourselves; and my daughter, Diana, for inspiring and spanning these pages, from the irrepressible girl on a school field trip at the United Nations to the young woman joyously taking charge of her world. "Things don't work out," acknowledged Grandma Diana, "and yet, they do."

NOTES ABBREVIATIONS

ABG	Anna Bulloch Gracie (*Paternal Great-Aunt*)
ARC	Anna Roosevelt Cowles (*Aunt*)
ARH	Anna Roosevelt Halsted (*Daughter*)
ARHR	Anna Rebecca Hall Roosevelt (*Mother*)
ARL	Alice Roosevelt Longworth (*Cousin*)
AW	Arthur Willert
BWR	Belle Willard Roosevelt
CBD	Curtis Bean Dall (*Son-in-law*)
CDP	Caroline Drayton Phillips
CRAC	Corinne Robinson Alsop Cole (*Cousin*)
CRR	Corinne Roosevelt Robinson (*Aunt*)
DDB	Dorothy Dow Butturff
DG	David Gurewitsch
EBR	Elliott Bulloch Roosevelt (*Father*)
EFM	Elinor Fatman Morgenthau
EHM	Edith Livingston "Pussie" Hall Morgan (*Aunt*)
EKR	Edith Kermit Roosevelt (*Aunt*)
EL	Esther Lape
ELHM	Elizabeth Livingston "Tissie" Hall Mortimer (*Aunt*)
EM	Earl Miller
E2	Elliott Roosevelt (*Son, 3rd*)
ER	Eleanor Roosevelt
ER2	Eleanor Roosevelt Wotkyns
FDR	Franklin Delano Roosevelt (*Spouse; 32nd U.S. President*)
FDR2	Franklin D. Roosevelt, Jr. (*Son, 4th*)
FP	Frances Perkins
FSW	Florence S. Willert
GD	George Draper, MD
GHR	Gracie Hall Roosevelt (*Brother*)

HM2	Henry Morgenthau, Jr. (*U.S. Secretary of the Treasury*)
HM3	Henry Morgenthau III (*TV Producer*)
HST	Harry S. Truman
ISFGK	Isabella Selmes Ferguson Greenway King
JAR	John Aspinwall Roosevelt (*Son, 5th*)
JB	John Boettiger (*Son-in-law*)
JEL	James Elliott Lindsley
JH	James Halsted (*Son-in-law*)
JPL	Joseph P. Lash
JR	James Roosevelt (*Father-in-law*)
JR2	James Roosevelt (*Son, 1st*)
JRR	James Roosevelt "Rosy" Roosevelt (*Brother-in-law*)
JWA	Joseph Wright Alsop V
JWP	Justine Wise Polier
LAH	Lorena Alice Hickok
LMH	Louis McHenry Howe
MBR	Martha Bulloch "Mittie" Roosevelt (*Grandmother*)
MCS	Marie Claire Souvestre
MCT	Malvina Cynthia "Tommy" Thompson
MD	Marion Dickerman
MDS	Margaret "Daisy" Suckley
MHG	Maude Hall Gray (*Aunt*)
ML	Marguerite "Missy" LeHand
MLLH	Mary Livingston Ludlow Hall (*Grandmother*)
NC	Nancy Cook
RWL	Robert Williamson Lovett, MD
SDR	Sara Delano Roosevelt (*Mother-in-law*)
SLP	Susan Ludlow Parish (*Mother's Cousin*)
STE	Stephen T. Early
TR1	Theodore Roosevelt, Sr. (*Grandfather*)
TR	Theodore Roosevelt (*Uncle; 26th U.S. President*)
TR3	Theodore Roosevelt, Jr. (*Cousin*)
WSC	Winston Spencer Churchill
WW	Woodrow Wilson

Selected Archives and Manuscript Collections

AEMP	Agnes Elizabeth Ernst Meyer Papers, 1853–1972, Library of Congress Manuscript Division, LCMD
AERP	Anna Eleanor Roosevelt Papers, Part 1, 1884–1964, Franklin D. Roosevelt Library & Museum, FDRL
AFP	Alsop Family Papers, Houghton Library, Harvard University
AMSP	Arthur M. Schlesinger, Jr., Papers, 1922–2007, Manuscripts and Archive Division, the New York Public Library, NYPL
ARHP	Anna Roosevelt Halstead Papers, FDRL
AWP	Arthur Willert Papers, Manuscripts & Archives, Sterling Memorial Library, Yale University
BAP	Bernard Asbell Papers, University Archives, Pennsylvania State University Libraries, PSU
CDPP	Caroline Drayton Phillips Papers, Schlesinger Library, Harvard University
CRP	Curtis Roosevelt Papers, FDRL
CUOHROC	Oral History Research Office Collection, Columbia University
DDBP	Dorothy Dow Butturff Papers, George Washington University
DDGP	David Gray Papers
DSP	Dorothy Schiff Papers, NYPL
EJKP	E. J. Kahn Papers, NYPL
EROH	Eleanor Roosevelt Oral History Transcripts, FDRL
ERPP	Eleanor Roosevelt Papers Project, George Washington University
FDRL	Franklin D. Roosevelt Presidential Library & Museum
FFP	Ferguson Family Papers, Arizona Historical Society
FFSC	Frank Freidel, Small Collections, FDRL
GHP	Grace Halsell Papers, Texas Christian University
HBP	Henry Brandon Papers, LCMD
HM2P	Henry Morgenthau, Jr., Papers, FDRL
JARP	John Aspinwall Roosevelt Papers, FDRL
JPLP	Joseph P. Lash Papers, FDRL
JRP	James Roosevelt Papers, FDRL
KBRP	Kermit Roosevelt and Belle Roosevelt Papers, LCMD
LAHP	Lorena Alice Hickok Papers, FDRL
LCMD	Library of Congress Manuscript Division

NYPL	New York Public Library
RABP	Ruby A. Black Papers, LCMD
RCP	Raymond Clapper Papers, LCMD
RFPDC	Roosevelt Family Papers Donated by the Children of Franklin and Eleanor Roosevelt, FDRL
RJBP	Ralph J. Bunche Papers, UCLA
RHKP	Rita Halle Kleeman Papers, FDRL
RPP	Rosamond Pinchot Papers, LCMD
RWLP	Robert W. Lovett Papers, Boston Medical Library, Francis A. Countway Library of Medicine, CLM
STEP	Stephen T. Early Papers, FDRL
TRBA	Theodore Roosevelt Birthplace Archive, New York, NY
TRC	Theodore Roosevelt Collection

Selected Principal Reporting on ER

BF	Bess Furman
EJK2	E. J. Kahn, Jr.
JM	Joseph Mitchell
LAH	Lorena Alice Hickok
RAB	Ruby A. Black
RC	Raymond Clapper
SJW	S. J. Woolf

Selected Principal Scholarship on ER

AMB	Allida M. Black
AMS2	Arthur M. Schlesinger, Jr.
AS	Alfred Steinberg
BA	Bernard Asbell
BWC	Blanche Wiesen Cook
DKG	Doris Kearns Goodwin
FF	Frank Freidel
GCW	Geoffrey C. Ward
JPL	Joseph P. Lash
KSD	Kenneth S. Davis
BWC1, 2, 3	*Eleanor Roosevelt*, Vols. 1 (1992), 2 (1999), 3 (2016)

E&F	*Eleanor and Franklin: The Story of Their Relationship, Based on Eleanor Roosevelt's Private Papers* (JPL, 1971)
EYA	*Eleanor: The Years Alone* (JPL, 1972)
F-C	*A First-Class Temperament: The Emergence of Franklin Roosevelt, 1905–1928* (GCW, 1989)
MRSR	*Mrs. R: The Life of Eleanor Roosevelt* (AS, 1958)

Selected Published Works by ER

AUTO	*The Autobiography of Eleanor Roosevelt* (1961)
HBG	*Hunting Big Game in the Eighties* (1933)
IAE	*India and the Awakening East* (1953)
ISTM	*It Seems to Me* (1954)
IUTW	*It's Up to the Women* (1933)
IYAM	*If You Ask Me* (1946)
MBD	*The Moral Basis of Democracy* (1940)
OMO	*On My Own* (1958)
TIMS	*This Is My Story* (1937)
TIN	*Tomorrow Is Now* (1963)
TIR	*This I Remember* (1949)
TTW	*This Troubled World* (1938)
YLBL	*You Learn by Living* (1960)
YT&M	*Your Teens and Mine* (1961)

Selected Published Sources for ER's Writings

AVOF	*A Volume of Friendship: The Letters of Eleanor Roosevelt and Isabella Greenway, 1904–1953* (Kristie Miller, ed., 2009)
ERP1	*The Eleanor Roosevelt Papers: The Human Rights Years, Vol. 1, 1945–1948* (2007)
ERP2	*The Eleanor Roosevelt Papers: The Human Rights Years, Vol. 2, 1949–1952* (2012)
EWY	*Empty Without You: The Intimate Letters of Eleanor Roosevelt and Lorena Hickok* (Rodger Streitmatter, ed., 1998)
IYAM-EAER	*If You Ask Me: Essential Advice from Eleanor Roosevelt* (Mary Jo Binker, ed., 2018)
ISTM	*It Seems to Me* (1954)

M&D	*Mother & Daughter: The Letters of Eleanor and Anna Roosevelt* (BA, ed., 1982)
SLER	*It Seems to Me: Selected Letters of Eleanor Roosevelt* (2001)
WHLB	*What I Hope to Leave Behind: The Essential Essays of Eleanor Roosevelt* (1982)

Selected Diaries, Memoirs, Letters, Recordings

AFM	*Eleanor Roosevelt: A Friend's Memoir* (JPL)
AM	*Eleanor Roosevelt in Conversation with Arnold Michaelis* (1957)
AMD	Agnes Meyer Diaries, LCMD
BWRD	Belle Willard Roosevelt Diary, LCMD
CDPD	Caroline Drayton Phillips Diary, Schlesinger Library, Harvard University
CRACD	Corinne Roosevelt Alsop Cole Diary, H
EMR	*The Extraordinary Mrs. R.* (Levy and Russett)
FRPL1–3	*His Personal Letters*, Vols. 1–3 (E2, ed.)
HBD	Henry Brandon Diary, LCMD
JPLD	Joseph P. Lash Diary, JPLP
L,E	*Love, Eleanor: Eleanor Roosevelt and Her Friends* (JPL, ed.)
RCD	Raymond Clapper Diary, LCMD
RPD	Rosamond Pinchot Diary, RPD
SDRD	Sara Delano Roosevelt Datebook, FDRL
WOL	*A World of Love: Eleanor Roosevelt and Her Friends, 1943–1962* (JPL, ed.)

NOTES

PART I: GRANNY

1. Epigraph: *HBG*, 37.

CHAPTER ONE

1. "Matters About the City," *New York Times*, Feb. 15, 1884, 8.
2. *Brooklyn Daily Eagle*, four o'clock edition, Feb. 14, 1884, 4.
3. From among posthumous condolences to TR, quoted in Edmund Morris, *The Rise of Theodore Roosevelt*, 232.
4. TR quoted in Lorant, *The Life and Times of Theodore Roosevelt*, 184.
5. EBR quoted in Pringle, *Theodore Roosevelt: A Biography*.
6. Harry Hewitt to EBR, Oct. 15, 1884, in *HBG*, 158.
7. Elizabeth Norris G. Roosevelt to EBR and ARHR, Oct. 11, 1884. See also handwritten record of ER's birth; time, date, and place, along with christening record, Box 1, AERP.
8. Oct. 11, 1884: last quarter; moon rise. *Sadlier's Catholic Directory: Almanac and Ordo for the Year of Our Lord 1884* (New York: D. & J. Sadlier, 1884), 9.
9. *HBG*, 157.
10. *YLBL*, 33.
11. Elizabeth Norris G. Roosevelt to EBR and ARHR, Oct. 11, 1884.
12. Ibid.
13. Jukes Morris, *Edith Kermit Roosevelt*, 112.
14. GHR's birth, which took a brief three hours, was "very different" from ARHR's previous deliveries: EBR to MLLH, n.d. [1891], papers of EBR, RFPDC.
15. The first of the "Three Friends" authors, *In Loving Memory of Anna Hall Roosevelt*, 8.
16. *E&F*, 24.
17. ARHR to ARC, "Monday Morning," n.d. [1885], TRC.
18. EBR to ARC, Sunday, n.d. [Aug. 30], 1885, TRC.
19. *ISTM*, 176. She once said that she had known ever since she was six months old: *Cumberland Evening Times*, Aug. 16, 1920, 7.
20. *HBG*, 34.
21. *HBG*, 37.
22. *HBG*, ix.
23. ARHR quoted in Alsop, *FDR*, 39.

24. Henry Adams to Elizabeth Cameron, Jan. 26, 1902, in Levenson et al., *The Letters of Henry Adams*, 331.

25. Martha Strayer, "Eyes Dampened at First Lady's Recital of Her Physically Handicapped Youth," *Daily News* (Washington, DC), Oct. 6, 1933; clipping, RABP.

26. ER, fictional self-portrait; ER, "Ethics of Parents," unpublished article, 1927; cited in *E&F*, 46, 729.

27. "Representative Society Ladies—VIII. Mrs. Elliott Roosevelt," *Frank Leslie's Illustrated Newspaper*, Oct. 12, 1889, 168.

28. *HBG*, 37.

29. *YT&M*, 38.

30. Strouse, *Morgan: American Financier*, 215.

31. TR to Cabot Lodge, Oct. 8, 1894; in Morison, *The Letters of Theodore Roosevelt*, 400.

32. See Aldrich, *Old Money*, 56.

33. Tonnele's estate, valued at $500,000 in 1846, for which VGH was executor, and he and his wife, Susan Tonnele Hall, were two of six heirs; see judge's ruling of contested estate. So, roughly: $250K + [one-third of $500K] = $416K.

34. Aaron Ogden [cousin] to MLH, Nov. 9, 1883, RDPDC, Box 2. FDRL.

35. Rev. Canon JEL to DTM, Mar. 2, 1911.

36. Lash, *E&F*, 21. Before marriage, Elliott to Mittie in *Hunting Big Game*, 109: "I try not to go beyond my five hundred a month."

37. William T. Cobb, *The Strenuous Life: The "Oyster Bay" Roosevelts in Business and Finance* (New York: William E. Rudge's Sons, 1946), 65. See, also, 1989 New York Landmarks Preservation Commission Landmark Designation Report http://www.flickr.com/photos/emilio_guerra/5631200654/.

38. Quoted by Murray Kempton, "The Kindly Stranger," *New York Review of Books*, April 15, 1982.

39. Margaret Chanler interview by Mary Hagedorn. See Caroli, *The Roosevelt Women*, 70.

40. TR to ARC, Aug. 8, 1888, TRC.

41. ARHR to ARC quoted in *E&F*, 31.

42. ARHR to EBR, n.d., Box 4, RFP.

43. *HBG*, 123.

44. "Of all people in the world, he and Anna have fraternized with Browning!" TR to Cabot Lodge, Sept. 5, 1887, in Morison, *The Letters of Theodore Roosevelt*, Vol. 1, 131.

45. JER to Jean S. R. Roosevelt, Oct. 13, 1936; Jean Schermerhorn Roosevelt, notes on EBR, *91M-49, TRC.

46. EBR, "A Hunting Trip in India," in TR and George Bird Grinnell, eds., *Hunting in Many Lands*, 107–22.

47. Wharton, *The Age of Innocence*, 56.

48. Gardiner, *The History of the White Star Line*, 103.

49. See inquiry's findings on the ships' speeds: "Censuring Both Captains; the Blame for the Britannic-Celtic Collision," *New York Times*, June 10, 1887. See also Flayhart, *Perils of the Atlantic*, 125.

50. "Cut by the Celtic's Bow," *New York Times*, May 23, 1887, 1; see passenger lists, "In a Fog," *San Francisco Examiner*, May 23, 1887, 1.

51. Descriptions of decks and layout of ship, see "S.S. Britannic, White Star Line," http://www.norwayheritage.com/p_ship.asp?sh=brit1, accessed July 2012.

52. "My Day," June 21, 1938.

53. "Disaster in the Fog," *New York Sun*, May 23, 1887, 1.

54. "In a Fog—Huntington's Story," *San Francisco Examiner*, May 23, 1887, 1. See also "Cut by the Celtic's Bow," *New York Times*, May 23, 1887, 1; T. W. Bacchus, quoted in "The Celtic In," *Brooklyn Daily Eagle*, May 23, 1887, 6.

55. "The Celtic In."

56. Flayhart, *Perils of the Atlantic*, 118.

57. George B. Bernaard, quoted in "The Celtic In."

58. Daniel Hoey, cited in "The Celtic In."

59. Bernaard, in "The Celtic In."

60. "Cut by the Celtic's Bow."

61. ARHR quoted in *E&F*, 29.

62. Walker, *Mrs. Astor's Horse*, 14–15.

63. *TIMS*, 7.

64. "Fatal Collision at Sea," *New-York Tribune*, May 23, 1887, 1.

65. "The Imperiled Steamers," *New York Times*, May 24, 1887, 8.

66. See GCW, *Before the Trumpet*, 268n.

67. David Lavender (CPH biographer) quoted in Stanton Coblentz, "Collis P. Huntington, A Tempered View," *Los Angeles Times*, June 14, 1970.

68. Klein, *Dynastic America and Those Who Own It*, 4.

69. "Society Topics of the Week," *New York Times*, May 29, 1887.

70. John Paton (b. Scotland, 1831, d. 1901), obituary, *Banker's Magazine*, Vol. 62, Jan.–June, 1901, 640.

71. "Society Topics of the Week," *New York Times*, May 29, 1887.

72. GCW, *Before the Trumpet*, 268.

73. Ibid., 269.

74. *New York Times*, untitled editorial 1, May 23, 1887.

75. *TIMS*, 7.

76. *HBG*, 158.

77. CRAC autobiographical fragment in Hagedorn notes, R200.H12i, TRC.

78. Helen R. Roosevelt to Mary Hagedorn, Nov. 17, 1954; "Interview of Mrs. Theodore Douglas Robinson," R200.H12i, TRC.

79. James K. Gracie Residence, Oyster Bay, McKim, Mead, and White, architects, 1884. See Robert B. Mackay et al., *Long Island Country Houses and Their Architects 1860–1940*, 274.

80. ABG to CRR, Sept. 9, n.d. [1887], TRC.

81. ABG to CRR, quoted in *E&F*, 29–30.

82. *E&F*, 30.

83. EBR to ARC, June 19, 1887, in *HBG*, 159–60.

84. EBR to ARC, July 8, 1887, in *HBG*, 160–61.

85. Ibid.

86. ABG to CRR, quoted in *E&F*, 29–30.

CHAPTER TWO

1. *HBG*, 161.s.

2. Louie Vega, Dylan Meehan, Joncarlo Esquival, research paper at Woodland Middle submitted to New York State Archive Student Research Awards, June 2011, cited in David Weingrad, "Eleanor Roosevelt Slept Here," *Long Island Herald*, Apr. 23, 2014, http://liherald.com/eastmeadow/stories/Eleanor -Roosevelt-slept-here,54533.

3. EBR to ARC, July 14, 1888, RFP.

4. "Representative Society Ladies—VIII. Mrs. Elliott Roosevelt," *Frank Leslie's Illustrated Newspaper*, Oct. 12, 1889, 168.

5. "Meadow Brook Park Company," *New York Times*, Apr. 15, 1888, 5.

6. ER, quoted in *AFM*, 108.

7. EBR, quoted by ER in "Rubbing Noses Not New to Mrs. Roosevelt," *Decatur (IL) Herald*, Dec. 18, 1943, 1.

8. ARHR to EBR, "Thursday" n.d. [Aug. 1888], Box 1, RFP.

9. *YT&M*, 21.

10. ARHR to ER, "Tuesday" n.d. [Oct. 11], RFP.

11. Margaret Cutter to JPL, Aug. 13, 1966, Box 44, JPLP.

12. David Grubin, *FDR*, 1984, PBS.

13. *TIMS*, 13.

14. EBR to ARC, Oct. 13, 1888, *HBG*, 162.

15. EBR to ER, Oct. 9, 1892, Box 1, RFPDC.

16. *TIMS*, 6.

17. Ibid.

18. *YLBL*, 25.

19. ARHR to ARC, in GCW, *Before the Trumpet*, 274.

20. Letter appears as elided by Sylvia Jukes Morris, *Edith Kermit Roosevelt*, 534.

21. ARHR to EBR, n.d. [circa 1890], ARHR Papers, RFP.

22. *TIMS*, 6.

23. *ISTM*, 176.

24. "Amateur Circus: A Startling Fad—New York Sun," *Current Literature: A Magazine of Record and Review*, Vol. 2, Jan.–June 1889, 481–82; "Mrs. Roosevelt's Death," clipping, n.d. [Dec. 1892], AERP.

25. E to ALR, June 13, 1889, ER Family Papers, Box 1, FDRL.

26. *TIMS*, 8.

27. *E&F*, 32.

28. EBR to ER, Aug. 1, 1894, Box 1, RFP.

29. EBR to ARC, June 13, 1889, Box 1, RFP.

30. *E&F*, 33.

31. Erenberg, *Steppin' Out: New York Nightlife*, 36.

32. "It Will Be a Great Ball," *Brooklyn Eagle*, Dec. 29, 1889, 6.

33. "Happy 1,400!," *The World*, Jan. 3, 1890, 1.

34. "Laudanum, and Its Many Uses," *The Victorian Era* blog, Mar. 2, 2008, http://19thcentury.wordpress.com/2008/03/02/laudanum/.

35. GCW, *Before the Trumpet*, 271.

36. Ibid., 272.

37. TR to EBR, June 14, 1891, TRC.

38. TR to ARC, May 23, 1891, TRC.

39. *Rockland County Journal*, Aug. 22, 1891, 7. See also its source: Affidavits of Anna Roosevelt and Eleanor Roosevelt, submitted with petition of Theodore Roosevelt to Justice Bartlett of the Supreme Court, Queens County, Jamaica, NY, cited in "To Examine Him," *Brooklyn Eagle*, Dec. 3, 1891, 6.

40. CRAC to JPL, Apr. 27, 1966, Box 44, JPLP.

41. Ibid.

42. EBR to ER, Apr. 6, 1893, in *HBG*, 174.

43. *L,E*, 10.

44. Eleanor Biles to Edmund Morris, July 6, 1981, in Mann, *The Wars of the Roosevelts*, 25, 538n.

45. Pat Johnson to William J. Mann in *The Wars of the Roosevelts*, 25, 538n.

46. TR to EBR, June 14, 1891; TRC.

47. TR to ARC, n.d. [1890]; TRC.

48. FP, CUOHROC.

49. ER, quoted in Turner and Russett, *The Extraordinary Mrs. R*, 143.

50. CRR, *One Woman to Another*, 100.

51. Elizabeth Sherman Cameron to Henry Adams, in Jukes Morris, *Edith Kermit Roosevelt*, 135.

52. "Noted Vienna Surgeon to Be Visitor Here," *Los Angeles Times*, Apr. 4, 1931, A3.

53. ARC to CRR, Mar. 13, 1891; TRC.

54. Ibid.

55. Ibid.

56. TR to ARC, July 8, 1891; TRC.

57. TR to ARC, June 28, 1891; TRC.

58. ARC, "Story of the Roosevelt Family," unpublished memoir, section dictated Oct. 23, 1925; TRC.

59. TR to ARC, n.d. [1890]; TRC.

60. Dalton, *Theodore Roosevelt*, 140–41.

61. Elizabeth Winthrop, granddaughter of Corinne Robinson Alsop and author of *In Her Mother's House* (1988), modeled the incestuous sexual abuser in her novel after Eleanor's father.

62. ER to AS, in *MRSR*, 23.

63. ARHR, quoted by ER in "Eleanor as a Child and Young Girl," *My Husband and I.*

64. *TIMS*, 12.

65. *YT&M*, 21.

66. FP, CUOHROC.

67. *YLBL*, 18.

68. *Rockland County Journal*, Aug. 22, 1891, 7.

69. GCW, *Before the Trumpet*, 276.

70. Ibid.

71. Edgard Fournier, *Suresnes: Notes Historiques* (Paris: La Bourse de Commerce, 1890), 293–94.

72. "Elliott Roosevelt 'Insane,'" *New York Times*, Aug. 18, 1891, 8; Judge O'Brien, Affidavits of Anna Roosevelt and Eleanor Roosevelt, submitted with petition of Theodore Roosevelt to Justice Bartlett of the Supreme Court, Queens County, Jamaica, NY, cited in "To Examine Him," *Brooklyn Eagle*, Dec. 3, 1891, 6.

73. *New York Times*, Aug. 18, 1891, 8.

74. *Rockland County Journal*, Aug. 22, 1891, 7.

75. Ibid.

76. TR to ARC, "Jan 21st 91" [i.e., 1892]; TRC.

77. "Weeks Taken to New York," *Times-Picayune* (New Orleans, LA), Nov. 2, 1893, 3.

78. ALR to MLLH, Feb. 15, 1893, Box 2, RFPDC.

79. Leslie E. Keeley, MD, LLD, *Inebriety Is a Disease,* privately printed pamphlet, 2nd edition, 1897.

80. Charles S. Clark, *The Perfect Keeley Cure*, 3rd edition (Milwaukee: C. S. Clark, 1893).

81. William L. White, *Slaying the Dragon: The History of Addiction Treatment and Recovery in America* (Bloomington, IL: Chestnut Health Systems/Lighthouse Institute, 1998), 9. See also Cheryl Krasnick Warsh, "Adventures in Maritime Quackery: The Leslie E. Keeley Gold Cure Institute of Fredericton, NB," *Acadiensis* 17, No. 2, Spring 1988, 122–24.

82. W. K. Armistead, from Abingdon, Virginia, to Douglas Robinson, Jr., Nov. 5, 1883, Elliott Roosevelt, Virginia Property folder, ER Papers, Box 3, FDRL.

83. C. R. Boyd to Douglas Robinson, Jr., n.d., Elliott Roosevelt, Virginia Property folder, Box 3, AERP.

84. JWA, quoted in Hugh Davis Graham, "The Paradox of Eleanor Roosevelt: Alcoholism's Child," *Virginia Quarterly Review*, 62, No. 2, Spring 1987, 210–30.

85. EBR to MLLH, Aug. 17, 1892, papers of EBR in RFPDC.

86. ER to Carl Rowan, c. June 20–July 3, 1957, in Rowan, *Dream Makers, Dream Breakers*, 135.

87. "Three Friends," *In Loving Memory of Anna Hall Roosevelt*, 34.

88. Baroness Emily de la Grange to JPL, Jan. 12, 1967, Box 44, JPLP.

89. *TIMS*, 17.

90. ARHR, quoted in GCW, *Before the Trumpet*, 278.

91. *TIMS*, 16.

92. AHR to ER, Tuesday, n.d. [Oct. 11], ER Family Papers, FDRL.

93. *TIMS*, 33: "Lyman's" should be "Lynam's"; according to the Mount Desert Island Historical Society, there was no "Lyman's Hotel" at Bar Harbor, but rather a Lynam House, started in July 1881 by owner John Lynam. See also "Doings at Bar Harbor," *New York Times*, July 21, 1907: Lynam House "has always been a favorite with New Yorkers"; *Boston Evening Transcript*, June 2, 1915, 2.

94. EBR to MLLH, Aug. 17, 1892, papers of Elliott Roosevelt, Sr., RFPDC.

95. *TIMS*, 13.

96. *HBG*, 170n.

97. *YT&M*, 82.

98. *TIMS*, 16, 17; *YT&M*, 38–39.

99. *BWC*1, 72.

100. *YT&M*, 39.

101. Helen Cutting Wilmerding to JPL, Apr. 29, 1966, Box 44, JPLP.

102. *In Loving Memory of Anna Hall Roosevelt*, 27.

103. Ibid., 31.

104. Ibid., 29.

105. *TIMS*, 17.

106. *E&F*, 42.

107. *TIMS*, 17.

108. Helen Cutting to JPL, Apr. 29, 1966, Box 44, JPLP.

109. "Saunterings," *Town Topics: The Journal of Society*, Vol. 29, No. 1, Jan. 3, 1893, 6.

110. Susan Livingston Ludlow, born in NYC, June 19, 1866, daughter of Edward Philip Livingston Ludlow and Margaret Tonnele Hall Ludlow.

111. "Elliott Roosevelt Dead," *The World*, Aug. 16, 1894, 5; "News and Views," *Buffalo (NY) Express*, Aug. 17, 1894, 5.

112. *YT&M*, 22.

113. ER, Notes for Speeches and Articles, 1941, Box 1411, AERP.

114. *TIMS*, 19.

115. E2, *Eleanor Roosevelt, with Love*, 8.

116. *HBG*, vii.

117. *TIMS*, 20.

118. EBR to ER, Apr. 6, 1893, in *HBG*, 174.

119. *TIMS*, 20.

120. EBR to ER, July 24, 1893, Box 1, RFP.

121. ELHM, "Writings of Mrs. W. Forbes Morgan," section dated August 1892—Bar Harbor & Lenox, Box 1, RFP.

122. EBR to ER, Oct. 9, 1892, in *HBG*, 168.

123. "My Day," Feb. 6, 1936.

124. Douglas Robinson to CRR, June 2, 1893, AFP.

125. Ruby Black, "Overnite," United Press dispatch, Aug. 12, 1933, RABP.

126. Lillian Lloyd to ER, quoted in Steinberg, *Mrs. R*, 27.

127. Edith Hall Morgan, "Writings of Mrs. W. Forbes Morgan," section dated August 1892—Bar Harbor & Lenox, ER Family Papers, Box 1, FDRL.

128. ELHM to ARC, n.d. [1893], in RFPDC.

129. ARC, unpublished family memoir, 1924, typescript, Pt. 2, 10, TRC.

130. Douglas Robinson to CRR, May 26, 1893, AFP.

131. "This was a great blow to the father, and led to further excesses on his part," *Evening World*, extra two o'clock edition, Aug. 15, 1894.

132. ABG, Sept. 15, 1833–June 9, 1893.

133. EKR, quoted in Jukes Morris, *Edith Kermit Roosevelt*, 142.

134. "the noblest and 'truest' man that I know of in New York": Daniel P. Kingsford to ARHR, July 5, 1883, RFP.

135. MLLH to CRR, Aug. 25 [1894], Box 1, RFP.

136. TR to ALR, May 6, 1894; bMS Am 1834 (416), TRC.

137. EBR to ER, Jan. 19, 1894, Box 5, RFPDC.

138. EKR, quoted in Jukes Morris, *Edith Kermit Roosevelt*, 142.

139. Ibid., 144.

140. EBR to ER, Apr. 6, 1893, RLP.

141. ER, "Insuring Democracy," *Collier's Weekly*, June 15, 1940, 70.

142. Donn, *The Roosevelt Cousins*, 177: "Eleanor once observed that her father with his problems had reminded her of Jesus in Michelangelo's Pieta." See also "My Day," Mar. 21, 1955.

143. Adams, *Exploring Art*, 166.

144. TR to ALR, Aug. 18, 1894, bMS Am 1834 (430), TRC.

145. ER to EBR, July 30, 1894, AERP.

146. ELHM, "Writings of Mrs. W. Forbes Morgan," section dated August 1892—Bar Harbor & Lenox, Box 1, RFP.

147. *TIMS*, 34.

148. MLLH to CRR, Aug. 25 [1894], RFP, Box 1, AERP.

149. JEL, Rector of St. Paul's Church, Tivoli, NY, to JAR, May 12, 1980, JARP.

150. TR to ALR, Aug. 18, 1894, bMS Am 1834 (430), TRC.

151. *TIMS*, 34.

152. Dalton, *Theodore Roosevelt*, 145.

153. TR to ALR, Aug. 18, 1894, bMS Am 1834 (430), TRC.

154. Dalton, *Theodore Roosevelt*, 145.

155. *TIMS*, 34. Burial was in the afternoon on Friday, Aug. 17, 1894.

156. *YLBL*, 18.

CHAPTER THREE

1. ER, quoted in RAB, unpublished notes, Undated Biographical Data, Box 7, RABP.
2. *YLBL*, 18.
3. *TIMS*, 21.
4. ER, in George Roach interview, "Mrs. Franklin D. Roosevelt Talks about the Hall Family," Aug. 1962, AERP.
5. ER, in Charl Ormond Williams, "This I Believe About Public Schools: An Interview with Eleanor Roosevelt," in *WHLB*, 325.
6. ER to Arnold Michaelis on ERCAM.
7. FP, 531–43, CUOHROC.
8. ER to Arnold Michaelis on ERCAM.
9. *YLBL*, 26.
10. *YT&M*, 23.
11. ER, quoted in LAH, "War Started Mrs. Roosevelt on Her Career in Public Life," *Boston Globe*, Nov. 11, 1932, 11.
12. *YT&M*, 22.
13. *TIMS*, 40.
14. "My Day," Feb. 4, 1936.
15. ER, interviewed by George Roach, Aug.–Sept. 1962, "Mrs. Franklin D. Roosevelt Talks about the Hall Family," 5, AERP.
16. "Divorce for H. T. Sloane," *New York Times*, Apr. 29, 1899, 1.
17. *YT&M*, 177.
18. Ibid.
19. *TIMS*, 46.
20. The Sloanes' disintegrating marriage also became the basis for an Edith Wharton story, "The Line of Least Resistance," published the following October, 1890, in *Lippincott's Magazine*.
21. Wayne Craven, *Gilded Mansions: Grand Architecture and High Society* (New York: W. W. Norton, 2009), 341.
22. Henry Adams to Elizabeth Cameron, May 3, 1899, in *The Letters of Henry Adams, Vol. IV, 1892–1899*, edited by J. C. Levenson et al., (Massachusetts Historical Society, 1988), 716.
23. "Quite lively going isn't it?" a precocious Franklin D. Roosevelt remarked to his mother about the Sloane scandal on May 2; Sara Delano Roosevelt's sister Kassie had been married to a brother of Jessie Robbins Sloane. Eleanor's childhood could be one very small world.
24. "My Day," Nov. 23, 1959.
25. ER, "Mrs. Franklin D. Roosevelt Talks about the Hall Family," 7, interviewed by George Roach, Aug.–Sept. 1962; AERP; ER, "Wives of Great Men," *Liberty*, Oct. 1, 1932, 12; Speech and Article File, 1931–1933, Box 1397, AERP.
26. *TIMS*, 39. "Overhulse" is the correct spelling.

27. Annette Hunter, author interview, Sept. 2010.

28. Thomas Hunt, *A Historical Sketch of the Town of Clermont* (Hudson, NY: Hudson Press, 1929), 149.

29. "My Day," June 22, 1938; *TIMS*, 42.

30. *WHLB*, 345.

31. *YT&M*, 23.

32. "My Day," Dec. 3, 1953.

33. ELHM to MHG, May 16, 1935, RFP. Even after building a sixty-room Queen Anne–style manor on the Stanley Mortimers' hundred-acre estate in Old Westbury, Long Island, Tissie would still declare of Oak Lawn: "I could never love any place as well."

34. Deshler Welch, ed. *The Theatre: An Illustrated Weekly Magazine*, Vol. 4 (New York: Theatre Publishing, 1889), 373–74.

35. Honoria Livingston McVitty, EROH.

36. David Gray to Maude Gray, Apr. 3, 1921, David Gray Papers, FDRL.

37. JPL, *A Friend's Memoir*, 360.

38. ER to David Gray, May 4, 1937, David Gray Papers, FDRL.

39. *TIMS*, 38.

40. "My Day," Aug. 24, 1936.

41. *YT&M*, 169.

42. ER, "The Joy of Reading," *Coronet* 50, Sept. 1961, 74.

43. *TIMS*, 359.

44. Ibid.

45. Whenever they dramatized or made tableaux from whichever book Eleanor was reading, she "was always the principal character." ER, Introduction to *Alice in Wonderland*, July 1932, Speech and Article File, 1931–1933, Box 1397, AERP.

46. JWA, *FDR*, 40.

47. R. W. B. Lewis and Nancy Lewis, *The Letters of Edith Wharton* (New York: Scribner's, 1988), 54–55, 96–97.

48. ER, Introduction, *Alice in Wonderland*.

49. ER, Introduction, *John Martin's Book: Tell Me a Story*, Jacket Library edition, 1932; *E&F*, 939n.

50. "My Day," Sept. 27, 1941.

51. "My Day," Sept. 26, 1941.

52. *TIMS*, 11.

53. ER, "The Joy of Reading," *Coronet* 50, Sept. 1961, 74.

54. *TIMS*, 25.

55. *YT&M*, 30.

56. CRAC, quoted in *E&F*, 61.

57. *YT&M*, 32; *TIMS*, 50.

58. ER to Arnold Michaelis, ERCAM. All her life she remembered "being terrified of the water": "My Day," June 26, 1946.

59. ARL in Teague, *Mrs. L*, 42.

60. Dalton, *Theodore Roosevelt*, 558n.

61. "My Day," Jan. 6, 1944.

62. ER to Arnold Michaelis, ERCAM.

63. "My Day," Oct. 25, 1958.

64. *YT&M*.

65. "My Day," Sept. 29, 1950.

66. MLLH to ER, quoted in "Mrs. Roosevelt Still Insists on Being Herself," *Niagara Falls Gazette*, Nov. 9, 1944, 33.

67. *TIMS*, 48.

68. James, *The American Scene*, 148.

69. *YT&M*, 25.

70. "They were all out of our lives": CRAC to Hermann and Mary Hagedorn, Dec. 28, 1954, R200.H12i, TRC.

71. CRAC to JPL, Nov. 10, 1966, Box 44, JPLP.

72. "If ever their names were mentioned in the presence of the youngsters the conversation was quickly turned," recalled Nicholas Roosevelt, son of cousin J. West Roosevelt. "Every family has its black sheep, of whom the less said the better." Nicholas Roosevelt, *A Front Row Seat*, 20.

73. Monroe Robinson to ER, Feb. 1937, AERP.

74. CRR paraphrased in CRAC to JPL, Nov. 10, 1966, Box 44, JPLP.

75. *YT&M*, 16.

76. Merry, *Taking on the World*, 11.

77. Ibid.

78. ARL, quoted in Felsenthal, *Alice Roosevelt Longworth*, 179.

79. Teague, *Mrs. L*, 154.

80. *YT&M*, 204: "I was reassured to have my grandmother pass on to me what Franklin's mother reported to her. 'My son thinks Cousin Eleanor has a fine mind.'"

81. MS to MLLH, in *E&F*, 83.

82. *YT&M*, 26.

83. *YT&M*, 119.

84. MS, quoted in *E&F*, 81.

85. Quoted in *L, E*, 32.

86. "My Day," Mar. 27, 1942.

PART II: ORPHAN

1. Epigraph: ER, *AM*.

CHAPTER FOUR

1. *YT&M*, 40.

2. Ibid.

3. *YT&M*, 43.

4. Helen Gifford, London *Daily Mail*, Oct. 21, 1942.

5. "She was 'Totty' Roosevelt to British Schoolgirls," *Boston Globe*, Nov. 27, 1932, A52.

6. *YT&M*, 41–42.

7. *TIMS*, 65.

8. Brooks, *Boston and Return*, 41.

9. Helen Gifford to the London *Daily Mail*, n.d. [1942], in *L, E*, 27.

10. CRAC to CRR, n.d. [late May 1902], bMS Am 1785.8 (62), AFP.

11. Mildred Adams, "When T. R. gave his niece in marriage; it was thirty years ago that Eleanor married Franklin," *New York Times Magazine*, Mar. 17, 1935, 8. See also reviews by Ordway Tead and John M. Gaus in *Amherst Graduates' Quarterly* 12 (1922–23), 254–58.

12. Pakenham, *The Boer War*, 1.

13. ER, quoted in Eunice Fuller Barnard, "Mrs. Roosevelt in the Classroom," *New York Times Magazine*, Dec. 4, 1932, 2.

14. ER, "Wives of Great Men." *Liberty*, Oct. 1, 1932, 12, Speech and Article File, 1931–1933, Box 1397, AERP.

15. CRAC to CRR, June 2, 1902, bMS Am 1785.8 (62), TRC.

16. *YT&M*, 170.

17. CRAC to CRR, n.d. [late May 1902], bMS Am 1785.8 (62), AFP.

18. Brooks, *Boston and Return*, 39.

19. CRAC to CRR, n.d. [late May 1902], bMS Am 1785.8 (62), AFP.

20. CRAC to Douglas Robinson, Jr., n.d. [circa 1902], MS Am 1785.8 (450), TRC.

21. CRAC to CRR, n.d. [late May 1902], bMS Am 1785.8 (62), TRC.

22. CRAC to CRR, May 15, 1902, bMS Am 1785.8 (62), TRC.

23. Brooks, *Boston and Return*, 37–38.

24. "Schoolmates Predicted a President Husband for Mrs. Franklin Roosevelt," *Milwaukee Journal*, Nov. 28, 1932, 8.

25. *YT&M*, 42.

26. Ibid.

27. Ibid.

28. *TIMS*, 65.

29. Harper, *Around the World in Eighty Years on a Sidesaddle*, 12.

30. Helen Agnes Post, b. Jan. 1885: Edward Carpenter, *Samuel Carpenter and His Descendants* (Philadelphia: J. B. Lippincott, 1912), 243.

31. *TIMS*, 61.

32. Holthusen, *James W. Wadsworth, Jr.*, 72.

33. Ibid.

34. *TIMS*, 62. See also Cornelia Adair, *My Diary* (Austin: University of Texas Press, 1965), xxiv; Ernest Wallace, "My Diary," *Southwestern Historical Quarterly* 70 (Jan. 1967), 531–32.

35. *TIMS*, 61.

36. "American Peeresses," *The Lady's Realm: An Illustrated Monthly Magazine*, Vol. 15, Nov. 1903–Apr. 1904 (London: Hutchinson and Co.), 66.

37. Harper, *Around the World in Eighty Years on a Sidesaddle,* 12.

38. Baroness Emily de la Grange to JPL, Jan. 12, 1967, Box 44, JPLP.

39. Harper, *Around the World in Eighty Years on a Sidesaddle*, 12.

40. "Schoolmates Predicted a President Husband for Mrs. Franklin Roosevelt," *Milwaukee Journal,* Nov. 28, 1932, 8.

41. Ibid.

42. *TIMS*, 74.

43. MCS remarks, ER Report Card from Allenswood School, Jan.–Apr. 1900, Eleanor Roosevelt Significant Documents Collection, ER-1, Series 2, Box 2, AERP.

44. MCS to MLLH, Feb. 18, 1901, Box 2, RFPDC.

45. Ibid.

46. MCS to MLLH, Feb. 18, 1901, quoted in *E&F*, 74.

47. *TIMS*, 63.

48. Ibid.

49. Her husband succeeded to the title on the death of his brother, becoming the 8th Earl St. Germans in November 1942. See Oswald Frewen, *Sailor's Soliloquy* (London: Hutchinson, 1961), 62.

50. Helen Agnes Post Eliot; Mrs. Montague Charles Eliot, 8th Earl of St. Germans; second son, Montague Robert Vere Eliot, Page of Honour to King George VI, 1934–1940. Cracroft's Peerage: http://www.cracroftspeerage.co.uk/online /content/stgermans1815.htm, accessed July 26, 2015. Ancestry File. http://www .royalblood.co.uk/D744/I744875.html.

51. *TIMS*, 61.

52. *YT&M*, 154.

53. *TIMS*, 86.

54. *TIMS*, 84.

55. MCS to MLLH, Apr. 24, 1902, Box 2, RFPDC.

56. *TIMS*, 87.

57. EJK2, interview with ER, 67, Box 69, EJKP.

58. CRAC, quoted in *L, E*, 30.

59. *L,E*, 36.

60. "Schoolmates Predicted a President Husband for Mrs. Franklin Roosevelt," *Milwaukee Journal,* Nov. 28, 1932, 8; CRAC to Hermann and Mary Hagedorn, Dec. 28, 1954, R200.H12i, TRC.

61. *YT&M*, 132.

62. *MRSR*, 42.

63. *YT&M*, 26. See also "Mrs. F. D. R. Names 7 People Who Influenced Her Life," *Boston Globe*, June 5, 1951, 1.

64. After ER's death, Frances Perkins said, "In the next few days we are going to

hear a great deal about how much Mrs. R did for mankind. But the striking fact about Eleanor Roosevelt to those of us who knew her for many years was how much she did for herself in overcoming great difficulties." Dr. Christopher N. Breiseth, "The Frances Perkins I Knew," 1966, FDR American Heritage Center Museum, https://francesperkinscenter.org/wp-content/uploads/2014/04/The -Frances-Perkins-I-Knew-by-Christopher-Breiseth.pdf, accessed Apr. 30, 2020.

65.   EL to JPL, Feb. 24. 1970, Box 44, JPLP.

66.   "Mrs. Franklin D. Roosevelt Talks about the Hall Family, Recording made by George Roach, Aug/Sept 1962," transcript, 10, FDRL: "Always falling in love with the wrong people, very often with gentlemen who were already married . . ."

67.   Ibid.

68.   Ibid.

69.   Ibid.

70.   *TIMS*, 88.

71.   Ibid.

72.   ISFGK, quoted in BWRD, Aug. 12, 1942, KBRP.

73.   CDP, in *E&F*, 102.

74.   Ibid.

75.   *MRSR*, 40.

76.   *MRSR*, 41.

77.   *BWC*1, 88.

78.   U.S. Census, 1900: Elliott Mann, born March 1891; U.S. Census, 1930: Elliott R. Mann, age 39; WWI draft card, June 5, 1917: Date of birth: Mar. 11, 1891.

79.   Elliott Robert Mann draft card, June 5, 1917.

80.   Morris, *The Rise of Theodore Roosevelt*, 819.

81.   *YT&M*, 79.

82.   *MRSR*, 41.

83.   *YT&M*, 44.

84.   ER, quoted in Turner and Russett, *The Extraordinary Mrs. R*, 143.

85.   Teague, *Mrs. L*, 151.

86.   *TIMS*, 149.

CHAPTER FIVE

1.   *YT&M*, 184.

2.   "a cool Wedgwood blue": Anne O'Hare McCormick, "Still 'A Little Left of Center,'" *New York Times Magazine*, June 21, 1936, 2.

3.   Murray Kempton, "The Kindly Stranger."

4.   Bronson Winthrop "Bim" Chanler to David Grubin, *FDR*, David Grubin Productions, Boston: WGBH, *The American Experience*, 1994.

5.   FDR, quoted in Freidel, *The Apprenticeship*, 49.

6.   SDR, *My Boy Franklin*, 62.

7.   In *BWC*3, 399, 632n.

8.   Mary Newbold Morgan to JPL, May 24, 1967, Box 44, JPLP.

9.   SDR, quoted in SJW, *Here Am I*, 201–2.

10.   SDR, quoted in William T. McCleery, "Mrs. Roosevelt Says Son's Fame 'Seems Natural' Now," *North Adams [MA] Transcript*, May 12, 1934, 8; SDR, quoted in "My Day," May 21, 1937.

11.   Bradley, *The Imperial Cruise*, 29.

12.   Kienholz, *Opium Traders and Their Worlds*, n.p.

13.   "Springwood" appears listed in *Social Register, Summer, 1905* (New York: Social Register Association, June 1905), 362.

14.   "She was not afraid of anything, nor of anyone": Bottome, *From the Life*, 68.

15.   GCW, *Before the Trumpet*, 114.

16.   *MRSR*, 45.

17.   ER, *Franklin D. Roosevelt and Hyde Park*, 1.

18.   SDR to FDR and ER, Oct. 14, 1917, in *E&F*, 212.

19.   Ibid.

20.   Louise Tompkins, "Yours Truly," *Taconic Newspapers*, Jan. 27 and 28, 1982, 5.

21.   FDR, quoted in GCW, *Before the Trumpet*, 253.

22.   Alice Sohier, quoted in GCW, *Before the Trumpet*, 254.

23.   FDR to Robert D. Washburn, Aug. 18, 1928, FDRL.

24.   *TIMS*, 99.

25.   MLLH to MHG, July 30, n.d. [1913], David Gray Papers, FDRL.

26.   *TIMS*, 99.

27.   "A Dinner Suddenly Ended," *New York Times*, Mar. 17, 1893, 1.

28.   "Resignations in Order," *New York Times*, Mar. 18, 1893, 8.

29.   "A Dinner Suddenly Ended," *New York Times*, Mar. 17, 1893, 1.

30.   Ibid. See also, "Hall's Party on Trial," *New York Times*, Apr. 12, 1893, 5.

31.   "The Seed of Socialism," *Brooklyn Eagle*, Mar. 18, 1893, 4.

32.   "My Day," Dec. 11, 1944.

33.   "Son of Wealthy Widow in Custody," *Poughkeepsie (NY) Eagle-News*, Aug. 12, 1915, 5.

34.   Helen Cutting Wilmerding to JPL, interview, Apr. 29, 1966, Box 44, JPLP.

35.   ARC to CRR, n.d. [1903], TRC.

36.   ER quoted by ELHM to MHG, Jan. 14, n.d. [1942], DGP.

37.   "My Day," Aug. 24, 1936.

38.   "Society at Home and Abroad," *New York Times*, Nov. 2, 1902, 28.

39.   *YT&M*, 58.

40.   *Town Topics*, Dec. 8, 1904. See clipping, Algonac Diary. FDRL.

41.   ER quoted by JPL to JEL, letter, July 18, 1967, courtesy of JEL.

42.   MCS to ER, Oct. 5, 1902, quoted in *BWC*1, 122.

43.   Geoffrey T. Hellman, "Mrs. Roosevelt," *Life*, Feb. 5, 1940, 78.

44.   "New York Society," *New-York Tribune*, Feb. 4, 1903, 8.

45.   *TIMS*, 100.

46.   *TIMS,* 101.

47. *YT&M*, 26.

48. *YT&M*, 88–89.

49. CRR to CRAC, *L, E* 35.

50. *TIMS*, 102.

51. *TIMS*, 109.

52. JPL, in *A Centenary Remembrance*, 10.

53. ARC to CRR, n.d. [1903], TRC.

54. "Society and Personal Mention," *Washington Times*, Dec. 31, 1902, 7.

55. ARC to CRR, n.d. [1903], TRC.

56. "New Year's Reception at the White House," *Harrisburg (PA) Telegraph*, Jan. 1, 1903, 1, 3.

57. Adolf A. Berle, Jr., writing about the Henry Street Settlement, put this phrase in plural to describe all Lower East Side settlements; quoted in Berle, *A Life in Two Worlds: An Autobiography*, 72.

58. Helen Thayer Rand, *Blazing the Settlement Trail*, cited in Jane E. Robbins, "The First Year at the College Settlement," *Survey* 27, Feb. 24, 1912, 180.

59. *College Settlement Associations*.

60. Mary Kingsbury Simkhovitch, "East Side," *Neighborhood: My Story of Greenwich House* (New York: W. W. Norton, 1938), 60.

61. Ibid.

62. *TIMS*, 109.

63. *AUTO*, 413.

64. *YT&M*, 180–81.

65. FDR cast his first ballot in a presidential election for TR: see ARL to Jean van den Heuvel, in "The Sharpest Wit in Washington," *Saturday Evening Post*, Dec. 4, 1965, 33.

66. TR to SDR, quoted in *F-C*, 106.

67. ARL, quoted in Teague, *Mrs. L*, 156.

68. ARL quoted in *E&F*, 103.

69. Walt Whitman, *Complete Poetry and Collected Prose* (New York: Library of America, 1982), 384.

70. ER to FDR, quoted in *L, E*, 41.

71. Simkhovitch, *Neighborhood: My Story of Greenwich House*, 90.

72. *TIMS*, 111.

73. ER quoted in *E&F*, 107.

74. ER to SDR, Dec. 2, 1903, quoted in *E&F*, 110.

75. FDR to SDR, quoted in *E&F*, 109.

76. Harry Hopkins to Florence Kerr, quoted in Roll, *The Hopkins Touch*, 57.

77. ARC, quoted in *YT&M*, 31.

78. ER to FDR, Dec. 16, 1903, and Jan. 7, Jan. 18, 1904, AERP.

79. GCW, *Before the Trumpet*, 317.

80. ER to FDR, quoted in GCW, *F-C*, 17.

81. ER quoted in GCW, *Before the Trumpet*, 317.

82.   *E&F*, 123.

83.   *YT&M*, 68–69.

84.   *E&F*, 123.

85.   ER to FDR, Jan. 6, 1904, AERP.

86.   ER to FDR, quoted in *L, E*, 45.

87.   "Harvard Class Day Honors/President Roosevelt's Nephew Defeated—
      Brooklyn Man Class Odist," *New York Times*, Dec. 17, 1903, 1.

88.   ER to FDR, quoted in *L, E*, 45.

89.   *YT&M*, 186.

90.   ER, quoted in Pottker, *Sara and Eleanor*, 110.

91.   RABP, Biographical Data, Box 7, RBP.

92.   ER, quoted in Pottker, *Sara and Eleanor*, 110.

93.   SDR, quoted in Pottker, *Sara and Eleanor*, 110.

94.   SDRD, Box 68, RFPDC.

95.   TR to FDR, quoted in GCW, *Before the Trumpet*, 337–38.

96.   CRR, account of TR Inaugural 1905, Woman's Roosevelt Memorial Associa-
      tion Records, TRBA.

97.   ER, in "T. Roosevelt's Inauguration in Washington, DC," *My Husband and I*.

98.   "Social and Personal," *Ogdensburg (NY) Advance and St. Lawrence Weekly
      Democrat*, Dec. 22, 1904, 5.

99.   Edith, quoted in Jukes Morris, *Edith Kermit Roosevelt*, 289.

100. H. G. Wells, *Experiment in Autobiography: Discoveries and Conclusions of a Very
      Ordinary Brain (Since 1866)*, 679.

101. ER, in "Two Homes: Hyde Park and Campobello," *My Husband and I*.

102. "Folks: About the Big Town," *Cincinnati Enquirer*, Jan. 9, 1910, II, 1. See also
      "Roosevelts Wed 29 Years Today," *Wisconsin Rapids Daily Tribune*, Mar. 17,
      1934, 2.

103. "President Roosevelt's Program For Today," *Washington Times*, Mar. 17, 1905, 1.

CHAPTER SIX

1.   "60,000 in Parade Honor St. Patrick," *Evening World*, Mar. 17, 1905, 1.

2.   "Wedding Day Stirs Memory of the First Lady," *Pittsburgh Post-Gazette*,
     Mar. 17, 1934, 2.

3.   TR quoted in Morgan, *FDR*, 102.

4.   SDRD, quoted in Rita Halle Kleeman, *Gracious Lady*, typescript, 205, Small
     Collections, FDRL. See also *New York Times*, Mar. 18 1905, 1.

5.   Hall, *Social Customs*, 77–78.

6.   "Theodore Roosevelt and Franklin Delano Roosevelt, 26th and 32nd Pres-
     idents of the United States," American Heraldry Society, https://www
     .americanheraldry.org/heraldry-in-the-usa/arms-of-famous-americans/presi
     dents-of-the-united-states/theodore-roosevelt-and-franklin-delano-roosevelt
     -26th-and-32nd-presidents-of-the-united-states, accessed June 18, 2012.

7.   *YT&M*, 177–78. See also Mildred Adams, "When T. R. Gave His Niece in

Marriage: It Was Thirty Years Ago That Eleanor Married Franklin," *New York Times Magazine*, Mar. 17, 1935, 17.

8. RPD, Apr. 28, 1933, RPP.

9. *Town Topics*, Mar. 23, 1905.

10. CRACD, Mar. 17, 1905, bMS Am 1785.8 (505), AFP.

11. ER, "I Remember Hyde Park," *Reader's Digest*, June 1963, 95.

12. Tugwell, *The Democratic Roosevelt*, 65.

13. ER, quoted in GCW, *F-C*, 18.

14. Sherwood, *Roosevelt and Hopkins*, 9.

15. *YLBL*, 29.

16. Ibid.

17. ER, "Wives of Great Men," *Liberty* 9 (Oct. 1, 1932), 12.

18. SDRD, Mar. 25, 1905, typescript, "Surprising Years," 1, Small Collections, FDRL.

19. *TIMS*, 127.

20. Height and weight: *MRSR*, 79.

21. *TIMS*, 127.

22. GCW, *F-C*, 14–15.

23. ER to Ethel Roosevelt, in GCW, *F-C*, 412.

24. Dorothy Dix, "Dorothy Dix Talks: What Kind of a Man Makes the Best Husband," syndicated column, appearing in *Ogden (UT) Standard*, Sept. 3, 1919, 5.

25. See recollection of Spruille Braden in Benjamin Welles, *Sumner Welles: FDR's Global Strategist*, 274.

26. GCW, *F-C*, 14.

27. Freidel, *The Apprenticeship*, 14.

28. ER to SDR, in *FRPL2*, 19.

29. FDR to SDR, July 30, 1905, in *FRPL2*, 51.

30. FDR to SDR, June 23, 1905, *FRPL2*, 19.

31. LAH, *The Road to the White House*, 80.

32. FDR to SDR, Sept. 7, 1905, *FRPL2*, 84.

33. *AFM*, 356.

34. *MRSR*, 57; for FDR's thinking on immaturity, see George Johnson, *Eleanor Roosevelt*, 26.

35. ER to SDR, June 19, 1905, *FRPL2*, 12.

36. FDR to SDR, June 22, 1905, *FRPL2*, 17.

37. "Nelly Post" and "tickets for Ranelagh": ER to SDR, June 19, 1905, *FRPL2*, 12; "Ranelagh *v.* Hurlingham," Sat., June 17, 1905, in "Hurlingham Club, Programme for Season 1905," *The Bystander: An Illustrated Weekly*, Vol. 6, Apr. 19, 1905, supplement, 13.

38. "Honors for Another American Girl," *Spokesman-Review* (Spokane, WA), Jan. 28, 1911, 10.

39. *TIMS*, 132.

40. *TIMS*, 132. See also ER to SDR, June 19, 1905, *FRPL2*, 13.

41. Worksop appears in *TIMS* as "Workshop," ER's typo surviving in almost all subsequent Roosevelt literature.

42. Lord Hawkesbury, "Notes on Osberton, & etc.," Nottinghamshire History, http://www.nottshistory.org.uk/articles/tts/tts1901/osberton1.htm, May 2015.

43. John Lamberton Harper, *American Visions of Europe: Franklin D. Roosevelt, George F. Kennan, and Dean G. Acheson* (Cambridge and New York: Cambridge University Press, 1996), 9.

44. ER to JPL, in private conversation, JPL Diary, Jan. 1, 1941, JPL Papers, FDRL.

45. *TIMS*, 134; ER to LAH, in Hickok, *The Road to the White House*, 81.

46. "My Day," Mar. 5, 1962.

47. *TIMS*, 128: "everywhere we went." In the revised and condensed *Autobiography* (p. 51) the pronoun changed: "books, books, everywhere *he* went."

48. *YT&M*, 186.

49. ER to SDR, July 19, 1907, *FRPL2*, 98–99.

50. FDR, quoted by ER in Robert D. Graff, Robert Emmett Ginna, and Roger Butterfield, *FDR* (New York: Harper & Row, 1962), 192.

51. Ibid., 23. See also *YT&M*, 21.

52. ER to SDR, Aug. 23, 1905, *FRPL2*, 75; *E&F*, 123.

53. ER to SDR, June 29, 1905, *FRPL2*, 28.

54. FDR to SDR, July 8, 1905, *FRPL2*, 29.

55. *TIMS*, 129.

56. Elliott Roosevelt, ed., *FDR: His Personal Letters, Vol. II, 1905–1928*, 47.

57. Ibid., 56, 57.

58. ER to SDR, July 19, 1905, *FRPL2*, 39.

59. *YLBL*, 15.

60. ER to SDR, Sept. 5, 1905, *FRPL2*, 82.

61. FDR to SDR, Sept. 7, 1905, *FRPL2*, 83.

62. *YLBL*, 15.

63. *TIMS*, 136.

64. *YLBL*, 15.

65. ER, "Wives of Great Men," *Liberty*, Oct. 1, 1932, 13, Speech and Article File, 1931–1933, Box 1397, AERP.

66. *YT&M*, 104.

67. Ibid.

68. *YLBL*, 15.

69. TR, quoted in Jukes Morris, *Edith Kermit Roosevelt*, 259.

70. *YT&M*, 134; *TIMS*, 137.

71. *YT&M*, 150.

72. *YT&M*, 151.

73. *YT&M*, 151.

74. *TIMS*, 137.

75. ER, "Wives of Great Men," *Liberty*, Oct. 1, 1932, 13.

76. *YLBL*, 15.
77. Ibid.

CHAPTER SEVEN

1. Edith Roosevelt to Isabella Ferguson, Jan. 10, 1906, Ferguson Collection, Arizona Historical Society. See also Rowley, *Franklin and Eleanor*, 46, 306n.
2. SDRD, quoted in GCW, *F-C*, 45.
3. *YLBL*, 33.
4. *AUTO*, 56.
5. Caroline Astor, born Oct. 26, 1880.
6. CDPD, Nov. 17, n.d. 1915.
7. SDRD, quoted in GCW, *F-C*, 47.
8. *TIMS*, 142.
9. Ibid.
10. Ibid.
11. *BWC*1.
12. "a short, sturdy English nurse": GCW, *F-C*.
13. "My Day," Jan. 25, 1938.
14. ER, manuscript for *Eleanor Roosevelt's Book of Etiquette*, Books and Manuscripts, AERP.
15. *History of the St. Luke's Hospital [NY] Training School for Nurses*: Fiftieth Anniversary, May 28, 1888–May 28, 1938, 37.
16. "My Day," Jan. 18, 1945.
17. *IUTW*, 84.
18. SDRD, in *E&F*, 155.
19. J. West Roosevelt, M.D., *In Sickness and In Health*, 887.
20. SDR, quoted in GCW, *F-C*, 49.
21. *ISTM*, 45.
22. Laura Delano to JPL: "Eleanor was very close to my mother. When Eleanor became desperate about Aunt Sallie, she would take refuge with my mother," JPLP.
23. Ibid.
24. SDR, quoted in *E&F*, 160.
25. ER, quoted in *E&F*, 160.
26. FDR to ER, July 19, 1916, *FRPL2*, 310.
27. City Directory: 118 East 37th Street, Bayard Tuckerman and Annie Osgood Smith Tuckerman.
28. Lily Polk, quoted in *E&F*, 160.
29. Letter, n.d. [1940], from unnamed Scottish governess, quoted in JPLD, Jan. 1, 1941, JPLP.
30. *AUTO*, 59; *ISTM*, 92.
31. *TIMS*, 147.
32. FDR to SDR, quoted in *E&F*, 159.

33. *E&F*, 159.

34. SDRD: "I had Doe and Paul and Franklin for Xmas dinner. Hall went to Corinne's. He and Franklin and I lunched at Corinne's, 14 in all."

35. FDR to SDR, Aug. 22, 1905, in *FRPL2*, 72; SDR, *My Boy Franklin*, 65.

36. SDR "thought that our house was too small": *TIMS*, 152.

37. SDR to FDR and ER, Christmas 1905, facsimile of drawing on letterhead in *E&F*, 161.

38. SDR to Warren Delano, Apr. 15, 1908, Delano Family Papers, Cont. 49, FDRL.

39. The United States Census of 1930.

40. See Marks, *Still Counting: Achievements and Follies of a Nonagenarian*, 19. Edward B. Marks, Sr., owner of a popular music company, his wife Miriam, and a daughter and son lived at 53 East 65th Street. Edward B. Marks, Jr., future UNICEF executive and author, was born in 1911.

41. Laura Delano to JPL, JPLP.

42. Roosevelt and Shalett, *Affectionately, F.D.R.*, 29.

43. SDRD, Apr. 2, 1916, Box 68, RFPDC.

44. Standard Oil, United States Steel, the Morgan Bank, the American Tobacco Company: "Franklyn [*sic*] Roosevelt's Residence," *Poughkeepsie (NY) Eagle-News*, Oct. 28, 1910, 7.

45. SDRD, May 10, 1907, Box 67, RFPDC.

46. ER, recording made by John Cotter, Nov. 21, 1959, S-490, transcript, 18–19, FDRL.

47. "In the subsequent years I saw him wound members of his entourage who were more sensitive or had allowed themselves to become personally involved." Biddle, *In Brief Authority*, 5.

48. "She had a sense of the ridiculous, but not a sense of humor." Margaret Cutter to JPL, Aug. 13, 1966, Box 44, JPLP.

49. ER, "Insuring Democracy," *Collier's* 105, June 15, 1940, 70.

50. SDRD, Dec. 17, 1908.

51. ER, "I Remember Hyde Park: A Final Reminiscence," *McCall's*, Feb. 1963.

52. Curtis Dall Roosevelt on *Treasures of New York: Roosevelt House*, WLIW21 in association with WNET.Thirteen.org.

53. *TIMS*, 170–71.

54. Dorothy Ducas Herzog quoted in Janet Rems, "Former Newspaper Woman Remembers Mrs. Roosevelt," *New York Ledger*, Lewisboro Section, Nov. 14, 1984, 1.

55. David Gray to JPL, Apr. 14, 1966, Box 44, JPLP.

56. Mrs. Lucius Wilmerding to JPL, Apr. 29, 1966, Box 45, JPLP.

57. CRAC to JPL, Apr. 27, 1966, Box 44, JPLP.

58. Mrs. Lucius Wilmerding to JPL, Apr. 29, 1966, Box 45, JPLP.

59. FDR to ER, Sept. 14, 1911, *FRPL2*, 174.

60. Ibid.

61. Ibid.
62. *TIMS*, 162.
63. ER to SDR, Aug. 20, 1907, *FRPL2*, 122.
64. SDRD, Apr. 2, 1908.
65. *TIMS*, 162.
66. *AUTO*, 62.
67. Ibid.
68. Henry Gribbon, a Poughkeepsie doctor: SDRD, Oct. 22, 1909.
69. ER, quoted in SDRD, Oct. 31, 1909.
70. ER to ISFGK, Mar. 7, 1912, FFP.
71. *IYAM*, 141.
72. *TIMS*, 168.
73. FDR was named a director of the committee when it incorporated, Nov. 1910: "Consider the Farm Babies," *New York Sun*, Jan. 27, 1910, 3; "Milk Committee Incorporated," *New York Times*, Nov. 24, 1910, 8.
74. *TIMS*, 165.
75. GCW, *F-C*, 106.
76. W. A. Warn, "Senator F. D. Roosevelt, Chief Insurgent at Albany," *New York Times Magazine*, Jan. 22, 1911, 11.
77. *E&F*, 167. See also FDR's fellow law clerk Grenville Clark, in Smith, *FDR*, 59.
78. *TIMS*, 166.
79. Ibid.
80. "Political Advertising," *Poughkeepsie (NY) Eagle-News*, Nov. 19, 1910, 5.
81. SDR Diary in *E&F*, 169.

PART III: MISSUS

1. Epigraph: ER to LAH, n.d. [early 1933], in LAH, *Reluctant First Lady*, 88.

CHAPTER EIGHT

1. *MRSR*, 73; *TIMS*, 170.
2. *TIMS,* 171.
3. LMH, quoted in *MRSR*, 74.
4. Eunice Fuller Barnard, "Madame Arrives in Politics," *North American Review* 226, No. 5, Nov. 1928, 551–56.
5. ER, "The Life of the Wife of a Public Official," Apr. 5, 1935, Speech and Article File, Box 1401, AERP.
6. Weiss, *Charles Francis Murphy, 1858–1924*, 48. See also Freidel, *The Apprenticeship*, 109.
7. Tugwell, *The Democratic Roosevelt*, 78.
8. Dearstyne, *The Spirit of New York: Defining Events in the Empire State's History*, 181.
9. "After Two Months in Office," *New York Sun*, Mar. 13, 1911, 6.
10. *TIMS*, 173–74.

11. Edmund Terry, quoted in *E&F*, 172.
12. W. A. Warn, "Senator F. D. Roosevelt, Chief Insurgent at Albany," *New York Times Sunday Magazine,* Jan. 22, 1911, 11.
13. Freidel, *The Apprenticeship*, 118.
14. Tugwell, *The Democratic Roosevelt*, 75.
15. FDR to ER, July 14, 1911, in *FRPL2*, 165.
16. Tugwell, *The Democratic Roosevelt*, 75.
17. FDR, quoted in W. A. Warn, "Senator F. D. Roosevelt, Chief Insurgent at Albany," *New York Times Sunday Magazine,* Jan. 22, 1911, 11.
18. LMH quoted from *New York Herald* in GCW, *F-C*, 134.
19. Davis, *FDR*, Vol. 1, 251.
20. Tugwell, *The Democratic Roosevelt*, 79.
21. *MRSR*, 76.
22. "Brooklyn Standard Union," *Brooklyn Eagle*, May 11, 1911, 4. See also FDR and Sheehan and the Traction Trust, in Davis, *FDR*, Vol. 1, 251.
23. *TIMS*, 174.
24. *MRSR*, 76.
25. Ruby Black, *Eleanor Roosevelt*, 26–27.
26. *MRSR*, 76.
27. Tugwell, *The Democratic Roosevelt*, 80.
28. Ruby Black, *Eleanor Roosevelt*, 8.
29. *MRSR*, 77. Typical of the period: See Edwin Nye, "Heart to Heart Talks to a Housewife," *Sentinel* (Rome, NY), July 11, 1912, 5.
30. May 12, 1908.
31. May 14, 1908.
32. ER to FDR, Apr. 17, 1912, FDRL.
33. FDR to SDR, Apr. 22, 1912, *FRPL2*, 186–87.
34. ER to FDR, Apr. 17, 1912, FDRL.
35. FDR, quoted in GCW, *The Roosevelts*, 169.
36. "Sheehan Is Not Sure," *Indianapolis Star*, Jan. 18, 1911, 2.
37. Al Smith quoted in Smith, *FDR*, 79.
38. Rowley, *Franklin and Eleanor*, 58.
39. "Society to Give Vaudeville Show," *New York Sun,* June 2, 1912, III, 1.
40. ER to ISFGK, Jan. 29, n.d. [1912], FFP.
41. Elliott Stewart, grandson of GHR, EROH.
42. "My Day," Sept. 26, 1941.
43. GHR, Groton School report, Nov. 17, 1906, Box 19, Folder 5, RFPDC.
44. Mary Newbold Morgan to JPL, May 24, 1967, Box 44, Folder 42, JPLP.
45. "Elections to Phi Beta Kappa," *Harvard Crimson*, Nov. 26, 1912.
46. ER to LAH, Aug. 21, 1934, Box 1, LAHP.
47. GHR to ER, n.d. [1911], Box 19, Folder 7, RFPDC.
48. Margaret Cutter to JPL, Aug. 13, 1966, Box 44, JPLP.
49. Ibid.

50. GHR to ER, quoted in *BWC*1, 226.

51. James Malcom, "Boom in County for Roosevelt," *Knickerbocker Press* (Albany, NY), June 20, 1914, 1.

52. *TIMS*, 195.

53. Ibid.

54. Berg, *Wilson*, 233.

55. ER to Maude Gray, July 5, n.d. [1912], David Gray Papers, FDRL.

56. Ibid., 124–25.

57. *TIMS*, 191.

58. SDR to MHG, Tuesday night, n.d. [Oct. 15?, 1912], David Gray Papers, FDRL.

59. ELHM to MHG, n.d. [Oct. 1, 1912], David Gray Papers, FDRL.

60. Freidel, *Franklin D. Roosevelt: A Rendezvous with Destiny*, 22.

61. *E&F*, 168.

62. "One Suffrage Leader on T. R.," *San Bernardino Sun*, Oct. 6, 1912, 4.

63. "'Most Beautiful' to Lead," *Anaconda (Montana) Standard*, Jan. 22, 1913, 2.

64. Ellen Carol DuBois, *Suffrage: Women's Long Battle for the Vote*, 192.

65. Rowley, *Franklin and Eleanor*, 60.

66. "Sidelights on the Secretary of the Navy," *Brooklyn Eagle*, July 6, 1913, 3.

67. Ickes, *The Secret Diary of Harold Ickes*, Vol. 2, 22.

68. FDR, quoted in Daniels, *The Wilson Era*, 124.

69. Josephus Daniels, Mar. 6, 1913, in Cronon, *The Cabinet Diaries of Josephus Daniels, 1913–1921*, 4. See also Daniels, *The Wilson Era*, 126.

70. Berg, *Wilson*, 263.

71. Ibid., 264.

72. Daniels, *The Wilson Era*, 127.

73. Elihu Root, quoted in Berg, *Wilson*, 263–64.

74. ER to ISFGK, FFP.

75. ER to ARC, in *L, E*, 64.

76. Alsop and Platt, *"I've Seen the Best of It": Memoirs*, 30.

77. ARC, quoted in Caroli, *The Roosevelt Women*, 266.

78. ER to Isabella Ferguson, Mar. 12, n.d. [1913], FFP.

79. Jonathan Daniels, *The End of Innocence*, 120.

80. FDR to ER, in *BWC*1, 201.

81. ER to FDR, Mar. 17, 1913, AERP.

82. FDR to ER, Mar. 19, 1913, Elliott Roosevelt, ed., *F.D.R.: His Personal Letters, Vol. II*, 200.

83. "What a Roosevelt!/Assistant Secretary of Navy Fails to Start a War," *Washington Herald*, Mar. 20, 1913, 4.

84. Cronon, *The Cabinet Diaries of Josephus Daniels*, 10.

85. Aileen Tone to JPL, n.d., Box 45, JPLP, FDRL.

86. ER, "The Life of the Wife of a Public Official," AERP.

87. *TIMS*, 196.

88. Keyes, *All Flags Flying*, 149.

89. Baroness Emily de la Grange to JPL, Jan. 12, 1967, Box 44, JPLP.

90. ARL, "Some Reminiscences," *Ladies' Home Journal*, Jan. 1933, 6.

91. Keyes, *All Flags Flying*, 149; Keyes, *Capital Kaleidoscope*, 24–25.

92. CDPD, Feb. 27, 1917, CDPP.

93. Ibid.

94. Daniels was responsible, "more than any other individual, for the disenfranchisement of the state's African American citizens": Craig, *Josephus Daniels: His Life and Times,* xiv. See also: David Zucchino, *Wilmington's Lie: The Murderous Coup of 1898 and the Rise of White Supremacy* (New York: Atlantic Monthly Press, 2020).

95. Josephus Daniels, quoted by ER to JPL, recorded in JPLD, July 18, 1940. Lash omits the quote from *AFM*, 135.

96. Jonathan Daniels, *The End of Innocence*, 80.

97. *BWC*1, 204.

98. ARL, in Teague, *Mrs. L*, 154, 156–57.

99. *TIMS*, 169.

100. ER to SDR, Jan. 14, 1918, in Beasley, et al., *The Eleanor Roosevelt Encyclopedia*, 281.

101. ER to SDR, Jan. 16, 1918, in Beasley, et al., *The Eleanor Roosevelt Encyclopedia*, 281.

102. TR, quoted in Willert, *Washington and Other Memories*, 65.

103. ER to SDR, May 12, 1918, in Beasley, et al., *The Eleanor Roosevelt Encyclopedia*, 281.

104. Bowers, *My Life*, 75.

105. Quigley, *Just Another Southern Town*, 78.

106. WW, quoted in Norton et al., *A People and a Nation*, 558.

107. Aileen Tone to JPL, n.d., Box 45, JPLP.

108. Nathalie Colby, "Washington Pageant," *Harper's Magazine*, Sept. 1937, 393.

109. W. A. Warn, "Senator F. D. Roosevelt, Chief Insurgent at Albany," *New York Times Magazine*, Jan. 22, 1911, V, 11.

110. Franklin K. Lane to ER, Mar. 25 [1921], in Lane and Wall, eds., *The Letters of Franklin K. Lane*, 455–56.

111. CRAC to JPL, 1st interview, Apr. 27, 1966, Box 44, JPLP.

112. EM to JPL, Jan. 9, 1968, Box 44, JPLP. See also Kirke L. Simpson (who covered FDR in the Navy Department), "Roosevelt Made Reputation Early for Quick Decisions, Willingness to Take Responsibility for Them," *St. Louis Post-Dispatch*, Apr. 16, 1945, 1-B.

113. EM to JPL, Jan. 9, 1968, Box 44, JPLP.

114. Frank Freidel interview with Josephus Daniels, May 29, 1947, Freidel, Small Collections, FDRL.

115. Lane, quoted in Alter, *The Defining Moment*, 42.

116. WW, quoted in "Fifty Who Made the Difference: A Celebration of Fifty American Originals," *Esquire*, Dec. 1983, 471.

117. Margot Asquith, Countess of Oxford, quoted as "Margot Oxford" in Gunther, *Roosevelt in Retrospect*, 214.

118. Walter Camp, quoted in Jonathan Daniels, *The End of Innocence*, 232. See also "Cabinet Officers End Seven Weeks' Athletic Training," *Washington Times*, Sept. 7, 1917, 2.

119. "It was not at all unusual to hear references to Adonis," Keyes, *Capital Kaleidoscope*, 119.

120. Admiral W. Sheffield Cowles to FDR, Aug. 17, 1917, FDRL.

121. ARH to Bernard Asbell, interview transcript, 42, BAP.

122. FDR, quoted in GCW, *The Roosevelts*.

123. Drew Pearson and Robert S. Allen, "Daily Washington Merry-Go-Round," *San Mateo (CA) Times*, May 20, 1938, 8.

124. Haitian history counts no fewer than seventeen constitutions proclaimed up to 1918; Franklin was not among their authors.

125. FDR, quoted in Jonathan Daniels, *The End of Innocence*, 145.

CHAPTER NINE

1. *TIMS*, 238.

2. "Mrs. Wilson in the City," *Washington Herald*, Oct. 18, 1913, 5.

3. Elsie Cobb Wilson. Drew Pearson, "How Roosevelt's Love Affair Broke Up," *Washington Times-Herald*, Aug. 16, 1966, B11. See also Drew Pearson, "More Details on Roosevelt Romance," *Washington Times-Herald*, Sept. 22, 1966, B15.

4. Henry Jay Macmillan, quoted in Drew Pearson, "Mrs. Roosevelt Chose to Protect FDR's Career," *Gazette (Indiana, PA)*, Sept. 4, 1968, 6.

5. "Chat of Well-Known People," *Washington Post*, Apr. 28, 1908, 11.

6. "Burial of Maj. Mercer," *Washington Post*, Sept. 15, 1917, 8.

7. "Fair, slender, full-breasted, and smiling," as Eleanor's favorite son would describe her rival: Roosevelt and Brough, *An Untold Story*, 11.

8. Ibid., 78.

9. Aileen Tone to JPL, n.d., Box 45, JPLP.

10. Roosevelt and Brough, *An Untold Story*, 11.

11. Persico, *Franklin and Lucy*, 83; ARH interview, Box 70, ARHP.

12. Roosevelt and Brough, *An Untold Story*, 68.

13. SDR to ER, n.d. [Mar. 1915], Box 8, RFPDC.

14. FDR to ER, Aug. 1, 1914, in *FRPL2*, 233.

15. Smith, *FDR*, 139.

16. FDR to ER, Aug. 2, 1914, *FRPL2*, 238.

17. ER to FDR, Aug. 7, 1914, AERP.

18. Fiske, quoted in *New York Times*, Feb. 23, 1925, 32; Feb. 24, 1925, 18.

19. FDR and Daniels, quoted in Freidel, *The Apprenticeship*, 267.

20. James Malcom, *Knickerbocker Press* (Albany, NY), June 20, 1914, n.p.

21. Golway, *Machine Made*, 299.

22. *E&F*, 194.

23. *TIMS*, 311. FDR would later say that one of the reasons he decided to run was that when the Senate was in recess he would be able to spend the whole summer with his wife and children.

24. FDR to William Castle, Box 25, William Richards Castle, Jr. Papers, 1917–1969, Herbert Hoover Presidential Library.

25. ER to LAH, Aug. 21, 1934, Box 1, LAHP.

26. ER, "What Religion Means to Me," *The Forum*, Dec. 1932, 324.

27. *The Protestant Magazine* 3, No. 1 (First Quarter 1911): 69.

28. "A Live Issue," St. Thomas Parish Episcopal Church, Dupont Circle, Washington, D. C. NW, https://stthomasdc.org/welcome/our-history/, accessed August 22, 2016.

29. "My Day," Mar. 25, 1946.

30. SDR to FDR, Oct. 7, n.d. [1915], Box 8, RFPDC; "J. G. Webb Fuel Administrator," *Poughkeepsie (NY) Eagle-News*, Oct. 25, 1917, 6.

31. ER to FDR, in *E&F*, 216.

32. Isabella Ferguson Greenway to ER, July 14, 1913, FFP.

33. ER to FDR, *E&F,* 216.

34. ARL to Jean vanden Heuvel, "The Sharpest Wit in Washington," *Saturday Evening Post*, Dec. 4, 1965, 30.

35. CDP, Diary, Feb. 9, 1917, CDPP.

36. Roosevelt and Brough, *An Untold Story*, 94.

37. Ibid., 80.

38. Ibid., 94.

39. "Text of the President's Address" and "President Calls for War Declaration, Stronger Navy, New Army of 500,000 Men, Full Co-Operation with Germany's Foes," *New York Times*, Apr. 3, 1917, 1.

40. *TIR*, 239; Berg, *Wilson*, 435–38.

41. WW, quoted in GCW, *The Roosevelts*, 202.

42. "As You Like It, Celebs We Have Met: Josephus Daniels," editorial miscellany, *Lima (OH) Daily News*, Apr. 11, 1918, 6.

43. Keyes, *All Flags Flying*, 147.

44. Strawn, *Knitting America*, 98.

45. "The Point of View," *Scribner's Magazine*, Vol. 63, Jan. 1918, 249.

46. Ibid., 250.

47. ER, quoted in LAH, "War Started Mrs. Roosevelt on Her Career in Public Life," *Boston Globe*, Nov. 11, 1932, 11.

48. "Sixteen U. S. Battleships Equipped . . . ," *Washington Post*, Feb. 24, 1918, 12.

49. "Form Refreshment Unit," *Washington Herald*, Mar. 24, 1917, 2.

50. Hubert K. Clay and Paul M. Davis, *History of Battery "C" 148th Field Artil-*

lery, American Expeditionary Forces, Memorial Edition (Colorado Springs: Out West, 1919), 30.

51. *Report of War Relief Activities 1917–1919* (American Red Cross, 1920), 33. See also photos of American Red Cross canteen, Union Station, Washington, DC, Library of Congress Prints and Photographs Division, npcc 30779.

52. Helm, *The Captains and the Kings*, 52–53.

53. *Report of War Relief Activities 1917–1919*, 53.

54. Helm, *The Captains and the Kings*, 51–52.

55. "Mrs. Wilson Presides," *Washington Post*, Feb. 15, 1918, 2.

56. JR2 quoted in Russell Freedman, *Eleanor Roosevelt*, 58.

57. *E&F*, 215; E2, *Eleanor Roosevelt, with Love*, 33.

58. *Report of War Relief Activities 1917–1919*, 33.

59. ER to ISFGK, [n.d.] Apr. 2, 1918, FCAHS.

60. ER to ISFGK, [n.d.] Apr. 2, 1918, FFP.

61. Sept. 1917 to Sept. 1918.

62. Anderson, *Zigzagging*, 1.

63. ER to LAH, "War 'My Emancipation and Education,' Mrs. Roosevelt Says in Story of Childhood," *Austin American*, Nov. 12, 1932, 5.

64. ER to SDR, July 22, 1918, Box 13, RFPDC.

65. Helm, *The Captains and the Kings*, 53.

66. *Selective Service Regulations*, Second Edition (Washington, DC: Government Printing Office, 1918), 351.

67. *TIMS*, 252.

68. Daniels, *Editor in Politics*, 26–27.

69. TR, quoted by Edith Benham Helm in "Wilson Realized Role of Messiah, Writes Secretary," *Daily Northwestern* (Oshkosh, WI), July 11, 1930, 24.

70. SJW, "Mrs. Roosevelt's New Chapter," *New York Times Magazine*, Dec. 14, 1946, 52.

71. Lombard, *While They Fought*, 14.

72. GHR to ER, Mar. 3, 1917, Box 19, RFPDC.

73. Josephus Daniels quoted in Elizabeth Cobbs, *The Hello Girls: America's First Women Soldiers* (Cambridge, MA: Harvard University Press, 2017), 57.

74. Daniels, *The Wilson Era*, 211–12.

75. FDR, quoted in Roosevelt and Brough, *An Untold Story*, 11.

76. ER to FDR, [n.d.] July 1918, Box 13, RFPDC.

77. Baroness Emily de la Grange to JPL, Jan. 12, 1967, Box 44, JPLP. See also SLP to ARH in 1925: "This horrible thing had happened, this woman named Lucy Mercer almost run off with Father. And in those days you used the word, an 'affair.' And [said Cousin Susie to Anna] 'this had been very much gossiped about at the time' but that 'thank goodness, nothing had happened,' but that it had hurt Mother very deeply. There was no divorce, you see," ARH to Bernard Asbel, interview transcript, 41, BAP.

78. Vidal, "Eleanor Roosevelt," *United States*, 744.

79. Greenwald, *Women, War, and Work*, 34.

80. ER to FDR, quoted in Morgan, *FDR*, 205.

81. "How to Save in Big Homes," *New York Times*, July 17, 1917, 3.

82. FDR to ER, July 18, 1917, *FRPL2*, 349.

83. "How to Save in Big Homes," *New York Times*, July 17, 1917, 3.

84. ER quoted in GCW, *F-C*, 364.

85. Morgan, *FDR*, 204.

86. Ibid., 205.

87. FDR to ER, July 16, 1917, in *FRPL2*, 347.

88. WSC to FSW, Aug. 8, 1917, AWP.

89. ER to FDR, Aug. 15, 1917, FDRL.

90. Roosevelt and Brough, *An Untold Story*, 86.

91. ER to FDR, quoted in Persico, *Franklin and Lucy*, 106.

92. ARL quoted in Persico, 125.

93. ER to FDR, n.d. [1918], quoted in Rowley, *Franklin and Eleanor*, 79.

94. ER, quoted in Bess Furman, "First Lady Will Observe Fiftieth Birthday Today," Associated Press, San Bernardino *Daily Sun*, Oct. 11, 1934, 2.

95. ARH to SDR, Mar. 17, 1918, Anna Roosevelt Halsted Papers, Box 69, FDRL.

96. *TIMS*, 253.

97. ER Red Cross Documents, signed by Marie D. Gorgar for the Women's Volunteer Aid, and Edyth M. Horline, Commander General Women's Volunteer Aid, American Red Cross, District of Columbia, 1917, the Dobkin Family Collection of Feminism, Glenn Horowitz Bookseller.

98. Timothy C. Dowling, ed., *Personal Perspectives: World War I*, Vol. 1 (Santa Barbara, CA: ABC-CLIO, 2006), 217–20 .

99. ER to SDR, May 12, 1918, RFPDC, Box 13, FDRL.

100. *AUTO*, 94; Renehan, *The Lion's Pride*, 118–19.

101. BWR to Eleanor Alexander Roosevelt, Dec. 2, 1942, KBRP.

102. Fred Lockley, "Journal Man Abroad," *Daily Journal (Portland, OR)*, Aug. 7, 1918, 6.

103. Anne Emerson, "Who's She in War Work," *Forum*, June 1918, 745.

104. Robinson and Edwards, *The Memoirs of Ray Lyman Wilbur*, 256.

105. ER to SDR, May 12, 1918, Box 13, RFPDC.

106. ER to ISFGK, quoted in GCW, *F-C*, 389.

107. ER to FDR, quoted in GCW, *F-C*, 389.

108. Quentin Roosevelt, quoted in Franklin R. Egloff, *Theodore Roosevelt: An American Portrait* (Madison, WI: Vantage, 1980), 172.

109. Miller Biddle, *Flora Whitney Miller*, 16–17.

110. ER to SDR, July 23, 1918, Box 13, RFPDC.

111. TR, quoted in O'Toole, *When Trumpets Call: Theodore Roosevelt After the White House*, 391.

112. CRAC to Hermann and Mary Hagedorn, Dec. 28, 1954, R200.H12i, TRC.

113. "Douglas Robinson, Brother-in-Law of Col. Roosevelt, Dies," *New York Tribune*, Sept. 13, 1918, 9.

114. ER, quoted in GCW, *The Roosevelts*, 202.

115. Kirke L. Simpson, "Roosevelt Made Reputation Early for Quick Decisions, Willingness to Take Responsibility for Them," *St. Louis Post-Dispatch*, Apr. 16, 1945, 6-B.

116. Arthur S. Link, ed., et al., *The Papers of Woodrow Wilson*, Vol. 36 (Princeton, NJ: Princeton University Press, 1981), 120.

117. FDR, quoted in GCW, *The Roosevelts*, 213.

118. *Treaty of Peace and the Covenant of the League of Nations* (Philadelphia: John C. Winston, 1920), 50.

119. FDR telegram, quoted in GCW, *F-C*, 410.

120. Livingston Davis, Diary, Sept. 19, 1918, FDR Papers as Assistant Secretary of the Navy, Box 33, FDRL.

121. *TIMS*, 268.

122. GCW, *F-C*, 393.

123. *E&F*, 226. Lash, who probably heard most from ER directly about her discovery of her husband's feelings for Lucy Mercer, identifies what ER "came upon" while taking care of FDR's mail as "Lucy's letters," without qualifying anything about their number or presentation or what she did with them or what was in them.

124. Freidel, *Rendezvous*, 33; *BWC*1, 228; Persico, *Franklin and Lucy*, 11.

125. GCW, *F-C*, 412; Rowley, *Franklin and Eleanor*, 81.

126. Persico, *Franklin and Lucy*, 10.

127. Persico, *Franklin and Lucy*, 11; Flynt and Eisenbach, *One Nation Under Sex: How the Private Lives of Presidents, First Ladies and Their Lovers Changed the Course of American History*, 105.

128. *BWC*1, 228.

129. "Blanche Wiesen Cook on: Franklin's Affair with Lucy Mercer," Reference: Interview Transcripts, Boston: WGBH, The American Experience, 1999, https://www.shoppbs.pbs.org/wgbh/amex/eleanor/filmmore/reference/interview/cook06.html.

130. Asbell, *The F.D.R. Memoirs*, 228; Persico, *Franklin and Lucy*, 10–11; Flynt and Eisenbach, *One Nation Under Sex*, 105.

131. Bundle tied with a string, in Ken Burns's documentary series *The Roosevelts: An Intimate History*; in GCW, *The Roosevelts*, the "bundle" remains, but the tied string has been omitted.

132. Aileen Tone to JPL, n.d., Box 45, JPLP.

133. Roosevelt and Brough, *An Untold Story*, 68.

134. Bottome, *From the Life*, 64.

135. Ibid.

136. SDR, quoted by James Farley to Leonard Lyons, "The Lyons Den," *Amarillo (Texas) Daily News*, June 3, 1947, 8.

137. ARL to JPL, Feb. 6, 1967, JPLP. See also ARL to CRR, in *L, E*, 69.

138. Family sources include Aunt Corinne (offered to give him "his freedom") and ARL et al. The first time the story appeared in print, in 1946, Oliver Clapper reported that, at a private "conference," ER "offered to give her husband a divorce if the woman wished to marry him. A Catholic, the woman could not marry a divorced man." Olive Clapper, *Washington Tapestry*, 238.

139. ER to Raymond Corry, quoted in Roosevelt and Brough, *A Rendezvous with Destiny*, 33.

140. ARH to BA, interview transcript, 14, BAP.

141. Bottome, *From the Life*, 64.

142. Marton, *Hidden Power: Presidential Marriages That Shaped Our Recent History*, 54.

143. GCW, *Closest Companion*, 420.

144. ARH to BA, interview transcript, 14, BAP.

145. Freidel, *A Rendezvous with Destiny*, 34: ". . . he must promise never again to see Lucy. He agreed."

146. See Margaret Cutter to JPL, Aug. 13, 1966, Box 44, JPLP.

147. ARL to Henry Brandon, "A Talk with an 83-Year-Old Enfant Terrible," *New York Times Magazine*, Aug. 6, 1967, 70.

148. JPLD, Jan. 1, 1942, JPLP.

149. ER, quoted in *L, E*, 66.

CHAPTER TEN

1. *TIMS*, 271.

2. Burns, *Roosevelt*, 66.

3. FDR to Lathrop Brown, quoted in GCW, *F-C*, 417.

4. U.S. battle figures: Harvey Cushing, *From a Surgeon's Journal, 1915–1918* (Boston: Little, Brown, 1936), 502.

5. *TIMS*, 272.

6. Woodrow Wilson, quoted in Berg, *Wilson*, 469.

7. SDR, quoted in JR2, *My Parents*, 25–26.

8. ER, quoted in GCW, *F-C*, 416.

9. ER, Diary, quoted in Roosevelt and Brough, *An Untold Story*, 106–7.

10. "Dearest Honey . . .": see *BWC*1, 223–24.

11. ER, Dinner Seating Chart, n.d. [c. 1917], research copy courtesy of the Dobkin Family Collection of Feminism, Glenn Horowitz https://www.dobkinfeminism .org/item/45281D8F-D6D6-3F4A-9746-D8544034D143/, accessed Jan. 19, 2015.

12. JR2, *My Parents*, 29.

13. "Society," *Los Angeles Times*, Apr. 29, 1919, 19.

14. ER to FDR, in *L, E*, 74. Nb: "Bolshevik" lower case in original.

15. "Antis Won't Quit Fight on Suffrage," *Brooklyn Daily Eagle*, Jan. 27, 1918, 11.

16. *TIMS*, 297.

17. Jonathan Daniels, *The End of Innocence*, 273.

18. "I hated to go," she pretended, "but I was afraid to let Franklin go without me." ER to ISFGK, July 11, FFP.

19. *TIR*, 349.

20. Sheffield Cowles, to GCW in *F-C*, 430.

21. "My Day," Jan. 4, 1951.

22. Amos, *TR: Hero to His Valet*, 157.

23. FDR to reporters, quoted in GCW, *The Roosevelts*, 217.

24. ER, quoted in *MRSR*, 56.

25. MacMillan, *Paris 1919*, 460.

26. Daniels, *Washington Quadrille*, 156.

27. Smith, *Lady Macbeth in America*, 156.

28. "Precedent by Mrs. Wilson," *Washington Post*, July 20, 1919, 17.

29. See ER to Mama, *FRPL2*: Lunch criticism led by Eleanor Foster Lansing, wife of Wilson's secretary of state, Robert Lansing; including Mrs. House, Mrs. Benson.

30. ER to SDR, Feb. 8, 1919, *FRPL2*, 467.

31. ER to SDR, Jan. 11, 1919, *FRPL2*, 450.

32. Alice Draper to JPL, Mar. 27, 1967, Box 44, JPLP.

33. See Item 172 in Papers of ARC, MS AM 1834, TRC.

34. Elinor Glyn, quoted in MacMillan, *Paris 1919*, 146.

35. MacMillan, *Paris 1919*, 146.

36. Henry Adams, quoted in Harold Dean Cater, ed., *Henry Adams and His Friends: A Collection of His Unpublished Letters* (New York: Octagon Books, 1970), lxvii.

37. Ibid.

38. ER, quoted in *L, E*, 70.

39. Eden, *Another World 1897–1917*, 121.

40. ER to ISFGK, Jul. 11, 1919, FFP.

41. "the Cathedral is *always* destroyed": ER, quoted in *E&F*, 231.

42. ER to ISFGK, Jul. 11, 1919, FFP.

43. *TIMS*, 281–82.

44. ER to SDR, Jan. 20, 1919, Box 13, RFPDC.

45. "My Day," Oct. 19, 1940.

46. Barron Lerner, "Charting the Death of Eleanor Roosevelt," Fathom: The Source for Online Learning http://www.fathom.com/feature/35672/index .html, accessed June 18, 2012, archived at https://web.archive.org/web/2012050 4045424/http://www.fathom.com/feature/35672/index.html.

47. ER to SDR, Feb. 11, 1919, Box 13, RFPDC.

48. Berg, *Wilson*, 542.

49. Scott, *Self-Portrait of an Artist*, 171, 294–95.

50. *TIR*, 349.

51. ER to SDR, Feb. 11, 1919, Box 13, RFPDC.

52. ER, Diary, quoted in *MRSR*, 114.

53. Scott, *Self-Portrait of an Artist*, 171, 294–95.

54. GWC, *F-C*, 426–27.

55. ER to SDR, Jan. 29, 1919, Box 13, RFPDC.

56. SDR to FDR and ER, Feb. 3, 1919, Box 8, RFPDC.

57. GCW, *F-C*, 428.

58. JR2, *My Parents*, 101.

59. *TIMS*, 291.

60. *TIMS*, 291.

61. "My Day," Aug. 10, 1962.

62. CRAC to Hermann and Mary Hagedorn, Dec. 28, 1954, R200.H12i, TRC.

63. Ibid.

64. FDR to Harold Ickes, quoted in Robert A. Caro, *The Path to Power: The Years of Lyndon Johnson* (New York: Alfred A. Knopf, 1982), 449.

65. CRAC to Hermann and Mary Hagedorn, Dec. 28, 1954, R200.H12i, TRC. See also William B. Baskerville, "Mighty Welcome Given Wilson on His Return Home," *Portland (OR) Daily Journal*, Feb. 24, 1998, 1.

66. FDR's memory of Coolidge's speech in Boston in February 1919, recalled at a small White House dinner on February 12, 1944, cited in Jack Bernard Tate to Louise Sevestre Tate, Feb. 16, 1944, private collection, courtesy of Robert Wood Tate.

67. *Theodore Roosevelt, American*, also known as "the *famous* Roosevelt picture," in "At the Picture Shows Tonight," *Independence (KS) Daily Reporter*, Feb. 24, 1919, 1; *The Fighting Roosevelts* was the "Film All Americans Should See, It Will Make Them Better Americans" in "Screen Favorites . . . Arcadia," *Reading (PA) Times*, Feb. 24, 1919, 6.

68. Morgan, *FDR*, 193.

CHAPTER ELEVEN

1. "Mrs. Roosevelt Back," *Washington Times*, May 6, 1919, 10. c. Apr. 9 to c. May 6, with Daniels in France, Franklin served as secretary of the navy.

2. *TIMS*, 296.

3. United States, Dept. of the Interior, *Annual Report of the Department of the Interior*, 1920, Part 2, 814.

4. "War's Insane Suffer," *Washington Post*, June 22, 1919, 1.

5. "Suffer from Low Pay," *Washington Post*, Dec. 6, 1919, 19.

6. "Killed by a Maniac," *Washington Post*, Sept. 5, 1920.

7. N. O. Messenger, "Report Horrors at St. Elizabeth's," *Sunday Star* (Washington, DC), June 22, 1919, 1. See also Archibald MacLeish, *The Eleanor Roosevelt Story* (Boston: Houghton Mifflin, 1965), 30.

8. "Revise Salaries Upward," *Washington Herald*, Dec. 7, 1919, 6.

9. "Hearing on Hospitals," *Washington Post*, Sept. 1, 1919, 1.

10. *YLBL*, 30.

11. *TIMS*, 257.
12. "'Commotion' Cured Without Medicine," *Lansing (MI) State Journal*, Mar. 27, 1920, 3.
13. FKL to James M. Cox, July 25, 1920, in Lane and Wall, eds., *The Letters of Franklin K. Lane*, 346–49.
14. "Help St. Elizabeth's," *Washington Post*, June 24, 1919, 6.
15. "$72,000 For Teachers," *Washington Post*, June 11, 1919, 4.
16. United States, Dept. of the Interior, *Annual Report of the Department of the Interior*, 1920, Part 2, 794–97.
17. "St. Elizabeth's To Get $125,000 More," *Washington Times*, June 28, 1919, 14.
18. *YT&M*, 171.
19. United States, Dept. of the Interior, *Annual Report of the Department of the Interior*, 1920, Part 2, 794–97. See also ER to ISFGK in GWC, *F-C*, 449.
20. ER to SDR, Mar. 4, 1919, RFPDC, Box 13, Folder 7, FDRL.
21. Roosevelt and Brough, *An Untold Story*, 107.
22. ER to Isabella Ferguson, in GCW, *F-C*, 447.
23. *TIMS*, 295–96.
24. ER to SDR, summer 1919, *E&F*, 239.
25. "Sec. Daniels to Hear Navy Yard Minstrels," *Washington Times*, Dec. 15, 1919, 13.
26. Mrs. Charles Hamlin, "Some Memories of Franklin Delano Roosevelt," typescript, "ER & FDR: Reminiscences by Contemporaries," Small Collections, FDRL.
27. E. C. Drum-Hunt, "Society," *Washington Herald*, Aug. 13, 1919, 7.
28. December 18, 1919.
29. E. C. Drum-Hunt, "Society," *Washington Herald*, Dec. 18, 1919, 5.
30. JR2, *My Parents*, 44.
31. ER, quoted in Lowell Thomas, "Imperturbable Eleanor," *Reader's Digest*, Apr. 1937, 89.
32. *E&F*, 239.
33. ER to FDR, quoted in Asbell, *M&D*, 15.
34. ARH to BA, interview transcript, 14, BAP.
35. ER to ISFGK, July 11, 1919, FFP.
36. ER to FDR, July 23–25, 1919, AERP.
37. "Chicago Under State Control," *Chanute (Neosho County, Kansas) Daily Tribune*, July 31, 1919, 1.
38. Jami Bryan, "Fighting for Respect: African-American Soldiers in WWI," *On Point*, Army Historical Foundation, https://www.military.com/history/fighting-for-respect-african-american-soldiers-wwi.html, accessed Dec. 14, 2018.
39. Adrian E. Cook, "At the Gates of the White House: The Washington, D.C., Race Riots of 1919," in Rhodri Jeffreys-Jones and Bruce Collins, eds., *The Growth of Federal Power in American History* (Dekalb: Northern Illinois University Press, 1983), 88–101.

40. James Weldon Johnson, *Writings* (New York: Library of America, 2004), 658–59.

41. FDR to ER, July 24, 1919, *FRPL2*, 479–80.

42. Berg, *Wilson*, 610.

43. FDR, quoted in Freidel, *The Ordeal*, 30.

44. FDR to ER, July 22–23, 1919, *FRPL2*, 479.

45. *TIMS*, 300–301.

46. ER, Diary, Oct. 5, 1919, FDRL; quoted in *E&F*, 237.

47. Bruce Catton, "The Restless Decade," *American Heritage*, Vol. 16, No. 5, Aug. 1965, 5.

48. "Mrs. Edith Morgan, Children Die in Fire," *Los Angeles Times*, Feb. 5, 1920, 13.

49. Charles Cooper Nott, Jr., and A. Mitchell Palmer, quoted in "What Is Back of the Bombs?" *Literary Digest* 61, No. 11 (June 14, 1919): 9.

50. FDR to A. Mitchell Palmer, Mar. 22, 1919, printed in *Providence Journal*, Mar. 19, 1920, 1.

51. Harold Evans with Gail Buckland and Kevin Baker, *The American Century*, 174.

52. Franklin Knight Lane, Jan. 19, 1920, in Lane and Wall, eds., *The Letters of Franklin K. Lane*, 391.

53. ER to ISFGK, Oct. 26, 1919, FFP.

54. Ferber, *A Peculiar Treasure*, 259.

55. "The One-Half of One Per Cent Roosevelt," *Chicago Tribune*, Aug. 13, 1920, 6.

56. H. L. Mencken, June 1932, quoted in Terry Teachout, *The Skeptic: A Life of H. L. Mencken*, 263.

57. ER, in "Vice Presidential Nomination—1920," *My Husband and I*.

58. SDR, quoted in GCW, *The Roosevelts*, 222.

59. *Veepee Candidate FDR*, 1920 video, Budget Films, http://www.budgetfilms.com/clip/13258/, accessed June 28, 2018.

60. ER to FDR, Aug. 27, 1920, quoted in *L, E*, 76.

61. Beschloss, *Presidents of War*, 352.

62. "Campaign of 1920," in Shields-West, *The World Almanac of Presidential Campaigns*, 156.

63. ER, quoted in *MRSR*, 118.

64. "Democratic Leaders and Their Wives," *Chicago Tribune*, July 7, 1920, 3.

65. "First Lady Biography: Grace Coolidge," National First Ladies' Library, http://www.firstladies.org/biographies/firstladies.aspx?biography=31.

66. ER, quoted in *L, E*, 77.

67. LMH had nearly thirty years on the youngest advance man, Stephen T. Early; seven years on Marvin McIntyre, the scheduler, oldest of Franklin's former-newsmen Navy Department associates; and was a full decade senior to the AP reporter and Spanish-American War veteran Kirke L. Simpson.

68. "Asst. President Is Astute and Devious," *Transcript* (North Adams, MA), May 9, 1934, 6.

69. ER, quoted in *MRSR*, 120.

70. Lotridge Levin, *The Making of FDR*, 50–51.

71. "Home and Politics Chief Interests, Mrs. Franklin D. Roosevelt Tells Eagle," *Poughkeepsie (NY) Eagle-News*, July 15, 1920, 2.

72. *TIMS*, 311.

73. Simpson was quoting Ohio Republican Harry Daugherty.

74. Ruby Black, *Eleanor Roosevelt*, 45. See also Betty Houchin Winfield, *FDR and the News Media* (New York: Columbia University Press, 1994), 13; Stanley W. Prenosil, 1895–1967, obituary, *Press (Asbury Park, NJ)*, Apr. 13, 1967, 2; Kirke L. Simpson, 1881–1972; obituary, *New York Times*, June 17, 1972.

75. ER, "Women in Politics," in Allida Black, ed., *What I Hope to Leave Behind*, 253.

76. Ibid.

77. ARH interview, Box 44, JPLP.

78. ER to SDR, Oct. 19, 1920, Box 13, Folder 11, RFPDC.

79. *TIMS*, 318.

80. A few of FDR's 1920 campaign speeches were "carried on the radio in a pioneering effort": "Franklin Delano Roosevelt's Desk, Working in New York City, 1921–1928," Roosevelt House at Hunter College website.

81. Jonathan Daniels, *The End of Innocence*, 319.

82. "Popguns and Duds of Politics," *Oregon Statesman*, Sept. 15, 1920, 2.

83. "The First Award for Harding," *St. Louis Times* credited with story in *Lincoln (NE) Evening Journal*, Sept. 20, 1921, 4.

84. Turner Catledge to Richard Reeves, in "John F. Kennedy, 1961–1963," Wilson, ed., *Character Above All*, 95.

85. ARL to Jean vanden Heuvel, "The Sharpest Wit in Washington," *Saturday Evening Post*, Dec. 4, 1965, 33.

86. See multiple articles around the U.S., including *Lima (OH) News*, May 8, 1920, 4; Morgan, *FDR*, 229–30.

87. *Minneapolis Tribune* editorial re-run as "Mr. Roosevelt and Haiti," *Wichita (KS) Beacon*, Sept. 7, 1913, 12.

88. "Crowd at Roosevelt Meeting Jeers Laudatory Reference to President," *Butte (MT) Daily Bulletin*, Aug. 18, 1920, 2.

89. Jonathan Daniels, *The End of Innocence*, 319.

90. Hatch, *Franklin D. Roosevelt*, 124–25.

91. "3 Die in Gas Explosion at Niagara Falls," *Democrat and Chronicle* (Rochester, NY), Oct. 22, 1920, 1.

92. "Plans to Harness Niagara Power and Not Mar Beauty," *Wichita (KS) Daily Eagle*, Oct. 6, 1920, 8.

93. Five feet six inches: Alfred B. Rollins, "Notes for *Roosevelt and Howe*: Hartley Howe comments on mss," Small Collections, FDRL.

94. Roosevelt and Brough, *An Untold Story*, 126.

95. *TIMS*, 314.

96. Ibid.

97. LMH quoted in Fenster, *FDR's Shadow*, 147.

98. ER, quoted in Faber, *Life of Lorena Hickok*, 281.

99. "Campaign of 1920," in Shields-West, *The World Almanac of Presidential Campaigns*, 159.

100. Stanley Prenosil's reporting from Salina, Kansas, in "'Twas Very Possible!" *Daily Capital* (Topeka, KS), Nov. 11, 1920, 5.

101. James M. Cox, editorial, *Atlanta Journal*, Apr. 14, 1945, quoted in "Cox Thinks Yalta Meeting Broke F.D.R.'s Health," *St. Louis Post-Dispatch*, Apr. 15, 1945, 4A. Cox recalled FDR: "He was sure the common people of the country loved him."

102. Jonathan Daniels, *The End of Innocence*.

103. ER, "The Life of the Wife of a Public Official," Apr. 5, 1935, ERPP.

104. SDR, 1920 Datebook, Nov. 2, 1920, Papers of SDR, Roosevelt Family Papers, Box 68, FDRL.

CHAPTER TWELVE

1. ER, quoted in ER and LAH, *Ladies of Courage*, 262.

2. Howard A. Shiebler, "Franklin D. Roosevelt, Who Seeks to Make 'Al' Smith President," *Brooklyn Daily Eagle*, June 1, 1924, 5.

3. "Bok Peace Contest Ruled 3 Women; One Was Dictator," *Brainerd (MN) Daily Dispatch*, Jan. 25, 1924, 1.

4. Esther Lape to JPL, interview, Feb. 24, 1970, JPLP.

5. Ibid.

6. *E&F*, 264.

7. FDR quoted in Freidel, *The Ordeal*, 93.

8. ER, quoted indirectly in Roosevelt and Brough, *An Untold Story*, 133.

9. "Governor Cancels Date to Address Women Voters," *New-York Tribune*, Jan. 23, 1921, 3.

10. Esther Lape to JPL, interview, Feb. 24, 1970, JPLP.

11. Kleeman, *Gracious Lady*, 134.

12. "My Day," Dec. 15, 1943.

13. ER to EL, quoted in *BWC2*, 518.

14. ER, quoted in Roosevelt and Brough, *An Untold Story*, 132.

15. Esther Lape to JPL, *E&F*, 261.

16. Edith Wharton, "The Touchstone," *Scribner's*, Mar., Apr. 1900, reprinted in Wharton, *The Touchstone*, 51.

17. June Hamilton Rhodes, "Woman Praises Mrs. Roosevelt for Her Qualities of Leadership," *Louisville Courier-Journal*, Oct. 9, 1932, 3.

18. EL to JPL, Mar. 3, 1970, Box 44, JPLP.

19. Elizabeth Read to Narcissa Vanderlip, quoted in *BWC1*, 298.

20. ER to FDR, Apr. 11, 1921, quoted in *E&F*, 264.

21. ER, quoted in *E&F*, 263.

22. ER to FDR, Apr. 11, 1921, in *E&F*, 264.

23. ER to Edna Gellhorn, Dec. 17, 1940, Edna Gellhorn Collection, Series 4, Box 12, Folder 25, University Archives, Department of Special Collections, Washington University Libraries, Washington University in St. Louis. See also Lisa Marie Lillie, "Votes for Women: Edna Gellhorn and the Social Networks of American Suffragettes," Mar. 8, 2017, https://library.wustl.edu/edna-gellhorn -suffragettes/, Oct. 19, 2017.

24. "My Day," Aug. 25, 1945.

25. "God Calling Women to Guide World to Peace, Says Mrs. Catt," *Pittsburgh Daily Post*, Apr. 14, 1921, 7.

26. "Order Deportation Soviet Chancellor," *Salt Lake City Telegram*, Jan. 21, 1921, 2.

27. ER, quoted in *E&F*, 263. Cunningham: "Take an active part in what was happening to your country as a whole."

28. "Women Censure Coolidge," *New York Times*, May 25, 1921, 10.

29. "Coolidge Is Censured by Club Women," *Poughkeepsie (NY) Eagle News*, May 24, 1921, 1.

30. ER, quoted in *BWC*1, 303.

31. EL to JPL, Mar. 3, 1970, Box 44, JPLP.

32. Jukes Morris, *Edith Kermit Roosevelt*, 451.

33. *TIMS*, 330.

34. "Burns Tells Story of Plot to Throw 1919 World Series," *New York Times*, July 20, 1921, 1.

35. ER to FDR, July 22, 1921, AERP.

36. "Lay Navy Scandal to F. D. Roosevelt," *New York Times*, July 20, 1921, 4.

37. Ibid.

38. FDR, quoted in Fenster, *FDR's Shadow*, 143.

39. Oursler, *Behold the Dreamer*, 374–77.

40. "I was head of the Boy Scouts in my part of the State. I was on five State committees. I was on seven committees in the State legislature. I was interested in all sorts of relief and social work. I was tied up with the Legion, with biographies that were being written about President Wilson, with all sorts of interesting things going on in Washington, Albany, and New York, and I had a law practice." FDR to Marie M. Meloney, Dec. 11, 1938, quoted in Marie M. Meloney interview notes, "Sunday, December Eleventh, 1938," Marie M. Meloney Papers, Box 34, Columbia University Rare Book and Manuscript Library.

41. MLH to ER, Aug. 23, 1921, Family/Business/Personal Correspondence File, FDRL.

42. FDR, quoted in Looker, *The American Way: Franklin Roosevelt in Action*, 134.

43. ER to JRR, Aug. 14, 1921, *FRLP*2, 524.

44. FDR, "A History of the Case in Franklin D. Roosevelt's Own Words," *Journal of the South Carolina Medical Association* 45, No. 1, Jan. 1945.

45. Gareth Williams, *Paralyzed with Fear: The Story of Polio*, 2. See also "Nation's Anti-Polio Fight Began 25 Years Ago in Vermont, Where Scourge First Struck Hard," *Burlington (VT) Free Press*, Oct. 20, 1939, 10. Statistically nothing like

the global predator that influenza or even diphtheria had become in the previous decade. "Fears No Infantile Paralysis," *Boston Post*, Jan. 3, 1921, 4.

46. Donald G. McNeil, Jr., "In Reaction to Zika, Echoes of Polio," *New York Times*, Aug. 30, 2016, D3.

47. Tobin, *The Man He Became*, 159.

48. Algeo, *The President Is a Sick Man*, ix.

49. FDR, "A History of the Case in Franklin D. Roosevelt's Own Words."

50. "Fears No Infantile Paralysis," *Boston Post*.

51. FDR, quoted in Marie M. Meloney interview notes, "Sunday, December Eleventh, 1938," Marie M. Meloney Papers, Box 34, Columbia University Rare Book and Manuscript Library.

52. "Fears No Infantile Paralysis," *Boston Post*, Jan. 3, 1921, 4.

53. GD to RWL, Sept. 9, 1921, RWLP.

54. *AUTO*, 278.

55. Conrad Black, *Franklin Delano Roosevelt*, 138; H. W. Brands, *Traitor to His Class*, 148.

56. "Franklin D. Roosevelt Reported Better," *Boston Post*, Aug. 28, 1921, 10.

57. Roosevelt and Brough, *An Untold Story*, 153.

58. JAR to Nina Roosevelt Gibson, in Pottker, *Sara and Eleanor*, 221.

59. "Franklin D. Roosevelt on Road to Recovery," *(Burlington, VT) Free Press*, Sept. 15, 1921, 1.

60. "F. D. Roosevelt Ill of Poliomyelitis," *New York Times*, Sept. 16, 1921, 1.

61. See AW to FSW, Nov. 6, 1921, Box 6, Folder 233, AWP: "Afterwards I went to the Roosevelts', Franklin being back in their house. He is better. [Colonel] House [had] told me that he understood that he would never walk again!"

PART IV: STATE-WOMAN

1. Epigraph: *TIMS*, 297.

CHAPTER THIRTEEN

1. GD quoted in Freidel, *The Ordeal*, 101.

2. "What Is Infantile Paralysis?" *Boston Globe*, June 4, 1922, 61.

3. SDR to ER, Sept. 4, 1921, quoted in Pottker, *Sara and Eleanor*, 216.

4. FF interview with ER, July 13, 1954, FFSC.

5. FDR to Margaret "Daisy" Suckley, quoted in GCW, *Closest Companion*, xvii.

6. "Treat Victims of Infantile Malady with New Method," *Danville (VA) Bee*, Aug. 13, 1927, 6.

7. EL to JPL, Feb. 24, 1970, *L, E*, 120.

8. ER to JRR, quoted in *E&F*, 272.

9. "Democrats Gain in Four States from Election," *Democrat Chronicle* (Rochester, NY), Nov. 10, 1921, 1; "Democrats Carry Off All Honors in 'Off Year' Election Down in Metropolis," *Democrat Chronicle* (Rochester, NY), Nov. 9, 1921, 1; Burns, *Roosevelt*, 91.

10. "What Is Infantile Paralysis?," *Boston Globe*, June 4, 1922, 61.

11. Ibid.

12. ER and LMH, quoted in GCW, *F-C*, 616–17.

13. "Franklin Roosevelt, Cripple, Launches Drive for Memorial to Wilson, Casualty of War," *Austin American*, Jan. 16, 1922, 1.

14. *TIMS*, 341.

15. FDR, quoted in GCW, *F-C*, 606.

16. "Joffre Sails Today, Happy at Tributes," *New York Times*, Apr. 29, 1922, 18.

17. SDR, *My Boy Franklin*, 101.

18. FDR Jr. and ER, quoted in GCW, *The Roosevelts*, 228.

19. JAR, EROH, Nov. 10, 1977, EROH.

20. Edna Rockey appears in diaries, letters, and accounts of Franklin's recovery as a "looker" or a "knockout."

21. *History of United States Army Base Hospital No. 20* (Philadelphia, PA: University of Pennsylvania, 1920), 145–46; "Real Marital Preparedness," *Pennsylvania Gazette*, Mar. 16, 1917, 321.

22. Kathleen Lake quoted in GCW, *F-C*, 622.

23. Kathleen Lake to RWL, Jan. 22, 1922, RWLP.

24. GD to RWL, May 2, 1922, RWLP.

25. LMH quoted in *Roosevelt and Brough: An Untold Story*, 205; Kathleen Lake quoted in Pottker, *Sara and Eleanor*, 220.

26. FP, Pt. 2, Session 1, 328, CUOHROC.

27. "Women Democrats Plan State Machine," *New York Times*, May 12, 1922, 15.

28. MD to JPL, Jan. 30, 1967, JPLP.

29. *YT&M*, 94.

30. *YT&M*, 94, 98.

31. "My Day," May 30, 1936.

32. Herbert Claiborne Pell, "Roosevelt vs. Landon," *Daily Argus* (Mount Vernon, NY), Oct. 22, 1936, 4.

33. ER, *The Wisdom of Eleanor Roosevelt*, 106; cited in *E&F*, 277–78.

34. FF, *FDR: The Ordeal*, 110.

35. CDPD, Apr. 1, 1932, 232–37, CDPP, folder 14.4.

36. Vesta Kelling, "Mrs. Henry Morgenthau, Kin of Lehman, One of First Lady's Warmest Friends/Nancy Cook Also Ranks High on List," *Knickerbocker News* (Albany, NY), May 22, 1941, A1.

37. SDR to ER, quoted in Dall, *F.D.R.*, 45.

38. RP, Apr. 28, 1933, Box 1, RPP.

39. JWP, EROH.

40. LMH, quoted in Looker, *The American Way: Franklin Roosevelt in Action*, 166.

41. Lucia McCurdy McBride, quoted in "Women Want Facts in Politics, Says Citizenship School Leader," *Tribune (Bismark, ND)*, Sept. 2, 1920, 5.

42. LMH quoted in "My Day," Feb. 19, 1955.

43. ER quoted in "Says Miller Angers Women," *New York Times*, Aug. 7, 1922, 10.

44. ER, quoted in Rose Feld, "Women Are Slow to Use the Ballot," *New York Times*, Apr. 20, 1924, IX-1.

45. ER to EM, *L, E*, 92.

46. "The Reminiscences of Marion Dickerman," 1973, 15, CUOHROC.

47. EL to JPL, Jan. 16, 1970, JPLP.

48. Ann V. Masters, "Out of Rich Life, Headmistress Recalls Rare Friendship with Eleanor, FDR," *Post (Bridgeport, CT)*, Dec. 15, 1974, 83.

49. MD to JPL, Jan. 30, JPLP.

50. *L,E*, 96.

51. "Women Advance Upon Syracuse," *Poughkeepsie (NY) Eagle-News*, Sept. 27, 1922, 1; "State Convention Opens at Syracuse," *Olean (NY) Times-Herald*, Sept. 27, 1922, 2.

52. "Democrats See Victory with Alfred E. Smith," *Ithaca (NY) Journal-News*, Sept. 30, 1922, 7.

53. "sinister figure": "Murphy Will Name Leader of Democrats," *Syracuse (NY) Post-Standard*, Sept. 24, 1922, 1.

54. Warner, with Daniel, *The Happy Warrior*, 135.

55. "Many Rumors at Syracuse," *Poughkeepsie (NY) Eagle-News*, Sept. 29, 1922, 1.

56. "Reminiscences of Herbert Claiborne Pell," Vol. 2, 312, CUOHROC.

57. Ibid.

58. This was Franklin's first run-in with the imperious public-works prodigy Robert Moses, but even this future nemesis of Eleanor's, the neighborhood-destroying master-builder of Greater New York, couldn't kill the delight Franklin took from foresting parkway medians with native trees and building overpasses and filling stations with native stone facings—a signature FDR fusion of progress and preservation. Ghee and Spence, *Taconic Pathways: Through Beekman, Union Vale, LaGrange, Washington, and Stanford*, 9–11.

59. Hall to ER, Nov. 9, 1922, quoted in *E&F*, 279–80.

60. "Reminiscences of Jonathan Worth Daniels," 1972, 37, CUOHROC.

61. "It was a certain gambling spirit in him": ER to FF, July 13, 1954, FFSC.

62. Roosevelt and Shalett, *Affectionately, F.D.R.*, 181.

63. ER to FF, interview transcript, 4, FFSC.

64. FDR, quoted in Gallagher, *FDR's Splendid Deception*, 92.

65. "Many Besieging Come for Advice He Seeks a Rest," *Franklin (PA) News-Herald*, Jan. 6, 1923, 1.

66. "The Compressed Air Cure," *Windsor (Ontario, Canada) Star*, Sept. 1, 1920, 12.

67. *MRSR*, 136.

68. Beran, *The Last Patrician*, 51.

69. "Science's New Sun-and-Water Cure for 'Hopeless Cripples,'" *Morning Call* (Allentown, PA), Jan. 11, 1925, 31.

70. FDR to ER, Oct. 1924, quoted in Gallagher, *FDR's Splendid Deception*, 34.

71. C. Vann Woodward, quoted in Kennedy, *Freedom from Fear*, 19.

72. Durr, *Outside the Magic Circle: The Autobiography of Virginia Foster Durr*, 183.

73. *TIR*, 27.

74. Ibid.

75. FP, *The Roosevelt I Knew*, 68.

76. "Local Brevities," *Farmers' Advocate* (Steuben, NY), June 6, 1923, 5.

77. "Meeting Is Arranged for Democratic Party Women," *Saugerties (NY) Telegraph*, Aug. 24, 1923, 4.

78. ER quoted in William H. Chafe, "Eleanor Roosevelt (1884–1962)," in G. J. Barker-Benfield and Clinton, eds., *Portraits of American Women: From Settlement to the Present*, 469.

79. "Social Notes," *New York Times*, Feb. 9, 1923, 15.

80. "Roosevelt Home Afire; Servants Soon Quench It," *New York Daily News*, Feb. 26, 1923, 43.

81. "Louis McHenry Howe, One of Strangest Behind Scenes in American History /How He 'Drove' Franklin D. Roosevelt from Invalidism to White House," *Boston Globe*, Apr. 25, 1954, 128.

82. FP, oral history interview, part 2, session 1, p. 330, CUOHROC.

83. Roosevelt and Brough, *An Untold Story*, 228.

84. SDR quoted by Rita Halle Kleeman, unpublished notes, 1938–1941, Box 1, RHKP.

85. *L,E*, 101.

86. *YLBL*, 67.

87. ER to FDR, n.d.c. Dec. 1926], *L, E*, 101.

88. *TIMS*, 336.

89. Quoted in *E&F*, 274.

90. JR2, *My Parents*, 67.

91. JH to BA, Jan. 26, 1980, transcript, 9–10, BAP.

92. Ibid.

93. Nancy Cook to Dorothy Schiff, recorded in notes, July 9, 1985, Box 64, DSP.

94. *TIMS*, 338.

95. Gore Vidal, author's interview, Dec. 2, 2010.

96. "Reminiscences of Anna Roosevelt Halsted," 1973, 9, CUOHROC.

97. ARH to JPL, Box 44, JPLP.

98. "Reminiscences of Anna Roosevelt Halsted," CUOHROC.

99. ARH to JPL, June 22, 1966, JPLP.

100. Helen Roosevelt Robinson to CDP, Feb. 13, 1936, CDPD.

101. LMH to Grace Howe, July 10, 1922, Howe Papers, FDRL.

102. ARH, "Reminiscences of Anna Roosevelt Halsted," 1973, 9, CUOHROC.

103. "New York Society," *Chicago Tribune*, July 31, 1924, 19.

104. ARH to ER, *M&D*, 33.

105. ARH, Box 44, JPLP.

106. ARH to BA, interview transcript, 3, Pt 2, BAP.

107. Ibid.
108. Ibid., Pt. 3.
109. Chafe, *Private Lives, Public Consequences*, 13.
110. ER quoted in Rowley, *Franklin and Eleanor*, 133.
111. Claudia Hatch Stearns, Vassar College, Class of 1929. Her parents, fellow *Mayflower* descendants of SDR, had a place in Saugerties.
112. Claudia Hatch Stearns quoted in Kisseloff, *You Must Remember This*, 137.
113. Bottome, *From the Life*, 68.
114. Quoted in *E&F*, 304.
115. EL to JPL, Mar. 12, 1970, Box 44, JPLP.
116. ER to FDR, quoted in Freedman, *Eleanor Roosevelt*, 81.
117. *L,E*, 100.
118. SDR to FDR, quoted in *L, E*, 100.

CHAPTER FOURTEEN

1. Log of the *Larooco*, Feb. 5, 1924, in Chase, ed., *FDR on His Houseboat*, 16.
2. ER to FDR, Feb. 6, 1924, AERP.
3. "New York Pays Homage to Memory of Wilson," *Marion (OH) Star*, Feb. 6, 1924, 1.
4. Ibid.
5. "Chain of Appeals on World Court," *Wilmington (DE) News Journal*, Aug. 22, 1925, 5.
6. Ibid.
7. "Meet Busy Mrs. Roosevelt," *Bismarck (ND) Tribune*, Dec. 24, 1928, 5.
8. *BWC*1, 243, citing *Women's Democratic News*, July 1927.
9. ER to FDR, Feb. 6, 1924, AERP.
10. Gabrielle Forbush interview, Small Collections, Oral History, Interviews A–O, FDRL, 8.
11. ER to FDR, Feb. 6, 1924, AERP.
12. ER quoted in GCW, *The Roosevelts*, 150.
13. ER quoted in *L, E*, 87.
14. FDR, quoted in "Silent Strength Held Murphy Dominant Over Tammany for 22 Years," *Brooklyn Eagle*, Apr. 25, 1924, 2.
15. Allowing only 2 percent of all entrants from any one country: See Johnson, *A History of the American People*, 670.
16. Harry Laughlin, Eugenics Records Office, testifying to Congress, 1924; quoted in Carl Zimmer, *She Has Her Mother's Laugh: The Powers, Perversions, and Potential of Heredity* (New York: Penguin Random House, 2019), 93.
17. FDR, editorial, *Telegraph* (Macon, GA), Apr. 30, 1924.
18. "Coolidge Signs the Immigration Bill," *New York Times*, May 27, 1924, 1.
19. "My Day," Jan. 23, 1939.
20. "Coolidge Signs the Immigration Bill," *New York Times*, May 27, 1924, 2.

21.   "Fiery Cross Illumines Hillside," *Hopewell (NJ) Herald*, June 4, 1924, 1.
22.   "American Vatican Under Way," *Yellow-Jacket* (Moravian Falls, NC), Oct. 1, 1924, 6.
23.   "Jersey Klan Endorses Republican Nominees," *New York Times*, Nov. 3, 1924, 2.
24.   "Roosevelt Claims Strength of Smith Is Rapidly Increasing," *Republic* (Phoenix, AZ), June 28, 1924, 1.
25.   Clinton W. Gilbert, "Mirrors of Washington: A Fine Nominating Speech to Deaf Ears," *Nashville Tennessean*, July 3, 1924, 4.
26.   Ibid.
27.   *Brooklyn Daily Eagle*, July 8, 1924, 1.
28.   Fenster, *FDR's Shadow*, 205–7.
29.   JR, quoted in Stephen Hess, *America's Political Dynasties: From Adams to Clinton*, 201.
30.   ER, indirectly quoted in caption, *Daily Argus* (Mount Vernon, NY), July 9, 1924, 3.
31.   Krock, quoted in Brown, *Setting a Course: American Women in the 1920s*, 21.
32.   Maxine Davis, "Women Delegates Take Convention as Grave Affair," *Syracuse (NY) Journal*, July 2, 1924, II-1.
33.   James Farley to Nancy Joan Weiss, Nov. 7, 1964, in Weiss, *Charles Francis Murphy, 1858–1924*, 120.
34.   "Biggest 'Teapot' Gunners for Dems in New York," *Nevada State Journal*, Nov. 1, 1924, 7. See also Gidlow, *The Big Vote*, 180.
35.   Dwight Lowell Dumond, *Roosevelt to Roosevelt: The United States in the Twentieth Century* (New York: Holt, 1937), 378–79.
36.   "Oil's Well! Miss Roosevelt Chases Teapot Dome Bubbles," *New York Daily News*, Oct. 22, 1924, 11.
37.   ISFGK to John C. Greenway, Oct. 20, 1924, quoted in *AVOF*, 200.
38.   ARL in Pietrusza, *1920: The Year of Six Presidents*, 430–31.
39.   ARH to JPL, Box 44, JPLP.
40.   ER to MD, *L, E*, 101.
41.   Margaret Cutter to JPL, Aug. 13, 1966, Box 44, Folder 13, JPLP.
42.   Dall, *F.D.R.: My Exploited Father-in-Law*, 43–44.
43.   Ibid.
44.   ER, quoted in Esther A. Coster, "Mrs. Franklin D. Roosevelt: Political Woman and Old-Fashioned Wife and Mother," *Brooklyn Daily Eagle*, Oct. 19, 1924, 79.
45.   John Auwaerter and Laura Roberts, *Cultural Landscape Report for Eleanor Roosevelt National Historic Site, Hyde Park, New York*, Vol. 2 (Boston: Olmsted Center for Landscape Preservation, National Park Service), 2019, 5–6, http://www.nps.gov, accessed Oct. 3, 2019.
46.   "My Day," Oct. 13, 1937.
47.   MD to JPL, Feb. 26, 1968, JPLP.
48.   ARH to JPL, June 22, 1966, JPLP.

49. ER to FDR, May 4, 1926. *FRPL2*, 611.

50. ER quoted in Rowley, *Franklin and Eleanor*, 136.

51. ER to FSW, July 21, 1932, Box 6, Folder 224 (I. Correspondence), MS 720, AWP.

52. ER to FSW, Jan. 19, 1933, Box 6, Folder 224 (I. Correspondence), MS 720, AWP.

53. See ER, "Building Character," *Parents' Magazine*, June 1931, 17.

54. EL to JPL, Mar. 12, 1970, JPLP.

55. EL to JPL, Mar. 30, 1970, Box 44, JPLP.

56. CBD to Jeanette and Curtis Roosevelt, Jan. 19, 1977, CRP, Box 8, FDRL.

57. EN: EL to JPL, Apr. 7, 1970, Box 44, JPLP.

58. ARH to JPL, Box 44, JPLP.

59. ER, quoted in GCW, *F-C*, 748.

60. SDR to ER quoted in Rowley, *Franklin and Eleanor*, 136.

61. Albin Krebs, "Anna Roosevelt Halsted, President's Daughter, Dies," *New York Times*, Dec. 2, 1975, 42.

62. ER to ISFGK, Jan. 1, 1927, FFP.

63. ER to FDR, quoted in GCW, *F-C*, 784.

64. FDR to Emil Ludwig, in Flynn, *Country Squire*, 36.

65. Kirke L. Simpson, "F. D. as I Knew Him," *Pantagraph* (Bloomington, IN), Apr. 19, 1945, 8.

66. Will Durant, quoted in *Windsor (Ontario, Canada) Star*, Dec. 3, 1930, 4.

67. Pauline Morton Sabin, her Republican Party counterpart, an outspoken advocate of Prohibition repeal, daughter of Uncle Ted's secretary of the navy, and heiress to the Morton salt fortune, was the other.

68. Anne O'Hare McCormick, "Enter Woman, the New Boss of Politics," *New York Times Magazine*, Oct. 21, 1928, 3.

69. Freeman, *A Room at a Time: How Women Entered Party Politics*, 297n.

70. Editorial, *Corvallis (OR) Gazette-Times*, Oct. 12, 1928, 2.

71. FDR, quoted in "Southeastern States Strong for Governor, Says Roosevelt," *Ithaca (NY) Journal*, Oct. 4, 1928, 1.

72. "This Year's Woman Vote to Set a High Record," *New York Times*, Oct. 21, 1928, 8.

73. Anne O'Hare McCormick, "Enter Woman, the New Boss of Politics," *New York Times Magazine*, Oct. 21, 1928, 3.

74. LAH, "Two Women Leaders Shape Plans for Active Campaign," *Lansing (MI) State Journal*, Aug. 16, 1928, 9. See also LAH, "Women Active in '28 Campaign/Mrs. Franklin D. Roosevelt and Mrs. Charles H. Sabin Lead Two Rival Parties," *Shreveport (LA) Times*, Aug. 16, 1928, 15.

75. FP, III, 13, CUOHROC.

76. June Hamilton Rhodes, "Woman Praises Mrs. Roosevelt for Her Qualities of Leadership," *Louisville Courier-Journal*, Oct. 9, 1932, 3.

77. Ibid., 1.

78. FP, III, 16, CUOHROC. See also FP, quoted in Elisabeth Israels Perry, *Belle Moskowitz*, 152–53.

79. June Hamilton Rhodes, "Woman Praises Mrs. Roosevelt for Her Qualities of Leadership," *Louisville Courier-Journal*, Oct. 9, 1932, 1.

80. Henry James called TR a "wonderful little machine." Eleanor's tendency to take action for wrongs done others would increasingly remind political observers of Uncle Ted: "She is his reincarnation." Walter Johnson, ed., *Selected Letters of William Allen White, 1899–1943* (New York: Henry Holt, 1947), 403.

81. June Hamilton Rhodes, "Woman Praises Mrs. Roosevelt for Her Qualities of Leadership," *Louisville Courier-Journal*, Oct. 9, 1932, 1.

82. "My Day," Mar. 23, 1948. See also Paul Comly French, "Mrs. Pinchot Joins Strikers at Sweatshop," *Pottstown (PA) Mercury*, May 5, 1933, 1.

83. Editorial, *Corvallis (OR) Gazette-Times*, Oct. 12, 1928, 2.

84. June Hamilton Rhodes, "Woman Praises Mrs. Roosevelt for Her Qualities of Leadership," *Louisville Courier-Journal*, Oct. 9, 1932, 3.

85. ML to FDR, quoted in AMS2, *The Age of Roosevelt*, Vol 1, 382.

86. Ibid.

87. ER to June Hamilton Rhodes, quoted in "Our New First Lady," *Des Moines (IA) Register*, Nov. 13, 1932, 67.

88. "Why Mrs. Roosevelt Did Not Object," *Boston Globe*, Dec. 16, 1928, A-53.

89. "A 'Flattering' Campaign," *New York Times*, Oct. 17, 1928, 28.

90. "Why Mrs. Roosevelt Did Not Object," *Boston Globe*, Dec. 16, 1928, A-53.

91. Ibid.

92. LAH, "Mrs. Roosevelt Is 'Whirlwind' in Vitality, Spartan in Her Habits," *Lincoln (NB) State Journal*, Nov. 12, 1932, 4.

93. "Mrs. F. D. Roosevelt a Civic Worker," *New York Times*, Nov. 9, 1932, 9.

94. "Mrs. F. D. Roosevelt's Religion," *Brooklyn Eagle*, Oct. 21, 1928, 6.

95. "Democrats of Three Counties Hear Campaign Discussion by Mrs. Franklin D. Roosevelt," *Jamestown (NY) Evening Journal*, Sept. 15, 1928, 5.

96. Ibid.

97. Ibid.

98. "Roosevelt Sharp on 'Intolerance,'" *New York Times*, Oct. 21, 1928, 29.

99. Gunther, *Roosevelt in Retrospect*, 95.

100. ER to FSW, Jan. 19, 1933, Box 6, Folder 224, AWP.

101. One reason why actors later had such trouble with the earlier FDR: Where was this predator's leer coming from?

102. H. L. Mencken, June 1932, quoted in Teachout, *The Skeptic: A Life of H. L. Mencken*, 263.

103. Roosevelt and Shalett, *Affectionately, F.D.R.*, 200.

104. Lord Chancellor of London, Lord Sankey, quoted in "Rita Halle Kleeman, 85, Dead; Wrote Life of Young Roosevelt," *New York Times*, May 17, 1981.

105. ER to EFM, *L, E*, 112.

106. "Busy Mrs. Roosevelt Finds Time for One More Big Job," *Milwaukee Journal*, Dec. 26, 1928, 16.

CHAPTER FIFTEEN

1. FDR, quoted in Conrad Black, *Franklin Delano Roosevelt*, 249.
2. LAH, *Reluctant First Lady*, 59.
3. Ibid.
4. *TIR*, 74.
5. NCL dinner, Nov. 15, 1928, in Florence Kelley to Alice Hamilton, Nov. 22, 1928, in Sklar and Palmer, eds., *The Selected Letters of Florence Kelley, 1869–1931*, 439.
6. KSD, *Invincible Summer*, 107–8.
7. *Selma (AL) Times-Journal*, Oct. 18, 1932, 1.
8. *Sioux City Journal*, Nov. 10, 1932, 13.
9. *Knoxville News-Sentinel*, Nov. 9, 1932, 8.
10. Rodger Streitmatter, ed., *Empty Without You: The Intimate Letters of Eleanor Roosevelt and Lorena Hickok*, 8.
11. Warner B. Ragsdale to Doris Faber, Dec. 13, 1978, the Papers of Doris Faber relating to *The Life of Lorena Hickok, E.R.'s Friend*, 1971–1989, Box 2, FDRL.
12. LAH, Associated Press clippings, [n.d.] Sept. 1932, LAHP.
13. LAH, *Reluctant First Lady*, 10.
14. Ibid.
15. Ibid.
16. Herbert Hoover, *Public Papers of the Presidents of the United States, 1929* (Washington, DC: United States Government Printing Office, 1974), 383.
17. Herbert Hoover, *Congressional Record*, Vol. 75 (Washington, DC: United States Government Printing Office, 1974), 9771.
18. HH and FDR quoted in "Rival Prophets," editorial, *Baltimore Sun*, May 5, 1930, 21.
19. ER quoted in "Mrs. Roosevelt—America's Most Unusual Woman," *Cairns (Queensland, Australia) Post*, Sept. 4, 1943, 2.
20. "Servant Union Urged by Mrs. Roosevelt," *Hamilton (OH) Journal News*, June 16, 1930, 4.
21. "My Day," Oct. 17, 1955.
22. ER quoted in "First Lady Sees Chance for U.S. to Prove Democracy," *York (PA) Gazette and Daily*, Nov. 15, 1939, 5.
23. "Poor Find Champion in Mrs. Roosevelt," *New York Times*, July 2, 1932, 7.
24. ER, quoted in Cain, *Quiet: The Power of Introverts*, 139.
25. ER, quoted in "Eleanor Roosevelt's Health Secrets," *Healthful Living Digest* 19, No. 2 (Spring–Summer 1959): 5.
26. Ibid.
27. Harry Houdini, *The Right Way to Do Wrong: An Exposé of Successful Criminals* (Boston: Harry Houdini, 1906), 94.

28. Esther A. Coster, "Mrs. Franklin D. Roosevelt—Political Woman and Old-Fashioned Wife and Mother," *Brooklyn Sunday Eagle Magazine*, Oct. 19, 1924, 13.

29. JEL, author's interview, Mar. 5, 2011.

30. ER to EFM, Apr. 29, 1927, Box 512, HMP, FDRL.

31. EM's account of putting Vallie under restraint: "As I wrestled him down, the cords stood out in his head." *L, E*, 119.

32. ER to EFM, Apr. 29, 1927.

33. *L,E*, 254.

34. ER, n.d., unsigned typescript, 1948, JRP, FDRL.

35. Claude Bowers, *My Life*, 252.

36. Earl Miller to JPL, Feb. 8, 1968, Box 44, JPLP.

37. "Farley to Go West with Roosevelt/Wedding of Bodyguard at Hyde Park Gives the Candidate an Interlude from Politics," *New York Times*, Sept. 9, 1932, 3.

38. Ibid.

39. ER, n.d., unsigned typescript, 1948, JRP, FDRL.

40. EM, quoted in Cal Campbell, "Little Known Characters in America," *Journal Gazette & Times-Courier* (Mattoon, IL), Nov. 7, 2016, 4.

41. *L,E*, 245.

42. MD to JPL, Feb. 26, 1968, Box 44, JPLP.

43. Rhoda Lerman, in Henry Mitchell and Megan Rosenfeld, "Eleanor Roosevelt and the Styles of Friendship," *Washington Post*, Oct. 23, 1979.

44. ER, n.d., unsigned typescript, 1948, JRP.

45. ER to LAH, in *BWC*2, 405.

46. LAH quoted in Kenneth S. Lynn, *The Air-line to Seattle*, 154–55.

47. David Kaszuba, "'Auntie Gopher': Lorena Hickok Tackles College Football," *Minnesota History* 60, No. 3, Fall 2006, 100–12.

48. LAH to Virginia Safford in *Minneapolis Star*, June 6, 1941, 25.

49. Ibid.

50. Ibid.

51. Vesta Kelling, "Many of Mrs. FDR's Closest Friends Have Stained Their Fingers with Printer's Ink," *Danville (VA) Bee*, May 22, 1941, 10.

52. Ibid.

53. Abe Altrowitz, "Lorena Hickok's Newspaper Career Was Colorful, Vital—Memories of Her Abound," *Minneapolis Star*, May 16, 1968, 4B. LAH also recalled as "a legend in Minneapolis newspaper circles": "Mrs. Roosevelt Faces Busy Twin Cities Day," *Minneapolis Star Journal*, June 3, 1941, 19.

54. David Kaszuba, "'Auntie Gopher': Lorena Hickok Tackles College Football," *Minnesota History* 60, No. 3, Fall 2006, 101.

55. LAH, "Mrs. Roosevelt in Night Flight over New York," *Danville (VA) Bee*, Nov. 30, 1932, 3.

56. LAH, *Reluctant First Lady*, 48.

57. Ibid., 49.

58. "Mrs. Roosevelt's Activities," *Herald-News* (Passaic, NJ), Jan. 30, 1933, 8.

59. "Mrs. Roosevelt Says Drys Made Tipplers of Girls," *New York Daily News*, Dec. 10, 1932, 26.

60. ER, Dec. 9, 1932, quoted in "Murphy Flays Gov. Dickinson for Criticism," *Buffalo Courier-Express*, July 21, 1939, 2.

61. Norman Vincent Peale, quoted in "W.C.T.U. Wildly Applauds Attack on Mrs. Roosevelt," *New York Daily News*, Jan. 15, 1933, 38.

62. Gerald Eskenazi, "Morey Wins Seniors Golf For Third Year in a Row," *New York Times*, June 9, 1977, Sports Section, 93.

63. Norman W. Getsinger, interviewed by Charles Stuart Kennedy, Jan. 19, 2000, 4, Association for Diplomatic Studies and Training, Foreign Affairs Oral History Project, https://www.adst.org/OH%20TOCs/Getsinger,%20 Norman%20W.toc.pdf, accessed Nov. 4, 2016.

64. Roth, *Portnoy's Complaint*, 237.

65. William Crowninshield Endicott, Aug. 1, 1933, AER & FDR Reminiscences by Contemporaries, Small Collections, FDRL.

66. "New First Lady," *Nashville Tennessean*, Feb. 7, 1933, 4.

67. "Dr. Pruette Answers Charge Women Do Not Know Executive Technicalities," *Pittsburgh Press*, Jan. 8, 1933, 36.

68. Aaron, *The Inman Diary*, 527.

69. Maxwell E. Perkins to V. F. Calverton, in Berg, *Max Perkins*, 213–14.

70. Nancy Astor, MP, quoted in "Anything to Live!," *Cincinnati Enquirer*, Dec. 14, 1932, 10.

71. "Mrs. Roosevelt Displays Furniture in Town House," *New York Daily News*, Dec. 5, 1932, 17.

72. "Eleanor, Frances, and Martha," *Sioux City (IA) Journal*, Mar. 28, 1935, 8.

73. ER quoted in Ruth Reynolds, "It's So Hard to Say No: But Mrs. Roosevelt Will Curtail Her Fund Raising," *New York Daily News*, Jan. 22, 1933, 5.

74. ER, "How to Take Criticism," *Ladies Home Journal*, Nov. 1944, 171.

75. ER quoted in LAH, "Mrs. Roosevelt Dreads 'First Lady' Role," *Milwaukee (WI) Sentinel*, Nov. 10, 1932, 22.

76. Ibid.

77. Golay, *America 1933*, 31.

78. Damon Runyon, "Serious Throngs See Leader Inducted," for Universal Service, in *Sunday Light* (San Antonio, TX), Mar. 5, 1933, 1.

79. ER, quoted in Muller, *Adlai Stevenson*, 37.

80. Nicolson, ed., *Diaries and Letters of Harold Nicolson*, 140.

81. AMD, Mar. 6, 1933, Box 2, AEMP.

82. "President Reject," *Time*, Nov. 14, 1932, 31.

83. Ibid.

84. *TIR*, 78.

85. ER, quoted in LAH, "New Deal Pledged for White House," *Louisville Courier-Journal*, Mar. 5, 1933, 1.

86. Runyon, "Serious Throngs See Leader Inducted."

87. ER, quoted by Martha Gellhorn in introduction, *Eleanor Roosevelt's My Day*, xii.

88. Julia Blanchard, "Tour of the New White House," *Dunkirk (NY) Evening Observer*, Mar. 11, 1933, 8.

89. Parks, *A Family in Turmoil*, 5.

90. Edmund Wilson, *Travels in Two Democracies* (New York: Harcourt, Brace, 1936), 45.

91. RPD, Mar. 4, 1933, RPP.

92. Fields, *My 21 Years in the White House*, 46.

93. ER, quoted in AMD, Mar. 6, 1933, Box 2, AEMP.

PART V: MRS. ROOSEVELT

1. ER to servicemen overseas: "Mrs. R's Travels," in *My Husband and I*.

CHAPTER SIXTEEN

1. ER to LAH, Mar. 5, 1933, Box 1, LAHP.

2. E2, quoted in Felsenthal, *Alice Roosevelt Longworth*, 180.

3. ER to LAH, Mar. 9, 1933, Box 1, LAHP.

4. Length of FDR's time in office: 4,422; factor in the many days/nights when ER was traveling.

5. See ER to LAH, Mar. 6, 1933, Box 1, LAHP.

6. ER, quoted in BF, *Washington By-Line*, 220.

7. ER, quoted in Graff, Ginna, and Butterfield, *FDR*, 192.

8. Ibid.

9. "Would-Be Assassin Opens Fire as Roosevelt Finishes Brief Speech," *Salt Lake City (UT) Tribune*, Feb. 16, 1933, 12.

10. "Woman Who Saved FDR Buried Same Day as His Wife," *Ocala (FL) Star-Banner*, Nov. 11, 1962, 25.

11. Ibid.

12. RCD, 1933, Box 8, Folder 4, RCP. See also "Rumor-Mongers Busy," *Minneapolis Star*, Mar. 6, 1933, 6.

13. FDR, quoted in Smith, *An Uncommon Man: The Triumph of Herbert Hoover*, 152.

14. "Franklin D. Roosevelt (Assassination Attempt)," Department of Government Information and Special Formats, Otto G. Richter Library, Miami University, 2002, http://digital.library.miami.edu/gov/FDRAssn.html, archived at https://web.archive.org/web/20110115190422/http://digital.library.miami.edu/gov/FDRAssn.html, accessed Apr. 30, 2020.

15. ER to Mary E. Patten, Feb. 17, 1933, http://www.amazon.com/ELEANOR-ROOSEVELT-TYPED-LETTER-SIGNED/dp/B0099SYVAY, accessed Aug. 21, 2014.

16. LAH, quoted in *EMR*, 151.

17. ER to LAH, Mar. 7, 1933, Box 1, LAHP.

18. CDPD, April 26, 1932–June 25, 1933, MC 560, folder 15.1, 1897–1961.

19. FDR quoted in Roger Daniels, *Franklin D. Roosevelt: Road to the New Deal, 1882–1939* (Champaign: University of Illinois Press, 2015), 150.

20. Errol Lincoln Uys, *Riding the Rails: Teenagers on the Move During the Great Depression* (New York: Routledge, 2003), viii.

21. Harry Hopkins, quoted by Susan Ware, *Beyond Suffrage: Women in the New Deal*, 106.

22. See H in Forrest Anderson Walker, "The Civil Works Administration: An Experiment in Federal Work Relief, 1933–1934," PhD diss., University of Oklahoma, 1962, 39–40.

23. HH quoted in "Many Jobs," *Semi-Weekly Light (Corsicana, TX)*, Nov. 21, 1933, 5.

24. See Ware, *Beyond Suffrage*, 107.

25. Shelby, "Giving Her A Lift To Town," Dec. 2, 2014, incorrectly dates the John L. Knott cartoon, which was published in the *Dallas Morning News*, Wed, Nov. 22, 1933. "Language and Humor in Archives," University of Texas Libraries, University of Texas at Austin, http:www/blogs.lib.utexas.edu/nonaka /category/fall2014/, archived at https://web.archive.org/web/20171024071142 /http://www.blogs.lib.utexas.edu/nonaka/category/fall2014/, accessed Apr. 30, 2020.

26. ER to LAH, Aug. 3, 1933, LAH typescript, Box 1, LHP.

27. Ibid.

28. "My Day," Apr. 1, 1939.

29. ER to LAH, Dec. 25, 1933, LAHP.

30. ARH to JPL, Box 44, Folder 22, JPLP.

31. *L,E*, 137.

32. JPLD.

33. JB to ER, Aug. 13, 1943, BAP.

34. Associated Press, "President's Daughter Is Enjoying Honeymoon After Secret Marriage in N.Y. to Chicago Newspaperman," *Gloversville (NY) Morning Herald*, Jan. 19, 1935, 8.

35. Alice Behrendt, b. Oct. 31, 1899, d. Aug. 1980. "Boettiger a Suicide In 7-Floor Plunge," *New York Times*, Nov. 1, 1950, 38.

36. JH to BA, Pt. 26, BAP.

37. JH to BA, Jan. 26, 1980, BAP.

38. ER to LAH, Aug. 3, 1933, LAH typescript, Box 1, LHP.

39. ER to LAH, May 16, 1933, Box 1, LHP.

40. Stephen R. Ortiz, *Beyond the Bonus March and GI Bill: How Veteran Politics Shaped the New Deal Era* (New York: New York University Press, 2010), 100.

41. See *Corpus Christi Caller-Times*, Nov. 16, 1952, 13.

42. "Mrs. Roosevelt's Pearls," *Cairns Post* (Queensland, Australia), May 23, 1940, 9.

43. SDR quoted in Pottker, *Sara and Eleanor*, 283.

44. CBD to ARH, Sept. 10, 1948, Box 8, CRP.

45. SDR, quoted in "My Day," Mar. 29, 1958.

46. AMS2, notes, typescript, Jan. 20, 1947, AMSP, NYPL.

47. Belle Willard Roosevelt, Diaries, n.d. [Aug. 1942], LOC.

48. ER to LAH, Mar. 8, 1933, Box 1, LAHP.

49. ER to LAH, May 27, 1933, LAH typescript, Box 1, LAHP.

50. ER to LAH, May 31, 1933, Box 1, LAHP.

51. Elliott's attitude about his parents is similar to that of Tony Soma, known as "Broadway Tony," who ran a speakeasy in the late twenties and early thirties, a favorite hangout for writers and theater people. "Roosevelt changed the country back into the United States today. We are still adventurous today. I would give credit not to F.D.R., but to Mrs. Roosevelt. She was the genius of that family. He was a vain man." See Terkel, *Hard Times*, 175.

52. E2 to ER, n.d. [c. 1932–33], Tucson, AZ, JARP.

53. "First Lady to Start Coast Flight Today," *Washington Post*, June 4, 1933, 12.

54. "Aged Woman Who Invited Herself Is Roosevelt Guest," *Miami (OK) News-Record*, June 4, 1933, 1.

55. *Popular Aviation*, Apr. 1934, 228.

56. *New York Times*, quoted in *BWC2*, 44.

57. *Chicago Daily News*, Dec. 1, 1937, II, 2A.

58. Steve Early memo, Folder 1932–33, AERP.

59. "First Lady Takes Test to Be Pilot," *(NY) Daily News*, Nov. 20, 1933, 25.

60. ER to Amelia Earhart, Dec. 4, 1933, Amelia Earhart Papers, George Palmer Putnam Collection, Libraries and School of Information Studies, Purdue University. See also: ". . . foolish since we do not have a ship and we can't afford to buy one just now": ER, quoting FDR in Joan Thomas, "The Aero-Sportswomen," *Popular Aviation*, Apr. 1934, 228.

61. Will Rogers, "Mr. Rogers Lists First Lady As New Heroine in Aviation," *New York Times*, June 8, 1933, 17.

62. See ER to Amon G. Carter, June 13, 1933; Amon G. Carter to ER, June 25, 1933; ER Papers, Series 100, FDRL.

63. "All-American Woman," editorial, *Fort Worth Star-Telegram*, June 16, 1933, 12.

64. Elliott Roosevelt, *Murder and the First Lady*, 173.

65. Quoted in ER to LAH, Aug. 3, 1933, LAH typescript, Box 1, LHP.

66. ER to LAH, Aug. 3, 1933, LAH typescript, Box 1, LHP.

67. ER to LAH, June 8, 1933, LAH typescript, Box 1, LHP.

68. Parks, *The Roosevelts*, 142.

69. ER to LAH, June 8, 1933, LAH typescript, Box 1, LHP.

70. Ibid.

71. ER to LAH, June 14, 1933, typescript, Box 1, LHP.

72. ER to LAH, Mar. 7, 1933, typescript, Box 1, LHP.

73. ER to LAH, Mar. 11, 1933, Box 1, LHP.

74. LAH to ER, Aug. 15, 1933, Box 1, LAHP.

75. LAH to ER, Sept. 21, 1938, in "'The Big One': Hurricane of September 21, 1938," Ken Spooner, Spooner Central, http://www.spoonercentral.com/2007/Hurricane.html, accessed Mar. 9, 2020.

76. LAH to ER, Aug. 15, 1934, Box 1, LAHP.

77. LAH to ER, Dec. 5, 1933, Box 1, LAHP.

78. ER to LAH, Dec. 17, 1935, Box 2, LAHP.

79. ARL quoted in Paul Horgan, "Mrs. L," *A Certain Climate: Essays in History, Arts, and Letters* (Middletown, CT: Wesleyan University Press, 1988), 180–81.

80. Phillips, *From the Crash to the Blitz*, 474.

81. MCT, Introduction, ER, *My Days*, 7.

82. By 1938, sixty-two papers (circulation 4,034,552): Margaret Marshall, "Columnists on Parade: Eleanor Roosevelt," *Nation* 146, No. 14 (Apr. 2, 1938): 386.

83. "Fill her up Mrs. Roosevelt?" blog post, *Scranton Times Tribune*, Apr. 27, 2012, http://blogs.thetimes-tribune.com/pages/index.php/2012/04/, archived at https://web.archive.org/web/20150320084904/http://blogs.thetimes-tribune.com/pages/index.php/2012/04/, accessed Apr. 8, 2016.

84. See Roberts, *A History of New York in 101 Objects*, 74–76.

85. *Gloversville (NY) Morning Herald*, May 10, 1933.

86. Frederic J. Haskin, "Answers to Questions," *Kokomo Tribune* Information Bureau, Washington, DC, *Kokomo (IN) Tribune*, Feb. 4, 1937, 4.

87. Kathleen McLaughlin, "Mrs. Roosevelt Goes Her Way," *New York Times Magazine*, July 5, 1936.

88. ER, quoted in Steinberg, *Mrs. R*, 231–32.

89. ARL, "The Ideal Qualifications for a President's Wife," *Ladies' Home Journal*, Feb. 1933, 9.

90. Miss Gladys Eleanor Key to ER, June 25, 1959, ER Papers, Box 3576, FDRL.

91. May Thompson Evans, Jan. 30, 1978, EROII, FDRL.

92. "So This Is Washington!," *Daily Northwestern* (Oshkosh, WI), June 13, 1933, 7.

93. ER's 1957 pistol application, FDRL, indicates that she had previously been granted a pistol license in 1933.

94. "My Day," Mar. 13, 1937.

95. ER to FDR quoted in Page Smith, *Redeeming the Time: A People's History of the 1920s and the New Deal* (New York: McGraw Hill, 1987), 478.

96. Ibid.

97. Ibid.

98. Douglas, *Go East, Young Man*, 317.

99. Farley to John H. Sharon, in Sharon, *The Psychology of the Fireside Chat*, Vol. 1.

100. Perkins, *Roosevelt As I Knew Him*, 90.

101. Sharon, *The Psychology of the Fireside Chat*, Vol. 1.

102. Clipping, June 19, 1934, RABP.

103. ER, "In Defense of Curiosity," *Saturday Evening Post*, Aug. 24, 1935, 8. See Box 1402, AERP.

104. Penix, *Arthurdale*, 10.
105. ER, "Address to the Chicago Civil Liberties Committee," Mar. 14, 1940, ER Papers Project.
106. Henry Ward, "First Lady Secretly Tours Coal Mining," *Pittsburgh Press*, Aug. 18, 1933, 1.
107. "First Lady Makes Secret Mine Visit," *Pittsburgh Press*, Aug. 18, 1933, 5.
108. ER, quoted in United States Department of the Interior, National Register of Historic Places fact sheet on Arthurdale, Section 8, page 2, https://npgallery.nps .gov/GetAsset/e18ab861-5a2b-4e46-b1c1-8dca2c8cbffe, accessed Feb. 16, 2017.
109. "First Lady Secretly Tours Coal Mining Area to Learn Facts," *Pittsburgh Press*, Aug. 18, 1933, 1.

CHAPTER SEVENTEEN

1. Sam Stack, "Elsie Ripley Clapp and the Arthurdale Schools," 1999, https://www .semanticscholar.org/paper/Elsie-Ripley-Clapp-and-the-Arthurdale-Schools .-Stack/a33eac1f37efc7299fe30303246b23160163cf16, accessed Jan. 11, 2012.
2. Sadovnik and Semel, eds., *Founding Mothers and Others*, 101–2.
3. Joseph Mitchell, "Anna Eleanor Roosevelt," *New York World-Telegram*, May 20, 1935, 1.
4. *Time*, source for "Editorial of the Day," *Olean (NY) Times Herald*, Mar. 23, 1942, 10.
5. "A Trip Through Time: Grand Rapids Furniture History," The Woodshop, McLure Tables, Grand Rapids, Michigan, 2015, https://shuffleboardmcclure tables.com/a-trip-through-time-grand-rapids-furniture-history/, accessed Oct. 19, 2018.
6. Vandenberg, quoted in Meijer, *Arthur Vandenberg*, 85.
7. "Mrs. Roosevelt Uses Radio Pay to Help Needy," *Asheville (NC) Citizen-Times*, Mar. 4, 1935, 10.
8. Sulmasy and Brick, "Too Busy to Be Sick."
9. ER, "In Defense of Curiosity," *Saturday Evening Post*, Aug. 24, 1935, 9.
10. "Caring for Husband Is Better Than Own Career," *Wilkes-Barre (PA) Evening News*, Nov. 2, 1934, 16.
11. Ibid.
12. JPL, *L, E*, 91.
13. George Gallup, "First Lady's Popularity Tops F.D.R.'s," *Louisville Courier-Journal*, Jan. 15, 1939, III-1.
14. Fields, *My 21 Years in the White House*, 60.
15. ER quoted in Patrick Shaughnessy, "Mrs. Roosevelt Visits the Palisades," *The Palisades News: A Newsletter of The Palisades Citizens Association*, Vol. 13, No. 1, October 2001, 7–8.
16. Speer, *Inside the Third Reich*, 365.
17. "Why Not a Party for Black and White Virgins," *Time*, May 25, 1936.
18. "My Day," Feb. 4, 1937.

19. ARH to BA, interview transcript, 28, BAP.

20. "Louis M. Howe, Roosevelt's Aide And Friend, Dies," *Montgomery (AL) Advertiser*, Apr. 19, 1936, 1.

21. ARH to BA, interview transcript, 28, BAP.

22. FDR, quoted in *MSR*, 235.

23. "Wife of President Speaks Today for Friend, Mrs. O'Day," *Brooklyn Eagle*, Oct. 25, 1934, 15.

24. ER, quoted in "Mrs. Roosevelt Will Make Five Campaign Talks," *Freeport (IL) Journal-Standard*, Oct. 15, 1934, 1.

25. "First Lady Assumes Stump Speaker Role," *Louisville Courier-Journal*, Oct. 24, 1934, 2.

26. Ibid.

27. "Mrs. Roosevelt In Contest," *Great Falls (MT) Tribune*, Oct. 26, 1934, 1.

28. Beasley et al., eds., *The Eleanor Roosevelt Encyclopedia*, 89.

29. Pickett, *For More Than Bread*, 49.

30. Ibid.

31. Ickes, *The Secret Diary of Harold Ickes*, Vol. 1, 143–45.

32. Beasley et al., eds., *The Eleanor Roosevelt Encyclopedia*, 89.

33. ER to STE, Aug. 8, 1935, FDR Papers, Box 1336, FDRL.

34. Ibid.

35. FDR quoted by Walter White, *A Man Called White*, 169.

36. Thurgood Marshall to Carl Rowan, in Rowan, *Dream Makers, Dream Breakers*, 131.

37. Ibid.

38. King, *Devil in the Grove*, 30–31.

39. ER to LAH, while collaborating on *Ladies of Courage*, cited in JPL, *Years Alone*, 264.

40. "U.S. Worse Than Hitler, Baron Tells H.U. Head," *Baltimore Afro-American*, Feb. 17, 1934, 15.

41. "From the Land of the Lynchers," *Das Schwarze Korps*, the weekly newspaper of the SS, German Propaganda Archive, Calvin College, http://research.calvin.edu/german-propaganda-archive/sk.htm.

42. Mann, *Diaries*, 244.

43. "German Official Blames Jews," *West Palm Beach (FL) Post*, Oct. 5, 1935, 1.

44. FDR quoted in "Roosevelt Asks U.S. Join World Court at Once," *Brooklyn Daily Eagle*, Jan. 16, 1935, 2.

45. FDR, Message to the Senate, quoted in "Adherence to Court Requested," *Moberly (MO) Monitor-Index*, Jan. 16, 1935, 1.

46. EL to ER, Jan. 15, 1935.

47. "20,000 Cheer Coughlin's Attack on Bonus Veto," *New York Daily News*, May 23, 1935, 3, 10.

48. Charles Edward Coughlin, quoted in "Backs World Court Entry," *Windsor (Ontario, Canada) Star*, Jan. 28, 1935, 14.

49. Ibid.

50. ER, "World Court Broadcast," Jan. 27, 1935, 10:45–11:00 p.m., NBC Red Network, in Smith, ed., *The First Lady of Radio*, 70–73.

51. "Senate Beats World Court . . . ," *New York Times*, Jan. 30, 1935, 1.

52. "Protests Flood Wires," *Philadelphia Inquirer*, Jan. 28, 1935, 3.

53. Hiram Johnson, quoted in *E&F*, 559.

54. FDR to Joseph T. Robinson, Jan. 30, 1935, in Elliott Roosevelt, ed., *F.D.R.: His Personal Letters, Vol. III*, 450.

55. Ickes, *The Secret Diary of Harold L. Ickes*, Vol. 1, 284–85.

56. FDR to Mary Caperton Bingham, Oct. 1944, quoted in Freidel, *Franklin D. Roosevelt*, 547.

57. See Ickes's biographical notes, "A Reader's Guide to People," in *The Secret Diary of Harold L. Ickes*, Vol. 1, 5.

58. ER to Elinor Morgenthau, n.d. [Apr. 1936], HM2P, Box 512, FDRL.

59. ER to LAH, Apr. 19, 1936, Box 2, LAHP.

60. ER to LAH, Nov. 11, 1940, Box 2, LAHP.

61. ER to LAH, Nov. 15, 1940, Box 2, LAHP.

62. Smith, *The Gatekeeper*, 89.

63. ER to LAH, Apr. 19, 1936, Box 2, LAHP.

64. "No Banjo Stunt on Roosevelt Tour; He Rejects Wife's Plan," *Chicago Tribune*, June 3, 1936, 4.

65. Ibid.

66. ER to LAH, see Hoff-Wilson and Lightman, *Without Precedent*, 21.

67. ER to LAH, Apr. 27, 1935, Box 2, LAHP.

68. Mary E. Woolley, "Because Wars Waste Human Life," from *Why Wars Must Cease*, quoted in Isabel M. Ellis, "Women—And What They Are Doing," *The (Camden, NJ) Morning Post*, Jan. 26, 1935, 12.

69. ER, Carrie Chapman Catt et. al., *Why Wars Must Cease* (New York: Macmillan, 1935), 28.

70. Sen. Homer T. Bone, "News of the Week," *Phoenix (AZ) Republic*, Aug. 25, 1935, 9.

71. "Germany Backing Roosevelt's Bid for World Peace," *West Palm Beach (FL) Post*, Oct. 4, 1935, 1.

72. *TIR*, 162.

73. *Jim Farley's Story*, 225.

74. Joseph Mitchell, "Anna Eleanor Roosevelt," *New York World-Telegram*, May 20, 1935, 1.

75. "Table 8.—Population of Voting Age (21 Years and Over) by Sex, Color, Nativity, and Citizenship: 1930 and 1920," *Fifteenth Census of the United States: 1930, Population Bulletin, 2nd Series, United States Summary* (Washington, DC: United States Government Printing Office, 1931), 9.

76. "Oracle," *Time*, Apr. 17, 1939, 21–22.

77. Editorial, *Baltimore Afro-American*, May 23, 1936.

78. Rayford W. Logan, quoted in Weiss, *Farewell to the Party of Lincoln*, 122.

79. Leuchtenburg, *The White House Looks South*, 132, 458n.

80. This list comes from ER to Carl Rowan, c. June 20–July 3, 1957, quoted in Rowan, *Dream Makers, Dream Breakers*, 1993, 140.

81. "Mrs. Roosevelt Objects to Coal Bins and Wash Tubs in the Same Room," *Lawrence (KS) Journal-World*, Nov. 12, 1936, 1.

82. Ibid.

83. ER, "Some of My Best Friends Are Negro," *Ebony*, Feb. 1953, 17.

84. Carl T. Rowan, "The Life of Eleanor Roosevelt," *New York Post*, Mar. 20, 1958, 24.

85. "Eleanor Club Quest Fails," clipping, Sept. 22, 1942, in ER FBI File. See also Carl T. Rowan, "The Life of Eleanor Roosevelt," *New York Post*, Mar. 20, 1958, 24, and Leuchtenburg, *The White House Looks South*, 133.

86. JM, "Anna Eleanor Roosevelt," *New York World-Telegram*, May 20, 1985, II-15.

87. "Opinion Of Mrs. Roosevelt On Hauptmann Verdict Is Debated," *Wilmington (CA) Daily Press Journal*, Feb. 25, 1935, 1.

88. "The League and Gas," *Montgomery (AL) Advertiser*, Apr. 21, 1936, 4.

89. See AMS's account of the 1936 convention in Schlesinger, *The Age of Roosevelt*, Vol. 3, *Politics of Upheaval*, 583–84.

90. Clapper, *Washington Tapestry*, 112.

91. "Navy Plans Air Armor on Warship," *Hartford Courant*, Mar. 28, 1937, 10.

92. Inaugural Address, in Rosenman, ed., *Public Papers and Addresses of Franklin D. Roosevelt*, Vol. 6, 2.

93. "My Day," Aug. 17, 1937.

94. Joseph Mitchell, *New York World-Telegram*, May 21, 1935, II-1.

95. "Our First Lady's First Epithet," *Baltimore Afro-American*, Apr. 17, 1937, 4.

96. George B. Murphy, Jr., to ER, Apr. 28, 1937, Box 843, AERP.

97. MCT to George B. Murphy, Jr., May 3, 1937, Box 843, AERP.

98. TR, *Autobiography*, 12.

99. MCT to George B. Murphy, Jr., May 3, 1937, Box 843, AERP.

100. "Our First Lady's First Epithet," *Baltimore Afro-American*, Apr. 17, 1937, 4.

101. ER to John Flyner, Dec. 1935, in JPL, *E&F*, 522.

102. ER, "Some of My Best Friends Are Negro," *Ebony*, Feb. 1953, 17.

103. Mrs. Margaret Hawkins to ER, May 7, 1937, Box 843, AERP.

104. E. Birdie Smith to ER, May 3, 1937, Box 843, AERP.

105. LAH to ER, Sept. 8, 1937, Box 2, LAHP.

106. ER to LAH, Jan. 27, 1934, Box 1, LAHP.

107. LAH, *Reluctant First Lady*, 157–61.

108. *L,E*, 218: "Of course you should have had a husband & children & it would have made you happy if you loved him & in any case it would have satisfied certain cravings & given you someone on whom to lavish the love & devotion you have to keep down all the time. Yours is a rich nature with so much to give that the outlets always seem meagre."

109. ER to LAH, May 13, Box 2, LAHP.

110. Lowitt and Beasley, *One Third of a Nation*, 220–21.

111. LAH, in Lowitt and Beasley, *One Third of a Nation*, 221.

112. E2 to ER, n.d. [June 1933], JARP.

113. ER to LAH, Apr. 27, 1935, Box 2, LAHP.

114. ER to LAH, n.d. [Feb. 1935], Box 2, LAHP.

115. LAH, quoted in "Mrs. Roosevelt Faces Busy Twin Cities Day," *Minneapolis Star Journal*, June 3, 1941, 19.

116. Charles S. Johnson, "More Southerners Discover the South," *The Crisis*, Jan. 1939, 14.

117. ER quoted in "First Lady Gives Example of Tact," *Louisville Courier-Journal*, Nov. 27, 1938, 35.

118. Ibid.

119. "My Day," Feb. 27, 1939.

120. ER to Walter White, cited in AMB, "Championing a Champion: Eleanor Roosevelt and the Marian Anderson 'Freedom Concert,'" *Presidential Studies Quarterly* 20, No. 4 (Fall 1990): 719–36.

121. ER to Mrs. Henry M. Robert, Jr., Feb. 26, 1939, AERP.

122. *E&F*, 526.

123. Endicott Peabody to ER, in *E&F*, 526.

CHAPTER EIGHTEEN

1. "My Day," June 21, 1939.

2. Donna Akers Warmuth, *Abingdon, Virginia* (Charleston, SC: Arcadia, 2002), 24.

3. "So This Is Washington!" *Daily Northwestern* (Oshkosh, WI), June 13, 1933, 7.

4. "Finding Time for Writing Worries Mrs. Roosevelt," *Harrisburg (PA) Telegraph*, Feb. 17, 1937, 6.

5. Evelyn Perkins Ames to JPL, July 30, 1968, Box 44, JPLP.

6. Dorothy Ducas Herzog, quoted in Janet Rems, "Former Newspaper Woman Remembers Mrs. Roosevelt," *Lewisboro (NY) Ledger*, Nov. 14, 1984, 1.

7. Society columnist for *Columbia (SC) State*, quoted in "Society," *Aiken (SC) Standard and Review*, Nov. 2, 1938, 5.

8. Lorania K. Francis, "Mrs. Roosevelt Quits the Front Page," *Los Angeles Times*, June 23, 1935, H3.

9. Ibid.

10. RABP, 1941 Biographical Data, Box 7, LCMD.

11. Ann Landers, quoted in Christopher Buckley, Profile, *New Yorker*, Dec. 4, 1995, 83.

12. Rosamond Pinchot, Apr. 28, 1933, Box 1, RPP, LCMD. See also Brendan Gill, *A New York Life: Of Friends and Others* (New York: Poseidon Press, 1990), 75–76.

13. Rosamond Pinchot, Apr. 28, 1933, Box 1, RPP, LCMD.

14. Gill, *A New York Life*, 75–76.

15. Ibid.

16. Brandon, *Special Relationships*, 16.

17. "So This Is Washington!," *Daily Northwestern* (Oshkosh, WI), June 13, 1933, 7.

18. West and Kotz, *Upstairs at the White House*, 14.

19. Victor Rodriguez, "An Intriguing Love Story," Amazon Reader Report on Ellen Feldman, *Lucy*, May 23, 2003, https://www.amazon.com/gp/customer -reviews/R3LTN6S271Y32A/, accessed Sept. 17, 2016.

20. Tony Soma, quoted in Terkel, *Hard Times*, 175.

21. May Thompson Evans, Jan. 30, 1978, EROH, FDRL.

22. Reilly and Slocum, *Reilly of the White House*, 81–82.

23. Ina Hill Chandor to Betty Beale, "Capital Capers," *Toledo Blade*, Feb. 13, 1966, E6.

24. *Florence (AL) Times*, Nov. 18, 1937, 5.

25. Christopher Lynch, *When Hollywood Landed at Chicago's Midway Airport: The Photos and Stories of Mike Rutunno* (Charleston, SC: History Press, 2012), 51.

26. ER quoted in "Visit Is Paid to Boys' Club," *Muncie (IN) Star Press*, Oct. 26, 1939, 4.

27. "Sees No Danger of Nation's Youth Becoming Communistic," *Muncie (IN) Star Press*, Oct. 26, 1939, 4.

28. Lutz Kaelber, "Eugenics: Compulsory Sterilization in 50 American States," paper presented at the annual conference of the Social Science History Association, Vancouver, Nov. 1–4, 2012, https://www.uvm.edu/~lkaelber/eugenics/.

29. "Anti-Semitism Is Here," editorial, *Nation*, 147, Aug. 25, 1938, 167.

30. "The Failure of Evian," *Guardian*, July 14, 1938.

31. The psychologist Gordon Allport made these findings, cited in Leonard Dinnerstein, "Anti-Semitism Exposed and Attacked, 1945–1950," *American Jewish History* 71, No. 1 (Sept. 1981). 134.

32. Hazel Gaudet Erskine, "The Polls: Religious Prejudice, Part 2: Anti-Semitism," *Public Opinion Quarterly* 29, No. 4 (Winter, 1965–1966): 649.

33. Roper had predicted FDR's 1936 re-election landslide to within a single percentage point.

34. Samuel H. Flowerman and Marie Jahoda, "Polls on Anti-Semitism," *Commentary*, Apr. 1946, 83; Bruce Bliven, "U.S. Anti-Semitism Today," *New Republic*, Nov. 3, 1947, 19.

35. Quoted in Digby B. Whitman, review of Allan R. Bosworth, *American Concentration Camps*, documentary film, *Chicago Tribune*, Feb. 26, 1967, 141.

36. Coughlin response after Pearl Harbor, see: United States Holocaust Memorial Museum, https://encyclopedia.ushmm.org/content/en/article/charles-e-coughlin.

37. "Kuhn Promises Queens Bund He'll Drive Jews from U.S.," *Hackensack (NJ) Record*, Nov. 19, 1938, 1.

38. GCW, *F-C*, 254.

39. EM, quoted in Shedd, *Thank You, America*, 75.

40. Ibid.

41. *E&F*, 323. See also ER to FDR, Nov. 13, 1928, FDRL.

42. Sept. 7, 1948: Office memorandum from Dorothy Schiff Thackerey to her husband, Theodore Thackerey: "I was shocked to read the attached by Eleanor Roosevelt from the current Ladies Home Journal in which she favors the partition of Palestine but repeatedly refers to the Jews as a 'race.' I think you have done some research on this subject and probably would be a better person to answer it than I would be. However, would be delighted to discuss with you." Dorothy Schiff Thackerey to Theodore Thackerey, Sept. 7, 1948, office memorandum, DSP, Box 64, NYPL.

43. ER, "Mrs. Roosevelt Answers Mr. Wells on the Future of the Jews," *Liberty*, Dec. 31, 1938, 5.

44. JPLD, July 17, 1940.

45. ER, in ibid.

46. ER to Elinor Morgenthau, July 14 [1936], HM2P, Box 512, FDRL.

47. ER to Elinor Morgenthau, Feb. 2 [1926], HM2P, Box 512, FDRL.

48. *L,E*, 229.

49. See Box 1411, AERP.

50. ER, "Mrs. Roosevelt Answers Mr. Wells on the Future of the Jews," *Liberty*, Dec. 31, 1938, 5.

51. FDR, STE, quoted in Sandifer, *Mrs. Roosevelt as We Knew Her*, 5.

52. ER to Carl Rowan, c. June 20–July 3, 1957, quoted in Rowan, *Dream Makers, Dream Breakers*, 140.

53. Quoted in Joseph Mitchell, "Anna Eleanor Roosevelt: The President's Partner," *New York World-Telegram*, May 22, 1935, II–15.

54. Joseph Mitchell, "Anna Eleanor Roosevelt: The President's Partner," *New York World-Telegram,* May 22, 1935, II-15.

55. "Probers Praise Industrial Home," *Washington Times*, May 13, 1919, 3.

56. Ibid.

57. "Mrs. Roosevelt Sets Precedent in Appearing Before House Unit," *Salt Lake City (UT) Telegram*, Feb. 9, 1940, 4.

58. "My Day," Jan. 15, 1937.

59. Thomas M. Rives, *The History of the District of Columbia Jail*, unpublished report, Dec. 12, 1941, Records of Phi Mu, Special Collections, University of Maryland Library. "One of the extremely undesirable features up to the present year [1941] was the fact that electrocutions took place in the mess hall. Now, with the advent of the remodeling of the jail, they will be held in the Administration Building."

60. Sanford Bates (director, Bureau of Prisons, Dept. of Justice, Washington) to ER, Jan. 17, 1934, Box 1401, AERP.

61. Annys Shin, "Ten Things to Do Before Closing a Prison," *Washington City Paper*, Mar. 9, 2001.

62. "'Chair' in Dining Room Shocks Mrs. Roosevelt," *New York Post*, Jan. 14, 1937.

63. Rives, *The History of the District of Columbia Jail.*

64. See John W. Kelly, "Kelly Says—Mrs. Roosevelt Big News Maker," *Daily Capital Journal* (Salem, OR), Mar. 22, 1940, 4.

65. "Oracle," *Time*, Apr. 17, 1939, 21–22.

66. Donovan, *Madame Chiang Kai-shek: Face of Modern China*, 95.

67. Pamela Harriman, quoted in Purnell, *Clementine*, 241.

68. Clementine Churchill to WSC, Dec. 19, 1941, quoted in Weintraub, *Pearl Harbor Christmas*, 10.

69. Gallup poll found ER more popular than FDR: "But Most Voters Object to Post with Son's Firm," *Lincoln (NE) State Journal*, Jan. 15, 1939, 7.

70. Hunter College speech, Feb. 19, 1941, "Mrs. Roosevelt's Visit," *Hunter College Alumnae News* 48, No. 3 (Mar. 1941): 1–4.

71. ER quoted in Alice Frost Lord, "Subversive Groups Small Says Mrs. Roosevelt," *Lewiston (ME) Evening Journal*, Oct. 31, 1940, 7.

72. "Lectures Bore First Lady; Believes in Visual Education," *Los Angeles Times*, Jan. 23, 1939, 11.

73. "Address by Mrs. Franklin D. Roosevelt—the Chicago Civil Liberties Committee," Mar. 14, 1940, Voices of Democracy: The U.S. Oratory Project, National Endowent for the Humanities, University of Maryland.

74. "First Lady Backs Move to Open U.S. to 20,000 Exiles," *Washington Post*, Feb. 14, 1939, 1. See also Breitman and Lichtman, *FDR and the Jews*, 149.

75. Greg Siskind, "Peter Pan and Helen Hayes—Lessons from Past Child Refugee Crises," July 7, 2014, http://blog.ilw.com/gregsiskind/2014/07/07/peter-pan-and-helen-hayes-lessons-from-past-child-refugee-crises/, accessed Mar. 9, 2020.

76. Contrary to popular belief, there was no specific or official order by President Roosevelt refusing entry of the *St. Louis* refugees. State Department memorandum of conversation written by J. Butler Wright, U.S. ambassador to Cuba, concerning his meetings in Havana with the Cuban president and secretary of state about the SS *St. Louis*, June 8, 1939, Sumner Welles Papers, Office Correspondence, File: Wright, J. Butler, April–June 1939, Box 57, http://www.fdrlibrary.marist.edu/archives/pdfs/holocaust.pdf.

77. Israel, ed., *The War Diary of Breckinridge Long*, 283.

78. Richard J. Garfunkel, "St. Louis, Cuba, and the Quotas," "The Advocates on WJUP," May 10, 2009, http://www.theadvocatesradio.com/feed.xml.

79. JWP, Sept. 14, 1977, EROH, 19.

80. Breckinridge Long, "Immigrants," U.S. Dept. of State memorandum (National Archives and Records Administration, College Park, MD), posted in "Americans and the Holocaust," https://exhibitions.ushmm.org/americans-and-the-holocaust/personal-story/breckinridge-long, accessed Mar. 9, 2020.

81. Isenberg, *A Hero of Our Own: The Story of Varian Fry*, 11.

82. JPLD, June 9, 1940, JPLP.

83. Karl Boromäus Frank to ER, quoted in Isenberg, *A Hero of Our Own: The Story of Varian Fry*, 11.

84. Robert N. Rosen, *Saving the Jews: Franklin D. Roosevelt and the Holocaust* (New York: Thunder's Mouth, 2006), 509.

85. Israel, ed., *The War Diary of Breckinridge Long*, 130.

86. Shankar Vedantam, "Brain Bonus: Magic Brain," *Hidden Brain* podcast, Oct. 2, 2015, NPR.

87. "The Columnists' Song," *Music Box Revue of 1938–1939*, in *The Complete Lyrics of Irving Berlin* (New York: Alfred A. Knopf, 2001), 328.

88. "Mrs. Roosevelt Replies to Nazi Paper's Attack on Her Writing," *West Palm Beach (FL) Post*, Feb. 10, 1939, 13.

89. "Nazi Jibe Ignored by Mrs. Roosevelt," *Pittsburgh (PA) Press*, Feb. 8, 1939, 2.

90. "My Day," Apr. 5, 1939.

91. Robert A. M. Stern et al., *New York 1930: Architecture and Urbanism Between the Two World Wars* (New York: Rizzoli, 1987), 689–90.

92. Ulric Bell, "Mrs. Roosevelt Is Calmest in Capital—President's Wife Stays Herself," *Louisville Courier-Journal*, June 7, 1939, 16.

93. Ibid.

94. "My Day," June 14, 1939.

95. William Lyon Mackenzie King, Diaries, June 10, 1939, 677, Item 20424, Library and Archives Canada, https://www.bac-lac.gc.ca/eng/discover/politics -government/prime-ministers/william-lyon-mackenzie-king, accessed June 26, 2017.

96. Trude Belle Feldman, "Eleanor Roosevelt's Last Trip: Science, Birds, Lemonade—It Was All in Day's Jaunt," *Amarillo Globe-Times*, Feb. 26, 1963, 9.

97. Representative Hamilton Fish, quoted in "Fish Praises Royalty—But," *Poughkeepsie (NY) Eagle-News*, June 10, 1939, 1.

98. Gallup Poll, November 1941.

99. *TIR*, 198.

100. "My Way," Aug. 26, 1939.

101. FDR, quoted in caption accompanying "Finest Ship the U.S. Ever Built Is Launched at Newport News," *Life*, Sept. 11, 1939, 72.

102. FDR to ER, quoted in Steinberg, *Mrs. R*, 266.

103. See William L. Shirer, "At Dawn This Morning Hitler Moved Against Poland," in *Reporting World War II*, Part 1 (Library of America, 1995), 19.

104. "My Day," Sept. 2, 1939.

105. Ibid.

106. "My Day," June 19, 1940.

107. "My Day," Sept. 2, 1939.

108. Charles A. Lindbergh, quoted in Berg, *Lindbergh*, 396.

109. Hugh S. Johnson, quoted in "Columns Crash on Lindbergh," *Plain Speaker* (Hazleton, PA), Oct. 20, 1939, 8.

110. FDR quoted in "Can U.S. Keep Out?" *Pittsburgh (PA) Sun-Telegraph*, Sept. 1, 1939, 1.

111. ER to Carola von Schaeffer-Bernstein, Sept. 6, 1939, quoted in *E&F*, 583–84.

112. FDR, quoted from minutes of the Casablanca Conference, Jan. 1943, in Richard Cohen, *Israel: Is It Good for the Jews?* (New York: Simon & Schuster, 2014), 146.

113. S. J. Perelman, letter, 1940, in *Don't Tread on Me: The Selected Letters of S. J. Perelman* (New York: Penguin, 1988), 23–24.

114. Martin Dies quoted in "More of the Dies Committee?" *Coshocton (OH) Tribune*, Oct. 24, 1939, 2.

115. "Don't Trample Aliens, Says First Lady," *Madison (WI) State Journal*, Oct. 25, 1939, 8.

116. ER, quoted in *AFM*, 63.

117. "My Day," Feb. 13, 1940.

118. Ibid.

119. Eugene G. Schwartz, ed., *American Students Organize: Founding the National Student Association After World War II* (Westport, CT: American Council on Education/Praeger, 2006), 16.

120. ER to ARH, Feb. 21, 1940, in *M&D*, 116.

121. Straight, *After Long Silence*, 149.

122. Richard Norton Smith, "No First Lady Like Eleanor Roosevelt," *Wall Street Journal*, Oct. 28, 2016, https://www.wsj.com/articles/no-first-lady-like-eleanor -roosevelt-1477677417.

123. Fulton Lewis, Jr., quoted in David Holbrook Culbert, *News for Everyman: Radio and Foreign Affairs in Thirties America* (Westport, CT: Greenwood, 1976), 165.

124. Hellman, "Mrs. Roosevelt," *Life*, Feb. 5, 1940, 71.

125. "My Day," Aug. 4, 1944.

126. "My Day," May 13, 1940.

127. Same as the pattern set in 1917: from nowhere people coming to extraordinary power. Lenin had been a penniless exile in Switzerland in spring 1917, grinding out one more brilliant bitter article. By November he was sitting in the palaces of Saint Petersburg.

128. ER to Ralph Bunche, in "Memo on Interview with Mrs. Franklin D. Roosevelt at the White House," May 15, 1940, 18, Ralph J. Bunche Papers, Dept. of Special Collections, UCLA Library.

129. June 5, 1941: see full scene in James Farmer, *Lay Bare the Heart: An Autobiography of the Civil Rights Movement* (New York: Arbor House, 1985), 68–69.

130. ER to Ralph Bunche, in "Memo on Interview with Mrs. Franklin D. Roosevelt at the White House," May 15, 1940, 19–20.

131. Ibid.

132. FDR to ER to JPL, quoted in JPL Diary, June 3, 1940, JPLP.

133. *TIR*, 350–51.

134. See caption of Hitler portrait: "Hitler, the Conquerer?" in "First Year Ends— HITLER CONQUEROR?—What Comes Next?" *Akron (OH) Beacon Journal*, Sept. 1, 1940, 5.

135. Elliott Roosevelt to Doris Kearns Goodwin, in Goodwin, *No Ordinary Time*, 88.

136. MCT to ARH, June 17, 1940, Box 75, ARHP.

137. Ibid.

138. Dallek, *Defenseless Under the Night*, 154–55.

139. *Constitution of the United States of America*, Article II, Section 2.

140. ER, quoted in "Mrs. Roosevelt," *Minneapolis Sunday Tribune and Star Journal*, June 8, 1941, 5.

141. Laurence Rees, *World War II: Behind Closed Doors: Stalin, the Nazis, and the West*, BBC/KCET Hollywood Production, 2009.

142. F. H. Hinsley, C. F. G. Ransom, R. C. Knight, and E. E. Thomas, *British Intelligence in the Second World War*, Vol. 2 (Cambridge: Cambridge University Press, 1981), 67.

143. ER ARH, June 12, 1941, AERP.

144. "Rev. Wilson Says Roosevelt Had Premonition of Death," *Poughkeepsie New Yorker*, Sept. 8, 1941, 10.

145. JPLD, JPLP, June 4, 1941, JPLP.

146. "Rev. Wilson Says Roosevelt Had Premonition of Death," *Poughkeepsie New Yorker*, Sept. 8, 1941, 10.

147. Frank Place, *Gazetteer of the State of New York*, 1860, 272.

148. Mike F. Reilly, as told to William J. Slocum in Slocum, *Reilly of the White House*, 84.

149. Douglas B. Cornell, "Roosevelt Funeral Services Today; Will Be Simple," *Independent Record* (Helena, MT), Sept. 9, 1941, 1.

150. ER to ARH, Sept. 10, 1941, Proposal, 3, BAP.

151. Douglas B. Cornell, "Burial Services Held for Mother of the President," *Paris (TX) News*, Sept. 9, 1941, 1.

152. ER to ARH, Sept. 10, 1941, Proposal, 3, BAP.

153. ER to Arnold Michaelis, on recording, *Eleanor Roosevelt in Conversation with Arnold Michaelis* (1957).

154. Elliott Stewart, grandson of Hall Roosevelt, EROH.

155. ER to LAH, June 8, 1933, LAH typescript, LAHP, Box 1, FDRL.

156. Eleanor Wotkyns, June 12, 1978, EROH, FDRL.

157. ER to ARH, Sept. 17, 1941, AERP.

158. Davis, *FDR*, 283.

159. JR2, *My Parents*, 113.

160. Thomas Fleming, *The New Dealers' War*, 105.

161. *TIR*, 230.

162. Ruth Cowan, "Elinor for Eleanor Is Washington Recipe," *(Dayton, Ohio) Journal Herald*, Nov. 16, 1941, 11.

163. Scott Hart, *Washington at War: 1941–1945* (Englewood Cliffs, NJ: Prentice-Hall, 1970), 81.

164. Gilbert Harrison, "Liberal Perspectives," oral history interview by Joel Gardner, UCLA Oral History Program, 1982.

165. Ibid.

166. Curtis B. Munson, report to John Franklin Carter and FDR, Nov. 7, 1941, quoted in *Personal Justice Denied: Report of the United States Commission on Wartime Relocation and Internment of Civilians* (Washington, DC: U.S. Government Printing Office, Dec. 1982), 52.

167. Curtis B. Munson, preliminary report to John Franklin Carter, Oct. 1941, quoted in Greg Robinson, *By Order of the President: FDR and the Internment of Japanese Americans* (Cambridge, MA: Harvard University Press, 2001), 66.

168. Curtis B. Munson, "Japanese on the West Coast," in *American Concentration Camps: Vol. 1, July 1940–December 31, 1941*, edited with an introduction by Roger Daniels (New York: Garland, 1989), http://www.michiweglyn.com/wp-content/uploads/2010/06/Munson-Report.pdf, archived at https://web.archive.org/web/20150907173312/http://www.michiweglyn.com/wp-content/uploads/2010/06/Munson-Report.pdf.

169. ER quoted in Greg Robinson, "Eleanor Roosevelt," *Densho Encyclopedia*, http://encyclopedia.densho.org/Eleanor_Roosevelt/, accessed Mar. 10, 2020.

170. ER, "Town Hall Meeting of the Air," Box 1411, ARH, Sept. 17, 1941, AERP.

171. "Aliens of Good Record Need Not Fear Concentration Camps in USA, Says Mrs. Roosevelt." Jewish Telegraphic Agency, Dec. 5, 1941, http://www.jta.org/1941/12/05/archive/aliens-of-good-record-need-not-fear-concentration-camps-in-usa-says-mrs-roosevelt, accessed Jan. 16, 2015.

172. ER and Judge Jerome Frank, quoted in Geoffrey R. Stone, *Perilous Times: Free Speech in Wartime from the Sedition Act of 1798 to the War on Terrorism* (New York: W. W. Norton, 2004), 289.

173. Pan American Coffee Bureau Program #11, Dec. 7, 1941, Box 1411, AERP.

174. Grace Tully's diary and the stenographer's diary show that the message asking Congress for a Declaration of War on the Japanese was delivered at 12:30 p.m. Pare Lorentz, FDRL.

175. Pan-American Coffee Bureau Series #11, Dec. 7, 1941, Box 1411, AERP.

176. Henry Morgenthau Diaries, Dec. 7, 1941; Presidential Diary, Vol. 4, Mar. 1, 1941–Dec. 31, 1941, Part Two, 1939, FDRL.

177. Hoehling, *Home Front, USA*, 7.

178. FDR, quoted in Williams, *City of Ambition*, 302–3.

179. Manners, *Patience and Fortitude: Fiorello La Guardia*, 257.

180. Jonathan Daniels, "Thursday Afternoon," in Crane, ed., *The Roosevelt Era*, 620.

181. Drew Pearson and Robert S. Allen, "Merry-Go-Round," *Salt Lake City (UT) Telegram*, Aug. 12, 1941, 6.

182. Lee McCardell, "D.C. Air Wardens Ready; City Has Semi-Blackout," *Baltimore Evening Sun*, Dec. 8, 1941, 2.

183. *TIR*, 234.

184. 1941 Biographical Data, Box 7, RABP, LCMD.

PART VI: AGITATOR

1. Epigraph: *TIR*, 349.

CHAPTER NINETEEN

1. Gilbert Harrison, "Liberal Perspectives," oral history interview by Joel Gardner, UCLA Oral History Program, 1982.
2. Biographical Data, 1941, Box 7, RABP, LCMD.
3. ER, quoted in Goodwin, *No Ordinary Time*, 296.
4. "Mayor Sees U.S. On Brink of War," *New York Times*, Nov. 1, 1941, 4.
5. Dallek, *Defenseless Under the Night*, 176.
6. FL, quoted in "LaGuardia at Frisco to See Raid Defenses," *New York Daily News*, Dec. 11, 1941, 10.
7. "Mayor Sees U.S. On Brink of War," *New York Times*, Nov. 1, 1941, 4.
8. FL, quoted in "LaGuardia at Frisco to See Raid Defenses," *New York Daily News*, Dec. 11, 1941, 10.
9. ER, quoted in *New York Times*, Dec. 15, 1941, 9.
10. "Rodent Exterminators," *Time*, July 5, 1943: "The ordinary unreasoning Jap is ignorant. Perhaps he is human. Nothing . . . indicates it."
11. ER, quoted in Thomas J. Hamilton, "Japanese Seizure Ordered By Biddle," *New York Times*, Dec. 8, 1941, 6.
12. ER, quoted in Dallek, *Defenseless Under the Night*, 142.
13. "Chick Sexers Are American Citizens," *Cullman (AL) Democrat*, Jan. 1, 1942, 1.
14. "My Day," Dec. 16, 1941.
15. "White House Handshakes," AP, June 9, 1937.
16. Sherwood, *Roosevelt and Hopkins*, 205. See also Beasley, *Eleanor Roosevelt: Transformative First Lady*, 63.
17. Drew Pearson and Robert S. Allen, "The Washington Merry-Go-Round," *Wilkes-Barre Record*, May 1, 1942, 22.
18. *TIR*, 248–49.
19. Martin Dies quoted in "Root Out the Disturbers," *Muncie (IN) Star Press*, Sept. 30, 1939, 10.
20. Adolf Hitler: Speech Declaring War Against the United States (December 11, 1941), Jewish Virtual Library, https://www.jewishvirtuallibrary.org/hitler-s-speech-declaring-war-against-the-united-states, accessed, Mar. 21, 2019.
21. ER to JPL, Dec. 24, 1941, in *L, E*, 366.
22. ER to JPL, quoted in *L, E*, 367.
23. "My Day," Dec. 24, 1941.
24. Alonzo Fields, in Goodwin, *No Ordinary Time*, 300; see also, Fields, *My 21 Years in the White House*, 81.
25. WSC, quoted in Weintraub, *Pearl Harbor Christmas*, 5.
26. WSC, *The Second World War: The Grand Alliance*, 662.
27. As WCS did during lunch at the White House in September 1943.

28. ER, Broadcast for December 28, 1941, Speech and Article File, 1941, Box 1411, AERP.

29. ER to ARH, Jan. 4, 1942, AERP.

30. "If I can epitomize in one word the lesson I learned in the United States, it was 'China.'" WCS, quoted in Ricks, *Churchill and Orwell*, 158.

31. FDR, quoted in ER2, *As He Saw It*, 37.

32. Mencken, *The American Language, Supplement Two*, 786.

33. FDR to WSC, Apr. 16, 1942, quoted in Thorne, *Allies of a Kind*, 6.

34. Mabel Irwin to BA, Pt. 19, BAP.

35. *Fantasy Review*, Issues 87–97 (Florida Atlantic University, 1986), 27.

36. JPLD, Dec. 26, 1941, JPLP.

37. ER to ARH, Jan. 4, 1942, AERP.

38. Ibid.

39. ER, quoted in Goodwin, *No Ordinary Time*, 297.

40. Paul Moke, *Earl Warren and the Struggle for Justice* (Lanham, MD: Lexington Books, 2015), 68.

41. Walter Lippmann, "Today and Tomorrow," *Washington Post*, Feb. 12, 1942, 10.

42. Westbrook Pegler, quoted in Biddle, *In Brief Authority*, 217–18.

43. Miller quoted in Reeves, *Infamy*, 99.

44. Biddle, *In Brief Authority*, 218.

45. Ibid., 219.

46. Geoffrey S. Smith, notes, "Racial Nativism and Origins of Japanese American Relocation," in Daniels, Taylor, and Kitano, eds., *Japanese Americans*, 86.

47. John L. DeWitt, quoted in David A. Neiwert, *Strawberry Days: How Internment Destroyed a Japanese American Community* (New York: Palgrave Macmillan, 2005), 125.

48. ER, "A Challenge to American Sportsmanship," *Collier's*, Oct. 16, 1943, 21, 71; Speech and Articles Files, Box 1414, AERP.

49. ER, "A Challenge to American Sportsmanship," ibid.

50. SDR, *My Boy Franklin*, 43.

51. FDR to Sir Ronald Campbell; Campbell to Sir Alexander Cadogan; Aug. 6, 1942, quoted in Thorne, *Allies of a Kind*, 167n.

52. Thorne, *Allies of a Kind*, 8.

53. HBD, Dec. 22, 1941, Box 1, HBP.

54. The eugenicist Madison Grant had helped Hrdlicka raise money to start the *American Journal of Physical Anthropology*, the editorial board of which Hrdlicka packed with fellow eugenicists.

55. "Wake Up in Time," *Baltimore Sun*, Feb. 13, 1942, 11.

56. Kashima, *Personal Justice Denied*, 112.

57. Norman Thomas quoted in Greg Robinson, *The Great Unknown: Japanese American Sketches* (Boulder: University Press of Colorado, 2016), 127.

58. Monroe Deutsch to Frankfurter, Mar. 28, 1942, quoted ibid., 113.

59. Kashima, *Personal Justice Denied*, 113.

60. Biddle, *In Brief Authority*, 219.

61. Harrison, *Parts of a Past*, 59.

62. Milton S. Eisenhower, *The Preident Is Calling* (Garden City, NY: Doubleday, 1974), 98.

63. ER, "My Day," Mar. 29, 1942.

64. Earl Warren, Feb. 21, 1942, testifying before a House committee on "National Defense Migration," quoted in G. Edward White, *Earl Warren: A Public Life* (New York: Oxford University Press, 1982), 71.

65. Greg Robinson, "Eleanor Roosevelt: In Defense of Japanese Americans," https://encyclopedia.densho.org/Eleanor%20Roosevelt/. Accessed Aug. 29, 2018.

66. ER to JPL, July 11, 1943, in WOL, 38.

67. "My Day," June 21, 1940.

68. FDR, quoted in GCW, *The Roosevelts*, 400.

69. "Mrs. Roosevelt Follows Course Planned Long Ago, Say Friends," *Herald Statesman* (Yonkers, NY), Aug. 28, 1943, 5.

70. Gardner Jackson quoted in Henry A. Wallace, Diary, Aug. 28, 1943, quoted in Blum, ed., *The Price of Vision*, 243.

71. "Zoot Riots Race Problem, Says 1st Lady," *New York Post*, June 16, 1943, 2.

72. "My Day," June 17, 1943.

73. Blum, ed., *The Price of Vision*, 243n.

74. Quoted in Luis Alvarez, *The Power of the Zoot: Youth Culture and Resistance During World War II*, American Crossroads Series, No. 24 (Berkeley: University of California Press, 2008), 150.

75. "My Day," Sept. 26, 1944.

76. Ibid.

77. JPL to ER, July 10, 1943, V-Mail, JRP.

78. FDR, quoted by BWRD, July 13, 1943, KBRP.

79. Freidel, *Rendezvous*, 509; also quoted in Persico, *Franklin and Lucy*, 275.

80. MCT to ARH, Aug. 11, 1943, Box 75, ARHP.

81. Emma Bugbee to JPL, Box 44, JPLP.

82. "A.R.C. Uniforms Only, Mrs. Roosevelt's Wardrobe," *Sydney Morning Herald*, Sept. 3, 1943, 3; 29,945 miles: "Mrs. Roosevelt Arrives in N.Y. Aboard Bomber," *Nashville Tennessean*, Sept. 25, 1943, 3.

83. "Soldiers' Poll Shows They're Most Willing To Fight For Mother," *Gazette and Daily (York, PA)*, May 8, 1942, 23.

84. GI joke quoted in Hoehling, *Home Front*, 129.

85. Brawley and Dixon, *Hollywood's South Seas*, 107: *Yank* (published "Down Under"), Sept. 24, 1943), reported: "Mrs. Roosevelt has been photographed from Fiji to Canberra tying on grass skirts and strings of native beads over the Red Cross uniform she is wearing on the tour."

86. "A.R.C. Uniforms Only, Mrs. Roosevelt's Wardrobe," *Sydney Morning Herald*, Sept. 3, 1943, 3.

87. Captain Nikolai Stevenson, USMC, Guadalcanal, to Diana Tead, Nov. 20, 1942, author's collection.

88. Sledge, *With the Old Breed: At Peleliu and Okinawa*, 157.

89. Halsey and Bryan, *Admiral Halsey's Story*, 166–67.

90. Ibid.

91. ER to MCT, Aug. 26, 1943, AERP.

92. JPL to ER, Sept. 7, 1943, JRP.

93. ER to MCT, Aug. 26, 1943, AERP.

94. Halsey and Bryan, *Admiral Halsey's Story*, 135.

95. ER quoted in DKG, *No Ordinary Time*, 463; see also, "Auckland Greets Mrs. Roosevelt," *New York Times*, Aug. 28, 1943, 13.

96. Capt. Robert M. White, II, "Changed His Mind About Mrs. Roosevelt," *Des Moines Register*, Oct. 24, 1943, 42.

97. Halsey and Bryan, *Admiral Halsey's Story*, 136.

98. JPL to ER, July 18, 1943, JRP.

99. ER to JPL, Sept. 18, 1943, JRP.

100. Ibid.

101. "International Bill of Rights Urged by Leading Americans," *Evening News Paterson (NJ)*, Dec. 15, 1944, 10.

102. "My Day," Dec. 20, 1944.

103. FDR, "Address of the President," Dec. 24, 1944, 2, Box 52, STEP.

104. William L. Shirer, *End of a Berlin Diary* (New York: Rosetta Books, 2016), electronic edition, location 378.

105. Unnamed London newspaper quoted Feb. 12, 1945, in Shirer, *End of a Berlin Diary*, location 365.

106. Herbert Hoover quoted in Shirer, *End of Berlin Diary*, location 365.

107. FDR, address to Congress, Mar. 1, 1945, in GCW, *The Roosevelts*, 446.

108. Ibid.

109. *M&D*, 184.

110. *TIR*, 439.

111. Ibid.

112. ER, in *My Husband and I*.

113. Quoted by GCW, *The Roosevelts*, 448.

114. Bruenn, in *M&D*, 184.

115. *M&D*, 184.

116. GCW, ed., *Closest Companion*, 418.

117. Anonymous source, quoted in *M&D*, 185.

118. *TIR*, 344.

119. GCW, ed., *Closest Companion*, 419.

120. Pogue, *George C. Marshall*, 557–58.

121. ER, overseas cable, quoted in Asbell, *When F.D.R. Died*, 94.

122. ER and HST, quoted in GCW, *The Roosevelts*, 452.

123. Edward Robb Ellis, *New York World-Telegram*, Apr. 12, 1960.

124. ER quoted in Klara, *FDR's Funeral Train*, 61.

125. Pogue, *George C. Marshall*, 557–58.

126. E. B. White, *The Wild Flag*, 76.

127. Frank Lloyd Wright, quoted in Carleton Smith, unpublished memoir, 64–65, cited in Brendan Gill, *Many Masks: A Life of Frank Lloyd Wright* (New York: G. P. Putnam's Sons, 1987), 417.

128. *TIR*, 348.

129. "5,000 Turn Out for City Demonstration," *Poughkeepsie (NY) Eagle-News*, July 14, 1920, 1.

130. See Louise Tompkins, "Yours Truly," Taconic Newspapers, Jan. 27 and 28, 1982, 5: Norman Lane, of Millbrook, NY, worked as a gardener for the Roosevelts for thirty years, dug FDR's grave, Fala's and Chief's graves.

131. E2, *Eleanor Roosevelt, with Love*, 103.

132. See *EYA*, 322: "her veins cut (because she had an irrational fear of waking up with piles of earth on top of her)." See JPLD, Mar. 16, 1960, JPLP.

133. FDR, quoted in "My Day," Apr. 20, 1945.

134. Vidal, *Screening History*, 74.

135. James Agee, "A Soldier Died Today," *Time*, Apr. 23, 1945. See also Tugwell, *The Democratic Roosevelt*, 682.

136. ER to JPL, Apr. 19, 1945, in *WOL*, 189.

137. "Mrs. Roosevelt Explains Duties in White House to Mrs. Truman," *St. Louis Post-Dispatch*, Apr. 16, 1945, 1.

138. ER to LAH, Apr. 16, 1945, Box 3, LAHP.

139. Fecher, ed., *The Diary of H. L. Mencken*, 359.

140. "Mrs. Roosevelt Leaves White House/Bids Farewell at Tea Party," *Munster (IN) Times*, Apr. 20, 1945, 6.

141. BWRD, n.d. [Apr. 1945], 1–2, KBRP.

142. Ibid.

143. ER to LAH, Apr. 19, 1945, Box 3, LAHP.

144. E2, *Murder and the First Lady*, 12.

145. ER to LAH, Apr. 19, 1945, in Box 3, LAHP.

CHAPTER TWENTY

1. "My Day," Feb. 19, 1947.

2. ER to DG, Dec. 13, 1947, Box 53, JPLP.

3. "My Day," May 29, 1945.

4. ER to ARH, Sept. 10, 1941, Proposal, 4, BAP.

5. E2, *Eleanor Roosevelt, with Love*, 104.

6. ER to JPL, Aug. 9, 1945, quoted in *EYA*, 26.

7. Ibid.

8. ER to MG, May 9, n.d. [1945], DGP.

9. "Buchenwald: Report from Edward R. Murrow, April 16, 1945," Jewish Virtual Library. https://www.jewishvirtuallibrary.org/report-from-edward-r-murrow

-on-buchenwald, Feb. 23, 2020. See also, Holocaust Encyclopedia, "Buchenwald," United States Holocaust Memorial Museum, https://encyclopedia .ushmm.org/content/en/article/buchenwald: "The SS murdered at least 56,000 male prisoners in the Buchenwald camp system, some 11,000 of them Jews."

10. Sidney Olson, "Foreign News: Dachau," *Time,* May 7, 1945.

11. "My Day," Apr. 30, 1945.

12. Ibid.

13. Ibid.

14. "My Day," May 31, 1956.

15. "My Day," Aug. 7, 1945.

16. Kennedy, *Freedom from Fear*, 381.

17. *EYA*, 35.

18. ER, quoted in *MRSR*, 316–17.

19. "My Day," Feb. 13, 1947.

20. ER, quoted in Ruth Millett, "Story Is Not 'Over' Yet for Widow of President, Millett Believes; She Can Be Guide to Other Widows," *Helena (MT) Independent-Record*, May 15, 1945, 4.

21. FDR, from two speeches. "Peace-loving nations": post-Yalta speech to Congress; "an end . . .": speech in spring 1945; quoted in GCW, *The Roosevelts*, 446, 451.

22. Ralph J. Bunche, "First General Assembly Meeting (First Half)—London— Jan. 1946," Book I (Dec. 30–Jan. 21), unpublished handwritten notes, Sun., Dec. 30, 1945, RJBP, Box 281, Folder 8.

23. Urquhart, *Ralph Bunche*, 130.

24. Ralph J. Bunche, "First General Assembly Meeting (First Half)—London— Jan. 1946," Book I (Dec. 30–Jan. 21), unpublished handwritten notes, Sun., Dec. 30, 1945, RJBP, Box 281, Folder 8.

25. S. J. Woolf, "The New Chapter in Mrs. Roosevelt's Life," *New York Times Magazine*, Dec. 15, 1946, 8.

26. *OMO*, 40.

27. *M&D*, 201; FDR2, on Paul Noble, *We Remember Eleanor*.

28. "My Day," Jan. 5, 1946.

29. ER, press conference, Jan. 3, 1946, quoted in *EYA*, 38.

30. Hiss, *Recollections of a Life*, 141.

31. *MRSR*, 320.

32. Theodore Bilbo, quoted in F. Ross Peterson, "Glen H. Taylor and the Bilbo Case," *Phylon* (4th quarter 1970): 346. See also Bartlett, *Wrong on Race*, 90.

33. HST to ER, Feb. 21, 1949, in Neal, ed., *Eleanor and Harry*, 161.

34. MCT to ARH, Mar. 11, 1946, Box 75, Folder 9, ARHP.

35. ER quoted in Durward V. Sandifer, oral history interview by Richard D. McKinzie, Mar. 15, 1973, Harry S. Truman Library, https://www.trumanlibrary .gov/library/oral-histories/sandifer, accessed June 18, 2019.

36. Ralph J. Bunche, "First General Assembly Meeting (First Half)—London—

Jan. 1946," Book I (Dec. 30–Jan. 21), unpublished handwritten notes, Jan. 12, 1946, RJBP, Box 281, Folder 8.

37. Hiss, *Recollections of a Life*, 141.

38. Urquhart, *Ralph Bunche*, 129.

39. *OMO*, 47.

40. *OMO*, 43–44.

41. Sandifer, oral history, Truman Library, https://www.trumanlibrary.org/oral hist/sandifer.htm#65.

42. Alger Hiss, quoted by Durward Sandifer in Oral History, Truman Library, https://www.trumanlibrary.org/oralhist/sandifer.htm#65.

43. ER, quoted in *EYA*, 50.

44. "American Divorce," *Guardian*, Feb. 16, 1946, 6; "British Wives Jilted by GI's Seek Intercession," *Lincoln (NB) State Journal*, Feb. 12, 1946, 7.

45. "G.I.s Call on Mrs. Roosevelt," *Guardian*, Jan. 12, 1946, 5.

46. ER, statement made before Committee 3 of the UNO General Assembly (Lake Success, NY), Nov. 8, 1946, "U. S. Position on International Refugee Organization," *Department of State Bulletin*, Nov. 24, 1946, 936.

47. Urquhart, "Mrs. Roosevelt's Revolution," *New York Review of Books*, Apr. 26, 2001.

48. Vishinsky, quoted by ER in "The Russians Are Tough," *Look*, Feb. 18, 1947, 65–69, in *WHLB*, 549.

49. ER, speech, "Is America Facing World Leadership?," May 6, 1959, Ball State U., Muncie, IN. Eleanor Roosevelt Speech Collection, Ball State University Digital Media Repository. https://dmr.bsu.edu/digital/collection/ElRoos, Feb. 23, 2020.

50. *OMO*, 57.

51. Paul-Henri Spaak, quoted in Hiss, *Recollections of a Life*, 142.

52. ER, press conference, Jan. 3, 1946, quoted in *EYA*, 38.

53. John Foster Dulles to ER, quoted in Maury Maverick, Jr., *Texas Iconoclast* (Fort Worth: Texas Christian University Press, 1997), 228.

54. Drew Pearson, "The Daily Washington Merry-Go-Round," Feb. 28, 1946, *Atlantic (IA) News-Telegraph*, 2.

55. Vidal, *United States*, 761.

56. Vandenberg, quoted in Donie Carmack, "Francis Wilcox, Back from U.N. . . ." *Louisville Courier-Journal*, Mar. 24, 1946, 26.

57. FDR2, indirectly quoted by STE to ER, May 16, 1946, Box 15, STEP.

58. STE to ER, May 16, 1946, Box 15, STEP.

59. The number depends on which historian you read; by any count, an incomparable contrast to Americans killed and missing: 400,000.

60. Allport, *The Nature of Prejudice*, 204.

61. WSC, "Alliance of English-Speaking People," Mar. 1946, *The Annals of America*, 365.

62. Ibid., 366.

63. Sandifer, *Mrs. Roosevelt as We Knew Her*, 27.
64. Ibid., 28.
65. ER to STE, May 18, 1946, Box 15, STEP.

PART VII: WORLDMAKER

1. Epigraph: ER, quoted in Freedman, *Eleanor Roosevelt*, 185.

CHAPTER TWENTY-ONE

1. "My Day," Nov. 29, 1947.
2. Ibid.
3. As of Christmas 1932: LAH, "None More Welcome Than Santa Claus," *Daily Northwestern* (Oshkosh, WI), Dec. 9, 1932, 16.
4. *OMO*, 77.
5. "My Day," Feb. 20, 1947.
6. Carol Anderson, *Eyes Off the Prize: The United Nations and the African American Struggle for Human Rights, 1944–1955* (New York: Cambridge University Press, 2003), 87.
7. Ibid.
8. Walter White to ER, Sept. 18, 1946, Box 3338, NAACP, 1945-1947, AERP.
9. *ERP1*, 634.
10. *ERP1*, 976.
11. EJK2, interview with Richard Winslow, 44, Box 69, EJKP.
12. MCT to LAH, Dec. 6, 1947, Box 17, LAHP.
13. EJK2, Winslow, 44, Box 69, EJKP.
14. MCT to LAH, Dec. 6, 1947, Box 17, LAHP.
15. Nemone, born May 27, 1906.
16. "My Day," Jan. 29, 1940.
17. *Report*, Vols. 75–79, Presbyterian Hospital, New York, NY, 1943, 72. See also "Hot Baths Found Best in Treatment of Polio," *Miami (FL) News*, May 9, 1947, 1.
18. First meeting of the United Nations Human Rights Commission: AP story, Dec. 1, 1947, called it the "second session"; "My Day," Dec. 5, 1947, "the first meeting."
19. "Mrs. Roosevelt Able to Leave Eire After Delay of Two Days," *Chicago Tribune*, Dec. 2, 1947, 22.
20. Ibid.
21. ER, Diary, typescript by MCT, Nov. 30, 1947, Box 17, LAHP.
22. ER to LAH, June 24–25, 1933, Box 1, LAHP.
23. See DG to ER, Sept. 8, 1948, misfiled in David Gray folder in John Roosevelt Papers, FDRL.
24. MG to DG, July 8, 1950, quoted in Moorehead, *Gellhorn*, 287.
25. EJK2, interview with Sandifer, 56, Box 69, EJKP.
26. "Mrs. Roosevelt Reaches Geneva for UN Meeting," *Wilkes Barre (PA) Record*, Dec. 2, 1947, 1.

27. EJK2, interview with Eleanor Hendrick, 52, Box 69, EJKP.

28. "My Day," Dec. 9, 1947.

29. James Hendrick to JPL, interview, May 5, 1970, JPLP. See also *EYA*, 71–72.

30. ER to DG, Dec. 4, 1947, Box 53, JPLP.

31. ER to DG, Dec. 8, 1947, JPLP.

32. See Moorehead, *Gellhorn*, 288.

33. ER to DG, Dec. 13, 1947, Box 53, JPLP.

34. *EYA*, 71–72. See also Hendrick, quoted in Richard Henry, *Eleanor Roosevelt and Adlai Stevenson*, 26.

CHAPTER TWENTY-TWO

1. EJK2, interview with ER, 69, Box 69, EKJP.

2. "My Day," Feb. 20, 1947.

3. "Truman Approves Mrs. FDR as Vice-Pres. Candidate," *Naugatuck (CT) Daily News*, July 1, 1948, 1.

4. Martin Flaherty, Richard N. Gardner, Blanche Wiesen Cook, and Oscar Schachter, "The Genesis of the Declaration: A Fresh Examination," *Pace International Law Review* 11, No. 1 (Spring 1999): 31.

5. ER, "In Defense of Curiosity," *Saturday Evening Post*, Aug. 24, 1935, 8. See Box 1402, AERP.

6. Spellman, quoted in "Bishop Scores Cardinal on Use of Word," *Long Branch (NJ) Daily Record*, June 23, 1949, 2.

7. Ibid.

8. "Archer Hits at Catholics," *New York Times*, June 23, 1949, 18.

9. Spellman, quoted in "Bishop Scores Cardinal on Use of Word," *Long Branch (NJ) Daily Record*, June 23, 1949, 2.

10. "My Day," June 23, 1949.

11. John Updike, *Couples* (New York: Alfred A. Knopf, 1968), 279.

12. Justine Wise Polier, interviewed by Dr. Thomas F. Soapes, Sept. 14, 1977, 29, EROH, FDRL.

13. Spellman, quoted in Sheed, *Clare Boothe Luce*, 112.

14. Sheed, *Clare Boothe Luce*, 112.

15. Stephen Rutledge, "#LGBTQ: The Twisted Tale of the Closet Case Cardinal," *The WOW Report*, May 5, 2018, https://worldofwonder.net/lgbtq-the-twisted -tale-of-the-closet-case-cardinal/, accessed Nov. 14, 2019.

16. Jacqueline Bouvier Kennedy to AMS2, Mar. 23, 1964, in Beschloss, ed., *Jacqueline Kennedy*, 105.

17. Michelangelo Signorile, quoted in Rutledge, "#LGBTQ: The Twisted Tale of the Closet Case Cardinal."

18. John C. Bennett, quoted in Steven R. Weisman, ed., *Daniel Patrick Moynihan: A Portrait in Letters of an American Visionary* (New York: PublicAffairs, 2010), 87.

19. "My Day," July 14, 1950.

20. HM3, author's interview, Mar. 16, 2010.

21. "Mrs. Roosevelt Dies in New York . . . ," *Hartford Courant*, Nov. 8, 1962, 1.

22. Details of Spellman's Aug. 18 visit to Val-Kill: JWP, interviewed by Dr. Thomas F. Soapes, Sept. 14, 1977, EROH.

23. JWP to JPL, Nov. 20, 1968, Box 44, Folder 47, JPLP.

24. "My Day," Dec. 29, 1950.

25. See ER to Bertrand Russell, Sept. 22, 1960, in Russell, *Autobiography*, 187.

26. Russell, *Autobiography*, 146–47.

27. Allida Black, quoted in Julia Baird, "The Real Eleanor Roosevelt: Smart, Disciplined, Strong," http://www.newsweek.com/real-eleanor-roosevelt-smart-disciplined-strong-94321, accessed Aug. 26, 2015.

28. ARH to BA, Anna Roosevelt interview, Side One, 42, BAP, PSU.

29. Eulalie Salley to Gladys Hinckley Werlick, n.d. [1966], printed in Emily L. Bull, *Eulalie* (Aiken, SC: Kalmia, 1973), 123.

30. Stephen E. Ambrose, *D-Day, June 6, 1944: The Climactic Battle of World War II* (New York: Simon & Schuster, 1994), 279.

31. ER, "The Struggle for Human Rights," Oct. 10, 1948, in *Department of State Bulletin*, Vol. XIX, No. 483, Oct. 3, 1948, 457.

32. E. B. White, editorial, *New Yorker*, Mar. 31, 1945, in E. B. White, *The Wild Flag*, 69.

33. Ibid., 187.

34. "In Our Hands," Speech delivered on the tenth anniversary of the Universal Declaration of Human Rights (New York, NY: United Nations, 1958).

35. HBD, Dec. 10, 1948, Box 1, HBP.

36. Ibid.

37. Philip Roth, *American Pastoral* (Boston: Houghton Mifflin, 1997), 40–41.

38. Asbjørn Eide, "Economic and Social Rights," quoted in Rhodes, *The Debasement of Human Rights*, 33.

39. FDR, State of the Union address, Jan. 11, 1944, in Rosenman, *Public Papers and Addresses of FDR*, Vol. 13, 41–42.

40. ER, quoted in Glendon, *A World Made New*, 186.

41. Rhodes, *The Debasement of Human Rights*, 178.

42. EL to JPL, Jan. 11, 1972, Box 44, JPLP.

43. DG to Grace Halsell, Notes, Dec. 14, 1972, GHP.

44. ER to DG, n.d. [June 1962], Box 53, JPLP.

45. Grace Halsell: "He insists that he called her 'Mrs. Roosevelt,' and I find this very sad. Dean Acheson called Harry Truman 'Mr. President' but I think he did it out of his (Acheson's) strength, and I think DG called her by that formal name because he was not strong enough to say Eleanor." Notes, Feb. 8, 1973, GHP.

46. ER to DG, Feb. 8 n.d. [1956], Box 53, JPLP.

47. ER to DG, Aug. 20 n.d. [1950], Box 53, JPLP.

48. Grace Halsell, Notes, Dec. 17, 1972, GHP.

49. Adlai Stevenson interview, Jan. 24, 1947, AMS Jr. Papers, Box 472, Folder 3, NYPL.

50. Jay I. Meltzer, MD, author's interview, May 4, 2011.

51. Thomas Louis Stix, "Mrs. Roosevelt Does a TV Commercial," *Harper's*, Nov. 1963, 104–6.

52. DG to JPL, interview, Dec. 4, 1971, Box 44, JPLP.

53. Lloyd, *William Walton: Muse of Fire*, 305.

54. JPL, Dec. 4, 1971, Box 44, JPLP.

55. DG, typescript, 6, GHP.

56. *OMO*, 96.

57. Harold B. Minor to ER, quoted in Edna Gurewitsch, *Kindred Souls*, 60.

58. MCT to ARH, Feb. 28, 1952, Box 75, Folder 12, ARHP.

59. MCT to ARH, Feb. 10, 1952, Box 75, Folder 12, ARHP.

60. ER, quoted in Ivan H. Peterman, "'Do-Good' Envoys Seen Timid on Boosting U. S.," *Philadelphia Inquirer*, May 14, 1952, 47.

61. MCT to DDB, Nov. 9, 1951, DDBP.

62. *IAE*, 92.

63. *IAE*, 96.

64. Ibid.

65. RAB, manuscript, "This Woman: Mrs. Roosevelt," RABP.

66. DG typescript, 5, GHP.

67. DG, typescript, 6, GHP.

68. Ibid.

69. Devi, *A Princess Remembers*, 247–48.

70. Karin Ebeling, "Holi, a Nepali and Indian Festival, and Its Reflection in English Media," in *Die Ordnung des Standard und die Differenzierung der Diskurse: Akten des 41: Linguistischen Koloquiums in Mannheim*, 2006, part 1, eds. Beate Henn-Memmesheimer and Joachim Franz (Frankfurt am Main: Peter Lang, 2009), 107.

71. DG, typescript, 8, GHP.

72. Ibid.

73. Maureen Corr to JPL, Dec. 7, 1971, Box 44, JPLP.

74. See letters from Srinagar, *HBG*.

75. *IAE*, 171.

76. ER to William Turner Levy, quoted in Levy and Russett, *The Extraordinary Mrs. R*, 39.

77. *IAE*, 168–69.

78. *IAE*, 169.

79. Levy and Russett, *The Extraordinary Mrs. R*, 39.

80. DG, *Eleanor Roosevelt: Her Day*, 29.

CHAPTER TWENTY-THREE

1. Jacqueline Kennedy to ER, May 31, 1962, AERP.

2. Gellhorn to Adlai Stevenson, Oct. 11, 1962, quoted in Moorehead, *Gellhorn*, 326.

3. Maureen Corr to JPL, quoted in *EYA*, 312.

4. Robert M. Krim, "Lowenstein: The Making of a Liberal 1968," *Harvard Crimson*, Jan. 8, 1968, http://www.thecrimson.com/article/1968/1/8/lowenstein-the -making-of-a-liberal/?page=2.

5. Hendrik Hertzberg, "The Second Assassination of Al Lowenstein," *New York Review of Books*, Oct. 10, 1985, http://www.nybooks.com/articles/1985/10/10 /the-second-assassination-of-al-lowenstein/.

6. Tom Lowenstein to author, July 6, 2015, quoting Jennifer Littlefield: ER to Allard Lowenstein.

7. ER's "basic values" in this period: see John Roosevelt Boettiger, "My Grandmother, Eleanor Roosevelt: A Conversation with John Roosevelt Boettiger and Susan Ives," Apr. 3, 2015, https://livingnewdeal.org/full-interview-my-grand mother-eleanor-roosevelta-conversation-with-john-roosevelt-boetti ger-and-susan-ives/, accessed Nov. 12, 2017.

8. ER, "Tolerance Is an Ugly Word," *Coronet*, July 1947, 118.

9. *Who's Who in the East* (Chicago: Marquis—Who's Who, 1953), 962.

10. *WOL*, 7.

11. *IYAM*, 54.

12. Ibid.

13. ER to William Turner Levy, *EMR*, 4.

14. *YLBL*, 85.

15. *IYAM-EAER*, 106.

16. ER to Grace Tully, Aug. 27, 1953, Tully Papers, Box 3, FDRL.

17. Betsy Prioleau and Elizabeth Stevens Prioleau, *Seductress: Women Who Ravished the World and Their Lost Art of Love* (New York: Penguin, 2004), 142.

18. Ibid.

19. Benfey, *American Audacity*, 105.

20. ER, quoted in Moorehead, *Gellhorn*, 100.

21. MG, quoted in Moorehead, *Gellhorn*, 285.

22. MG to ER, Jan. 23, 1952, Box 6, AHRP.

23. Prioleau and Stevens Prioleau, *Seductress*, 142.

24. According to a 1948 poll by *Woman's Home Companion*, cited in EJK2, Profile, *New Yorker*, June 12, 1948, 30.

25. Allport, *The Nature of Prejudice*, 204.

26. "My Day," Aug. 9, 1946.

27. ER quoted in "Texas Today," *Pampa (TX) Daily News*, Mar. 17, 1946, 16.

28. Kissinger, on Paul Noble, *We Remember Eleanor*.

29. ER to DG, n.d. [Sept. 1954], Box 53, JPLP.

30. MG to Adlai Stevenson, Nov. 8, 1962, in Moorehead, ed., *Selected Letters of Martha Gellhorn*, 296.

31. Harry Ashmore anecdote in Henry, *Eleanor Roosevelt and Adlai Stevenson*, 95–96.

32. Adlai Stevenson quoted in HM3, "Eleanor Roosevelt at Brandeis: A Personal Memoir," *Brandeis Review*, Vol. 4, No. 1, Fall 1984, 6.

33. ER, quoted in JPLD, Oct. 28, 1953, in Henry, *Eleanor Roosevelt and Adlai Stevenson*, 57.

34. Ibid.

35. Robert Allen, "Mrs. Roosevelt Rakes Truman Over Coals," *Idaho State Journal*, Aug. 17, 1956, 4.

36. See ER to Grace Tully, Nov. 28, 1952, Grace Tully Papers, FDRL.

37. William F. Buckley, Jr., "Buckley: 'Liberal' Thought Produces Uncertainty," *Phoenix (AZ) Republic*, Dec. 10, 1961, 7.

38. Paul Simon quoted in Ash Carter and Sam Kashner, eds. *Life Isn't Everything: Mike Nichols, as Remembered by 150 of His Closest Friends* (New York: Henry Holt, 2019), 132.

39. Emblidge, ed., *My Day*, ix.

40. "Mrs. Roosevelt Can't Find Sponsor To Air Program On World Affairs," *Gazette and Daily* (York, PA), Mar. 11, 1959, 2. See also, Haskin, "Question and Answers," *Times* (Munster, IN), Feb. 20, 1964, 33.

41. Edna Gurewitsch, *Kindred Souls*, 88.

42. Ibid., 89.

43. ER to DG, Feb. 15, 1958, Box 53, JPLP.

44. Maureen Corr to JPL, Dec. 7, 1971, Box 44, JPLP.

45. EL to JPL, Jan. 11, 1972, Box 44, JPLP.

46. ER to ARH, Dec. 2, 1959, BAP.

47. Ibid.

48. ER to Arthur Axelman, Aug. 17, 1959, courtesy of Robert Nedelkoff.

49. Barbara Kerr to AMS2, Jan. 20, 1947, "BWK comments on Mrs. Roosevelt," AMSP, NYPL.

50. "My Day," Aug. 22, 1958.

51. HM3, author's interview, Mar. 16, 2010; Paul Noble, author's interview, Feb. 13, 2010; see also: HM3, "Eleanor Roosevelt at Brandeis: A Personal Memoir," *Brandeis Review*, Vol. 4, No. 1, Fall 1984–Spring 1985, 3; Connie Cass, "43 Years Later, a Blacklisted Name is Cleared," AP, Mar. 8, 1996, https://apnews.com/809181bce8f688ab7c505d7304b54c38, accessed Mar. 15, 2020.

52. ER, press conference, Mar. 10, 1959, quoted in "Mrs. Roosevelt Changes Mind—Urges Stevenson-Kennedy Ticket," *Bend (OR) Bulletin*, June 15, 1960, 7.

53. ER to reporters, Dec. 1959, quoted in "Mrs. Roosevelt Changes Mind—Urges Stevenson-Kennedy Ticket," *Bend (OR) Bulletin*, June 15, 1960, 7.

54. Ibid.

55. Dallek, *An Unfinished Life*, 12.

56. ER, quoted in Robert Dallek, *John F. Kennedy*, 13.

57. ER, quoted in Rovere, *Senator Joe McCarthy*, 18.

58. Troyan, *A Rose for Mrs. Miniver*, 288.

59. Mailer, *The Presidential Papers*, 36.

60. Reeves, *President Kennedy*, 432–33.

61. David Lilienthal to JPL, July 28, 1970, JPLP, Box 44, FDRL.

62. *EYA*, 295–96.

63. Nannine Joseph to JPL, May 4, 1966, JPLP, Box 44, FDRL.

64. ER to Adlai Stevenson, Aug. 11, 1960, FDRL.

65. Walton Oral History, cited in Smith, *Grace and Power*, 138.

66. "My Day," Aug. 16, 1960.

67. Nina Roosevelt Gibson, Aug. 14, 1979, ER Oral History, FDRL.

68. "House Calls," photo caption, *New York*, Nov. 7, 1977, 89.

69. William Walton, "JFK and Mrs. Roosevelt," *John Fitzgerald Kennedy: As We Remember Him* (New York: Atheneum, 1965), 88.

70. "My Day," Sept. 28, 1960.

71. John O'Hara, *My Turn* (New York: New American Library, 1965), 84.

72. Ibid.

73. "Demo 'Show' Broadway Hit," *Austin American*, Nov. 6, 1960, 1.

74. Florence Mary to ER, June 18, 1960, ER Papers, Box 3576, AERP.

75. Paul Noble, author's interview, Feb. 13, 2010.

76. Paul Noble, email to author, Sept. 5, 2012.

77. Edna Gurewitsch told the story on WNYC radio on Nov. 10, 1962, hosted by Lee Graham. "Remembering Eleanor, 1962," Number 30, Nov. 7, 2011, WNYC Archives, http://www.wnyc.org/story/169067-remembering-eleanor/.

78. ER to Stella K. Hershan in 1962, quoted in Hershan, *A Woman of Quality*, 14.

79. Edna Gurewitsch on WNYC, Nov. 10, 1962.

80. Philip A. Mackowiak, MD, *Diagnosing Giants*, 196.

81. James A. Halsted, 1906–1984. Halsted would die of leukemia. He practiced medicine from 1936 to 1950 in Boston and Dedham, where he pioneered in establishing group practices. See "Dr. James Halsted, Medical Researcher," *Herald-News* (Passaic, NJ), Mar. 5, 1984, 24.

82. JH to BA, Jan. 26, 1980, transcript, 4, BAP. See also, JH to JPL, in *WOL*, 528–29. Halsted emphasized to Bernard Asbell: "[David Gurewitsch] was a very neurotic man. His relationship to Mrs. Roosevelt was something of a greatly emotional character—emotionally beneficial to his own ego, among other things. . . . He shouldn't have taken care of her—he was too close to her emotionally, for one thing. Here was a potentially fatal illness, which actually turned out to be, and he was—doctors don't like to take care of their own close people, their families. He was so close to her he shouldn't have done it because objectivity was nil."

83. ER, quoted by Jim Halsted to Bernard Asbell, Jan. 26, 1980, Pt. 25, BAP.

84. ER to ARH, June 20, 1955. See *WOL*, 429.

85. ER, "To My Executors [unnamed]," unsigned copy of document, June 21, 1955, JRP, FDRL.

86. ER, quoted in Gureswitsch, *Kindred Souls*, 236.

87. Morrison, *Mathilde Krim and the Story of AIDS*, 100–101.

88. "Elinor [*sic*] Says Adlai Hopeful," *Indiana (PA) Gazette*, June 16, 1960, 20.

89. Suzanne Roosevelt Kloman to Sally Bedell Smith, in Smith, *Grace and Power*, 138.

90. Mary Ellen Gale, "East House Hears Mrs. Roosevelt on Politics, Peace Marches, Morals," *Harvard Crimson*, May 21, 1962.

91. Ibid.

92. June 13, 1961: farm machinery team to Havana; June 23, 1961: committee disbands; July 8, 1961: contributions returned.

93. Gore Vidal, author's interview, Dec. 2, 2010.

94. James Wechsler to Dorothy Schiff, Office Memorandum, *New York Post*, Feb. 3, 1954, Box 64. DSP.

95. ER to David Gray, Nov. 18, 1954, cited in *EYA*, 274.

96. Jaker, Sulek, and Kanze, *The Airwaves of New York*, 157.

97. ER, quoted in *AFM*, 329.

98. ER to Gore Vidal, quoted by Murray Kempton in William Safire, *The New Language of Politics: A Dictionary of Catchwords, Slogans, and Political Usage* (New York: Collier Books, 1972), 564; see also, ER to Vidal: "When Mr. di Sapio did what he did to my Franklin, I vowed that I would bide my time and then—one day—I would *get* him. And I have!" quoted in Vidal, *Palimpsest: A Memoir* (New York: Penguin, 1996), 344.

99. HM3 to Paul Noble, in Noble, *We Remember Eleanor.*

100. Gordon Ball, ed., Allen Ginsberg, *Journals, Early Fifties, Early Sixties* (New York: Grove, 1977), 167–68.

ENVOI

1. Helen Agnes Post Eliot; Mrs. Montague Charles Eliot: Cracroft's Peerage, http://www.cracroftspeerage.co.uk/online/content/stgermans1815.htm, accessed July 26, 2015; Ancestry File, http://www.royalblood.co.uk/D744/I74 4875.html, accessed July 26, 2015.

2. *New York: A Guide to the Empire State*, America Guide Series (New York: Oxford University Press, 1940), 610.

3. JAR to FDR2, Apr. 24, 1980, JARP.

4. JEL to JAR, May 12, 1980, JARP.

5. JEL to JPL, Aug. 22, 1967, JPLP.

6. JEL, author interview, Mar. 2, 2011.

7. "Catholic Paper Criticizes Mrs. Roosevelt," *Owensboro (KY) Messenger-Inquirer*, Dec. 10, 1951, 2.

8. JEL to JPL, Aug. 22, 1967, JPLP.

9. JEL to Maureen Corr, Nov. 8, 1962, Box 6, Papers of Maureen Corr, FDRL.

10. Edward I. Koch to Stella K. Hershan, Jan. 26, 1983, quoted in Hershan, *The Candles She Lit*, 60.

11. The show, taped by WGBH-TV, Channel 2, a presentation in the *NET Perspectives* series, was shown on Oct. 8; see "JFK Urged: Tell Radiation Facts," *Boston Globe*, Sept. 24, 1962, 1.

12. Gurewitsch, *Kindred Souls*, 275.

13. ER to William Levy, Oct. 1, 1962, AERP.

14. JH to JR2, quoted in *EYA*, 331n.

15. Barron H. Lerner, MD, author's interview, June 23, 2011.

16. Edmund N. Goodman, *A Surgeon's Story: An Odyssey Through Medicine 1928–2003*, privately published memoir, courtesy of Stacy Goodman, Feb. 22, 2014.

17. Lerner, "Charting the Death of Eleanor Roosevelt," accessed June 18, 2012.

18. Jay I. Meltzer, author interview, May 4, 2011.

19. Lalit Kant, "Using Fluoroquinolones for Shortening SCC," *Indian Journal of Tuberculosis* 49, No. 3 (July 2002).

20. Lerner, "Charting the Death of Eleanor Roosevelt."

21. Kant, "Using Fluoroquinolones for Shortening SCC," *Indian Journal of Tuberculosis* 49, No. 3 (July 2002).

22. Lerner, "Charting the Death of Eleanor Roosevelt."

23. C. C. J. Carpenter, MD, author interview, Mar. 1, 2012.

24. DG to press, quoted in *EYA*, 331.

25. Lerner, "Charting the Death of Eleanor Roosevelt."

26. Maureen Corr witnessed the scene and gave at least two interviews on the subject: see Gurewitsch, *Kindred Souls*, 285; Collier, *The Roosevelts*, 469.

27. Lerner, "Charting the Death of Eleanor Roosevelt."

28. "Mrs. Roosevelt Can't Vote, Even As Absentee," *Miami News*, Nov. 6, 1962, 4B.

29. ARH to David Gray, Nov. 1, 1962, David Gray Papers, FDRL.

30. Daniel P. Sulmasy, Christopher Brick, Philip A. Mackowiak, "Eleanor Roosevelt's Last Days: A Bioethical Case Study," *American Journal of Medicine* 128, No. 4, 437–40, http://dx.doi.org/10.1016/j.amjmed.2014.11.006, accessed Oct. 2, 2015.

31. Barron H. Lerner, "Final Diagnosis," Feb. 8, 2000, *Washington Post*, reprinted in: "Charting the Death of Eleanor Roosevelt," see B. H. Lerner, "Revisiting the Death of Eleanor Roosevelt: Was the Diagnosis of Tuberculosis Missed?" *International Journal of Tuberculosis and Lung Disease* 5, no. 12 (Dec. 2001), 1080–85.

32. Lerner, "Charting the Death of Eleanor Roosevelt."

33. DG to JPL, notes on ER's final illness, Box 55, JPLP.

34. Helen Gavin to JPL, Apr. 7, 1970, Box 44, JPLP.

35. ER to LAH, Dec. 19, 1935, Box 2, LAHP.

36. Roosevelt and Brough, *Mother R: Eleanor Roosevelt's Untold Story*, 270.

37. ER to LAH, Dec. 19, 1935, Box 2, LAHP.

38. Jacqueline Kennedy to ARH, Nov. 11, 1962, Box 61, ARHP.

39. Ralph Bunche, "Notes on Funeral for Mrs. Eleanor Roosevelt/Hyde Park—November 10, 1962," Box 3, Folder 5, Brian Urquhart Papers, Dept. of Special Collections/UCLA Library.

40. Jacqueline Kennedy to ARH, Nov. 11, 1962, Box 61, ARHP.

41. Ibid.

42. "My Day," Apr. 8, 1959.

43. FDR memo, "In the event of my death in office as President of the United States," Dec. 26, 1937, Box 61, ARHP. In 1937 FDR specified its dimensions in a handwritten memo as follows: *Length 8 feet. Width 4 feet. Height 3 feet.*

44. AMS2, *Journals, 1952–2000*, 180.

45. Rev. Gordon Kidd, quoted in *New York Times*, Nov. 12, 1962, 1.

46. Margaret Logan Marquez to Nancy Alden, "Across the Spectrum," *Pine Plains (NY) Register Herald*, Oct. 17, 2002, A4.

SELECT BIBLIOGRAPHY

Archival Sources

Asbell, Bernard. Papers, 1950–2000. University Archives. Pennsylvania State University Libraries. University Park, PA.

Bethune, Mary McLeod. Papers. Bethune Foundation Collection, 1914–1955; Bethune-Cookman College Collection, 1922–1955. Digital Collections. Princeton University Library. Princeton, NJ.

Bingham, Mary Caperton and Barry. Papers, 1929–1953. Schlesinger Library. Radcliffe Institute. Harvard University. Cambridge, MA.

Black, Ruby A. Papers, 1916–1976. Library of Congress Manuscript Division. Washington, DC.

Brandon, Henry. Papers, 1939–1994. Library of Congress Manuscript Division. Washington, DC.

Bunche, Ralph J. Papers, 1927–1971. Library Special Collections. Charles E. Young Research Library. UCLA. Los Angeles, CA.

Butturff, Dorothy Dow. Papers, 1933–1985. Booth Family Center for Special Collections. Lauinger Library. Georgetown University. Washington, DC.

Clapper, Raymond. Papers, 1908–1962. Library of Congress Manuscript Division. Washington, DC.

Daniels, Josephus. Papers, 1829–1948. Library of Congress Manuscript Division. Washington, DC.

Dreier, Mary Elisabeth. Papers, 1797–1968. Schlesinger Library. Radcliffe Institute. Cambridge, MA.

Eichelberger, Clark M. Papers, 1920–1991. Manuscripts and Archives Division. The New York Public Library. New York, NY.

Eleanor Roosevelt Papers Project. George Washington University. Washington, DC.

Ferguson Family Papers, 1870–1940. Arizona Historical Society. Library and Archives. Tucson, AZ.

Furman, Bess. Papers, 1728–1967. Library of Congress Manuscript Division. Washington, DC.

Gellhorn, Edna. Collection. University Archives. Department of Special Collections. Washington University Libraries. Washington University in St. Louis. St. Louis, MO.

Halsell, Grace. Papers. Manuscript Collections. Mary Couts Burnett Library. Texas Christian University. Fort Worth, TX.

Harrison, Gilbert Avery. Papers, 1902–1978. Library of Congress Manuscript Division. Washington, DC.

Hopkins, Harry Lloyd. Papers, Pt. 1, 1890–1946. Lauinger Library, Georgetown University. Washington, DC.

Kahn, E. J. (Ely Jacques). Papers, 1916–1994. The New York Public Library. New York, NY.

Lovett, Robert Williamson. Papers. Boston Medical Library, Francis A. Countway Library of Medicine. Boston, MA.

Meyer, Agnes Elizabeth Ernst. Papers, 1853–1972. Library of Congress Manuscript Division. Washington, DC.

National Association for the Advancement of Colored People, 1842–1999. Records. Library of Congress Manuscript Division. Washington, DC.

National Women's Trade Union League of America. Records, 1903–1950. Library of Congress Manuscript Division. Washington, DC.

Pegler, James Westbrook. Papers, 1845–1969. Manuscript Collections. Herbert Hoover Presidential Library and Museum. West Branch, IA.

Phillips, Caroline Drayton. Papers, 1897–1961. Schlesinger Library. Radcliffe Institute. Cambridge, MA.

Pinchot, Rosamond. Papers, 1918–1955. Library of Congress Manuscript Division. Washington, DC.

Roosevelt, Anna Eleanor. Main File. Reference File. The Federal Bureau of Investigation. Washington, DC.

Roosevelt, Franklin Delano and Eleanor. Collection, 1911–1970. Robert D. Farber University Archives and Special Collections. Goldfarb Library. Brandeis University. Waltham, MA.

Roosevelt, Kermit, and Belle Wyatt Willard Roosevelt. Papers, 1725–1975. Library of Congress Manuscript Division. Washington, DC.

Roosevelt, Theodore. Collection. Houghton Library, Harvard University. Cambridge, MA.

Roosevelt, Theodore, Jr., Papers, 1780–1962. Library of Congress Manuscript Division. Washington, DC.

Roosevelt Family Collection, 1911–1959. Special Collections. Seeley G. Mudd Manuscript Library. Princeton University Library. Princeton, NJ.

Schiff, Dorothy. Papers, 1904–1989. The New York Public Library. New York, NY.

Schlesinger, Arthur M., Jr. Papers, 1922–2007. The New York Public Library.

Stevenson, Adlai Ewing. Papers, 1861–2001. Special Collections. Seeley G. Mudd Manuscript Library. Princeton University Library. Princeton University. Princeton, NJ

White, Walter Francis, and Poppy Cannon White. Papers, 1910–1956. Beinecke Rare Book and Manuscript Library. Yale University. New Haven, CT.

Willert, Arthur. Papers, 1907–1973. Manuscripts & Archives. Sterling Memorial Library, Yale University. New Haven, CT.

Wilson, Edith Bolling Galt. Papers, 1833–1961. Library of Congress Manuscript Division. Washington, DC.

Manuscript Collections at Franklin Delano Roosevelt Presidential Library & Museum, Hyde Park, NY

Dewson, Mary W. "Molly," Papers. 1898–1961.

Early, Stephen E. Papers, 1933–1951.

Freidel, Frank. Small Collections.

Halsted, Anna Roosevelt. Papers, 1886–1976.

Hickok, Lorena. Papers, 1913–1962.

Howe, Louis McHenry. Papers, 1912–1936.

Kleeman, Rita Halle. Papers. Small Collections.

Lape, Esther. Papers, 1925–1978.

Lash, Joseph P. Papers, 1934–1978.

Morgenthau, Henry, Jr. Papers, 1866–1960.

Roosevelt, Anna Eleanor. Papers, Pt. 1, 1884–1964.

Roosevelt, Curtis. Papers, 1951–1982.

Roosevelt, James II. Papers, 1918–1966.

Roosevelt, John Aspinall. Papers, 1916–1987.

Roosevelt, Sara Delano. Papers.

Roosevelt Family Papers, 1469–1962.

Roosevelt Family Papers Donated by the Children of Franklin and Eleanor Roosevelt, 1686–1959.

Tully, Grace. Collection, 1907–1977.

Women's Division of the Democratic National Committee. Papers, 1933–1944.

Oral History Transcripts, Published Interviews, and Recordings

Beasley, Maurine Hoffman, ed. *The White House Press Conferences of Eleanor Roosevelt*. New York: Garland, 1983.

Columbia University Oral History Research Office Collection. Butler Library. Columbia University, New York, NY.

Eleanor Roosevelt Oral History Transcripts. FDR Presidential Library & Museum.

ER, "Mrs. Franklin D. Roosevelt Talks about the Hall Family." Recording made by George Roach, Aug/Sept 1962. FDR Presidential Library & Museum.

Eleanor Roosevelt in Conversation with Arnold Michaelis: A Recorded Portrait. Vinyl LP. Recorded Communications, 1957.

My Husband and I: Eleanor Roosevelt Recalls Her Years with FDR. Sony BMG Music Entertainment, 1964.

Teague, Michael. *Mrs. L: Conversations with Alice Roosevelt Longworth*. New York: Doubleday, 1981.

Published Letters

Asbell, Bernard, ed. *Mother & Daughter: The Letters of Eleanor and Anna Roosevelt*. New York: Coward, McCann & Geoghegan, 1982.

Lash, Joseph P., ed. *Love, Eleanor: Eleanor Roosevelt and Her Friends*. Garden City, NY: Doubleday, 1982.

———. *A World of Love: Eleanor Roosevelt and Her Friends, 1943–1962*. Garden City, NY: Doubleday, 1987.

McClure, Ruth K., ed. *Eleanor Roosevelt, An Eager Spirit: Selected Letters of Dorothy Dow, 1933–1945*. New York: W. W. Norton, 1984.

Miller, Kristie, and Robert H. McGinnis, eds. *A Volume of Friendship: The Letters of Eleanor Roosevelt and Isabella Greenway, 1904–1953*. Tucson: Arizona Historical Society, 2009.

Neal, Steve, ed. *Eleanor and Harry: The Correspondence of Eleanor Roosevelt and Harry S. Truman*. New York: Scribner, 2002.

Roosevelt, Elliott, ed. *F.D.R.: His Personal Letters*. 4 volumes. New York: Duell, Sloan and Pearce, 1947–1950.

———. Vol. 1. *Early Years*. 1947.

———. Vol. 2. *1905–1928*. 1948.

———. Vols. 3 and 4. *1928–1945*. 1950.

Schlup, Leonard C., and Donald W. Whisenhunt, eds. *It Seems to Me: Selected Letters of Eleanor Roosevelt*. Lexington: University Press of Kentucky, 2001.

Streitmatter, Rodger, ed. *Empty Without You: The Intimate Letters of Eleanor Roosevelt and Lorena Hickok*. New York: Free Press, 1998.

Published Books by ER

Roosevelt, Eleanor. *Mrs. Alfred E. Smith as I Knew Her*. New York: Democratic National Committee, 1928.

———, ed. *Hunting Big Game in the Eighties: The Letters of Elliott Roosevelt, Sportsman*. New York: Scribner, 1933.

———. *When You Grow Up to Vote*. Boston: Houghton Mifflin, 1932.

———, and Michelle Markel. *It's Up to the Women*. New York: Frederick A. Stokes, 1933.

———. *A Trip to Washington with Bobby and Betty*. New York: Dodge, 1935.

———. *This Is My Story*. New York: Harper & Brothers, 1937.

———. *My Days*. New York: Dodge, 1938.

———. *This Troubled World*. New York: H. C. Kinsey, 1938.

———. *Christmas: A Story*. New York: Alfred A. Knopf, 1940.

———. *The Moral Basis of Democracy*. New York: Howell, Soskin, and Company, 1940.

———, and Frances Cooke Macgregor. *This Is America*. New York: G. P. Putnam's Sons, 1942.

———. *If You Ask Me*. New York: D. Appleton-Century, 1946.

————. *The Human Factor in the Development of International Understanding*. Hamilton, NY: Colgate University Press, 1949.

————. *This I Remember*. New York: Harper & Brothers, 1949.

————. and Helen Ferris. *Partners: The United Nations and Youth*. Garden City, NY: Doubleday, 1950.

————. *India and the Awakening East*. New York: Harper & Brothers, 1953.

————, and William DeWitt. *UN: Today and Tomorrow*. New York: Harper, 1953.

————. *It Seems To Me*. New York: W. W. Norton, 1954.

————, and Lorena A. Hickok. *Ladies of Courage*. New York: G. P. Putnam's Sons, 1954.

————. *On My Own*. New York: Harper & Brothers, 1958.

————. *You Learn by Living*. New York: Harper & Brothers, 1960.

————. *The Autobiography of Eleanor Roosevelt*. New York: Harper & Brothers, 1961.

————. and Helen Ferris. *Your Teens and Mine*. Garden City, NY: Doubleday, 1961.

————. *Eleanor Roosevelt's Book of Common Sense Etiquette*. New York: Macmillan, 1962.

————. *The Wisdom of Eleanor Roosevelt: Eleanor Roosevelt Writes About Her World*. New York: McCalls, 1962.

————. *Eleanor Roosevelt's Christmas Book*. New York: Dodd, Mead, 1963.

————. *Tomorrow Is Now*. New York: Harper & Row, 1963.

————. *Eleanor Roosevelt's My Day: Her Acclaimed Columns, 1936–1945*. Introduction by Martha Gellhorn. New York: Pharos Books, 1989.

————, et al. *Universal Declaration of Human Rights*. Bedford, MA: Applewood Books, 2001.

Albion, Michele Wehrwein, ed. *The Quotable Eleanor Roosevelt*. Gainesville: University Press of Florida, 2013.

Binker, Mary Jo, ed. *If You Ask Me: Essential Advice from Eleanor Roosevelt*. New York: Atria Books, 2018.

————. *What Are We For? The Words and Ideals of Eleanor Roosevelt*. Foreword by Nancy Pelosi. New York: Harper Perennial, 2019.

Black, Allida M., ed. *What I Hope to Leave Behind: The Essential Essays of Eleanor Roosevelt*. Brooklyn, NY: Carlson, 1995.

————. *Courage in a Dangerous World: The Political Writings of Eleanor Roosevelt*. New York: Columbia University Press, 1999.

Emblidge, David, ed. *My Day: The Best of Eleanor Roosevelt's Acclaimed Newspaper Columns, 1936–1962*. Boston: Da Capo, 2001.

Smith, Stephen Drury, ed. *The First Lady of Radio: Eleanor Roosevelt's Historic Broadcasts*. Foreword by Blanche Wiesen Cook. New York: New Press, 2014.

Woloch, Nancy, ed. *Eleanor Roosevelt: Her Words: On Women, Politics, Leadership, and Lessons from Life*. New York: Black Dog & Leventhal Publishers, 2017.

Online Sources for ER's Writings

The Eleanor Roosevelt Papers Project. George Washington University. Columbian College of Arts & Sciences. Washington, D.C. https://erpapers.columbian.gwu.edu/.

———. Comprehensive Digital Edition of ER's "My Day" columns.

———. Comprehensive Digital Edition of ER's monthly column, "If You Ask Me."

Memoirs and Diaries

Aaron, Daniel, ed. *The Inman Diary: A Public and Private Confession*. Cambridge, MA: Harvard University Press, 1985.

Abell, George, and Evelyn Gordon. *Let Them Eat Caviar*. New York: Dodge, 1936.

Abell, Tyler, ed. *Drew Pearson Diaries, 1949–1959*. New York: Holt, Rinehart, and Winston, 1974.

Alsop, Joseph. *FDR: A Centenary Remembrance*. New York: Viking, 1982.

———, and Adam Platt. *"I've Seen the Best of It": Memoirs*. New York: W. W. Norton, 1992.

Anderson, Isabel. *Zigzagging*. Boston: Houghton Mifflin, 1918.

Anderson, Marian. *My Lord, What a Morning: An Autobiography*. New York: Viking, 1956.

Anderson, Mary, and Mary Nelson Winslow. *Woman at Work: The Autobiography of Mary Anderson*. Westport, CT: Greenwood, 1951; Minneapolis: University of Minnesota Press, 1973.

Baruch, Bernard. *Baruch*. 2 vols. New York: Holt, Rinehart and Winston.

———. *My Own Story*, 1957.

———. *The Public Years*, 1960.

Belafonte, Harry. *My Song: A Memoir*. New York: Alfred A. Knopf, 2011.

Berle, Beatrice Bishop. *A Life in Two Worlds: An Autobiography*. New York: Walker, 1983.

Biddle, Flora Miller, et al. *Flora Whitney Miller: Her Life, Her World*. New York: Whitney Museum of American Art, 1987.

Blum, John Morton. *From the Morgenthau Diaries*. 3 vols. Boston: Houghton Mifflin, 1959–1967.

———. *The Price of Vision: The Diary of Henry A. Wallace, 1942–1946*. Boston: Houghton Mifflin, 1973.

Boettiger, John R. *A Love in Shadow*. New York: W. W. Norton, 1978.

Bottome, Phyllis. *From the Life*. London: Faber and Faber, 1944.

Bowers, Claude. *My Life: The Memoirs of Claude Bowers*. New York: Simon & Schuster, 1962.

Bowles, Chester. *Promises to Keep: My Years in Public Life, 1941–1969*. New York: Harper & Row, 1971.

Brandon, Henry. *Special Relationships: A Foreign Correspondent's Memoirs, From Roosevelt to Reagan*. New York: Atheneum, 1988.

Brinkley, David. *Washington Goes to War*. New York: Alfred A. Knopf, 1988.

Brown, Claude. *Manchild in the Promised Land*. New York: Macmillan, 1965.

Bull, Emily L. *Eulalie*. Aiken, SC: Kalmia, 1973.

Clapper, Olive Ewing. *Washington Tapestry*. New York: Whittlesey House, 1946.

Cronon, Edmund David, ed. *The Cabinet Diaries of Josephus Daniels, 1913–1921*. Lincoln: University of Nebraska Press, 1963.

Dall, Curtis B. *F.D.R.: My Exploited Father-in-Law*. Tulsa, OK: Christian Crusade Publications, 1967.

Daniels, Josephus. *Editor in Politics*. Chapel Hill: University of North Carolina Press, 1941.

Davis, Kenneth S. *Invincible Summer: An Intimate Portrait of the Roosevelts Based on the Recollections of Marion Dickerman*. New York: Atheneum, 1974.

Delano, Frederic A. *Warren Delano (II) 1809–1898 and Catherine Robbins (Lyman) Delano 1825–1896: A Memoir*. Privately printed, 1928.

Devi, Gayatri. *A Princess Remembers: The Memoirs of the Maharani of Jaipur*. New Delhi: Rupa Publications India, 1995.

Douglas, Helen Gahagan. *The Eleanor Roosevelt We Remember*. New York: Hill and Wang, 1963.

———. *A Full Life*. Garden City, NY: Doubleday, 1982.

Durr, Virginia Foster. *Outside the Magic Circle: The Autobiography of Virginia Foster Durr*. Edited by Hollinger F. Barnard. Tuscaloosa: University of Alabama Press, 1985.

Farley, James Aloysius. *Behind the Ballots: The Personal History of a Politician*. New York: Harcourt, Brace, 1938.

———. *Jim Farley's Story*. New York: McGraw-Hill, 1948.

Fields, Alonzo. *My 21 Years in the White House*. New York: Coward-McCann, 1961.

Furman, Bess. *Washington By-Line: The Personal History of a Newspaperwoman*. New York: Alfred A. Knopf, 1949.

Galbraith, John Kenneth. *A Life in Our Times: Memoirs*. Boston: Houghton Mifflin, 1981.

Graham, Katharine. *Personal History*. New York: Alfred A. Knopf, 1997.

———. *Katharine Graham's Washington*. New York: Alfred A. Knopf, 2002.

Gurewitsch, A. David. *Eleanor Roosevelt, Her Day: A Personal Album*. New York: Quadrangle, 1974.

Gurewitsch, Edna P. *Kindred Souls: The Friendship of Eleanor Roosevelt and David Gurewitsch*. Introduction by Geoffrey Ward. New York: St. Martin's, 2002.

Hancock, Noelle. *My Year with Eleanor: A Memoir*. New York: HarperCollins, 2011.

Harper, Harriet Wadsworth. *Around the World in Eighty Years on a Sidesaddle*. New York: Spiral, 1966.

Harper, John Lamberton. *American Visions of Europe: Franklin D. Roosevelt, George F. Kennan, and Dean G. Acheson*. New York: Cambridge University Press, 1996.

Harrison, Gilbert. *Parts of a Past*. iUniverse, 2009.

Height, Dorothy. *Open Wide the Freedom Gates: A Memoir*. New York: PublicAffairs, 2003.

Helm, Edith Benham. *The Captains and the Kings*. Foreword by Eleanor Roosevelt. New York: G. P. Putnam's Sons, 1954.

Hepburn, Katharine. *The Making of The African Queen*. New York: Alfred A. Knopf, 1987.

Hiss, Alger. *Recollections of a Life*. New York: Seaver Books, 1988.

Hobbins, A. J., ed. *On the Edge of Greatness: The Diaries of John Humphrey, First Director of the United Nations Division of Human Rights*. 2 Vols., 1948–1951. Montreal: McGill University Libraries, 1994.

Hoover, Irwin Hood. *Forty-Two Years in the White House*. Boston: Houghton Mifflin, 1934.

Humphrey, John P. *Human Rights & the United Nations: A Great Adventure*. Ardsley, NY: Transnational, 1984.

Israel, Fred L., ed. *The War Diary of Breckinridge Long: Selections from the Years 1939–1944*. Lincoln: University of Nebraska Press, 1966.

Keyes, Frances Parkinson. *All Flags Flying: Reminiscences*. New York: McGraw-Hill, 1972.

Kiplinger, W. M. *Washington Is Like That*. New York: Harper & Brothers, 1942.

Krock, Arthur. *Memoirs: Sixty Years on the Firing Line*. New York: Funk & Wagnalls, 1968.

Lash, Joseph P. *Eleanor Roosevelt: A Friend's Memoir*. Garden City, NY: Doubleday, 1964.

Levy, William Turner, and Cynthia Eagle Russett. *The Extraordinary Mrs. R: A Friend Remembers Eleanor Roosevelt*. New York: John Wiley & Sons, 1999.

Listowel, Judith. *This I Have Seen*. London: Faber and Faber, 1943.

Mann, Thomas. *Diaries, 1918–1939*. New York: Harry N. Abrams, 1982.

Marks, Edward B., Jr., *Still Counting: Achievements and Follies of a Nonagenarian*. Lanham, MD: Hamilton Books, 2005.

McArthur, Judith N., and Harold L. Smith. *Minnie Fisher Cunningham: A Suffragist's Life in Politics*. New York: Oxford University Press, 2003.

Meyer, Agnes E. *Out of These Roots: The Autobiography of an American Woman*. Boston: Little, Brown, An Atlantic Monthly Press Book, 1953.

Murray, Pauli. *Song in a Weary Throat: An American Pilgrimage*. New York: Harper & Row, 1987.

Nesbitt, Henrietta. *White House Diary: F.D.R.'s Housekeeper*. Garden City, NY: Doubleday, 1948.

Nicolson, Nigel, ed. *Diaries and Letters of Harold Nicolson*. 3 vols. New York: Atheneum, 1966, 1967, 1968.

Parks, Lillian Rogers, and Frances Spatz Leighton. *My Thirty Years Backstairs at the White House*. New York: Fleet, 1961.

———. *The Roosevelts: A Family in Turmoil*. Englewood Cliffs, NJ: Prentice-Hall, 1981.

Perkins, Frances. *The Roosevelt I Knew*. New York: Viking, 1946.

Pickett, Clarence E. *For More Than Bread*. Boston: Little, Brown, 1953.

Reilly, Michael F., and William J. Slocum. *Reilly of the White House*. New York: Simon & Schuster, 1947.

Robinson, Edgar Eugene, and Paul Carroll Edwards, eds. *The Memoirs of Ray Lyman Wilbur, 1875–1949*. Palo Alto, CA: Stanford University Press, 1960.

Roosevelt, Curtis. *Too Close to the Sun: Growing Up in the Shadow of My Grandparents, Franklin and Eleanor*. New York: PublicAffairs, 2008.

Roosevelt, David B., and Manuela Dunn-Mascetti. *Grandmère: A Personal History of Eleanor Roosevelt*. New York: Warner Books, 2002.

Roosevelt, Elliott. *Eleanor Roosevelt, with Love: A Centenary Remembrance*. New York: E. P. Dutton, Lodestar Books, 1984.

Roosevelt, Grace L. *We Owed It to the Children*. New York: Coward-McCann, 1935.

Roosevelt, Hall, and Samuel Duff McCoy. *Odyssey of an American Family: An Account of the Roosevelts and Their Kin as Travelers, from 1613 to 1938*. New York: Harper & Brothers, 1939.

Roosevelt, James, and Sidney Shalett. *Affectionately, F.D.R.: A Son's Story of a Lonely Man*. New York: Harcourt, Brace, 1959.

Roosevelt, James, with Bill Libby. *My Parents: A Differing View*. Chicago: Playboy, 1976.

Roosevelt, James, and Sam Toperoff. *A Family Matter*. New York: Simon & Schuster, 1980.

Roosevelt, Sara Delano, Isabel Leighton, and Gabrielle Elliot Forbush. *My Boy Franklin*. New York: Ray Long & Richard R. Smith, 1933.

Rosenman, Samuel. *Working with Roosevelt*. New York: Harper & Brothers, 1952.

Sandifer, Irene Reiterman. *Mrs. Roosevelt as We Knew Her*. Silver Spring, MD: Mrs. Durward Sandifer, 1975.

Schlesinger, Arthur M. *Journals, 1952–2000*. Edited by Andrew Schlesinger and Stephen Schlesinger. New York: Penguin Press, 2007.

Scott, Anne Firor, ed. *Pauli Murray and Caroline Ware: Forty Years of Letters in Black and White*. Chapel Hill: University of North Carolina Press, 2006.

Scott, Kathleen Bruce. *Self-Portrait of an Artist: From the Diaries and Memoirs of Lady Kennet, Kathleen, Lady Scott*. London: Arthur Murray, 1949.

Shedd, Charlotte. *Thank You, America*. Riverside, CA: Ariadne, 1997.

Shoumatoff, Elizabeth. *FDR's Unfinished Portrait: A Memoir*. Pittsburgh, PA: University of Pittsburgh Press, 1990.

Slayden, Ellen Maury. *Washington Wife: Journal Ellen Maury Slayden from 1897 to 1919*. New York: Harper & Row, 1963.

Smith, A. Merriman. *Thank You, Mr. President: A White House Notebook*. New York: Harper & Brothers, 1946.

Smith, Margaret Chase. *Declaration of Conscience*. Edited by William C. Lewis, Jr. Garden City, NY: Doubleday, 1972.

Somerville, Mollie D. *Eleanor Roosevelt as I Knew Her*. McLean, VA: EPM Publications, 1996.

Starling, Edmund W., and Thomas Sugrue. *Starling of the White House*. New York: Simon & Schuster, 1946.

Straight, Michael. *After Long Silence*. New York: W. W. Norton, 1983.

Swing, Raymond. *"Good Evening!": A Professional Memoir*. New York: Harcourt, Brace & World, 1964.

"Three Friends." *In Loving Memory of Anna Hall Roosevelt*. New York: privately printed, 1893.

Tully, Grace. *F.D.R.: My Boss*. New York: Charles Scribner's Sons, 1949.

Truman, Harry S. *Memoirs*. 2 vols. Garden City, NY: Doubleday, 1955–1956.

vanden Heuvel, William J. *Hope and History: A Memoir of Tumultuous Times*. Ithaca, NY: Cornell University Press, 2019.

Wallace, Henry A. *The Price of Vision: The Diary of Henry Wallace, 1942–1946*. Boston: Houghton Mifflin, 1973.

Ward, Geoffrey C., ed. *Closest Companion: The Unknown Story of the Intimate Friendship Between Franklin Roosevelt and Margaret Suckley*. Boston: Houghton Mifflin, 1995.

Wells, H. G. *Experiment in Autobiography: Discoveries and Conclusions of a Very Ordinary Brain (Since 1866)*. New York: Macmillan, 1934.

West, J. B., and Mary Lynn Kotz. *Upstairs at the White House: My Life with the First Ladies: 1941–1969*. New York: Coward, McCann, & Geoghegan, 1973.

White, Walter F. *A Man Called White: The Autobiography of Walter White*. Athens: University of Georgia Press, 1995.

Willert, Arthur. *Washington & Other Memories*. Boston: Houghton Mifflin, 1972.

Wilson, Edith Bolling. *My Memoir*. Indianapolis: Bobbs-Merrill, 1939.

Wood, Laclaire Traver. *Barefoot at Val-Kill*. USA: Xlibris Corporation, 2006.

Wotkyns, Eleanor Roosevelt. *With Love, Aunt Eleanor: Stories from My Life with the First Lady of the World*. Petaluma, CA: Scrapbook, 2004.

Biographies and Historiography of Eleanor Roosevelt

Beasley, Maurine Hoffman. *Eleanor Roosevelt and the Media: A Public Quest for Self-Fulfillment*. Urbana: University of Illinois, 1987.

———. *Eleanor Roosevelt: Transformative First Lady*. Lawrence: University Press of Kansas, 2010.

Beasley, Maurine Hoffman, ed. *The White House Press Conferences of Eleanor Roosevelt*. New York: Garland Press, 1983.

———, Holly C. Shulman, and Henry R. Beasley, eds. *The Eleanor Roosevelt Encyclopedia*. Westport, CT: Greenwood, 2001.

Bell-Scott, Patricia. *The Firebrand and the First Lady: Portrait of a Friendship: Pauli Murray, Eleanor Roosevelt, and the Struggle for Social Justice*. New York: Alfred A. Knopf, 2016.

Berger, Jason. *A New Deal for the World: Eleanor Roosevelt and American Foreign Policy*. New York: Columbia University Press, 1981.

Black, Allida M. *Casting Her Own Shadow: Eleanor Roosevelt and the Shaping of Postwar Liberalism*. New York: Columbia University Press, 1996.

Black, Ruby. *Eleanor Roosevelt: A Biography*. New York: Duell, Sloan and Pearce, 1940.

Burns, Ric. *New York: A Documentary Film*. Public Broadcasting Service, 1999.

Cain, Richard. *Eleanor Roosevelt's Val-Kill*. Charleston, SC: Arcadia, 2002.

Caroli, Betty Boyd. *The Roosevelt Women: A Portrait in Five Generations*. New York: Basic Books, 1998.

Cook, Blanche Wiesen. *Eleanor Roosevelt*. 3 Vols. New York: Viking.

———. Vol. 1: *The Early Years,* 1884–1933. 1992.

———. Vol. 2: *The Defining Years, 1933–1938*. 1999.

———. Vol. 3: *The War Years and After, 1939–1962*. 2016.

Dallek, Matthew. *Defenseless Under the Night: The Roosevelt Years and the Origins of Homeland Security*. New York: Oxford University Press, 2016.

Eaton, Jeanette. *The Story of Eleanor Roosevelt*. New York: William Morrow, 1956.

Eighty-Eighth Congress (1st Session). *Anna Eleanor Roosevelt: Humanitarian, Stateswoman, Diplomat, Author*. U.S. House of Representatives, Joint Committee on Printing, 1963.

Eleanor Roosevelt on Her Own: Personal Papers and Objects of Mrs. Roosevelt, Photographs by Dr. A. David Gurewitsch. Eleanor Roosevelt Memorial Foundation, 1963.

Fleming, Candace. *Our Eleanor: A Scrapbook Look at Eleanor Roosevelt's Remarkable Life*. New York: Atheneum Books for Young Readers, 2005.

Flemion, Jess Stoddart, and Colleen M. O'Connor, eds. *Eleanor Roosevelt: An American Journey*. San Diego, CA: San Diego State University Press, 1987.

Freedman, Russell. *Eleanor Roosevelt: A Life of Discovery*. New York: Clarion, 1993.

Gerber, Robin. *Leadership the Eleanor Roosevelt Way: Timeless Strategies from the First Lady of Courage*. Englewood Cliffs, NJ: Prentice-Hall, 2002.

Ghee, Joyce C., and Joan Spence. *Eleanor Roosevelt: A Hudson Valley Remembrance*. Charleston, SC: Arcadia, 2005.

Glendon, Mary Ann. *A World Made New: Eleanor Roosevelt and the Universal Declaration of Human Rights*. New York: Random House, 2001.

Golay, Michael. *America 1933: The Great Depression, Lorena Hickok, Eleanor Roosevelt, and the Shaping of the New Deal*. New York: Free Press, 2013.

Hareven, Tamara K. *Eleanor Roosevelt: An American Conscience*. Chicago: Quadrangle Books, 1968.

Harrity, Richard, and Ralph G. Martin. *Eleanor Roosevelt: Her Life in Pictures*. New York: Duell, Sloan and Pearce, 1958.

Henry, Richard. *Eleanor Roosevelt and Adlai Stevenson*. New York: Palgrave Macmillan, 2010.

Hershan, Stella K. *A Woman of Quality*. New York: Crown, 1970.

———. *The Candles She Lit: The Legacy of Eleanor Roosevelt*. Westport, CT: Praeger, 1993.

Hickok, Lorena A. *The Story of Eleanor Roosevelt*. New York: Grosset & Dunlap, 1959.

————. *Eleanor Roosevelt: Reluctant First Lady*. New York: Dodd, Mead, 1962.

Hoff-Wilson, Joan, and Marjorie Lightman, eds. *Without Precedent: The Life and Career of Eleanor Roosevelt*. Bloomington: Indiana University Press, 1984.

Jacobs, William Jay. *Eleanor Roosevelt: A Life of Happiness and Tears*. New York: Coward-McCann, 1983.

Jencks, Penelope. *Eleanor Roosevelt on Riverside Drive*. Middletown, DE: privately printed, 2015.

Johnson, George. *Eleanor Roosevelt: The Compelling Life Story of One of the Most Famous Women of Our Times*. New York: Monarch Books, 1962.

Kearney, James R. *Anna Eleanor Roosevelt: The Evolution of a Reformer*. Boston: Houghton Mifflin, 1968.

Knapp, Sally. *Eleanor Roosevelt: A Biography*. New York: Thomas Y. Crowell, 1949.

Lash, Joseph P. *Eleanor and Franklin: The Story of Their Relationship, Based on Eleanor Roosevelt's Private Papers*. New York: W. W. Norton, 1971.

————. *Eleanor: The Years Alone*. New York: W. W. Norton, 1972.

————. *"Life Was Meant to Be Lived": A Centenary Portrait of Eleanor Roosevelt*. New York: W. W. Norton, 1984.

————. *Dealers and Dreamers: A New Look at the New Deal*. New York: Doubleday and Company, 1988.

Mackowiak, Philip A., MD. *Diagnosing Giants: Solving the Medical Mysteries of Thirteen Patients Who Changed the World*. New York: Oxford University Press, 2013.

Noble, Paul. *We Remember Eleanor*. Documentary. New York: WNET-TV, 1984.

O' Farrell, Brigid. *She Was One of Us: Eleanor Roosevelt and the American Worker*. Ithaca, NY: Cornell University Press, 2010.

Peyser, Marc, and Timothy Dwyer. *Hissing Cousins: The Lifelong Rivalry of Eleanor Roosevelt and Alice Roosevelt Longworth*. New York: Anchor Books, 2016.

Pottker, Jan. *Sara and Eleanor: The Story of Sara Delano Roosevelt and Her Daughter-in-Law, Eleanor Roosevelt*. New York: St. Martin's, 2004.

Quinn, Susan. *Eleanor and Hick: The Love Affair That Shaped a First Lady*. New York: Penguin Press, 2016.

Roosevelt, Elliott. *Murder and the First Lady*. New York: St. Martin's, 1984.

Roosevelt, Elliott, and James Brough. *An Untold Story: The Roosevelts of Hyde Park*. New York: G. P. Putnam's Sons, 1973.

————. *A Rendezvous with Destiny: The Roosevelts of the White House*. New York: G. P. Putnam's Sons, 1975.

————. *Mother R: Eleanor Roosevelt's Untold Story*. New York: G. P. Putnam's Sons, 1977.

Rowley, Hazel. *Franklin and Eleanor: An Extraordinary Marriage*. New York: Farrar, Straus & Giroux, 2010.

Scharf, Lois. *Eleanor Roosevelt: First Lady of American Liberalism*. Boston: Twayne, 1987.

Smith, Harold Ivan. *Eleanor: A Spiritual Biography*. Louisville, KY: Westminster John Knox Press, 2017.

Somervill, Barbara A. *Eleanor Roosevelt: First Lady of the World*. Minneapolis: Compass Point Books, 2006.

Steinberg, Alfred. *Mrs. R: The Life of Eleanor Roosevelt*. New York: G. P. Putnam's Sons, 1958.

Sulmasy, Daniel P., and Christopher Brick. "Too Busy to Be Sick." Poster presented at the Historical Clinicopathological Conference, University of Maryland School of Medicine, Baltimore, May 2, 2014.

Watrous, Hilda R. *In League with Eleanor: Eleanor Roosevelt and the League of Women Voters, 1921–1962*. New York: Foundation for Citizen Education, 1984.

Wigal, Donald. *The Wisdom of Eleanor Roosevelt*. New York: Citadel, 2003.

Williams, Sue. *Eleanor Roosevelt*. Boston: WGBH, *The American Experience*, 2000.

Wilson, Emily Herring. *The Three Graces of Val-Kill: Eleanor Roosevelt, Marion Dickerman, and Nancy Cook in the Place They Made Their Own*. Chapel Hill: University of North Carolina Press, 2017.

Youngs, J. William T. *Eleanor Roosevelt: A Personal and Public Life*. 2nd edition. New York: Pearson Longman, 2006.

Biographies and Historiography of FDR

Alter, Jonathan. *The Defining Moment: FDR's Hundred Days and the Triumph of Hope*. New York: Simon & Schuster, 2006.

Asbell, Bernard. *The F.D.R. Memoirs: A Speculation on History*. New York: Doubleday, 1973.

Black, Conrad. *Franklin Delano Roosevelt: Champion of Freedom*. New York: Public Affairs, 2003.

Brands, H. W. *Traitor to His Class: The Privileged Life and Radical Presidency of Franklin Delano Roosevelt*. New York: Anchor Books, 2009.

Breitman, Richard, and Allan J. Lichtman. *FDR and the Jews*. Cambridge, MA: Harvard University Press, 2013.

Brinkley, Alan. *Franklin Delano Roosevelt*. New York: Oxford University Press, 2010.

Burns, James MacGregor. *Roosevelt: The Lion and the Fox, 1882–1940*. New York: Harcourt, Brace, 1956.

———, and Susan Dunn. *The Three Roosevelts: Patrician Leaders Who Transformed America*. New York: Grove, 2001.

Carmichael, Donald Scott, ed. *F.D.R., Columnist: The Uncollected Columns of Franklin D. Roosevelt*. Foreword by Eleanor Roosevelt. New York: Pellegrini & Cudahy, 1947.

Chase, Karen, ed. *FDR on His Houseboat: The Larooco Log, 1924–1926*. Albany: State University of New York Press, 2016.

Dallek, Robert. *Franklin D. Roosevelt and American Foreign Policy, 1932–1945*. 2nd edition. New York: Oxford University Press, 1995.

———. *Franklin D. Roosevelt: A Political Life*. New York: Viking Penguin, 2017.

Daniels, Josephus. *The Wilson Era: Years of Peace—1910–1917*. Chapel Hill: University of North Carolina Press, 1944.

Davis, Kenneth S. *FDR*. 5 vols. New York: Random House, 1972–2000.

Flynn, John T. *Country Squire in the White House*. Garden City, NY: Doubleday, Doran, 1940.

Fogel, Nancy A., ed. *F.D.R. at Home*. Hyde Park, NY: Dutchess County Historical Society, 2005.

Freidel, Frank. *Franklin D. Roosevelt*. 5 vols. Boston: Little, Brown.

————. Vol. 1. *The Apprenticeship*, 1952.

————. Vol. 2. *The Ordeal*, 1954.

————. Vol. 3. *The Triumph*, 1956.

————. Vol. 4. *Launching the New Deal*, 1973.

————. Vol. 5. *A Rendezvous with Destiny*, 1990.

Gallagher, Hugh Gregory. *FDR's Splendid Deception*. New York: Dodd, Mead, 1985.

————. *Black Bird Fly Away: Disabled in an Able-Bodied World*. Foreword by Geoffrey Ward. St. Petersburg, FL: Vandamere, 1998.

Goldberg, Richard Thayer. *The Making of Franklin D. Roosevelt: Triumph Over Disability*. Cambridge, MA: Abt Books, 1981.

Goodwin, Doris Kearns. *No Ordinary Time: Franklin and Eleanor Roosevelt: The Home Front in World War II*. New York: Simon & Schuster, 1994.

Graff, Robert D., Robert Emmett Ginna, and Roger Butterfield. *FDR*. New York: Harper & Row, 1963.

Grubin, David. *FDR*. David Grubin Productions. Boston: WGBH, *The American Experience*, 1994.

Gunther, John. *Roosevelt in Retrospect: A Profile in History*. New York: Harper & Brothers, 1950.

Hamby, Alonzo L. *Man of Destiny: FDR and the Making of the American Century*. New York: Basic Books, 2015.

Hatch, Alden. *Franklin D. Roosevelt: An Informal Biography*. New York: Henry Holt, 1947.

Hickok, Lorena A. *The Road to the White House: FDR, The Pre-Presidential Years*. New York: Scholastic Book Services, 1962.

Hoffman, Nancy. *Eleanor Roosevelt and the Arthurdale Experiment*. New Haven, CT: Linnet Books, 2001.

Hoopes, Townsend, and Douglas Brinkley. *FDR and the Creation of the U.N.* New Haven, CT: Yale University Press, 1997.

Ickes, Harold LeClair. *The Secret Diary of Harold L. Ickes*. 3 vols. New York: Simon & Schuster.

————. *The First Thousand Days, 1933–1936*. Vol. 1. 1953.

————. *The Inside Struggle, 1936–1939*. Vol. 2. 1954.

————. *The Lowering Clouds, 1939–1941*. Vol. 3. 1954.

Jackson, Robert H. *That Man: An Insider's Portrait of Franklin D. Roosevelt*. New York: Oxford University Press, 2003.

Kaiser, David. *No End Save Victory: How FDR Led the Nation into War*. New York: Basic Books, 2014.

Kennedy, David M. *Freedom from Fear: The American People in Depression and War, 1929–1945*. Oxford History of the United States. New York: Oxford University Press, 1999.

———. *Freedom from Fear: The American People in World War II*. New York: Oxford University Press, 1999.

Klara, Robert. *FDR's Funeral Train: A Betrayed Widow, a Soviet Spy, and a Presidency in the Balance*. New York: Palgrave Macmillan, 2010.

Lelyveld, Joseph. *His Final Battle: The Last Months of Franklin Roosevelt*. New York: Alfred A. Knopf, 2016.

Leuchtenburg, William E. *Franklin D. Roosevelt and the New Deal, 1932–1940*. New York: Harper & Row, 1963.

———. *The White House Looks South: Franklin D. Roosevelt, Harry S. Truman, Lyndon B. Johnson*. Baton Rouge: Louisiana State University Press, 2005.

———. *In the Shadow of FDR: From Harry Truman to Barack Obama*, 4th edition. Ithaca, NY: Cornell University Press, 2011.

Meacham, Jon. *Franklin and Winston: An Intimate Portrait of an Epic Friendship*. New York: Random House, 2003.

Miller, Nathan. *F.D.R.: An Intimate History*. Garden City, NY: Doubleday, 1983.

Morgan, Ted. *FDR*. New York: Simon & Schuster, 1985.

Oursler, Fulton. *Behold This Dreamer!* New York: Macaulay, 1924; reprint, Boston: Little Brown, 1973.

Pederson, William D., ed. *A Companion to Franklin D. Roosevelt*. Malden, MA: Wiley-Blackwell, 2011.

Persico, Joseph E. *Franklin and Lucy: Mrs. Rutherfurd and the Other Remarkable Women in Roosevelt's Life*. New York: Random House, 2008.

Roosevelt, Eleanor. *Franklin D. Roosevelt and Hyde Park: Personal Recollections of Eleanor Roosevelt*. U. S. Department of the Interior, National Park Service, 1949.

Roosevelt, Elliott. *As He Saw It*. New York: Duell, Sloan and Pearce, 1946.

Roosevelt, Franklin D. *Whither Bound? A Lecture at Milton Academy on the Alumni War Memorial Foundation, May 18, 1926*. Boston: Houghton Mifflin, 1926.

Roosevelt, James, and Sidney Shalett. *Affectionately, F.D.R.: A Son's Story of a Lonely Man*. New York: Harcourt, Brace, 1959.

Roosevelt, Nicholas. *A Front Row Seat*. Norman, OK: University of Oklahoma Press, 1953.

Rosenman, Samuel, ed. *The Public Papers and Addresses of Franklin D. Roosevelt*. 5 vols. New York: Random House, 1938.

———. Vol. 1. *The Genesis of the New Deal, 1928–1932*.

———. Vol. 2. *The Year of Crisis, 1933*.

———. Vol. 3. *The Advance of Recovery and Reform, 1934*.

———. Vol. 4. *The Court Disapproves, 1935*.

———. Vol. 5. *The People Approve, 1936*.

———. *The Public Papers and Addresses of Franklin D. Roosevelt*. 5 vols. New York: Random House, 1938. New York: Macmillan, 1941.

————. Vol. 6. *The Constitution Prevails, 1937.*

————. Vol. 7. *The Continuing Struggle for Liberalism, 1938.*

————. Vol. 8. *War—and Neutrality, 1939.*

————. Vol. 9. *War—and Aid to Democracies, 1940.*

————. Vol. 10. *The Call to Battle Stations, 1941.*

————. Vol. 11. *Humanity on the Defensive, 1942.*

————. Vol. 12. *The Tide Turns, 1943.*

————. Vol. 13. *Victory and the Threshold of Peace, 1944–45.*

Schlesinger, Arthur, Jr. *The Age of Roosevelt.* 3 vols. Boston: Houghton Mifflin, 1957–1960.

Sharon, John H., *The Psychology of the Fireside Chat.* 2 vols. Princeton Senior Thesis, Class of 1949. Seeley G. Mudd Manuscript Library. Princeton University Library. Princeton University.

Sherwood, Robert E. *Roosevelt and Hopkins: An Intimate History.* New York: Harper Brothers, 1948.

Shesol, Jeff. *Supreme Power: Franklin Roosevelt vs. the Supreme Court.* New York: W. W. Norton, 2010.

Smith, Jean Edward. *FDR.* New York: Random House, 2007.

Stevens, Ruth. *"Hi-Ya Neighbor."* Atlanta, GA: Tupper and Love, 1947.

Sutton, Antony C. *Wall Street and FDR.* New York: Arlington House, 1975.

Tobin, James. *The Man He Became: How FDR Defied Polio to Win the Presidency.* New York: Simon & Schuster, 2013.

Tugwell, Rexford G. *The Democratic Roosevelt: A Biography of Franklin D. Roosevelt.* Garden City, NY: Doubleday, 1957.

————. *The Brains Trust.* New York: Viking, 1968.

————. *In Search of Roosevelt.* Cambridge, MA: Harvard University Press, 1972.

————. *Roosevelt's Revolution.* New York: Macmillan, 1977.

Ward, Geoffrey C. *Before the Trumpet: Young Franklin Roosevelt, 1882–1905.* New York: Harper & Row, 1985.

————. *A First-Class Temperament: The Emergence of Franklin Roosevelt.* New York: Harper & Row, 1989.

————. *Closest Companion: The Unknown Story of the Intimate Friendship Between Franklin Roosevelt and Margaret Suckley.* New York: Houghton Mifflin Harcourt, 1995.

————, and Ken Burns. *The Roosevelts: An Intimate History.* New York: Alfred A. Knopf, 2014.

Weingast, David E. *Franklin D. Roosevelt: Man of Destiny.* New York: Julian Messner, 1952.

Weintraub, Stanley. *Young Mr. Roosevelt: FDR's Introduction to War, Politics, and Life.* Boston: Da Capo, 2013.

Williams, Gareth. *Paralysed with Fear: The Story of Polio.* New York: Palgrave Macmillan, 2013.

Winik, Jay. *1944: FDR and the Year That Changed History*. New York: Simon & Schuster, 2015.

Zevin, B. D., ed. *Nothing to Fear: The Selected Addresses of Franklin Delano Roosevelt, 1932–1945*. Cambridge, MA: Riverside Press, Houghton Mifflin, 1946.

Biographies and Historiography of Theodore Roosevelt and Edith Kermit Roosevelt

Amos, James E. *TR: Hero to His Valet*. New York: John Day, 1927.

Dalton, Kathleen. *Theodore Roosevelt: A Strenuous Life*. New York: Alfred A. Knopf, 2002.

Donn, Linda. *The Roosevelt Cousins: Growing Up Together, 1882–1924*. New York: Alfred A. Knopf, 2001.

Gould, Lewis L. *Edith Kermit Roosevelt: Creating the Modern First Lady*. Lawrence: University Press of Kansas, 2013.

Hale, William Bayard. *A Week in the White House with Theodore Roosevelt: A Study of the President at the Nation's Business*. New York: G. P. Putnam and Sons, 1908.

Longworth, Alice Roosevelt. *Crowded Hours: Reminiscences of Alice Roosevelt Longworth*. New York: Charles Scribner's Sons, 1933.

Lorant, Stefan. *The Life and Times of Theodore Roosevelt*. Garden City, NY: Doubleday, 1959.

Morison, Elting E., ed. *The Letters of Theodore Roosevelt*, Vol. 1. Cambridge, MA.: Harvard University Press, 1951.

Morris, Edmund. *The Rise of Theodore Roosevelt*. New York: Coward, McCann, & Geoghegan, 1979.

——. *Theodore Rex*. New York: Random House, 2001.

——. *Colonel Roosevelt*. New York: Random House, 2010.

Morris, Sylvia Jukes. *Edith Kermit Roosevelt: Portrait of a First Lady*. New York: Coward, McCann, & Geoghegan, 1980.

O'Toole, Patricia. *When Trumpets Call: Theodore Roosevelt After the White House*. New York: Simon & Schuster, 2005.

Pringle, Henry F. *Theodore Roosevelt: A Biography*. New York: Harcourt, Brace, 1956.

Renehan, Edward J., Jr. *The Lion's Pride: Theodore Roosevelt and His Family in Peace and War*. New York: Oxford University Press, 1998.

Rixey, Lilian. *Bamie: Theodore Roosevelt's Remarkable Sister*. New York: McKay, 1963.

Robinson, Corinne Roosevelt. *My Brother Theodore Roosevelt*. New York: Charles Scribner's Sons, 1921.

Roosevelt, Theodore. *New York*. London: Longmans, Green, 1891.

——. *African Game Trails*. New York: Charles Scribner's Sons, 1910.

Roosevelt, Theodore, and George Bird Grinnell, eds. *Hunting in Many Lands: The Book of the Boone and Crockett Club*. New York: Harper & Brothers, 1914.

Books

Adamic, Louis. *Dinner at the White House*. New York: Harper & Brothers, 1946.

Adams, Laurie Schneider. *Exploring Art*. London: Laurence King, 2002.

Agar, Herbert. *The People's Choice, from Washington to Harding: A Study in Democracy*. Boston: Houghton Mifflin, 1933.

Albright, Madeleine. *Fascism: A Warning*. New York: Harper, 2018.

Aldrich, Nelson W., Jr. *Old Money: The Mythology of America's Upper Class*. New York: Alfred A. Knopf, 1988.

Algeo, Matthew. *The President Is a Sick Man: Wherein the Supposedly Virtuous Grover Cleveland Survives a Secret Surgery at Sea and Vilifies the Courageous Newspaperman Who Dared Expose the Truth*. Chicago: Chicago Review Press, 2012.

Allport, Gordon W. *The Nature of Prejudice*. 25th Anniversary Edition. New York: Basic Books, 1979.

Anderson, Jervis. *A. Philip Randolph: A Biographical Portrait*. Berkeley: University of California Press, 1986.

Anthony, Carl Sferrazza. *First Ladies*, Vol. 1. New York: William Morrow, 1990.

Arsenault, Raymond. *The Sound of Freedom: Marian Anderson, the Lincoln Memorial, and the Concert That Awakened America*. New York: Bloomsbury, 2009.

Ashburn, Frank D. *Peabody of Groton: A Portrait*. New York: Coward-McCann, 1944.

Barker-Benfield, G. J., and Catherine Clifton. *Portraits of American Women: From Settlement to the Present*. New York: Oxford University Press, 1998.

Bartlett, Bruce. *Wrong on Race: The Democratic Party's Buried Past*. New York: St. Martin's, 2008.

Bates, Josephine White. *Mercury Poisoning in the Industries of New York City and Vicinity*. National Civic Federation New York and New Jersey Section, 1910. Reprinted: Miami, FL: HardPress, 2017.

Begley, Louis. *Why the Dreyfus Affair Matters*. New Haven, CT: Yale University Press, 2009.

Bell, Margaret. *Margaret Fuller*. Introduction by Eleanor Roosevelt. New York: Charles Boni, Jr., 1930.

Bellow, Saul. *It All Adds Up: From the Dim Past to the Uncertain Future: A Nonfiction Collection*. New York: Viking, 1994.

Benfey, Christopher. *American Audacity: Literary Essays North and South*. Ann Arbor: University of Michigan Press, 2008.

Beran, Michael Knox. *The Last Patrician: Bobby Kennedy and the End of American Aristocracy*. New York: St. Martin's, 1998.

Berenbaum, Michael. *The World Must Know: The History of the Holocaust as Told in the United States Holocaust Memorial Museum*. Baltimore, MD: Johns Hopkins University Press, 1981.

Berg, A. Scott. *Max Perkins: Editor of Genius*. New York: E. P. Dutton, Thomas Congdon Books, 1978.

———. *Goldwyn*. New York: Alfred A. Knopf, 1989.

————. *Lindbergh*. New York: G. P. Putnam's Sons, 1998.

————. *Kate Remembered*. New York: G. P. Putnam's Sons, 2003.

————. *Wilson*. New York: G. P. Putnam's Sons, 2013.

————, ed. *World War I and America: Told By the Americans Who Lived It*. New York: Library of America, 2017.

Beschloss, Michael. *Kennedy and Roosevelt*. New York: W. W. Norton, 1980.

————. *The Crisis Years: Kennedy and Khrushchev, 1960–1963*. New York: Harper-Collins, 1991.

————. *The Conquerors: Roosevelt, Truman and the Destruction of Hitler's Germany, 1941–1945*. New York: Simon & Schuster, 2002.

————. *Presidents of War: The Epic Story, from 1807 to Modern Times*. New York: Crown, 2018.

————, ed. *Jacqueline Kennedy, Historic Conversations on Life with John F. Kennedy: Interviews with Arthur M. Schlesinger, Jr.* Foreword by Caroline Kennedy. New York: Hyperion, 2011.

Biddle, Francis. *In Brief Authority*. Garden City, NY: Doubleday, 1962.

Bradley, James. *The Imperial Cruise: A Secret History of Empire and War*. New York: Little, Brown, 2009.

Brandt, Clare. *The Livingstons: An American Aristocracy*. Garden City, NY: Doubleday, 1986.

Brawley, Sean, and Chris Dixon. *Hollywood's South Seas and the Pacific War: Searching for Dorothy Lamour*. New York: Palgrave Macmillan, 2012.

Breitman, Richard, and Allan J. Lichtman. *FDR and the Jews*. Cambridge, MA: Belknap Press, 2013.

Brinkley, Alan. *Voices of Protest: Huey Long, Father Coughlin and the Great Depression*. New York: Vintage Books, 1983.

————. *The End of Reform: New Deal Liberalism in Recession and War*. New York: Alfred A. Knopf, 1995.

————. *Liberalism and Its Discontents*. Cambridge, MA: Harvard University Press, 1998.

————, Andrew Huebner, and John Giggie. *The Unfinished Nation: A Concise History of the American People*. 8th edition. New York: McGraw-Hill Education, 2018.

Brooks, Gladys. *Boston and Return*. New York: Atheneum, 1962.

Brown, Dorothy Marie. *Setting a Course: American Women in the 1920s*. Boston: Twayne, 1987.

Buchanan, Rachel. *A Débutante in New York Society: Her Illusions and What Became of Them*. New York: D. Appleton, 1888.

Buckley, William F., Jr., and James Rosen, eds. *A Torch Kept Lit: Great Lives of the Twentieth Century*. New York: Crown Forum, 2016.

Butler, Susan. *Roosevelt and Stalin: Portrait of a Partnership*. New York: Alfred A. Knopf, 2015.

Cain, Susan. *Quiet: The Power of Introverts in a World That Can't Stop Talking*. New York: Crown, 2012.

Caro, Robert. *The Power Broker: Robert Moses and the Fall of New York*. New York: Alfred A. Knopf, 1974.

Cash, W. J. *The Mind of the South*. New York: Alfred A. Knopf, 1941.

Chace, James. *Acheson: The Secretary of State Who Created the American World*. New York: Simon & Schuster, 1998.

———. *1912: Wilson, Roosevelt, Taft & Debs—The Election That Changed the Country*. New York: Simon & Schuster, 2004.

Chafe, William H. *The Paradox of Change: American Women in the 20th Century*. New York: Oxford University Press, 1991.

———. *Never Stop Running: Allard K. Lowenstein and the Struggle to Save American Liberalism*. New York: Basic Books, 1993.

———. *Privates Lives/Public Consequences: Personality and Politics in Modern America*. Cambridge, MA: Harvard University Press, 2005.

Charles River Editors. *Executive Order 9066: The History of President Franklin D. Roosevelt's Controversial Decision to Intern Japanese American Citizens during World War II*. Amazon Digital Services, 2016.

Churchill, Winston S. *The Second World War: The Grand Alliance*. Boston: Houghton Mifflin, 1950.

Cohen, Robert. *When the Old Left Was Young: Student Radicals and America's First Mass Student Movement, 1929–1941*. New York: Oxford University Press, 1993.

Collier, Peter. *The Roosevelts: An American Saga*. New York: Simon & Schuster, 1994.

Cordery, Stacy A. *Alice: Alice Roosevelt Longworth, from White House Princess to Washington Power Broker*. New York: Penguin Books, 2008.

Craig, Lee Allan. *Josephus Daniels: His Life and Times*. Chapel Hill: University of North Carolina Press, 2013.

Daniels, Jonathan. *The End of Innocence*. Philadelphia: J. B. Lippincott, 1954.

———. *The Time Between the Wars: Armistice to Pearl Harbor*. Garden City, NY: Doubleday, 1966.

———. *Washington Quadrille: The Dance Beside the Documents*. New York: Doubleday, 1968.

Daniels, Roger, Sandra C. Taylor, and Harry H. L. Kitano, eds. *Japanese Americans: From Relocation to Redress*. Revised edition. Seattle: University of Washington Press, 1991.

Dawidoff, Robert. *Making History Matter*. Philadelphia: Temple University Press, 2000.

Dearstyne, Bruce W. *The Spirit of New York: Defining Events in the Empire State's History*. Albany: State University of New York Press, 2015.

Debnam, W. E. *Weep No More, My Lady: A Southerner Answers Mrs. Roosevelt's Report on the "Poor and Unhappy" South*. Raleigh, NC: Graphic Press, 1950.

Dies, Martin. *Martin Dies' Story*. New York: Bookmailer, 1963.

Dietz, Ulysses Grant, and Sam Watters. *Dream House: The White House as an American Home*. New York: Acanthus Press, 2009.

Dinnerstein, Leonard. *Antisemitism in America*. New York: Oxford University Press, 1994.

Doctorow, E. L. *Ragtime*. New York: Random House, 1975.

Dodworth, Allen. *Dancing and Its Relations to Education and Social Life*. New York: Harper & Brothers, 1900.

Donovan, Sandy. *Madame Chiang Kai-shek: Face of Modern China*. Minneapolis: Compass Point Books, 2007.

Douglas, William O. *The Autobiography of William O. Douglas*. 2 vols. New York: Random House, 1974, 1980.

Dowling, Timothy C., ed. *Personal Perspectives: World War I*. Vol 1. Santa Barbara, CA: ABC-CLIO Inc., 2006.

Downey, Kirstin. *The Woman Behind the New Deal: The Life of Frances Perkins, FDR's Secretary of Labor and His Moral Conscience*. New York: Nan A. Talese/Doubleday, 2009.

Dray, Philip. *At the Hands of Persons Unknown: The Lynching of Black America*. New York: Random House, 2002.

DuBois, Ellen Carol. *Suffrage: Women's Long Battle for the Vote*. New York: Simon & Schuster, 2020.

Du Maurier, George. *Peter Ibbetson*. Myna Classics, 2010.

Dumond, Dwight Lowell. *Roosevelt to Roosevelt: The United States in the Twentieth Century*. New York: Henry Holt, 1937.

Dyja, Thomas. *Walter White: The Dilemma of Black Identity in America*. The Library of African American Biography. Chicago: Ivan R. Dee, 2008.

Eden, Anthony. *Another World, 1897–1917*. London: Allen Lane, 1976.

Egerton, John. *Speak Now Against the Day: The Generation Before the Civil Rights Movement in the South*. New York: Alfred A. Knopf, 1994.

Equal Justice Initiative. *Lynching in America: Confronting the Legacy of Racial Terror*. Montgomery, AL: Equal Justice Initiative, 2015.

Erenberg, Lewis A. *Steppin' Out: New York Nightlife and the Transformation of American Culture, 1890–1930*. Westport, CT: Greenwood, 1981.

Evans, Harold, Gail Buckland, and Kevin Baker. *The American Century*. New York: Alfred A. Knopf, 1998.

Faber, Doris. *The Life of Lorena Hickok: E.R.'s Friend*. New York: William Morrow, 1980.

Fahey, James J. *Pacific War Diary, 1942–1945: The Secret Diary of an American Sailor*. Boston: Houghton Mifflin, 1963.

Fairlie, Henry. *The Life of Politics*. New York: Basic Books, 1968.

Fecher, Charles A., ed. *The Diary of H. L. Mencken*. New York: Alfred A. Knopf, 1989.

Felsenthal, Carol. *Alice Roosevelt Longworth*. New York: G. P. Putnam's Sons, 1988.

Fenster, Julie M. *FDR's Shadow: Louis Howe, the Force That Shaped Franklin and Eleanor Roosevelt*. New York: Palgrave Macmillan, 2009.

Ferber, Edna. *A Peculiar Treasure*. New York: Doubleday, Doran, 1939.

Ferrell, Robert H. *Off the Record: The Private Papers of Harry S. Truman*. New York: Harper & Row, 1980.

Flayhart, William H., ed. *Perils of the Atlantic: Steamship Disasters, 1850 to the Present*. New York: W. W. Norton, 2003.

Flint, Anthony. *Wrestling with Moses: How Jane Jacobs Took On New York's Master Builder and Transformed the American City*. New York: Random House, 2009.

Flynt, Larry, and David Eisenbach. *One Nation Under Sex: How the Private Lives of Presidents, First Ladies and Their Lovers Changed the Course of American History*. New York: Palgrave Macmillan, 2011.

Freeman, Jo. *A Room at a Time: How Women Entered Party Politics*. Lanham, MD: Rowman & Littlefield, 1999.

Fromkin, David. *A Peace to End All Peace: The Fall of the Ottoman Empire and the Creation of the Modern Middle East*. New York: Henry Holt, 1989.

————. *In the Time of the Americans: FDR, Truman, Eisenhower, Marshall, MacArthur—The Generation That Changed America's Role in the World*. New York: Alfred A. Knopf, 1995.

Galbraith, John Kenneth. *Letters to Kennedy*. Edited by James Goodman. Cambridge, MA: Harvard University Press, 1998.

Gardiner, Robin. *The History of the White Star Line*. Surrey, England: Ian Allan, 2001.

Gardner, Deborah S. *Roosevelt House at Hunter College: The Story of Franklin and Eleanor's New York City Home*. New York: Gilder Lehrman Institute of American History & Hunter College, City University of New York, 2009.

Gellerman, William. *Martin Dies*. New York: John Day, 1944.

Gentry, Curt. *J. Edgar Hoover: The Man and the Secrets*. New York: W. W. Norton, 1991.

Ghee, Joyce C., and Joan Spence. *Taconic Pathways: Through Beekman, Union Vale, LaGrange, Washington, and Stanford*. Charleston, SC: Arcadia, 2000.

Gidlow, Liette. *The Big Vote: Gender, Consumer Culture, and the Politics of Exclusion, 1890s–1920s*. Baltimore: Johns Hopkins University Press, 2004.

Gilmore, Glenda Elizabeth, and Thomas J. Sugrue. *These United States: A Nation in the Making, 1890 to the Present*. New York: W. W. Norton, 2015.

Golway, Terry. *Machine Made: Tammany Hall and the Creation of Modern American Politics*. New York: W. W. Norton, 2014.

————. *Frank and Al: FDR, Al Smith, and the Unlikely Alliance That Created the Modern Democratic Party*. New York: St. Martin's, 2018.

Goodier, Susan, and Karen Pastorello. *Women Will Vote: Winning Suffrage in New York State*. Ithaca, NY: Cornell University Press, 2017.

Gordon, John Steele. *An Empire of Wealth: The Epic History of American Economic Power*. New York: Harper Perennial, 2004.

Graubard, Stephen. *Command of Office: How War, Secrecy and Deception Transformed the Presidency, from Theodore Roosevelt to George W. Bush*. New York: Basic Books, 2004.

Greenwald, Maurine Weiner. *Women, War, and Work: The Impact of World War I on Women Workers in the United States*. Ithaca, NY: Cornell University Press, 1981.

Gruber, Ruth. *Haven: The Story of 1,000 World War II Refugees and How They Came to America*. New York: Putnam, 1983.

Hahn, Emily. *Once Upon a Pedestal*. New York: Thomas Y. Crowell, 1974.

Hall, Florence Howe. *Social Customs*. Boston: Dana Estes, 1911.

Hall, Valentine Gill. *Lawn Tennis in America*. New York: D. W. Granbery, 1889.

Halsey, William F., and J. Bryan III. *Admiral Halsey's Story*. New York: Whittlesey House, 1947.

Hansen, Chris. *Enfant Terrible: The Times and Schemes of General Elliott Roosevelt*. Tucson, AZ: Able Baker, 2012.

Harper, John Lamberton. *American Visions of Europe: Franklin D. Roosevelt, George F. Kennan, and Dean G. Acheson*. Cambridge: Cambridge University Press, 1994.

Heffner, Richard D., and Alexander B. Heffner. *A Documentary History of the United States*. 10th edition. New York: Signet Classics, 2018.

Height, Dorothy. *Open Wide the Freedom Gates: A Memoir*. New York: PublicAffairs, 2003.

Heilbut, Anthony. *Thomas Mann*. New York: Alfred A. Knopf, 1995.

Hess, Stephen. *America's Political Dynasties: From Adams to Clinton*. Washington, DC: Brookings Institution Press, 2015.

Hillman, James. *The Soul's Code: In Search of Character and Calling*. New York: Random House, 1996.

Hoehling, A. A. *Home Front, USA*. New York: Thomas Y. Crowell, 1966.

Holthusen, Henry F. *James W. Wadsworth, Jr.: A Biographical Sketch*. New York: G. P. Putnam's Sons, 1926.

Hurd, Charles. *The Compact History of the American Red Cross*. Portland, OR: Hawthorn Books, 1959.

Isenberg, Sheila. *A Hero of Our Own: The Story of Varian Fry*. New York: Random House, 2001.

Jaker, Bill, Frank Sulek, and Peter Kanze. *The Airwaves of New York: Illustrated Histories of 156 AM Stations in the Metropolitan Area, 1921–1996*. Jefferson, NC: McFarland, 1998.

James, Henry. *The American Scene*. New York: Charles Scribner's Sons, 1946.

Johnson, James Weldon. *Writings*. New York: Library of America, 2004.

Johnson, Paul. *A History of the American People*. New York: HarperCollins, 1997.

Kaiser, Charles. *The Cost of Courage*. New York: Other Press, 2015.

Kaiser, Philip M. *Journeying Far and Wide: A Political and Diplomatic Memoir*. New York: Scribner, 1993.

Kanfer, Stefan. *Groucho: The Life and Times of Julius Henry Marx*. New York: Alfred A. Knopf, 2000.

Kaplan, James. *Sinatra: The Chairman*. New York: Doubleday, 2015.

Kaplan, Paul M. *Lillian Wald: America's Great Social and Healthcare Reformer*. Gretna, LA: Pelican, 2018.

Kashima, Tetsuden. *Personal Justice Denied: Report of the Commission on Wartime Relocation and Internment of Civilians*. Seattle: University of Washington Press, 1997.

Katznelson, Ira. *Fear Itself: The New Deal and the Origins of Our Time*. New York: W. W. Norton, 2013.

Keiler, Allen. *Marian Anderson: A Singer's Journey*. New York: Scribner, 2000.

Kempton, Murray. *Rebellions, Perversities, and Main Events*. New York: Times Books, 1994.

———. *Part of Our Time: Some Ruins and Monuments of the Thirties*. Introduction by David Remnick. New York: New York Review of Books, 2012.

Kendi, Ibram X. *Stamped from the Beginning: The Definitive History of Racist Ideas in America*. New York: Nation Books, 2016.

Kennedy, Caroline. *A Patriot's Handbook: Songs, Poems, Stories, and Speeches Celebrating the Land We Love*. New York: Hachette Books, 2003.

Keyes, Frances Parkinson. *Capital Kaleidoscope: The Story of a Washington Hostess*. New York: Harper & Brothers, 1937.

Kienholz, Mary L. *Opium Traders and Their Worlds: A Revisionist Exposé of the World's Greatest Opium Traders*. Vol. 1. iUniverse, 2008.

King, Gilbert. *Devil in the Grove: Thurgood Marshall, the Groveland Boys, and the Dawn of a New America*. New York: HarperCollins, 2012.

Kisseloff, Jeff. *You Must Remember This: An Oral History of Manhattan from the 1890s to World War II*. New York: Harcourt Brace Jovanovich, 1989.

Kleeman, Rita Halle. *Gracious Lady: The Life of Sara Delano Roosevelt*. New York: Appleton-Century, 1935.

Klein, Henry H. *Dynastic America and Those Who Own It*. New York: Henry H. Klein, 1921.

Klibaner, Irwin. *Conscience of a Troubled South: The Southern Conference Education Fund, 1946–1966*. New York: Carlson, 1989.

Krugler, David F. *This Is Only a Test: How Washington, D.C. Prepared for Nuclear War*. New York: Palgrave Macmillan, 2006.

Lagemann, Ellen Condliffe. *A Generation of Women*. Cambridge, MA: Harvard University Press, 1979.

Lane, Anne Wintermute, and Louise Herrick Wall, eds. *The Letters of Franklin K. Lane: Personal and Political*. New York: Houghton Mifflin, 1922.

Lash, Jonathan, et al. *Joseph P. Lash*. Chilmark, Massachusetts, Community Center, 1987.

Layton, Thomas L. *The Voyage of the "Frolic": New England Merchants and the Opium Trade*. Palo Alto, CA: Stanford University Press, 1997.

Lee, Alfred McClung, and Norman D. Humphrey. *Race Riot*. New York: Dryden, 1943.

Lepore, Jill. *These Truths: A History of the United States*. New York: W. W. Norton, 2018.

Levenson, J. C., Ernest Samuels, et al., eds. *The Letters of Henry Adams, Vol. V: 1899–1905*. Massachusetts Historical Society, 1988.

Levin, Linda Lotridge. *The Making of FDR: The Story of Stephen T. Early, America's First Modern Press Secretary*. Amherst, NY: Prometheus Books, 2008.

Levy, Paul. *The Letters of Lytton Strachey*. New York: Farrar, Straus and Giroux, 2005.

Lewis, Sinclair. *Main Street: The Story of Carol Kennicott*. New York: Harcourt, Brace and Howe, 1920.

Lloyd, Stephen. *William Walton: Muse of Fire*. Woodbridge, Sussex, England: Boydell, 2001.

Lomazow, Steven, and Eric Fettmann. *FDR's Deadly Secret*. New York: PublicAffairs, 2009.

Lombard, Helen. *While They Fought: Behind the Scenes in Washington, 1941–1946*. New York: Charles Scribner's Sons, 1947.

Longstreet, Abby Buchanan. *Social Etiquette of New York*. New York: D. Appleton, 1896.

Looker, Earle. *The American Way: Franklin Roosevelt in Action*. New York: John Day, 1933.

Louchheim, Katie, ed. *The Making of the New Deal: The Insiders Speak*. Cambridge, MA: Harvard University Press, 1983.

Lowenstein, Allard K. *Brutal Mandate: A Journey to Southwest Africa*. Foreword by Eleanor Roosevelt. New York: Macmillan, 1962.

Lowitt, Richard, and Maurine Beasley. *One Third of a Nation: Lorena Hickok Reports on the Great Depression*. Urbana: University of Illinois Press, 1983.

Lunardini, Christine Anne. *From Equal Suffrage to Equal Rights: The National Women's Party, 1913–1923*. Princeton, NJ: Princeton University Press, 1983.

Lynn, Kenneth S. *The Air-line to Seattle: Studies in Literary and Historical Writing About America*. Chicago: University of Chicago Press, 1983.

Mackay, Robert B., Anthony K. Baker, and Carol A. Traynor. *Long Island Country Houses and Their Architects, 1860–1940*. New York: W. W. Norton, 1997.

MacMillan, Margaret. *Paris 1919: Six Months that Changed the World*. New York: Random House, 2001.

Mailer, Norman. *The Presidential Papers*. New York: Bantam, 1964.

Manchester, William. *The Last Lion: William Spencer Churchill*. 2 vols. Boston: Little, Brown, 1983, 1988.

———, and Paul Reid. *The Last Lion: Winston Spencer Churchill, Defender of the Realm*. Boston: Little, Brown, 2012.

Mann, William J. *The Wars of the Roosevelts*. New York: Harper, 2016.

Manners, William. *Patience and Fortitude: Fiorello La Guardia—A Biography*. New York: Harcourt, Brace, Jovanovich, 1976.

Marton, Kati. *Hidden Power: Presidential Marriages That Shaped Our Recent History*. New York: Pantheon Books, 2001.

Mathews, Jane DeHart. *The Federal Theatre, 1935–1939: Plays, Relief, and Politics*. Princeton, NJ: Princeton University Press, 1967.

McCullough, David. *In the Dark Streets Shineth: A 1941 Christmas Eve Story*. Stevens Point, WI: Shadow Mountain, 2010.

———. *Mornings on Horseback*. New York: Simon & Schuster, 1981.

———. *Truman*. New York: Simon & Schuster, 1992.

McWhorter, Diane. *Carry Me Home: Birmingham, Alabama—The Climactic Battle of the Civil Rights Revolution*. New York: Simon & Schuster, 2001.

Meijer, Henrik. *Arthur Vandenberg: The Man in the Middle of the American Century*. Chicago: University of Chicago Press, 2017.

Mencken, H. L. *The American Language, Supplement Two*. New York: Alfred A. Knopf, 1948.

Merry, Robert W. *Taking on the World: Joseph and Stewart Alsop, Guardians of the American Century*. New York: Viking, 1996.

Miller, Kristie. *Isabella Greenway: An Enterprising Woman*. Tucson: University of Arizona Press, 2004.

Miller, Merle. *Plain Speaking: An Oral Biography of Harry Truman*. New York: G. P. Putnam and Sons, 1974.

Moorehead, Caroline, ed. *Gellhorn: A Twentieth-Century Life*. New York: Henry Holt, 2003.

———. *Selected Letters of Martha Gellhorn*. New York: Henry Holt, 2006.

Morgenthau, Henry III. *Mostly Morgenthaus: A Family History*. New York: Ticknor & Fields, 1991.

Morrison, John. *Mathilde Krim and the Story of AIDS*. New York: Chelsea House, 2005.

Morse, Arthur. *While Six Million Died: A Chronicle of American Apathy*. New York: Overlook Books, 1983.

Morsink, Johannes. *The Universal Declaration of Human Rights: Origins, Drafting, and Intent*. Philadelphia: University of Pennsylvania Press, 1999.

Moscow, Warren. *Politics in the Empire State*. New York: Alfred A. Knopf, 1948.

———. *The Last of the Big-Time Bosses: The Life and Times of Carmine DeSapio and the Rise and Fall of Tammany Hall*. New York: Stein and Day, 1971.

Muller, Herbert J. *Adlai Stevenson: A Study in Values*. New York: Harper & Row, 1967.

Myrdal, Gunnar. *An American Dilemma: The Negro Problem and Modern Democracy*. New York: Harper & Brothers, 1944.

Nevins, Allan. *Herbert H. Lehman and His Era*. New York: Scribner's, 1973.

Nissenson, Marilyn. *The Lady Upstairs: Dorothy Schiff and the* New York Post. New York: St. Martin's, 2007.

Norton, Mary Beth, et al. *A People and a Nation:, A History of the United States,* Vol. II: *Since 1865*. 10th edition. Boston: Cengage Learning, 2008.

O'Hara, John. *My Turn*. New York: New American Library, 1965.

Olson, Lynne. *Citizens of London: The Americans Who Stood with Britain in Its Darkest, Finest Hour*. New York: Random House, 2010.

Pakenham, Thomas. *The Boer War*. New York: Random House, 1979.

Pakula, Hannah. *The Last Empress: Madame Chiang Kai-shek and the Birth of Modern China*. New York: Simon & Schuster, 2009.

Palmer, Charles F. *Adventures of a Slum Fighter*. Atlanta, GA: Tupper and Love, 1955.

Penix, Amanda Griffith. *Arthurdale*. Charleston, SC: Arcadia, 2007.

Perry, Elisabeth Israels. *Belle Moskowitz: Feminine Politics and the Exercise of Power in the Age of Alfred E. Smith*. New York: Oxford University Press, 1987.

Phillips, Cabell. *From the Crash to the Blitz, 1929–1939*. The *New York Times* Chronicle of American Life. New York: Macmillan, 1969.

Pietrusza, David. *1920: The Year of Six Presidents*. New York: Carroll & Graf, 2007.

Pogue, Forrest C. *George C. Marshall: Organizer of Victory, 1943–1945*. New York: Viking, 1973.

Potter, Jeffrey. *Men, Money & Magic: The Story of Dorothy Schiff*. New York: Coward, McGann, & Geoghegan, 1976.

Powe, Lucas A., Jr. *The Supreme Court and the American Elite, 1789–2008*. Cambridge, MA: Harvard University Press, 2009.

Prioleau, Betsy, and Elizabeth Stevens Prioleau. *Seductress: Women Who Ravished the World and Their Lost Art of Love*. New York: Penguin Books, 2004.

Purdum, Todd. *An Idea Whose Time Has Come: Two Presidents, Two Parties, and the Battle for the Civil Rights Act of 1964*. New York: Henry Holt, 2014.

Purnell, Sonia. *Clementine: The Life of Mrs. Winston Churchill*. New York: Viking, 2015.

Quigley, Joan. *Just Another Southern Town: Mary Church Terrell and the Struggle for Racial Justice in the Nation's Capital*. New York: Oxford University Press, 2016.

Redel, Victoria. *The Border of Truth: A Novel*. New York: Counterpoint, 2007.

Reeves, Richard. *President Kennedy: Profile of Power*. New York: Simon & Schuster, 1993.

———. *Infamy: The Shocking Story of the Japanese American Internment in World War II*. New York: Henry Holt, 2015.

Rhinevault, Carney, and Shannon Butler. *Hyde Park in the Gilded Age*. Charleston, SC: Arcadia, 2019.

Rhodes, Aaron. *The Debasement of Human Rights: How Politics Sabotage the Ideal of Freedom*. New York: Encounter Books, 2018.

Ricks, Thomas E. *Churchill and Orwell: The Fight for Freedom*. New York: Penguin Books, 2017.

Roberts, Sam. *A History of New York in 101 Objects*. New York: Simon & Schuster, 2016.

Robinson, Corinne Roosevelt. *One Woman to Another, and Other Poems*. Charles Scribner's Sons, 1914.

———. *The Poems of Corinne Roosevelt Robinson*. New York: Charles Scribner's Sons, 1921.

Roediger, David R. *Working Toward Whiteness: How America's Immigrants Became White: The Strange Journey from Ellis Island to the Suburbs*. New York: Basic Books, 2005.

Roll, David L. *The Hopkins Touch: Harry Hopkins and the Forging of the Alliance to Defeat Hitler*. New York: Oxford University Press, 2013.

Rollins, Alfred B. *Roosevelt and Howe*. New York: Alfred A. Knopf, 1962.

Roosevelt, Elliott. *Murder and the First Lady*. New York: St. Martin's, 1984.

Roosevelt, J. West, MD. *In Sickness and In Health: A Manual of Domestic Medicine and Surgery, Hygiene, Dietetics, and Nursing*. New York: D. Appleton, 1912.

Ross, Lillian. *Adlai Stevenson*. Philadelphia: J. B. Lippincott, 1966.

Rosskam, Edwin. *Washington—Nerve Center: The Face of America*. Introduction by Eleanor Roosevelt. New York: Alliance Books, 1939.

Roth, Philip. *Portnoy's Complaint*. New York: Random House, 1967.

Rothstein, Richard. *The Color of Law: A Forgotten History of How Our Government Segregated America*. New York: Liveright, 2017.

Rouse, Jacqueline, et al. *Women in the Civil Rights Movement: Trailblazers and Torch-bearers, 1941–1965*. Brooklyn, NY: Carlson, 1990.

Rovere, Richard H. *Senator Joe McCarthy*. New York: Harcourt, Brace, Jovanovich, 1959.

Rowan, Carl. *Dream Makers, Dream Breakers: The World of Justice Thurgood Marshall*. New York: Little, Brown, 1993.

Russell, Bertrand. *The Autobiography of Bertrand Russell, 1944–1969*. New York: Simon & Schuster, 1969.

Russell, Jan Jarboe. *The Train to Crystal City: FDR's Secret Prisoner Exchange and America's Only Family Internment Camp During World War II*. New York: Scribner, 2015.

Sadovnik, A. R., and S. F. Semel, eds. *Founding Mothers and Others*. New York: Palgrave Macmillan, 2002.

Scarry, Elaine. *Thinking in an Emergency*. New York: W. W. Norton, 2011.

Schlesinger, Arthur M., Sr., Dixon Ryan Fox, and Mark C. Carnes. *A History of American Life*. Edited by Arthur M. Schlesinger, Jr. New York: Scribner, 1996.

Shapiro, Laura. *What She Ate: Six Remarkable Women and the Food That Tells Their Stories*. New York: Viking, 2017.

Sheed, Wilfrid. *Clare Boothe Luce*. New York: Dutton, 1982.

———. *In Love with Daylight: A Memoir of Recovery*. New York: Simon & Schuster, 1999.

Sherman, Richard B. *The Case of Odell Waller and Virginia Justice, 1940–1942*. Knoxville: University of Tennessee Press, 1992.

Shields-West, Eileen. *The World Almanac of Presidential Campaigns*. New York: Pharos Books, 1992.

Simkhovitch, Mary Kingsbury. *Neighborhood: My Story of Greenwich House*. New York: W. W. Norton, 1938.

Sklar, Kathryn Kish, and Beverly Wilson Palmer, eds. *The Selected Letters of Florence Kelley, 1869–1931*. Champaign: University of Illinois Press, 2009.

Sledge, E. B. *With the Old Breed: At Peleliu and Okinawa*. New York: Oxford University Press, 1990.

Smith, Amanda. *Hostage to Fortune: The Letters of Joseph P. Kennedy*. New York: Viking, 2001.

Smith, Gay. *Lady Macbeth in America: From the Stage to the White House*. New York: Palgrave Macmillan, 2010.

Smith, Kathryn. *The Gatekeeper: Missy LeHand, FDR, and the Untold Story of the Partnership That Defined a Presidency*. Touchstone/Simon & Schuster, 2016.

Smith, Richard Norton. *An Uncommon Man: The Triumph of Herbert Hoover*. New York: Simon & Schuster, 1984.

Smith, Sally Bedell. *Grace and Power: The Private World of the Kennedy White House*. New York: Random House, 2004.

Speer, Albert. *Inside the Third Reich: Memoirs*. New York: Macmillan, 1970.

Srodes, James. *On Dupont Circle: Franklin and Eleanor Roosevelt and the Progressives Who Shaped Our World*. Berkeley, CA: Counterpoint, 2012.

Stacton, David. *Tom Fool*. London: Faber and Faber, 2014.

Stearns, Alfred E., et al., eds. *The Education of the Modern Boy*. Boston: Small, Maynard, 1925.

Stiles, Lela. *The Man Behind Roosevelt: The Story of Louis McHenry Howe*. Foreword by Eleanor Roosevelt. Cleveland: World, 1954.

Stone, Oliver, and Peter Kuznick. *The Untold History of the United States*. New York: Gallery Books, 2012.

Strachey, Dorothy. *Olivia: A Novel*. London: Hogarth, 1949.

Strawn, Susan M. *Knitting America: A Glorious Heritage from Warm Socks to High Art*. St. Paul, MN: Voyageur, 2007.

Strouse, Jean. *Morgan: American Financier*. New York: Random House, 1999.

Swift, Will. *The Roosevelts and the Royals: Franklin and Eleanor, the King and Queen of England, and the Friendship That Changed History*. Hoboken, NJ: John Wiley & Sons, 2004.

Takei, George, Justin Eisinger, Steven Scott, and Harmony Becker. *They Called Us Enemy*. Marietta, GA: Top Shelf Productions, 2019.

Tarr, Rodger L., ed. *As Ever Yours: The Letters of Max Perkins and Elizabeth Lemmon*. University Park: Pennsylvania State University Press, 2003.

Teachout, Terry. *The Skeptic: A Life of H. L. Mencken*. New York: Harper Perennial, 2002.

Terkel, Studs. *Hard Times: An Oral History of the Great Depression*. New York: New Press, 1986.

Thorne, Christopher. *Allies of a Kind: The United States, Britain, and the War Against Japan, 1941–1945*. New York: Oxford University Press, 1978.

Troyan, Michael. *A Rose for Mrs. Miniver: The Life of Greer Garson*. Lexington: University Press of Kentucky, 1999.

Updike, John. *Couples*. New York: Alfred A. Knopf, 1968.

Urquhart, Brian. *Ralph Bunche: An American Life*. New York: W. W. Norton, 1993.

Vidal, Gore. *The Best Man: A Play About Politics*. Boston: Little, Brown, 1960.

———. *Screening History*. Cambridge, MA: Harvard University Press, 1992.

———. *United States: Essays 1952–1992*. New York: Random House, 1993.

von Hesse, Elisabeth Ferguson. *So To Speak: A Practical Training Course for Developing a Beautiful Speaking Voice*. Philadelphia: J. B. Lippincott, 1959.

Walker, Stanley. *Mrs. Astor's Horse*. New York: Frederick A. Stokes, 1935.

Wallace, Henry A. *Democracy Reborn*. New York: Reynal and Hitchcock, 1944.

Ware, Susan. *Beyond Suffrage: Women in the New Deal*. Cambridge, MA: Harvard University Press, 1987.

———. *Partner and I: Molly Dewson, Feminism, and New Deal Politics*. New Haven, CT: Yale University Press, 1987.

———. *Notable American Women: A Biographical Dictionary*. Cambridge, MA: Belknap Press of Harvard University Press, 2004.

———. *American Women's Suffrage: Voices from the Long Struggle for the Vote, 1776–1965*. New York: Library of America, 2020.

Warner, Emily Smith, with Daniel Hawthorne. *The Happy Warrior: The Story of My Father, Alfred E. Smith*. Garden City, NY: Doubleday, 1956.

Weiner, Tim. *Enemies: A History of the FBI*. New York: Random House, 2012.

Weintraub, Stanley. *Pearl Harbor Christmas: A World at War, December 1941*. New York: Da Capo, 2011.

Weiss, Nancy Joan. *Charles Francis Murphy, 1858–1924: Respectability and Responsibility in Tammany Politics*. Northampton, MA: Smith College, 1968.

———. *The National Urban League, 1910–1940*. New York: Oxford University Press, 1974.

———. *Farewell to the Party of Lincoln: Black Politics in the Age of FDR*. Princeton, NJ: Princeton University Press, 1983.

Welles, Benjamin. *Sumner Welles: FDR's Global Strategist*. New York: St. Martin's, 1997.

Wharton, Edith. *The Age of Innocence*. New York: D. Appleton, 1920.

———. *A Son at the Front*. New York: Charles Scribner's Sons, 1923.

———. *The Touchstone*. Hoboken, NJ: Melville House, 2004.

White, E. B. *The Wild Flag: Editorials from the* New Yorker *on Federal World Government and Other Matters*. Boston: Houghton Mifflin, 1946.

Whitman, James Q. *Hitler's American Model: The United States and the Making of Nazi Race Law*. Princeton, NJ: Princeton University Press, 2017.

Widmer, Ted. *Ark of the Liberties: America and the World*. New York: Hill & Wang, 2008.

———, ed. *American Speeches: Political Oratory from Patrick Henry to Barack Obama*. New York: Library of America, 2011.

Williams, Juan. *Thurgood Marshall: American Revolutionary*. New York: Three Rivers Press, 1998.

Williams, Mason B. *City of Ambition: FDR, La Guardia, and the Making of Modern New York*. New York: W. W. Norton, 2013.

Wills, Garry. *Certain Trumpets: The Call of Leaders*. New York: Simon & Schuster, 1994.

Wilson, Edmund. *The American Earthquake: A Documentary of the Jazz Age, the Great Depression, and the New Deal*. Garden City, NY: Doubleday Anchor Books, 1958.

Wilson, Robert A., ed. *Character Above All: Ten Presidents from FDR to George Bush*. New York: Simon & Schuster, 1995.

Wilson, Sondra Kathryn, ed. *In Search of Democracy: The NAACP Writings of James Weldon Johnson, Walter White, and Roy Wilkins (1920–1977)*. New York: Oxford University Press, 1999.

Winthrop, Elizabeth. *In My Mother's House: A Novel*. New York: Doubleday, 1988.

Woloch, Nancy. *A Class by Herself: Protective Laws for Women Workers, 1890s–1990s*. Princeton, NJ: Princeton University Press, 2015.

Woods, Robert A., and John M. Gaus. *The Neighborhood in Nation Building*. Boston: Houghton Mifflin, 1923.

———, and Albert J. Kennedy. *The Settlement Horizon: A National Estimate*. New York: Russell Sage Foundation, 1922.

Woolf, S. J. *Here Am I*. New York: Random House, 1941.

Wyman, David. *The Abandonment of the Jews: America and the Holocaust, 1941–1945*. New York: New Press, 1984.

Young, Nancy Beck. *Lou Henry Hoover: Activist First Lady*. Lawrence: University Press of Kansas, 2004.

Zangrando, Robert L. *The NAACP Crusade Against Lynching, 1909–1950*. Philadelphia: Temple University Press, 1980.

ILLUSTRATION CREDITS

ENDPAPER:

1. Getty/Corbis Historical
2. Getty

INSERT 1:

1. Bettmann
2. Eleanor Roosevelt/Charles Scribner's Sons, 1932
3. Culver Pictures
4. *Harper's Weekly*, May 28, 1887; "The 'Celtic'—'Britannic' Disaster," by Fred Schiller Cozzens, after sketches by George Allen Rudd, passenger on the *Britannic*
5. Corbis Historical
6. Bettmann
7. Bettmann
8. Universal History Archive
9. Newspaper Enterprise Association (NEA)/George Moffett
10. Franklin D. Roosevelt Presidential Library
11. Getty/Corbis-Historical
12. Getty
13. Munsey's Magazine
14. Getty/Corbis Historical
15. Franklin D. Roosevelt Presidential Library
16. Getty/Corbis Historical
17. Wladyslaw T. Benda, for the American Red Cross, 1918. Library of Congress, Prints and Photographs
18. Getty/Bettmann
19. Getty/Corbis Historical
20. Getty/Hulton Archive
21. Getty/Bettmann
22. Corbis Historical

23. FDRL
24. Getty/Bettmann
25. Getty
26. FDRL
27. Getty/New York Daily News
28. Getty/Bettmann
29. Associated Press
30. Getty/Bettmann
31. United Feature Syndicate/United Media
32. Handbill, presented by the Women's Organization of Bryden Road Temple, 1938, author's collection
33. Getty/Bettmann
34. Wide World
35. Associated Press
36. Getty/Bettmann
37. Newspaper Enterprise Association (NEA)
38. AP Images
39. Getty/Corbis Historical
40. Thomas D. McAvoy/The LIFE Picture Collection
41. Detroit Mirror photo, ID HS8069, Frank Murphy Papers, Bentley Historical Library, University of Michigan
42. Getty/Irving Haberman
43. Getty/Thomas D. McAvoy
44. Getty
45. Getty
46. Getty/PhotoQuest
47. Getty
48. Bettmann
49. Getty
50. Getty
51. Bettmann
52.   Getty/Corbis Historical
53. Getty/Bettmann
54. National Park Service
55. FDRL
56. Leo Rosenthal/The LIFE Images Collection
57. Getty
58. Bettmann

59. Bettmann
60. Getty/ullstein bild

THROUGHOUT:

INDEX

Page numbers beginning with 555 refer to notes.